A LIBRARY OF LITERARY CRITICISM

A Library
of Literary Criticism

VOLUME I

A-L

 Frederick Ungar Publishing Co., New York

MODERN LATIN AMERICAN LITERATURE

Compiled and edited by
DAVID WILLIAM FOSTER
Professor of Spanish
Arizona State University

VIRGINIA RAMOS FOSTER
Professor of Spanish
Phoenix College

103302

*Selections in these volumes
are quoted with the approval of the copyright owners
and may not be reprinted elsewhere without their consent.
The exact source is given at the end of each selection.
For acknowledgments see p. 465 of Volume II.*

Library of Congress Cataloging in Publication Data
Foster, David William.
    Modern Latin American literature.
    (A Library of literary criticism)
    CONTENTS: v. 1. A-L.—v. 2. M-Z.
    1. Latin American literature—20th century—Book
reviews. I. Foster, Virginia Ramos, joint author.
II. Title. III. Series.
PQ7081.F63 1975   860'.9   72-81713
ISBN 0-8044-3139-6

INTRODUCTION

Latin American literature is at last coming into its own as one of the great literatures of the Western world. The richness and diversity of this writing have been acclaimed in the United States and in Europe. When the critic Roger Caillois returned to France from Buenos Aires after World War II he announced the "discovery" of "the literature of the future." Since then, the increased flow of translations and the revolution in communications have helped to create a wider audience for this impressive literature. And the emigration of many noted writers because of political oppression has allowed cultural institutions in Europe and the United States direct access to some of the most important and influential Latin American writers of our time.

In the United States the literature of Latin America has had an increasing vogue since the early 1960s. In colleges and universities courses on contemporary Latin American writing are now attracting more student interest than courses on modern Spanish and Portuguese literature. In the early decades of the century there was only minor awareness of the literature to the south, which was then hardly known in Europe. *The New York Times Book Review* would occasionally assess a translation of a Latin American novel. Somewhat later such magazines as *The Nation, The New Republic*, and a handful of others also published reviews from time to time. With the appearance in the 1920s of *Books Abroad*, which aimed to cover the world's literature, the first permanent forum for commentary on current Latin American writing came into being. Special issues of this journal, as well as symposia it has sponsored in recent years, have focused on contemporary literature in Latin America. In 1972 the *Books Abroad*/Neustadt International Prize was awarded to Gabriel García Márquez, author of the highly praised novel *One Hundred Years of Solitude*.

As translations into English mount, even the nonacademic press in the United States is beginning to acknowledge the achievements of

Latin American literature, although earlier preconceptions often persist. One magazine review in the mid-1960s began with a sentence certain to raise the hackles of Latin Americanists: "While Argentina does not have a literary tradition," it stated confidently, "it does have Borges." Yet many very competent reviews and articles in such publications as *The New York Times, The New York Review of Books, The New Yorker, Saturday Review,* and others have been exposing the general reader to an increasing array of Latin American novelists, short-story writers, and—to a lesser degree—poets, essayists, and dramatists. Many of the reviews continue to be written by professors of Latin American literature, but perceptive analyses by writers such as John Updike (on Cabrera Infante, for one), Edmund Wilson (on Mujica Láinez), John Barth (on Borges), and Anthony West (on Carpentier)—all represented in these volumes—attest to a growing interest outside the academic community.

Special issues of such journals as *TriQuarterly* and *Studies in Short Fiction* have contributed to a growing awareness of Latin American literature by English-speaking academics. And *Review*, published by the Center for Inter-American Relations in New York, which started as a digest of reviews in English of Latin American literature, has developed into a distinguished forum for the new Latin American writing and for other arts as well.

This compilation of international critical commentary on Latin American literature, the first of its kind, is intended as further testimony to the importance of that literature today. *Modern Latin American Literature* follows the format of other volumes in Ungar's "Library of Literary Criticism" series (American, British, German, Slavic, to name some) in presenting twentieth-century Latin American writers through the eyes of leading critics in their own countries and abroad, with particular stress on their reception in the United States.

Approximately half of the critical excerpts are translations from the Spanish and Portuguese. Some of these originate in the writer's native country, others elsewhere in Latin America and in Spain and Portugal. Still others are taken from American journals written either wholly or partly in Spanish or Portuguese, such as *Hispania, Revista iberoamericana,* and *Luso-Brazilian Review*; many of the contributors to these journals are American professors writing in Spanish or Portuguese.

The other half of the excerpts come mainly from English-language sources. Most of these were selected judiciously from a wide variety of American publications; British critics, too, are well represented. There is also a sampling taken from French, German, Italian, and Swedish sources to give some indication of the range of interest in what may indeed turn out to be the "literature of the future." Of its achievements and vitality, there is no longer any doubt.

A few words about the criteria for inclusion of the 137 writers represented. The guidelines called for (1) living writers and those who died after 1900 whose major work or influence belongs to the twentieth century; (2) among essayists, only those who have an important place in literature; (3) writers important in the formation and development of a Latin American literary tradition; those who have had temporary vogue, or no lasting influence, have been excluded (for example, Argentina's Hugo Wast); (4) those who have attracted sufficient serious (and worthwhile) critical commentary to allow for a representative selection (which excludes many promising younger writers); those on whom sufficient criticism was available in the United States; many Brazilian periodicals, for example, are simply impossible to obtain here, even through loan services; and (6) writers who continue to hold a place in or have begun to become part of the programs of American universities, or who have attracted serious attention in the nonacademic American press.

Clearly, the extent to which a writer has been translated was a major factor in selection, especially since this largely determines the standing of a writer beyond the romance-language departments of colleges and universities. On the other hand, we have accorded extensive coverage to traditional writers like Rómulo Gallegos, who may not be appreciated by readers of contemporary experimental fiction but who continue to hold a secure position in Latin American literary history and, therefore, in academic programs. It is true that the criticism devoted to the dozen or so most important writers who have become prominent in the last twenty years rivals the amount of critical comment available on the "patriarchs." Nonetheless, one aim of this work is to reflect the variety of critical approaches throughout the years on all major writers.

Other factors also influenced the final list of authors. It is not difficult to come up with a core list of about fifty major writers, writers of international stature, who must be covered in any overview of twentieth-century Latin American literature. But the editors' aim has been to offer a broader picture. The abundance of good "minor" writers, of promising novelists and poets, of old-guard traditionalists, made the final choice a difficult one, and the editors' personal judgment had to be the ultimate arbiter.

Some remarks about the omissions are in order. As mentioned above, we were limited in some cases by the lack of criticism or by inadequate criticism. The literature of post-revolutionary Cuba, for example, has been abundant; yet we could not find enough usable criticism on such writers as Manuel Brunet, Heberto Padilla, and Reinaldo Arenas to warrant their inclusion. Because of the same lack, we have regretfully not included Ernesto Cardenal and Violeta Parra among Latin American poets.

A desire for balance between the old and the new as well as among genres led us to limit the number of "new novelists." Among the second rank of "new novelists" there are some worthy writers: Enrique Lafourcade, Silvina Bullrich, Juan García Ponce, Sergio Pitol, José Emilio Pacheco, to name only a few. These writers, representing this very popular contemporary movement, were omitted so that a balanced presentation could be achieved.

Drama continues to struggle for recognition in Latin America. Playwrights generally receive only marginal support at home from a public that prefers to see movies, foreign plays in translation, and pseudo-Broadway musicals. Since the appearance in 1967 of *Latin American Theatre Review*, sponsored by the University of Kansas, Latin American drama has been gaining considerable academic attention in this country, and a good share of the drama criticism selected comes from this journal. Among dramatists not included, those who deserve more critical attention than they have thus far received are Egon Wolff, Jorge Díaz, Ricardo Monti, and Emilio Carballido.

For the 137 writers represented here, selections have been culled from monographs on individual writers and single works, books dealing with a specific subject or theme in the work of several writers, literary histories and encyclopedias, introductions to single works and collected editions, academic periodicals, literary reviews, and book-review sections of newspapers and general-interest magazines. The excerpts were assembled with the aim of giving a balanced perspective on each writer's achievements and development. Where appropriate, we have included extended remarks on individual works such as García Márquez's *One Hundred Years of Solitude*, Carpentier's *The Lost Steps*, and Güiraldes's *Don Segundo Sombra*. Selections are arranged chronologically; a special effort was made to include early reactions to a writer's work as well as more recent criticism. The current critical standing of a writer in the United States was a determining factor in the allotment of space to each writer.

The authors are presented alphabetically, with nationality noted. A list arranged by country precedes the text. The reader of this work has the option of using it in two ways. He can, for example, compare Mario Vargas Llosa to other "new novelists" or to other Peruvian novelists. Moreover, the reader will find national, supranational (that is, Spanish American or Latin American), and international orientations among the many critics included. All critics, and the authors they cover, are listed in the Index of Critics at the end of Volume II.

One word of caution for the reader still relatively new to Latin American writing. The word "modernism," frequently used in the excerpts, has a different meaning in Brazil than it does in Spanish America. Spanish American modernism began at the turn of the century as a development of French symbolism and Parnassianism; Brazilian modernism, introduced during the 1920s, was derived from Italian futurism and German expressionism. The approximate Spanish American equivalent of Brazilian modernism is called "ultraism," while the Brazilian counterpart of Spanish American modernism is called Parnassianism.

Many of the selections included here have been translated into English for the first time—not only from Spanish and Portuguese but from other languages as well; these are marked with a dagger after the credit line. The translating of so much material from Spanish and Portuguese proved to be an extremely demanding task. Hispanic prose style continues to be markedly hypotactic, with clauses within clauses within clauses. The critic's tone is often less neutral or objective than is usual in English-language criticism, and there is greater reliance on personal or subjective criteria. Moreover, Hispanic criticism often seems to rival the text it is discussing in its use of difficult syntax or in its display of lexical variety. When translated into English, such writing yields an impressionism or theatricality American critics generally deplore. We have aimed to present such Latin American criticism in more concrete, less rhetorical English. In a few instances, however, we have selected examples of the criticism we consider to be objectionable in approach because it is indicative either of the type of analysis a particular writer has attracted or of a trend of impressionistic criticism that continues to be published, despite the efforts of those Latin American critics who insist on rigorously defined premises and methods.

For the sake of uniformity and clarity, one literal translation has been used consistently for each title mentioned in the critical passages. This avoids the confusion of having the same work referred to by different critics' literal translations and by different published translations. For the original Spanish or Portuguese title, as well as information about published English translations, the reader should consult the lists of works mentioned in the back of each volume.

We have also imposed a uniformity on Brazilian orthography, still not completely standardized. We chose the more prevalent form of each Brazilian writer's or character's name and used that form throughout. In credit lines, however, the orthography of both authors' names and titles is that to be found on the title page of the work itself.

Modern Latin American Literature is intended as a reference tool for students, scholars, librarians, and researchers—the first such compilation on twentieth-century Latin American literature in any language. It is hoped that this work will provide, in addition to critical portraits of 137 important writers, a selective, annotated bibliography that will guide the reader to the books, articles, and journals themselves, so that he can pursue the writings of those critics who seem particularly interesting to him. The book can also be indirectly useful to scholars and critics in pinpointing those writers whose works call for more serious critical study or translation. We also hope that interested nonspecialists will find here much to satisfy their curiosity about an ever more important literature and that they will be stimulated to pursue further the work of individual writers.

This book has been several years in the making, and many people, too numerous to single out, have helped in many ways. Without the cooperation of so many copyright holders this book could not have been published. (Only in a very few instances did a copyright holder's refusal or unreasonable demands necessitate the exclusion of a selection.) Our editor, Leonard S. Klein of the Ungar staff, offered valuable assistance and advice during all phases of the preparation of the manuscript. Professor Gary L. Brower greatly assisted with materials. The Center for Latin American Studies of Arizona State University and our academic departments gave us much support. Finally, the staff of the Hayden Library at Arizona State University offered invaluable professional assistance.

D.W.F.
V.R.F.

AUTHORS INCLUDED

VOLUME I

Adonias Filho
    (pseud. of Adonias Aguiar)
Aguilera Malta, Demetrio
Agustín, José
    (pseud. of José Agustín Ramírez)
Agustini, Delmira
Alegría, Ciro
Amado, Jorge
Amorim, Enrique
Anderson Imbert, Enrique
Andrade, Carlos Drummond de
Andrade, Mário de
Andrade, Oswald de
Aranha, José Pereira de Graça
Arciniegas, Germán
Arévalo Martínez, Rafael
Arguedas, Alcides
Arguedas, José María
Arlt, Roberto
Arreola, Juan José
Asturias, Miguel Ángel
Azuela, Mariano
Ballagas, Emilio
Bandeira, Manuel
Barrios, Eduardo
Benedetti, Mario
Benedetto, Antonio di
Bilac, Olavo Braz Martins dos
    Guimarães
Bioy Casares, Adolfo
Borges, Jorge Luis
Caballero Calderón, Eduardo
Cabrera Infante, Guillermo

Cardoso, Lúcio
Carpentier, Alejo
Carrera Andrade, Jorge
Carvalho, Ronald de
Casaccia, Gabriel
    (pseud. of Gabriel Bibolini)
Castellanos, Rosario
Chocano, José Santos
Coelho Neto, Henrique
Conti, Haroldo
Cortázar, Julio
Cunha, Euclydes da
Darío, Rubén
    (pseud. of Félix Rubén García
    Sarmiento)
Díaz Mirón, Salvador
Díaz Rodríguez, Manuel
Donoso, José
Edwards Bello, Joaquín
Elizondo, Salvador
Freyre, Gilberto
Fuentes, Carlos
Gallegos, Rómulo
Gálvez, Manuel
Gámbaro, Griselda
García Márquez, Gabriel
Girri, Alberto
Gomes, Alfredo Dias
González Martínez, Enrique
González Prada, Manuel
Gorostiza, José
Guillén, Nicolás

Güiraldes, Ricardo
Henríquez Ureña, Pedro
Herrera y Reissig, Julio
Huidobro, Vicente
Ibarbourou, Juana de
Icaza, Jorge
Jaimes Freyre, Ricardo

Leñero, Vicente
Lezama Lima, José
Lispector, Clarice
Lobato, José Bento Monteiro
López Velarde, Ramón
Lugones, Leopoldo
Lynch, Benito

VOLUME II

Machado de Assis, Joaquim Maria
Mallea, Eduardo
Marechal, Leopoldo
Marqués, René
Martínez Estrada, Ezequiel
Martínez Moreno, Carlos
Meireles, Cecília
Mendes, Murilo
Mistral, Gabriela
        (pseud. of Lucila Godoy
        Alcayaga)
Molinari, Ricardo E.
Moraes, Vinícius de
Moyano, Daniel
Mujica Láinez, Manuel
Murena, H. A.
Nalé Roxlo, Conrado
Neruda, Pablo
        (pseud. of Neftalí Ricardo
        Reyes)
Nervo, Amado
Novo, Salvador
Onetti, Juan Carlos
Ortiz, Adalberto
Palés Matos, Luis
Parra, Nicanor
Payró, Roberto J.
Paz, Octavio
Pellicer, Carlos
Picón-Salas, Mariano
Puig, Manuel
Queiroz, Rachel de
Quiroga, Horacio
Ramos, Graciliano

Rebêlo, Marques
        (pseud. of Eddy Dias da Cruz)
Rêgo, José Lins do
Reyes, Alfonso
Reyles, Carlos
Ricardo, Cassiano
Rivera, José Eustacio
Roa Bastos, Augusto
Rodó, José Enrique
Rojas, Manuel
Romero, José Rubén
Rosa, João Guimarães
Rulfo, Juan
Sábato, Ernesto
Sáenz, Dalmiro
Sainz, Gustavo
Salazar Bondy, Sebastián
Sánchez, Florencio
Sanín Cano, Baldomero
Sarduy, Severo
Solórzano, Carlos
Soto, Pedro Juan
Spota, Luis
Storni, Alfonsina
Suassuna, Ariano
Torres Bodet, Jaime
Usigli, Rodolfo
Uslar Pietri, Arturo
Vallejo, César
Vargas Llosa, Mario
Verbitsky, Bernardo
Veríssimo, Érico
Villaurrutia, Xavier
Viñas, David
Yáñez, Agustín

LIST OF AUTHORS BY COUNTRY

ARGENTINA

Anderson Imbert, Enrique
Arlt, Roberto
Benedetto, Antonio di
Bioy Casares, Adolfo
Borges, Jorge Luis
Conti, Haroldo
Cortázar, Julio
Gálvez, Manuel
Gámbaro, Griselda
Girri, Alberto
Güiraldes, Ricardo
Lugones, Leopoldo
Lynch, Benito
Mallea, Eduardo

Marechal, Leopoldo
Martínez Estrada, Ezequiel
Molinari, Ricardo E.
Moyano, Daniel
Mujica Láinez, Manuel
Murena, H. A.
Nalé Roxlo, Conrado
Payró, Roberto J.
Puig, Manuel
Sábato, Ernesto
Sáenz, Dalmiro
Storni, Alfonsina
Verbitsky, Bernardo
Viñas, David

BOLIVIA

Arguedas, Alcides

Jaimes Freyre, Ricardo

BRAZIL

Adonias Filho
Amado, Jorge
Andrade, Carlos Drummond de
Andrade, Mário de
Andrade, Oswald de
Aranha, José Pereira da Graça
Bandeira, Manuel

Bilac, Olavo Braz Martins dos
     Guimarães
Cardoso, Lúcio
Carvalho, Ronald de
Coelho Neto, Henrique
Cunha, Euclides da
Freyre, Gilberto

CHILE

COLOMBIA

CUBA

DOMINICAN REPUBLIC

ECUADOR

GUATEMALA

Arévalo Martínez, Rafael
Asturias, Miguel Ángel

Solórzano, Carlos

MEXICO

Agustín, José
Arreola, Juan José
Azuela, Mariano
Castellanos, Rosario
Díaz Mirón, Salvador
Elizondo, Salvador
Fuentes, Carlos
González Martínez, Enrique
Gorostiza, José
Leñero, Vicente
López Velarde, Ramón
Nervo, Amado

Novo, Salvador
Paz, Octavio
Pellicer, Carlos
Reyes, Alfonso
Romero, José Rubén
Rulfo, Juan
Sainz, Gustavo
Spota, Luis
Torres Bodet, Jaime
Usigli, Rodolfo
Villaurrutia, Xavier
Yáñez, Agustín

NICARAGUA

Darío, Rubén

PARAGUAY

Casaccia, Gabriel

Roa Bastos, Augusto

PERU

Alegría, Ciro
Arguedas, José María
Chocano, José Santos
González Prada, Manuel

Salazar Bondy, Sebastián
Vallejo, César
Vargas Llosa, Mario

PUERTO RICO

Marqués, René
Palés Matos, Luis

Soto, Pedro Juan

URUGUAY

Agustini, Delmira
Amorim, Enrique
Benedetti, Mario
Herrera y Reissig, Julio
Ibarbourou, Juana de
Martínez Moreno, Carlos

Onetti, Juan Carlos
Quiroga, Horacio
Reyles, Carlos
Rodó, José Enrique
Sánchez, Florencio

VENEZUELA

Díaz Rodríguez, Manuel
Gallegos, Rómulo

Picón-Salas, Mariano
Uslar Pietri, Arturo

PERIODICALS USED

Where no abbreviation is indicated, the periodical references are used in full.

	Alcor (Asunción)
	America (New York)
ABC	American Book Collector (Chicago)
Amer	American Mercury (New York)
	Américas; English edition (Washington, D.C.)
	The Americas (Washington, D.C.)
ArQ	Arizona Quarterly (Tucson)
AyL	Armas y letras (Monterrey, Mexico)
	Asomante (Río Piedras, Puerto Rico)
	Atenea (Concepción, Chile)
At	The Atlantic Monthly (Boston)
	Atlas (New York)
BBB	BBB: Boletim bibliográfico brasileira (São Paulo)
	La biblioteca (Buenos Aires)
BAAL	Boletín de la Academia Argentina de Letras (Buenos Aires)
BLM	Bonniers litterära magasin (Stockholm)
BW	Book Week (New York)
BA	Books Abroad (Norman, Okla.)
BH	Bulletin hispanique (Paris)
BHS	Bulletin of Hispanic Studies (Liverpool)
BRMMLA	Bulletin of the Rocky Mountain Modern Language Association (Boulder, Col.)
	Cahiers de L'Herne (Paris)
CarR	Caribbean Review (Miami)
	The Carleton Miscellany (Northfield, Minn.)
	Casa de las Américas (Havana)
	Chasqui (Madison, Wis.)
CSM	The Christian Science Monitor (Boston)
	Cithara (St. Bonaventure, N.Y.)
Cmty	Commentary (New York)

Com	Commonweal (New York)
CompD	Comparative Drama (Kalamazoo, Mich.)
CLS	Comparative Literature Studies (College Park, Md.)
CSSH	Comparative Studies in Society and History (New York)
CR	Contemporary Review (London)
	Critique (Minneapolis)
CA	Cuadernos americanos (Mexico City)
CCLC	Cuadernos del Congreso por la Libertad de la Cultura (Paris)
	Cuadernos del idioma (Buenos Aires)
CHA	Cuadernos hispanoamericanos (Madrid)
	Davar (Buenos Aires)
DQ	Denver Quarterly (Denver)
	Diálogos (Mexico City)
	Discourse (Moorhead, Minn.)
DA	Dissertation Abstracts (Ann Arbor, Mich.)
DHR	Duquesne Hispanic Review (Pittsburgh)
Enc	Encounter (London)
	Et caetera (Guadalajara)
	Ficción (Buenos Aires)
Forum	Forum, Ball State University (Terre Haute, Ind.)
Harper's	Harper's Magazine (New York)
	Hispania (Baltimore, etc.)
HR	Hispanic Review (Philadelphia)
	Horizontes (Mexico City)
	Ínsula (Madrid)
IPNA	Instituto Peruano-Norteamericano (Lima)
IAM	Inter-American Monthly (Washington, D.C.)
	Itá-Humanidades (Rio de Janeiro?)
JIAS	Journal of Inter-American Studies (Coral Gables, Fla.)
KFLQ	Kentucky Foreign Language Quarterly (Lexington)
	Kirkus Reviews (New York)
	Lateinamerika (Rostock, East Germany)
LALR	Latin American Literary Review (Pittsburgh)
LATR	Latin American Theatre Review (Lawrence, Kan.)
	Leitura (Rio de Janeiro)
LetN	Les lettres nouvelles (Paris)
LJ	Library Journal (New York)
List	The Listener (London)
LA	Living Age (Boston)
London	The London Magazine (London)
LBR	Luso-Brazilian Review (Madison, Wis.)
	Mainstream (New York)
MD	Modern Drama (Lawrence, Kan.)
MLF	Modern Language Forum (Los Angeles)
MLN	Modern Language Notes (Baltimore)
MLQ	Modern Language Quarterly (Seattle)

MLR	The Modern Language Review (Cambridge)
MNu	Mundo nuevo (Paris/Buenos Aires)
	La nación (Buenos Aires)
Nation	The Nation (New York)
NLr	The New Leader (New York)
NMQ	New Mexico Quarterly (Albuquerque)
NR	The New Republic (Washington, D.C.)
NSo	New Society (London)
NS	New Statesman (London)
NSN	The New Statesman and Nation (London)
NYHT	The New York Herald Tribune Book Review (New York)
NYR	The New York Review of Books (New York)
NYT	The New York Times Book Review (New York)
NY	The New Yorker (New York)
NWR	Northwest Review (Eugene, Ore.)
	Nosotros (Buenos Aires)
NRF	La nouvelle revue française (Paris)
	Novel (Providence)
	Nueva crítica (Buenos Aires)
	Nuevos Aires (Buenos Aires)
	Ocidente (Lisbon)
PAUB	Pan-American Union Bulletin (Washington, D.C.)
PSA	Papeles de Son Armadans (Palma de Mallorca)
PLL	Papers on Language & Literature (Edwardsville, Ill.)
PMLA	PMLA: Publications of the Modern Language Association of America (New York)
	Poetry (Chicago)
	Prévues (Paris)
PPNWCFL	Proceedings: Pacific Northwest Conference on Foreign Languages (Seattle, etc.)
	Punch (London)
	Review (New York)
RBF	Revista brasileira de folclore (Rio de Janeiro)
RCu	Revista cubana (Havana)
RA	Revista de América (Bogotá)
RBA	Revista de Bellas Artes (Mexico City)
RCB	Revista de cultura brasileña (Madrid)
RCCE	Revista de la Casa de la Cultura Ecuatoriana (Quito)
RUM	Revista de la Universidad de México (Mexico City)
RLAI	Revista de literatura argentina e iberoamericana (Mendoza, Argentina)
RdL	Revista do livro (Rio de Janeiro)
RHM	Revista hispánica moderna (New York)
RI	Revista iberoamericana (Pittsburgh)
RIL	Revista iberoamericana de literatura (Montevideo)
RIB	Revista interamericana de bibliografía/Inter-American Review of Bibliography (Washington, D.C.)

RML	Revista mexicana de literatura (Mexico City)
RNC	Revista nacional de cultura (Caracas)
RPC	Revista peruana de cultura (Lima)
RomN	Romance Notes (Chapel Hill, N.C.)
RR	Romanic Review (New York)
SR	Saturday Review (New York)
SAJ	The South American Journal (London)
SoR	The Southern Review (Baton Rouge, La.)
Spec	The Spectator (London)
	St. Louis Post-Dispatch (St. Louis)
SSF	Studies in Short Fiction (Newberry, S.C.)
	Sur (Buenos Aires)
Sym	Symposium (Syracuse, N.Y.)
TR	La table ronde (Paris)
TM	Les temps modernes (Paris)
TQ	The Texas Quarterly (Austin)
Thesaurus	Thesaurus: Boletín del Instituto Caro y Cuervo (Bogotá)
TLS	The Times Literary Supplement (London)
	La torre (Río Piedras, Puerto Rico)
	TriQuarterly (Evanston, Ill.)
TC	Twentieth Century (London)
USF	Universidad (Sante Fe, Argentina)
	Universidad de Antioquia (Antioquia, Colombia)
WSCL	Wisconsin Studies in Contemporary Literature (Madison)
YR	The Yale Review (New Haven, Conn.)

ADONIAS FILHO (1915–   )

BRAZIL

It is a truly frightening world, the one Adonias Filho presents before our
startled eyes in the course of three novels: *The Servants of Death*,
Memories of Lazarus, and *Body Alive*. It is a terrifying world, but at the
same time a real and perfectly "possible" one from the point of view of
the human condition. . . .

Without light and without horizon—at least this is how we see the
sinister bulks evolve in *The Servants of Death*—almost all of [his char-
acters] are marked indelibly by the curse of madness and drunkenness,
by a crime that has already been performed or is about to be. Then,
opening up the horizon, letting the light in, in *Memories of Lazarus*,
he makes us collide with the deaf, unyielding hostility of nature,
adverse, crushing, one that envelops men, dominates them completely,
returns them to an almost animallike condition. Finally, in *Body Alive*,
we rediscover these men, armed and outside the law, hurling themselves
against nature, struggling with it, attacking it, violating it, in order finally
to triumph, by making use of it, by bringing about a violent collision of
evil and human pettiness . . . in an ending of epic desperation rarely
equaled in dramatic intensity. Cajango and Malva disappear in the
primeval forest, impenetrable to the eye and to power of human evil.

Upon this terrible and at times Dantesque panorama, the figures
take shape, take form, project themselves onto our sharpened and
almost always tormented imaginations. . . . Evidently, this is a complete
world of large, vital figures, tremendous in their almost barbaric
instincts, slaves of egoism and of evil, if not of madness and death—
tragic, terribly tragic figures. The whole world he creates gives him an
uncommon stature, fundamentally different from that of our other great
novelists, whom he rarely resembles. . . . His whole world fascinates us;
we cannot stop admiring it, although there are times that we may not

1

want to accept its totality, perhaps because of its exaggerated pessimism. This whole world confers upon its creator the position of a great novelist. . . .

Octávio de Faria. *BBB*. 9, Oct., 1962, pp. 265–66†

The diabolical surrealist and the Christian novelist joined hands in *The Servants of Death, Memories of Lazarus*, and *Body Alive*, a trilogy woven from the fabric of damnation and despair. . . . In them, not only do we have the man from Bahia; we have universal man traveling the telluric road. The novels are only circumstantially stories of Bahia, they are essentially histories of the collective hallucination of a world in panic, stories of the ancestral blemish, narrated impressionistically. . . .

In deforming his characters, admitting, like Kafka, that "facts are legitimate because they are guided by legitimate ideas," Adonias Filho, like Kafka, embraces a philosophy of despair, which indicates his relationship to Kierkegaard. Hence the obsessive primacy of the idea of sin in his fiction is an idea that in its entirety often links him to Faulkner, who stays within the limits of traditional Christian thought. . . .

The admirable technique of the novelist, especially in his two latest novels, makes possible—through direct dialogues and cinematographic scenes—a vigorous and dramatic action, which at first glance conceals the revelation or even the suspicion of the submerged metaphysical thread. His style, so admirably sober, made all of "muscles and nerves," derives, without a doubt, from a morbid imagination, but paradoxically one of a vigorous Christian novelist, preoccupied with the infinite evil of men, with the ancestral blemish, with the condemned heritage.

Oliveiros Litrento. *Leitura*. No. 63, 1962, p. 13†

In [*The Fort*] Adonias Filho presents a magical-realist vision of the world, which seems to me to be one of the most valid approaches to the exploration of life. This approach is radically opposed to the pseudorealism—naturalism without any other adornment—that tempts a number of contemporary novelists. Being a realist does not mean chronicling the appearance of life and describing it without seeing complications. On the contrary, being a realist presupposes a commitment to the effort to find true reality, the one beyond easily graspable appearances. *The Fort*, seen superficially, may seem like a fantasy. But it will not seem thus for anyone who is aware of the force exercised on an individual life by history and the traditions from which life derives. Adonias Filho, in this novel, by means of an artistic process that, as it should, sharpens every reflection on the theme, underlines the force of the collective on the individual and points toward an understanding of a world in which materialism is so acute that it comes to be confused with spirituality, or vice-versa. . . .

Perhaps the key to the success of *The Fort* is its immersion in—or better, its derivation from—a specific local situation. It may well be that this story of transmigration would be excessively intellectualized, or ultimately false, if it were placed in a setting other than a Brazilian one—and, more specifically, that of Bahia. Life in Bahia presupposes a popular belief in spiritualism and transmigration, the inclination to accept the marvelous and the magical.

Pilar Gómez Bedate. CHA. No. 193, Jan., 1966,
pp. 184–85†

[Adonias Filho uses] localisms and regional expressions in a way so as not to "upset" the traditional linguistic system very much. But he does create his own artistic language. Like the best of the renovational romantics, he also questions language, he puts it in doubt, so as to draw his own positive results. Thus, his world appears to be new, and his language new. The overall result is a new form for the Brazilian novel.

Language, in the hands of the artists—like marble, wood, iron, ink—has infinite possibilities of renovation. . . . [The artist] improves and expands the resources of the linguistic system. It is he who forges new terms and expressions. The grammarian comes along later and "gathers" the result and incorporates it into the system.

The reverse side of what Adonias Filho has done is the work of João Guimarães Rosa. Rosa "upsets" the linguistic system in such a way that he either falls into the pure and simple creation of words and expressions or he uncovers "antiquated" expressions that have been long lost in the interior of Brazil. His is without a doubt another way of renovating the language, of enriching it. I must stress, however, that Rosa's method is scarcely an integral aspect of his creation, while in Adonias Filho it is intimately linked to the fable and to the creative ideas in his work. Both work, we could say, with different "gradations" of inquiry into the linguistic system in order to achieve the result that they desire—the artistic form, the world seen from their "reality."

Assis Brasil. Adonias Filho, ensaio (Rio de Janeiro,
Organização Simões, 1969), pp. 17–18†

Though no critic has understood the value of the telluric in Brazilian literature better than he, Adonias Filho's own evolution led away from realism: "I continue to believe too much in man, and in the possibilities of his intelligence, to accept reality as the life blood of the modern novel"—reality is various and changing, and there is something in man that is superior to it. In the mid-thirties he tore up a documentary novel he had written and rejected another that he was later to rewrite and publish [as *Body Alive*] . . . in 1962. He had also begun to think of another work in his "cocoa cycle," but it was not to reach definitive form until 1952, as the present *Memories of Lazarus*. Part of the same cycle and perhaps the least notable artistically, *The Servants of Death* was the first of his novels to be published, in 1946.

The end of World War II, in which Brazil participated actively, brought significant changes in political, social, and intellectual life, especially in the direction of greater individual freedom. A new literary generation had arisen, the so-called generation of 1945, which was vanguardist, experimental, and interested in the implications of modern art for literature. Joyce, Proust, Kafka, Virginia Woolf, and later the French writers of the *nouveau roman* were major influences; so, particularly for Adonias Filho, were Faulkner, Jouhandeau, Jakob Wassermann, Henry James, and Hermann Hesse's *Steppenwolf*. Adonias Filho has been one of the leaders of the new movement, along with Clarice Lispector, whose first novel had appeared in 1944, and João Guimarães Rosa, whose first collection of short stories was published in 1946. . . .

[In *Memories of Lazarus*] the Ouro Valley is disquieting, if not terrifying, in its strangeness. Since specific links with reality are often dissolved, Alexandre's narration quickly transcends the local; time becomes a function of his hallucinations. In creating the Ouro Valley, its look, its atmosphere, its inner "feel," Adonias Filho has eliminated all but a few specific features—for example, the slough, the searing wind, Jeronimo's cavern, the dusty road, the earth's hot crust, the black sky. Men are described with a similar laconism in their simple lives and in their primitive society. As a matter of technique, Adonias Filho has depended upon the observation of gesture, facial expression, or other movement to convey inner states and upon a few physical details to establish outward appearance. Constant repetition of these details serves to give an almost sculptural quality to his characters. The author is "visual without being a landscape painter," in the words of Rachel de Queiroz, speaking of Adonias Filho's newest work, *Promised Leagues*, a collection of tales of the same Itajuipe Territory.

Fred P. Ellison. Introduction to Adonias Filho,
Memories of Lazarus (Austin, University of Texas Press,
1969), pp. x–xiii

One of the foremost postwar literary figures of Brazil and director of its National Library, Adonias Aguiar ("Adonias Filho") was born in 1915 in the state of Bahia, the setting for most of his novels and short stories. His regionalism is somewhat akin to Faulkner's—close to the native soil but with the sense of another, mythical country. [*Memories of Lazarus*], the second of his four novels and the first to be translated into English, places its doomed narrator Alexandre against the almost lunar landscape of the backlands of Bahia. The bleak and windswept, peopled by near-savage peasants, the desolate valley torments and repels Alexandre, finally luring him back to his death after a cycle of rapes, mutilations, and a particularly grisly killing of a leper by vultures. The stench of evil is overwhelming, evoked through a spare stylistic technique which alternates between realism and recollection, narrative and symbol. Ellison [the translator] does an admirable job of recreating the novel's nightmare imagery.

Rosemary Neiswender. *LJ*. 94, Oct. 1, 1969, p. 3465

[*The Fort*] achieves a synthesis of backlands and coast, of Rosa and Amado. Out of the interpenetration and ultimate fusion of the brooding and archaic metaphysics of the harsh prairie world of the interior and the vibrant, colorful world of legends of the coast, there emerged the crystalline narrative so typical of Adonias Filho. The structure of his works partakes of techniques of the *nouveau roman*, most successfully realized in *The Fort*, a small book but one whose content embraces the human spiritual topography of a whole world—focused, as if through a burning glass, on the old town of Bahia de Todos os Santos (the Salvador of today) and its legendary fort.

The action is strikingly simple; it tells the story of a handful of people who live and die in the shadow of the fort. There is no suspense, because whatever happens is placed at such a remove by Adonias Filho that it seems to take on the character of a medieval altarpiece, thereby achieving a timeless validity. The interest of the book is thus not what happens but how it happens—its language, its inner rhythm, its elevation of everyday occurrences to archetypal images.

Both theme and language in *The Fort* are developed on two constantly overlapping temporal and psychological planes. Facts and memories flow together to create a new perspective of reality, which exceeds all limits to achieve a magical unity of events in which the living and the dead alike are actors in an unfathomable play whose protagonist is the menacing silhouette of the fort, yesterday a feudal bastion, today a lovers' hideout. This synthesis of threat and idyll, of symbols of violence and hope, of superstition and religious belief, is wrought into an exquisitely poetic portrait not only of Bahia but of all Brazil and its history.

Günter W. Lorenz. *Die zeitgenössische Literatur
in Lateinamerika* (Tübingen, Horst Erdmann Verlag,
1971), p. 243†

[*Body Alive*] evolves through a series of narrative fragments that substitute for a more traditional "plot line," a sort of evocative impressionism where we first "sense" that something is happening before we actually understand its true nature. Ambiguous or vague references, elliptic transitions, ill-defined dialogue contexts all contribute to the creation of the highly "poetic" prose associated with magical realism. Certain characters, of course, assume an outstanding importance, despite the fact that in a novel of this sort, aside from the one central character, it is often difficult to identify with accuracy who the principal characters are. . . .

Seen as a whole, the novel most immediately represents another example of the eternal triumph of the all-powerful forces of the jungle and of primitivism. However, the importance of Adonias Filho's work does not stem from the theme as it is here presented. Inuri is the image of the jungle and the consummate essence of the latent primitivism and cruelty hidden in the depths of the animal-man. He is, in other words, the "call of the wild." When Cajango and Inuri emerge from the jungle, it is Inuri who speaks for them both: Cajango has become little more than an extension of Inuri.

The author's attempt to penetrate the curtain of mystery surrounding the actions of these men and the interplay in at least the souls of Cajango and Malva of human good and primitive evil becomes the most significant goal of the novel. Toward this goal, the novel lifts the veil of indisputable reality in order to bring into view the unconscious motives of men, and the man whose motives are most important here is Cajango. The theme of the novel, as represented by Inuri, is the primitive destiny which he sees Cajango as called upon to fulfill: the avenging of the spilt blood of his kin. . . .

The social context of *Body Alive* is a familiar one. But being a limited social one, it must be defined in terms of its customs and distinctive characteristics and the novel must observe these in order to be credible. The novelist could have chosen any one of a number of social contexts; his option is naturally for his own. Seen in this light *Body Alive* is more than merely a Brazilian novel with a socio-anthropological orientation. It is a human document of the highest order which sets up in a handful of quasi-mythical persons the whole panorama of the suffering soul of mankind that is the common inheritance of all humanity. Cajango is a neo-Adam, but not in any allegorical or mystery-play sense. Indeed, one would be hard put to explain allegorically all of the details of his story. Rather, Cajango assumes the role of Adam through Adonias Filho's sustained endeavor—an endeavor carried out within an unabashedly moral and Christian frame of reference—to make him stand out from the vague shadows of the novel's background. In so standing above or beyond his physical world, he incarnates man trapped by evil in a world of atavism which he did not create but which relentlessly works his fall, a fall from which he must, with the help of woman's love, extricate himself and seek his personal, and fatal, redemption.

David William Foster. *LALR*. 1, 2, Spring, 1973,
pp. 44–45, 50

AGUILERA MALTA, DEMETRIO (1905–   )

ECUADOR

In the very diversified literary work of Aguilera Malta, his short stories included in the collection *They Who Go Away* and his "great novels," *Don Goyo* and *The Virgin Isle*, definitely hold a predominant position. The rest of his extensive work . . . forms a kind of varied and pulsating background against which the above-mentioned works stand out. In this background, there is great variety, from spirited, lively reports on Madrid and the Canal Zone . . . to biographies clearly destined to become scenarios for motion pictures, like *Manuela, Knightess of the Sun*, which concerns the life of Manuelita Sáenz, the mistress of Simón Bolívar. . . .

They Who Go Away . . . is a youthful work filled with vigor, a collection of stories about the peasants of the coast told with originality, harshness, and virility. Aguilera Malta's own stories in this [collaborative] collection are almost poems. They are very sensitive, full of suppleness, sadness, tenderness, and color. . . .

Ángel F. Rojas, in his magnificent preface to *The Virgin Isle*, points out the domination of the land, the jungle, the vegetal earth over the human will, and he places the work of Aguilera Malta in the line of great American novels describing the defeat of man by the virgin land: *The Vortex* by Rivera and *Toá* by Uribe Piedrahita. . . . In Aguilera Malta's view, the virgin earth has a will superior to that of man, a panicky will that absorbs and dominates him, shapes his life, and punishes those who dare rebel against it.

Aguilera Malta writes well, constructs well. His talents as a painter (which have not been developed) and as a poet (which are confined to his original book of sonnets) have helped to contribute to a flexible, colorful, almost lyrical prose, which lends itself marvelously to describing the jungle, a mystical subject surrounded by superstition, magic, and ancient fatalism.

Diccionario de la literatura latinoamericana: Ecuador
(Washington, D.C. Unión Panamericana, 1962),
pp. 76–77†

Demetrio Aguilera Malta, because of his excellence as a writer and his exemplary character, has achieved a secure place in the literary history of Latin America. A member of the so-called Group of Guayaquil, he has used modern themes and techniques in his novels, plays, short stories, and poetry in order to make the sordid and relatively unknown way of life of his native region come alive. At the same time, the Ecuadorian writer has been able to overcome the repetitiousness of a single theme and setting, and his works, like his personal presence, have made him a pan-American writer.

The pan-American scope of Aguilera Malta has given him the inspired idea of creating a novelistic mural that would encompass in its thematic range all of Latin America. The title *American Episodes* (a title chosen by Editorial Guadarrama that makes us think immediately of the *National Episodes* of Benito Pérez Galdós) covers a series of historical novels, of which three have already appeared, which pursue profoundly Americanist and democratic goals. There can be no disputing the claim that the Latin American nations share similar native and European cultural traditions. Nevertheless, there is a growing realization today that these bonds and the "common obstacles" of our societies will only be coincidental until we are able to integrate the institutions and cultural patterns of Latin America. Researchers note the economic and political urgency of creating an authentic extranational sentiment, which requires the familiarization with both the historical and the contemporary circumstances of all of Latin America. This sentiment, moreover, should include the culminating events of our history and its symbolic figures, not only in their local or regional significance but also as integral parts of *one* future and perhaps accessible Latin America. Aguilera Malta, certainly impelled by the "repertory of convictions" of our age, has utilized the entire gamut of devices of the contemporary novel (interior monologue, flashback, thematic parallelism, and so forth) in the service of the Latin American people, recreating the historical moments that belong to all of Latin America in a simple prose, a formal structure, offering a study of social and psychological realities ... within the grasp of all readers.

Saúl Sibirsky. *RI.* 32, Jan.–June, 1966, pp. 176–77†

There have been books on the Green Hell of the jungles. [*Black Hell*] is a two-act play about the Black Hell endured by Negroes in a white man's world. . . .

Aguilera Malta is best known for his novels, though his great love is the theater. His recent short dramas have been bitter commentaries on social conditions. The present play is not for squeamish readers. Its mood can best be judged by the initial quotation from Nelson Rockefeller: "When a Negro child has his nose and ears eaten by rats, his family loses hope in society."

Black Hell with symbolic masked characters takes place in Nylónpolis to an accompaniment of African music and with quotations from contemporary poets as part of the dialogue. In flashbacks the career of Hórridus Nebus is presented, beginning with his burial and eulogy of his accomplishments in purifying the white blood and solving the Negro problem, accomplished by founding a sausage factory to use their flesh. Resurrected by the blacks for a trial, Nebus is condemned to be the "wandering Negro," living among white people until the establishment of a blood brotherhood.

A reader may wonder where this combination of gruesomeness and poetry might be performed, but other plays more upsetting have reached the stage. *Black Hell* would engender some arresting thoughts in anyone witnessing the performance.

Willis Knapp Jones. BA. 42, Summer, 1968, p. 410

Despite the variety of themes treated by [Aguilera Malta], his vision of man and society has remained basically the same. However, the same thing has not occurred in the form of his works. In fact, his development as a practitioner of theatrical form implies a long journey and can be divided into three major periods according to dominant stylistic methods. . . .

The first period corresponds to a realistic conception of art, that is to say, a primarily mimetic conception, which takes the form in the theater of a faithful copy of an exterior observation of reality that is verisimilar, rational, and phenomenally probable. . . . Right after comes a cycle of transitional works, in which one can clearly see Aguilera Malta's desire to search for new stylistic directions. . . . The third and latest period in the formal evolution in the theater of Demetrio Aguilera Malta shows a definite bent toward expressionism. The expressionist writer abhors above all the mimetic representation of reality, and he strives for a much more creative and imaginative approach.

Gerardo A. Luzuriaga. LATR. 3, 2, Spring, 1970,
pp. 39, 42†

In Santorontón [in *Seven Moons and Seven Serpents*], where "the Devil still dances on the tip of his tail," the perennial contest between good and evil emerges in the tropical atmosphere of coastal Ecuador which inspired [Aguilera Malta's] earlier gems, *Don Goyo* and *The Virgin Isle*. Although the novel has a telluric flavor similar to Aguilera Malta's first works about the native *cholo*, the content and structure are more complex, more universal in significance.

Lust for blood, sex, and money—the stuff that maintains Satan's hold on Everyman—is the motivating force of the characters who are threatened by spiritual or physical death. Salvation is interpreted in rhythmic, onomatopoeic lyricism, earthy dialogue, and stream-of-consciousness technique molded into an admixture of African, Indian, and Christian myths. Heroes and anti-heroes are surrealistically and expressionistically presented according to their vices or passions, and zoomorphic typology is frequent: a caymanesque Candelario Mariscal sows homicide and rape along a marine and terrestrial course toward perdition; Crisóstomo Chalena, self-consuming and batrachian, makes a pact with Lucifer for money; and the flowering Dominga sallies forth each night to perform the somnambulant ritual of burying the serpent that threatens her virginity.

The characters of *Seven Moons and Seven Serpents* are vibrantly human, including the spiritual or preternatural advisers whose role it is to aid the afflicted. The two priests, Cándido and Gaudencio, must relearn the principles of humility and mercy, and the black medicine man Bulu-Bulu, working to "exorcise" Candelario, decides marriage to his daughter Dominga would be the best cure. Perhaps the most human participant is the Burned Christ (who needs to be "saved" himself when the church is set afire), for he refuses to perform any miracle beyond that of chatting with Cándido and occasionally descending from his cross.

Clementine Rabassa. BA. 45, Spring, 1971, p. 285

AGUSTÍN, JOSÉ (1944–   )

MEXICO

Pretending that I Dream is a "drama in four acts" comprised of six stories and a bit of prose. The first act is "It is a Fact that She Lived in France," which consists of statements of Julie Christie's converted into a fine example of stream of consciousness, which integrates the personality of the actress in a short story a bit beyond what would be possible in the best news report. This is what makes us have a keen feeling for the young, emancipated, confused, amorous, and adorable English girl. . . . The typography emphasizes, dilutes, and separates themes. . . .

After the intermission, there is the prose "How Did Your Eye Turn Out (Dear Gervasio)," which is a pathetic, incisive, and comical sketch; then there follow two short stories whose common denominator is a profound and rigorous moral attitude. "Closed" is about a strange triangle. It is a sordid and terrifying story. . . . The three characters end up playing cards, as in the film *Viridiana*. . . . "Mourning" is not less terrifying but somewhat less sordid. Here the device of telling what someone told is handled with virtuosity. . . . The third act, "What Is Going On?," was written, according to Agustín himself, to get rid of games and obsessive jokes. The game almost becomes separated from the text, gratuitous and therefore boring. But unlike someone like Cabrera Infante (one of his epigraphs is included), Agustín knows how to play: he is not an exhibitionist but a sincere experimentor. . . .

This is one of the most important, unsettling, mature, and ambitious works of recent years.

Juan Tovar. *RBA*. No. 22, July–Aug., 1968, pp. 59–60†

"I Can't Get No Satisfaction." The song by the Rolling Stones serves as an epigraph for José Agustín's *Pretending that I Dream* and at the same time offers the best and most conclusive criticism of the seven stories that make up the book. The title of the book, its front cover . . . and the table of contents seem to indicate that the reader is on the point of embarking on a "magical and fantastic trip." Actually, the key lies on the back cover—an action shot of José Agustín with an Arriflex in hand. The medium is the message. *Pretending that I Dream* is a game of cinematic-narrative techniques: zoom in, pull back, tilt up, slow pan to a medium shot to photograph the surrounding reality, the world of young people of the capital. The objective, impersonal, and at times playful camera—the author stops the action, comments on it, winks his eye at the reader, and continues filming—tenaciously pursues the characters to the point of revealing to us their inner drama, surprising them during moments in which they pretend to be dreaming. They dream about action without being able to attain it. . . .

In a decade in which Latin American writers—Cortázar, Fuentes, Lezama Lima, García Márquez, Sarduy—have gone forth in search of new forms and structures, José Agustín's attempt deserves our admiration, although the experimentation in *Pretending that I Dream* accomplishes more in intention than in substance.

Francisco Pabón. *RBA*. No. 22, July–Aug., 1968, pp. 60–61†

Precocious and by nature somewhat brash, José Agustín might be called the "enfant terrible" of contemporary Mexican letters. If any two of the [young Mexican novelists] were to be compared for the similarities in their works, they would undoubtedly be José Agustín and Gustavo Sainz, principally for their treatment of post World War II youth and for their exposure of what they consider outmoded, hypocritical conventions and attitudes. Still there are marked differences between the two. Whereas Sainz portrays a limited segment of the lower middle class, José Agustín's characters encompass a wide range of social strata —from upper middle to the working classes. Moreover, although Sainz reveals occasional flashes of humor, José Agustín is infinitely funnier, more satirical and spontaneous, and less preoccupied with structure.

[Agustín's] first novel, *The Tomb*, describes in lineal form the dissolute lives led by a group of wealthy Mexican juveniles whose conduct derives at least in part from their debauched parents. In contrast to the pessimistic tone of *The Tomb*, his second novel, *From the Side*, seems amusing and gay, although tinged with malice and cynicism. This work portrays the family life of the teen-age narrator as well as his drinking bouts, sexual exploits, street fights, pseudo-intellectual bull sessions and his hilarious initiation into politics at the "preparatoria." Like [Sainz's] *Gazapo, From the Side* depicts the confused psychic world of juveniles with its intricate melange of reality and imagination woven into its complex temporal realm. José Agustín's novel, again like Sainz's, illustrates the gulf between adults and rebellious youths who, having rejected the obsolete code of ethics and conformity of their elders, seek new ideals and modes of behavior.

José Agustín has been severely criticized, with some justification, for his excessive use of slang and obscene language. Nevertheless, his original and dynamic presentation of what might be termed "the universal youth crisis of the 1960's" makes *From the Side* the best Mexican novel of 1966.

George R. McMurray. *Hispania.* 51, Sept., 1968,
pp. 534–35

Among the critical commentaries that greeted the publication of José Agustín's second novel, *From the Side*, in 1966, there was one, by Fausto Castillo, whose title, "At Last Someone Who Laughs . . .," indicates Agustín's characteristic that most attracts our attention. I realize the possible injustice in stressing joking in novels as serious as are those of this young writer. Nevertheless, humor is so rare a quality in the Mexican novel that it turns out to be more attractive than the other elements, elements that evoke Joyce's *Ulysses*. That some readers are reminded of Joyce probably arises from the novel's pseudoautobio-graphical effects, from its linguistic innovations, and from its scandalous elements (pornography or realism, depending on the point of view of each reader).

Approaching the laughter more profoundly, one can observe that it arises from the author's point of view, or, more precisely, from his manner of seeing reality (visible objects and people and also their visi-ble way of getting tangled). In the introduction to José Agustín's auto-biography [*José Agustín (Autobiography)*] Emmanuel Carballo speaks of "his very personal way of looking at men and things, in which tender-ness and coolness, love and hate, humor and hostility, become inter-mingled. . . ." Carballo recognized Agustín's individuality from the very beginning. He had seen it in *The Tomb*, the writer's brief first novel, published in 1964 when he was only twenty years old. This book did not have a large readership until its second edition, published after *From the Side*. The second novel is more comprehensive and polished.

Because of his great capacity to reproduce, with absolute accuracy, the speech and attitudes of individuals (and it is important to note that they are individuals) who belong to various social classes, the novelist has demonstrated that his work is something more than mere autobiog-raphy.

John S. Brushwood. *Et caetera*. 2nd series, No. 14,
March–April, 1969, pp. 7–8†

Abolition of Property, which is difficult to classify according to standard literary genres, belies one characteristic of contemporary Mexican fic-tion in general: constant experimentation to arrive at an appropriate if not always original expression. The very structure of this latest book is indicative of such experimentation. The work is neither novel nor drama, nor exactly TV or movie script. It is obvious, however, that the author had in mind a script for performance when he wrote *Abolition of Property*. Through the dialogue of two young people, Everio and Norma, Agustín presents the conflict of two generations (one of his favorite themes). The entire dialogue is anticipated by tape recordings and movie projections which give the work a quality of unreality. Norma, a student of political science and the younger of the two, is caught up in every new ideology which bucks the establishment. Everio, the opposite, a white-collar worker, once married, who considers him-self the more mature of the two, is the more passive in accepting the status quo. The point Agustín seems to be making through the conflict between Everio and Norma is that today's youth, moving in a real yet unreal world, is attempting to identify itself, to find understanding, not only of itself but of the world in which it is caught. The contemporary aspect of this universal problem is accentuated by mention of present-day ills such as the Vietnam war and Mexican *machismo* (an exaggerated sense of masculinity), the use of pop songs, and the general structure of the work which suggests a type of psychedelic short movie.

The language in *Abolition of Property* is milder and more correct by comparison with earlier works of Agustín. The author has been criticized for excessive use of slang and obscene language, both of which he considers indispensable in his treatment of contemporary youth, their problems and conflicts. Considering his age and the fact that José Agustín is a writer of much talent and promise, many such criticisms can be overlooked in these formative works.

Fred M. Clark. BA. 44, Spring, 1970, p. 274

By the time [Agustín] was twenty-two years old he had published his first two novels and his autobiography, had been twice married, and had received a scholarship from the Centro Mexicano de Escritores. Brash and outgoing by nature, he has more than once been referred to as "L'enfant terrible" of present-day Mexican letters. Along with his running mate and mentor of sorts, Gustavo Sainz (four years his senior), he has spearheaded the youngest crop of Mexican writers, which is sizeable, serious, talented, and articulate—to say nothing of unabashed. Of the whole group, José Agustín is the one who has produced the most and at this point shows the most likelihood of maturing into a first-rate writer. . . .

Cut generally from the same cloth as *The Tomb* [his first novel, *From the Side*] is considerably longer, more mature and ambitious, and it puts the author's sense of humor delightfully on display. *From the Side* also has more front-line characters and explores a wider range of the narrator's existence (family life with his parents and younger brother, the goings-on at school, and philosophical discussions with his friends). Despite the fact it is in part satire and that its viewpoint is anything but impartial, this novel possesses a documental essence. It is, to use the Spanish word, highly *testimonial*. And despite too its excessive fondness for the colloquial speech of the teen-agers and its disdain for proper grammar and syntax, *From the Side* is fresh enough and dynamic enough to make one serious critic label it the best Mexican novel of 1966. On the other hand, Juan Rulfo passed a more restrained and sobering judgment of this young novelist. After naming José Agustín first among a few young fiction writers that he felt showed promise, Rulfo went on to say: "He has great talent, although it still is not reflected in his work." Continuing, he said that these youngsters are still producing "adolescent literature for adolescents and I think they cannot go on with that literature forever."

Walter M. Langford. *The Mexican Novel Comes of Age*
(Notre Dame, University of Notre Dame Press, 1971),
pp. 200–202

[*The Tomb*], as well as *From the Side* by the same author, and *Gazapo* by Sainz, deal with life among adolescents in Mexico City. Both writers are representative of this movement [called "La Onda"], which is characterized by an informal attitude, by the use of the language of the adolescents, by the interest in popular forms of expression, such as rock and roll music, and by an attitude of disdain towards the culture of those over thirty-five. They write a type of narrative that rejects and denounces the established way of life. . . .

In his third book, *Pretending that I Dream*, José Agustín experiments with form; the six stories are united in a dramatic structure; six acts, the first and the last separated by an interlude and a promenade. The last act, "Game of Points of View," has the form of a television script, with a list of characters, technical instructions, and even canned applause. In this last act the author foreshadows the structure of his next novel, *Abolition of Property*, in which we find, besides the dramatic form, two worlds, the world of the two principal characters, and the world reproduced by the machines, in this case the tape recorder, the movie projectors, the slides, the closed circuit, and the monitors. The protagonists are two; a man and a woman. Norma, who is the narrator and reveals to us her states of consciousness, is a free-thinking liberated woman who denies history, laws, and all types of norms. Everio, on the other hand, is a young man who accepts the rules of life, who believes that progress depends on those rules. The ironic thing is that Norma accepts the possibility of the existence of other worlds, of other realities, while Everio rejects them. This short novel represents Agustín's greatest effort in the art of fiction. In it he has given expression with accuracy to the mechanized world in which we live.

Luis Leal. In Harvey L. Johnson and
Philip B. Taylor, Jr., eds., *Contemporary Latin
American Literature* (Houston, University of Houston,
Office of International Affairs, 1973), pp. 42–43

AGUSTINI, DELMIRA (1886–1914)

URUGUAY

Critics are haunted by the need to find traces of influences in literary works, and the need has caused some to find in Delmira's poetry influences of Darío, D'Annunzio, Baudelaire, and Poe. Should I affirm it or deny it? It may be that she read them and that she slept with their books beneath her pillow. But I suspect that if this were so, she was nonetheless inspired first by an intellectual fervor and then by a physical fervor toward those men who moved her sensitivities and whom she undoubtedly wanted to encounter along the way, encounter them really, in the flesh. In any case, if they in part nurtured the deep roots of her inspiration, it is difficult to recognize the contribution of each one, for a genius knows how to incorporate all sources without showing them.

Of course, it is true that Delmira followed the dominant tastes of her age . . . and she could be classified with the decadents. But she was no slave to line or rhythm, nor did she trap her verses in the bonds of meter. . . . When she attempted to find her own door to passion, fearful that all would be lost, she found a violent escape, like any unprincipled girl, through the window. And she did not find her escape from the tower down medieval stairways or drawbridges, or even in secret; she fled wildly out into the open, shouting aloud, demanding from life what she had expected of it. Drunk with herself—"I am a bacchante, I am a bacchante"—she ran yelling down the road and then brought it all to her poetry. She was as sincere in the way she lived as in the way she wrote. Her "originalities" scandalized the Uruguayan bourgeoisie to which Delmira belonged, and that bourgeoisie looked askance at her. So much the better for her: she ceased to have anything to do with dull people. She limited her daily life to her family circle and gained enough time and space to develop her mind.

E. Labarca. *Atenea*. No. 110, Aug., 1934, pp. 314–15†

The truth about [Agustini] herself, the deepest reality of her being, is love, which is also the reality of the universe and of men—poets, philosophers—who have arrived at this idea by a process of exaltation, idealization and depuration of its physical, corruptible and perishable elements. But in the poetry of this young woman love is an exclusive and all-absorbing emotion which leaves room for no other, or which is the reason-for-being of all the rest. It appears in her in a spontaneous manner, as a product of her organic physiology. And she never feels ashamed of it, nor sees it as different from her highest spiritual aspirations. Body and soul are an absolute identity in her poetry. The modern poets, notably Rubén Darío, have also looked for the unity of the antithetical aspects of love: the physical and spiritual; but the peculiar thing about Delmira is that for her there is no such antithesis, for both are one and the same thing. This affirmation of pure sexuality as the only reality, and its projection upon the universe, is the true character of the poetry of Delmira Agustini, which, we believe, represents a modality of spirit which is typically feminine.

Sidonia Carmen Rosenbaum. *Modern Women Poets of Spanish America* (New York, Hispanic Institute in the United States, 1945), p. 164

The unending appearance of the physical love theme makes one inclined to believe that Delmira had many lovers. But no poetry should ever be taken to mean that the author does everything that is mentioned or suggested. Outside of Manuel Ugarte, a witness at her wedding, with whom she was reported to have been in love, there is no other name linked with hers prior to marriage. Just as Sor Juana Inés de la Cruz wrote great love sonnets in the seventeenth century without a lover, so also Delmira Agustini wrote violent and sensual love poetry of the postmodernist period without actual experiences. Of the two kinds of experience, actual and imaginary, the imaginary was always more real to Delmira.

Delmira lighted the torch for present-day feminine poetry. Almost immediately in rapid succession appeared Gabriela Mistral, Alfonsina Storni, and Juana de Ibarbourou. The veneration they all felt for Delmira and the debt they owed her is expressed by Juana de Ibarbourou . . . "Delmira Agustini is the secular saint of Latin women who write poetry." . . .

Death very frequently enters the poems of Delmira. She speaks of death with calm naturalness, even familiarity—and at times with eagerness, as of something for which she is yearning. . . . The feeling of fear and awe which pervades most people when speaking of death is totally absent in her. Death may well have been that last road over which she chose to travel in her intense pining for the transcendental, superhuman love for which she was constantly yearning.

Madeleine Simonet. *Hispania.* 39, Dec., 1956, pp. 400, 402

The renovation that the women poets brought to modernism included the appearance of themes that had not yet been developed in [Latin]

American poetry. Not only are personal, romantic feelings exalted; the women poets bare their souls and embrace as frequent themes over-whelming passion, disenchantment, the unrealized life. . . .

Delmira Agustini was one of the most representative figures of this period, which I, echoing Federico de Onís, would label post modern-ism. If we examine [four traditional poetic subjects—God, nature, love, death] in the poetry of Agustini, we will note that she does not develop the theme of God, perhaps because of her secular cultural background. And nature does not attract this poet. When she does describe it, she describes not real nature but rather a nature that belongs more to the realm of visions, raptures, or ecstasies, one which, in any case, has no correspondence with surrounding reality. This fact can be explained by her naturally introverted nature.

On the other hand, love and death, above all love, are frequent themes. Love . . . is her dominant theme, the lyrical expression of a sex-ual pantheism. For Delmira Agustini, the poem is nothing more than an obligatory form, an inevitable ordering, given her necessity to con-template her own feelings. She seeks after lyrical expression because it is the form that best lends itself to that exaltation which is most private, individual, and feminine—Agustini herself. To this extent, the short lyrical form, which reveals the significant details briefly, which con-denses the emotion in them, is the genre most suitable to the presenta-tion of erotic themes.

Roberto Bonada Amigo. *Delmira Agustini en la
vida y en la poesía* (Montevideo, Librería Técnica, 1964),
pp. 53–54†

Delmira Agustini has been presented as a creature tortured since child-hood by visions that dragged her toward the chasms of her dreams, wresting her from her own human reality, cutting her loose from her physical surroundings in order to lead her through an oneiric and erotic jungle, transforming her into a somnambulent lover capable, through the strength of her intuition, of singing about what she should not have known about because of her lack of experience. There has also been the desire, especially among those who would make of her a myth and keep her safe from more revealing conclusions, to present Delmira in a symbolic perspective that could change into mysticism what at a first glance appears to be eroticism.

Either of these two versions, if taken literally, goes beyond Delmira's own limits. It is very difficult, in any case, to believe in either of these versions after having read her surprising poem "The Swan," which documents a sick, obsessed sensibility rather than a metaphysical or mystical attitude. Because the swan of the poem is not, as in the myth of Leda, the transformation that the lover is subjected to in order to reach her, but a simple device Delmira's imagination uses to give free rein to her eroticism. . . .

Angelina Gatell. *CHA*. No. 174, June, 1964,
pp. 584–85†

How inaccurate is the perspective of one who would look only at the texture of form [in Agustini's poetry] in order to attempt to grasp it in its profundity! Her forms are generally uneven, at times defective. There are words, entire verses, that at first seem to be in bad taste. . . . But it turns out—and this is disconcerting—that these false verses, these worn words, do not at all compromise the authentic poetry that passes like a powerful and perfectly discernible current through them. . . . We are dealing with a literary work, constructed therefore with words and with all the complexity of sound. And we find meaning in these very words, a meaning we can grasp, although in a confused way. We sense also that the primordial and decisive meaning of the poem, that something which leaves one trembling, does without those very words, even without those that, in context, are removed from what we understand as conventional language.

Amanda Berenguer. *Alcor*. No. 31, July–Aug.,
1964, p. 2a†

[Agustini's] intellectual—we could say philosophical—intuition . . . became apparent, in the introspective mystery of her solitude, when, shut up in her room, "La Nena" [the little girl] transformed herself into a poet, like the chrysalis into a butterfly—but one that became a chrysalis again the next day, when it came into contact again with real life, with the daily reality of a middle-class young lady and a spoiled child. This distinctly poetic intuition, which she expressed exclusively in a language of images, symbols, allegories, and dreams, became intensi- fied in the poems in her second book [*Morning Songs*], written between 1907 and 1910. She overcame a certain literary ingenuousness present in her first book [*The White Book*], and she descended, so to speak, from the platonic region in which she moved to a consciousness of carnal reality now quite a bit more painful, and at times more somber. She was evolving toward her third book [*The Empty Chalices*], in which we find originality and the brilliant fusion of sexuality with thought, of the physical side of the erotic with the abstract side of the conceit. But she achieved this without losing her purely poetic nature and language. On the contrary, she increased her powers of vision and symbol, which is, as has been recognized, what makes the erotic poetry of Delmira both unique and valuable, different from all other examples of erotic poetry: its transcendence, its sense of the beyond.

And all of this occurred without her ever ceasing to be, on the exterior, in her daily life, the young middle-class lady and the spoiled child who wrote idiotic letters and in whose "favorite, homey little nook" (as her own family put it) she played mother to that doll that we have seen [in a picture]: blonde, dressed in baby-blue satin, with its porcelain smile, looking like Delmira herself.

Clara Silva. *Genio y figura de Delmira Agustini*
(Buenos Aires, Editorial Universitaria de
Buenos Aires, 1968), p. 32†

ALEGRÍA, CIRO (1909–1967)

PERU

[*The Golden Serpent*], by the author of the prize-winning *Broad and Alien Is the World*, is a slighter, more poetic, gayer work. *Broad and Alien Is the World* was a social novel of the Peruvian highland, its protagonist an Indian village destroyed by avarice backed by governmental force. *The Golden Serpent* (originally written in 1935) is a collective novel, too, with the protagonist once more a village. But the villagers are the sunny, laughter-loving cholos (half breeds) of the exuberant lowlands, where life is easy except when the river is wild. The evil is not the evil done by man to man, unnecessary and therefore vile, but the evil done by almighty nature to man, inevitable and therefore morally indifferent. The songs in this book are sunny, ribald and defiant songs, and the people are garrulous and gay. Human injustice is a far-off rumored thing that only occasionally descends upon the valley, and then the whole valley unites to ward it off. The jungle, too, puts up defenses for the valley folk. When an engineer comes from Lima thinking he can tame this wild and luxuriant river with map and compass and prospector's kit and bonds and shares, the river mocks him, the cliff claims his horse, the rains rust his equipment, he learns to chew cocoa leaves and half absorbs the native superstitions and beliefs.

Several tales are filled with the excitement of a raft on the treacherous river, a feeble little structure poised above roaring waters and jagged rocks, on it, kneeling as if in adoration, a man of the Marañón staking his life as on the toss of a coin. Other stories deal with the men who cross the river at Calemar, state troopers hunting for victims that, of course, no villager has seen, highland Indians who come down for cocoa, red pepper, bananas and, though they go right back, get chills and fevers and terrible running sores and shiver like dogs in the wind or die far from home. But most are tales of joy and laughter. . . . Many deal with fiesta time and the folklore of the valley, like the one about the magical blue puma who turns out to be a wild cat of common flesh and blood or the priest who came for the annual marryings and masses for the dead but, joining too heartily in the festivities, drank up all the sacramental wine and was run out of town.

The translation by Harriet de Onís is admirable, catching all the subtle overtones of poetry and humor and making us forget that we are dealing with an alien tongue.

Bertram D. Wolfe. NYHT. Dec. 12, 1943, p. 4

In this century a group of Latin American novelists has arisen that is preoccupied with both private and social problems. In the preceding century the Latin American writers who dealt with social problems did so in a picturesque or touristic manner. But this generation has moved into the problems; it attempts to live them. Despite his relative youth (he was born in 1909), the best representative of this group is Ciro Alegría, *the* novelist of Peru. In his three novels communal and private emotions . . . surge forth, and the novelist suffers, attempting at each step to find solutions for the problems he raises.

Although Alegría was born in Peru and lived there until he was twenty-five, his three novels were written in exile in Chile, where he emigrated for political reasons. His first novel, *The Golden Serpent*, was created by expanding one of his stories, "The Balsa," which he had sent to a Buenos Aires newspaper for which he was a stringer at fifty pesos a month. But the story was quite long and was not published. This rejection made him decide to convert the story into a novel of 120 pages, first called *Marañón*, which was also rejected by two publishers. Finally, he found out about the inauguration of the contest Consurso Nascimento and decided to submit a work. Because a minimum of 200 pages was necessary, he expanded the original *Marañón*, and the novel won the first prize under its new name, *The Golden Serpent*.

This novel is addressed to the river Marañón itself, seen as winding and unwinding from above, giving the appearance of a great serpent, called golden for its live-giving powers. . . . The novel is a series of interesting episodes revolving around the daily struggle for existence by the people who live on the banks of the Marañón River. Some of these episodes are light and colorful, for example, the one in which Arturo, the man of the river, makes love to the beautiful Lucinda. Others are pathetic and sad, such as the one about the *utosos* [people suffering from uta, a disease like leprosy; also used metaphorically]. Others are full of violent emotion: in one, two brothers of the river attempt to shoot the rapids during a flood and are trapped by the whirlpools and the currents until their balsa is caught on a protruding rock, where they must spend several days. . . .

The people who live on the banks of the Marañón never try to fathom its deep mysteries; they accept them as they are, even though the river keeps them in constant terror. . . . Although the people may curse the river at times, they never leave it, because they have learned to take life as it is. Their life is the river; it is like their own blood, and they must respect it. . . .

Faye L. Bumpass. IPNA. No. 14, Jan.–June, 1950,
pp. 44–45†

Broad and Alien Is the World is an epic portrayal of the Andean Indians of northern Peru. As the story unfolds, this hitherto little known people emerges *in toto*, as a massive sculpture slowly takes shape out of a block of granite under the artist's hands. This graphic, collective representation is vivid and poignant, and readers all over the world have been captivated by the Indians' simple, industrious way of life and their ideally democratic government. Whether or not their model community will be destroyed by Don Alvaro Almenábar, through the connivance or indifference of the rulers of the land, forms the suspense in the plot of *Broad and Alien Is the World*, which can be as readily classified among the novels of social protest as among those of local custom. There is a yet deeper note of protest in this book, sounded in Chapter Twenty, in which Demetrio Sumallacta meets the three *futres* [dandies]. That the significance of the chapter has not always been fully understood is shown, for example, in the fact that the English translation does not include this chapter. Demetrio is certainly one of the most important characters in *Broad and Alien Is the World*—not in his actual participation in the Rumi plot but in the aggregate portrait of these Indians as a people. . . .

In delineating the personality of Demetrio Sumallacta—with his perceptive appreciation of music, art, and poetry—Alegría has created a unique figure among the Indians in fiction. The indigenous peoples of America have often been depicted as susceptible to musical stimuli; an unforgettable example is the scene in [Azuela's] *The Underdogs* in which Demetrio Macías, the rough leader, has to turn his face away so that no one sees the tears in his eyes after listening to Valderrama sing. But generally *indianista* literature has limited itself to showing that the Indian is human, whereas his oppressors think of him as an animal. *Broad and Alien Is the World* contains this message, but it goes further.

In showing the artistic and intellectual faculties of the untutored flutist, Alegría points to a double abuse; not only do the Almenábars of America exploit the Indians and deprive them of their inalienable social rights; in addition, through their intransigent arrogance they commit an equally grave injustice in relegating the Demetrios to an inferior position and suppressing a personality so vital to society—the artist. These overlords allow native talent to go unrecognized, whereas they should have seen it as their duty to promote and develop the Indians' potential aesthetic contribution. Because of their greed and indifference, a rich source of artistic values and creativity has remained unknown and untapped, to the impoverishment of culture in the nation and in the world.

This is the distinctive mark of Ciro Alegría's protest, and it makes *Broad and Alien Is the World* the culmination of all that has been achieved by the novels written to vindicate the Indians and to indict their oppressors.

Richard J. Callan. Hispania. 45, Sept., 1962,
pp. 419, 421†

Ciro Alegría is one of the younger of that gifted group of novelists Latin America began to produce in the nineteen-twenties, which includes writers like Ricardo Güiraldes of Argentina, Rómulo Gallegos of Venezuela, José Eustasio Rivera of Colombia, José Lins do Rêgo and Jorge Amado of Brazil, and so many others. Their artistic purpose was to discover and give expression to the reality of their own land and people. This world of the Marañón is one Alegría knows as intimately as do the boatmen of whom he tells. . . . "I have never forgotten the life I lived there," he writes, "nor my experiences traveling the thin-aired trails of the uplands, the suffering I saw, the tales I heard. My first teachers were my parents, but the people of all Peru finally molded me in their own likeness, and made me understand their sorrows, their joys, their great and overlooked gifts of intelligence and fortitude, their creative ability, their capacity for endurance." . . .

Alegría is too great a writer to make his protest against the injustice and neglect under which so many of his countrymen live mere social tracts whose value is circumscribed to a moment in history. Like one of his literary progenitors, the Inca Garcilaso de la Vega . . . Alegría's books will stand as a vision of and tribute to the courage, endurance, and rectitude of his countrymen when the circumstances which elicited his protest have disappeared. He has created a world peopled by beings teeming with life, with their sorrows and joys, their aspirations and defeats, and all suffused with that poetry which comes from emotion recalled in tranquillity.

And when progress has spanned the turbulent Marañón with bridges, has dammed and channeled its treacherous waters, and the boatmen of Calemar have disappeared, their work done, *The Golden Serpent* will remain as a monument to the days when it ran free and bold, tamed only by brave men.

Harriet de Onís. Afterword to Ciro Alegría,
The Golden Serpent (New York, New American
Library, 1963), pp. 187–90

In Latin America ever since 1920 there has been a very strong trend known, generically, as the *corriente indigenista*, or Indianist movement. In addition to its political cast, Indianism includes artistic expression in painting, sculpture, and literature, but especially in the novel. Taking the human problems of the Indian as its main theme, among the difficulties that face the Indian it has emphasized the theme of the land. . . .

In *The Golden Serpent*, his first book, Alegría rejected the simplification of the traditional Indianist novel. As a result, there is not sufficient contrast between the "good men" (the Indians) and the "bad men" (the great proprietors), and he refrained from using landscape merely as setting. In contrast, the plot focuses upon a type of man—the man of the Eastern valleys, a region distinct from both the coast and the Andean zone; and in developing the story he makes use of events in contrasting the psychological make-up and the material situation of his character, the *balsero* (raftman), with the equivalent aspects of the Westernized man from the capital and with the Andean dweller. . . .

There are two factors that the author will develop in the rest of his work with notable mastery. One is the image of the small and personal world in which man struggles with the natural forces, comes to know himself, and finally imposes his human standards upon it. The other is a decisive portrait of a kind of man who is not the Indian of the traditional versions; who is instead anthropologically identified as a *cholo*, an acculturated person whose native language is Spanish, although it is spoken with a strongly regional accent and reveals the influence of Quechua. Both factors, strongly developed, operate actively in the novel; they sustain the positive, optimistic tone that flows from living and building unceasingly, and demand that the reader respond not with pity but with admiration.

In this understanding originates the literary process that culminates in *Broad and Alien Is the World*, where it is expressed with sympathy and comprehension. The author's works form a cycle; each of his later books is, in a certain fashion, implicit in its predecessors, and the vision the whole presents is formed of elements mentioned or implied earlier.

The guiding principles, the play of composition, the lights or shadows on people and actions, the narrative technique, the bringing together of the experiences of a great many observers, have been tried, polished and decanted in *The Golden Serpent* and *The Hungry Dogs* before taking their place in the epic mural of *Broad and Alien Is the World.*

Therefore, if *The Hungry Dogs* is judged as an isolated work, it could be thought of as a less forceful book. Nevertheless, its relation to *The Golden Serpent* demonstrates the extent of the creative effort that renews man's struggle with nature, seen in terms of Indian animism, and links this theme with the oppression exercised by certain social institutions. It deals with the battle against drought and its impact on the farmer's means of subsistence which finally upsets his vital equation. What was incidental in *The Golden Serpent* (the relation with the police, military service, the clashes with the mestizos who seize property and control the countryside from the villages) is more sharply outlined in *The Hungry Dogs*, since all the dramatic tension and internal dynamics of the work are based on examining both factors, comparing them, inclusively, in terms of their transitory nature.

Alberto Escobar. *Américas.* 15, 2, Feb., 1963, pp. 7–9

If we were to place Ciro Alegría's novels into a scheme of concentric [thematic] circles, the first circle would frame the telluric or anthropological matter; the second, the social, economic, and legal issues; the third, the ontological, metaphysical superstructure.

The key to the first circle lies in the laconic definition of a character in *The Golden Serpent*, which brings together river, jungle, and Andean mountain into one telluric unity that Peruvian man challenges, suffers, and overcomes. Alegría's characters reveal the dimension of their grandeur by fighting intensely against the adverse forces of nature, be they the fury of the River Marañón in *The Golden Serpent*, the drought in *The Hungry Dogs*, or the barren and rocky land on which the commune members are cast after being dispossessed of Rumi in *Broad and Alien Is the World*. The struggle against nature, against the telluric, clarifies and defines them. Struggle as a vital decision is their sign and their essence. The man of the interior is placed in a hostile natural setting, and his existence and survival are linked to his decision to fight, to his rebellion against what nature imposes upon him or what is superimposed by the actions of men.

The second circle of Alegría's work is socioeconomic conflict. We see the annihilation of a form of communal agrarian property whose origins reach back in time to the Inca ayllus. This annihilation put in relief the continuity of organized injustice against the indigenous peasant, initiated during the Spanish domination.

The third circle transcends purely national issues and places the drama of the indigenous peasant within the context of the human condition as a whole. The Indian is a fallen being, whose authentic existence is rendered impossible. He needs a myth which could effect a total integration within a higher order, which could make possible an authentic existence for him, which could redeem him from the condition of "having been cast forth into the world," to borrow Heidegger's terms.

Mario Castro Arenas. La novela peruana y la
evolución social (Lima?, Ediciones: Cultura y
Libertad, 1964?), pp. 233–34†

Perhaps *The Hungry Dogs* is the best of Alegría's novels. It is a novel of the puna—the high range—as his previous work [*The Golden Serpent*] was of the trans-Andean valley. The appropriateness of its fictional details, its controlled tenderness, its treatment of the problem of the land from both a poetic and a realistic point of view make this work one of the most vivid examples of typical indigenist fiction. There are no proclamations; it is a story of realities. But it is told with emotion and imagination in the service of literature. . . . The Vergilian opening, with shepherds and their flocks . . . changes into tragedy, with the pitiless drought that parches men and beasts. The life of the man of the puna, attached to his hut, his small parcel of land, and his cattle, moves toward a violent climax. The four sheepdogs whose lives are traced throughout the novel parallel their owner's conflicts. . . .

Along with the drought there are other problems—highway construction, military conscription, the nearby landowner who tramples the rights of the Indians—all dominated by a feeling for the land, which molds the character of the native protagonists of this transcendental event of the drought, which destroys their routine existence. Pathos is always at the side of drama, seen in the death of the child and in the novel's female figures, in whom we see maternity, conjugal love, quiet and submissive daughterhood, and the awakening of instinct. Arturo del Hoyo has said of *The Hungry Dogs*: "It gives the impression of a total maturity and artistic perfection." As in *The Golden Serpent*, the narrative is based on diverse episodes that make up something like isolated stories linked together by a finely executed framework. [1965]

Augusto Tamayo Vargas. Literatura peruana
(Lima, Universidad Nacional Mayor de San Marcos,
1967), pp. 1102–3†

Few elements or devices in *Broad and Alien Is the World* reveal so much about the nature of the Indians as their relationship to animals. . . . Animals are not employed by Alegría merely as an embellishment, as an element haphazardly thrown into the novel, but are integral to characterization, setting, and style. . . .

The Indian as portrayed by Alegría is a simple person who feels deeply the ties that unite him to his home and the nature that surrounds him. This picture is derived not so much from descriptions of his actions or scenes of his relationships with his family and friends as from knowledge of how he feels about his animals. . . . The Indians' deep sorrow that accompanies loss of their animals and their respect for the good qualities these friends possess are explicit. . . . Implied also are the Indians' sentiments toward their human friends. Because Alegría leads us to this understanding indirectly, through the use of animals, we are given a knowledge not only of the sentiments themselves but also of the Indians' reticence in expressing them overtly. We recognize that these people hold their strong feelings within themselves, reluctant to manifest them directly.

The Indians' concept of time is, as one might expect, dependent upon natural phenomena. Here again the animal is indispensable. When a new day appears, it is never introduced with a statement such as "It is six o'clock," but usually by mentioning that the cocks are crowing and the birds are singing, and one soon realizes the irrelevance of clock-time to these people. They live their days as they are defined by nature, not by clocks. . . .

Since the Indian's existence is a simple one, there is little to distinguish him from the other animals of the earth. Naturally he is close to these creatures with whom he has so much in common, and much of the quality of his life is captured and expressed in his relationship to them. Aware of this relationship, Alegría has carefully exploited it as a means of character portrayal, and in so doing he has captured the essence of Indian life.

Valeria Endres. Hispania. 48, March, 1965, pp. 67–69

Perhaps the best way to begin our study of Alegría's use of the short story form is to recognize its presence within the general framework of his novels. On examining the unusual structures of these three prize-winning works, we find that it is possible to pick out a series of episodes which, though forming integral parts of the main narrative, could be considered and appreciated as stories in their own right. *The Golden Serpent*, for example, comprises nineteen chapters, each of which has its own unity. Naturally, these chapters, and for that matter all of the events of the novel, are linked together harmoniously so that they have an overall unity and interrelationship; nevertheless, considered individually, many of the episodes possess both the necessary independence, character development, and dramatic force to stand alone. . . .

The structure of *The Hungry Dogs* shows further interesting relationships between the short and long narrative forms. Intercalated at strategic points of the novel are five folktales told by two characters. Again, though the tales are specifically and skillfully designed to further the main action of the narrative, they could be extracted from its framework and read individually without loss of meaning.

Finally, *Broad and Alien Is the World*, which was inspired in part by one of the incidents in *The Hungry Dogs*, contains several portions which have the attributes of independent short narratives, particularly those episodes in the section following the destruction of the Indian community of Rumi. . . .

Alegría's regular short stories are neither numerous nor very well-known. For many years his stories remained unpublished or dispersed in anthologies and in the literary sections of Latin American newspapers. In fact, it was not until 1963, with the appearance of *Gentleman's Duel* that any of his stories became available in collected form. The collection is quite complete and has been highly acclaimed in Peru; but unfortunately, it was published in such a limited edition that it failed to attract much attention outside of the country. The majority of Alegría's short stories have a rural setting. . . . He has also written narratives with urban settings and with humble city dwellers as the main characters. Finally, his legendary tales, which he has especially adapted for children, can be considered as a separate category.

Alegría's profound understanding of his humble characters and their environment comes through as strongly in his short narratives as it does in his novels. This is particularly true in his stories of the sierra in which he studies the psychology of the Indians, capturing their beliefs, values, and special view of nature with a sensitivity not found in previous Indianist fiction. . . .

Earl M. Aldrich, Jr. *The Modern Short Story in Peru*
(Madison, University of Wisconsin Press, 1966),
pp. 117–19

[*Broad and Alien Is the World*] bids well to be the last as well as perhaps the best *indigenist* novel ever written. It is to be doubted that any present or future writer will improve on the sweeping panoramic view that Alegría presents in this narrative. The novel could have been called The Life and Death of a Peruvian Indian Community. That in essence is what it is. . . .

Alegría shows an amazing knowledge of the mind, soul, and emotions of the *Quechua* Indians of Peru. The *Quechuas* are in Peru what the Aztecs are in Mexico, only much more so. Whereas in Mexico the remaining Aztecs perhaps do not even approach a million souls, in

Peru the remaining Quechuas are perhaps in excess of five or six million individuals. . . .

Alegría describes the slow but inexorable erosion of the only cherished possession of the true sedentary Indians of the Americas, the land. For the North American Indian, it was the "hunting grounds," the vast acreage that constituted the ground over which the buffalo roamed, that was his "living space." . . . The Peruvian and Mexican civilized Indian had almost a European idea of land. It was a small area around the village where he was born, lived, and died without having travelled beyond its confines or, very seldom, to the next village or community. Land was held and tilled as a precious and communal possession. Maqui, the Indian elder of *Broad and Alien Is the World*, feels that both his wife and the land of the community are of the same ilk, and both are cherished and treated in like manner.

Alegría projects a time setting in the present century, although time has stopped for the Quechua after the Spanish conquest. The same conditions and human or inhuman relations that obtained in the 16th century after swineherd conqueror Francisco Pizarro conquered the empire of the Inca are the ones that operate today. . . .

The rather rapid and one-generation process of erosion of Rumi, the Indian community chronicled by Ciro Alegría, is presented in great detail. Each and every man, woman, and child is subjected to the effects of the despoiler's rapacity which culminates in a violent and armed takeover by the army sent to back the "just" claims of the man who has coveted the good lands of the Indians of Rumi.

José Vázquez Amaral. *The Contemporary Latin American Narrative* (New York, Las Américas, 1970), pp. 76–77, 79

Confined to a sanatorium where he was undergoing treatment for tuberculosis, and further burdened by other aches and pains that caused him amnesia, Alegría was paradoxically counseled by a doctor to write in order to regain control over his memory. And, in fact, by making associations to the barking of some dogs he heard in the night, Alegría found reborn in his mind . . . the memory of the dogs he had heard in his childhood and in his youth in and about the Peruvian farms. His imagination, thus enlivened, did the rest, and he proceeded to gather together the images of the mountain life of the men and animals—harried alike by every kind of hardship—the bits of earth that move, which fill the pages of *The Hungry Dogs*.

While writing this novel, he already had begun work on his next novel, his most outstanding and famous one. He had already written the title of one of its chapters, "Broad and Alien Is the World," and suddenly this sentence revealed to him a wealth of possibilities. He replaced his original title with this sentence, and, overwhelmed by a rush of ideas, his imagination began to give form to the conception of a new work whose uniqueness and transcendence were foreshadowed by the intuition of that sentence: *Broad and Alien Is the World*. By completing this work, he was shortly to create the capstone of his cyclical unified work and to ensure his position as a great novelist, who, by moving away from the limited area [of his earlier novels] to the farms in the outskirts of the Marañón, by fleshing out his world, was able to transmute his work into a totalizing, panoramic vision of the Peruvian people tied body and soul to their Andean lands.

Raimundo Lazo. *La novela andina, pasado y futuro*
(Mexico City, Editorial Porrúa, 1971), pp. 60–61†

AMADO, JORGE (1912–   )

BRAZIL

[*Cocoa* and *Sweat* were] published during 1934 by a brilliant young proletarian writer who is obviously animated by a distinctly revolutionary intention. . . . Both are powerful novels, of a kind that would doubtlessly be described by many readers as "revolting." In the prefatory note to his *Cocoa*, however, Sr. Amado frankly confesses that his aim is to write "with a minimum of literature and a maximum of honesty"; and he adds the query: "Is mine a proletarian novel?"

Cocoa deals with the life and the all but indescribable condition of the workers on the great cocoa plantations of northern Brazil, a subject with which the author possesses a first-hand acquaintance. The book is a grim one, but it is not as grim as *Sweat*, which is, by the way, a splendid example of the collective story in its pure form, being a depiction of life in a horrible tenement of Bahia, in which the tenement itself becomes in a manner the protagonist. In its collocation of horrors, this work is almost stylized.

Samuel Putnam. *BA*. 9, Spring, 1935, p. 166

A novelist since the age of nineteen, filled with the euphoria of public success, almost unanimously well-received and even eulogized in the course of his literary life, Jorge Amado has been quite careless about the artistic, literary, and technical details of his craft. He would seem to want to construct his works using only his immense talent as a storyteller, along with his ability to portray feeling and emotion. . . . But does

Amado want to construct only a work of folklore, or a personal work of literature? Does he want his instrument to be oral language, or the literary style of writers?

Even his best books, such as *Jubiabá* or *Lands without End*, leave serious doubts. They are uneven books, in which good and terrible material exists side by side. . . . He does what he wants to and succeeds efficiently when he is dealing with characters of primary feelings, instinctive and simple beings, when he describes men in their most direct and most immediate relationship with their environment. On the other hand, he falters and becomes confused, falling into the unreal, into the grossly artificial, when faced with complex beings, with feelings full of psychological nuance which demand analysis and accuracy.

His taste also strikes one as quite dubious. Not only does he lapse at times into bad taste, which happens even to writers of a more artistic bent; he also indicates that he is incapable of distinguishing bad taste from good taste. [1943]

Álvaro Lins. *Sagas literárias e teatro moderno do Brasil*
(Rio de Janeiro, Tecnoprint Gráfica, 1967), p. 42†

This young man is a born storyteller. He has no love or respect for grammar: he writes as he pleases. But how! His prose is fluent, picturesque, and expressive. A poet at heart, sometimes his pages are pure poetry. His stories are tinged with a manly kind of lyricism. His characters are generally rough folk, stevedores, fishermen, farmers, tramps, whores, bandits; and he has special liking for Negroes. His half a dozen excellent novels describe the life of these people. The slums of Bahia are pictured in *Sweat*, and the cocoa plantations in *Cocoa*. He tells a tale of fishermen in *Dead Sea*, and of abandoned street urchins in *Beached Captains*. His *Jubiabá* is the story of Baldo, the Negro, an ex-prize fighter, a tramp, a rhapsodist, and an ebony Casanova. It is a delightful book swept by the winds of adventure. Last year Amado published the saga of the cocoa plantations of his state, *Lands without End*, a panoramic novel full of pathos and drama. It is in my opinion one of the most daring and impressive novels ever published in Brazil. It is a barbaric parade of heroes and bandits, potentates and underdogs, whores and saints, common people and ghosts. The book is at the same time a prose poem, a folkloric tale, a crude story, a libel, and a work of art.

Érico Veríssimo. *Brazilian Literature: An Outline*
(New York, Macmillan, 1945), p. 154

The European as well as the Brazilian vogue of Amado has often been the result of political rather than literary qualities. He reacted violently to his times, and some of his books have been marred by extreme parti-sanship to the left. Nevertheless, he is a novelist, and an important one. Brazilian literature would be deprived of several impressive works should critics decide to rule out his writings as political. . . .

In plot construction, characterization, and other phases of novel-istic technique, the author's *parti pris* leads him to commit errors. In his effort to prove the thesis that the masses are unjustly exploited and should unite against their oppressors, Amado gives to his novels a broad sameness that permits the reader to predict with accuracy the final out-come of nearly any plot situation. Aside from *Carnival Land* and *Lands without End*, both of which are unrepresentative (one because of its weakness, the other because of its strength), the story pattern of the novels is generally that of *Cocoa*, in which the workers, after long enduring their economic servitude, are driven to collective action in a strike or some act of violence. . . .

The continual intervention of the author's political animus, the frequent homilies on class solidarity and the need for action, the fact that most of the novels end in a strike, all count against the reader's interest. . . .

In the works of this most controversial of modern Brazilian writers, unevenness is the salient characteristic. Amado seems to write solely by instinct. Of conscious art intellectually arrived at, the result of reflec-tion and high craftsmanship, there is relatively little. Yet his novels have a mysterious power to sweep the reader along. Serious defects in artistry are overcome by the novelist's ability to weave a story, to con-struct vivid scenes, and to create fascinating characters. "An incomplete and mutilated novelist," as Álvaro Lins has well characterized him, he offers the "spectacle of a great talent for creating fiction in contrast with enormous deficiencies as a writer and as an intellectual." Though his literary career now covers more than twenty years, Jorge Amado is barely forty years old. No writer holds out a greater promise, and his future works will be eagerly read by those who expect the promise, made manifest in *Lands without End* some day to be fulfilled.

Fred P. Ellison. *Brazil's New Novel* (Berkeley,
University of California Press, 1954),
pp. 83, 102, 104, 107–8

Occasionally Jorge Amado in *Lands without End* . . . searches beneath the exterior of his characters to reveal their inner thoughts and conflicts. There is one particularly powerful scene near the beginning of the novel describing the fears of Damião, a black *jagunço* [member of a fanatic revolutionary group], the most dreaded professional killer of the region. His carefree childlike nature has never before questioned the rightness or wrongness of killing, but has obeyed his master's command without hesitation or afterthought. Ordered to assassinate a small plantation owner who stands in the way of his master's desires, Damião begins for the first time to experience doubts. . . . Then he sees the kindly face of Dona Teresa, his intended victim's wife, white and tortured, her eyes fixed on him accusingly, her voice choked with fear, gasping the words of Sinho Badaró: "Do you enjoy killing people? Don't you feel anything inside?" In his hallucination he imagines her to be pregnant. He is terrified that he will cause her death and the child's too, for she will have a miscarriage and die of shock and grief when she learns of her husband's murder. The usually stolid *jagunço* works himself up to a high pitch of hysteria: completely unnerved now by his train of thought and by the dark forest screaming eerily round about him, tears streaming down "his black cheeks from the blue eyes of Dona Teresa," he shoots wildly, missing his mark.

Amado has disclosed with tremendous impact the tormenting fears and indecision which torture the naive and superstitious Damião. *Lands without End* would be a far better novel if Amado had treated his other characters with similar care, for in truth, many of them are little more than names on the page. Amado has also cluttered his tale in historical novel fashion with too many characters, with the result that few of them are memorable. . . .

With the exception of a few scenes like that describing Damião's inner strife, *Lands without End* does not measure up. . . . Its action is too unrestrained and its characters are for the most part unreal. But Amado does succeed in maintaining interest in his story. He has a gift for narration and his prose has an unquenchable vitality, an exuberance and extravagance that are in keeping with the Brazilian character. This is probably the reason for his great popularity and charm.

George D. Schade. Hispania. 39, May, 1956,
pp. 392, 394–95

Jorge Amado is, in a popular sense, the leading contemporary Brazilian novelist. Érico Veríssimo may sell as many books; João Guimarães Rosa is perhaps more profound and excitingly experimental. But Amado, a member of the Brazilian Academy of Letters, has achieved a worldwide reputation for his poetic realism, his leisurely, well-made verisimilitude, and his sociological implications. In *Gabriela, Clove and Cinnamon* he shows himself to be the Brazilian Balzac of the twentieth century.

The title of the novel is applicable to the heroine, to her performance in the kitchen and in bed. Gabriela, an earth goddess from the backlands of Bahia (a Brazilian state that is ninety per cent negroid), has the cinnamon body of an amoral Venus and the clove scent of spicy cooking and lovemaking. In the course of her ingenuous romance with Nacib, the Arab bar owner and restaurateur, she moves from servant to mistress to wife to outcast to servant to mistress, in a beautiful artistic circle which proves that only the squares are foolish enough to kill over the eternal triangle and that no man should marry his grand passion: Respectability is the beginning of boredom and the end of love.

The mystery of love, in fact, as symbolized by the childlike innocence of Gabriela, is perhaps the key theme of Amado in this novel. And that theme says that love is not to be equated with either legality or fidelity, terms introduced into the game by the overly possessive and property-ridden hand of civilization. Love is rather prodigal and lavish, no respecter of persons or of moral codes. Thus the unworthy dandy who sleeps with Gabriela is blessed by the same principle that assures the eleventh-hour worker of his parabled penny. . . .

By novel's end . . . a relative modernity is in Ilhéus to stay, but Brazil remains Brazil—that is to say, drought continues to force the *sertanejos* (backlanders) into migration, grinding poverty, or slavery; the double standard persists in the pansexual world of the tropical lover; the Latin preference for unintelligible eloquence goes on haunting the culture-vulture meetings of the would-be intellectuals; male control of all things legal remains absolute; a naïve and enthusiastically adolescent corruption eats away at the heart of *Order and Progress* (the national motto of Brazil). To extend the list any further would be to give a tragic overtone to what Amado intends to keep basically comic.

Like Brazilian revolutionaries (frustrated lovers) lingering over their *cafezinhos* or a bottle of *pinga* (sugarcane brandy), this novel enjoys the leisurely pace of the nineteenth-century novel. For the Anglo-Saxon world, it demonstrates an anti-puritanical vision that is utterly charming, universally Latin, and transcendental to its somewhat antiquated style. If the book could be strengthened by a reduction of one-third of its wordage, it still boasts a mastery of conflict, local color, characterization, dialogue, and implicit philosophy—a mastery that puts to shame many a sleeker moded contemporary American or European fictionalist. In his study of sensual love, for example, Amado accepts—in the manner of Chaucer—those details which do not need the self-conscious panegyrics of a D. H. Lawrence to give them value. Nor does the Brazilian intellectualize, as though Egyptian veils, the ground of experience away in the manner of Lawrence Durrell. On the couch of reality, Amado is neither sentimental nor clinical.

John Nist. *ArQ*. 19, Spring, 1963, pp. 79–80

[*Gabriela, Clove and Cinnamon*] is a long book but broken down into easily assimilated sketches; the pattern formed by this mosaic is completely successful. Viewed through European eyes the characters may seem larger than life, but even today a visit to that part of Brazil would soon convince one of the plausibility of all of them except possibly of Gabriela herself. Jorge Amado seems to have created her as the amalgam of all the physical attractions attributed to the Brazilian female of mixed blood, the *mulata,* and she is a somewhat improbable creation. Her romantic adventures with the Arab Nacib, apart from exemplifying the racial tolerance practised in Brazil, provide a useful thread in the narrative and some funny episodes. The essence of the book, however, lies in its detailed account of a few months in the life of a small town groping its way to civilization. In the original [Portuguese] the author displays his virtuosity in the use of the vernacular and his skill in adapting the rhythm of his prose to any situation or description. . . .

The corpus of Jorge Amado's work aims to draw attention to social injustice; pathos is the keynote. In one or two instances there has been an excessive preoccupation with extreme left-wing propaganda and the characters have not been drawn objectively enough. *Gabriela, Clove and Cinnamon* strikes a new note. While conveying atmosphere succinctly and, where necessary, dramatically, it is written in a more tolerant vein. Compared with the harsh black-and-white quality of his other novels, this one is like a burst of Technicolor illumined by geniality.

TLS. Aug. 30, 1963, p. 653

One of the happiest developments in world literature during the past few years has been the mellowing of the Brazilian novelist Jorge Amado. Always a gifted storyteller, with an appeal so universal that he has been published in thirty-one languages, Amado nevertheless used to suffer under the self-imposed handicap of a preoccupation with violence and with the misery resulting from economic and social "conditions." An avowed Communist, he sometimes sacrificed literary values to ideology. Then, in 1958, came *Gabriela, Clove and Cinnamon*, which achieved critical and popular success in both Brazil and the United States, followed in 1961 by *The Whole Truth Concerning the Redoubtful Adventures of Captain Vasco Moscoso de Aragão, Master Mariner*. These novels give us a radically new and improved Amado, humorous, gently ironic, broadly human.

Vasco . . . is an undistinguished somewhat ineffectual man of inherited wealth. At the age of sixty he moves to a suburb of Salvador, the capital of Bahia, and lets it be known that he is a retired sea captain. He has a master mariner's certificate to prove it, fraudulently obtained for him years before by his influential friends when they discovered that he envied them their titles of colonel, doctor, and so on. With his Mitty-like fantasies about a captain's life and his heroic but benevolent manner, he becomes the idol of the community—until a jealous skeptic discovers his landlubber past, including adventures not as a romantic lover in exotic ports but as a sort of frustrated playboy in and out of the brothels of Salvador.

To make matters worse, "Captain" Vasco is pressed into service to command a coastal passenger ship in the emergency caused by its master's death. It is Vasco's first sea voyage. But fate intervenes, and the débacle is transformed into a triumph that reinforces the imposture. The story here becomes a bit contrived; but this is not a book of stark realism, and the contrivance is all part of the fun.

The narrative is related long after the event by an amateur historian, who interrupts it from time to time to philosophize on the nature of truth or to tell us about his affair with the playfully amorous mulatto mistress of a retired judge. This device contributes to the ironic detachment that seems to be an essential element in the new Amado and which, in paradoxical combination with his affection for his characters, gives his work a special charm—that of an indulgent, tropical, heart-warming smile at the human comedy.

William L. Grossman. SR. March 28, 1964, p. 43

The Brazilian novelist Jorge Amado has produced a delightful piece of classical comedy in *The Whole Truth Concerning the Redoubtful Adventures of Captain Vasco Moscoso de Aragão, Master Mariner. . . .* [The title] suggests the point about the book; like so much fiction in the Spanish and Portuguese traditions, it derives its manner and its high style from the original comic novel—*Don Quixote.* The narrator, a lustful local poet seeking prestige through his story telling, interrupts and comments on his narrative; the action deals with snobbery and hypocrisy, those basic themes of classical fiction; and in its oblique way the book takes a cool hard look at the social pattern of provincial Brazilian society. At the same time, it takes an enormous joy in the fact of its being fiction, and a similar joy in the lies and self-delusions of men. The hero is a classic comic figure; the grandson of a wealthy merchant, he has money but no title, and, since titles bring prestige in this rigid society, he gets, through a friend, a mastermariner's certificate. Buttressed by this, he carries on a rumbustious life in the brothels and the smart society of coastal Brazil until finally, one day, he is compelled to take command of a ship whose captain has died. Like all comic heroes he is blessed with good fortune to reward his good heart, and all comes out well, as it must. . . . Vasco, derivative though he may be, has the attributes of a major comic hero.

Malcolm Bradbury. *Punch*. Jan. 20, 1965, p.108

Senhor Amado does not exemplify, these days, the vanguard of Latin American literature. Yet his work is exemplary in another sense: he bridges the gulf between a certain *naturalisme plat* [flat or documentary naturalism] that was the breeding ground of the basic literary evidences of Latin America and the highly complex books being written today by Alejo Carpentier, Julio Cortázar, José Donoso, Mario Vargas Llosa and Gabriel García Márquez. . . .

In the implacable fight between Colonel Horácio and the Badaró family [in *Lands without End*] for the lands of Sequeiro Grande, there is a mythological flavor that the American reader will recognize; for it also belongs to the Western saga. One might go further and identify it with the tone of the ageless chronicle . . . of antiquity, whose purpose was to keep alive the deeds of Gods and men; the medieval *minnesinger*, the folksingers of the Mexican *corridos*, the lonely *payadores* of the vast Argentine plain. Once again, in Amado, one feels this urgency of a story that must be sung and remembered.

Colonel Horácio, Juca and Sinho and Don'Ana Badaró are all mythical, larger-than-life figures; they are part of an epic, told by Amado, at its most evident level, with snatches of folksong, eye-witness accounts and even malicious gossip and police reports. There is a second level, however, where the novelist steps in and supplies another vision. In it, will is set against destiny. The classic power of this novel is in an implied, inner struggle, in which men and women are set as a part of the epic rush that drives on to its predetermined fate, but still refuse to abdicate a personal freedom that can express itself only in a will to tragedy. If destiny is fatal, all will can do is precipitate it, thwart its temporal design and meet it before its own time. The violent succession of deaths is the tense and fascinating act of an implicit play where the men of the Badarós willfully trick the fate of Colonel Horácio's men and these, in their turn, quicken the destiny of the men of Badaró.

Carlos Fuentes. *BW*. July 11, 1965, pp. 4, 15

The Two Deaths of Quincas Wateryell is a raucous, impudent little book. Hardly more than a long short story, its dimensions, like its scope, are admirably calculated. The demonstration may be rowdy, but the form is as strict and composed as a theorem in Euclid—whence much of the ironic charm of the narrative. On the surface it would appear to be a tall tale in the familiar American manner—the outrageous exaggerations, the tough talk, monstrous felicities of booze and bumming: an urban proletarian pastoral.

Its hero, too, is familiar enough: the "successful" middle-class citizen, respectable and predictable, who reverts to nature, goes wild. Here, however, Nature is not a matter of Thoreau-like communion with chipmunks and toadstools, but the low bars and devoted-drunken stevedores and fishermen of the waterfront, where our Prodigal Father lives in the odor of scandal. Lives, and dies; for the story hardly gets under way before his wake, when his methylated pals circumvent the decorous family mourners and kidnap the corpse. They have the confused impression that the dead man revived; and such is the strength of the swaying, swaggering prose—even in translation!—that the reader half falls under the same spell. . . .

The immediate effect is that of the tall tale, the frontier tale, as I have said. On this level, the story is convincingly irresponsible, a fine specimen of its kind. Perhaps inevitably, but none the less unhappily, much of the apparatus is deployed in such a way as to enforce a recognition of symbols. The tall tale is also a social parable. What is unhappy about it is not the parable impulse itself, the diving below the surface. Rather it is the fact that the symbols themselves so often turn out to be worn counters, the clichés of thought. The drunken paterfamilias, the outraged prim wife, the scandalized relatives; the whore, a battered but loving mistress, with the heart of gold; the ragged, redolent, credulous, faithful companions of the bottle, likewise hearts of gold; the middle class shown bankrupt, the proletariat triumphant—all well and good; but how tired, how done to death, these types, these portents!

Dudley Fitts. NYT. Nov. 28, 1965, p. 5

Amado does not accept man [in *Lands without End*] in his role of the *conquistador*, a term that today symbolizes greed, oppression, exploitation and slaughter for the Latin American cultural nationalist. Amado's characters don't see or feel the spirit of the land because they have come only to grab its riches and fight among themselves over the spoils. Amado's forests remain inviolate and aloof, superior to their supposed human victims as a potential source of cultural inspiration. The tropical land is grim and basically Darwinian, and the nightly cries of the frogs in the snake's mouth prove it; but the human invaders erected too many whipping posts and pest houses; they enslaved and mutilated each other too much; and they forced too many children and orphans into brothels.

The way of Amado's human predators raise some disturbing questions: What was the historical mission of these so-called pioneers?

Did their cultivation of the northeastern coastal strip, that infinitesimal fraction of Brazil's virgin land, justify their crimes? Is it enough to emulate the Faustean claim of nature's treasures or must it be done by substituting evil with some form of humanistic idealism?

If Amado were less of a Latin American and more of a European writer, the multiple confrontation of man, nature and evil that fills this novel would probably have moved him towards ontological explorations. As it stands, he offers—implictly at least—the realization that economic development and the proliferation of man-made societies without idealistic conceptions are more futile than the laws and mutations of nature.

H. Ernest Lewald. *The Carleton Miscellany*.
7, Fall, 1966, p. 106

Any critical appraisal of Jorge Amado's novels invariably means a discussion of social consciousness, historical documentation, and poetic prose. Critics will apologetically mention Amado's lack of psychological penetration and then hasten to point out his lyricism and prowess as a story-teller. They may also apologize for the early politically oriented works, but they will certainly praise Amado's dramatic forcefulness and his identification with the common man. Unfortunately, in its enthusiasm, this criticism often passes lightly over the significance of the Bahian author's interpretation of Brazilian reality. Most commentators on his works limit themselves to a few preliminary remarks on his popular or folkloric sources without seeing a definite pattern in his use of certain Brazilian institutions. In spite of the fact that many students of Brazilian literature will agree that Jorge Amado is a serious regionalist and not merely a reporter on local color, much of what appears in the pages of such novels as *Jubiabá* and *Dead Sea* receives the label of picturesque.

Amado's use of Afro-Brazilian religious cults is a case in point. Most will agree that Afro-Brazilian culture imparts an exotic effect to Amado's works, but many make the mistake, first, of considering this as so much folklore, and, second, of not realizing the extent of Amado's involvement in the religious cults—an involvement that becomes more and more apparent with each novel. . . .

Jorge Amado gives Afro-Brazilian customs some of the glorification associated with nineteenth century indianism, while at the same time he sees *candomblé* [an Afro-Brazilian cult] with all the intensity and authenticity of realism. He first saw the sect as primitive beauty and a means of social protest. In later works the primitiveness, with its uninhibited sensualness, serves to defy established attitudes, while social protest is translated into group and individual identity. When

Amado's novels lose much of the early political and social idealism, *candomblé* remains as an artistic expression of Brazilian nationalism, and Jorge Amado's attitudes toward Afro-Brazilian customs compare with modern African *negritude*, without, of course, the philosophy of anti-Occidentalism and spiritual racism. The cultural and spiritual values which Jorge Amado seeks out in Brazil's African heritage are an integral part of this country's reality.

Russell G. Hamilton. Hispania. 50, May, 1967,
pp. 242, 250–51

Amado's early books were renowned for the militant socialist realism he brought to bear as a member of the Communist party and follower of Luis Carlos Prestes. The relative permissiveness of the Soviet thaw radically altered his writing over the last 13 years. In 1958, he wrote *Gabriela, Clove and Cinnamon*, an ebulliently exotic book in which social postures were abandoned and characters were paraded with more emphasis on their eccentricities than their suffering. *Dona Flor and Her Two Husbands*, a novel about sex and gambling, is in much the same vein.

The problems of the North-East are scarcely mentioned. . . . In his new novel, we see the North-East from the inside, through the eyes of its humbler inhabitants, people whose primary interests are the latest film at the local movie house, the prospects of success at roulette or with a handsome *mulatta*, the latest serial on the radio—and, not least, the marriage, widowhood and remarriage of everyone's favorite neighbor Dona Flor dos Guimarães.

The novel's villain is Dona Rozilda, Dona Flor's mother, and her villainy lies in the fact that she is a scheming social climber. The hero is Dona Flor's reckless first husband, a handsome rogue named Vadinho, whom no *mulatta* has ever been known to resist, who is so charming that no man can refuse to lend him money. Usually, he lavishes the loan on a game of baccarat. If he wins, he throws a party; if he loses, that's too bad; another creditor will be found. When he dies, he dies dancing the samba. . . .

In the past few decades the shamanistic traditions of Latin America (usually in countries where there is a strong Negro influence or a living Indian culture) have been skillfully exploited in literature. Fantasy in many Latin American novels is a real, active dimension in the characters' lives—and, just as the characters themselves ignore the boundaries between reality and imagination, so for the reader, too, real events slip almost imperceptibly into magic. In *Dona Flor and Her Two Husbands* it is the Devil-God Exu who resuscitates the body of Vadinho and restores it to Dona Flor, to distract her from her second husband. . . .

It is easy to see that the Yoruba deities of Brazil have done a therapeutic service to Dona Flor in resurrecting Vadinho and removing her deceitful inhibitions—a service performed by classical deities in much modern literature. Magic plays another role, that of wish-fulfilling retributions. Just as in Miguel Ángel Asturias's novel *Strong Wind* a cyclone summoned by the local shaman levels the exploiting American banana plantations of Guatemala, so in *Dona Flor and Her Two Husbands* the magic of Exu is deployed to avenge the exploitation of the local roulette wheel. During his lifetime, Vadinho lost a small fortune on his favorite number, 17. With magical powers acquired in death, he is able to ruin the casino by causing 17 to come up with miraculous regularity, after whispering to his cronies that they should stake every cent they can borrow on it.

David Gallagher. *NYT*. Aug. 17, 1969, p. 3

In Amado's novels one finds in glorious melee all the characters of the lore of Northeast Brazil. There are bandits, religious fanatics, fat Bahian cooks, officiating priests of the Macumba cult, drunken bums and prostitutes from the wharves of Salvador, police, soldiers, autocratic cocoa lords, the cream of Bahian society, and the most important, the *gentinho*—the little people who form the substance of the population of the Northeast. In this sense, Amado writes novels of custom, in which he describes in vivid detail the day-to-day life of the region he knows so well. . . .

In Amado's "new" novels there is a change from the emphasis on the collective spirit to the careful development of the individual character. Gabriela [in *Gabriela, Clove and Cinnamon*] and Dona Flor [in *Dona Flor and Her Two Husbands*] are outstanding examples. Amado introduces optimism where before he was pessimistic. He describes a changing Ilhéus; Flor is able to overcome her inhibitions about having two husbands; Quincas Wateryell [in *The Two Deaths of Quincas Wateryell*] achieves the ultimate in individual liberty by overcoming death. In the new novels, Amado still romanticizes the lower classes, and he continues to attack the Establishment. However, the poor are no longer pictured as groveling in impossible filth and deprivation, and Amado's weapon for criticizing the Establishment is no longer unbridled animosity, but rather a sly smile and a subtle wit. Amado begins to show the lighter side of the lives of the poor; he describes their merry-making as well as their suffering. The theme of sex is treated playfully—it is no longer ugly or harsh, and Amado's characters now enjoy it immensely. . . .

Thus in *Gabriela, Clove and Cinnamon, The Two Deaths of Quincas Wateryell*, and *Dona Flor and Her Two Husbands* we see the "new" Amado. He is still the rebel of the days of *Cocoa* and *Sweat*, but he has now remoulded the methods of his criticism. In Amado's "new" novels we still see social protest, but it is now expressed with humour and poetry. Life and death, love, liberty, and truth are themes which are as important to these novels as the hard life of the poor and the hypocrisy of the rich. *Macumba* mysticism weaves its way through the "new" novels, just as it did in the old, giving them the particular Bahian flavour for which Amado's work is famous.

Elizabeth Schlomann Lowe. *LBR*. 6, 2, Dec., 1969,
pp. 73, 82

AMORIM, ENRIQUE (1900–1960)

URUGUAY

For one who knows Enrique Amorim's previous literary work, there are no surprises in *Peasant Aguilar*, although it does reinforce the already proven gifts of the author, such as they may be. . . . In the themes, the techniques, the depth of rural feeling, in the geographic setting in the Río de la Plata area, even in certain Freudian concerns for sex, Amorim continues to pursue the same interests as in his best-known stories and novels. He is the same agile narrator, abrupt in his brevity, a narrator of firm and vivid outlines. He is the portrait painter and the contemplative man, at times a poet but always a storyteller. He even continues to be the fragmentary writer as in his earlier works. . . .

In *The Cart* we find the immediate antecedent of *Peasant Aguilar*. A novel about *quitanderas* [plains prostitutes] and vagabonds, according to the author's subtitle, it could not of course represent exemplary ethics. . . . . *The Cart* is at some remove from the taste of demanding observers. . . . When the description of human pettiness is not illuminated by a ray of idealism to purify it—as is the case with *The Cart*—burning misery cannot be transformed into the authentic fire of art. . . . *The Cart* does not go beyond being an uneven presentation of the degenerate and vicious creatures that spread lust about the countryside.

Juan B. González. *Nosotros*. 2nd series, No. 4,
July, 1936, pp. 440–41†

Like most good South American fiction I have read, *The Horse and His Shadow* is a revolutionary novel but unlike the revolutionary fiction of our own country, it is subtle, fluid, based deep in the drama of human relationships. The action moves between the *estancia* [cattle ranch] of Nico Axara, outside Montevideo, and the community of Polish refugees and poor natives who live on the fringes of Nico's lands; on the *estancia* itself there is every shade of political opinion. In addition to the peons at the one extreme, and the arrogant Nico at the other, there is Adelita, Nico's wife, an aristocrat of decent liberal opinions; there is Bica, her servant but also her illegitimate half-sister, who lives in lonely severity among the men ranchers; there is Marcelo, Nico's brother sought by the government for his part in smuggling refugees into Uruguay.

Mr. Amorim, however, measures neither the decency and courage nor the weakness of these people by the familiar yardstick of their social-political views. If it is Marcelo who brings to the *estancia* the gift of the stallion, Don Juan, symbol of life-creating powers, and Marcelo who gives the stricken family of refugees permission to cross his brother's lands, it is also Marcelo who seduces Bica and then calmly goes on his way, leaving her pregnant. Again, Nico is the dark force of reaction in the book who, by refusing his neighbors access to the road across his fields, precipitates the tragedy with which the book ends; but the stallion knows Nico for his master, and in the duel in which Nico loses his life, the horse allows his body to be used as a barricade by his owner; Nico's death itself, for that matter, is a display of the kind of heroism which fiction likes to reserve for heroes.

Even the poor people in Mr. Amorim's novel, the gauchos and the struggling refugees, are shown quite naked of grandeur in an amazing scene in which two of their number steal the services of Don Juan for a broken down mare. What Mr. Amorim is saying is what is too seldom said in fiction these days, that it is from the new and the old, from the mixture of good and evil, of the progressive and the retarding, that society must advance, and he says it is the only way fruitful for the novelist—by drama and even by melodrama.

It is of course dangerous to use the larger animals symbolically in fiction: one slip and the whole business becomes laughable. But unlike the stallion, say, in D. H. Lawrence's *St. Mawr,* the horse whose shadow is so pervasive in Mr. Amorim's novel is never absurd because it is not only a sexual symbol but also an economic symbol, indeed an economic fact. This play between symbolisms and between symbol and reality strikes me as a fine complication in a novel of revolution. It almost makes us forgive Mr. Amorim's wretched writing.

Diana Trilling. *Nation.* Sept. 4, 1943, pp. 273–74

From *The Cart*, which is really a group of stories tied together by a common motif, through his best novel, *The Horse and Its Shadow*, one can see that Amorim is at his best in the story-episode. . . . In *Peasant Aguilar*, for example, the scene of the flooding of the river, which carries men and cattle along in its waters, or another scene dealing with the drunks and the banter of reciprocal amiability, can be read by themselves with very little alteration. The same is true of *The Horse and Its Shadow*, in which there are episodes that, without upsetting the harmony of the whole, are not woven into the overall plot, such as the story about Don Ramiro's blindness, which is one of the novel's most vivid segments. In *The Moon Was Made from Water* the story of the savage punishment suffered by the guide Gregorio Lanza could stand independently, while the episode of the salting house Britannia in *The Uneven Age* almost clashes with the whole out of a lack of integration.

Amorim is, in short, an excellent storyteller. And one cannot speak of his novels without alluding to his stories, in which one can find the key to his creative aptitude. His "stories with birds" provide excellent examples, whether he is describing the picturesque naughtiness of a young thief of nests, who is left hanging from a tree with his forearm caught in a hollow of a tree made by the birds, in "The Carpenters"; or whether, in "The Carriages" he shows the delicate tenderness that exists behind the ferocity of a gunman from the Upper Uruguay [River], who refuses to destroy the nest that stands in the way of the advance of his raft in order not to hinder the innocent pair of birds in the labor of their instinct. These brief scenes always exhibit, through man's reactions and the indirect intervention of the birds, Amorim's charm, his simple grace, and his profound yet tender observations on nature and its beings.

Alicia Ortiz. Las novelas de Enrique Amorim
(Buenos Aires, Compañía Editora y Distribuidora
del Plata, 1949), pp. 56–57†

No other Uruguayan writer of the twentieth century possesses the amazing vitality of Enrique Amorim. . . . I have known Amorim for thirty years, and I have always recognized his capacity for renovation, the constant freshness of his art, and the beautiful mixture of fantasy and reality that flows through his novels and short stories. A profound master of the themes of rural Uruguay, he has also found the sources of creativity in other subjects, subjects that demand psychological maturity, mental sophistication, and technical sagacity. . . .

Lately [Amorim] has taken a revolutionary stance, and his vision of society involves a bold revision of traditional values. But his art eschews clichés and mottos, except during one brief period. . . . In

Everything Can Happen he describes with great subtlety the story of two loves in the seaside setting of Punta del Este. Although he satirizes the social group that frequents the elegant spa, what dominates the book are his narrative instinct and his knowledge of the human heart in his presentation of the characters of Martín Durond, Laura, and Eva. The passages portraying Eva show Amorim at his most refreshing and most human—something very different from the completely tragic atmosphere of *The Backwoods Men* or *Open Corral.* [1959?]

Ricardo Latcham. Carnet crítico (Montevideo,
Editorial Alfa, 1962), pp. 135, 139–40†

Since the publication of Domingo Faustino Sarmiento's *Facundo* in 1845 the vast, desolate pampa of Argentina and Uruguay has played a significant role in the literature of the lands bordering the Río de la Plata. . . . Successive generations of essayists, poets, and novelists have sought to interpret the pampa in a variety of manners. Some, like Ricardo Güiraldes, have emphasized the exotic, legendary aspects of gaucho life while others have sought a solution to the complex sociological and economic problems of the region.

One of the outstanding leaders of the latter group is the contemporary Uruguayan novelist, Enrique Amorim, whose rural novels present a panoramic view of the vast area. Amorim never confines himself to a mere description of its exotic aspects but attempts to interpret the gradual changes which slowly destroy the forces of barbarism in the wake of advancing civilization. Much of his writing is based on personal experiences from his childhood on a large *estancia* in northern Uruguay near the Brazilian border. There at his father's side he became interested in the destinies of the sad, passive, frugal people who toiled in the fields. The gauchos he describes do not resemble the familiar, romantic figures of Uruguayan literature but are workingmen of the plains, frequently unable to cope with the responsibilities of a harsh, fierce land. Although he deals with brutal and sometimes sordid realities of rural life, Amorim writes with a delicate style tempered by a sympathetic understanding of the plains people and an appreciation of the spectacular beauty of the motionless landscape.

Harley D. Oberhelman. BA. 34, Spring, 1960, p. 115

Without attempting to analyze his work—his narratives, his poetry, his political writings—I should point out that Enrique Amorim abandoned Río de la Plata creolism, which some writers favored so much, and united in his books the positive values of surrounding nature with his own private sensitivity to capture nature and to capture, as part of that same nature, the individuals that move through *The Horse and Its Shadow*, *Peasant Aguilar*, and *The Cart*.

From these first works of realism . . . [he] derived the concept, which was to be refined with time, of a novel in which ideology and plot are mixed together. . . . His technique reached a true peak in the *Unmasked Assassin* and in the poemlike story, *Birds and Men*. For Amorim's spirit was dominated, more than by the political ideas of a leftist, by the calling of the deep-seated poetry that sprang from his soul, along with a bit of the peasant that was hidden in him. To confirm this, one only has to observe him, as I myself have many times, in the great European cities or in Buenos Aires, where he always seemed to be just passing through, like a peasant who comes in to do some buying and who must return as soon as possible to his fields.

Miguel Ángel Asturias. *Ficción*. No. 28,
Nov.–Dec., 1960, p. 54†

The two fundamental images that penetrated the soul and the intellect of Amorim were the Río de la Plata countryside, which inspired novels like *The Cart* and *The Backwoods Men* . . . and the suffering that this century of iron, cruel and unjust, inflicts on the dispossessed, of which Amorim wanted to be an eloquent and an X-ray-like spokesman. That the great Uruguayan storyteller may have been more objective in presenting nature and less so in social problems, that he may have attained the highest level of his literary career in the domain of nature (the political *Nine Moons over Neuquén* is not the work of the great writer of *Peasant Aguilar*) . . . stems from the fact . . . that literature that does not want to be literature unfortunately obscures objectivity and ends up with a subjectivity that can often be puerile. . . .

Enrique Amorim has achieved his position in American literature because of *The Horse and Its Shadow* . . . because of *Trap in the Straw Patch*, in which he masterfully developed sadness and despair . . . because of *Peasant Aguilar*, in which he presented the American plains, the character of its men, in a style of variegated color and perfect sobriety. . . .

Amorim, aside from being an extraordinary painter of the landscape and soul of the Uruguayan countryside and a portraitist in fire of the misery of the exploited, the bitterness of the persecuted, and the patience of the hopeful . . . is, most importantly . . . one of the initiators of a literary aesthetic that fired the last shot against the petrified literature, varicosed and dandruffed, that was solidly entrenched, like a wedge, during the second decade of our century. . . .

Bernardo E. Koremblit. *Ficción*. No. 28,
Nov.–Dec., 1960, pp. 56–57†

If Amorim had merely pointed out and denounced, if Amorim had merely raised the veils, pulled back the curtains on our rural and urban conditions, his work, although valuable as a document, would only be that. It would serve the ends of history, not those of literature. But Amorim knew how to transmute documentary material into art in the best of his ten novels (although not in all of them). He was successful in many of them in bridging the gap that separates social or political testimony from full literary creation. This is evident if we examine two elements from a pair of important novels, written twenty-five years apart. I refer to the *quitanderas* of *The Cart* and to the rebellion of the plague victims in *Open Corral.* . . .

Amorim took the word *quitandera* from Portuguese, in which it refers to a woman who hawks candy. But he added a new meaning to it, that of prostitute. And here we can precisely see how a novelist works over the material he takes from real life. Anyone who knows our countryside, the countryside of years ago as well as the countryside of today, agrees that these wagons [with prostitutes] never existed except in the imagination of the novelist, that these *quitanderas* never existed in the sense in which Amorim uses the word. . . . Nevertheless, Amorim's invention is so powerful, so convincing in its description, so believable in the human situation it postulates, that these *quitanderas* of his imagination have ended up by imposing themselves upon reality. . . .

I do not mention this anecdote now to make an ironic commentary on the labyrinthine paths of art and men. I mention it to show to what extent this writer, superficially a realist, this minute observer of a concrete reality, is a creator, an inventor, an artificer who converts fantasy into his "real-life material." What does this traveling wagon mean, and what do those women who offer their bodies for a bit of money mean? In Amorim's novel they are symbols of all the dreams of full sexual union, frustrated by the solitary life of our countryside. They are dreams that only find liberation in the familiar formulas of casual concubinage or in bestial coupling. They are the symbols of something that material, visible reality cannot offer. . . .

Emir Rodríguez Monegal. *Narradores de esta América*,
2nd ed. (Montevideo, Editorial Alfa, 1969–74),
Vol. I, pp. 145–47†

Amorim's passion for truth underlies, and in turn is largely directed by, a powerful sympathy, especially for the proletarian masses and underdogs. A comparison with the report of the Rural Federation's survey to which reference was made above would help to point up this quality. The report speaks of the degraded position of the woman of the *rancherío* [settlement] as a beast of pleasure but views her operating as a factor of dissolution on the men folk. This is natural since the members of the Federation regarded the peasant as little more than a beast of burden. Amorim, on the contrary, views the *quitandera* [plains prostitute] as a noble reliever of loneliness and pent-up hungers. This basic human sympathy, which very early showed itself as a trait of character, brought a social passion to Amorim's writing before his Socialist affiliation and, to some degree, was bigger than a monolithic conception of Communism. For, in his later work, Amorim is still a Communist as far as that represents a directional force of redemption of the masses, but resists any tenet that tries to confine the human being in an overrestrictive, common mould. This social passion, combined with his vehement temper, often impaired the quality of Amorim's art.

In spite of this, his work towers above that of the men most often mentioned as belonging to his Uruguayan generation—Montiel Ballesteros, Juan José Morosoli, Francisco Espínola, and Felisberto Hernández—because of his immense vision and his creation of a vast narrative world. Some of these writers are Amorim's superiors in aesthetic discipline, but when this occurs, their production, probably because of lack of publishing opportunities and their own economic situation, is so reduced as to rob the fact of a comparative virtue. Further, they are all better short story writers than novelists.

K. E. A. Mose. *Enrique Amorim, the Passion of a Uruguayan* (New York, Plaza Mayor Ediciones, 1972), pp. 211–12

ANDERSON IMBERT, ENRIQUE (1910–   )

ARGENTINA

[Anderson Imbert's] new collection, *The Proof of Chaos*, gathers fantastic stories . . . various essays . . . fantasies or caprices . . . brief tales. . . . Although of various genres, all the pieces have the stamp of difficulty, which the writer establishes and then resolves. There is an obvious effort on his part to avoid usual themes. For this reason, because he flees from facileness, a few passages are very dense. And sometimes he plays capriciously with recurrent themes—the detective plot, for example—which undermines his customary enchantment. . . . We often hear the sound of his voice: in Alicia [in "The Determinist Goblins"], the child confused by the attempt of the King who could not dehumanize his fairies; in José [in "The Prodigal Son"], the unexpected prodigal son who returns defeated by life and reveals to his brother his tremendous inner desolation; in that obsessive fantasy called "The Phantom." Irony, when present, does not derive from skepticism but from the intentional contrast of a very literary theme and a language that has the difficulty yet ease of colloquial speech.

Julio Caillet-Bois. Sur. No. 100, Jan., 1946, p. 100†

Argentina is a country without conversation, Anderson Imbert says; of course, what he means is without good conversation. There is a lack of talkers; even more, anyone who wants to make an effort to attain a degree of polish in expression must struggle along, for years and years, amidst the foolery of the rest. Hence, when we write, he says, we are unable to escape from the hovel. "The ear is an opening that is invaded by imbecility, vulgarity, and falseness from the outside. Without sight, without books, without those links stretching out to Europe, our national vulgarity would drown us."

Bad education, which makes us lose years and years traveling the wrong roads (two or three timely words of advice would have saved us from this), this bad education, as I said, results from a conception of Argentine life in which the intellectual aristocracy is a myth that no longer has any force. The curriculum, "free of arts, spirit, and humanism" thus resulted from this evident decline of the spiritual life of Argentina, which, around 1930, motivated the essays of Anderson Imbert, the novels of Roberto Arlt, Martínez Estrada's *X-ray of the Pampa*, Manuel Gálvez's novel *Men in Solitude*, and Eduardo Mallea's first writings.

The young Anderson Imbert was truly implacable: "The teachers are accomplices. The textbooks are terrible, and we poor autodidacts are therefore the result: we know a few points intensely but are ignorant of the continuity of literature and its essential lessons." [His] essays, as can be seen, are crisscrossed by a concern that is ethical, not just literary or expressive.

Enrique Zuleta Álvarez. La biblioteca. 9, 5, 1961, p. 80†

The title story of [*The Book of Magic*] sums up almost the entire work of fiction of Anderson Imbert, or at least the best of it. . . . The writer . . . refers to an enchanted book, illegible at first sight. It is legible, but one cannot read the selections separately or turn back or interrupt the reading. One must seize the initial word and not let go until he finishes it, lest it become indecipherable. To read it is to undertake a magic flight. To read it is to feel that the book is devouring the reader. At the end of the story, Rabinovich, its protagonist, before losing consciousness, thinks that he is the Wandering Jew, writer of the magic book; he feels totally identified with it. He believes that he is the protagonist, "as in a detective novel—so perfect that one could not even conceive it—in which the murderer turns out to be . . . the reader himself."

Isabel C. Ruiz. RLAI. 3, Dec., 1961, p. 69†

Anderson Imbert, like everyone, has his sources and his influences. By the nature of his themes, few could be Spanish. If we take a passage from his prologue [to *The Book of Magic*] we can find a confession: "My literary sources are those of the English library of my house; my vision of life—from solipsism to existentialism—was formed thanks to the philosophers that old [Alejandro] Korn [the Argentine philosopher] made me read." . . . Probably many of these readings were the same as those that led to blossoming of the contemporary Anglo-American short story—some extraordinarily narrated—in which terror and cruelty are fundamental ingredients.

Nevertheless—and this is our first surprise—although he uses these same elements, Anderson Imbert does not fall into any "tremendism" [that is, literature of violence and the shocking] or into an exploitation of his ability, his mastery of his craft, so as to shake the reader. It seems that he has written the stories for himself, for himself as a reader and not for himself out of a narcissism charged with self-satisfaction. He has enjoyed himself by writing them, and for this reason he entertains us when we read them. There is a certain poetry in his way of telling a story. But this is not the easy poetry of saying that someone's eyes are filled with light or butterflies . . . but rather a way of feeling the theme lyrically and of controlling, with the same meaning, the feelings that make it up.

Very prominent in Anderson Imbert's art is the idea of telling as a game, which shows that he possesses one of the fundamental attributes of a good storyteller. Thus, his stories must be repeated in his own words: it is not enough to tell the plot. . . . This game, to be sure, is derived from the very character of the writer, who has relied on good models: "My strategies in the art of telling stories began as exercises learned in humble O'Henry and in the not-so-humble Chesterton." These models did not serve him as material for scenes as plots but rather as game-playing strategies with which to control his own movements. . . .

Jorge Campos. Insula. No. 184, March, 1962, p. 11†

[The short fiction in *The Book of Magic*], like the novels, essays, and critical studies by Anderson Imbert, are created out of a complex conception of the world, full of nuances, vibrantly linked to the contemporary spirit. . . . Anyone who can understand the unifying themes in the work of our compatriot will find in *The Book of Magic* many subtle reinforcements. Erudition, fantasy, originality, the tension of speculation, lyricism, and the persistent nuance of melancholy—all are almost always present, regardless of how different subject and technique are from story to story. . . .

Whether within a strict intellectual game (above all in the sparkling "Cases and More Cases") or in very refined psychological examinations ("Like the Taste of Lipstick") or in simple tales like the one about a boy from Santiago del Estero [in the desert] trapped by the sea ("The Voyage"), the flow of experience is always associated with the internal world of his characters. Even in stories in which technique is his greatest concern, man, often the man of our country and our time, stands before the artist. But local man also has a magical, poetic, alogical, and unintelligible side, which the local-color realists customarily overlooked. . . .

Anderson Imbert's stories round out and add profundity to the dimension of his oeuvre. Expressed with the techniques and thought of contemporary art, they successfully move from limited, *précieux* exercises to testimonies of anguished vigil of man in the shadows. Immanence and transcendence, free lyrical caprice and fervent intimacy, imagist abstraction and the concrete presentation of Argentina . . . all this is filtered through a very personal atmosphere of precise fantasy, one of rich and enriching beauty.

Antonio Pagés Larraya. *Ficción*. No. 40,
Nov.–Dec., 1962, pp. 59–61†

The stories in *The Book of Magic* go all the way from apparent realism to pure fantasy. Apparent realism because Anderson is not a realistic writer: the stories that seem most realistic—"Tsantsa," "The North American Woman" [translated title: "Mishina,"] "Taste of Lipstick," "The Wall"—have surprise endings that bring the reader up short, make him rearrange his whole concept of the story's situation. What he had been trustingly following was a false reality, a playing with reality. There is poetic realism, as in "The Queen of the Wood," and *casos* ("cases") which make no pretense, from the very beginning, of having anything to do with the real world. But most typical of Anderson's fiction is magic realism; a story will begin with a perfectly realistic situation that is developed with rigorous logic to an utterly fantastic conclusion. Someone once asked me, talking about one of the stories, "Where does the magic begin?" My reply was to point out a line in the text that indicated the very moment when the magic began. This moment is clearly marked in each story, but not always in such a way that the reader can see it at first reading. . . . Everything seems so logical that the reader does not say, "This is impossible." He realizes it later.

The blending of the real and the fantastic is reflected in the author's style, a blending of the colloquial and the poetic. And in the matter-of-fact way in which the supernatural is accepted into the natural world: it is interesting to see an angel at a cocktail party, but not at all surprising. . . . Wishes are granted by both angels and devils, always ironically.

Because irony is another principal characteristic of these stories. The monk who longed for sanctity as union with God finds that it is precisely his sanctity that has separated him from God; the perfect crime planned to vanquish the intelligence of the police is itself vanquished by the lack of intelligence of the police; a man's desperate attempts to kill himself succeed only in killing other people; the noisy celebration of the birth of a prince causes the infant's death; a child with wings is afraid to use them because people will laugh at him.

This stifling of originality by a rigid society is a recurrent motif in these stories. It is the theme of "The Determinist Goblins": a superimposed conformity destroys the best that is in us. Both in his criticism and in his fiction, Anderson Imbert's emphasis is always on the individual: a language does not exist, only those who speak it; a book does not exist as a book except when someone is reading it (there are often flashes of idealist philosophy in these stories); more important than literary movements, schools of thought, national groups, etc. are the individual writers who form them; the image is superior to the concept, the particular to the general, the concrete to the abstract. What counts, always, is the individual. And the freedom of the individual. "All of us aspire to a life at least as free as our imagination," says Alicia to the restrictive King of the Goblins.

Isabel Reade. Introduction to Enrique Anderson Imbert,
The Other Side of the Mirror: El Grimorio
(Carbondale, Southern Illinois University Press,
1966), pp. xi–xiii

One of the most interesting recent phenomena of contemporary Argentine literature has been the increasing cultivation of the short-short story form. One is tempted to add even one more "short-" to the denomination, since many of these brief tales, or "micro-stories," or "small short stories," as they have been variously termed, do not exceed one hundred words in length.

Cameo sketches of this sort have always appeared here and there, in one guise or other; a representative anthology of micro-stories could span five centuries of Spanish-language literature and would surely include some of the most august names in the literatures of the New and Old Worlds alike. It is difficult to say just how this current vogue started in Argentina, but it is worth noting that, once Jorge Luis Borges began producing abbreviated prose pieces, other writers began doing the same thing.

The most prolific and artistic cultivator of the micro-story is the Argentine teacher, author, and critic, Enrique Anderson Imbert. His *estampas* ["images"] have been appearing in the literary supplement of *La nación* and in other publications for more than two decades. The first group collected in book form is found in *The Proof of Chaos*. These were subsequently reprinted along with other new *casas* ["cases"] (as Anderson Imbert originally termed them) and a number of short stories in *The Book of Magic*. Now we have a harvest of some 150 new pieces in *The Cheshire Cat*.

This volume is not for reading at a single sitting. It is for sampling. In this fashion the work will achieve its greatest aesthetic effect. *The Cheshire Cat* offers a privileged glimpse into the whimsical, elastic, highly intellectualized mind of a widely respected teacher and literary artist. Here are dazzling games with time and existence played not on the regulation checkerboard, but on the magical, fantastic, and invisible patterns of one of the squares.

Donald A. Yates. BA. 41, Winter, 1967, p. 74

ANDRADE, CARLOS DRUMMOND DE (1902–   )

BRAZIL

After a century of romantic subjectivity, which ended up in mockery, mere decoration, decadence, and desperation, we [in Brazil] are rediscovering the objective role of poetry. The poetry of Carlos Drummond de Andrade, although the very personal expression of a soul, is objective. . . .

A personal, psychological analysis, at best impractical in the case of living poets, is out of the question for Carlos Drummond de Andrade, who has so rigorously separated his private life and his poetry. Such a "dissociation of the personality," a state of mind always fruitful for poetry, cannot help but appear odd to "normal" men. Hence the "strangeness" of all of Carlos Drummond de Andrade's poetry. It is a reflection of great anguish and a key to the dramatic tension and conflict that have never been resolved and still persist. The formal coefficient of this conflict, which excludes harmony either of the soul or of the spheres, is the lack of rhyme. . . .

The poetry of Carlos Drummond de Andrade, while of great percision, is a poetry without music. . . . One needs a catholic taste . . . to appreciate contemporary lyricism, which contrasts with that of different periods from the past. Carlos Drummond de Andrade, representative of a new lyrical expression, is quite a distinctive poet, and ill-educated "good taste" is not enough to interpret his poems properly, poems he has put together with the fine precision of a superior intelligence. It is not a poetry of images, to which many are accustomed; it is a poetry of conceits, somewhat comparable to the conceptualist poetry of the baroque period. Like baroque poetry, and like conceptualist poetry in general, this kind of verse is open to two dangers: it can become bookish, like the poetry of T. S. Eliot; or it can fall into a lack of formal discipline, like that of E. E. Cummings and Wallace Stevens. Andrade is saved from these pitfalls by the unusual coexistence in him of rustic ingenuousness and the most vigorous intellectual discipline.

He will never be sentimental, in any sense. Thus, he has taken decisive steps from the melancholy of his "prehistoric" period to true anguish, out of which the true poet Carlos Drummond de Andrade was born late. Since then, he has guarded the position it cost him so much to attain with the supreme weapon of self-defense of the individual— satiric humor, humor that remains incidental in his poetry, but which is nonetheless a significant index of his inner drama. [1943]

Otto Maria Carpeaux. In Carlos Drummond de
Andrade, *Obra completa* (Rio de Janeiro, Companhia
Aguilar Editôra, 1964), pp. 33–34†

[*The People's Rose*] reveals the conflict of an authentic revolutionary who nevertheless wishes to remain faithful to the call of his art; of a human being who wants to identify himself with problems of the people without abandoning his artistic personality, which is of an aristocratic nature. Thus, the revolutionary feeling of Carlos Drummond de Andrade's poetry is not of the type that leads art to meld itself with the masses, to exalt them, to help them to acquire an awareness of their own wretchedness and needs, but of the sort that transfigures feelings of unconformity and revolt so that they can move the so-called intellectual elite.

The writer of *The People's Rose* and Castro Alves are the two poets in the history of our literature who have produced works of the clearest social stamp and revolutionary tendency. In Castro Alves, however . . . the poetic inspiration derived from the people and was returned to them in forms that were correspondingly popular. In Carlos Drummond de Andrade the inspiration of some popular themes never comes to him intact; rather, their structure is a transformation predetermined by the original vision of the poet and the creative processes of modern art, and the poem never gets back to the people because it is written in an aristocratic style. . . . An inspiration—of thoughts, ideas, or feelings—that is revolutionary (and therefore contains an element that is in part popular) lodges together with a form that is difficult and makes no concessions to the general public. A shiver of that duality—the aristocracy of expression and the generous effort to comprehend the people—can be felt in all of these sober, dry, and ascetic poems, which are nonetheless impregnated with passion and sentiment. [1945]

Álvaro Lins. In Carlos Drummond de Andrade,
Obra completa (Rio de Janeiro, Companhia Aguilar
Editôra, 1964), pp. 35–36†

In our poetry, the most typical representative of the men of Minas Gerais is Carlos Drummond de Andrade. The real Minas people are endowed with the qualities of careful reflection, mistrust of hasty enthusiasm, a taste for double meanings, and pessimistic reserve, all elements that generate irony. Every time this *mineiro* temperament coincides with a fine sensitivity or the gift for poetry, an ironist with real style results. Carlos Drummond de Andrade is the most notable example of this happy combination. With moved and moving feeling in every line he writes, the poet almost never abandons the ironic attitude, even in the tenderest moments. In his poetry, tenderness and irony generally play an automatic game of see-saw; there is never a false motion in this marvelous lyric apparatus. The poet does not expect much of mankind: "Except for two or three, they are all going to hell." Like the Jesus in the poem "Pilgrimage," he must dream, when he is tired, of "another humanity." His judgment of his own country could not be more bitter: "It was my people and my land that made me like this"; "It is stupid to long for Europe; here at least the people know that it's all one single rabble, they read their newspapers, criticize the government, complain about life, and everything turns out all right in the end." Love? The eternal tune: "Fight, forgive, fight."

Manuel Bandeira. *Américas*. 6, 11, Nov., 1954, p. 19

It is fascinating to notice the changes thirty years have wrought in [Carlos Drummond de Andrade's] work. As the jacket blurb of *Tiller of Air, and Poems up to Now* points out, Andrade has "come a long way from his former anecdotal style and now seeks to interpret, as purely as possible, the meaning of things, feelings, and moods."

His anecdotal style helped a great deal toward making him

famous. Actually, "anecdotal" is not an adequate word to describe his unique brand of sly, often wry, dry, unsentimental humor, which remains quite recognizably [his own] despite the general use of surrealistic humor by other contemporary poets. It consists in the most unexpected word combinations, delightfully comic images, used sometimes to put across a tragic thought or a melancholy mood. Though there is no great *joie de vivre* in his work, neither is there despair; the poet looks philosophically at life, expecting no great happiness from it, but at the same time finding it immensely interesting and worthwhile. Occasionally an element of bitterness creeps in, as in the long, socially conscious "Song to the Man of the People: Charlie Chaplin." But even here, the last words are of hope: "Oh Charlie, my and our friend, your shoes and your mustache walk on a road of dust and hope." It is worth noting that when this poem first appeared, sometime in 1945, it was considered "subversive" by a number of people.

Armando S. Pires. *Américas.* 7, 4, April, 1955, p. 45

Carlos Drummond de Andrade began to publish when the new order was already established; for him, modernism was no longer a revolt, if even a challenge (soon transformed from a literary challenge to a political one). In 1930, with *Some Poetry* Carlos Drummond did not need to exclaim as did Manuel Bandeira, "I am fed up with well-tempered lyrics/With well-behaved lyricism," but instead presented his new poetics in the form of an ambiguous figure: "In the middle of the road was a stone."

From then on . . . Carlos Drummond de Andrade grew by accretion: each collected edition of his poems ended one phase and introduced another. . . . Thus, the volume *Poetry* in 1942 temporarily brought to an end his lyric phase and marked the beginning of a phase of politically committed poetry, of which *The People's Rose* (1945) was the best example. The 1947 anthology *Poetry up to Now* was an account of the political phase that it brought to a close. What came next, in 1951, was the first presentation, in *Clear Enigma*, of the "pure" poetry that was to follow, an attempt to reconcile fixed form with the liberties introduced by modernism. . . .

By 1945, Andrade had already revealed his profundity. From then on, he perfected his poetic instrument and enriched his inspiration. Nothing strikingly new has been added to his essence. . . .

Wilson Martins. *O modernismo* (São Paulo, Editôra
Cultrix, 1956), pp. 270–71†

[Carlos Drummond de Andrade's native] Itabira assumes a mythic role in his poetry. It represents a body of traditional values. . . . Andrade is recognized today throughout Brazil as one of the poets who best speaks both our eternal language and the language of our own times. Successful in his pursuit of the simple and the everyday, he is the interpreter of the common man, who feels close to his universe, notwithstanding the distinct stamp of the poet that his world bears.

At times a mixture of personal lyricism and social concerns, his poetry is notable in its attention to craftsmanship, in the conscientiousness with which he labors over his verbal instrument and the structure of his poems. All the while he is quite personal, having created for his exclusive use a specific technique suitable to the needs of his expression and his thematic preoccupations.

His personality and his lyrical work have a clear outline and evolution. His first book, *Some Poetry*, reveals the timidity, humility, and awkwardness of a poet who was already showing a tendency toward communion in the "world's feeling" and toward flight to symbolic levels. Later, in *Swamp of Souls*, a note of humor appears, which was to become a constant in his poetry (and prose). In *Sentiment of the World* and *The People's Rose* he reacted to the collective pain and the misery of the modern world, a mechanistic, materialistic, and inhumane world. This phase enriched his essentially lyrical and emotional nature. Through his profound artistic conscience, he attained plenitude, fulfillment, and humanization in a soft and tender form. The native of Itabira submerged himself deeply in his native region and his ancestors in order to comprehend, with a feeling of broad fraternity, the workings of the world, the anguish of his time, the uprooting of contemporary man.

Skilled as a poet, Drummond is also a prose writer of rare excellence, whether as a short-story writer, a writer of memoirs, or a journalist. His prose combines a light touch of humor and a penetrating feeling of disenchantment with the things of life, in a style in the tradition of Machado de Assis.

Afrânio Coutinho. In Carlos Drummond de Andrade,
Obra completa (Rio de Janeiro, Companhia Aguilar
Editôra, 1964), pp. 11–12†

I have always believed that our great poet's verses—of extreme intellectual density—were meant to be read in private and silently. Read aloud, they should be uttered as the author himself would say them, not recited. Even if gesticulation and declamation would not falsify these poems, they would add nothing to them, for Andrade's poetry does not depend on rhetorical or musical values; its value derives from the original way simple, conventional words are brought together and invested with a singular evocative power. This power can awaken in us the multiple meanings of these lusterless words. . . .

In all of these poems it seems that the lyrical element, some personal motive, is lacking. The nucleus is a daily fact, probably read in some newspaper. "The Death of the Milkman," for example, describes an event that took place in Rio some years ago, which was commented on in the press for a few days: someone, hearing the early-morning steps of the milkman at his door, takes him for a thief and shoots him dead. One could claim that the direct voice of the poet can still be found in this poem in the guise of commentary. But in "The Case of the Dress" the speaker is a woman of the people, who tells her daughters how her husband humiliated and abandoned her for another, and how the other woman, years later, abandoned in turn, came to beg forgiveness, leaving her dress as a token; at the end, the steps of the returning husband are heard. In "Death in an Airplane" the speaker is the victim, who relives the day before the catastrophe, interpreting it in light of the tragic event. [1965]

Paulo Rónai. In Carlos Drummond de Andrade,
José & outros (Rio de Janeiro, Livraria José Olympio
Editôra, 1967), p. xvii†

Among younger Brazilian artists, writers, poets, and critics, Carlos Drummond de Andrade—even more than world-famous sociologist Gilberto Freyre—is undoubtedly the most admired intellectual of his generation. . . . After a generation of constant literary growth, Andrade has achieved a complete fusion of sensibility and reason: that is the history of his genius.

In his first volume, *Some Poetry*, published in Belo Horizonte in 1930, Carlos Drummond de Andrade represented the general aesthetic position, accepted in Brazil ever since the Symbolists, of opposition to the cliché, stylized "poetic" diction, and "appropriate" literary convention. Like the Modernists, however, in his work he united the universal with the intimately personal, without permitting "any musical, rhythmical, conceptual, social, or euphemistic limitation." Believing at this time that rhyme is useless unless the words agree in an association of ideas, Andrade dropped his new approach into the Modernist Movement like the stone he saw "In the Middle of the Road." . . . As the most popular of present-day Brazilian novelists, Érico Veríssimo, has said, the reaction to Andrade's stone lying in the middle of the road was to call its author mad from schizophrenia. The Modernists who came to the defense of Andrade, however, hurled back their contention that the poem is psychologically sound. For them, it represented the "drama of obsessing ideas."

Much of the poetry of Carlos Drummond de Andrade moves upon

the drama of obsessing ideas, for he is possessed with several convictions of the perfectionist: That he is impossible. That language is absolutely insufficient for the needs of communication. That life is ineffable. That the social order is filled with an injustice for which there is no final resolution. That even though love turns out to be useless, one must live in order that existence may become its own essence. . . . In a poem ["Secret"] that illustrates the thesis, "You cannot communicate poetry," Andrade says, "Everything is possible, only I am impossible." . . .

From the frustration of the perfectionist who saw what immense passion abides potentially in language and which was lacking in his own account because of his failure to master that language, Andrade took up the tactics of combative affirmations in that "aggression of one who accepts defeat in the social realm because he is only interested in victory in the individual." To further the cause of that victory, the vocabulary of Andrade became increasingly colloquial, realistic, almost naïve, and full of verbal repetition. . . . More impressive than any technical virtuosity in his poetry is Andrade's utterly courageous and incorruptible honesty with the human situation, the word, and himself.

John Nist. *The Modernist Movement in Brazil*
(Austin, University of Texas Press, 1967),
pp. 129–31, 134, 140

Announcing the publication of his *Lesson of Things* and *Poetic Anthology*, Carlos Drummond de Andrade wrote in a column of his, referring to the two poems in the last part of *Lesson of Things,* that the "poet explores the word as sound and sign, in its approximations, contrasts, defoliations, distortions, and enraged interpenetrations," and he concluded, "Judge for yourselves."

One of the poems to which he was referring was "This Is That" . . . which represents the latest results of Carlos Drummond de Andrade's investigations in rhyme. . . .

Explore the word as sound and sign. . . . Sometimes there appears to be more to the poem: complicated metaphors, semantic revelations, occult suggestions linking one word to another, evocative effects, an unleashed process of association, which in some cases reminds one of the charm of surrealistic poetry. Indeed, some of these associations appear to belong to the same family as those that gave special nuances to his metaphors in [the early collections] *Some Poems, Swamp of Souls*, and *Sentiment of the World*.

In an article that appeared soon after the publication of *Lesson of Things*, Mário Chammie made some observations about "This Is That" . . . that transcend the narrow limits of textual explication and penetrate the realm of the broad comprehension of the poet. He says: "Above all, it is necessary to understand the reticent Andrade, the man who, insulating himself in an irony and bitterness of an intelligence that goes beyond his feelings toward the world, sees the gratuitousness of things: heads and tails, this is that."

Hélcio Martins. *Rima na poesia de Carlos Drummond de Andrade* (Rio de Janeiro, Livraria José Olympio Editôra, 1968), pp. 123–26†

It is no longer possible to speak of modern Brazilian poetry without mentioning Carlos Drummond de Andrade, and it is impossible to speak of Carlos Drummond de Andrade without mentioning his poem "In the Middle of the Road," since this poem has come to be, for various reasons, the most intriguing, the most recited, and the most discussed of the poet's works. . . . Ever since its first publication, the poem, just a little poem [it contains only ten lines], has had . . . the effect of scandalizing readers, if not . . . irritating and revolting them. And such reactions have occurred, first, because these readers could not believe, out of deference to the poetic conventions of the 1920s and 1930s, that a theme of the evident commonness of a "stone in the middle of the road" could be the subject of a poem. And what is more, the recurrent sentence which expresses this commonness . . . introduced a grammatical "mistake" (the use of the verb *ter* for *haver* [to mean "there is"]). . . .

In the second place, the poem itself was shocking because although it was written using the element of poetry—that is, with verses, strophes, and a curious process of repetition or parallelism—nonetheless, in terms of the subject and the language, it seemed to display a lack of knowledge of what was always held to be poetic expression. It also had the audacity (which the young poet from Minas Gerais appeared to take pride in) of showing off ostentatiously that lack of knowledge and of supposing that the public would be impressed by such behavior.

In the third place, the poem was scandalous, irritating, and revolting because people could not attach any meaning to it. It contained a profound but enigmatic meaning: What could "middle of the road" and "stone" mean for the poet? Why would he "never" forget that happening? What "happening" was this? Perhaps, they felt, it was merely a poetic sketch, so in favor with the futurists, the dadaists, the surrealists, and the modernists, with whose revolutionary or even anarchic tendencies the poet identified.

Antônio Soares Amora. In Hans Flasche, ed., *Litterae hispanae et lusitanae* (Munich, Max Hueber Verlag, 1968), pp. 33–34†

Repetition, in its many forms, seems to have its origin in [Andrade's] anxious desire to go beyond the unspeakable. The poet knows that he could say much beyond the limits of the word, but he must subordinate himself to it. But at the same time he rebels. He readjusts the elements of language, he combines them in a particular system of signs, he attributes to them other possible values and meanings, and he is able to impose on the text a profound vision and comprehension of life, of men, of things, and of the world. He reveals to us things we did not know or could not grasp directly, for we lack the intuitive force necessary to perceive them and the expressive capacity to reveal them.

Thus, if on the one hand he has always achieved the aesthetic victory of the creative energy of man over the structures of language, on the other hand his victory is incomplete, since a great part of the vitality of his poetic world must continue to be trapped, suffocated in his throat or, as another poet would have it, strangled "in the grip of a paralytic language." Andrade himself . . . has not concealed his pessimism about the problems of expression, and—another indication of his modernity—all his books contain poems whose very content is the presentation of a poetic concept or the anguished reference to the struggle for expression. We could say that the poet has his *metalanguage*, his *metapoems*.

Gilberto Mendonça Teles. *Drummond, a estilística da repetição* (Rio de Janeiro, Livraria José Olympio Editôra, 1970), p. 179†

Carlos Drummond de Andrade's work up until now . . . can be summarized as the constant investigation of poetic devices, with an interest in what is new, in discovery. His poetry possesses the stamp, the flavor, of the people: it is the poetry of the everyday, as someone has already noted. Day-to-day facts are present, showing the poet's preoccupation with his province, with his recollections and his memories, with man and his destiny, with wars. He is the occasionally stubborn anti-lyricist and also the most subtle ironist. He is the poet of free verse, narrative and prosaic, and also the neoclassic poet and the experimental poet. He is the poet concerned with the outcome of the war and also the disenchanted poet. . . .

José Guilherme Merquior, in a study of the poem "The Machine of the World," speaks of a "third" Andrade, one who emerged with the publication of *Clear Enigma* in 1951: "After the early humorist and the 'social poet' of *Sentiment of the World* and *The People's Rose*, he must have become a neoclassical pessimist, fleeing from society, removed from concrete struggles, not believing in anything or anybody." . . .

For a better clarification of Drummond's career, we can divide his "odyssey" into the following stages: (1) a portrait of the province, with sarcasm and irony, even with some wisecracking, the inheritance from the first phase of modernism . . . (2) the movement from the preoccupation with his province and its individuals to the concern for the world— a feeling of solidarity with humanity . . . (3) the reassertion of the lyricist (contained until now, with a certain feeling of disenchantment toward the world . . . (4) an increased disenchantment with the world, together with a cultivation of more classical forms. . . . In summary, his poetry has moved from free verse to metered verse, whether classical or not, ending up with the experimentalism of concrete verse, as for example when he subverts syntax with great vigor and undoes words in the search for new forms of expression.

> Assis Brasil. *Carlos Drummond de Andrade, ensaio*
> (Rio de Janeiro, Livros do Mundo Inteiro, 1971),
> pp. 99–101†

ANDRADE, MÁRIO DE (1893–1945)

BRAZIL

What we should take note of first in Mário de Andrade is his originality. He created his own place in his own way, and in an unmistakable way. Alongside this intrinsic originality, however, there exists another, less apparent one: the personality that he sought to create with his technique. Thus, we can explain how a poet of so much personality is also a poet of many artifices. His best accomplishments are those he has achieved by giving himself over naturally to his originality. His weakest or falsest passages are those in which he becomes involved in the search for an artificial expression.

Two levels of concern, two kinds of motives, are dominant in Andrade: the feeling for his land and his intimate feeling as a man. In his books of poetry both levels alternate. . . . In his early works, the feeling for the land dominates, while in his later books it is the intimate feeling. In *Auction of Ills* we perceive the best confluence of the two currents.

Nevertheless, this feeling toward the land is not the same toward all its aspects. A feeling of love toward natural life is accompanied by a feeling of rebellion toward social life. One cannot ask for a position from an artist that is loftier or more legitimate. And the feeling of revolt comes to him spontaneously from three sources: his temperament, his youth, and the literary movement he belonged to. He externalized this feeling with a courage, an artistic purity, and a complexity that are truly exemplary. [1942]

Álvaro Lins. *Poesia moderna do Brasil* (Rio de Janeiro, Tecnoprint Gráfica, 1968), p. 50†

[Some argue] that Mário de Andrade's poetry is contaminated by "erudite blemishes." . . . Perhaps they would demand that a poet, when he writes poetry, do away with his scholarly exterior, so that his poetry is accessible to ignoramuses. Is a poet responsible if his readers do not have the knowledge to understand the subjects and themes of his poetic work? Perhaps a poet is obliged always to speak of canaries, full moons, moonlight and parks, just because the reader doesn't know Dom Rodrigo de Castel Branco or Brigadier Jordão. Is the poet supposed to make a deal with the reader not to use Brazilian dialect in his poems because the readers think he should speak "lawful" Portuguese?

Fernando Mendes de Almeida. *Mário de Andrade* (São Paulo, Conselho Estadual de Cultura, Comissão de Literatura, 1958?), p. 17†

The same reasons that led Mário de Andrade to become more interested than most writers in the problems of language also attracted him to folklore, that other form of expression of national culture. In the desire to know the Brazilian people and in the quest for authenticity for the literary work are to be found the motives for the intense passion of the scholar.

His clear intellectual honesty, a sign of his personality . . . constitutes the key to his approach. . . . In a lecture given in Belo Horizonte he recalled how he was prepared to scar his own body as part of his method of participation, in order to deepen his understanding of this aspect of folklore. He always pursued exactness.

Naturally, he wrote a considerable amount on popular traditional culture, particularly in *Dramatic Dances of Brazil*, in which he gathered together outstanding essays conceived and developed with a deep love for the people and a very firm belief in the existence of Brazil as something alive (these being other gifts of the good folklorist). . . .

One can see the omnipresence of folklore in *Macunaíma*, "a hero without character" (this subtitle is his own, but there was a decision to omit it in the edition of 1942).

Aires de Mata Machado Filho. In Fábio Lucas, ed., *Mário de Andrade* (Belo Horizonte, Edições MP, 1965), pp. 13–14†

A preoccupation with language and poetical style, quite apart from content, but not separated from it, is one of the distinctive contributions of Andrade and one of the primary characteristics of the modernist movement to which he belonged. The poetry which emerges as a result of this intense movement of cultural renovation for Brazil represents an attempt to break away from traditional poetic style and traditional poetic form, an attempt which continues today in Brazilian poetry, as Cassiano Ricardo's article in [the journal] *Invenção* so adequately demonstrates. One of the characteristics of such an attempt to renovate the poetic form is the renunciation of the standard poetic unities (in Brazil, those of Parnassianism) based upon verse, rhyme, and stanzaic format, i.e., meter. This introduction has had as its primary purpose to indicate through an extended analysis of a representative body of poetry how Mário de Andrade, for one, attempts to fill that void left by such a renunciation. The poet finds, due to the intrinsic nature of poetry—its limited, intense and controlled perspective of the universe—that he must seek new forms of poetic unity and cohesion to replace those he has abandoned.

David William Foster. *LBR*. 2, 2, Dec., 1965, pp. 94–95

[Andrade] was a writer who lacked a sense of cosmic drama and who did not feel, unless it was a landscape or picturesque point of view, any mystery of living as a man before the universe. The great archetypal themes of love, death, time, life, and God . . . did not arouse his passions in any way. Instead, he made of his work the domain of passing instants in which life seems to be a lovable complement of the landscape. The misery of the human condition—whether in the Christian sense of the recognition of original sin or in the atheistic sense of the absolute permissiveness regarding imaginable earthly pleasures—did not bother him. A poet of the everyday, he does not make any references in his work to day and night in the genuinely metaphysical sense. . . .

Despite the commendable feeling for the world that shines through so many poems in *São Paulo Lyre*, we cannot accept the claim—so often repeated—that Mário de Andrade resolved the political problem of his art by according to it an almost partisan position, turning it into a means for understanding the rest of mankind. This in my opinion is the most violent distortion possible of the writer from São Paulo, a self-serving falsification of the nature of his thought, since the aesthete of *The Little-Bird Stuffer* never was able to attain the balance that would provide him with a direction and an emphasis for his work. . . .

Mário de Andrade's work is the adventure of a rigidly developed style . . . within the heart of the modernist movement, carried out in an atmosphere of common research and investigation, a sense of liberty that led the writers of 1922 [the year of the Modern Art Week] to formulate an aesthetic revolution of national discovery, although their best weapons were imported from France and Italy.

Lêdo Ivo. *Poesia observada* (Rio de Janeiro, Orfeu, 1967), pp. 224–26†

Mário de Andrade was not content merely to embalm the ghosts of an earlier literary movement. He had to affirm what he believed as well as negate what he opposed. . . . Mário developed aesthetic ideas that were to form the basis of revolt in the first phase of Modernist Brazilian poetry, in which the emphasis was on originality, spontaneity, liberty, expressiveness, inspiration, and emotional strength. These ideas may be summarized as follows:

1. Art is not solely concerned with the fashioning of beauty; indeed the fashioning of beauty is not even the major end of art.

2. Art arises from the need of man to express himself.

3. It was the original desire of man to express feelings and thoughts of lyrical value that led him to create the arts.

4. True art, then, is the expression of feelings and thoughts by way of the vehicle of a concrete beauty.

5. Young writers should create, as artists, with the sense of life and liberty.

6. Above all else, young poets and novelists must develop their own personal artistic principles; the rest is application by study and practice. . . .

Mário summed up his aesthetic position with one short sentence which stressed three key words: "A *Hymn* to *Life* and *Joy*." These three "marvelous and beautiful words," he thought, constituted a criticism of his own work. They certainly formed the basis of his Catholic happiness. He wished "the young writers my happiness: Hymn, Life, and Joy. But they should not confuse Hymn with a toast, Life with a brothel, Joy with a binge." Within the responsible limitations of religious decency, art was an exciting adventure for Mário de Andrade. . . .

In the final stages of the intensifying campaign that would result in the victory of the Modern Art Week, Mário de Andrade supplied what the Modernist Movement needed: a coherent rationale, an inexhaustible enthusiasm, and high-minded bravado.

John Nist. *The Modernist Movement in Brazil* (Austin, University of Texas Press, 1967), pp. 68–69

Although Andrade was essentially a poet, his novels created a greater sensation than his verse. *Macunaíma* has a place in Brazilian literature equivalent to that of *Ulysses* in English literature. It is not exactly a novel. Though in prose, it has some of the characteristics of the epic poem in that its hero is a mythical figure who is supposed to symbolize the Brazilian spirit and to incorporate in his psyche the collective unconscious of his compatriots, just as the style, which is permeated with linguistic innovations, is supposed to be based on the speech of all Brazil.

Andrade's other fiction is satirical and humorous and very much concerned with urban São Paulo, with its national groups and its first and second generations of immigrants.

Raymond S. Sayers. In Encyclopedia of World Literature
in the 20th Century (New York, Frederick Ungar,
1967), Vol. 1, p. 49

Hallucinated City is a slender volume of twenty-two poems preceded by a short dedication from the poet to the poet and an "Extremely Interesting Preface," as Mário immodestly qualified his foreword. This preface, often called the bible of Brazilian Modernism, in reality constitutes the first formal poetics of the Movement. As such, it is largely responsible for the direction which the Brazilian lyric took after 1922. Rather than bible, the "Extremely Interesting Preface" might more justly be termed missal: text of the proper thing to write, rubric directing the creator as to how he shall write it. The poet himself, however, would have objected to the term "missal." It smacks of school, and he hated the rigidity of the literary school. . . . With customary tongue-in-cheek, Mário states that in order to prove his divorcement from [Italian] Futurism he will found his own school: Hallucinism. Next week he will found another.

This, in itself, is not to be taken seriously. What the Brazilian admired in Marinetti was the liberated word: "the suggestive, associative, symbolic, universal, and musical power of the liberated word." He did not, however, appreciate the petrification of the liberated word in a modern poetic system. This is the gulf that separates Mário from the Italian Futurist. This freedom from the stricture of school points always, in Mário, away from Futurism and toward Modernism. Unlike the Futurists, Mário writes of modern things only because they are part of his world; they are neither to be systematized nor to be deified. . . .

Owing to the nature of its genesis, it is not surprising that, like all the representative lyrical works of the first decade of Brazilian Modernism, *Hallucinated City* is, to a certain extent, a flawed book. It represents perhaps too much the impassioned outcry of the moment, notwithstanding Mário's definition of Art. This verse frequently lacks philosophical depth; it often reveals a want of simple meditation. On the other hand, it is legitimately the portrait of a young poet with all the baggage of his sincerity weighing lightly on his back. Later, in 1931, Mário was to write that, in his opinion, youths under twenty-five should be prohibited by law from publishing books of poetry! His final word on that point.

Nonetheless, if the poems which figure in the *Hallucinated City* had been deeply meditated and meditative, the work would have lacked the agitated revolutionary spirit so essential to the renovation of Brazil's fading Parnassianism. It is not foolhardy, then, to declare that this small volume of poetry was effectively instrumental in changing the direction of Brazilian letters for all time. After *Hallucinated City* and the Modernist revolution followed the more durable and mature Modernist spirit. Brazilian Portuguese became once and for all a fitting tool for the composition of the lyric and the novel. The sociological prose fiction of the Northeast, largely a product of the thirties, would not have been possible without the literary housecleaning of the poets of the twenties. Because Mário de Andrade sang a vehement hymn of love to his São Paulo—and by extension to his Brazil—the path was opened to all Brazilian writers to compose such hymns, each in his way, with varying degrees of profundity. And so they did.

> Jack E. Tomlins. Introduction to Mário de Andrade,
> *Hallucinated City* (Nashville, Vanderbilt University
> Press, 1968), pp. xiii, xvi–xvii

Alceu de Amoroso Lima, in an article written after the appearance of *Macunaíma*, does not really undertake a critical study. Instead, he tries to analyze and comment on the two prefaces, something that allowed him to set readers straight who might be thinking about plagiarism. In trying to place the work, he writes that this is "not a novel, or a poem, or an epic. I would call it, rather, a cocktail, a mixture of whatever was at hand of the basic elements of our 'psyche,' as the sociologists say. It is one of these half-portraits in which there is a superimposition of several different photographs and which· ends up not looking like any of them."

Mário himself was not sure how to classify the book. First he called it a "history" in one of the prefaces, thereby wanting to point out what it had in common with popular stories. But this was not an exact title, and he remembered calling it a "rhapsody." Indeed, *Macunaíma* presents, like musical rhapsodies, a variety of popular motifs, which Andrade arranges, on the basis of the affinities among them, linking them, giving the impression of unity, adding segments of his own creation so that the transition from one motif to another would not be apparent. . . .

Later the book was submitted as a "novel" to a literary contest. The idea was not Andrade's, but he did not object. And he would not have agreed to this classification if he could not justify it. It is, in fact, a novel or romance in the old sense of the life and deeds of a hero, like those of Gil Blas, Gargantua. . . . *Macunaíma* approximates the medieval epic as well. . . . It is beyond space and time. . . .

M. Cavalcanti Proença. *Roteiro de "Macunaíma"*
(Rio de Janeiro, Editôra Civilização Brasileira, 1969),
pp. 10–11†

With their rebelliousness, their scorn of normality, their disparate imagery, and their sense of the integrity of the alienated and dissociated personality, these 22 poems [in *Hallucinated City*] and their "Extremely Interesting Preface" shocked Brazilian poetry into the 20th century in 1922. Andrade in Brazil, like Eliot in England and America, remained the masterly presence in Brazilian poetry until his death in 1945.

The modern reader will find echoes of Gautier ("Nocturne"), Whitman—or is it Francis Jammes?—("Ode to the Bourgeois Gentleman"), and Apollinaire ("The Troubadour"). But more important is the voice of Andrade accommodating the clashing images of São Paulo, his "harlequin city," to the beating of his "harlequin heart":

São Paulo! tumult of my life . . .

The tumult of the world of appearances provokes an analogous commotion of images within Andrade's interior self. What is most notable and most un-Eliot-like is Andrade's eager acceptance of all experience in its unresolved disharmony. The poems are laden with rebelliousness —prosodic revolution, which readers of the English version will not be able to sense; thematic revolution, for Andrade was the first to turn squarely toward the Brazilian scene; and personal revolt, as Andrade crucifies the mediocrity, blindness, and dullness of the Brazilian middle class.

Tomlins' renderings are presented *en face*, with an excellent, informative introduction, but without notes, which they sometimes need badly. Unfortunately, the very "accurate" translations are wilted by a dull pedestrianness I had thought difficult for a translator to achieve when working with open patterns that actually yield the translator a freedom for which he should be grateful. The chief awkwardness here derives from Tomlins' decision to follow the order of imagery too closely. I can appreciate the reasons for such a choice, but even in poetry whose prosody is not bound by stanzaic patterns, rhythm still determines the shaping of the whole effect. I think Tomlins should have been more sensitive to the collaboration of rhythm and imagery. . . .

Leland H. Chambers. DQ. Winter, 1969, pp. 127–28

That inextricable interpenetration of genres, which harmonize finally to constitute Andrade's admirable personality, cannot be torn apart if we wish to understand him in his authenticity and in his true greatness. In my opinion, those who take pains to show that in him the poet was greater than the critic or the critic more interesting than the fiction writer are in error. Although he himself, as we shall see, has fallen into that trap, it is not possible to consider his protean qualities as other than an indissoluble unity. So thoroughly is this true that we find him in all his spontaneity in each of the genres that he practiced, and his qualities as a writer and artisan are always the same. Even more: in a general way, all his several qualities are balanced when seen as a whole. It is impossible and evidently wrong to see in Mário de Andrade a poet who by accident practiced the other genres or a critic gnawed by the ambition to write creative literature. In such cases the difference in quality between the "vocationed" pages and the others immediately tells the truth about a writer. With Mário de Andrade, that difference simply does not appear. He is always the same: in his short stories, in his criticism, in his poetry. He is not a Victor Hugo attempting to write a novel, nor a Sainte-Beuve trying his hand at poetry, nor a Balzac attempting criticism. His creative impulse—whatever his limitations may be—is genuinely the same in all his books and on all his pages. . . .

[Andrade's] human presence is still too strong, too moving, for us to approach him with the cold instruments of critical analysis. There is no Brazilian writer of these last forty years who has not felt his human presence outside of literature. And here we pinpoint a fact that is essential for the proper comprehension of his historical role. It is that Mário de Andrade was also, more than any other Brazilian writer of any period, a *presence*. The presence of a man identified by his warmth, by his winning laughter, by that kind of angelic innocence which was observed in him on one occasion. A presence that, without the slightest intention of indulging in literary "politics," sacrificed to this end an enormous amount of time that might better have been spent on personal tasks, prompted by a sensibility which led him to write long letters to obscure or unknown beginners; or to discuss with his companions in literary adventure, in letters no less extensive, the crucial problems at that time heatedly debated.

Wilson Martins. *The Modernist Idea* (New York, New York University Press, 1970), pp. 245–46

Mário de Andrade sets [*To Love, an Intransitive Verb*] within a bourgeois family in São Paulo, regulated by convention. He stresses this aspect in a synthesizing caricature: "As for the tone of life, you already know too well that photograph: the mother is seated with the little ones around her lap. The father, standing, protectively rests his honorable hand on her shoulder. . . ." It is the portrait of pretentious mediocrity. . . .

The economic position of the father reflects the emergence of the São Paulo business community, the urban middle class that aspired to power in a society still politically dominated by the rural aristocracy, banded together in oligarchic groups. Since Brazilian industry was established as a result of the abundance of agricultural activity, it was common for industrialists also to be landowners. The culture, as can be seen, was modeled along lines of patriarchal and conservative customs. . . .

In essence, *To Love, an Intransitive Verb* is the cruel portrait of a society that denies room to love in favor of other values held to be more basic. What the Sousa Costa family is after is the stability of its interests in light of the style of existing life, interests cloaked in hypocrisy and deceit. . . .

In Brazilian literature, the theme of the colonization by Germans also found special analysis in Aranha's novel *Canaan*. Mário de Andrade attempts to explore the encounter between the two cultures, the German and the Brazilian, in the "idyll" *To Love, an Intransitive Verb*. Fräulein [whose love for the family's son threatens their bourgeois stability] is portrayed as a woman of conflicting impulses. Reason and passion collide in her psychology in the manner of baroque aesthetics. We are presented the Teutonic sensibility, with its love of rationality and affection for science, on the way to becoming Latin— that is, on the way to giving itself over to the primacy of emotion.

Fábio Lucas. *LBR*. 8, 2, Dec., 1971, pp. 70–71†

ANDRADE, OSWALD DE (1890–1954)

BRAZIL

In its style, its technique, and its psychology, *Zero Boundary* is a contemporary extension of [Oswald de Andrade's earlier] *The Damned*. It shows the same preference for uncommon adjectives, the same quest for the powerful sentence, for the unexpected image, the same sort of cinematographic technique, which in 1922 was a sensational novelty, the same summarial psychology, tending toward caricature. All the things which made Oswald such a personality during the Semana de Arte Moderna [Week of Modern Art], which stamped it with originality and gave it an almost violent polish, reappears here in an even more concentrated form.

A rapid survey of Parnassian devices in the distinctive style of the author makes me want to compare him not to the great muralists of whatever period [he called *Zero Boundary* a "mural novel"] but to surrealists like Salvador Dalí. . . . His delight in striking contrasts, without landscapes and half-tones, [makes] Oswald not a bourgeois Flaubert or even a populist Zola, but a Satanic Baudelaire, a Rimbaud of the novel, a great novelist astray in a modern functional classicism. This is not meant to limit the author, but only to situate him in time so that his work will be better understood and so that we can see why he is not a writer with a large audience. . . . His total irreverence for language irritates the reader used to seeing some matters handled with reserve. In its ability to upset, Oswald de Andrade's work possesses quite a strong revolutionary quality. . . . *Zero Boundary* occupies an odd position, out of the reach of the masses because of its literary and artistic refinement, but yet unacceptable to the intelligentsia because of its separatist revolutionary sentiment, which has long been passé. . . .

Sérgio Milliet. *Diário crítico (1940–1943)* (São Paulo,
Editôra Brasiliense, 1944), pp. 250–51†

The [Pau-Brazil] movement, whose manifesto was published in 1923, found its expression in [Oswald de Andrade's] book *Pau-Brazil* [literally, Brazil-Stick] with a preface by Paulo Prado. This group had as its program the liberation of verse, in a creative phase that could succeed the futurist destruction, and nationalism, which ought to free us "from the baneful influences of the old civilizations in decadence." Oswald desired a primitive poetry, one that would correspond to European exoticism, for which he would opt to reject cubism and surrealism. And he realized his aims in *Pau-Brazil* and in *First Student Notebook of Poetry.*

Péricles Eugênio da Silva Ramos. In Afrânio Coutinho,
ed., *A literatura no Brasil* (Rio de Janeiro, Livraria
São José, 1959), Vol. 3/1, pp. 511–12

The most combative and polemical figure among the Paulista [São Paulo] Modernists, Oswald de Andrade had read the Italian Marinetti's *Futurist Manifesto* in Paris—a document upon which Mussolini based his program of fascism in 1919. The Italian announced that literature was in favor of the new technical civilization, that it was against academicism, bric-a-brac, and museums. Marinetti furthermore exalted the cult of "words in freedom." The *Manifesto,* together with the crowning of Paul Fort as the prince of French poets, stirred Oswald. In fact, Fort's influence on the Brazilian was much stronger than Marinetti's. Oswald reveled in the fact that Fort had never written either stanzas or sonnets. Free verse opened up a whole new realm of possibilities, for as Oswald admitted, "I could never count syllables. Metrics was a thing to which my intelligence could not adapt, a subordination which I completely refused."

Clinging to the word *Futurist* from Marinetti's manifesto with a cultural cry that "the modern world needs poets above all else," and wanting to enliven the Brazilian Academy of Letters, which was living on its past glories, Oswald campaigned to have Amadeu Amaral [a Parnassian poet] elected a member. By this time, of course, the giants Machado de Assis and Euclides da Cunha were both dead. Neither had left a successor worthy of his substance or style. Oswald was convinced that Brazilian literature had grown musty, stale, out-of-date. The country had not yet renounced its cultural past: writers still had to obey the rules, and poets were judged on the basis of their metrics. To modernize Brazilian literature and culture in general, Oswald constantly called for a transfusion from foreign sources, but "that did not imply that he wanted to renounce Brazilian sentiment" [Mário da Silva Brito].

John Nist. *The Modernist Movement in Brazil*
(Austin, University of Texas Press, 1967), p. 21

In *Sentimental Memories of João Miramar . . .* and *Seraphim Big Bridge* Oswald de Andrade devoted himself to social satire and to the renovation of narrative language, adopting procedures then common to both Brazilian and European writers (an exceedingly exaggerated aspect of his style, in all his works, is the unchecked animism with which he referred to all objects, a systematic anthropomorphism, by means of which he attempted to give a touch of modernity to his work).

A man of imposing presence, a fearless agitator of ideas, and a sarcastic destroyer of persons and institutions, Oswald de Andrade created a national expectation for the publication of his last work of fiction, *Zero Boundary*, the first volume of which, *The Melancholic Revolution*, he offered with this explanation: "*Zero Boundary* tends toward social fresco. It is an attempt at a mural novel."

In effect, the two volumes of the work, *The Melancholic Revolution* and *Plains,* can be compared to an immense painting, patiently executed with a detailed use of color—nothing less alive and functional. Here we have everything: the difficulties and the struggles for the survival of the people of the clearings; the relationship between the humble and the powerful; the authorities, the haciendas, businesses, where there appear Turks, Japanese, and blacks; communism, which one overhears being discussed . . . the involved games of politicians; the São Paulo vision of the Getúlio Vargas era. The central themes of Oswald de Andrade are also here: the decadence of Christianity, the proximity of a world revolution that will transform everything. At the end of *The Melancholic Revolution* he says: "The Church of Christ, which presided over the formation of the society of the West and which formed the medieval collectives, drew back from the struggle, like a businessman who makes his profit and then retires to private life. The Church in the service of the bourgeoisie, subordinated to it, abstained from being present at the tremendous debate of the contemporary world." . . .

Fábio Lucas. O caráter social da literatura brasileira
(Rio de Janeiro, Editôra Paz e Terra, 1970), pp. 76–77

ARANHA, JOSÉ PEREIRA DA GRAÇA (1868-1931)

BRAZIL

The exotic still dazzles even the greatest wits. Otherwise Anatole France could never have called *Canaan* "the great American novel." For as a piece of writing, due allowance being made for a wretched translation, the book is amorphous in a curiously old-fashioned way. In spirit and structure it goes back to the first generation of the romantic writers.

It smacks of Chateaubriand and of the romantic novelettes of the Germans; it is filled with futile and high-flown discussions. . . .

The theme and fable of the book are scarcely less early-romantic in character than its style and structure. Milkau, a young German idealist, the son of a university professor, has wearied of the cruelty and corruption of Europe—quite as the sons of the late eighteenth century did or thought they did—and sets out to find

> In happy climes the seat of innocence
> Where Nature guides and virtue rules.

He does not desire to stay in the commercial colonies of his country-men in Brazil, but with his somewhat harder headed friend Lentz settles in the virgin forest. A modern note steals into the narrative with the gradual disillusionment of Milkau. He finds himself soon enough in a situation which is anything but primitive and idyllic. On the one hand he sees the decay of the older Brazilian civilization and on the other a new and harsh and quite European struggle for the possession of the resources of the country. The ugly moral passions and prejudices of Europe are also projected into the book through the episode of Mary Perutz, which is horrible in a semi-romantic, semi-naturalistic way. But the end of the story is quite true to form. Milkau rescues Mary and wanders with her into the mountains, consol-ing himself with a long series of vague and melancholy and, in the original no doubt, sonorous reflections. We are given no hint as to any practical adjustment between the disillusioned man and his world.

What gives its value to the book . . . is the picture which, largely by means of discussion, Aranha presents of the Brazilian civilization of today. How correct that picture is a complete outsider cannot pre-sume to say. But the author's profoundly and helplessly romantic tem-perament should be taken into account. His strongest feeling is one of a vast dreariness in the present fate of his country. . . .

Aranha does not succeed in communicating to the reader a very strong sense of [the] hope which he nourishes. Joca, the mulatto who dances his folk-dance and sings his Portuguese folk-song as a protest against the influence of the strangers, is a picturesque and pathetic figure. But he has neither energy nor mind. Yet he symbolizes the theme and intention of the book on its best side. Its weaker side is illustrated by the absurdly unreal description of the foreigner's behavior on the same occasion. Aranha's protest is poetic and appealing. But in its intellectual character it is futile, since his romanticism has not even permitted him to grasp the nature of the forces which he would assault.

Nation. March 13, 1920, p. 337

The most striking politico-economic phenomenon of current history—the simultaneous Europeanization of America and Americanization of Europe—is woven into the background of [*Canaan*] and is interpreted as a single step in this progress. The Americas, of both continents, Senhor Aranha says, are being Europeanized by the dissolvent action of the hordes of immigrants who cross the Atlantic, bringing with them the shadows of their several gods; the New World is, in turn, hastening the decomposition of the old European social structure by the force of its example.

Brazil is chosen as typical of this change in all the countries of the Americas. And Brazil's tragic loss of identity as a nation in her truceless struggle against the tides of immigration is pictured as an example of the metamorphosis through which the entire New World is passing.

Europe's influence on the Americas and humankind's quest for the ever-fading land of Canaan are both symbolized by giving the individual history of Milkau, a German immigrant into Brazil, a profound social and philosophical significance. . . .

In content, presentation and significance Aranha's novel is worthy of Anatole France's enthusiastic estimate of it as "the great American novel." Its author's charity for weakness, his great compassion for sorrow and pain, wherever found and whatever their cause, is akin to Dostoyevski's sympathy for the world's misfits; but as an artist Aranha suffers at the expense of the philosopher in him. His present novel is vouched for by its publishers as "the masterpiece of Brazilian literature." But for pure literature the book must take a lower rank than it commands as a work of philosophy. It requires too attentive reading for Simon-pure fiction. The author's canvas is overcrowded with ideas. He uses so much of the pigment of raw thought that we sometimes lose sight of the picture in the philosophical background. There is ample material in the book for two separate novels—one on the historical phenomenon of changing America, and another on man's quest for the chimera of the ideal.

This lack of proportion between the elements of drama and philosophy is the outcome of Senhor Aranha's preoccupation with his central idea. He is dominated by his desire to preach the doctrine of salvation through love. (He uses the term "love" as synonymous with man's acceptance of his first duty as sympathy for humankind.)

No observant reader can doubt that this absorption in his message has made the author artistically careless of proportions. For no reader of this remarkable novel can escape Senhor Aranha's abilities as a descriptive and dramatic writer of exceptional calibre. His book is notable for the purity of its psychological analysis, for its powers of characterization, for the vivid beauty of its descriptive passages and for its scenes of tremendous dramatic power as much as it is for the light it throws into the depths of an unusually reflective mind.

NYT. April 11, 1920, p. 174

In this novelized document upon Brazil's racial problems and popular customs [*Canaan*] a certain and facile symbolism seems to inhere. Milkau is . . . the blend of Christianity and Socialism—two concepts which, for all their recent historic enmity, are closely related, though by no means identical, in philosophical background. Lentz is the apostle of Nietzscheanism. Mary is the suffering land, a prey to the worse elements. The pot that melts the peoples melts their philosophies. So are they fused in this book, which terminates in a cloud, as of the first smoke to rise from the crucible.

Canaan is not, for all its novelty and substantiality, the "splendid alliance of artistic perfection and moral grandeur" that one of its countless panegyrists has discovered it to be. Neither does it contain that mixture of Ibsen, Tolstoi, Zola, Sudermann, Maeterlinck and Anatole France which was found in it by an editorial writer in the *Journal do commercio*. Even [José] Veríssimo, it seems to me, exaggerated the artistic importance of the novel in his enthusiasm—a rare thing in Veríssimo—over the newness and the social significance of the book. . . . Its historic importance is less to be questioned, though it has not created a school. . . .

The philosophy of Aranha . . . is a philosophy of hope, of intoxication, before the glorious majesty of nature; it is like a magnificent flower of dream, life, desire, aspiration toward happiness, which returns incessantly to the august bosom of the eternal Pan. Man passes on, he is a particle of dust that is blown for a moment across the earth. His whole struggle aims to merge him with nature, through religion, through love, through philosophy. It is this unceasing anxiety to dissolve into something superior to ourselves that produces the great mystics, the great lovers or the great philosophers; yet, at bottom, life in itself is worth what the dust is worth that glitters for an instant in the sun's rays. . . . Such surely is the philosophy of Aranha; a sunflower gilded by thought, it turns eternally toward fleeting happiness, in a perpetual desire to merge with it and drink in the light through its petals.

Isaac Goldberg. *Brazilian Literature* (New York, Alfred A. Knopf, 1922), pp. 240–41, 246–47

Aranha conceived of a unity of beauty—a reality both aesthetic and sensory—by making emotion the central point of his world view. As a result, any discussion of ideas was governed by their strict relationship to sensory reality. In this way, Aranha created a universe colored by the possibilities for stimulation of the senses, so as to demonstrate the absorption of man into the splendor of that reality.

Toward accomplishing this program, he aimed at expressing the universe as in permanent change, which makes possible the appearance and sustenance of emotional states. Therefore, he wanted to populate his novels with characters who possessed an acute capacity for feeling and the ability to identify their emotional states quickly when they appeared. In short, Aranha tried to create a reality that would objectify his aesthetic principles and to fill that reality with elements that would give form to the artistic and human ideals that served as the writer's point of departure. . . . He was successful in achieving forms to produce the states of wonderment he sought, and he demonstrated those qualities of beauty that were necessary for the awakening of man's understanding of his setting, of the surrounding atmosphere.

José C. Garbuglio. *O universo estético-sensorial de Graça Aranha* (São Paulo, Faculdade de Filosofia, Ciéncias e Letras de Assis, 1966), pp. 137–38†

[Aranha] was a Symbolist (after Ibsen and Maeterlinck) in the time of Expressionism, in a generation of Expressionists. He was a student of Recife-style positivism who wrote a Symbolist novel, perhaps the only Symbolist novel of any merit in all of Brazilian literature. However, *Canaan* will also be for some time to come the nationalist breviary of a rhetorical generation. Aranha was an open spirit, open not to novelty (like Oswald de Andrade) but to youth, to all that was young; the Modernist generation, ungrateful in the extreme, was nevertheless for him a fountain source of rejuvenation. . . .

Because he saw himself as "revolutionary by heredity," his natural place in 1922 was on the side of the Modernists. Besides, the first number of the *Estética* opened with an inaugural article by him. . . . He put forth therein his favorite ideas, according to which a new esthetics would be born out of a civilization of iron and concrete, "the expression of all modern energy," an esthetics which is a philosophy of youth "because only youth can conquer Terror and transform everything into Joy." At the same time, however, taking an anticipatory position against [Freyre's] *The Masters and the Slaves*, he condemned the "new man" identified with the mestizo: "the plague, scourge, and shame of Brazilian society."

Wilson Martins. *The Modernist Idea* (New York, New York University Press, 1970), pp. 210–11

Canaan has been singled out as a precursor of modernism, a movement to which Aranha aligned himself with a great deal of fanfare twenty years later. Since *Canaan* is a work of the turn-of-the-century period, it shows the influences of naturalism and symbolism, reflected in the descriptions and in the exaltation of tropical nature, which serves as the background for the work. The novel also reflects the taste for philosophical discussions, which Aranha, a disciple of Tobias Barreto, developed from his contact with the famous School of Recife.

A female character plays a very important role in this novel, although it does not directly turn on her. The unhappy fate of the German-Brazilian Maria moves the reader, who responds to the suggestions of serene nobility in her suffering and humiliation. Most of the rest of the book contains neither action nor narration but ideological debate.

Santos Moraes. *Heroínas do romance brasileiro*
(Rio de Janeiro, Editôra Expressão e Cultura, 1971),
p. 159†

ARCINIEGAS, GERMÁN (1900–   )

COLOMBIA

Germán Arciniegas is one of the most gifted minds of the new crop of Spanish American writers. Balanced in his expression and profound in thought, he is as little tropical as is possible. Besides, he is a man who has read vastly and has assimilated his reading, yet he is free of that very Hispanic-American defect of overwhelming the reader with pompous bibliographies. Nor does he bring to his works the eagerness of the teacher of the seminary or of the institutions of higher learning—the accumulation of the opinions of others in order to mask or to hide his own.

All of these positive qualities, which contribute toward making him a serious and lofty figure in our literature, seem at times obscured by a certain partisanship. This would not be reproachable on balance—who does not exalt his own feelings even without wanting to?—if the objectivity of his studies did not suffer because of it. To adopt current assessments without examining them critically, just because they serve to support the thesis set forth, when one should not ignore the serious works that invalidate it, to affirm roundly as facts things that the most immediate reality denies—these are certainly not commendable methods.

Emilio Suárez Colimano. *Nosotros.* 2nd series,
No. 40, July, 1939, p. 267†

The fecundity and the popularity of Germán Arciniegas, recently appointed Colombian Minister of Education, are among the most hopeful signs on the horizon of Spanish American letters. With *Germans in the Conquest of America*, Arciniegas carries one step further a cycle begun with *The Communes* and *Jiménez de Quesada*. These books represent one of the first attempts to exploit the rich vein of history and biography offered by the centuries between the Conquest and the attainment of independence in northern South America. . . .

The principal actors in these pages are all German: Charles V, the Fuggers, the Welsers, Ambrosio Elfinger and his brothers, Federmann, Hohermuth, von Hutten. The action takes place largely in the eighteen years during which the House of Welser dominated the colony of Coro, and what is now Venezuela. Wisely Arciniegas does not try, as some romantic historians do, to build for us a personality out of whole cloth. Some of these sixteenth century characters remain names only—as they must in the hands of an honest historian—for lack of dependable material. The mighty Federmann, the vacillating Hohermuth, and his loyal friend Bartolomé Welser are felt and known, however, as real human beings. And this in itself is a notable contribution to the field of novelized history in which category this book belongs.

There is a continuity throughout the work of Arciniegas; he seems determined that each successive volume shall propagate in some manner or fashion his own liberal beliefs.

IAM. May, 1942, p. 23

Most biographers of the conquistadors study their subject in relation to European social, political, religious, and ethical values. Señor Arciniegas [in *The Knight of El Dorado*] sees his men as detached from Europe and transplanted to the teeming soil of America where their virtues, their sins, and their weaknesses must flourish in a freer and wilder fashion. His fresh point of view is combined with a fine sense of proportion and a delightful sense of humor to offer us candid pictures of men of the conquest, as they would have appeared at the time to the eyes of a keen aboriginal observer.

Señor Arciniegas—*rara avis*—is an unbiased historian. Whether his book supports or contradicts the "black legend" of Spain, it would be difficult to determine. *The Knight of El Dorado* is a serene appraisal of some of the human ingredients that destiny took from the medieval Spain of Doña Juana la Loca and mixed with native stock to form the basic elements of the future man of Hispano America.

Eduardo Cárdenas. *SR*. June 6, 1942, p. 7

A strange and sinister story of German marauders in South America is told by Señor Arciniegas, an important South American writer [in *Germans in the Conquest of America*]. It is a tale of adventures that seem fabulous in the barbaric wealth they disclose and in the romantic and mysterious lands they explore. In point of fact, these adventures belong among the most tragic pages of South American and European history. . . .

Señor Arciniegas' book reads like the most incredible and breathless of detective stories. Sometimes one feels that this is a picaresque novel—certainly the rogues and rascals are legion—and all the other ingredients are there, rich beyond the dreams of a Gil Blas. And then, one realizes that this is the raw stuff of history—that the villains Señor Arciniegas pins down on his pages are all too real. . . .

The German banking houses drained the wealth from South America and Spain, but it slipped through their fingers in loans that were not repaid and in fantastic commercial enterprises that finally collapsed. The Welsers and the Fuggers ended in bankruptcy.

There was a curse of futility on all these men. Theirs was "a futile trek, making wars, burning villages, shackling Indians, in order to arrive nowhere." Several of them stop just short of the rich, fabulous lands they were seeking. One lands to get drinking water and has his head broken by rocks hurled at him from ambush. One dies of a poisoned arrow. One has his fleet dispersed by storms. A treasure ship blows up and sinks. The most fantastic of all, Ulrich Schmidl, forgets his mission and wanders about for twenty years, then returns with a few parrots and is cast into prison where he consoles himself by writing a bizarre book of his adventures.

Alvaro da Silva. NYT. Oct. 17, 1943, p. 22

Biography of the Caribbean is at first glance a jumble of unrelated fights and voyages, discoverers, conquerors, smugglers, and dictators. Too often the student and the casual reader have had to absorb it this way and to try vainly to fit their own order to the myriad chaos. Germán Arciniegas has pretty much succeeded in weaving the entire history of the "Sea of the New World" into a single pattern.

The binding thread of the Caribbean's multicolored tapestry is the sea itself. The author believes the Caribbean is to the New World what the Mediterranean was to the old. Here, as there, the interests of nations met in strife. Their struggles always centered around the great trade routes. In the New World this story of the sea parallels the main currents of history. . . .

The success of this book and its ultimate justification is that it ties the tale of the Caribbean so well together and, at the same time, holds the interest of the reader with a breezy, informal style. The author does not, like too many historians, think that one must speak in hushed tones of people and deeds of the past. In his pages the rugged adventurers of our tropic sea live again with all their bravery, their lust, their sins, and their faith. The faults lie, as is often the case with summary histories compiled largely from secondary sources, in many inaccuracies and mistakes in emphasis. . . .

Strangely enough, this Colombian scholar is at his best when writing not of the Spanish conquistadors but of the English pirates Hawkins, Drake, and Morgan. Perhaps it was their half-official, half-bandit status and the indelible mark their ways and deeds left on the sea of the New World that really inspired the whole. Certainly his tales of these men and of Florin, Lafitte, and lesser lights (for some reason he says little of the great Dutchman, Piet Heyn) are the most racy portions of the book. In these exciting adventures he can let go with his breezy style, his excellent sense of timing and contrast. The last part of the volume, devoted increasingly to more organized and intellectual concerns, does not fit well in the adventurous pattern. He left out the twentieth century because it would have required more detailed handling. Perhaps it would have been as well to cover the nineteenth and part of the eighteenth century in this later study.

Albert Harkness, Jr. SR. July 6, 1946, pp. 10–11

Germán Arciniegas, a master historian and biographer, as he has demonstrated in many works, has come to rest . . . in the smiling and turbulent but seductive waters of the novel. And he has just written one that is like a collection of biographies, written in the manner painters do their great works, bringing together sketches and vivid colors, which come to constitute the admirable canvas that is *Halfway along the Road of Life.* . . .

How has he conceived his novel? In the most simple of ways. He pretends that before setting out on a trip from Genoa to New York aboard a freighter, he extends an invitation to the people who will be his sailing partners to join him at a meal. There are twelve passengers: the Arciniegas couple (the professor and his wife), a woman from Milan, a Salesian priest, the captain with the bushy eyebrows, four Jews (a couple and their children), an English couple, and a man from Brooklyn of Neopolitan origin. Also invited to the meal are the captain of the ship and his officers, along with the crew: servants, cabin boys, the carpenter, the cook, the scullion. All good people. Arciniegas uses his brush strokes to portray them from the very first page. . . .

The writer begins to explain the purpose of his invitation, and the plan he proposes to follow in the writing of a novel during the crossing. The book, he says, will include on the back of its title page a note saying that all of the characters of the work are fictitious, that all of the situations are of his invention, that any coincidence to be found between them and real persons is purely accidental. He tells them that he does not want to mix any of them in his pursuits, that they can do whatever they want, that what he says later will be the novel. Everything must happen as if it were his own invention. Besides, he observes, whatever will happen must be so real that people will not believe it. They will say that it is absurd, and they will think that it is a novel. This is, he says correctly, the most significant truth of the novel—events that seem to us to be fantasies because they are so real.

Federico Córdova. *Vida y obras de Germán Arciniegas*
(Havana, Publicaciones del Ministerio de Educación,
1950), pp. 369–71†

Amerigo Vespucci, still a vague figure in schoolbook history, is dealt with in lively fashion in [*Amerigo and the New World*], apparently the first biography of the singular Florentine whose name our two continents bear. There is good reason—aside from his being an interesting character—why he should be better known. It was he, not Solís, who actually discovered the Río de la Plata (which he called the Jordan), while on a voyage that took him to about 52 degrees south latitude, all along our Patagonian coast and within a short distance of the strait through which Magellan was to pass thirteen years later. . . .

To Arciniegas, Columbus is a man still tied to the Middle Ages. Vespucci—familiar with the ideas of Toscanelli, a contemporary of Botticelli, Ghirlandaio, Leonardo, and Michelangelo; a friend of Columbus—is a man of the Renaissance. Arciniegas brings to life this world of the Italian cities, especially Florence, where modern commerce and industry were being born and where the bourgeoisie was rising as a class, introducing a new period of history. In this environment, in which echoes of Dante and Petrarch mingle with political and financial ambitions and with wars and intrigues, commercial navigation filled the imaginations of all and the New World seemed to take on existence before it appeared. Vespucci was up to the minute in science and art, and Arciniegas is certainly correct when he says: "In part, Amerigo owed the immediate success of his letters to his literary art." . . . Arciniegas, for his part, makes it clear to us that he did not attempt here to confirm a preconceived idea. He builds on facts gathered in strict and diligent research, and his biography provides virtually a definitive picture. The reader also profits from his command of an expressive and racy Spanish—the style best suited to give life to his subject and to the bustling environment in which it is set.

Bernardo Verbitsky. *Américas*. 9, 11, Nov., 1957, p. 40

The work of Germán Arciniegas—from *The Student of the Round Table* through *Amerigo and the New World*—is characterized by profoundly American and democratic sentiments. His concern for matters regarding America is very well reflected in his excellent anthology *The Green Continent*, which contains one of the best panoramic visions of Latin American culture. Through various selections of the most representative writers of different countries, Arciniegas presents to us man and his environment, the different periods of historical development, the leaders and the heroes, the cities and the most picturesque areas of each region.

Although all his works are filled with exhaustive documentation, Germán Arciniegas knows how to transcend exclusively bibliographical limitations, by giving a fresh dimension to historical events and by enlivening facts with literary creation. He does not fragment historical reality but captures it through a kind of Bergsonian intuition. He is a synthesizer, not an analyst. The pictures he draws are filled with life; the settings he describes are admirable evocations with a very special atmosphere. Therefore, imagination takes precedence in his books over mere reproduction or cataloguing of facts.

The Cuban critic Medardo Vitier, in an excellent study on this Colombian writer, has expressed the following judgment: "Arciniegas is an excellent essayist. . . . In his books there is such a beautiful fusion of genres that one could well vacillate before labeling the genre. . . . Arciniegas does not subject himself to aesthetic categories. Fiction often bursts right into historical portrayal. . . . He has some of the aptitudes of the novelist, like an empathy that makes him have the same thoughts and feelings of the men and things of long ago, an imagination capable of reconstructing bits of the collective life, a sensitivity to psychology . . . and, finally, a clear perception of the dramatic, the essence of life. He also employs a direct and rapid style, which can be a possible characteristic of the essay but is more inherent to narrative prose."

Diccionario de la literatura latinoamericana: Colombia (Washington, D.C., Unión Panamericana, 1959), pp. 141–42†

In a well-thought-out introduction [to *The Continent of Seven Colors*], Arciniegas develops concisely his concept of the "four Americas" and draws some useful distinctions between North American and Ibero-American cultures. The remainder of this book [contains] a wealth of information on such subjects as the pre-Columbian civilizations, the conquest, the period of colonization, the influence of the Enlightenment, the struggle for independence and the socio-political and intellectual currents which followed independence. . . . This work does not ignore or pass over contemporary situations. The presence of Fidel Castro and the current status of the Monroe Doctrine, to cite just two examples, are discussed by the author.

Especially noteworthy are the chapters on Haiti and Brazil—in the case of Haiti because that country is so frequently overlooked in books of this nature and in the case of Brazil because of Arciniegas' concise but interesting account of Brazilian history and culture. Such matters as its discovery and colonization, its periods of independence under an emperor and as a republic, its unusual geographical features, and its distinctive cultural traits are presented in a fascinating and useful way.

Less successful are the chapters which Arciniegas devotes to Latin American belles lettres.

Earl M. Aldrich, Jr. Hispania. 52, March, 1969,
pp. 176–77

ARÉVALO MARTÍNEZ, RAFAEL (1884–   )

GUATEMALA

Surprisingly, Arévalo Martínez sees animal characteristics in his friends. Hence his many stories on this theme. When he began to write, he conceived of an "animal cycle," which he thought he would finish in a few years, but he ended up spending thirty years on it. . . .

Animals that seem to represent man in his instinctual life can be found in many ancient fables and in all later European versions. . . . In these works there is a form of anthropomorphism, by which human characteristics and customs are attributed to animals, who nonetheless keep their instincts and natural qualities. Arévalo Martínez's stories do not belong to this form of literature. Nor are they like Kafka's stories, in which there is a complete metamorphosis: Kafka changes Gregor Samsa into an enormous insect. Instead, Arévalo Martínez's animal cycle presents a zoomorphism, that is to say, the attribution of animal characteristics to man. In this way, man, without ceasing to be man, behaves like an animal. He lolls his head, stretches his neck, moves his arms, licks his hand, and so on, just like the animal he represents would. In this sense Arévalo Martínez could well be compared to the famous Dutch painter Bosch. . . .

Arévalo Martínez wrote *The Man Who Looked Like a Horse* during his adolescence, when he was "somewhat romantic and did not know anything about life." The neurasthenia he suffered in adolescence could be explained as the result of the solitary life that he led. Like every adolescent who suffers from neurasthenia, he undoubtedly lacked vitality; he was always tired, meditative, and voluntarily withdrawn. During adolescence there is also quite commonly a period during which there is an attraction to a person of the same sex, often an attraction to an older person. When he was eighteen, Arévalo Martínez met a young Colombian poet, very famous in Guatemala . . . whose name discretion prevents me from revealing. . . . *The Man Who Looked Like a Horse* is the story of this incident, taken from the life of the writer. Señor Aretal, the "man who looked like a horse," represents that Colombian poet; Arévalo Martínez appears in the story as the narrator. . . .

Alberto R. Lopes. *RI.* 4, Feb., 1942,
pp. 324–25†

[Arévalo Martínez] has created a type of cerebral introspective novel very much his own. Although Huysmans was his predecessor in this genre, Arévalo Martínez approached it in an original way. The most famous of these novels, *The Man Who Looked Like a Horse* (with its complement, *The Colombian Troubadour*), is the psychological portrait of that contradictory and strange man Miguel Ángel Osorio. . . . In Arévalo Martínez's novel the merely episodic is discarded: there are no incidents and there is no action. There is only observation and dialogue, which leads to the dissection of a character. . . .

[Arévalo Martínez's] first [novel of political fantasy] was *Orolandia's Office of Peace*, which alludes to North American imperialism. Those that followed also involve political ideas and concepts, not through concrete cases of international life but through a thesis that he symbolically casts in an imaginary world: *The World of the Maharachías* and *Trip to Ipanda*. [1954]

Max Henríquez Ureña. *Breve historia del modernismo*,
2nd ed. (Mexico City, Fondo de Cultura
Económica, 1962), pp. 400–401†

Arévalo Martínez belongs to the group of [Guatemalan] modernists who held sway during the dictatorship of Manuel Estrada Cabrera. His modernism, however, shines through not so much in a *précieux* language as in the sickly sensitivity of his soul. . . . Like most of the modernists, Arévalo Martínez felt himself unable to struggle against life. . . . One of the most constant themes in all Arévalo Martínez's works is the preoccupation with virility. . . .

Toward the end of *A Life* the narrator emerges from the Colegio de Infantes covered with [academic] prizes but judged incapable of living. In *Manuel Aldano* the protagonist begins to earn a living by working as an apprentice in a store and later in an office. He suffers everywhere from his timidity and his relative erudition. Finally it seems as if he is going to make his way. He gets a job in a bank, where his industriousness and intelligence earn him the respect of the owners. But excessive work wears him down. He becomes sick and is forced to resign. When he gets a little better, he strolls through the city, thinking about his country. He is critical of the indolence and inertia caused by the tropics, and, like many of the modernists, he criticizes the Indians. . . . At the same time as he damns the "lax mass that is the Indo-Latin population." . . . He laments the foreign exploitation of his country: the railroads, the mineral rights, the banana trees, and the coffee.

Faced with the material progress of the United States, Arévalo Martínez, like José Enrique Rodó in *Ariel*, defends Latin culture. . . . In his vision of his tropical homeland, Manuel Aldano attributes the evil of tyranny to the sickness of malaria. He sees a Guatemala stifled by the burden of a million Indians and feels sorry for their political status. In order to incorporate the political theme into his autobiographical story, Arévalo Martínez identifies Manuel Aldano with Guatemala; "My case, the clinical case of Manuel Aldano, seemed to me the emblem of the suffering nation of the tropics: it was a country in need of a doctor."

The analysis Arévalo Martínez makes of the sicknesses of his homeland illustrates the disquietude of the modernists in the face of Yankee imperialism and places him alongside Soto-Hall, Rodó, Darío, and Blanco Fombona, who all had likewise pointed out the danger. What distinguishes *Manuel Aldano* from other works like it is the direct style, agreeable and a little *précieux*. . . . In his subsequent novels Arévalo Martínez tried to efface himself so he could better express his political ideas.

Seymour Menton. *Historia crítica de la novela guatemalteca* (Guatemala City, Editorial Universitaria, 1960), pp. 140–42†

Among contemporary Guatemalan writers, Arévalo Martínez is the one who has had the greatest reputation throughout Latin America, with the possible exception of Miguel Ángel Asturias. He has excelled in poetry, the novel, the short story, and especially the philosophical essay. His poetry occupies a place within modernism although it has a profoundly personal tone. . . . Immersed in an atmosphere of mystic fervor and symbolist suggestiveness, it displays an ironic prosaicness. . . .

His fame began, nevertheless, with his psychological stories, a genre of which he was the initiator in Latin America. . . . In these stories, Arévalo Martínez has tried to describe the overt and hidden correspondences between men and animals. The most famous of these, a book that went through many editions, is *The Man Who Looked Like A Horse*, which presents a caricature of the great Colombian poet Miguel Ángel Osorio . . . a model of equine man both physically and psychologically. In this introspective study, Arévalo Martínez reveals to us both the exterior appearance and the interior world of Mr. Aretal, the protagonist, which have incredible similarities to those of the horse. . . . Arévalo Martínez is unquestionably one of the most outstanding representatives of psychological and fantastic fiction in Latin America. . . .

Diccionario de la literatura latinoamericana: América Central (Washington, D.C., Unión Panamericana, 1963), Part 1, pp. 87–89†

Arévalo Martínez [was] a precursor of the literature of the Absurd. Considered an independent and unique personality in Hispano-American letters, he was likewise a preoccupied and anguished man. In *Manuel Aldano*, a semibiographical novel of his early youth, he himself defines his life stance in a way that fits marvelously well with present-day sensibility. This novel is subtitled *The Fight for Life* and the author tells us in the prologue that after a hesitation of many years he gave it to the public without reconsidering or correcting it, but gave it as consolation for the lonely and the sick. The Manuel Aldano of the book is Arévalo Martínez, who, finding himself every day more irritable, more useless, more tired, went to consult a doctor, who diagnosed his case as "a classic type of degenerate" mainly for the following reasons: his failure to adapt himself to environment, his exaggerated sensitivity, his intense emotions, the sheer pain of being alive that bordered on what the doctor called melancholia. Aldano accepts the psychiatric catchword, but considers that to take it as such, accepting the diagnosis as partially true, "is only to shift the location of the dark problem of existence" because, as he says to the doctor, "whoever wants to explain man has to explain the insanity of the man. . . . It's so easy to classify those people who sick from the evil of the absolute ask the meaning of existence like dark mystics, like reasoning madmen or like examples of that strange caste of the sick you doctors present as people exhausted by the systematic doubt, who put an eternal question-mark beside life."

If Arévalo Martínez had limited himself to asking "for the meaning of existence" he would be just one more Modernist, but such is not the case; rather, in all of his work the human being is cast as absurd. . . .

Arévalo Martínez was a poet, as is Ionesco, and like Ionesco worked with the Absurd in literary forms other than poetry. In almost all of his stories and novels the sense of the Absurd is patent. . . . In his novel *Mr. Monitot*, to mention one of the better known, the main character is a man-elephant and there are a man-serpent, a man-mole, and man-birds. The worlds of Arévalo Martínez are also absurd creations. In *The World of the Maharachías*, for example, the inhabitants, men with tails, from a superior race, are destroyed by the race of men without tails.

Graciela Palau de Nemes. Américas. 17, 2,
Feb., 1965, p. 9

Rafael Arévalo Martínez, indisputable master among the prose modernists . . . won literary fame with two or three very brief stories which embody the quintessence of the modernist ideal and which represent a genuine nexus between the artistic novel of the end of the century and the psychological novel of the twentieth century. . . .

He intensely develops symbols and myths. His work is a complex mechanism in which the subtleties of hothouse literature are mixed with underground native elements. Dynamic, in an unusual way that borders on morbidity, his fantasies evoke a diabolical atmosphere, which perhaps results from his able handling of the subconscious zones of his characters' minds. The Indians of his country believe that every man has a double that accompanies him, visibly or invisibly, through his whole life and that that double—an animal—participates in the very essence of his life. Arévalo Martínez, an ultracivilized man . . . seems to have submitted the totem beliefs of his ancestors to the magician's sleight of hand, from which they emerge with a symbolic structure and the somewhat disquieting appearance of a bold treatise on psychozoology. . . .

Fernando Alegría. Historia de la novela
hispanoamericana, 3rd ed. (Mexico City, Ediciones De
Andrea, 1966), pp. 129–30†

[My father, Rafael Arévalo Martínez,] was reared in a Catholic boarding school and was therefore a Catholic throughout his childhood. But when he entered adolescence, in the first two years of secondary school, 1900–1901, at the age of seventeen, after a series of unsupervised readings of all kinds, he became an agnostic. And he remained one until 1902 when he had the first of what he called "his four contacts with the supernatural," which consisted of a spiritualist session at which the medium was my Aunt Teresa. . . . Convinced by her "that there are more things between heaven and earth than philosophy explains," and, above all, understanding that what is most valuable to a man—more than sexual love, glory, and riches—is a knowledge, insofar as it is possible, of the cosmos and of his place in it, he set about studying systems and philosophies. But this time he did not do it randomly, but with rigorous mental discipline, since his own mind was not scientific. He put himself to theosophy . . . but without ever accepting it completely. On the other hand, his reading of the *Lives of the Saints* made him return to his early Catholic faith, whose doctrines had been taught him, assiduously and lovingly, by his parents in the home from tender infancy. . . .

Perhaps one of the problems people have in understanding Arévalo Martínez's mysticism is that mystics are considered to be saints. People do not understand that a sinner—like my father was—can also become a saint. This is a mistake. All of my father's books of poetry published in Guatemala, from the first, *Mayan*, to the latest . . . exhibit a mystic quality. . . .

Teresa Arévalo. *Rafael Arévalo Martínez: Biografía de 1884 hasta 1926* (Guatemala City, Tipografía Nacional, 1971), pp. 362, 368†

ARGUEDAS, ALCIDES (1879–1946)

BOLIVIA

If I had to speak about Arguedas's ideology, frankly I would not know what to say. He is neither a fascist nor a socialist. His liberalism is more utopian than realistic. Perhaps one could say that he resembles the English democratic tradition, because Arguedas, like Joseph Conrad, like Wells and Kipling, is a supporter of the law. . . .

Race of Bronze, the great novel of Bolivia . . . is a harsh, realistic, and bitter exposé of realism and bitterness, in which he suggests the inevitability of a class struggle, making one reflect on the meaning of racial conflicts. . . . The author, without beating around the bush and even with a certain sadistic satisfaction, pries into the ayllu and shows it naked, to the world in all its tragedy, not out of scorn but out of a wish that something be done. . . .

There is no exaggeration or sentimentality; if this is obsession, it is a lacerating obsession that lies beyond the writer's will. . . . *Race of Bronze* foreshadowed other, [similar Latin] American works. . . . its pathos and its nativist slant became more developed later in *Doña Barbara, The Underdogs*, and other American works. . . . Arguedas is not the master of the Bolivian novel; he is simply one of the initiators of a literary movement. . . .

Hugo Vilela. *Alcides Arguedas y otros nombres en la literatura de Bolivia* (Buenos Aires, Kier, 1945), pp. 24, 26–27†

One perceives in Arguedas's book [*A Sick People*] the paradox of the conservative reformer. His entire ideological tendency was to reform Bolivia and to change the course of all aspects of national life. He was a doctor who analyzed all of the sicknesses, all of the calamities of Bolivia, while being a proponent of ideals and patriotic dreams. He believed in the coming of the good dictator, enlightened and informed. And, basing himself on arguments of [the French critic] Paul Bourget, he claimed that in Bolivia it was necessary to restrict freedom of the press. In his works Arguedas always shows a passion for morality but not for liberty. In Arguedas liberalism found a traditional expression but his thought more closely approached Comte's conservative formula —love, order, and progress—rather than the ideals of democratic liberalism of the French Revolution.

Gustavo Adolfo Otero. *RCCE*. 2, 4, Jan.–July, 1947, pp. 192–93†

[Arguedas's] anguish over the circumstances of his country did not stem from a philosophy of pessimism. Arguedas did not believe that humanity was incapable of progress and perfection. On the contrary, a good positivist, he was convinced that humanity was progressive and was destined for a future that would become gradually better and more nearly perfect. He admired the advances of the civilized towns of the land. He believed that work, education, and culture formed learned men. It was precisely his faith in man's possibilities that made him lash out against the deficiencies of Bolivia. His country agonized him. . . .

For the first time, in the work of Arguedas, the conscience of the country was examined, and it was made to realize that its backwardness and its misfortunes were not the result of external causes—foreign influences and exploitation—as the politicians wanted to make people believe, but rather of its own insufficiency and its own defects. Arguedas violently insisted that the people of the country look to their own souls. . . .

Arguedas's observations on Bolivian reality can be categorized into three fundamental areas: the psychology of the races, politics, and history.

Guillermo Francovick. *El pensamiento boliviano en el siglo XX* (Mexico City, Fondo de Cultura Económica, 1956), pp. 44–45†

[Arguedas] shattered the tradition of romantic fiction [in Bolivia] by confronting social reality through a realistic technique. He introduced realism into the Bolivian novel and was the first to write a novel about the Bolivian Indian, whom he presents with moving realism in his miserable, unalterable condition of servitude. . . . Arguedas's sense of humor does not go beyond the most elementary—a biting and somber sarcasm. He is a stranger to irony. . . . He offers instead—with seriousness, arrogance, and a certain inflexibility—sincerity and moralizing commitment.

Diccionario de la literatura latinoamericana: Bolivia
(Washington, D.C., Unión Panamericana, 1958), p. 7†

If the novelist's job is to describe the society of his time, Arguedas was successful to a rarely equaled degree. . . . One gets an idea of what the society of Bolivian landowners was like at the beginning of this century. Arguedas gives us a description of the three elements of this society: the white man . . . the mestizo, and the Indian. . . . In several passages of [*Race of Bronze*] he deals with the serious problem of the confusion produced in the Indians by the collision of their own culture with that brought by the Spaniards. . . . Anyone who would understand the way of thinking of upper-class Bolivians [and their racial prejudices] and the forms taken by this thinking has a limitless source in Arguedas.

Hugo Lijerón Alberdi. *Hispania*. 46, Sept., 1963,
pp. 530, 532†

Arguedas narrates from the outside, in the third person. Constantly he intervenes with moralizing and political judgments. . . . The prose, always carefully wrought, tends to be poetic. . . . These poems in prose are not discordant with the somber picture: Arguedas's modernism is sufficiently ample to accept naturalist procedures. Schooled in positivist philosophy, but taking an attitude that was more moralistic than scientific, Arguedas decided to tell the truth about Bolivia. The result was a denunciation of national evils which, according to him, stemmed from the psychology of the race and from its political corruption and disastrous history. . . .

Enrique Anderson Imbert. *Spanish-American
Literature, a History*, 2nd ed. (Detroit, Wayne State
University Press, 1969), p. 396

Arguedas's attack [in *Race of Bronze*] is directed mainly against the cruelty and indifference of whites and *ladinos*, and it is cruelty rather than economic exploitation alone which leads the Indians to rebel. At the same time, the author is at pains to show how different is his approach from that of the Modernists. He even introduces a poet, Suárez, who visits the landowner's estate in order to write about the Indians; one of Suárez's works is included in the novel and is clearly a parody of Modernist writing. Influenced by Marmontel's book, *The Incas*, Suárez idealises Indian civilisation and is without the training necessary to observe the Indians around him. The idealised Indian legend that he writes is reproduced in the chapter preceding the attempted rape of Wata-Wata as a deliberate contrast. Yet is Arguedas's picture of the Indian any more true? Though he makes a valiant attempt at interpreting Indian thoughts and speech, the study of anthropology was still in its infancy, and [one can find sentences that] merely transpose the author's own thoughts into the mind of the Indian. . . . However, the novel marks an important stage in the growing awareness of the Indian problem and foreshadows the Indianist novels of the 30's and 40's.

> Jean Franco. *An Introduction to Spanish-American*
> *Literature* (Cambridge, Cambridge University
> Press, 1969), pp. 186–87

ARGUEDAS, JOSÉ MARÍA (1911–1969)

PERU

During the years when he was a boy growing into young manhood, José María Arguedas . . . traveled on horseback with his father, a judge, to the remote towns and districts in the Andes. . . . His mother having died when he was three years old, he had lived, until he was old enough to accompany his father, with various relatives in different parts of the highlands, and had been a great favorite with the Indians at the haciendas where he stayed. He enjoyed taking part in their fiestas, and learning their songs to sing with them. Although Spanish was the language of his home, the sound of Quechua was in his ears throughout his childhood and youth. In Apurímac, for example, ninety percent of the population spoke only Quechua.

Fortunately his affection for the Indian did not vanish at the touch of European culture when he moved, at the age of twenty, to Lima to attend the University of San Marcos; instead, seeing the spasmodic knowledge in Peru concerning such a major portion of their inhabitants, his interest increased, so that he decided to devote his life to their folklore. He had the obvious advantage, moreover, of a good start in the Quechua tongue, as well as the invaluable confidence of many of the Quechua people. Since then, he has watched and noted their rites and customs, he has collected music and lore, he has written down their songs in Quechua while listening to the Indians sing them, all with meticulous care. It is in the songs, he says, that the truest clue to the Quechua nature is found. In them, the Indian speaks for himself, from his heart. . . .

In the essay by Arguedas near the end of [*Songs and Tales of the Quechua People*], he tells how he and Lira [a parish priest] collected the songs and tales from the lips of the Indians, of the infinite patience needed, and of how they worked together to bring the lore with its oral flavor into written Spanish.

> Ruth Stephan. Introduction to José María Arguedas,
> *The Singing Mountaineers: Songs and Tales of the*
> *Quechua People* (Austin, University of Texas
> Press, 1957), pp. 18–20

José María Arguedas has made one of the most important contributions to the literature of Peru of recent decades. After Ciro Alegría, Arguedas is the man most responsible for developing the Peruvian novel, bringing to it lasting significance and universal meaning. It is probably not accidental that these two creators . . . came from the harshest region of our country, from the semifeudal Sierra; nor is it accidental that they have reached the heights of creativity precisely by having distanced themselves from the salons, from the vices of a certain kind of Peruvian literature.

In any case, no one else among the living writers in Peru has revealed as much as the author of *Water* and *The Deep Rivers* . . . about the trials of life in the Peruvian Andes, the struggle for existence, the body and soul of the Indians who inhabit this large region of our country. Or about the snow-covered heights, the deep rivers, the valleys dotted with lakes, the storms. Or about the birds and trees and songs.

Nevertheless, I have been plagued by the fear that Arguedas has thus far only incompletely reflected the powerful drama that is to be found in our Sierra. To speak clearly: Arguedas's books have not yet caught the essence of the most recent, advanced, and vigorous form of the peasant struggle, which marches on full of grandeur and hope for the future, no matter how frustrated the efforts may seem at the present. [Despite this shortcoming of Arguedas's,] younger generations—and I am not referring only to writers—will turn time and again to the pages of this artist, who makes us feel, with a spirit of understanding but not always of acceptance, love for a sad Peru. And I believe that these generations will seek, with increasing insistence, the signs of the new times in Arguedas's works and will be able to distinguish the positive and productive aspects from the incomplete and the hesitant.

To what can we attribute the limitations that seem to exist in Arguedas's novels and stories? Is it an optical and ideological short-coming of the author's? Is it the narrowness of the country's social and political life? The answers to such questions are not easy to find and must be sought in the life and the works of the writer. [1960]

> César Lévano. *Arguedas: Un sentimiento trágico de la vida* (Lima, Librería Juan Mejía Baca, 1969), pp. 45–46†

The Deep Rivers contains eleven titled chapters, placed in straight-forward chronological order, each one more or less autonomous. From a formal point of view, the book has the structure of a classical novel. There is a main action—chronological, coherent, centered on the experiences of Ernesto—around which move several secondary actions . . . with their intrinsic, almost independent value in terms of the main action. Among the events experienced by Ernesto during his stay in Abancay are two key episodes, each of which could almost constitute a separate story: the revolt on the *chica* establishments, and the typhus epidemic.

Throughout the entire book events are linked together naturally, without artificial connections. The transitions are gradual, so that the novel's course continues steadily to a conclusive ending. Ernesto abandons the Colegio de Abancay because of the epidemic, and this departure also signals the end of a period in his life. The objective action, the external facts, is tied to a subjective action, which subtly familiarizes us with the inner life of a child who is becoming an adolescent. . . .

[Arguedas] chose a vantage point from which he could place in the foreground the changes in his protagonist, and through this pro-gress we can enter into the life of an entire people. One could say that this book, like all of Arguedas's work, offers a key for understanding the problems of Peru. But most immediately, *The Deep Rivers* is a literary work, without doctrinaire interruptions or ideological bag-gage. . . .

> Saúl Yurkievich. *CA*. No. 130, Sept.–Oct., 1963, pp. 276–77†

The Deep Rivers is interesting in its distinct literary focus, for its view of the highlands Peruvian town is developed through the sensitive eyes of a fourteen-year-old boy of criollo background. There is a dramatic contrast between the boy's childhood—he had been raised partly by

Indians on a communal ayllu—and the events of the novel, as he is exposed to the harshness of a new pueblo, in a valley dominated by haciendas. On the one hand he is shocked and alienated by the atmosphere of struggles, hatreds, immorality and cruelty among the boys at his Catholic boarding school. On the other hand he is equally anguished by the outside world of Abancay, to which he turns for solace. His natural instincts, and his experience as a boy in Indian and cholo villages, lead him to identify with the underdog groups in Abancay. He sympathizes with the women who rebel against commercial outrages. Similarly, he feels a spiritual identity for the Indian colonos [settlers] on a nearby hacienda, although he finds them to be submissive, cowed and childlike. Cut off from their traditions and relegated to an existence of fear, they are totally unlike the Indians he had known, who had maintained their sense of dignity and cultural heritage. . . .

The story is recounted in a straight, rarely unbroken chronological line, in the first person singular—a form difficult to sustain without relief. Action of the plot is frequently slowed by intercalation of static descriptive passages, or folkloric sections explaining the meaning or nature of a particular Indian expression. Much of the *costumbrismo* [local customs] in these passages, as well as the *huaynos* [a type of indigenous Quechua song] which are presented both in Quechua and Spanish texts, provides a rich background for the plot. It often alternates with the sequence of events, however, rather than being integrated and assimilated.

In style, José María Arguedas ranges from a subjective lyrical tone, capturing the poetic character of the boy's subtle reactions to nature, to one of detailed and realistic naturalism. The latter style aptly conveys the world of nascent sex, repressed emotions and self-degradation which marks much of boarding school life. The author interpolates occasional Quechua words and expressions which impregnate the novel with the flavor of the language in which most of the characters usually communicate.

Joseph Sommers. JIAS. 6, April, 1964, pp. 254–55

If Arguedas knew that a literary Spanish was not the answer, he also was certain that Quechua would not serve as an alternative because it was understood by so few. How then was he to convey authentically the Indians' mentality and manner of speaking in a language not their own? After painstaking experimentation, he reached a solution: a special language based on fundamental Spanish words incorporated into Quechua syntax. . . . In order to achieve maximum effectiveness from this unusual form of expression Arguedas employs monologue and dialogue to a large extent. The result is startling. For the first time we begin fully to realize that though we may have previously been supplied with rare insights of the Indians' attitude toward their tradition and present day reality, we have never before shared so completely their inner thoughts and their vision of the white man, the village, the landscape, the animals, and other Indians. In other words, the Indian has seemed largely "inscrutable" because our vision has been largely external. . . .

Unusual effects are created by the short, sometimes abrupt, phraseology as brief sentences are interspersed with longer ones containing several thoughts. The thoughts themselves, though coming in rapid succession, fall into logical patterns. The mode of expression is thus uncomplicated without in any way being an exaggerated sort of pidgin Spanish; thus, while capturing the speaker's essential simplicity of character, his dignity and native intelligence are preserved.

Earl M. Aldrich, Jr. *The Modern Short Story in Peru*
(Madison, University of Wisconsin Press, 1966),
p. 129–31

One of José Carlos Mariátegui's many correct observations was that "Indigenous literature cannot give us a rigorous portrait of the Indian. One has to idealize him or stylize him; one cannot give us his soul." This was obvious in 1928, when Mariátegui wrote *Seven Essays in Interpretation of Peruvian Reality*; it remained obvious in *Broad and Alien Is the World*, in which Ciro Alegría tried to get into the depths of the Indian soul. Arguedas, although not an Indian himself, presented the Indian speaking from within his culture.

In the introduction to *Diamonds and Stones,* Arguedas, speaking in the third person, says: "This contains two works written by a man who learned how to speak Quechua." What is the goal he set forth? It was precisely to transcribe faithfully the life of the mountain Indians with whom he had shared his childhood life, and in whose idiosyncracies he was steeped to the point that they formed part of his deepest being. He was afraid of betraying them and betraying himself after having lived with, loved, and been taught by the gentle and fascinating Quechuas.

Arguedas resolved the problem by creating for them a "special Spanish." But he realized that this was artificial, that the authenticity he wanted took a long time to achieve.

G. R. Coulthard. *MNu.* No. 19, Jan., 1968, p. 74†

In describing the social degradation of a traditional culture in the process of change [in *All the Bloods*] Arguedas, with inviolate and magnificent force, shows the indigenous element in the act of entering social destiny. . . . This poetic exploration is neither a romantic residue nor an anachronistic indigenist position. . . . Arguedas continued a cultural dialogue that was probably initiated in Peru by the Inca Garcilaso, one that Vallejo had carried on. Arguedas's answer is Latin American, one of the last replies a Latin American can make to the pillaging invasions of dependence and depersonalization brought on by the modern world.

It is no accident, therefore, that the critical framework of this novel is Peruvian underdevelopment. Within the miseries of dependence (the successive dependences of the social classes, of economic and political powers, of the entire country to imperialism), the liberating desire of poetry finds the last possibility of justice in the indigenous world, still intact but marginal and humiliated. Thus, criticism turns into desire, consciousness into the dream of another reality, literature into the poetic search for another history.

Arguedas's work is a profound anthropology that resolves itself in poetry. He shows us the social conflicts of a country in the process of change, but his greater dream is personalization, the construction of a human entity that will, basing itself on its own values, attain its own history. Yet nothing in [All the Bloods] is programmatic. On the contrary, its cultural debate is an adventure which challenges simple rationalism, which opens into a poetic amplification of reality.

Cortázar has written that great literature in some way implies a dream of paradise. And indeed, our best novels presuppose a lost paradise that refracts human deeds: *Pedro Páramo, Hopscotch, Paradiso, One Hundred Years of Solitude* all in different ways speak to us of that loss or of that search. In the same way, poetry in other works becomes the longing for a utopia. But no longer is it the utopia of a prodigal America; rather, it is the tattered utopia of a Latin America with a history. And the emptiness of that history leads to a poetic exploration, an agonized desire. This agony is found throughout Arguedas's work. The common destiny leads him to a long, impassioned debate—between despair and rebellion, between magic and longing. What makes Arguedas special is that his exploration recognizes the imminence of death, the shadow of desire. Thus, like Vallejo, Arguedas is a tragic writer.

Julio Ortega. *Figuración de la persona* (Barcelona, Edhasa, 1971), pp. 281–82†

Arguedas' last novel [*All the Bloods*] is a vast sociological document which focuses on the latent unrest in all social strata of Peruvian society. The scenes shift from the Andean environment of haciendas, villages, Indian "communities," mining centers; to a provincial capital; to Lima, from its abject "slums" to the elegant Monterrico. Thus *All the Bloods* is the completion of Arguedas' social mission. Originally cast in the regional mold, his work has retained only its outlines as Arguedas follows the path of Peruvian reality. . . .

All the Bloods goes beyond tragedy to explore solutions. To emphasize his intent, Arguedas suppresses the intimate, nostalgic air of past works. The novel is explicit and penetrating, and for these reasons it will contribute principally to the literature of its own nation. The foreign reader will be more moved by the beauty and pathos of *The Deep Rivers*. He will reach a greater degree of understanding of Peru's complex situation in *All the Bloods*, although he may consider himself an outsider. A beautiful melody is universally inspiring, even if only the musician grasps the beauty in the mechanics of the orchestration.

Peru, like other Latin American countries, is now beset with the social phenomenon of congested cities painfully swollen by a steady influx from the provinces. The new generation of Peruvian writers has found its source material in the sub-human misery of the sordid slums tacked onto the city. It cannot be claimed that Arguedas evolved all the way into the current urban novel; but within the framework of Peruvian literature *All the Bloods* does belong to the periphery of the urban novel because it deals with many of the factors occurring in the provinces which are responsible for the flight into the large cities.

Phyllis Rodríguez-Peralta. *Hispania.* 55, May, 1972,
pp. 227–28

ARLT, ROBERTO (1900–1942)

ARGENTINA

Roberto Arlt's *The Rabid Toy* is a good novel. Instinct guides the author securely through the intricacies of his narrative. Because of this, the book is spontaneous and extraordinarily interesting. Arlt is vivid in his depictions, discreet in his manner, although not always temperate in his expression. The underworld slang he places in the mouths of his characters is not false, as is the case in all previous attempts in novels of the city [of Buenos Aires]. Arlt handles these expressions naturally and with the goal of advancing the portrait of a character. . . . The characters in *The Rabid Toy* reflect their environment, breathe the air of our streets, and, finally, speak current language, since they are not simply bookish characters.

Leónidas Barletta. *Nosotros.* No. 211, Dec., 1926,

p. 553†

Roberto Arlt had talent, but he was undisciplined and could not produce a solid work, only the suggestion of what he could have been as a novelist. In *The Rabid Toy*, his first and most artistically successful novel, he drew his characters carefully and created settings reminiscent of those of Gorki, such as the hovel of Don Gaetano, the old bookseller. . . .

Arlt's best creations are the stories comprising *The Little Hunchback*, in which, as in his novels, he treats humble and victimized people. . . . His style is not his strength. Reading his works, one has the impression that an anguished urgency impelled him to write hurriedly so that he could get down on paper the torrential flow from his mind. Perhaps he had a presentiment that he would die young, and he wanted to leave behind something to be remembered by. He has left the world the shameless creatures in his feverish writing.

Germán García. *La novela argentina: Un iternario*

(Buenos Aires, Editorial Sudamericana, 1952),

pp. 216–17†

The anxiety of the characters of Arlt is a phenomenon of his time and class. Badler and Erdosain [in *The Seven Madmen* and *The Flame Throwers*] are definitely "period" characters; they belong to the middle class of Buenos Aires in the year 1930 and to no other time or place. The anxieties, the frustrated hopes that lie behind all of Arlt's works have a definite relationship to the economic crisis that shattered the middle class. After 1890 residents of Buenos Aires, caught up in the myth of National Progress, did not ask themselves about ultimate goals. In 1930 the wheels brusquely ground to a halt, and people saw they were going nowhere. From this "social complex" the themes of Arlt originate: the helplessness and immorality of man, the absurdity of the world, the anxiety of action without reason. . . . The collapse [of the middle class] revealed new aspects of the human condition to Arlt, which led him to profound metaphysical intuitions.

Marx was right when he asserted that man is a product of his times, his country, and his environment . . . and not of an eternal and unchangeable human nature. Arlt could not have written *The Seven Madmen* if he had been born in another country or if he had belonged to a different social class. . . . It is also true that Arlt's bold books reflect a tormented childhood, the tyranny of a cruel father. But his background does not explain why he became a creator rather than, like so many unfortunates, a victim of society. . . .

Juan José Sebreli. *Sur.* No. 223, July–Aug., 1953,
pp. 110–11†

Roberto Arlt is more than a tortured man; he is a man gripped by despair. What makes him humiliate, persecute, and destroy himself is both awareness and lack of awareness of his despair. . . . This despair leads to arbitrary conceptions, violent responses, meandering philosophizing. . . . It also causes his constant uneasiness, his almost morbid compulsion to grasp everything with avidity, impatience, and only slight penetration.

His books move rapidly, stamped with the vehemence of one who feels himself fevered and overburdened with impressions he must discharge quickly. Moreover, the inner vertigo that makes him dizzy and possesses him has made him come to believe more and more in improvisation . . . in intuition rather than knowledge. But despite his intense desire for rapidity in all he does and how he lives, Roberto Arlt has a great capacity for work. . . . Nothing and no one can drag him from his work: neither the uproar of the editorial office [of the newspaper where he worked], nor the instability of his spirit, nor the desolation of his love life. . . .

Nira Etchenique. *Roberto Arlt* (Buenos Aires,
La Mandrágora, 1962), pp. 10–11†

To mention Roberto Arlt in a specific study of fantastic literature may seem to be a distortion because the writer of *The Rabid Toy* is thought of as a persistent and even obsessive realist, a witness to a cruel, passion-driven world. But if one rereads his works without this preconception, one will begin to admit that beneath or alongside his undeniable interest in realism, Arlt nurtured a strong tendency to use fantasy as an hallucinatory counterpoint to the portrayal of reality.

The Seven Madmen is, to be sure, one of the most vigorous novels of social criticism ever written in Argentina before 1930. Arlt impressively depicted the disorientation and the anguish of the petite bourgeoisie of [Buenos Aires], pulverised by the economic crisis that followed World War I. . . . Arlt showed a sure talent in his accurate representation of types, in his ability to express dominant ideas and phobias. And by including his own tensions in the composition of the picture, he made it a documentary of misery. . . . The insertion of elements of fantasy into a realistic novel, the unusual importance these elements are given, and the writer's desire to use the same technique to develop two contrasting planes perhaps explain the confusion the average reader usually has when confronting this novel—a feeling that the world is a phantasmagoria, a frightening creation conceived by a madman. . . . [1963]

Adolfo Prieto. Introduction to Roberto Arlt,
Un viaje terrible (Buenos Aires, Editorial
Contemporáneo, 1968), pp. 10–13†

[The protagonists of Arlt's plays] change suddenly through the impact of a conflict, which in turn gives rise to the unexpected leap toward the unreal. The antagonists determine the course of the action. In *Saverio the Cruel* it is set in motion by the encounter of the sane, simple, and good Saverio with the evil, crazy middle-class characters, led by the twisted, demented Susana. In *The Deserted Isle,* the opposition is provided by the routine minds of the office workers . . . colliding with the dreamy, libertarian spirit of Cipriano.

Those unfamiliar with Roberto Arlt's plays will find in these two dramas keys to his work in general. They move from the possibilities for human liberty to the flight from reality, and from the flight from reality to negation itself. This movement is paralleled in form by the switch from realism to farce (with symbolist and expressionist overtones) and back to realism again. Symbolism may be seen in the personification of social forces in concrete individuals. Expressionism appears in an implicit moral consciousness, which denounces the injustice of a society of machines, commerce, and science, a society that looks on indifferently as the last chances for man are lost. . . .

Mirta Arlt. In Roberto Arlt, *Saverio el cruel/ La isla
desierta* (Buenos Aires, Editorial Universitaria de
Buenos Aires, 1964), pp. 7–8†

The following are the major features of the theater of Roberto Arlt:

1. Using the rehearsals and the performances as drawing-boards for giving final shape to the plays. . . .

2. A simplicity of themes. . . .

3. A duality of planes, an alternation between dreaming and consciousness, reality and fantasy, by virtue of which the plots become varied and complex.

4. A projection . . . of experiences, desires, frustrations, scruples or remorse, as a result of which he approached the methods of the

"theater within a theater," the mirrored theater, and the theater of the grotesque.

5. An evident tendency toward sadomasochism in some characters who delight in humiliation.

6. The prominent position of social criticism in all the plays, although without a definite and explicit purpose.

7. A deliberate refusal to localize the geography of the action, with the concomitant tendency toward universality.

8. A concept of the theater as both catharsis and magical game, as a means of both evading and presenting personal problems in a spectacle that does not exclude the tragic.

9. A somber action in a drama whose essence is fatality. The dominant farcical tone is accompanied by a tragic denouement, facilitating the transition from the particular to the universal, from personalization to depersonalization.

10. The use of the chorus, which, in the Greek manner, leads to a transcendent theater.

11. The constant use of surprise, the striving for unexpected effects . . . and the presentation of abrupt clashes between dreams and reality.

Raúl H. Castagnino. *El teatro de Roberto Arlt*
(La Plata, Argentina, Universidad Nacional de la
Plata, 1964), pp. 88–89†

In Arlt's work each social class is given its own specific value. The lowest classes, perhaps the people he most loved, are unreproachable. Here we have the *déclassés*, the prostitutes, the servants, and so on. To his highest class belong those people who maintain the loftiest values—especially beauty. The individuals belonging to this class do not appear directly in Arlt's work. They are distant and inaccessible beings, as pure as if they were ideas. The proletariat, the workers, does not appear either.

This leaves the class whose essential attribute seems to be the most blatant grossness in its daily conduct and the most profound ridiculousness in all its beliefs—the middle class. Arlt had to stretch his imagination to give an account of a fear, an annoyance, a boredom he knew too well—that is to say, the particular affectations of a man of this class. . . . To present this class subjectively, Arlt used the most surprising means of expression, developing an unusual style that mixes the penny-novel, the metaphysical novel, the police report, and plain ridicule. This style does not absorb his narrative prose but is fused with it. The result is his constant attention . . . to the class that obsesses him. When he invades the life of some malefactor, what he is really doing is nothing more than introducing himself into the inner life of a class that [in reality] is not at all evil-acting. . . .

Oscar Masotta. *Sexo y traición en Roberto Arlt*
(Buenos Aires, Jorge Álvarez Editor, 1965), pp. 43–44†

Roberto Arlt, an enigmatic figure, the son of German immigrants [was] by temperament and disposition obscurely marked for misfortune. Family difficulties, childhood misery, revolt against militaristic paternal discipline, early escape from home, years of penury and dereliction in the big city, were, in good Freudian fashion, some of the factors that inclined him toward the twilight zone. He knew the life of the down-and-out, the city's lunatic fringe, its Dostoevskian underworld. What he found there he portrayed with brilliant gutter humor in a series of works—culminating with *The Seven Madmen* and *The Flame-throwers*—that were at once a complete rogues' gallery of marginal characters and a map of a city's spiritual slum areas.

Arlt was working at a time of disenchantment in Argentine history that coincided with the rise to political power of militarist groups, starting with the 1930 government of President Uriburu. But, just as his spotty culture—he was considered a hack writer in his day —was self-taught, his true sufferings were self-inflicted. He was an outcast by nature, one of the downtrodden of the world. His crackpot idealists, deluded theologians, emasculated pimps and pariahs were inner figments, imaginative projections of a private vision of things. For Arlt the human predicament was not essentially social but philosophic and astronomical. This realization, the fruit of an absolute discomformity, helped him to cut deeper into the soul of his society than any other writer of his day.

He was not a literary man in the superficial sense of the word, and indeed in the realm of pure "literature" his work has great lacks. It is short-winded, full of misconceptions and malapropisms, and it falls apart for lack of structure. Yet Arlt has an instinct for buried treasure. He is ignorant, but never innocuous or insipid. He is a man who has come to grips with the world. He used to ask his intellectual friend, Ricardo Güiraldes, whose poetizations of reality, for all their finesse, he could never take much to heart, when he would start writing "seriously."

Luis Harss and Barbara Dohmann. *Into the Mainstream*
(New York, Harper & Row, 1967), p. 16

Arlt's fiction centers on two themes: the Oedipal conflict and death. . . . The Oedipal conflict has specific manifestations in Arlt's work, which includes dissociation from the heterosexual incestuous object (the mother or maternal representatives) . . . strong castration anxieties that dominate even attraction to the partner of the opposite sex, the intensity of jealousy, and so forth. The theme of death also takes specific form in Arlt's fiction. Generally there is a tense search for self-destruction or destruction of others, which culminates in death or an equivalently violent outcome. . . .

Little by little, one can establish elements common to most of Arlt's fiction. His protagonists seem to share a feeling of basic lack, of unsatisfied—at times intolerable—longing for an object. The search for this object always fails. In Arlt's fiction this failure is determined by the very nature of the object sought—an idealized woman, nonexistent, whom the character believes he possessed once and has lost. Without [this idealized figure] the character falls into a world of robberies, of feuds arising from vengeful grudges, of twisted hypocrisies arising from envy.

David Maldavsky. *Las crisis en la narrativa de
Roberto Arlt* (Buenos Aires, Editorial Escuela, 1968),
pp. 37–38†

ARREOLA, JUAN JOSÉ (1918–   )

MEXICO

Of all the stories collected in *Confabulario* the best seems to be "Verily, Verily I Say Unto You," a story with a scientific background, in which Arreola humorously presents a researcher who has discovered a way to make a camel pass through the eye of a needle. At heart, the work seems to be a veiled criticism of scientists who, instead of working for the benefit of society, sell their discoveries for personal gain. "Small Town Tale" is reminiscent of the zoomorphic tales of Arévalo Martínez, and the images of "Notes of an Angry Man" recall the world of Neruda. "Baby H. P." is a satire based on an advertisement for an apparatus to convert the energy of children into power to drive machines. . . . That Arreola's stories do not have purely Mexican themes in no way means that he is not a national writer. As [Emmanuel] Carballo observes, "His nationalism doesn't lie in anecdote but in the way in which he treats anecdote: his nationalism is more one of reaction than action."

Luis Leal. *El cuento mexicano* (Mexico City,
Ediciones De Andrea, 1955), pp. 131–32†

The epigraph of *Confabulario* is the key to its understanding: ". . . mute I do my spying while someone voracious in turn watches me." The Mexican Arreola's wide knowledge of literature makes him a true man of the twentieth century, an eclectic, who at will can draw upon the best of all who have preceded him in order to create truly masterful works of art which in turn will be seized upon by others. The contrast between the adjectives *mute* and *voracious* . . . indicates the precarious position of the sensitive artist in this fiercely mechanized and commercialized society. After thus defining his position, Arreola presents the reader with a collection of thirty short stories whose variety in both theme and style exemplify the attainments of this genre in the twentieth century.

In no other story is Arreola's literary credo better expressed than in "The Disciple," which takes place in Florence, probably during the Renaissance. The master painter criticizes his pupil's work. "There is not a single line missing in your sketch, but there are a lot of extra ones." In order to drive his point home even more forcibly, he tells his pupil that he is going to teach him how to destroy beauty. He sketches an outline of a beautiful figure and says, "This is beauty." Then after he finishes the picture, and the pupil stands enthralled before it, the maestro says that he has just destroyed beauty. He tears up the picture and throws it into the fire. . . . Arreola's message is, of course, that true beauty lies in suggestion only. Once a work of art goes beyond suggesting beauty, it loses its charm. . . .

Pervading all of these stories is Arreola's sense of humor, which is in the tradition of the best Mexican authors and at the same time is very much his own. Like Lizardi, Romero and many other Mexicans, Arreola has a cynical outlook on life which is tempered by stoicism. Basically he ridicules human failings not with the mordant wit of a Voltaire nor with the sense of utter despair of a Sartre, but with a somewhat benevolent feeling of commiseration. Notwithstanding his falling within this Mexican tradition, Arreola has a touch which is all his own. This touch may be defined as a keenness of mind combined with a vast literary culture expressed with the greatest subtlety. . . .

In our rapid review of *Various Inventions*, certain marked similarities with *Confabulario* have become apparent: the author's eclectic spirit; the existentialist's despair tempered by the Mexican's magic realism; the burlesquing of erudition and science; the reaction against the excessive commercialization of the world; the dim view of marriage; the symbolic use of animals; the interest in portraying people and events from all periods of history with a variety of styles —all of these things presented with the subtle touch which is so characteristic of Arreola. In spite of the great similarities between *Various*

Inventions and *Confabulario*, they can definitely be distinguished from one another. *Confabulario* represents the perfection of Arreola's art, most of whose elements may be perceived in *Various Inventions*, but with impurities.

Seymour Menton. *Hispania.* 42, Sept., 1959,
pp. 295, 300, 302, 305

One notes a constant feature in the art of Arreola, which gives it its special quality—wit. As a matter of fact, when the writer's only purpose is to present a humorous portrayal of a rhinoceros, or of a toad, or an owl or an ostrich, or when he decides to tell a rather brief story, he always demonstrates a subtle, paradoxical, and humorous wit, which both delights and surprises the reader because of the unexpectedness of its turns. The entire volume [*Total Confabulario*] is presented to us as a *tour de force....*

Hugo Rodríguez-Alcalá. *RHM.* 29, April, 1963, p. 181†

[*Total Confabulario*] is difficult to classify. Some of the pieces—like "The Switchman," "The Crow Catcher," "Private Life"—are clearly short stories in the modern mode, ranging widely in technique and style; a great many others, as the title would indicate, are fables; still others are sharp, satiric, one-page vignettes, and can hardly be called short stories. The tone and language vary considerably according to the subject. . . . For example, in "Baby H.P." and "Announcement" Arreola parodies the commercial world of advertising, using jargonistic terms and a breathless tone with excellent effect. But the same marvelous invention and wit, the same trenchant satire, and impish, impudent humor run throughout the collection.

Arreola is an accomplished satirist. He is very good at finding chinks in the armor, attacking his subjects in their most vulnerable spots and sometimes in places where they probably did not realize they were vulnerable. Bourgeois society and all its false values, rampaging twentieth-century materialism, the bomb, the cocktail party are just a few of his targets. With mordant descriptions, pungent attacks, or sly irony, he shows how silly mankind is, how outrageous man's behavior and antics are, how one is at the mercy of a world and society that more often seems to care for what is trivial and ephemeral than for what is essential. Arreola jabs at complacency and ruthlessly exposes pompous and hypocritical attitudes.

He takes a depressing view of most human relationships, and in large numbers of his stories and satires he chips away at love and its illusions. Like the celebrated seventeenth-century Spanish satirist Quevedo, Arreola is particularly hard on women and marriage. According to him, women are given to treachery and adultery, and the impossibility of finding happiness in marriage is a recurring theme and echo in his work. Whatever the subject of his satire, Arreola most often achieves his effects by a deliberate jumbling of phantasy and reality, a mingling of the logical and the absurd, a blend of imaginative frivolity and Orwellian grimness. . . .

Endowed with a resilient mind that skims swiftly from point to point, Arreola is also a gifted stylist. His imagery and language, except in some of the earliest stories, are tart and fresh, his choice of words sometimes startling the reader, at other times stinging him, frequently delighting him. His writing is crisp with sentences that tend to be short and closely packed, yet there is no jerky or jolting effect. It is all perfectly under control, balanced and rhythmic.

George D. Schade. Introduction to Juan José Arreola,
Confabulario and Other Inventions (Austin, University
of Texas Press, 1964), pp. viii–x

In 1962, Juan José Arreola published in Mexico City his *Total Confabulario*. It was, in a sense, his "Collected Works," since it brought together most of his short stories, including some of the earliest, which date back to 1941; his latest short sketches or fables (from which the book takes its title); his *Bestiary* of 1958, a satirical, anti-U.S. play, and all of his most recent prose pieces. . . .

The most polished and the most given to verbal and conceptual play of his "generation" of Mexican writers . . . Arreola performs generally in the guise of satirist—a curious type of satirist whose professed pessimism is more cultivated than convincing. . . .

Arreola's target is man and his entanglements with logical absurdities: but the paradox inevitably interests him more than the plight. "The Switchman," wherein the fantastic mismanagement and downright arbitrary deceptiveness of an imaginary national railroad system acquires, over the space of a few pages, the stature of a magnificent allegory of the human condition, is possibly his finest short story; it also happens to be one of his gaiest. The originality of Arreola's satire provokes surprise together with delight: he suggests that if all the rich men of the world were to pour their joint wealth into the construction of an inconceivably complicated and expensive machine designed to disintegrate a camel and zip him through the eye of a needle, then they would indeed most likely come to pass through the gates of Heaven. . . .

The most disconcerting feature of this book . . . must be charged to Arreola himself, who arranged the contents of the Mexican edition in such a way that his most recent fiction comes first in the book and his earliest, least controlled, and least impressive work appears last. The reader gets the odd impression that he is witnessing a gifted writer irrevocably and unaccountably losing his touch right before his eyes.

Donald A. Yates. *SR*. Aug. 1, 1964, p. 32

This long awaited novel [*The Fair*] by the author of *Various Inventions* and *Confabulario* retains several qualities which have established Arreola as a major figure in modern Mexican fiction.

The author continues to view society with the same perceptive skepticism, tempered by a compassionate understanding of man's foibles. It is this artistic view, detached enough to be objective, yet ultimately committed to humanism, which enables Arreola to fashion a literary mosaic of contemporary Mexico from multicolored bits and pieces of its everyday reality.

Just as his "tales" defy rote definitions of the short story, *The Fair* challenges traditional conceptions of the novel. There are no developed characters, with individual personalities. Nor is there a plot in the sense of conflict, climax, resolution. Instead of the usual chapters or larger subdivisions, the book consists of juxtaposed fragments of conversations, narration, letters, diaries, or recollections. Yet the totality of the work has body, literary development, and novelistic scope, for it synthesizes Arreola's vision of the human dimensions of Zapotlán, an imagined *pueblo* in southern Jalisco. . . .

Typical Arreola symbolism is suggested in the Zapotlán fair which, as one character points out, is a summation of the village's year round life process. It ends when a giant fireworks display is ignited by anonymous incendiaries, exploding in futility and destruction and killing many bystanders. Their bodies lie strewn in disorder, "like the dead on a false field of battle."

If this symbolism implies anguish and cynicism, these qualities are mediated by the author's understanding and sympathy for the complexity of human problems—qualities which he demonstrates in the subtlety and precision of his style. His sensitive use of language to underline human contradiction and his wry tone of bitter humor are the basis for the literary unity of this novel.

Joseph Sommers. *BA*. 38, Autumn, 1964, pp. 412–13

The Fair depicts the life of Arreola's home town, Zapotlán, from the colonial period through our own time. The plot is fragmented into innumerable pieces. Some of them can be knit together easily and, when arranged in order, present several individual stories. . . . The pieces left over fulfill a different function in the context of the work:

they furnish the information that permits Arreola to develop a broader story, that of the town itself. . . .

This novel breaks with some of the so-called basics of the novel form: it does not present characters: often the reader does not even know their names, their occupations, or their purposes. It does not sketch the scene where the action occurs, and it is not precise about the order in which the events take place. The work's architecture reminds one of a child's picture puzzle. Yet I am tempted to feel that Arreola did conceive of the novel traditionally, as a unified whole in which actions and characters were clearly and coherently set down. But he proposed to divide the plots into numerous little fragments. Anyone capable of putting them all together—and there are obvious clues to use in doing it—will assemble a novel that hides behind its "dislocated" cover a logical order and a classical harmony. . . .

The Fair is ingenuousness regained, a scrap of life snatched from oblivion thanks to the power of words: the Arreola who *is*—I am thinking of Hebbel's phrase—salutes with nostalgia the Arreola who could have been. If he had not left his home town . . . he would have known only one hemisphere of the universe. *The Fair*, in a sense, can be seen as an elegy: Arreola goes to his fair . . . and reencounters a noble and idealistic image of himself—the image of being young in a small town.

Emmanuel Carballo. *Diecinueve protagonistas de la literatura mexicana del siglo XX* (Mexico City, Empresas Editoriales, 1965), pp. 402–4†

Arreola discovers the literary matter of his short stories in the depths of a symbolic and imaginative meditation on history and reality: on occasions he openly operates on reality. . . . Arreola's mannerisms, shielded in humor, and his predisposition to write with great care, molding his materials, come together magically at the moment of creation, producing the tiny but marvelous works of art (most of them at least) that are his stories. . . . He takes from the boundaries of the unreal some germinal idea that obssesses him or impresses itself on his mind, and he strings together images, frequently surrealistic, with the stubborn and paradoxical logic of free association. . . .

Arreola is original in the way he treats his problems and in his technique which, as has been said, is not reducible to an exercise in the minor art of Kafka but goes back to a literary tradition extending beyond the Spanish baroque, finding inspiration in medieval allegories, fables, apologues, and bestiaries, in which human defects were cast in the form of animals. Arreola speaks of . . . Guillaume de

Machault, Ronsard, and Góngora's epistles with the same facility with which he speaks of . . . the atomic bomb. . . .

If this Mexican has a literary relative, that relative most likely is Borges. A distant relation . . . the one philosophical and elliptical, the other a graceful moralist and better poet. Both writers laugh a great deal, but we ourselves laugh more freely at the caricatures of Arreola.

Javier Martínez Palacio. Ínsula. 21, Nov., 1966, p. 16†

[Arreola] sets forth the absurdity of man's condition before him. He does this by contrasting an apparently logical premise—the flight from the happiness of others in "Sketches"; a tranquil journey in "Autrui"—and the violence caused by the sudden eruption of an inevitable paradoxical situation. The flight has brought an incomprehensible imprisonment within four walls; the tranquil journey ends in an unexplainable labyrinth of alleys. This is the device through which Arreola develops the meaning of his fantasies: a perfectly comprehensible, logical situation yields to a second, irrational situation. "There is in Zapotlán a plaza called Ameca, who knows why" ("Ballad"). The irrational element abruptly explodes onto something which has been presented to us as perfectly normal and understandable. There is a contradiction here that we have to accept, because the explanation is a confession of irrationality: who knows why? But the irrational leaves us dissatisfied and with a sense of anguish. Besides the dissatisfaction thus established, there also comes the doubt and the possibility of other unusual situations. The following sentence, when it comes, no longer surprises us: "A wide and paved street runs into a massive wall, parting it in two." The image now holds something of despair: again the logical and the absurd are contrasted, but this time with a clear and intentional violence that reflects misfortune.

Ángel González-Araúzo. RI. 34, Jan.–April, 1968,
pp. 105–6†

ASTURIAS, MIGUEL ÁNGEL (1899–1974)

GUATEMALA

Asturias is a writer who, like Neruda, surely owes much to his reading of Quevedo, under whose light, in more than a few aspects, his literary self must have been formed. From the great Spanish satirist he has taken a preoccupation with and a consciousness of style. From him he has learned to subordinate language at every step along the way to the crea-

tive function. Asturias knows how to overcome every stylistic pit-
fall. He can make his style lean, can create expressions to fill the
needs of the moment. . . . At times he has sacrificed the sonority,
ease, and perfection that pleases the ear—beauty itself. . . .

[*Mr. President*] is written in a lively and vital style, nourished by
itself (it avoids, in general, any devices which are *not* original), shun-
ning imitation. Asturias has done away with anything that could have
been affectation, and his book has such ease and communicativeness,
such rhythm and throbbing, that Gabriela Mistral was led to exclaim: "I
can't imagine where this unique novel has come from, written as it is
with the very ease of breathing and the movement of blood through the
body. The famous 'conversational language' that Unamuno demands at
the top of his voice, tired of our poor and pretentious rhetoric, is present
here to an extent that Unamuno could not have believed. . . . This
phenomenal work . . . is not going to 'pass away'—it is a cure, a purgation, almost a penitential need. Because I know that the author has
suffered in undertaking such an operation. Some will not take to it kindly. But let them listen and do likewise." Of course, the book is a purgation and a cure. It is a cure for American readers, tired of the repetitions from one writer to the next, of shameful "literary borrowings."
And it is a purgation—let us hope they understand that—for the writers
themselves. . . .

Juan Loveluck. *Atenea*. No. 310, April, 1951,
pp. 50–51†

Asturias the novelist does not see the drama of his people from the
outside, as a dilettante or as a witness, but from the inside, as a participant. This intimate participation of the novelist in life, in the trials,
in the impressions of his characters, is expressed in his language. The
colloquial language, in dialogue form, in Asturias's novels is the language spoken every day by the various classes of Guatemalan society.
For the first time the local language has been promoted to a level of
literary dignity. The true ring of the style contributes to placing the
reader within the setting of the novel. . . .

Asturias is a writer involved with daily events, a writer who takes a
position, always with vehemence. . . . A man of convictions, the ambassador of Arbenz's government to El Salvador, Asturias had the honor
of being the first Guatemalan diplomat to be relieved of his functions by
the new "Mr. President" imposed by the United Fruit Company and its
"Green Pope." And Asturias has raised his voice in anger at the tragedy of the betrayal of the people. . . .

Manuel Tuñón de Lara. *TM*. No. 107, Nov., 1954,
pp. 656–57†

The repulsive omniscience of the state in *Mr. President* might be thought only an imaginary world out of *1984* were it not for its historical model in the fantastic regime of Estrada Cabrera (1898–1920). Many of its incidents are real and may be read elsewhere in the few annals available today.

This work contains no hero and no heroine. Its only characters are so-called "flat characters" which enter and leave at the will of the author. If we look for a thesis, it is difficult to locate and harder still to express. Nevertheless, in a philosophical sense, Asturias has eloquently affirmed the validity of individual experience. Placed within the huge frame of reference of the state, our most frequently viewed character, Cara de Ángel, struggles to affirm his absolute existence and to relate this to an authentic self. So also do Asturias' entire pitiful chamber of beggars, idiots, prostitutes, generals, and hirelings blindly grope for the means to assert the validity of self and to anchor this individuality in a nightmare which constantly faces it with black nothingness.

Asturias has created in brilliant fashion a grotesque and asphyxiating conception of the total state. Running the whole gamut of literary devices, he has mixed essence and form to overcome a difficult task in a very effective manner. On the one hand there is poetic exploration into the innermost recesses and realities of the human mind. On the other, there is the material content of an urban mass caught in the grip of an iron regime. The synthesis of these two disparate elements into a unified literary whole is a real contribution to the novelistic genre of America.

Asturias' accomplishment has had antecedent efforts and similar examples. José Eustacio Rivera in his *The Vortex* attempted much the same thing in both stylistic effect and theme. Rivera depicted the ruthless power of the rubber interests; Asturias is concerned with the ruthless totality of the state. Both use highly impressionistic poetic styles to convey the effects of these forces upon the human mind, e.g. the surrealistic use of nightmares and dreams. Both create a stifling and intensely suffocating atmosphere. In the one, the rain forest closes in upon the mind in a nervous anthropomorphism. In the other, the total state and the city oppress and fill the mind with terror.

Richard L. Franklin. *Hispania*. 44, Dec., 1961, p. 683

The basic literary features of *Men of Maize* differ sharply from earlier Latin-American novels on the Indian. For this reason many studies in the field pay it little or no attention. But the novel's outstanding qualities—its poetic and stylistic exuberance, its emphasis on myth and its blend of reality and irreality—are factors which break new ground. They reflect the author's background as a youthful poet in Paris during the period of vanguardist experimentation, as well as his anthropological studies on Maya civilization under Georges Raynaud, translator of the *Popol Vuh*.

The underlying plot line of *Men of Maize* might well have served as the basis for an *indigenista* [indigenous/Indian] novel of the 1930's. It treats the economic and cultural clash between the highlands Indians of Guatemala and the *mestizo* peasants and *entrepreneurs* who invade Indian land in order to exploit it economically. The former resist not only to preserve their land, but also because of their cultural belief that man, having been created in the beginning from corn, must venerate it almost as a part of himself, and as a pillar of his existence. In the light of Indian belief, to commercialize corn is roughly equivalent to blasphemy.

But what might have been a conventional sequence of events disappears before an elaborate, frequently obscure interplay of the legends which Indian psychology structures as a result of the clashes. The reader sees briefly and fleetingly the concrete situation which gives rise to myth. Then, in a gradual transition from real events to a world of semi-fantasy, he witnesses the formation of legends, as the novel traces their spread and elaboration into full-fledged folklore, with roots in the timeless traditions of the Maya-Quiché. . . .

Men of Maize is not without its weaknesses, most of which, in the minds of many literary critics, overshadowed its strengths and its significance. Its structural form at times is completely hidden, and the reader is hard put to grasp the relationship between parts. The author is overly given to the use of expressive but difficult localism, so that for anyone but residents of rural Guatemala, frequent interruptions are necessary to consult the extensive vocabulary inevitably added at the end of the book. Even without this problem, the baroque profusion of imagery often strains the reader's capacity for absorption and comprehension.

Weaknesses notwithstanding, *Men of Maize* marks a new point of departure for the Indian-oriented novel, transcending the former stereotype of superficial realism and frequently elementary social protest. An enlarged concept of the Indian is created, including his own peculiar world-view. For the first time in the novel, the technique of surrealism is introduced in treating this theme. It is unquestionably in accord with the author's aim to penetrate beneath the surface of Indian consciousness. . . .

Joseph Sommers. JIAS. 6, April, 1964, pp. 250–51, 253

At times the symbolic and poetic forms [of *Mr. President*] are difficult, which is perhaps unavoidable in working with such tools: upon
abandoning rational language, which best duplicates observable reality,
an author runs the risk of entering an area of such obscurity that it
conveys meaning only to himself. Such extremism borders on a purely
automatic form of writing which lacks creative control. Asturias skil-
fully avoids degenerate surrealism by synthesizing two universes of
forms: rational, discursive language; plus a world of imagery which
reveals a deeper reality, rooted in the human psyche. It is the equilibrium of these two separate and distinct spheres of communication that
prevents excessive excursion into regions of such extreme obscurity.
Where it has been necessary to paint abysmal and unfathomable anguish, Asturias rises above the limited natural appearance of reality.
Where it has been necessary to return to these appearances, he employs
only a minimum of transformation through language. In the balance
and integration of the two lies the success of his style.

When the reader puts down the novel, he does so with a feeling
of compassion and, at the same time, relief that he has not had to live
through similar circumstances. The undercurrent of violence throughout
has kept the reader alert; yet a feeling of freshness and intensity en-
hances its social context. Just as Cara de Ángel sowed the seeds for
his own destruction, so will all these other figures destroy themselves.
If they really form a "damned people," then they will be the authors
of their own ultimate damnation. The political message is simply that
a society which does not know its rights and duties will have to learn
them the hard way, just as the English people learned them in the seventeenth century and the North American later on. After the past fifteen
years, the Guatemalan people are much wiser and more expressive of
their demands.

We might say that Asturias' message is stronger than his art; he
depends on detailed plot and active dialogue, neglecting description,
sustained development or analysis of character. The author has
achieved in a splendid manner a grotesque and almost asphyxiating
conception of the total state as this has developed in the small unitary
republics of Central America. Through a whole gamut of literary devices, he has mixed essence and form in such a way that he has solved
a difficult task in effective fashion: on the one hand, there is his poetic
exploration into the recesses and realities of the human mind; on
the other, there is the material picture of an urban mass manipulated
by its iron regime. Through Asturias, we manage to understand the
tribulations of those small republics which have had to solve their political problems through harsh experience which affects the entire citizenry,
high and low. The synthesis of these literary achievements into an

eloquent whole is Miguel Ángel Asturias' contribution to the art of the novel in America.

T. B. Irving. *RIB*. 15, April–June, 1965, pp. 139–40

In Paris Miguel Ángel Asturias met Unamuno, Barbusse, and Valéry, and established friendships with the surrealists Desnos, Breton, Péret, and Tzara, who also contributed to the review *Imán*, which Asturias founded together with Alejo Carpentier. He often saw Picasso, Braque, Utrillo, Stravinsky, and Cocteau. Among the Latin American artists and writers who resided in the French capital, Asturias became friends with Vallejo, Uslar Pietri, the García Calderón brothers, Luis Cardoza y Aragón, Pita Rodríguez, Alfonso Reyes, and the Guatemalan caricaturist Tono Salazar, who later was to illustrate the Buenos Aires edition of *Legends of Guatemala*. . . .

Legends of Guatemala, Asturias' first book, clearly revealed his qualities as a writer, qualities that were to attract the attention of the highest level of critics. The work is a charming incursion into the magic world of the past; reality and legend fuse into a single mood of poetry. . . .

Valéry's evaluation, accompanying the French edition of *Legends of Guatemala* and added as an appendix to later editions in the original language, neatly grasped the atmosphere and the suggestive force of the book, defined by the poet as a collection of "history-dream-poetry" in movement. The fabular grandeur of the past seemed to Valéry strongly operant in Asturias' creation and gave him the impression of a mysterious world in continuous change. . . .

The spirit of sacred native books, the *Popol Vuh* in particular, intimately permeates *Legends of Guatemala*. In this sense Asturias reveals himself to be essentially a poet, a magical creator of evanescences, of images and of structures that, at the very moment of becoming reality, dissolve into the ambiguity of the legend. Full of profound insights into the spiritual complexity, the poetry, and the conditions of a people, *Legends of Guatemala* achieved an immediate goal for the writer, that of freeing the world of Guatemala from the narrow limits of a geography that had condemned it to oblivion, bringing suddenly to the attention of Europe its most complex spiritual substance. . . . [1966]

Giuseppe Bellini. *La narrativa de Miguel Ángel Asturias* (Buenos Aires, Editorial Losada, 1969), pp. 20–22†

Asturias first began to play a part in the political life of his country when he was a student. After writing a dissertation on *Guatemalan Sociology: The Social Problem of the Indian* he went to Paris to study the ethnology of the Mayas and thus became acquainted with an important part of the cultural heritage of his people. As a result of his studies and partly under the influence of surrealism he wrote *Legends of Guatemala* in which he explores the cultural wealth of Guatemala in the spiritual heritage of its Indian peasant masses. This work is closely connected with the attempts, which became apparent throughout Latin America in the nineteen-twenties, to seize the essential character of the nation and make use of it as the basis for literary creation and the formation of national consciousness. . . .

Immediately after [*Men of Maize*] he turns to the portrayal of the central problem of Guatemalan society—exploitation by the United Fruit Company. According to his own account the three novels [of the "banana trilogy"] portray the destruction of the small planters, the domination of the whole life of the nation by the banana trust, and liberation by means of organized struggle on the part of the workers and peasants. To this extent the conception and structure of the sequence is complete in itself. Analysis shows, however, that from *Strong Wind* through *The Green Pope* to *The Eyes of the Interred* the author himself undergoes a far-reaching process of recognition and in many ways basically changes his conception. Here the relation between myth and reality plays an important part.

The conceptual basis of the whole sequence is a view of man derived from Bergsonian spiritualism developed by representatives of the Latin American national bourgeoisie. The meaning of life is seen as the creative realization of the self and an extension beyond the self. Asturias sums this up in the sentence: "Plant a tree and have a son."

Despite the metaphysical guise in which this is presented it must be said that Asturias is able by this means to bring a basic human and historical category within his grasp, namely the realization of the human being as a productive force.

Adalbert Dessau. Lateinamerika. 1966, pp. 49–50
[English summary appended to German text]

Though touched by Naturalism—or the tropical variety, the kind that has been known to produce the worst results—[Asturias's] work is closer in tenor to the morality tale and the medieval fable. It is part pantomime, part ventriloquism. Many threads meet in it: the myth and magic of Indian lore, the Spanish dream-world tradition stemming from Quevedo, the pamphlet and the picaresque, the phantasmagoric demonology of Goyaism, the enchantment and conjury of Surrealism. Whether in the realm of pure legend or that of social protest, he creates an atmosphere of otherworldliness sometimes uncomfortably close to soap opera or the cartoon but at best inhabited by a gentle whimsy and a tenderness for the creatures of this earth that can enliven the crudest caricature;

Asturias is a puppeteer whose fairy tales are a sort of divine comedy made of hellish visions and nightmarish realities. . . .

Luis Harss and Barbara Dohmann. *Into the Mainstream*
(New York, Harper & Row, 1967), pp. 69–70

This year [the Nobel Prize] was won by Miguel Ángel Asturias of Guatemala. He is a fine writer, but clearly there were two, possibly three writers greater than he who did not get the prize. . . . If one runs down the list of winners over the past sixty-odd years, one does get an uneasy sensation that the conscientiousness displayed by the Swedish Academy, the judges of the prize for literature, is sometimes more in the realm of geography than literary quality. . . .

Asturias's three-volume trilogy excoriating the activities of the United Fruit Company in Guatemala and his savage exposé of Latin American dictatorships in the already-translated *Mr. President* were probably the prime movers for the Nobel award. Both the trilogy and the novel have some spectacular moments, but ironically they are not Asturias at his best. It is a stroke of good luck that Asturias's latest novel, *Mulata So-and-So* has just been published here in a magnificent translation by Gregory Rabassa. It is an unleashed, freely associative novel that is at once a retelling of an old Guatemalan fable and a surrealistic gloss of that same fable: the marriage of the sun and the moon.

As Asturias remembers it, "the sun and the moon cannot share the same bed because if they did, the sun as a male and the moon as a female would breed monstrous children." But the marriage and the breeding goes on, spawning a series of enigmatic monsters right out of Goya. The book is full of dwarfs, dancers in the form of wild boars, elves and demonized priests. In this underworld, sex is regressive, perverse and thwarted, a bad joke on the creator—his children reflect less the glory of the Christian God brought over by the Spaniards than an atavistic thrust back into pre-Columbian aeons.

Mulata So-and-So is, in essence, layers of myths making up a grand final myth. Beginning with the unnatural marriage, Asturias sends his creatures down into a fantastic land of Dali-esque optical distortions, a Coney Island of the unconscious. The old gods do well down there, but Christianity gets plenty of lumps—a seedy priest wanders through the novel carrying the Apocalypse as light reading, while the Christians propagate in a pious way only to have their children carried off to Hell by Satan. As a final bang, Asturias conjures up a Götterdämmerung that levels this astigmatic world to post-atomic nothingness.

Mulata So-and-So is the work of a joker with words who doesn't at all mind letting them take over for whole chapters at a time—more the free flow of a drunkard than that of a conscious artist. But Asturias really does dig in, taking more chances with automatic writing than any other Latin American novelist writing today. A bad flaw, probably fatal for most American readers, but at the same time therein lies his triumph. Along the road to Stockholm, he has managed somehow cheerfully to exorcise the irrational and subhuman demons of a whole continent.

Alexander Coleman. NYT. Nov. 19, 1967, pp. 1–2, 8–9

Men of Maize could have provided an excellent springboard to further penetration into the freshness of native themes, but instead Asturias promptly announced a trilogy to expose the evils of North American intervention in his country. To *Strong Wind, The Green Pope,* and *The Eyes of the Interred*, the three novels, Asturias added *Weekend in Guatemala*, a collection of seven short stories, to complete the accusation. The novels predict a great wind which will rise up and efface the power of the Green Pope, a Chicago businessman, unmistakably the head of the United Fruit Company. The wind comes in the form of revolution, justice is eventually wrought, and the dead at last close their eyes in peace. So political and vindictive are these works, condemning supposed North American intervention, that they are frequently reviewed in Latin American political science journals rather than in literary publications. They are almost completely ignored in the United States.

The novels and short stories compose half of Asturias' prose output. They are the most translated, into thirty languages, and in some countries the only known works of the author. But from a standpoint of good literature of real artistic value, they are by far the weakest of the author's production. The names of the North Americans are often those of stereotyped characters. Jinger *Kind*, obviously, is sweet and understanding of the Indians, George *Maker* is solely interested in production and accomplishment. Characters are flat, lifeless, and unconvincing. Bobby Maker Thompson, as an example, is shown in only one role throughout the novel—he is playing baseball each time the narrator visits him. [The boy is the "Green Pope's" son.] The plots of the three novels are repeatedly ruptured by unnecessary digressions as the narrator rambles back to a previous novel to complete the present scene. Sex is present, not as an integral part of the prose but as an attention-arouser, extraneous to theme and plot. Unlearned, passive men are stimulated to action by idealistic speeches that more strongly reflect the author than the characters of the work. The short stories, especially, appear to be hastily and even carelessly written. The polished balance and closely watched style of the earlier prose are absent. But most serious, in the range of Asturias' prose, is their limited temporal scope. Concerned with one specific problem in a definite period, they lack the timeless universality and the mythical qualities of *Mr. President, Men of Maize*, and later prose. They will some day lose veracity as the urgent but temporary social situation changes. . . .

Thomas E. Lyon. *BA*. 42, Spring, 1968, pp. 184–85

Mr. President and *Men of Maize* represent Asturias' best contribution to Spanish-American fiction, as they blend mythical and social elements, whereas his later works suffer from a preoccupation with social realism.

Asturias justified his novels of social concern by saying that the Latin-American novel should reflect the social, political, and economic conditions of the continent. Latin-American literature, he has said, has always been a literature of protest. Bernal Díaz del Castillo, in the sixteenth century, wrote his famous *True History of the Conquest of Mexico* to complain to the King that after all his years of service to the Crown he had been forgotten. And Sarmiento during the nineteenth century wrote his *Facundo* to complain and denounce the death of Quiroga at the instigation of the dictator Rosas, the prototype of all Latin-American strong men. Asturias' own novel, *Mr. President*, belongs to the tradition of *Facundo*; it is a protest against one of the greatest evils that plague Latin America, that is, the presence of the dictators. . . .

The suffering his family had undergone at the hands of the dictator Manuel Estrada Cabrera had left an indelible impression on Asturias' mind. Asturias then met Estrada Cabrera while the dictator, fallen from power, was being tried for the many crimes he had committed. At that time, Asturias was serving as Secretary of the Tribunal, saw Estrada Cabrera every day, and was able to prove, he has told us, that men of Estrada Cabrera's type have a special power over the common people: " 'No,' they would say, 'that is not Estrada Cabrera. The real Estrada Cabrera has escaped. This must be a poor old man they have imprisoned to fool us.' " And this is the way in which Asturias presents Estrada Cabrera in his novel: as a man who has become a myth. His dictator is unlike that of don Ramón del Valle Inclán, whose novel *The Tyrant Banderas* (1926) presents a grotesque tyrant, a true *esperpento* [figure of wondrous fright or horror]. Nor is his dictator like that painted by the Guatemalan Rafael Arévalo Martínez, the first to make Estrada Cabrera a character in a work of fiction. In Arévalo Martínez's short story "Tropical Beasts," a work completed in January of 1915 but for obvious reasons not published until 1922, the dictator José de Vargas is a ferocious tiger more than a human being. The social impact of the story is further diluted by making Don José governor of an imaginary country, Orolandia. This, of course, was necessary for political reasons, but it destroys the emotional appeal which is so effective in *Mr. President*. It is true that in Asturias' novel the name Guatemala is never mentioned, but there is no question that the novel takes place in that country, a fact that can be determined by a study of the realistic motifs, as well as by the speech of the characters.

Luis Leal. CLS. 5, Sept., 1968, pp. 240–41

The brief, intense narrative [*Strong Wind*] begins at a time when North Americans are undertaking to clear great tracts of coastal land and plant the banana groves. To their successors, the corporate officials, those first engineers and managers will seem visionaries, pursuing their grandiose project out of some demanding ideal inflicted upon them by their puritan creed of justification by works. Almost at once, the generation of ascetic pioneers is replaced by expatriate clerks whose business it is to administer the new, industrialized agriculture and, indirectly, the country's economy and politics. As the home office in Chicago may direct, they also advance seed and credit to independent growers, and they buy or refuse to buy the crop.

During this period the people of the coast have undergone a reciprocal evolution, from depressed peasantry to agricultural proletariat. A few have prospered to the extent of owning their own plot of ground. These are the independent growers, but their lives are as subject to the vagaries of a distant market as are those of the laborers who work directly for Tropbanana....

The novel's inspiration is baroque. Its scenes generally have surreal elements, whether because of explicit symbolism, heightened language, hallucinatory episodes, or a deliberately disjointed and fragmentary quality. That is true whether Mr. Asturias is dealing with the impoverished rustic gentry of the highlands, the laborers and overseers of the banana groves, or the company officials, Yankee and Latin, whose work and recreation are a kind of routinized violence. The effect is one of brilliant impressionism. The country steams and shimmers by day, and is seen at night as if in flashes of lightning. The style of the novel is greatly varied. It offers the colloquial speech of the workers, and the speech of the company executives that is sometimes mannered as in drawing-room comedy, and sometimes philosophic or poetic as in eclogue. Finally, there is the perfervid tone and luxuriant vocabulary of the narrative proper, recalling some French writer of the *fin de siècle*, and has exotic preoccupations—say, Pierre Loti or Maurice Barrès. That varied utterance and the novel's hectic, episodic scenes convey the sense of time passing swiftly, of a land made over but presenting a shape that cannot endure.

Emile Capouya. Nation. Feb. 17, 1969, p. 213

The theater of Asturias is above all poetic and fanciful, and we know from Surrealism and from psychology that fantasy and poetry are often more real than outward reality. As in the case of his novels, it is difficult to distinguish any single, decisive meaning for his plays or their symbols; various interpretations present themselves. . . . Inasmuch as the plays are about processes occurring in the psyche, their ambiguity turns out to be intensely realistic; perhaps we might better say that they are super-realistic. . . .

Asturias' poetic gifts are essentially perceptive and he prefers to communicate experience as he receives it, through the senses. Even in his novels and tales he tends to stage his material, presenting it by means of intense visual images, through vibrant word harmony, and heightening its impact on the senses by devices normally reserved for poetry. He has known how to adapt this quality to stage requirements. There is an occasional lapse into fiction in *Dry Dike*, where the novelist, not the dramatist, writes that the mariner hides the femur bone from Jemmy's sight "out of superstitious fear of the Negro's glance"; but the play does not hang on these instructions, and they do elucidate the scene behind the literal scene. The author's novel use of light and sound has more than a decorative value; it forwards the action. The various dances, the byplay, the humorous mime, all contribute magnificent scenic entertainment. Furthermore, these highly theatrical plays have the virtue of addressing themselves directly to the spectators' unconscious. This is the reverse of dream procedure, whereby the unconscious tries to communicate with consciousness.

In this respect, I believe that Asturias' plays constitute an entirely new experiment in theater, although it may only be a return to something that is very old. They do not emphasize plot or character in the customary sense. Their matter is chiefly psychological, not by means of conventional character analysis, but in the concealed manner that we have seen. In breaking new ground and applying to the stage the peculiar strategy he has used in fiction, Asturias may be laying the foundations for a new form of theater.

Richard J. Callan. Miguel Ángel Asturias (New York,
Twayne, 1970), pp. 148–49

For the first time since the publication of *Mr. President*, Asturias [in *Good Friday*] has returned to the Guatemala City of Dictator Estrada Cabrera. However, the purpose of his new novel is not to ex-

coriate the nefarious dictator but rather to recreate somewhat nostalgically university student life. . . . In keeping with Judas's betrayal of
Jesus, the novel's principal theme is treachery. The protagonist and
main culprit is Ricardo Tantanis (cf. the mythological Tantalus), a
law student who betrays his companions because of a desire to move up
the social ladder. . . .

In spite of its relatively simple plot, *Good Friday* is much less
tightly structured than *Mr. President*. The whole first fourth of the novel
has nothing at all to do with the celebration of Good Friday but is
rather a census of all the picturesque bars near the national cemetery
frequented by gravediggers, coachmen, mourners and poets, including
the thinly disguised Rafael Arévalo Martínez. This whole section as
well as several other individual grotesque scenes based on sex and
drunkenness provide Asturias with a wonderful opportunity to revel in
his favorite pastime of punning. . . . Unlike *Mr. President*, social protest and plot are overshadowed by the highly Guatemalan-flavored puns
linking *Good Friday* to [Cabrera Infante's] *Three Trapped Tigers* and
other linguistic novels of the 1960s.

Seymour Menton. *BA*. 47, Spring, 1973, pp. 330–31

AZUELA, MARIANO (1873-1952)

MEXICO

The scenes [of *The Underdogs*] have the brutality of Gorki. Azuela
is the Mexican Chekhov only in so much as he is a doctor; in all else
he is close to Gorki, with a touch of Gorki's terrific pessimism but none
of Gorki's revolutionary optimism.

The style is crisp; it burns like the flash on a gun-muzzle close
to the skin. Azuela knows the *Underdogs*. He has seen the revolution;
he has smelled it; he has felt it. His language is the language of
reality . . . crude, often vile, truculent, fiendish.

Prostitutes . . . and others come and go. One is shot through the
belly. Women are taken on and cast off, like old trappings. A country
girl, kind to Demetrio, is sent for. The leech Luis, whom she loves,
tricks her into the arms of his chief. . . .

Old scores are settled, savagely, murderously, two eyes for one,
two teeth for one. And orgies, vivid as Carlyle and the French revolution. Broken wine casks. People licking up aged wine from gutters.
Abysmal violence. "If I could catch Pascual Orozco alive, I'd rip off

the soles of his feet and make him walk for a full day over the mountains."

And if there is gold and jewels stored in the houses of the prelates, why not steal them. . . . When the grabbing is good, grab; for "if there are days when the duck swims other days there is not even water to drink." It is a great release. An eruption of submerged passions, the explosion of sealed-up desires, lusts, rapacities. Now every underdog can roar out his mind, "without hairs on the tongue." If necessary, even if not necessary, just for sport's sake, he draws quick and shoots quick. It is enough for these underdogs to feel life, to let their repressions loose, to follow the gust of desire wherever it leads.

Here again in Azuela, is the terrible disillusion, the Götterdämmerung: "What a colossal failure would we make of it, friend, if we, who offer our enthusiasm and lives to crush a wretched tyrant, become the builders of a monstrous edifice holding one hundred or two hundred thousand monsters of exactly the same sort! . . . People without ideals. A tyrant folk. . . . Vain bloodshed. . . . The psychology of our race condensed into two words: *Robbery! Murder!"*

Carleton Beals. Preface to Mariano Azuela,
The Underdogs (New York, Brentano's, 1929),
pp. xi–xiii

The Underdogs . . . is a very remarkable book grown out of the soil of the Mexican revolutions. To appreciate it fully one should know the Mexican people of the lowest classes, who were released from a rule practically amounting to slavery, about twenty years ago. Since the days of the Aztecs the Mexicans have been fighters, and when the flame of revolution broke loose in 1910 practically everybody started his own private fight. Some fought purely for the pleasure of fighting, others for the little valley in which they lived, and many just fought and didn't know why. . . . Many idealists joined these hordes and in long and flowery speeches, so dear to the Latin people, they preached revolution, liberty, and social advancement.

Azuela has given us a most vivid picture of these fighters of low caste. In simple language he paints one phase of the Mexican turmoil of fifteen years ago so truly that his book is not only good literature, but also a historical document. We follow Demetrio Macías on his career from his first scrimmage with federal troops, through victories, lootings, and debauches, until he finally becomes a federal general and meets his defeat from a band similar to the one with which he started. Luis Cervantes, a young medical student, begins with idealistic dreams, but as the looting progresses he develops a greed for gold worthy of an old Spanish Conquistador. These characters are surrounded by a small band that grows into an army, an army of cut-throats and spoilers. . . . One who has seen several revolutions of that period can tell you that every word is true.

Frans Blom. SR. Sept. 28, 1929, p. 179

The Mexican Revolution has been conspicuously devoid of literary self-expression. . . . An outstanding exception to this dearth of literary expression, however, was a slender volume [*The Underdogs*] . . . by Mariano Azuela, first published at El Paso in 1918 but not "recognized" as a work of art until its republication nine years later. A physician in Mexico City, Azuela was caught up in the revolutionary whirl. Graphic, terrible, true, his portrayal of what he saw is the most important human document that has come out of the Revolution. Some of the horrors have been depicted elsewhere, notably in Fr. Francis Clement Kelley's *The Book of Red and Yellow*, a terrific indictment of the revolutionists of 1914–1915, and more recently in an extraordinarily able narrative of the Revolution, Martín Luis Guzmán's *The Eagle and the Serpent*. But in neither of these is found a presentation from the standpoint of the underdogs who both made and suffered the horrors of the Revolution. Father Kelley wrote in unsparing condemnation of the Revolution's leaders. Guzmán, one of them, while writing dispassionately, sees the Revolution through its leaders' eyes. Azuela writes of the peons who, equipped with machete and rifle, found release from a lifetime, indeed from generations, of oppression by reckless fighting, roving, killing.

In this book all the sordidness, all the baseness of these human dregs is shown faithfully, but wholly without propagandist purpose. It is a record starkly realistic in its simplicity and unsparing truth. It is for the Mexican Revolution a work which combines the qualities of Zola's *La débacle* in relation to the Franco-Prussian War and a composite of such fiction as *Soldiers Three, What Price Glory, Sergeant Grischa*, and *All Quiet on the Western Front* for the World War.

Ernest Gruening. Nation. Dec. 4, 1929, pp. 689–90

That life in Mexico is full of turbulent imprudence, is often vicious and always more or less a haphazard incident, may be the reason why the native writers are far inferior to the artists. The rich tales of the country are told and sung at fiestas to the tune of a guitar or they are painted on the walls of Cortez palaces, but they are seldom put into the form of a novel. Mariano Azuela, a still practicing physician who was an army surgeon during the revolution of 1910–1920, is one of the few exceptions. His tales might almost be case histories; his plots are taken from real life, or at least give that impression; they are scarcely important, but his people have the sardonic humor of a Daumier.

In [*The Weed*, his] second book to be translated into English, there is Marcela, who has the careless love life of any wild animal. She gives her body to Don Julián, not because she loves him, but because she is a peasant and, for generations before she was born, female slaves had lived soft lives if they were loved by the master of the big house. Marcela's life isn't very soft. Her lover kills one of her admirers, tries to kill another, succeeds in killing the only pure love of her life and then kills Marcela herself for her knowledge of his transgressions. The book, as Waldo Frank says in his foreword, "is a class-conscious melodrama; but it is much more. It is a portrait—accurate, racy, true— of Mexican life; of that depth of Mexican life which revolution has not really altered."

Peggy Baird. NR. Dec. 14, 1932, p. 143

The Firefly is a psychological novel, but it is also a faithful description of the customs of different social classes. In it we find an exact portrait of provincial life, reeking of incense, vague and boring in its monotony. We see some little old ladies with vituperative tongues spending their time listening to Mass every morning and gossiping at the expense of mankind. We also see the interminable parade of government and municipal employees, of lawyers, doctors, priests, soldiers, the great phalanx of parasites, swollen by the Revolution, eternal bloodsuckers always bleeding the workers. And in the capital, where to succeed one must be a politician or carry a rifle in each hand, we see another parade —of magistrates, generals, heads of worker parties—all opportunists, all corrupt, always climbing, always thriving, thanks to the Revolution, which made everything equal, which leveled everything. . . .

Azuela continues to use a fragmented style. His story moves backwards, goes forward. At times the author speaks; at other times, the characters. The principal narrator is Dionisio, always tormented by his sensitivity, which has been made more acute by marijuana and pulque. During feverish states cinematographic visions of his life pass through his head, and, unable to control them, he speaks so as to get rid of them, deforming and exaggerating them in the process. They emerge in the story as monstrous, torturing, like infinite nightmares.

The Revolution holds no secrets for Azuela. He understands that all of Mexico now belongs to the generals and to the politicians, as it had belonged before to the aristocracy. Who has benefited by the change? The Indian, the peasant, the worker? No, for they continue to be the victims of the powerful. And Azuela, almost like an apostle, thus continues his ministration of justice, of purification, and of social improvement.

Arturo Torres-Ríoseco. RCu. 11, Jan., 1938, pp. 62–63†

Nothing new or surprising can be found in the liberalism of Azuela. In general, his ideas are in the great liberal tradition of the nineteenth and beginning of the twentieth centuries. Nevertheless, in these days of totalitarian or communist dictators, it can be both valuable and stimulating to read his novels. Azuela does not belong to the pitiful class of "library" or "intellectual" liberals, who loudly proclaim their liberal principles only to show themselves as cowards and hypocrites when the time comes. . . . Azuela quietly maintains the liberal tradition, the struggle for social and economic improvement as well as for political and individual liberty for the masses. He follows goals that can be found in the ideals, if not always in the actions, of men like Hidalgo, Juárez, Madero, Zapata and, today, Cárdenas. . . .

If one undertakes the study of the liberal ideas of Azuela, he must confront the difficulty that the great Mexican novelist rarely allows any one character's opinions to dominate to the exclusion of others. As some critics have already pointed out, in his novels Azuela rarely identifies himself with any one character in particular. The only exception to this rule, if it really is an exception, is the characterization of the great liberal Rodríguez in The Bosses. As a consequence, the reader wanting to interpret Azuela's ideas must balance the differing points of view expressed by the many characters that he presents.

Azuela's liberalism can be seen most clearly in the spheres of politics, sociology, economics, and religion, with a marked emphasis on the first three. In the area of politics, he censures all forms of corruption, especially excessive bureaucracy, favoritism, and bossism. Azuela's social liberalism is manifest in his hatred for class distinctions, in his condemnation of the economic misery of the masses, and in his satire of the superficial and hypocritical education the people receive. In the area of religion, Azuela attacks the excessive evils of the clergy, the impersonal coldness of institutional charity, and religious hypocrisy.

Francis M. Kercherville. RI. 3, May, 1941, pp. 381–83†

While The Failures lacks much as a novel from a technical and artistic point of view, it is significant in that it portrays the intolerable conditions in a Mexican town that gave rise to the brutality of the underlings when they rose a few years later against their masters. The pessimistic tone found not only here but consistently in most of Azuela's novels, evidently voices his own attitude. . . . Also set in a small town is another thesis novel, *Without Love,* which portrays more pleasingly the same bourgeois society. The bare mention of the new government under Madero suggests that no radical change had as yet occurred in Mexican social life. The well-developed narrative is decidedly a source of interest; the protagonist, a young woman, in comparison with Azuela's other characters who are generally of one fiber, is more complex; and the milieu, while amply set forth, is not overdone. . . .

In *Without Love* there is less portrayal, for their own sake, of manners and customs than in *The Failures,* yet the philosophy of life of the social group common to both the novels—the middle-class folk of a fair degree of culture—is effectively revealed. One senses the great gulf between those that have and those that have not; the resentment of the latter toward the former; and the scorn of the wealthy for the poor. Both the men and the women are represented as uncharitable and mercenary; the latter are hypocritical, sharp of tongue, backbiting; and the men, who spend most of their time in the public bars and houses of prostitution, are debauched. Some of the minor figures embody in a high degree vices that are more or less characteristic of the entire social group: Lidia, who instilled mercenary ideas into Ana María; Don Salustiano, the falsely pious money-lender and miser; and Escolástica Pérez, a type of Mexican bluestocking who desired to reform society, but who deceived her husband and was fond of drink.

The accuracy of the settings of both these novels shows that Azuela's knowledge of small town life resulted from first-hand observation. Equally intimate was his acquaintance with rural folk, with whom he had come in contact in his childhood on his father's hacienda near Lagos. . . .

Jefferson Rea Spell. *Contemporary Spanish-American Fiction* (Chapel Hill, University of North Carolina Press, 1944), pp. 73–75

So long, therefore, as the Mexican Revolution continues to have meaning and appeal for the generations to come, Azuela will be remembered and read. And judgments of him will vary widely as readers either acclaim his prophetic denunciation of the negative aspects of the movement or decry his failure to have grasped its full meaning and to have conveyed that meaning with true crusading spirit to the people of his age. Whatever the reactions of those yet to discover him through the more objective eyes of time, it appears reasonably clear now that through it all Azuela ever maintained a position singularly well-balanced and free of any particular bias for one faction or the other.

To the extremists, however, it would appear that ever since the Revolution began back in 1911—and there is ample evidence for this already in *Andrés Pérez, Madero Supporter*, his first novel on the Revolution—Azuela steadily lost sympathy for the Cause: perplexed in 1911, pessimistic after 1915, doubtful of any fruitful results as the twenties drew to a close, and out of touch with and incognizant of its more recent phases and developments, Azuela, they would charge, was too much of a reactionary to have been expected to comprehend and to condone the more exaggerated—and sometimes objectionable, they will admit—but necessary aspects of the Revolution. These extremists would allow, for example, that Azuela's novels on the war years are documents worthy of the Revolution, that in them Azuela writes whereof he knows, records what he himself experienced; but, they would contend, when he took up residence in the capital, he began to veer ever more sharply to the right as he himself soon settled down to the very type of bourgeois existence he had so severely satirized in his provincial novels. In short, he soon lost all direct personal contact with the revolutionary movement of later years. How else can one explain his attacks on the agraristas, on the anti-cristeros, on the labor movement, on the state itself that become the embodiment of the Partido Nacional Revolucionario. There is no attempt in any of his novels in which he condemns the excesses of those charged with the program, to explain or to justify them in the light of ultimate objectives and basic principles of the Revolution. . . . He is, they conclude, no revolutionary after all; and the novels of his later period are convincing proof of his defection.

On the other hand, to those of the right Azuela's name is inseparably tied up with the Revolution; for them he was its mouthpiece; they recall his repeated attacks against the church, against the big landholders, against the bourgeoisie—neglecting, of course, to scrutinize carefully the nature of his satire, and in one blind sweep commit him and his works to inquisitorial flames. They have not yet understood—or even attempted to understand—the significant message of *The Underdogs*; for them it remains the epic apology of revolutionary madness.

John E. Englekirk. In *South Atlantic Studies for
Sturgis E. Leavitt* (Washington, D.C., The Scarecrow
Press, 1953), pp. 130–31

Azuela had already begun to think about the problems of Mexico—political "bossism," social and economic domination of peon by landowner, religious bigotry and intolerance. This we know from short stories written in the first years of the century and from the first three full-length novels. His concern is shown somewhat weakly in *Without Love*, becomes much stronger in *The Failures* and constitutes a real affirmation in *The Weed*. Then broke the storm of the Revolution. Azuela saw in a very short time quite a bit of gun-waving, proclaiming of loyalties, and political chicanery. Nauseated by the insincerity about him, he wrote a novel—a hard, nasty little novel about a cynical and spineless turncoat—*Andrés Pérez, Madero Supporter*. This raucous cry of protest is not pleasant reading and it is technically imperfect, but it has punch. It showed Azuela the possibilities of a kind of writing quite different from that of the pleasant garden of the Moreno house in Lagos. It made possible *The Underdogs*.

There is one novel between *Andrés Pérez, Madero Supporter* and *The Underdogs*. It is *The Bosses*, written in Lagos in 1914 under the Huerta domination and published in 1917, after Azuela had returned to Mexico from his brief exile. Azuela's most "Revolutionary" novel (in the sense of exalting the Revolutionary), in technique it is intermediate between the earlier novels and the masterpiece; it is far removed from the haphazardness of *Andrés Pérez* but lacks the epic sweep of *The Underdogs*. . . .

The designation of Azuela as "the novelist of the Mexican Revolution" does him only partial justice. Whoever reads his novels sees that his themes are broad. Actually, questions of a sociological and economic nature, and problems of human conduct, attract him much more than the specialized matter of the Revolution. This is strongly evident in his later novels, down to *Lost Paths*, his last. His long writing career has some anomalies, most obviously his mock flirtation with the Stridentist school in 1923–1932. In the long run, however, Azuela follows a consistent pattern. He is Man thinking about Mexico. His own emotions are often involved, and he is always aware of the high mission of the writer; yet he writes always as the novelist, and almost always as the objective manipulator of tools, working something out.

Azuela was oriented as was no other writer of our time in the life-complex of the Mexican people; and his receptiveness and his highly personal combination of literary resources give a great deal of his work an artistic status which promises permanence.

Robert E. Luckey. BA. 27, Autumn, 1953, p. 370

Naturally, in the limited scope of his short novel [*The Underdogs*], Azuela could not give the vast chaotic panorama of the struggle in which Mexico was engulfed for so many years. Nor did he attempt to. As the Spanish proverb says: "As a sample, a button will do." The incidents he describes, the atmosphere he creates, were the pattern which repeated itself throughout the country, like images endlessly reflected in facing mirrors. One need only read Martín Luis

Guzmán's *The Eagle and the Serpent*, that enthralling narrative of his own revolutionary experiences, to see that fiction and reality were almost indistinguishable. The protagonists of the Revolution were, with rare exceptions, counterparts of Azuela's hero, poor illiterate peasants, often turned outlaw because of clashes with the authorities or the police, and who, gathering to themselves others of their own kind, threw themselves into the struggle with only a dim perception of the objectives involved. Demetrio Macías is a bewildered actor on a stage so multiform as to make his role almost meaningless. When after two years he returns briefly to his little ranch and his wife asks him: "Why do you keep on fighting, Demetrio?" he answers, tossing a pebble into the depths of a canyon: "Look at that stone, how it keeps on going." . . .

The peasants who made up [the] armies, like Demetrio Macías and his followers, totally ignorant of the French Revolution, were living their Mexican version of "Arise ye prisoners of starvation" without ever having heard the name of Karl Marx—their songs were "La Adelita" or "La Valentina," that light, sinister music to which men have always marched to their death, as Hemingway puts it. Theirs was an autochthonous uprising, springing from centuries of servitude, exploitation, humiliation, affording an opportunity to settle long scores with landowners, masters, and the forces of authority, which they looked upon as agents of the ruling class. . . .

One of the remarkable features of Azuela's novel is that he should so early have grasped two of the human forces at work in the Revolution: its blind creators and those to whom the Revolution would be the ladder by which they mounted to success as typified by Luis Cervantes, the educated city man, who discerned in the rabble in arms the wave of the future.

Harriet de Onís. Foreword to Mariano Azuela,
The Underdogs (New York, New American Library,
1962), pp. viii–ix

Much less well known than *The Underdogs, The Trials of a Respectable Family* reveals new aspects of Azuela's literary gifts and of his ability to reflect the age in which he lived. In this novel the force and action of the Revolution are in the wings of the stage. The author centers attention on the impact of the Revolution on the people of the middle class and their reactions to their trials and tribulations. Seized with panic engendered by reports of the excesses of the revolutionaries, people of means fled to seek safety in the capital city. There through successive stages they descended to penury and hardship. Azuela undertakes to explore the ways in which the altered conditions affected the individuals concerned and how they reacted—how they revealed themselves.

His primary theme, he wrote, is as old as time but inexhaustible; that pain and suffering are the most fruitful source of noble deeds. Though many of the formerly favored class failed to meet the test imposed by the events of the Revolution, many found in it their "structure as men." . . . Such men were, he stated, in striking contrast to the crowd of grasping self-seekers suddenly in possession of power and riches "whose faces revealed their insatiable voracity."

The grossest error to Azuela of some of the revolutionaries consisted in their killing the best in themselves, forgetting their humble origins and simple habits formed in poverty and even in misery and "letting themselves be seduced by the mirage of power and money." In conformity with his own modest tastes and personal humility, Azuela denounced those who proposed as a "doctrine of salvation for our people the creation of wants they do not have" and held that they did more damage than "all revolutions put together." He extolled the simple life without "complexity or waste," pursuit of which he thought would solve all the worst ills of the time without "blood or tears." As long as anyone is hungry or needy, "he who wastes is a thief." In spite of the cruelty and destructiveness of suffering, when a spark of energy remained, it could revivify in man unexpected forces.

With these ideas in mind Azuela set about writing *The Trials of a Respectable Family*. Though founded, he said, in distressing events, it ended overflowing with hope and optimism. . . . His animosity was directed against the men "who corrupted everything," not against ideas. The excesses of the people of the Revolution did not, however, justify those of the days of Porfirio Díaz. Azuela wrote that he "put these words which expressed his ideas in the mouth of the protagonist," Procopio. . . .

Azuela indulges freely in this work in a propensity for satire and caricature, especially in his depiction of the unsympathetic characters. Though the effect is sometimes humorous, the principal consequence is to make them hardly believable as human beings, but admirably suited to demonstrate the despicable nature of the traits and attitudes he uses them to typify. In Procopio, the protagonist, he creates a distinctive personality who is more than a conveyance for Azuela's thoughts, though he serves that purpose, too.

Frances Kellam Hendricks. Introduction to Mariano Azuela, *Two Novels of the Mexican Revolution* (San Antonio, Texas, Principia Press of Trinity University, 1963), pp. xxv–xxvi

A half century after its publication, *The Underdogs* occupies a consecrated position in the Latin American novel. Nevertheless, like *Doña Bárbara, The Vortex, Don Segundo Sombra*, and other novels of the earth, Azuela's work has been somewhat overshadowed by those of more recent, more cosmopolitan writers. . . . [But] an analytical reading [of *The Underdogs*] reveals not only a justification for the favorable criticism of the past but also evidence to oppose the impression of many critics that the novel consists of a group of loose portraits and lacks a well-thought-out structure.

The key to an understanding of that structure lies in an interpretation of the novel as the epic of the Mexican Revolution and, in a certain sense, the epic of the Mexican people in general. Descendants of pre-Cortés Indians, Demetrio Macías and his men are condemned to wander blindly in space and time. . . . Like any good epic, *The Underdogs* is based on an historical event of transcendent national importance; it begins *in medias res*; it presents the deeds of a legendary hero and his friends; it confines itself to a chronological framework, with a structure reinforced by thematic motifs. And it uses various stylistic devices usually associated with epic poetry.

Although Azuela presents the actions of only a small group of revolutionaries, he never loses sight of the fact that they are participants in the Revolution that gave birth to the Mexico of the twentieth century. The division of the novel into three parts corresponds to three distinct historical phases of the Revolution. The fact that the first part is the longest—twenty chapters—and that it captures the idealistic spirit of the struggle against the reactionary forces of the usurper Victoriano Huerta leads one to reject the assertion of some critics that *The Underdogs* is an antirevolutionary novel. Nevertheless, one must realize that the simultaneity of the great revolutionary victory of Zacatecas and the death of the idealistic Solís at the end of the first part constitutes Azuela's ironic observation on the tragic destiny of his people. The fourteen chapters of the second part, which correspond historically to the political maneuverings of the various chiefs before the Convention of Aguascalientes, underlines the barbarianism of the revolutionaries. The third part, in seven chapters, begins with the downfall of Pancho Villa in the battle of Celaya and reflects the country in the process of readjustment.

Seymour Menton. Hispania. 50, Dec., 1967, pp. 1003–5†

The literature of the Mexican Revolution is the result of historical events that affected the lives of each individual and changed the face of Mexico. The revolutionary movement which began in 1910 and ended about 1940 was a struggle against the Díaz feudal regime and its social institutions. The new program favored a democratic form of government, social justice, land reforms, and a more equitable distribution of wealth. This struggle provided writers with materials to compose novels, short stories, memoirs, dramas, and poems in which they gave expression to the ideals of the revolution without overlooking the tremendous loss of lives, destruction of property, and human suffering. This body of writing soon came to be known as the literature of the Mexican Revolution. Its initiator and best exponent was Mariano Azuela.

The literature of the revolution, whether in the narrative, dramatic, or lyric form, has something in common besides subject matter. It breaks completely with the past and rejects the esthetic ideas of the modernists, who were mainly interested in creating exotic worlds while ignoring their immediate environment and the problems of the society of which they formed a part. At the same time, it does not imitate the forms prevalent in Europe at the time, which do appear in the works of the avant-garde writers.

Those writers identified with the revolutionary movement produced a social literature that reflects the world in which they lived, a literature that does not ignore, as do the works of the modernists first and the vanguardists later, Mexico's real problems. Alongside an art in which pure form prevailed, they placed one in which the contents are vital and dramatic and of interest to all the people, for it gives expression to their struggle on the battlefield, in the towns, and in the city halls.

Luis Leal. Mariano Azuela (New York, Twayne, 1971), p. 121

BALLAGAS, EMILIO (1908–1954)

CUBA

Those of us who were acquainted with Ballagas knew him to be profoundly Cuban . . . in his easy credulity, in his spontaneous tendencies toward religious syncretism, despite his conscious attempts to check himself. In his sonnet "To the Virgin of Copper for the Marvelous Oil" we have a testimony of his taste for the magical aspects of popular faith, which had the danger of making him a religious dilettante. But as we have seen, he had the strength, the sort of tremendous strength derived from weakness, to attain the realm of the spirit. From there he was able to say, with his sensuality transformed into another headiness, another "whiteness": "My thought possesses the sweet heaviness of a bunch of ripe grapes, but my heart is light. I can feel it beating white, supported by the eternal nothingness, suspended in the middle of my body" ("Revelation"). . . .

Ballagas's works summarize in their own way, through the microcosm of his personal experience, the development of our poetry from its origins to Martí: first, the senses, the Edenic, or the Arcadian in *Joy and Flight*; then the addition of typical characteristics in *Notebook of Black Poetry*; then the soul, the feelings in *Eternal Taste*; finally, spiritual life in *Hostage Heaven* and his last poems. With him we sense once again what . . . I have called the "mystery of weakness." Of an impressionable temperament, of a tenuous and ephemeral sensitivity, Ballagas seemed to give in to the merest suggestions of the poetic fashions of his time. Moreover, his poetic accent was slight and elusive. One could well assume that it was too undefined to produce an original style. Nevertheless, he did have an original style to a great degree. He is the mysterious, weak poet of his generation, the poet who bases himself on the imponderables of his voice, the poet who, always yielding, ends up defenseless but also intact and himself through the suggestive, quiet words. . . .

Cintio Vitier. *Lo cubano en la poesía* (Santa Clara, Cuba, Universidad Central de Las Villas, 1958), p. 337†

Baroque and popular like Góngora (I insist on the comparison), melodious and abstract like Valéry, suggestive and narrative like Mallarmé, subtle and complicatedly simple like Jiménez, tender like Béquer, and a great poet like no one but himself, Ballagas is not the sum of influences but rather a happy conjunction of other temperaments, facets of his own personality. . . . In Ballagas . . . Cuba possesses a voice rather than a throat, an inflection rather than a chord, a nuance rather than a color, a dream, a harbinger, an implacable oblivion of the immediate, an indispensable refuge in the implacable oblivion of the immediate, an indispensable refuge in the foreseen and unseen, a mysterious region in which man touches upon mystery with his own mystery, with his unfathomable and impregnable engima.

Luis Alberto Sánchez. *Escritores representativos de América, segunda serie* (Madrid, Editorial Gredos, 1963–64), Vol. III, pp. 244–45†

Ballagas made a notable contribution to [Afro-Cuban] poetry. Besides his *Notebook of Black Poetry*, he compiled two important anthologies of Afro-American poetry . . . and he published a critical work, *Situation of Black American Poetry*, in which he treated the subject extensively from the point of view not only of literature but also of history, ethnology, sociology, and dialectology. Ballagas also wrote many valuable essays and articles on Afro-American poetry. The quality of his own Afro-Cuban poems makes up for their small quantity: he only wrote two "diversions," as Vitier calls them, and fifteen poems, twelve of which were included in his *Notebook of Black Poetry*. . . .

Notebook of Black Poetry, a product of the first period of Ballagas's career, shows undeniable points of contact with [his even earlier] *Joy and Flight*. If I were to express those contacts in one word, I would say joy, the spirit of joy that brightens these two books. In *Joy and Flight* we already sense the multiple forms taken by joy. But while there are certain recurrences in *Notebook of Black Poetry*—Edenic, childlike, sensorial, and verbal joy—the differences are notable. In *Joy and Flight* Ballagas created his own extratemporal and spatial world, made of air and foam, in which the five senses are awakened in all their ingenuous happiness. The world of the *Notebook of Black Poetry* is also ingenuous in the sense of the infantile innocence of the primitive, but such a world is very far removed from abstractions and overflows with passionate, rhythmic life.

Argyll P. Rice. *Emilio Ballagas: Poeta o poesía* (Mexico City, Ediciones De Andrea, 1966), pp. 93–94†

The work of Emilio Ballagas, a white Cuban from Camaguey who earned his doctorate from the University of Havana, marked the beginnings of [Afro-Cubanism] in the mid-1930s. Ballagas began his career in 1931, with *Joy and Flight*, by following the techniques of "pure poetry" established in Spain by Juan Ramón Jiménez. But in *Notebook of Black Poetry* he added to this style direct references to the subjects and thoughts of the world of the Cuban Negroes, and even incorporated characteristic rhythms. From 1936 on . . . the elegiac element intensified into the religious feeling of *Our Lady of the Sea* and *Hostage Heaven*.

Ballagas's lullaby sung by a black mother to her baby is a good example of his emotional range and his style. His poetry is a special mixture of the Cuban-Negro dialect and the popular Iberian-Spanish *copla*, which he uses less as a metrical device than as an accompanying musical rhythm. . . . Ballagas's style, however, is "close to the people" only on the surface. It is actually the harmonious fruition of continuing aesthetic deliberations. . . .

> Rudolf Grossmann. *Geschichte und Probleme der lateinamerikanischen Literatur* (Munich, Max Hueber Verlag, 1969), p. 546†

BANDEIRA, MANUEL (1886–1968)

BRAZIL

A Gérard de Nerval with the gift of irony and sarcasm, an António Nobre who knows how to quit the tower of suffering and to love life after all, a Paul Valéry whose lot is to cry, a classicist who knows how to live profoundly all of the romantic raptures, and a modernist who loves the pleasure of turning out a beautiful strophe of rigorous geometry—this is how I would describe the Manuel Bandeira of *Fifty-Year Lyre*, if someone who did not know his poetry were to ask me to summarize it in a few words.

Manuel Bandeira has profoundly felt all the poetic "experiences" of the last twenty-five years, beginning with a tardy Parnassianism, which had a longer life in Brazil than anywhere else. He was to become . . . a sort of symbol and synthesis of all of modernism. At first glance, after a superficial, hasty reading, the careless could perhaps venture the word "versatility" in classifying him, particularly if he were to read only *Fifty-Year Lyre*. However, what should be noticed is the multiplicity of poetic planes and the persistence of each one of the chords that developed this lyre. Through constant enrichment and sustained concentration, Manuel Bandeira's poetry has never abandoned, from [his first book] *Ashes of the Hour*, a certain number of what I would call not so much themes as "existences" . . . existences that he proceeded to strip, little by little. . . .

Adolfo Casais Monteiro. *Manuel Bandeira*
(Lisbon, Editorial Inquérito, 1943), pp. 49–50†

Bandeira's Parnassian and symbolist poems alone (so little studied, as if most critics considered them only the promising beginnings of a poet and could not admit that artistic perfection could be present in a twenty-year-old) would be enough to give him a reputation as one of the best poets of the period. In his work we can find the historical sign of the moment of the break with an exclusive aesthetics of the traditional poem, the adoption of the so-called free-verse . . . and the modernist movement.

This break having been established, the second phase of his poetry was born, one in which the poet was to reveal himself as one of the best poets of our language. His outstanding work bears an inimitable personal stamp. Bandeira, although served by a respectable bookish practice and by a stupendous jongleurism, knows how to remain always honorably faithful to himself. . . . And this formidable fidelity is based on an immutable philosophy of life and on an uncompromising technical conception, which enables him to make the most daring experiments. . . .

"Etching" is one of Manuel Bandeira's key poems, since it reveals in each of its verses both his metaphorical and allusive method of composition—his aesthetics—and his particular vision of man in the face of the problems of life—his philosophy. [1955]

Lêdo Ivo. *Poesia observada* (Rio de Janeiro, Orfeu,
1967), p. 211†

"Before us, had anyone really discovered Brazil? No, no one."

These were the words with which Álvaro Moreya characterized his generation in 1946. This was the generation that included the poet Manuel Bandeira, its "starting point." "Manuel Bandeira, in everything, marks the age of 'our generation,'" he wrote, "a generation precisely without age." . . .

Did Manuel Bandeira see Brazil in such an unusual fashion that his friend could justly speak of a discovery? Geography used as a source of picturesqueness or national exaltation was not the discovery of any modern writer in Brazil, whose literature practically began with verses to the islands of Maré and Itaparica. Bandeira and his generation even rose up against the "multicolor poetry," deemed appropriate for recitation by children, which had been shortly before propagated by Olavo Bilac. . . . He learned no new ways of seeing things in the trip that brought him, sick with tuberculosis, to a Swiss village in 1913. Brazil was already inside his heart . . . as a complex of cherished memories—the sea, the beloved, his family.

Gerald M. Moser. RI. 20, Sept., 1955, p. 323†

Bandeira's early poetry is usually classified as symbolist. His first poems, nevertheless, tended toward a perfection of the line, a regular accent, which more properly belong to the Parnassian mold. This is what the poet calls "modest lyricism"—that is, conventionality. One could say that Bandeira found himself during the Semana de Arte Moderna [Week of Modern Art] in São Paulo in 1922, since he had already given signs of rebellion in *Carnival*. With the possible exception of Mário de Andrade, the great poet of São Paulo, Bandeira was the outstanding poet of this generation of great lyric voices. The titles of his modernist books, *Dissolute Rhythm* and *Libertinage*, reveal his negative attitude toward form—a constant preoccupation. He wanted to destroy form so as to free himself from a tyranny that had enchained him within routine molds. . . .

Arturo Torres Ríoseco. RHM. 22, April, 1956,
pp. 131–32†

Ever since *The Ashes of the Hours*, published in 1917, Manuel Bandeira has been a disrupter in our literature. Two years later, in *Carnival*, his voice became satirical in "The Toads," a poem that was to become sort of a national anthem for the modernists. When the modernists began to emerge, around 1921, they found that there was already a poet in their midst. Many attempted to tune their voices to his, and all recognized his distinction of being the first. Attracted almost unknowingly to the movement begun by a group of youths in São Paulo, which later was to have repercussions in Rio de Janeiro and in some of the states [of Brazil], he remained essentially the same solitary figure. His efforts at renovation, his "message," as it was then called, obeyed no definite program and did not lend itself to commitment.

If his early effort stood out . . . from the current orthodox concepts during the period in which *The Ashes of the Hours* appeared, this did not mean that it agreed in all its points with the concepts defended by the modernists. The popularity of Bandeira's poetry did not come quickly, since he adhered to an extremely cultivated technique. It did not aim at exterior effects, and it was often less directed at "feeling," at the "heart," than it was at the less-explored realms of the soul.

Because of these characteristics, Bandeira was particularly close to some of the tendencies of French symbolism (and German romanticism), precisely those tendencies that were not so influential in our poetry. Neither verbal richness, nor lyrical profusion, nor sleight of hand, nor picturesqueness, nor unusual images most attracts us in the symbolists.

Sérgio Buarque de Holanda. General Introduction to
Manuel Bandeira, *Poesia e prosa* (Rio de Janeiro,
Editôra José Aguilar, 1958), Vol. I, pp. xv–xvi†

Inspired by the example of the 1922 Generation, Bandeira found the means of reacting to [his] latent sentimentality. The ironic verses of Ronald de Carvalho, Oswald and Mário de Andrade, Murilo Mendes, Augusto Meyer and Vinícius de Moraes among others, led him to the discovery of a healthier channel of expression in which to assuage his grief. Humour and irony provided him with a new form of spiritual catharsis which comes from a spirit of acceptance rather than escape. In his own words "the disposition to laugh, or at least to smile, at things or situations which, if confronted seriously, would be too painful or revolting."...

Bandeira's entire approach to irony as a stylistic device starts from the basic concept of "a disassociation between two realities" —namely between what is actually thought and what is actually expressed. The inflections, however, are his own, and the variety of nuance he introduces into his ironic verse, like that of Carvalho's *Ironic and Sentimental Epigrams*, or Mário de Andrade's "*The Moral Fibrature of the Ipiranga*," gives some idea of the versatility of this "desentimentalized generation." The influence of these younger poets acted upon Bandeira's development in a very real way. In their verses he saw mirrored the facets of his own ironic nature all too long suppressed by his classical formation and the subsequent influence of Parnassian and Symbolist currents. Foreign influences also played their part in this new phase of development, and in his autobiographical essay *Pasárgada's Itinerary* the poet recalls his enthusiastic reaction to the anarchist poetry of the Italian *futuristi*, passed on by Ribeiro Couto....

Giovanni Pontiero. *Hispania*. 48, Dec., 1965,
pp. 844–45

There exists a relationship, quite a bit closer than might be apparent at first glance, between the heroic phase of Russian revolutionary literature, liquidated by Stalin—that is, between Russian futurism and creationism—and Brazilian concretism. And the concretist poets could find a lot of primary material in the documents, almost all practically unknown, of the two currents that Stalinism destroyed.

On the other hand, there is almost an abyss between concretism and surrealism, since, as Bandeira observes: "The enigmas of concrete poetry have this to be said for them: all of them are decipherable since all result from a conscious effort of the intelligence. It is not this way with the enigmas of surrealism, which are born already made, from the subconscious." . . .

In a biweekly column published in the *Jornal do Brasil*, Bandeira wrote a series of articles dealing with concrete poetry. I cannot understand how anyone, especially someone within the movement, cannot have appreciated the full importance of these papers, which, together with his concrete poems, should be gathered together in a small volume. This would not only establish Bandeira's role in concrete poetry; it would also demonstrate to how far a great poet can go in seeking new forms of expression. . . .

"The Key to the Poem" . . . can explain certain of Bandeira's poetic intentions, which until then had not been too clear. After announcing that he had not joined the ranks of concretism, Bandeira goes on to stress that his own concrete poetry is a matter of experimentation: "The three experiments that I made, inspired by the processes of the Campos brothers and by Décio Pignatari, cannot, I believe, be considered concrete poems. They may be para-concrete or pre-concrete, or whatever . . ."

Stefan Baciu. *Manuel Bandeira de corpo inteiro*
(Rio de Janeiro, Livraria José Olympio Editôra, 1966),
pp. 113, 119–20†

With his ability to enjoy simple things Manuel Bandeira has trained his ear to the voice of the people in Brazil. No other poet of his time has a better feel of the oral idiom of Brazilian Portuguese, or takes keener pleasure in the flavor of folk speech, whether it be African dialect or immigrant Orientalisms or Indian place-names or Carioca babytalk. When he joins this mastery of oral tradition with his selective cataloguing of some of the most simple and intense memories of childhood, the result is the elegiac masterpiece "Remembrance of Recife." The Recife that Bandeira loves is not the famous city of legend and history, the commercial heart of the Northeast and the center of the liberation revolutions. No, that Recife is too complex, too literary, therefore melodramatic, histrionic, and unreal. The Recife that Bandeira loves is a transcendent world of memory, a place where he once played crack-the-whip, broke the windows in one of his neighbors' houses, shouted in the game of rabbit-come-out, and listened to the singing voices of the rosebud girls who would die before womanhood. It is the Recife of fires in the night, of the delicious sins of sneaking off to smoke and to go fishing when one should be running errands or attending school. It is the Recife of that emotional vision which isolates objects into flashes of overwhelming reality. . . .

The tuberculous poet, who wanted either to die completely or to go to a mythic and fleshly paradise where he could have the woman he wanted on the bed that he would choose . . . comes finally to transfigure his agony into a hymn of praise for the eternal world where everything lost remains "Intact, suspended in air!" . . . It is a world where death intrudes not, a world where the memory of an old man blends with the experience of a six-year-old boy at the Feast of St. John to discover that the loved ones from the past—Grandmother, Grandfather, Totônio Rodrigues, Tomásia, Rosa—are merely, like the celebrants of the night before, all asleep, all lying down. . . . It is a compassionately triumphant world where the silk-paper balloon trimmed by the typesetter José rises on his consumptive gasps beyond the hisses, hoots, and thrown stones of hateful dead-end kids, beyond the pontificating sermons of officious busybodies, to fall at last "in the pure waters of the high sea." . . . It is the richest lyric world of modern Brazilian literature.

John Nist. *The Modernist Movement in Brazil* (Austin, University of Texas Press, 1967), pp. 124, 126–27

As a prose writer, translator and scholar Bandeira has a distinguished reputation. However, his fame rests chiefly on his poetry. His early poetry, *Ashes of the Hours, Carnival*, and *Dissolute Rhythm*, reveals the influence of symbolism in theme and Parnassianism in form. *Carnival,* however, also includes some poems that are suggestive of the new spirit of revolt that was brewing in Brazilian poetry, and a new freedom of rhythm and meter is apparent in *Dissolute Rhythm*. In this last volume the symbolist note is linked to the theme of personal reminiscence. . . .

Though Bandeira did not participate in the Week of Modern Art of 1922, which marked the official beginning of modernism, the poems published in his next volume, *Libertinage*, are modernist in manner and style; the language is colloquial, the form is free, and the choice and treatment of subject at times highly irreverent. The themes of reminiscence and nostalgia are developed exquisitely. In his next collection, *Morning Star*, further technical development is evident, and there are some poems in which he breaks the boundaries between verse and prose. In *Fifty-Year Lyre* . . . and *Pretty Pretty* he experimented with surrealism and published a poem that came to him during his sleep.

Since then he has continued to write and experiment, and though he still elaborates his early themes, the early tone of disillusionment that was due to his physical condition and to the influence of the symbolists has given way to a note of serenity and a stoical acceptance of his condition as a solitary human being. Now in his old age he is considered one of the greatest poets of the century.

Raymond S. Sayers. In *Encyclopedia of World Literature in the 20th Century* (New York, Frederick Ungar, 1967), p. 94

Manuel Bandeira has had what is probably the most durable reputation of any of the modernists. His life and his works have become a sort of national institution, and he is without a doubt Brazil's best-known literary figure. His importance is primarily as a poet, dating from the publication of his first collection in 1917. Since then, collections of his work have appeared regularly, and he has appeared widely in reviews and anthologies. Bandeira's earliest work is characterized by the dominant elements of the emerging modernist tradition: a preoccupation with experimentation in meter and poetic form, traces of a formalism and an interest in structure which, although reminiscent of the preceding generation, will underlie the best of the poetry to come and contribute significantly to the graphic, concretist poetry of the present generation, the symbolistic relationships expressed in daring and strikingly original images and metaphors. In addition, one is impressed by the interest in the problematics of poetic expression which is woven into the poem itself. Bandeira wrote in one of his "poetics": "There is no more poetry,/There *are* poetics"—implying that much if not all poetry is an attempt to formulate a poetic, an ideal implicit in the individual poems. Finally, Bandeira's poetry is colored by the ironic melancholy which is so much a feature of modern poetry—the expression of an emotional shock in the face of the unknowable, the incomprehensible, and the irreconcilable. In many cases the poet masks his emotions behind a playfulness and a humor which highlight a fanciful and imaginative perception of man and reality, particularly in man's relation to modern civilization. In its totality, Bandeira's poetry is the work of a modest man who seeks his inspiration in the acute apprehension and analysis of the complex states of emotion which are his burden as a man. His modernity lies precisely in his modesty as a *vates*, in his ironic melancholy, and in his uncompromising dedication to the art of poetry.

At seventy, Manuel Bandeira continues to represent the tenor of contemporary Brazilian literature. He and Cassiano Ricardo, another important poet who has had almost as much influence and popularity as Bandeira, are among the few surviving giants of the Semana de Arte Moderna. Both have been intimately connected with the latest movements in Brazilian poetry, testifying to their importance and to the continued validity of the principles of the movement of '22. . . .

David William Foster. BA. 41, Winter, 1967, p. 41

BARRIOS, EDUARDO (1884–1963)

CHILE

I do not agree with Manuel Gálvez's assertion that *A Lost One* is a typically realistic work, "which means that things take up greater space in it than does soul." In this novel, as in all of Barrios's novels, what concerns the writer most is the analysis of lives, the creation of characters. . . . If "things" are given special attention in *A Lost One*, they are there only to build a setting, so that the characters become more understandable through their contact with objective reality.

The solid construction of this novel and the balance the writer has been able to maintain among the different elements that compose it are very impressive. Although there is a great deal of lengthy description and vignettes of customs that can be of interest only to Chileans, leisureliness is not in itself a serious defect. And Barrios possesses the true novelist's gift of sensing the exact moment at which to change the mood; when too much descriptive detail brings him to the verge of monotony, he shifts to dialogue and analysis. Furthermore, even in his most realistic moments Barrios uses the soft shading of illusion to lighten the content somewhat.

A Lost One contains Barrios's most successful characterizations. Indeed, Lucho has even inspired clinical analysis by psychologists. Barrios is not too concerned with theorizing over the influences of heredity or environment, as are the naturalists. Rather, he presents his protagonist subjectively, perhaps drawing on incidents in his own life; there are undoubtedly common ties between Lucho, the boy who goes mad because of love, and Barrios himself. . . . Toward the end of the book, when Lucho surrenders to the inevitability of his destiny, bereft of both desire and will, it seems as if his life has achieved its logical fulfillment, that it has achieved its destiny. . . .

The whole spectrum of the population of Chile is presented in *A Lost One*, from the rich aristocratic lady to the most wretched bum, all professions and stations: miners, military men, doctors, government workers, painters, writers, pimps, whores, panderers, gamblers, criminals, theosophists, tramps, and thieves. Because of this, *A Lost One* is in part a novel of manners and customs; it is certainly *the* Chilean novel par excellence. . . . [1943]

Arturo Torres Ríoseco. *Grandes novelistas de la América Hispana* (Berkeley, University of California Press, 1949), Vol. II, pp. 34–37†

Brother Ass, truly a landmark in Latin-American fiction, has many of the characteristics of the new type of novel. Unlike *A Lost One*, it is brief. In the plot, there is very little physical action; but the soul struggle in Fray Lazaro and particularly in Fray Rufino is intense. The background, which is limited to the Franciscan monastery, is impressionistically interpreted. Barrios attains in this work his greatest perfection of style. Poetical figures are frequent; and both the short sentence and the repetition of words, phrases, and sentences are used effectively. The quality, perhaps, that distinguishes it most from his other works is the clearly detectable vein of quiet humor which enters into the presentation of the overzealous Fray Rufino.

From a literary point of view, Barrios seems to have almost completely spent himself in *Brother Ass*. In the collection *Pages of a Poor Devil*, there are only three new stories. . . . There is . . . a sense of the ludicrous in a rather gruesome situation in [the title story], which is by far the best of the three stories. Here, Barrios turns again to the confessional type of story and to his favorite character, a timid, hypersensitive, neurotic person—in this case a young man who wrote down his experiences and emotions during some months in which he was an employee in an undertaking establishment in Santiago. Among the excellent features of the story is the delineation of the undertaker who welcomed an epidemic and watched with great satisfaction a funeral procession if the coffin had been bought from him; if not, he turned aside in great disgust. There is throughout the story, too, a certain type of humor, which lies in the fact that the peculiar individual who wrote the memoirs was aware of his own peculiarity and of the incongruity between himself and the position he occupied.

With *Pages of a Poor Devil* Barrios' work came practically to an end. . . . In spite of the fact that literature has been an incidental matter in his life, it has been—on the other hand—a very personal matter. For Barrios' interest, literally speaking, is not in background or social problems, as is characteristic in general of Spanish-American fiction today, but in himself; and for his psychological analyses of those abnormal, self-centered characters in *The Child Who Went*

Crazy with Love and *A Lost One*, he drew, he confesses, upon himself. The latter novel contains much, too, of his own tempestuous life in Valparaíso, Iquique, and Santiago; and Fray Lazaro in *Brother Ass*— disillusioned, tired of the empty pleasures of the world and now philosophic—seems to reflect the middle-age attitude of Barrios.

In addition to his ability in psychological analysis, Barrios has a strong claim to fame for his style; in this, with the possible exception of Ricardo Güiraldes, he is without a peer among the writers of fiction in Spanish America. Nurtured on the rhythmical prose of the Spanish mystics, of the same literary tendencies as such contemporary Spanish "modernists" as Valle-Inclán, Ricardo León, Azorín, and Pérez de Ayala, Barrios attaches much importance to the pure music of style, without which "there are no sympathetic waves that enter the heart."

Jefferson Rea Spell. *Contemporary Spanish-American Fiction* (Chapel Hill, University of North Carolina Press, 1944), pp. 150–52

[Of Barrios's novels of the last ten years], *Tamarugo Grove* is the one that most closely follows the traditions of Chilean realism. The setting, the arid saltpeter region of northern Chile; some of the episodes, tragedies in the lives of the miners; and a character here and there, workers or employees of the mining company—all remind us of the realism of Baldomero Lillo or Manuel Rojas. There are also scenes that suggest the influence of Zola's *Germinal*, such as the episode about the *chanchero,* a miner who is crushed to death by the terrible jaws of the *chanchadora,* the machine that grinds the mineral from which the saltpeter is extracted. In this scene Barrios does not suppress a single detail that can contribute to the effect of horror and tragedy he wants to produce.

Yet if we examine not the details of the external setting but the inner worlds of the characters, we will find that similarities between Barrios's work and that of the orthodox realists and naturalists turn out to be quite superficial. It is worth remembering that Barrios at one time lived in the northern part of the country, as an employee of a saltpeter company; realistic elements in *Tamarugo Grove* seem to arise more from the personal experiences of the writer than from a conscious goal of imitating the subject matter of the realists.

The majority of Barrios's contemporaries who followed realism or naturalism did so undoubtedly because the techniques of these two schools were so well adapted to the goal of promoting social reform. Barrios, on the other hand, seems not to be very interested in society in general. . . . His creative faculties are always focused on the individual, on a man's soul, not on the collective. In *Tamarugo Grove* there is little polemics or preaching—no clamoring for justice for the miners exploited by the companies. Despite the realistic setting of the work, its drama is to be found in the lives of three or four individuals, in their feelings. . . .

Donald F. Fogelquist. RI. 18, Dec., 1952, pp. 14–15†

Critics have insisted on the autobiographical nature of Barrios's novels; some have even gone as far as to state that the Chilean novelist's works are not "psychological" fiction but rather exercises in self-psychoanalysis. To be sure, some of the writer's experiences have been translated into those of his characters. It should be borne in mind, however, that the first laboratory—and perhaps the only sure one—for the observation of the psychology of others is self-analysis. In *A Lost One* Barrios says in his "Autobiographical Notes" that "I have depicted sincerely the life of that school (the Military Academy of Santiago at the beginning of the century). Of course, I am not Lucho Bernales. Some have supposed that *A Lost One* is an autobiographical novel. This is untrue. But I accept the supposition as praise; it proves to me that my fiction is convincing." . . .

Barrios has unquestionably lived his material, but in the sense in which an artist lives, in the creative fantasy that produces its own reality, which is at times truer than ordinary reality, as Unamuno affirmed with regard to Don Quixote and his own character, Abel Sánchez.

The Child Who Went Crazy with Love certainly does reflect an emotional crisis in the youth of the sensitive and romantic Barrios. Yet, if the writer's experiences have resulted in the candid, sincere tone of the diary of the hurt child, only an artist could transform a childish episode into a poetic work vibrant with emotion.

Carlos D. Hamilton. CA. No. 85, Jan.–Feb., 1956,
pp. 283–84†

Barrios' dramatic production was enthusiastically received by Chilean critics and the public; it was not a lack of acceptance that led him to abandon the theater after *Living*. Barrios himself explained that the difficulties and irritating details of staging a play were responsible for his discarding the dramatic form in favor of the narrative genres. His decision was a wise one, since it would appear that the demands of drama for overt action as the vehicle of characterization are not in keeping with his peculiar talent for the narration of reverie and detailed self-analysis which reveals itself most effectively in his narrative works.

The social consciousness which pervades and, in part, dictates the composition of Barrios' dramas all but disappears from his works after 1916. As he abandons the theater he likewise sheds the somewhat ill-fitting garb of the social reformer and turns his attention entirely to the individual personality; society becomes simply an element of the larger adversary, life. Social institutions are no longer singled out for analysis; at best they serve as backdrops for the individual struggle.

The male characterizations in these dramas reflect the basic division which underlies Barrios' later portraits, in which there is a rather clear split between the aggressive, successful personality— the *fuerte* [he-man]—and the introverted, failure psychology of the *perdido* [down-and-outer] or *débil* [ruined, weak person]. The feminine figures do not reveal this division, however; they are usually composite personalities which reflect ideas current during Barrios' formative period: Olga, passion; María, procreation; María Rosa, the victim of society and the male ego; and Matilde, the maternal instinct. There is little doubt that Barrios was influenced by Ibsenesque ideas and techniques, and it is not unlikely that they came to him through the works of Florencio Sánchez, the Uruguayan playwright.

Ned J. Davison. *Hispania.* 41, March, 1958, pp. 62–63

Strong indications of the mastery Barrios was to develop in his later works can be found in the early *The Child Who Went Crazy with Love,* the anguished and lachrymose diary of a boy who falls in love with a friend of his mother's and ends up by losing his reason. Written in the first person, the novel reveals Barrios's audacity in confronting . . . the psychology of a child, which he presents knowingly and movingly. The boy is possessed by an adult passion he thinks he can handle. But ultimately the adult spirit in his fragile child's body destroys him. Barrios's style is at times lyrical, at times broken and halting, responding faithfully to the demands of this "ingenuous and painful picture," as the author himself has called it. . . .

Worthy of being anthologized, this early work of Barrios's, the fruit of a spontaneous flowering of sentiment, still retains—despite the years that have passed since its first publication, despite the changes in popular tastes and interests—its freshness and charm. It continues to elicit from readers that almost imperceptible shudder of sadness. . . .

Jaime Peralta. *CHA.* No. 173, May, 1964, pp. 360–61†

It is perhaps not surprising to find a strong vein of the grotesque running throughout Latin American literature when one considers that its cultural heritage has produced Goya, Velázquez and Cervantes. . . .

Working within this cultural framework and aware of existing and contradictory views regarding the natural order, Eduardo Barrios skillfully mastered the technique of the grotesque, stylistically as well as thematically.

In *Tamarugo Grove*, as in so many of Barrios' works, the grotesque is regularly invoked when the author is writing death scenes. This novel, which is Barrios' first attempt at the detailed analysis of a heroine, is concerned essentially with inhibited spiritual and physical love. It is set in the nitrate fields of Northern Chile. The major aspect of the novel is its *costumbrismo* [fiction based on customs]. Since the work is a study in pathos rather than social protest, the tone is extremely sentimental, and the reader's rational sense of the natural order, within the framework of the novel, is not prepared for the shock of the description of the suicide of Mr. Adams, an alcoholic friend of the protagonists. . . .

Barrios uses the grotesque to impress upon the reader the fact that human experiences have many facets and whether or not one conceives of the violent and bizarre as part of the natural order, their existence and effects must be admitted. Barrios employs the esthetically and thematically grotesque when the entire work creates an atmosphere of unfamiliarity and uncommon human experiences. He is also a master of the stylistically grotesque which is considerably more spectacular, since it is usually evident in unexpected and shockingly realistic deviations from the atmosphere previously established in the particular work. Whichever the case, Barrios is more than capable of disintegrating the reader's rational reality and of tilting, if not upsetting entirely, his sense of the natural order of things.

Jerry L. Benbow. Hispania. 51, March, 1968,
pp. 86–87, 91

BENEDETTI, MARIO (1920–   )

URUGUAY

[Benedetti's] purpose seems to be to close every possible optimistic exit with a dry and ruthless regularity. He denies his characters any poetic characteristics or any happy solution. Benedetti's microcosm is hostile, hopeless, and indifferent. It is reasonable to assume that it is also authentic; therefore, it introduces the average reader to a negative vision of society. . . . Among the characteristics of the fiction [of Benedetti and the Generation of '45 to which he belonged] . . . are anti-rhetoric and anti-romanticism, that is to say, the almost absolute hatred of poetic characteristics in style and of the sentimental reactions that abound in the morbid [stories of] Felisberto Hernández or in the short stories of Trielo Pays. . . . Some of this resentment is captured in the characters' attitudes, which can also be the direct consequence of the Montevidean social discontentment, of the impoverishment of the heretofore strong Uruguayan middle class and the decline of their standard of living because of the implacable inflation. It is important, therefore, to point out that Benedetti shows no sympathy or antipathy toward any political party, sect, or cause. His short stories do not make any social allegations, and his absolute objectivity removes them from commitment.

Nevertheless, sociologists of the present and the future will find in *Montevideans* an extraordinary document of our epoch, and they will be able to extract from its pages behavior and observations of major interest. . . . Ángel Rama, in discussing *The Truce*, said that sociologists will find material in the book for their search for the national essence. It is too bad that there still does not exist a work that tries to define the environment and psychology of Uruguay. Yet its short-story writers, even more than its novelists, have made outstanding contributions . . . to the comprehension of a people whom the men of the Pacific do not know or whom they analyze with the mindlessness of tourist propaganda.

Benedetti, more than anyone else, has focused on the analysis of urban man, especially the man who lives in the confining horizon of bureaucracy. . . . [1960–61]

Ricardo Latcham. Carnet crítico, ensayos (Montevideo, Editorial Alfa, 1962), pp. 142–43, 150†

Benedetti has published several volumes of stories . . . but the one that best represents him to date is *Montevideans*. It contains not only the themes and characters that have served to establish his fame; it also reveals a very personal focus on the society of the capital. . . .

Benedetti seems to have limited himself to the narrative, fictional examination of the bland and hedonistic creature that circumstances have caused to develop on the shores of the Río de la Plata. Wherever he may have been born—and the majority of Montevideans, like the protagonist of "The Fiancés," like the writer himself, like the critic who is writing these words, are from the interior—this person comes to Montevideo with his hopes of public employment and with his inevitable choices (of political party and soccer team) already resolved. . . .

Each of the stories in this book explores a zone of the Montevidean presence, although at times the writer does move about in search of distant roads or to project himself beyond this world. Each story por-

trays an archetypal character (the neighborhood boy, the faithful fiancée, the old grafter) or profiles a national institution. Yet it would not
be difficult to prove, if it were really necessary, that things are the same
all over the world, that the essential nature of the Montevidean merges
with the nature of man. . . .

Emir Rodríguez Monegal. *Literatura uruguaya del
medio siglo* (Montevideo, Editorial Alfa, 1966),
pp. 294–95†

Roundtrip owes its formal conception to two ideas repeated by a
Pirandellian dramatist obsessed with the subjective world of images:
(1) it is enough to imagine a person for him to be born into life; (2)
the character who is alive is autonomous and allows no one to impose
an order on him. The first concept functions like a premise for Benedetti's play; the second, like a conclusion. The development in between
—the ideological content—rests on situations and satirical references,
applicable not only to Uruguay but to all of Latin America. These
include the mockery of democracy, the obstacles in the way of a professional theater, the malignant infiltration of communism. In addition
to the vices of pseudoexistentialist youth (drugs, homosexuality),
Benedetti touches indirectly upon the problem of prostitution when he
refers to certain European women who make love "with erudition," in
contrast to some who still "improvise terrifically." With this remark he
would seem to suggest that improvisation, to the extent that it implies
sincerity, does indeed have a place in the sphere of human affection,
but never in the political sphere, where the laws must be strictly
observed. . . .

The structure of the work owes much to expressionism and particularly to Brecht, with its indirect exposition through a narrator as well as
its devices for distancing through sight and sound (expressionistic
sounds, changes of scene before the audience's eyes). Benedetti goes
the German dramatist one better by doing away with *all* illusionary
effects, beginning with his own imaginary "characters."

The Pirandellian "improvision" accentuates all that is trivial. In
addition, as happens in the works of the Italian master, this improvisation, with a very Latin American tenor, fails. . . .

The apparent ingenuity of *Roundtrip* hides an endless array of
underlying subtleties. With this avant-garde comedy Mario Benedetti
brings into focus the enormous changes in Uruguayan drama since the
days of naturalistic regionalism, at the beginning of the century, as in
the works of Florencio Sánchez, another Uruguayan who contributed
so much to the success of Río de la Plata theater.

Alyce de Kuehne. *Hispania*. 51, Sept., 1968, pp. 413–14†

Mario Benedetti for several years has been recognized as an important Uruguayan writer of fiction, principally short stories noted for a modified blend of comedy of manners with psychological novel. An extremely acute sense of the irony of daily existence has made his work compelling and often hilarious reading.

This most recent collection of nineteen stories [*Death and Other Surprises*] marks a significant departure for Benedetti in that few if any can be directly related to the social-irony orientation of his previous titles. Although some of the pieces are characteristically ironic and straightforwardly funny, the tone in general is much more serious, much more psychoanalytic, and, significantly, much more experimental, in line with the radical and audacious works published by vanguardistic Siglo Veintiuno. Sensitive to new directions in prose fiction, the Uruguayan chooses in the majority of the stories to focus on what can be called the "secret fetishes" of men: objects, behavior patterns, characteristics which, examined with ironic microscopic attention (bordering occasionally on magical realism), reveal a fundamental aspect of the individual, whether singular or universal in nature.

Being highly innovative, several of the stories fail to satisfy, either because the reader may not be equipped to understand their unique point of departure or because the author fails to give them extensive enough form to engage our understanding. The most successful, however, are those that probe, by way of a metonymic concentration on some feature or aspect so basic as to be the synthesis of meaning and personality. A case in point is the story dealing with the mysterious fraternity of Montevideo asthmatics, destroyed by the advent of a terrifying absolute cure for their affliction: the destruction of the bond that had related these men to each other in a secret and meaningful way is at the same time the destruction of their sense of identity and uniqueness. While this may be an extremely slender thread with which to weave an acceptable short story, it is significant in underlining an insistent feature of Benedetti's stories. If man does possess a coherency of personality, if he does possess a dignity of character, it is in terms of the slender threads with which he weaves for himself an acceptable existence. Examining these threads may reveal the impoverishment of his spirit, but, unfortunately or otherwise, it is the best we have got to work with.

David William Foster. *BA*. 43, Autumn, 1969,
pp. 565–66

Short, well-defined, built solidly on perceptions that are entered as notes in a diary, [*The Truce*] has something classic about it—it is the vehicle of a vision of life.

Santomé, the diarist, is a widower about to retire from his office in Montevideo. A new girl, much younger than he is, comes to work. She "doesn't seem overeager to work," he notes, "but at least she understands what one explains to her." Eventually he is able to explain himself to her, and more effectively than he had been able to explain himself in his diary. "I love you," she says, "because you're made of good stuff." Then she dies, and he enters a state of retirement made bleak by her absence. "After waiting so long, this is leisure. What shall I do with it?"

That is all. The story, like Santomé's whole life, has been without "irrational changes, or unusual and sudden twists." But it hasn't been without significant shape. Every element in the story functions, contributes to a theme which is its justification and its burden.

The theme is confidence: confidence as certainty and as the courage to confide; hence confidence as love's gift and animating force, which opens us to joy and leaves us defenseless against pain.

Nothing Benedetti's diarist treats fails to touch the question of confidence. The diary itself is the gesture of a man who isn't confident of his right to confide in others. The office is a place where a worker "takes an old file cover, crushes it in his fist and throws it in a wastebasket"—just as he seems on the edge of telling a "confidential story." Outside the office is Montevideo, an aging democracy where no one trusts the law to work without the assistance of a bribe. Above Montevideo is God. He exists, but He can't be trusted.

Taking form amidst such references, the love-story becomes a gathering of confidence and a giving of confidences, an illumination of the possibility of sincerity. Once the diarist had a good opinion of his body and entrusted it to his wife's. Now, as the diary begins, he makes love to strangers in the dark, fears ridicule, cultivates irony, expresses a "mania for equidistance," welcomes boredom and inertia as the best of defenses. But touched by the girl who comes to him "without defenses— meaning, defended only by me against myself," and surprised by his own capacity for emotion, he takes risks. The risks are small, but the novel makes them count for a lot. There is the risk of folly, of the shame of not satisfying, of the betrayals that ensue upon dependence. The novel persuades us that this is what love is: a taking of risks.

Arthur Gold. *NYT.* Oct. 19, 1969, p. 55

The Truce is one of the best novels to come out of Latin America in recent years. Its author, Mario Benedetti of Uruguay, is a polished professional writer. Unlike many other novels from that part of the world, *The Truce* is a conventional piece of writing. It is clear from start to finish. It does not shatter chronology or shuffle characters, episodes, physical reality, and interior monologues, as do so many of the Latin

American novels that have achieved success in the past two or three decades. Faulkner, John Dos Passos, and James Joyce were the mentors there. Benedetti, on the other hand, has produced a real classic with the old tools of the trade, which he has honed to a razor's edge. . . .

The search for a meaning to life has seldom been more movingly depicted. Benedetti focuses his attention on one moment of love that is a brief truce in the ugly and omnipresent war for human survival. It is this truce that makes life possible in a hostile universe. To love and to be loved is to risk everything and is worth everything, even if (as is inevitable) the prize is as suddenly withdrawn as it was unexpectedly offered. . . .

It is the stark language and probing mind of Benedetti that make this short novel memorable. Not a word is wasted. And it is the protagonist's absolute honesty that gives him dignity. He questions God, he deftly examines human nature and the eternal bureaucracy, he ponders about the same things that have caused men to ponder since the beginning of time, and he finds no answers. It is only his capacity to love that keeps his life from being a total waste on this unbright earth. . . .

John A. Crow. SR. Jan. 10, 1970, pp. 44–45

One of Uruguay's major contemporary writers, Mario Benedetti resides in Cuba where he founded the Centro de Investigaciones Literarias. His fourth and most avant-garde novel to date [*Juan Ángel's Birthday*] depicts brief episodes in the life of Osvaldo Puente from his eighth to his thirty-fifth birthday. Born into a conservative, middle class Uruguayan family, Puente gradually becomes so disenchanted with the false values of his nation's corrupt establishment that he sacrifices physical comfort and social prestige to join the Tupamaro movement (which christens him Juan Ángel) and, in the final pages, flees from the police through a sewer with a group of comrades.

Salient features of the book, written in blank verse entirely devoid of punctuation or capital letters, include stylistic innovations, structural complexities, and fervent political ideology. . . . A showcase for the author's personal obsessions as well as for the exposition of vital, universal themes such as individual alienation and solitude, the novel emerges as a highly readable, satiric tableau of stagnant bourgeois society under siege, a fusion of wry humor and tragedy, of lyric flights and earthy determinism.

George R. McMurray. BA. 46, Spring, 1972, pp. 270–71

BENEDETTO, ANTONIO DI (1922–   )

ARGENTINA

In 1956 something very similar [to the French "new novel"] was written thousands of kilometers from Paris. In Mendoza, Argentina, the novelist Antonio di Benedetto wrote a story, "Abandonment and Passivity," which belongs to what he himself has rightly called "experimental literature." After a long wait, this story was published in a bilingual, Spanish-English, edition by the Biblioteca Pública San Martín in Mendoza in 1958. Benedetto states in his "Clarification" that " 'Abandonment and Passivity' is composed only of things, but not things that are pretended to have life and language as in fables. The vase is a vase, and the letter is a letter. If a pane of glass and water wreak havoc, they do so in a merely passive function. The human drama turns out to be implicit." This clarification could well have been signed by Alain Robbe-Grillet. Yet so unknown was this French school to us that in the prologue to this volume the noteworthy critic Luis Emilio Soto does not even mention it.

By now this work by Antonio di Benedetto has enjoyed considerable impact in the interior of the country, particularly in the literary and university circles of Córdoba. But unfortunately it has gone unnoticed in Buenos Aires. If the author of *Zama*, a novel whose true value has yet to be appreciated, had published "Abandonment and Passivity" in Paris, it would already have worldwide fame. Even without having to go so far, if he had published it in our neighboring Brazil something similar would have happened. But in Argentina, as Eduardo Mallea recently said to me with a trace of bitterness, a writer's true social worth is not recognized.

Abelardo Arias. *Davar*. No. 100, Jan.–March, 1964,
pp. 68–69†

[Benedetto's] fiction, perhaps because most of it was published in limited editions in Mendoza . . . has not yet found the fame its notable relevance deserves, despite the eleven prizes the author has rightly won. Nevertheless, his recognition has begun, and the recent publication of his novel *Zama* by Centro Editor de América Latina proves it, as do the translations in Germany of his latest novels, *Zama* and *The Silencer*. . . .

To classify these two works, we need to point out a convergence of numerous literary currents, especially fantasy, Kafkaesque magic realism, and the metaphysical narrative, this last affiliation corroborated by Benedetto's declarations in his prologue to *Animal World*. . . . In addition, there is evidence of the influence of Quiroga, Borges, Cortázar, Sábato; of Poe, Hoffmann, Chekhov, Faulkner; of the philosophies of Nietzsche, Schopenhauer, Kierkegaard, Sartre; of the psychology of Freud and Jung. Finally, there is the overwhelming influence of the mass media, principally films and newspapers, and Benedetto has dedicated himself to journalism "in an essential and absorbing manner," in his jobs as editorial secretary of the Mendoza daily *Los Andes* and as a stringer for *La nación* in Buenos Aires.

The "zone of contact" [the tentative title of *The Silencer*] and all of its problems take on vital importance in the works of this writer. Conflicts result from a distorted relationship between the ego and the world around it. His protagonists are apparently ordinary beings, the anonymous "men on the street," but endowed with a hypersensitivity and a lucid awareness of their own marginality, which make them live in permanent conflict with their environment. The collective "other" invades them, assaults them, and diminishes them through thousands of subtle traps. . . . The protagonists internally resist these attacks, but they fail on the level of action. They are unable to impose themselves, to win friends, and they are perpetually solitary . . . without communication in the midst of a social monster that is out to trap them. . . .

Rosa Boldori. In Rogelio Barufaldi et al., *Moyano, Di Benedetto, Cortázar* (Rosario, Argentina, Ediciones Colmegna, 1968), pp. 38–40†

The literary work of Antonio di Benedetto occupies its own special place within contemporary Argentine fiction. He often adopts the economical form of the parable and consistently uses symbolism. The author himself has explained his purposes: "I seek . . . to make [the reader] enter into the mysteries of existence, which, if I cannot explain to him, I can suggest to his imagination."

Both his novels and his short stories tend to illustrate this proposition. . . . Without metaphysics or religion . . . Benedetto's characters find themselves "cast forth" into the world with a lacerating awareness of their finiteness. And the world in which these creatures move is always hostile. . . . Hemmed in by the horizon of death, an unavoidable constant of all of Benedetto's works that is well developed in the stories of *Animal World* and *The Suicides*, these men (there is no memorable figure of a woman in the works of this Mendozan writer) reveal their existence through anguish. And the cry, "I want to live," which at times they give vent to, is paradoxically a rejection, since living does not mean existing.

These men's lives do not project, do not flow toward the future. Thus, they seem cut off from the only dimension that is essentially human. Not even Zama [in the novel *Zama*], who is "waiting" for whatever is to come, projects. . . . The heroes of Benedetto's stories and novels, with the exception of Zama, are nameless, and this fact contributes to the sense of Benedetto's characters as immersed in a fog without faces—representatives therefore of general forms of existence. They are generic psychologies that deteriorate when placed in a natural time. At best, they develop mechanisms of defense, and they end up in crime or ambiguity. Absolutely isolated, there is no *you* that can complete them, nor do they constitute a solidary *we*.

Julieta Gómez Paz. Nueva crítica. 1, 1970, pp. 87–88†

Critics recognized in *Zama* a strong creative force, a carefully worked out style, imagination, details of humor, and a control over a language meant to reflect the degree of lucidity of the protagonist. Some critics have said that incarnate in *Zama* is the anguish of contemporary man, his blind and desolate searching, while others have made much of Benedetto's capacity to create characters and to explore their psychology and conduct. Juan Carlos Ghiano, discussing *Clear Stories*, grouped Benedetto with those writers of merit who have demonstrated that "wisdom in psychology is not opposed to flights of invention or to the renovation of expression" and also pointed out something that must be underlined when considering this writer: "In accord with his essential fidelity to his themes, he has a sustained interest in technique, and he thus seeks the only possible expression for each story." . . .

Jorgelina Loubet. Nueva crítica. 1, 1970, pp. 98–99†

Zama is a many-layered work. The book appears to be an historical and biographical novel, but the reader finds himself more and more drawn into a discussion of the timeless aloneness of man, a theme that, in the hands of Sábato and Cortázar, had become central to Argentine existentialism. The book also becomes a rendering of accounts—with Sartrian clarity—a presentation of the existentialist criteria by which, according to Benedetto, "many of us are measured at the end of a life full of love, adventure, trouble, deceit, and contradiction." *Zama* is dedicated to the "victims of waiting." It tells the simple story of a minor official who waits and hopes but in the end is overcome by resignation, desperation, and misery. . . .

Benedetto has a comprehensive vision and philosophy, and he

develops his varied themes with stylistic perfection. Although he is not dogmatic, the form of his novel is impressive in its logical progression. . . . Benedetto has received twelve literary prizes in Latin America alone. His works—a special blend of diary and chronicle, of confession and documentary—have won him a place immediately after Cortázar and Sábato in the esteem of Argentine literary circles. His success is the more surprising because Benedetto does not reside in Buenos Aires but works in the isolation of his native Mendoza. . . .

> Günter W. Lorenz. *Die zeitgenössische Literatur in*
> *Lateinamerika* (Tübingen, Horst Erdmann Verlag,
> 1971), pp. 156–57†

BILAC, OLAVO BRAZ MARTINS DOS GUIMARÃES (1865–1918)

BRAZIL

"His inspiration," wrote [the critic José] Veríssimo, considering the verse of Bilac, "is limited to a few poetic themes, all treated with a virtuosity perhaps unparalleled amongst us . . . but without an intensity of feeling corresponding to the brilliancy of the form, which always is more important in him. This is the characteristic defect of the Parnassian esthetics, of which Sr. Bilac is our most illustrious follower, and to which his poetic genius adjusted itself perfectly and intimately." I believe that Veríssimo was slightly misled by Bilac's versified professions. There is no doubt that Bilac's temperament . . . was eminently suited to some such orientation as was sought by those Parnassians who understood what they were about; there is as little doubt, in my mind, that his feeling was intense, though not deep. He may have spoken of the crystalline strophe and the etcher's needle—which, indeed, he often employed with the utmost skill—but there were moments when nothing but huge marbles and the sculptor's chisel would do. It was with such material that he carved "The Dawn of Love." "If Sr. Machado de Assis was," continues Veríssimo, "more than twenty-years previous to Bilac, our first artist-poet—if other contemporaries of immediate predecessors of Bilac also practised the Parnassian esthetics, none did it with such manifest purpose, and, above all with such triumphant skill. . . ."

I am not sure whether Veríssimo is right in having asked of Bilac a more contemporary concern with the currents of poetry. The critic grants that Bilac is perhaps the most brilliant poet ever produced by his nation, "but other virtues are lacking in him without which there can be no truly great poet. I do not know but that I am right in supposing that, conscious of his excellence, he remained a stranger to the social, philosophical and esthetic movement that is today everywhere renewing the sources of poetry. And it is a great pity; for he was amongst us perhaps one of the most capable of bringing to our anaemic poetry the new blood which, with more presumption than talent, some poets—or persons who think themselves such—are trying to inject, without any of the gifts that abound in him."

Bilac . . . did, toward the end of his life, become a more social spirit. But this was not necessary to his preeminence as a poet. He was, superbly, himself. Rather that he should have given us so freely of the voluptuary that was in him—voluptuary of feeling, of charm, of form, of language, of taste—than that, in a mistaken attempt to be a "complete" man, he should sprawl over the varied currents of the day and hour. For it is far more certain that each current will find its masterly spokesman in art, than that each artist will become a masterly spokesman for all of the currents.

Isaac Goldberg. Brazilian Literature (New York,
Alfred A. Knopf, 1922), pp. 208–9

Olavo Bilac understood the true meaning of Parnassianism. At first, however, attracted by the suggestiveness of the new literary canons, he reacted with unbridled excitement. As long as the fascination of the new school lasted . . . the fascination of a new approach that was so eloquent and aristocratic, Bilac allowed himself to be overwhelmed by unfamiliar lessons. And his temperament, his strong inclinations toward tranquillity, elegance, and aristocracy, found instant harmony with the spirit of the new school. . . .

For mediocre minds, the new school was an easy way to shine through form, since these writers could not shine through their ideas. But Bilac had a marvelous poetic genius to begin with, to which Parnassianism offered an impeccable form. The fecund energy of his dreaming soul—surrounded by the splendor of the stars in *Poems* and by the shadow of death in *Afternoon*—found an admirable mold for shaping itself.

But despite all his initial enthusiasm, Bilac did not finally embrace Parnassianism as a servile and self-effacing disciple. Once his period of enthusiasm was past, he began to react little by little against the exaggerations and the extravagances. Soon he would create poems that displayed a moderate, purified Parnassianism.

Affonso de Carvalho. A poética de Olavo Bilac
(Rio de Janeiro, Editôra Civilização Brasileira, 1934),
p. 39†

[Bilac] was a sort of Loïe Fuller of poetry, and he wrote poetry as she performed her celebrated luminous dances. There were some who said horrible things about him. One could find the iconoclasts of the younger generation proclaiming: "All the poems in *Burning Brambles* display a manifest case of verbal satyriasis. The writer does not go beyond being an erotic in the style of Catullus and the other rotten fruits of Roman society. Reading his work, one has the impression of a satyr who versified his bestial carnality. . . ." This judgment, my friends, comes from envy alone.

It is curious that when one hears the name of Bilac, one thinks of a man given over to fatal loves. But his loves sprang from literary sources; they were all in his head, purely cerebral. He never knew an ardent passion. Everything in his lyrical poetry was apparently simulated. And since these poems are always admirable, Bilac, without meaning to, gave ammunition to those critics who wanted to affirm that art is artifice and that the best muses an artist can have are unreal women, because of their vagueness, their indeterminateness.

This poet was truly an enchanting man! He had what it took to attract people, to command popularity. He was ugly, but he had an ugliness one could call fascinating, which impressed both men and women. His eyes squinted and his jaw protruded, but he offset his appearance through his intelligence, elegance, and grace. He was an enchanting reciter of poems, especially since a slight Lisbon accent (a petulant affectation) made his speech more picturesque. He conversed with ease, giving literary lectures on trifling subjects enriched by his imagination. He wrote newspaper articles, delightful ones, made out of nothing, like Mimi Pinson's clothes.

Agrippino Grieco. *Evolução da poesia brasileira*,
2nd ed. (Rio de Janeiro, Livraria H. Atunes, 1944),
pp. 64–65†

Bilac's creative life can be divided into three distinct phases. . . . In the first phase . . . he had the verve youths display when they sing of the love that seizes them in full adolescence. . . . If his thought seems puerile, the form already has the stamp of one predestined to be a poet. . . . He had a fine ear, "capable of hearing and understanding the stars." . . .

[His second phase began when,] steeped in the close reading of Leconte de Lisle, Hérédia, Baudelaire, Théophile Gautier, and so many other Parnassians of note, he came to understand the beauty of excellent work, the way of using the tireless chisel to give his style purity. . . . [In the last phase of his life] he crammed in as much as he could of philosophy and patriotism. In these waning years he contemplated human frailty and became almost mystical.

Henrique Orciuoli. Bilac: Vida e obra (São Paulo, Editôra Guaíra, 1944), pp. 103, 105, 109†

Olavo Bilac obsessively used (and sometimes abused) the image of stars, as is well known. By way of evidence, Elói Pontes, in his book on Bilac, reproduced about fifty excerpts from the volume *Poems* in which the unyielding image appears, sometimes in the very same terms. . . .

The metaphor of the star goes back, in Portugal, to the oldest songs. But it was Antero de Quental who gave this image what one could call verbal grace, an intense lyricism that was to influence Bilac. . . . A possible specific influence of Quental was the treatment of stars as sisters to enthrall the thought of the poet. The concept of virginal purity is implicit in this metaphor, fundamentally linked to the idea of metempsychosis, by which the pure maidens, when they die, are transformed into stars. . . .

There is no doubt that the ideas in "To Hear Stars" and, by extension, in "Dead Virgins" were implied in Antero de Quental's sonnets. But Bilac freely mixed together various influences. Thus, it is not improbable that the Brazilian poet, before he wrote the sonnet "Dead Virgins," had read Arsène Houssaye's sonnet "Ce qui disent les étoiles," published in his book *Poésies* in 1887.

Eugenio Gomes. Visões e revisões (Rio de Janeiro, Ministério da Educação e Cultura, 1958), pp. 142–44†

When Bilac was an adolescent, a climate of euphoria and heroic pride had succeeded the anguish of a half-decade of war. "This spectacle of heroism, dominating national life for many years and nourishing the sense of pride of the people, made my entire adolescence marvellous and thrilling." A similar military atmosphere, a bellicose enthusiasm and exaltation, came to dominate the premature sunset of his life, when he was barely fifty years old. . . . He was certainly stimulated by the enthusiasm awakened in Brazil and the rest of the world by the cause of the Allies. . . . France, along with Portugal, was one of the poet's great passions.

Thus did Bilac live and die, a South American Pindar who joined lyricism and patriotism into a celebratory war poetry, the kind of poetry World War II and the atomic age all but eliminated. Moreover, if we compare the military exaltation of Bilac between 1915 and 1917 with the fervent pacifism of a book like *Jaboti Clan*, published barely ten

years later by Mário de Andrade, we can see the abyss that the modernist revolution was to create between the two generations.

Alceu Amoroso Lima. Introduction to Olavo Bilac,
Poesia, 2nd ed. (Rio de Janeiro, Livraria Agir
Editôra, 1959), p. 7†

This book was born of my old admiration for Olavo Bilac. Not that I
consider him our greatest poet. But he was, without a doubt, an authentic poet in the most complete sense of the word. What fascinates me in
Bilac is his coherence, his sense of artistic destiny. He was a man who
detested vulgarity, who never betrayed the ideal. Now that the centenary of his birth is approaching, this book is offered to my countrymen
with the goal of paying homage to this noble artist.

It is still necessary to point out that Bilac was more than a virtuoso
in poetry and a writer of terse, elegant prose. Bilac loved Brazil as few
have. He tried to revitalize the energies of our people. A bachelor, he
married the country. And the country was always with him, in his
thoughts and activities. He profoundly wanted Brazil to be strong in
order to be good, armed in order to be just, and rich in order to be
generous.

In these absurd times, when the ignorant are venerated and citizens of talent and character are relegated to oblivion, when the great
men of our country are its soccer players, when the young show themselves to be stupid and lacking in fiber; in this Babylonian epoch, which
flaunts sex and transforms politics into a financial transaction; in these
times that are so dissolute and shameful; in these times of dastardliness,
anticulture, and opportunism—in these times it is especially comforting
to contemplate the figure of Olavo Bilac, who spent the last years of his
life attempting to awaken the sacrosanct flame of public spirit in the
breasts of Brazilians.

Fernando Jorge. *Vida e poesia de Olavo Bilac*
(São Paulo?, Livraria Exposição do Livro, 1963?),
pp. 16–17†

The sonnet "Dead Virgins" [was] composed when the aura surrounding the publication of [Hérédia's] *Les trophées* was still glowing. In
this sonnet Bilac took from [a similar Hérédia sonnet] an attachment
to life, changing the reference to living things to an explicit description
of physical love between human beings ("lovers, you who walk with
your mouths overflowing with kisses"). Both poets are similar in local-
izing the soul of the dead woman in a kind of pagan Hades. . . .

The originality of the Brazilian poet . . . was his change in the
response. In Hérédia, the young dead woman hangs on desperately

to the things of life; in Bilac, life is an insult to one who died unfulfilled. Love "offends" the dead virgins, is truly an affront to this eternal, involuntary purity (as it is to the stars).

Thus, the Brazilian poet, although he worked within a very rich tradition, was able to maintain his originality. At the same time, he showed his fidelity to the Parnassian movement by adopting a theme that the French master put back into vogue, which supplanted the gothic treatment of "dead virgins" during the romantic period. . . . Hérédia became the greatest influence both on Bilac's later work (especially in the sonnets of *Voyages* and in *The Seeker of Emeralds*) and on his awareness of his function as a poet within society.

Heitor Martins. *Ocidente.* 78, 1970, p. 154†

BIOY CASARES, ADOLFO (1914–   )

ARGENTINA

Around 1880 Stevenson observed that the adventure story was regarded as an object of scorn by the British reading public, who believed that the ability to write a novel without a plot, or with an infinitesimal, atrophied plot, was a mark of skill. In *The Dehumanization of Art* (1925) José Ortega y Gasset, seeking the reason for that scorn, said, "I doubt very much whether an adventure that will interest our superior sensibility can be invented today," and added that such an invention was "practically impossible." On other pages, on almost all the other pages, he upheld the cause of the "psychological" novel and asserted that the pleasure to be derived from adventure stories was nonexistent or puerile. That was undoubtedly the prevailing opinion of 1880, 1925, and even 1940. Some writers (among whom I am happy to include Adolfo Bioy Casares) believe they have a right to disagree. The following, briefly, are the reasons why.

The first of these . . . has to do with the intrinsic form of the adventure story. The typical psychological novel is formless. The Russians and their disciples have demonstrated, tediously, that no one is impossible. A person may kill himself because he is so happy, for example, or commit murder as an act of benevolence. Lovers may separate forever as a consequence of their love. And one man can inform on another out of fervor or humility. In the end such complete freedom is tantamount to chaos. But the psychological novel would also be a "realistic" novel, and have us forget that it is a verbal artifice, for it uses each vain precision (or each languid obscurity) as a new proof of verisimilitude. . . . The adventure story, on the other hand, does not propose to be a transcription of reality: it is an artificial object, no part of which lacks justification. It must have a rigid plot if it is not to succumb to the mere sequential variety of *The Golden Ass*, the *Seven Voyages of Sinbad*, or the *Quixote*.

I have given one reason of an intellectual sort; there are others of an empirical nature. We hear sad murmurs that our century lacks the ability to devise interesting plots. But no one attempts to prove that if this century has any ascendancy over the preceding ones it lies in the quality of its plots. Stevenson is more passionate, more diverse, more lucid, perhaps more deserving of our unqualified friendship than is Chesterton; but his plots are inferior. De Quincey plunged deep into labyrinths on his nights of meticulously detailed horror, but he did not coin his impression of "unutterable and self-repeating infinities" in fables comparable to Kafka's. Ortega y Gasset was right when he said that Balzac's "psychology" did not satisfy us; the same thing could be said of his plots. Shakespeare and Cervantes were both delighted by the antinomian idea of a girl who, without losing her beauty, could be taken for a man; but we find that idea unconvincing now. I believe I am free from every superstition of modernity, or any illusion that yesterday differs intimately from today or will differ from tomorrow; but I maintain that during no other era have there been novels with such admirable plots as *The Turn of the Screw, Der Prozess, Le voyageur sur la terre*, and the one you are about to read [*The Invention of Morel*] which was written in Buenos Aires by Adolfo Bioy Casares. [1940]

Jorge Luis Borges. Prologue to Adolfo Bioy Casares,
The Invention of Morel, and Other Stories
(Austin, University of Texas Press, 1964), pp. 5–6

The sorrowful characters who fill Bioy Casares's new book [*The Celestial Plot*], like all the characters subjected to an imaginary goal, do not appear motivated by natural causality but are moved by the severe, fantastic logic that each theme demands. But there is no doubt that the literary genre so honorably cultivated by Bioy Casares demands a rigid chaining of motives, a dialectical transparency, which the novelist who reflects only what is immediate and verifiable can leave aside. The writer who reproduces the world knows that many things can operate in the spirits of his characters, a great number of causes that are equivalent to gratuity and chance. This advantage, which permits him to dispense with the necessity to persuade, does not apply to the writer of fantastic fiction, in whose defined limits it is necessary to justify everything. . . .

Bioy Casares has been successful in tempering or correcting his fiction with the gradual introduction of circumstances and details of a "realistic" nature, which bring verisimilitude to his creations. And they gain in vigor and the power to influence in this way. This fortunate shift gives life to his complex plots, placing them with exactness in time and space. In this way . . . the bare plot does not suffer from simplicity or disintegrate into an unconvincing abstraction. . . . If a work is too simple or too schematized, it gives rise to humorous effects and therefore does not harmonize with the ambitions and goals of this literary genre.

Carlos Mastronardi. *Sur.* No. 179, Sept., 1949,

pp. 72–73†

The Invention of Morel is not one of those novels of the fantastic that one can read only once. On the contrary, one can reread it leisurely and enjoy the pleasure of perceiving its remarkable construction. This, by the same token, is no reason for the critic to deny the reader the pleasure of first reading this marvelous story innocently. Still, it is important to point out that this novel has as a preface a grand eulogy by Jorge Luis Borges, the author of the admirable *Fictions*. In short, *The Invention of Morel* is a remarkable adventure story, brief, dense, and to the point.

Michel Carrouges. *Prévues.* No. 23, Jan., 1953, p. 96†

Certain passages [of the stories in *A Prodigious Story*] are upsetting because of their probing of the dark strata of our minds. The first story, which gives the book its title, introduces us to the fundamental tone of uneasiness. The unusual is contained in motifs that are lucidly real in Argentine thought, thus demonstrating, through humor or satire, certain lapses of reason in our society, against which are projected the strange events and the unyielding perspectives of each story. The stories within the story appear coordinated by the ruthless possibilities of each subject dealt with, without pity for either character or reader.

The Dream of the Heroes, an intense novel published two years ago, which is perhaps his definitive work, confirms the extent to which Bioy Casares probes the innermost core of the people of Buenos Aires. He presents a tale of primitive courage and dreamed-of adventures that turns out to be the projection of the permanent anxieties of our youth. . . . Bioy Casares does without the easy tricks that certain writers repeat. . . . He avoids the easy invitation to terror and the equivocal security of the habitual.

Juan Carlos Ghiano. *Ficción.* No. 11, Jan.–Feb.,

1958, p. 164†

The work of Adolfo Bioy Casares, represented here in the novella, *The Invention of Morel* (which won the 1941 Primer Premio Municipal Award in Buenos Aires) and by six short stories originally collected in a volume entitled *The Celestial Plot*, [shows] an interesting mind at work, a mind involved with science, philosophy and psychology. His stories are adventures, albeit slow moving, in which time and space are mere mists through which he easily passes. The stories often verge on science-fiction, occasionally are tinged with the occult.

In the novella, the narrator-diarist tells of his experience on an island populated by a group—and especially one woman with whom he falls in love—who do not seem aware of him as he moves among them. They are fully-dimensioned projections of the cameras of the inventor Morel, who recorded a week's visit by the group to the island, years before the narrator's arrival. Morel's indestructible machines repeat that week over and over for all time. Eventually the narrator attempts to join his love in the projected reality.

In one of the short stories, "The Celestial Plot," Bioy Casares offers the existence of "infinite identical worlds, infinite worlds with slight variations, infinite different worlds" as a pilot takes off from one Buenos Aires and arrives at another. In "The Other Labyrinth" a man of the 20th century dies in the 17th century and "proves that successive time is a mere illusion of men and that we live in an eternity where everything is simultaneous."

It is plot, which reveals itself like a trip through a maze, which dominates this author's work. Though the stories are fully populated, the characters are secondary. Bioy Casares is not much concerned with the who, what and why of his people; they exist for him as needed guides to lead the reader through cerebral adventures.

That ultimately one leaves Bioy Casares without a feeling of enrichment is not his fault—but rather that of his publisher, who has done him the disservice of combining these six short stories and the novella into one volume. It is too much of a good thing. If the reader is at first fascinated by the way he "unpeels" a story, that same reader will be bored long before the book is finished.

Haskel Frankel. *NYT*. Nov. 15, 1964, p. 62

The Invention of Morel, and Other Stories by Adolfo Bioy Casares comes to us nearly a quarter of a century late (it won a Buenos Aires award in 1941), and in the wake of Jorge Luis Borges, compatriot and collaborator, who supplies its generous, yet characteristically discreet Introduction. Unlike Borges, whom he superficially resembles, Bioy Casares does not seem to have a sense of evil, so that his stories yield one a sense of ingenuity, rather than lucidity. There is, in each story, a progression of someone's mind toward the understanding of a situation. But some of the "plants" work out a little too cleverly, and most of the characters are a little too ordinary, to convince us that more is at stake than the functioning of a very clever machine.

It is handy to have Señor Bioy Casares's volume on the shelves because its limitations make clear the peculiar dry poetry of Borges—a poetry without which his fables would cut as shallow a furrow as do some of these. That is, perhaps, unfair, as close comparisons tend to be. By ordinary standards, Bioy Casares is ingenious in contriving an intellectual action; his prose as translated is strict, sinewy, and allusive and he will certainly exercise and entertain the reader who is willing to play his special game.

Robert M. Adams. NYR. Dec. 3, 1964, pp. 27–28

Undoubtedly the first Latin American novel to treat significantly the new social theme of aging, Bioy Casares' [*Diary of the War of the Pig*] is a superb example of the expressive potential of modern fiction. With the diary-like boundaries of one week, plus an epilogue, the novel explores, through the expressionistic hyperbole of a science-fiction war of extermination of the elderly (hence, the title), man's ultimate humble and humbling confrontation with himself. One's first impression is that the backdrop of mysterious incidents, set in a consciously insistent evocation of a suburb of northern Buenos Aires, concerns political disturbances, such as that during the closing days of the Perón regime. However, when events come into focus as they affect a closely-knit café group of elderly men, the reader realizes that Bioy Casares has interwoven a "real" setting and a fanciful circumstance in order to depict with touching irony one individual's total awareness of his fleeting and tenuous existence. This existence threatens to crumble under the weight of his dazed consciousness, if not from the cruel blows of the murderous gangs of youths.

Why the youth of the city should rebel during one week is never made clear. Several possibilities are implied in turn: a higher political need, overpopulation, a eugenic solution to the agony of aging, and a resentment for a world inherited from the elderly. Like most expressionistic narrative formulas, the circumstance, ostensibly meant to provide the basis of an explanation, results in further uncertainty for the reader. Here this uncertainty as to what, exactly, is happening and why—an uncertainty whose elaboration is the whole point of the novel—is metonymic of the central character's quite honest confusion in the face of the imponderable and intolerable demands of existence, not to mention old age itself.

David William Foster. BA. 45, Winter, 1971, p. 78

From ciphering to deciphering, Bioy Casares is a close friend and collaborator of Borges, and Borges's influence is very clear in his work (if we knew more about him, we might also say that his influence is very clear in Borges's work). He is in one sense more inventive than Borges, better able to create a plot and sustain a narrative. But he appears to lack Borges's eeriest and most important gift: the ability to suggest the uncanny lurking in the quietest, most unlikely corner of a house or a phrase. *Diary of the War of the Pig* has the logic of dream, or seems to invite such a logic, but it doesn't have the intensity of a dream, although it seems to be seeking it.

The young, we discover, have grown impatient with the old, and are killing them and beating them up and putting them away. A young man shoots an old man, and explains to the court that he was so irritated by the sight of a bald head, and by the old man's slow reflexes, that he just couldn't resist the temptation to kill him. The jury understands and he is acquitted.

What is interesting about the book is less its premise and the competent but uninspired execution of its consequences, than the psychology of the old men, who are busy either trivializing the whole thing, arguing about whether the war of the pig ought not to be called the war of the hog, or caving in wholesale to the arguments of the young, secretly agreeing to despise themselves, to feel ashamed at the course of nature. Bioy Casares is plainly thinking here of that damaging impulse so common in persecuted groups, and memorably dramatized in Kafka: the impulse to believe that your persecutors are in some sense right about you.

Michael Wood. *NYR.* April 9, 1973, p. 37

BORGES, JORGE LUIS (1899–   )

ARGENTINA

Jorge Luis Borges, in [*Fervor of Buenos Aires*], his first book, is correct in using the word "fervor"; perhaps nothing more was necessary. Buenos Aires in his book is changed completely into a spiritual flame: it is his alone. The panorama he has us see in his blank verse is not a panorama to which one could easily put a geographic name. Buenos Aires? Fine. It must be at the bottom of the poetic fervor we sense beating in each page of this book, which is less descriptive than any book that has ever been inspired by a city in the world. The title's evocation of the great Argentine city has only the value of a dedication. . . . Jorge Luis Borges's poems were intended to differ from those of all his other fellow writers through their rhythmic sureness, their verbal richness, their disdain for the new commonplaces. . . . *Fervor of Buenos Aires*, in its spiritual and rhythmic uniformity, accentuates these qualities. A constant invention of poetic expressions, of images, a new joining together of adjectives and nouns surprises us in each composition.

Enrique Diez Canedo. Nosotros. No. 178, March,
1924, p. 433†

Borges knows that all the facts and movements of human existence converge in eternity. His striving to reach eternal time and to anchor his thoughts in a kind of infinite extension of mankind's stay on earth can be traced throughout his poetry, a poetry that somehow keeps the freshness of a child's look at the present and the future.

Yet Borges came to realize that his mythology of Buenos Aires was nearing completion, that its spatial form was simple, and that he could grasp it by standing in his patio filled with the sky that was looking down, sensing that this spatial essence was being stretched to its outer limits and yet contained within the quiet suburban street up to the corner with its *almacén rosado*, the country store and inn, painted in the color of the sun that was just setting on the pampas. Borges indeed felt satisfied with his poetic creations, and with good reason. His three volumes of poetry—*Fervor of Buenos Aires, San Martín Notebook,* and *The Moon Across the Way*—established a perfect triangle in which all angles contain the proper measure. All that needed to be said was expressed, no more and no less than warranted by the subject. Borges did well to resist the temptation to plagiarize himself thereafter.

Eduardo González Lanuza. Sur. No. 98, Nov., 1942,
p. 59†

The new works of a writer are in many ways like cities that have been constructed on the ruins of previous ones: although in one sense they are new, they also provide a certain "immortality," assured by ancient legends and men of the same race with the same passions, eyes, and faces.

In turning now to *Fictions*, one might do well to do a little archeological research so as to find out how old myths keep on circulating in the veins of recent peoples. In doing excavation in the works of Borges, a number of unrelated fossils come to light: manuscripts of old heretics, tarot cards, Francisco de Quevedo and Robert Louis Stevenson, tango lyrics, mathematical equations, Lewis Carroll, Franz Kafka, labyrinths in Crete and old suburbs in Buenos Aires, John Stuart Mill, De Quincey, and the toughs who roamed the Río de la Plata shores around 1900. The mixture is quite constant and shows the same metaphysical preoccupations, although under a variety of colors and shapes: a card game could turn out to be immortality, a library can symbolize the eternal return, and a tough from Fray Bentos justifies the existence of Hume. Borges loves to confuse the reader: one thinks he is reading a detective story and suddenly meets God himself. The narrative techniques in this volume seem to have reached a state of perfection of the writer's potentialities. Thus, Borges's influence on Borges appears to be insuperable from now on. Will he be condemned, from here on, to copy himself?

Ernesto Sábato. *Sur.* No. 125, March, 1945, p. 69†

Other Inquisitions . . . leaves the reader with a strange sensation, which is hardly to be traced to the "fable-telling" aspect of Borges's writing. This sensation could be described as an illusion of power granted by the author. Yet it is far from easy to clarify this statement further. Borges not only takes the reader by the hand and submerges him in his peculiar world; he also wants the reader to discover the structure of this world for himself.

The first essay deals with the historical figure of Emperor Shih Huang Ti, who ordered the construction of the almost infinite Chinese Wall and at the same time decreed the burning of all books written before his time. Looking into the reasons that could have prompted each of these acts, Borges little by little eliminates all possible explanations and is finally left with a single statement to the effect that these acts or concepts of action are best to be considered *per se*, and that they, like all forms, are true and perfect within themselves beyond the reach of conjectural possibilities. From such an assumption Borges draws a consequent conclusion: "Music, happiness, a face ravaged by the passing of time, certain twilights or determined places are trying to tell us something or perhaps have told us something which we should not lose and in which lies the art of living."

Enrique Pezzoni. *Sur.* Nos. 217–18, Nov.–Dec., 1952, p. 123†

Borges is secluded within his own generation, although his contemporaries attribute to him the status of first among equals. Paradoxically, as far as I am concerned, he has yet to be born. . . . Borges is capable of performing the leap from one zone to another, of being born for us or of changing himself into a dead phantom. In the latter case, one should avoid phantomicide. The group around the review *Martín*

Fierro was, to a great extent, happy molesters of phantoms. I have already outlined the reasons why we reject this role [because of our more serious, existential stance]. To be anti-Peter, Ortega y Gasset once said, is to postulate a world in which Peter does not exist, to run the picture backward until Peter irremediably reappears. To declare oneself anti-Borges (besides the hasty and unjust anticipation of the phantom) is to postulate an Argentine literature without Borges, to run the picture backward until, after a certain amount of time, his figure appears again. In the case of a supposed Borges frozen by chance in his last known gesture, our obligation is to move the praiseworthy content of his work closer to the living organism of literature. . . . Borges's case can offer us at least these axioms: (1) ingenuity, erudition, and an excellent style do not guarantee great literature; (2) without knowing beforehand the itinerary one should not undertake the trip.

> Adolfo Prieto. *Borges y la nueva generación*
> (Buenos Aires, Letras Universitarias, 1954), pp. 85–86†

[Borges's] entire phantasmal world is expressed in highly original stories and essays which Borges decorates with those themes and situations which universal philosophy, theology, and literature make available. And all three should be placed on the same level because all interest him for the imaginative possibilities they offer and their capacity for stirring the deepest feelings. His work does not contain the coherent evolution of metaphysical thought nor a doctrine which he adopts as the single and real key to the universe because Borges is convinced that nothing in Man's destiny has any meaning. This incredulity incites him, nonetheless, to create a literature out of literature and philosophy in which the metaphysical discussion or the artistic problem constitutes the plot of the story. His literary creativity vitalizes what, a priori, would otherwise seem abstract, and he is capable of infusing drama and the throbbings of adventure into thoughts which in themselves lack narrative substance. . . . [1957]

> Ana María Barrenechea. *Borges the Labyrinth Maker*
> (New York, New York University Press, 1965), p. 144

Jorge Luis Borges is the outstanding writer of Spanish America today. He is best known abroad as the author of fantastic and ingenious short stories that are in their own enigmatic way the translucent expression of the spiritual crisis of the twentieth century. Of the several volumes of his short stories, the most varied and perhaps the most significant is *The Aleph*. The stories of *The Aleph* comprise a very small book; but, as the title implies, the little book is like a rare glass, strangely cut and painfully polished down by its author, to serve like the glass of a timeless telescope for probing the immense extent of the human past, and then, and at the same time, as a cosmic glass to be used for microscopic insight into the human present. A little book with an outrageous ambition for its size. But its contents are extremely interesting; they are the latest and best example of Borges' gifts as a storyteller. . . .

As a representation of the inner life of man, the labyrinth has always symbolized man's insecurity in the world and his attempts to propitiate, control, or possess the powers that seemingly decide his destiny. . . . In the stories of Borges the labyrinth, with all its multiple associations, symbolizes the consciousness of man in our time: his fears, which for all their dreadfulness do not seem to differ much from the ancient fears of primordial man; his frustrated will to power, that more than ever resembles the frustrated conjurations of magical formulas; his helplessness, his anxiety, his dread of death, and, above all, his despair. Not the least ironical point of this little book is that the resources of its highly sophisticated and esoteric art, the ingenuity and exotic erudition of its author, have as their purpose (in a manner curiously parallel to the "scientific" discoveries of anthropologists and psychiatrists) the revelation of the oldest, most primitive, and most constant despairs of man. From within the hollows of his labyrinths, Borges echoes that postscript of our age by which we manage to survive: not until now has man known himself to be such an odd creature that, in his deepest despair, despair may be a comfort to him.

L. A. Murillo. *MLQ*. 20, Sept., 1959, pp. 259, 266

A few years back the name of Jorge Luis Borges was associated almost exclusively with the *Ultraísta* [compare imagism] poets of Buenos Aires. Even very recently he still appeared regularly among the hard-bitten ranks of the vanguard poets in anthologies and handbooks of Hispanic American literature. It was not unusual to see his name along with those of the Chilean Huidobro, the Mexican Maples Arce, and the other champions of free verse and free imagery.

Today, however, Jorge Luis Borges has gained international repute as an inventive and fanciful storyteller. This reputation dates from 1944, when he published a collection of short stories and tales under the title of *Fictions*. Both critics and public at large agree in their enthusiasm for the new Borges and acclaim him as the most interesting contemporary Latin American prosist. Translations into English, French, German, and Italian are extending his fame beyond the frontiers of the Hispanic world. He is regarded as that most unusual phenomenon in letters: the vastly cultured and gifted writer who ventures along roads little traveled by those of his trade—metaphysics, mathematics, modern physics. Borges' short stories remind us on occasion of pages by Quevedo, Gracián, Unamuno, Dostoevski, Quiroga, Lugones, De Quincey, Browne, Poe, Anatole France, Kafka, Lord Dunsany, Chesterton, and even of The Arabian Nights, though this is not to say that they are imitations or even that they are inspired by these authors. Indeed, one of Borges' most notable characteristics is his strange originality, recognized today almost unanimously. . . .

Can there be, then, in the middle of the twentieth century, two themes so literary, so timely, so relevant for our life—even if we are locked in old ideological shells—as the exploration of the universe and its creator, or the search for the secret of the scarcely unveiled abysses of the human personality? Is there anything that matters to us as much as the mysterious rhythm of the development of that personality in that incomprehensible universe? These themes are eternal; they are the themes of philosophy, science, and religion. Why deny them to literature which has always had its own way of seeking man and God? . . .

Perhaps the literature of a man who makes use of the oldest and most effective of literary artifices to escape from his world, not in order to evade the anguish of the terrible present, but to confront it from new positions, may be the window on the literature of tomorrow. And perhaps this explains the absorbing interest with which we read Borges today. Though it is also possible that a literary output so contemporary may itself be only a fiction, a shadow, or a dream attracting us because it expresses our anxiety to have someone interpret authoritatively and artistically our misgivings, our tragedy, our grandeur, and our puniness.

Miguel Enguídanos. *TQ*. 4, 1961, pp. 118, 126–27

The narrations contained in *The Aleph* repeat a predominant theme: man's hallucinated search for the center of the labyrinth of his existence. We have also seen a suggestion that at the center lies something closely akin to the mystics' communion with the infinite, an experience which reveals the fundamental truths of existence, and which awakens a feeling of resignation and a willingness to accept death, possibly because the alternative, once perceived, is too horrible to accept. . . .

It can be seen that this concept of human life as being explained and justified by one moment pervades the various types of Borges' writing. What is this moment, really, but the center of the labyrinth? If human existence is justified and explained by one moment, this moment is the center of the labyrinth, the moment which virtually all Borges' characters seek. Examined in this light, the stories of *The Aleph* take on new meaning. Cartaphilus, perhaps more than any other, has come to understand the meaning of human existence and of his own life; he desperately seeks the mortality which will permit him to die. . . .

The vision underlying Borges' works is that of a chaotic universe, formless and without natural laws, within which man wanders in search of his destiny. In this search, man imposes intellectual constructions designed to aid him in the search by ordering reality. But upon penetrating to the center of his own creation, man realizes the falsity of this construction, penetrates the meaning of existence, and is left with no recourse but to die, resigned to the implacable fact of the universe: its total pointlessness.

Frank Dauster. HR. 30, April, 1962, pp. 144, 146, 148

The symbolism inherent in the labyrinth represents first of all an irrational universe whose multiplicity, or unknown factors, exemplifies a lack of order or apparent purpose. In the absence of a theological interpretation, these labyrinthic forces preclude any rational or positivistic analysis that might diminish man's bewilderment or frustration as he searches for some sense, order or purpose in the world around him. . . .

Borges, perhaps luckily, is not obsessed, or even concerned, with theological considerations when he probes into the world of phenomena. His labyrinth does not lead him to God, and the existence of a chaotic world does not constitute a proof to him that an incomprehensible divine power is lurking behind it. Borges' quest is one of knowledge and his speculations are largely concerned with epistemological problems. . . .

The labyrinth-stories serve the purpose of recreating a universe in miniature so that he, and the reader, can conveniently inspect it. The chaos and multiplicity of life lie within the dark corridors of the labyrinth; and it is here that Borges can show us his protagonists as they turn obscured corners. Herein lies the dramatic element of the stories, the only climax of Borges' chess game for the detached onlooker or reader who ironically watches the protagonists as they turn at each corner in a direction unknown to them. The absurdity of their decision resides in the fact that they, unlike the reader, do not see the labyrinth and its endless ramifications that escape any intellectual comprehension. Borges has given his characters tragic proportions by showing that they act under the illusion of possessing the necessary knowledge to lift their decision out of the category of futility. . . .

It is quite possible that Borges' rejection of epistemological and moral systems, whose foundations seem pragmatic and capricious to him, implicitly shows the idealist's yearning for a Lost Paradise. But Borges is no Unamuno. He has examined moral systems and their dreaded children: guilt and punishment. But, unlike most of his existentialist cousins in the field of literature, he went on to examine appearance and reality outside of the fields of ethics and culture. His deep concern for epistemology seems to have spared him the anguish that besets so many moralists in their desperate search for absolute values. Borges is used to living with his lack of knowledge which reduces the universe to an incomprehensible creation and prevents him from judging man's actions. Such a position is an honest one, especially in the light of the endless attempts throughout history to use this lack of knowledge to impose or justify a given set of more interpretations. Borges' labyrinth of time and space is more than a refuge. It is his sole certainty.

H. Ernest Lewald. *Hispania.* 45, Dec., 1962,
pp. 630–32, 635–36

One of the foremost quests in *Other Inquisitions* is for symmetries; two that are rediscovered throughout the book under various guises appear in the first two essays. In "The Wall and the Books" Borges evokes the Chinese emperor who both created the Great Wall and wanted all books prior to him burned. This enormous mystification inexplicably "satisfies" and, at the same time, "disturbs" Borges. His purpose then is to seek the reasons for "that emotion." (Note that the stimulus for the supposedly cerebral Borges is not an idea, that the satisfaction and disturbance are *one* feeling.) Various conjectures lead him to suggest that the aesthetic phenomenon consists in the "imminence of a revelation that is not yet produced"; a kind of expanding virtuality of thought, an unresolved yet centrally focussed multiplicity of views, which the essay's form as discussion, as tacit dialogue, has already reflected. The other essays also display, centrally or laterally, paradoxes or oppositions with analogous overtones. At the end of "Avatars of the Tortoise" the paradoxes of Zeno and the antinomies of Kant indicate for Borges that the universe is ultimately a dream, a product of the mind, unreal because free of the apparent limits of time and space we call "real." But the paradoxical confession with which "New Refutation of Time" ends—"it [time] is a fire that consumes me, but I am the fire"—must conclude that "the world, alas, is real; I, alas, am Borges." Extremes of fantastic hope and skepticism paradoxically coexist in Borges' thought. . . .

Stylistic uses of [Borges' "principle of identity"] are the paradoxical or near-paradoxical word pairs ("that favors or tolerates another interpretation," "our reading of Kafka refines and changes our reading of the poem") and also the ellipses and transferred epithets based on substitution of part for whole, whose possibilities for animation of the abstract and impersonal explain why Borges terms a typical example "allegorical" at the beginning of "From Allegories to Novels." . . . In general, the enumeration of sharply diverse yet somehow harmonizing parts that allude to some larger, static whole unnamable by any unilateral means is a common procedure underlying many features of Borges' style and form: the sentences that abruptly rotate their angular facets like cut stones, the succinct little catalogs that may comprise paragraphs and even whole essays, the allusions and generalizations that find echoes of the line of argument elsewhere and project it onto other planes, the larger confrontations of a writer with his alter ego (in himself or in another) or of the essay with its own revision or complement—all those series and inlays, in short, which are so much the curt mosaic design of this collection.

> James E. Irby. Introduction to Jorge Luis Borges,
> *Other Inquisitions* (Austin, University of Texas Press,
> 1964), pp. x–xii

It would be a mistake to think of Borges' work as being preoccupied with an effort, so common to much contemporary literature, at exploring and defining the individual self and its capacities for coping with a given private and social setting. If Borges represents the complexities and paradoxes of self, he does so with a mixture of melancholy and intellectual assurance. "Borges and I" represents the classic formulation of his conviction that the self is multifarious, that its countless reflections and projections give it reality as well as iridescence. Borges' self confronts his mirror-image, and little by little the living Borges yields to the other I, "well aware of his perverse habit of falsifying and exaggerating." . . .

Rimbaud's "moi, c'est l'autre," the dissociation of the self and the countervoice, or Musil's figure, in his *Mann ohne Eigenschaften,* of a mind constantly specifying its own indeterminacy, are echoed and paraphrased throughout Borges' work. He is the creator of fictions that momentarily fill the universal void, a poet who is a "calculating hallucinator" and who, like God, gives shape to his reflections upon an immeasurable void. . . .

Dreamtigers [that is, *The Maker*] is perhaps Borges' most appealing as well as his most characteristic work: of all his books, he confesses in the "Epilogue," "none . . . is as personal as the straggling collection mustered for this hodge-podge, precisely because it abounds in reflections and interpolations." Its original Spanish title, *El hacedor,* suggests the essence of his creative principle: the making of a work of art, of a book which, like Mallarmé's *Le livre*, is a mirror of life, a parable of the greater creation. It is altogether an account, in brief but radiant crystallizations of the mind, of that descent into memory "which seemed to him endless, and up from that vertigo he succeeded in bringing forth a forgotten recollection that shone like a coin under the rain, perhaps because he had never looked at it, unless in a dream" ("The Maker")

Whether in prose or poetry, it is Borges' ultimate purpose to a-chieve not a mystical and irrational surrender to an inscrutable chaos, but, on the contrary, the clarity of perception that comes from reflection as well as the meticulous making of models. What Borges offers us are poems and narratives that articulate the nature of our human situation. . . . He is a superb artist, who draws on life and books, on the sight of tigers and the moon, on the experiences of poets and phi-losophers: "Few things have happened to me more worth remem-bering than Schopenhauer's thought or the music of England's words," he writes in the "Epilogue."

Victor Lange. Introduction to Jorge Luis Borges,
Dreamtigers (Austin, University of Texas Press, 1964),
pp. xxi–xxii

It is necessary to realize that the word "labyrinth" covers two different and opposing conceptions. In the first, the path is interminable and tor-tuous, but obligatory. Hesitation is impossible. At each instant there is only one passage way indicated although it winds unendingly and is likely to give the impression to whoever takes it that it goes nowhere but back upon itself. . . . In the other kind of labyrinth there are inter-secting paths instead. Each bit of corridor begins at a crossing and leads to another crossing, identical to the first. . . . One has no way of finding out if the crossroads at which he ends up is not one of the ones he has passed through already. It is impossible for him to know if he is making progress or not.

I doubt that the labyrinths to be found in Borges's stories are of [the first] kind. He multiplies the universe with structures conceived in order to torture the reader with the incessant need to make uncertain choices, each one leading to, or back to, another. Caught within these inextricable ramifications, the prisoner turns around and around and seems unable to escape except by a lucky accident. But what is more likely is that he will die of exhaustion. . . .

Roger Caillois. *Cahiers de L'Herne*. No. 4, 1964,
pp. 214–15†

Probably because Borges is such a brilliant writer, his mirror-world is also profoundly, though always ironically, sinister. The shades of terror vary from the criminal gusto of *A Universal History of Infamy* to the darker and shabbier world of the later *Fictions*, and in *The Maker* the violence is even starker and more somber, closer, I suppose, to the atmosphere of Borges's native Argentina. In the 1935 story ["The Masked Dyer, Hákim of Merv"], Hákim the impostor proclaimed: "The earth we live on is a mistake, a parody devoid of authority. Mirrors and paternity are abominable things, for they multiply this earth." This statement keeps recurring throughout the later work, but it becomes much more comprehensible there. Without ceasing to be the main metaphor for style, the mirror acquires deadly powers—a motif that runs throughout Western literature but of which Borges's version is particularly rich and complex. In his early work, the mirror of art represented the intention to keep the flow of time from losing itself forever in the shapeless void of infinity.

Like the speculations of philosophers, style is an attempt at immortality. But this attempt is bound to fail. To quote one of Borges's favorite books, Sir Thomas Browne's *Hydrothapia, Urne-Buriall* (1658): "There is no antidote against the *Opium* of time, which temporally considereth all things. . . ." This is not, as has been said, because Borges's God plays the same trick on the poet that the poet plays on reality; God does not turn out to be the arch-villain set to deceive man into an illusion of eternity. The poetic impulse in all its perverse duplicity, belongs to man alone, marks him as essentially human. But God appears on the scene as the power of reality itself, in the form of a death that demonstrates the failure of poetry. This is the deeper reason for the violence that pervades all Borges's stories. God is on the side of chaotic reality and style is powerless to conquer him. His appearance is like the hideous face of Hákim when he loses the shining mask he has been wearing and reveals a face worn away by leprosy. The proliferation of mirrors is all the more terrifying because each new image brings us a step closer to this face.

Paul de Man. NYR. Nov. 19, 1964, p. 10

Vladimir Nabokov never lets his readers forget that he is the conjuror, the illusionist, the stage-manager, to whom his characters owe their existence; this flaunting of artifice, not merely as technique but also as theme, can perhaps be elucidated by a closer examination of one type of Nabokovian device, the book that, in whole or in part, explicitly imitates another book: a "discovered manuscript," a fictitious confession, a book about imaginary books, or a book that parodies such an already conventionalized structure as the detective story, the scholarly commentary, or the literary biography. Of the large number of contemporary writers employing such devices, Jorge Luis Borges, the Argentine poet, essayist, and author of disturbingly effective philosophical-fantastic tales, offers the closest and most illuminating parallels with Nabokov. Yet the similarity of their forms and structures brings into focus a fundamental difference in their premises about the relationship of art and reality.

Both Borges and Nabokov could be called "modern mannerists"; Borges, who said that "unreality is the necessary condition of art," has often been called "baroque" as well, a term that reminds us that *Don Quixote* is the father of the book-conscious-of-its-bookness. Both Borges and Nabokov exploit, for their own thematic purposes, all the narrative tricks and devices of the Gothic fantasy writers of the last two centuries, and they blend mannerism and Gothicism together in their single most important parodic pattern, the metaphysical detective story.

Borges' tales, rational and horrid, in the manner of Poe, yet paradoxical and philosophically teasing, in the manner of G. K. Chesterton, blend paradox, wonder and fear in a way that has often been compared with the nightmare logic of Kafka; the comparison is both obvious and justified. Both men see the world as a labyrinth of passages, a series of unopened doors, a thwarted or negated quest, a pointless wait separating the hero from a doubtfully existent Law, from a somehow menacing Judgment. Both authors are masters of the short poetic parable with much paradox and riddling in it, a form hovering somewhere between "fiction" and philosophic or even mythic tale-telling. But Borges, motivated by a passionate, highly intellectual curiosity, seeks to know what, if anything, is true; Kafka, motivated by a deep anxiety, seeks to know where, if anywhere, he belongs; the distortions of "laconic nightmares" seem more relevant to his quest than do the distortions of self-conscious and explicit artifice that charm both Borges and Nabokov. Even Nabokov's *Invitation to a Beheading*, so Kafkaesque in structure and effect, if not in intention, seems rather to lead back towards a world of the sane and normal, where something could perhaps be both real and beautiful at once.

Patricia Merivale. *WSCL.* 8, Spring, 1967, pp. 294–95

Two recurrent images are prototypical of Borges' art, being, as it were, its cornerstones, its master metaphors. There is, first, the labyrinth. We read, in various pieces, of the world as a labyrinth from which it is impossible to escape: of Ariosto's dreams weaving the skein of that illuminated labyrinth, his work; of a fugitive on horseback creating a labyrinth with his tortuous flight; of the sound of an invisible guitar in the next room creating for an invalid a "meager labyrinth infinitely winding and unwinding." Our dreams are labyrinths that reveal things we forget upon waking; a man, about to be executed, weaves within the last minute of his life a "lofty invisible labyrinth in time"; conversely, Borges' entire life is "the manifold labyrinth my steps/Wove through all those years since childhood." There is even a mysterious labyrinth in one of the tales "which is a single straight line."

What does this dominant image stand for? The maze is unreality in search of the real. The labyrinth is the frantic attempt to make sense of the jumble that surrounds us—whether it be the journey through life, sounds, and sights and movements that crowd us, or dreams and visions that, in the archaic word "maze" (i.e., bewilder) us. We try to run the maze from the beleaguering confusion toward the clear-cut, the unalterable, the real.

The second master image, fictions, is the other half of our story. In a poem, Borges writes that he "creates a fiction, not a living creature"; not, as he says elsewhere, "a mirror of the world, but simply one more thing added to the universe." All he can create as an artist is "my feeble translation/Timebound, of what was a single limitless World." For, as he again writes, the true work of art that summed up the world may have "consisted of a line of verse . . . of a single word." But this is lost; the legends that are handed down to us are "no more than literary fictions." There is a particular bitterness in that tautology "literary fictions." "Why," asks the rabbi who created the Golem, "did I decide to add to the infinite/Series one more symbol?" And one of the best known collections of Borges' works is entitled, redundantly, *Fictions*.

Fictions are the unreality of what we think most real: art. The author believes he has found his way out of the labyrinth into enduring, immutable reality, the work of art. And, behold, it is only a simulacrum, a verbose translation, one more knickknack added to the clutter of an overcrowded universe—a fiction rather than the Word that captures and mirrors all. At the end of the maze there is a fiction that makes the world even more labyrinthine, and merely extends our predicament.

John Simon. *BW*. April 23, 1967, p. 12

What makes Borges' stance, if you like, more interesting to me than say, Nabokov's or Beckett's, is the premise with which he approaches literature; in the words of one of his editors: "For [Borges] no one has claim to originality in literature; all writers are more or less faithful amanuenses of the spirit, translators and annotators of pre-existing archetypes." Thus his inclination to write brief comments on imaginary books: for one to attempt to add overtly to the sum of "original" literature by even so much as a conventional short story, not to mention a novel, would be too presumptuous, too naïve; literature has been done long since. A librarian's point of view! And it would itself be too presumptuous if it weren't part of a lively, passionately relevant metaphysical vision, and slyly employed against itself precisely to make new and original literature. Borges defines the Baroque as "that style which deliberately exhausts (or tries to exhaust) its possibilities and borders upon its own caricature." While his own work is *not* Baroque, except intellectually (the Baroque was never so terse, laconic, economical), it suggests the view that intellectual and literary history has been Baroque, and has pretty well exhausted the possibilities of novelty. His "fictions" are not only footnotes to imaginary texts, but postscripts to the real corpus of literature.

This premise gives resonance and relation to all his principal images. The facing mirrors that recur in his stories are a dual *regressus*. The doubles that his characters, like Nabokov's, run afoul of suggest dizzying multiples and remind one of Browne's remark that "every man is not only himself . . . men are lived over again." (It would please Borges, and illustrate Browne's point, to call Browne a precursor of Borges. "Every writer," Borges says in his essay on Kafka, "creates his own precursors.") Borges' favorite third-century heretical sect is the Histriones—I think and hope he invented them—who believe that repetition is impossible in history and therefore live viciously in order to purge the future of the vices they commit: in other words, to exhaust the possibilities of the world in order to bring its end nearer.

John Barth. *At.* Aug., 1967, pp. 33–34

For Beckett the mind is the curse of mankind. Perched at the top of a decaying body—in his most recent works almost totally decayed—this mind goes on and on being aware of its misery. If it could stop, the misery would stop. Thus the Cartesian *cogito, ergo sum* becomes the protracted torture of a malignant fate. Whereas for Borges the mind, since it is the source of perception, is everything. The body is only one, and by no means the most obtrusive, of its perceptions. Since the range of perceptions open to the mind is theoretically endless, the effect is a feeling of exhilaration, bordering on ecstasy. This is not to say that everything in the garden is lovely—much is nasty, brutish and short —but that everything is exciting. For Beckett, then, sunk in his heap of nauseous flesh, the telling of stories is a painful necessity against the hoped-for day of release, while, for Borges, to tell a story is the greatest pleasure and justification a man can ask for, which can even rise above the dire moment of extinction by setting it in the right context, by telling it right. . . .

Since as a philosopher Borges takes life to be nothing but the

perceptions of a central I, as a writer he must take life to be nothing
but the material of his art. Hence his emphasis on dreams: the man who
dreams is achieving effortlessly what the writer achieves by taking
pains, transmuting his random perceptions into a coherent whole, a
personal creation which both expresses himself and yet in a peculiar
and almost mystical manner becomes separate from himself and stands
apart. "The Circular Ruins," in which a man, by the effort of his
will, dreams another man into existence, only to discover that he himself is the dream of another, is Borges's most perfect artistic expression
of his own credo: the man who raises himself to a pitch becomes
an artist, the artist who raises himself to a pitch becomes a god, but
the god is almost certain to be reminded that he is a man.

The theme can be extended in all directions. As Borges owes
much to nearly every writer one can name and many one can't, so future and even contemporary writers—particularly the cloud of Latin
Americans, who are presently reviving international writing—are in
his debt. And the further refinement (as he himself points out in an essay on Kafka, not yet published in English) is that a writer even
modifies our reading of his predecessors.

Henry Tube. *Spec*. March 29, 1968, p. 406

Borges and Bioy Casares [in their collaboration] literally create a
combined writer, who could be baptized "Biorges," and in whom there
predominates a sharp sense of humor, a literary and social satire
which is more scathing than that which appears in their respective
"nonapocryphal" works, a delight in playing with language, in exploring its paradoxical possibilities and in breaking and re-creating its
oral structures. All this makes the almost nonexistent Bustos Domecq
[in *Six Problems for Don Isidro Parodi*] or Suárez Lynch [the pseudonym
Borges and Bioy Casares used for *A Model for Death*] or Biorges, one
of the most important Argentine prose writers of the epoch. Without
this prose writer, it is impossible to explain Leopoldo Marechal in his
best moments or Cortázar, especially in *Hopscotch*, when one starts to
talk about an invented Río de la Plata dialect. "Biorges was here" must
be inscribed on many pages of the most ingenious and inventive Río de la
Plata literature of these last thirty years.

Although it may be thought that [*The Chronicles of Bustos
Domecq*] is not the equal of their preceding collaborative books, it should
not be cast aside simply as a minor or erratic book. *The Chronicles of
Bustos Domecq* is a highly amusing and self-conscious document about
Argentine literary life of recent years. In twenty chronicles written in an
agile style, which parodies the corniness and pat sentences of provincial
journalism of thirty or forty years ago . . . Biorges clearly succeeds in

making fun of many literary superstitions held by his compatriots, reduces the true dimensions to a few pretentious nobodies whose work still circulates, and at the same time succeeds in creating some lasting texts. Although not all the parody—or satire—reaches important goals (there is a lot of in-joking . . .) in some chronicles, Biorges brilliantly attacks a number of the irrational critical concepts of our era.

Emir Rodríguez Monegal. *MNu*. No. 22, April, 1968, pp. 92–93†

In the large number of critiques and the several books on Borges, no consideration has yet been given, as far as I have seen, to the influence on him of Arabic philosophic thought and a certain quality of a given Arabic pattern of conceptualization. He has been among the most omnivorous readers of his generation, and in his critical and fictional works he has filled almost every page with reflections on more than 3000 years of world literature, the Islamic included. Borges himself points out the reading he considers most relevant to his work, but he never singles out any Arabic influence on himself. Perhaps he is so deeply affected by Arabic thought that he hardly notices it—just as, according to his own words (citing Gibbon), the Koran mentions no camels because the environment in which the Koran was written was saturated with the camel.

It may be that the Arabic element claims a larger share of Borges' intellectual make-up than he himself realizes—despite his conscious introduction of Islamic literary topics. Take, for instance, Borges' extraordinary use of paradox, and his wealth (by using multiple symbols) of intellectual puzzles. Borges confesses that all one's writing is, in the end, autobiographical and what he says of Nathanial Hawthorne seems particularly to define himself: he ascribes to Hawthorne the use of symbols open to many interpretations. I believe that Borges' contradictory style, his complexity and subtlety, is enhanced through his knowledge of Arabic—however imperfect that might be. He knows some of it at least, for he can write Arabic script.

Erika Spivakovsky. *Hispania*. 51, May, 1968, p. 223

Literary allusion is an inescapable characteristic of Borges' writing. Borges himself calls our attention to the pervasiveness of allusion in his work with footnotes, explanatory prefaces, and pages of notes at the end of stories and books. For Borges, allusion first of all expresses the collapse of time and the disintegration of personality. In an allusion, as in a metaphor, two distant things are brought together so that the reader is forced to become aware of their relationship or resemblance. Borges is such a master of these allusive equations that Marcial Tamayo and Adolfo Ruiz-Díaz have said: "This perfect adjustment induces one to believe that the quotation and the text obey a single creative process; that is, that the quotation does not proceed from a former exercise of choice but rather that in his esthetic elaboration Borges moves in a world of quotations." The perfect balance between allusion and text, making both appear the product of a single author, is precisely the goal Borges works toward. If we recall that a single repeated term is sufficient to deny succession and that a repeated idea denies the separate identities of the thinkers, then we can see that an allusion, as the embodiment of both these modes of repetition, denies both time and individuality.

Allusion unites text and reference in a point of time and space which eliminates both the separateness of the passages and of their authors. This union may be approximate, as in a footnote which indicates a parallelism of thought; it may be near perfect, as in a textual allusion which blurs the boundaries of the actual text and the cited work. In either case, Borges' technique destroys chronology and treats identical ideas as emanations of the same mind: to think the same is to be the same. To make allusions is to demonstrate the timeless universality of the human mind. Moreover, as Borges tries to show how all time and individuality may be compressed in the brief thought of a single mind, he attempts, too, to create a sense of the very diversity he compresses. The Aleph, we recall, is a single point containing all others; therefore, the literary work which aspires to the condition of the Aleph must itself be brief and unified but must also announce ontological variety. . . .

Allusion further serves Borges' intention by introducing an element of the fantastic into his writing. By allusion Borges introduces into his work other literary and philosophical writings which by their very appearance in a new and often unexpected context, create that disturbing quality of novelty and unreality which Borges understands as the source of our sense of the fantastic. But allusions used in this way and for this purpose lead us to a comforting symmetry: if Borges' text sometimes resembles a nest of Chinese boxes, his allusions point out that while each box is of a different size, all are always the same in essence. Thus allusion evokes in the work of Borges the systole and diastole of metaphysical, unified reality and fantastic, diversified appearance.

Ronald J. Christ. *The Narrow Act: Borges' Art of
Allusion* (New York, New York University
Press, 1969), pp. 33–35

The Symbolists made their poetry self-symbolizing, but perhaps took the matter too seriously. This is not to say that they damaged their poetry; but their seriousness affected adversely some of those who followed, creating a number of diverging and short-lived "isms." They looked for God through poetry; they tried to be mythic in order to restructure the universe. But Borges, both as poet and as fiction-maker, knows that modern man cannot be mythic, not really, and that imagination only confirms idealism as the nearest substitute for a mythic view; for in order to be mythic, the mind must lack a structured rationality. Only man's reason can call into question the hierarchy of reality it has created. The conceptual fluidity of the mythmaker can exist only as a mentality that radically doubts the validity of its own constructs, or as one which consciously forays into fancy without expecting to transcend or fulminate the vast system of practical fictions that men live by. Borges will not ride with Valéry on the seesaw of momentary subjective renewal followed by reentry into mundane reality; this smacks of psychedelic self-hypnosis, of religion, of escape. Borges will not lose psychic control over the game; he will remain the chess player as well as the pawn.

Carter Wheelock. *The Mythmaker: A Study of Motif
and Symbol in the Short Stories of Jorge Luis Borges*
(Austin, University of Texas Press, 1969), p. 17

Emerson? Many of Borges' other enthusiasms are equally dismaying, like the Russians' for Jack London, or the symbolist poets' for Poe; on the whole they tend to be directed toward obscure or marginal figures, to stand for somewhat cranky, wayward, even decadent choices; works at once immature or exotic, thin though mannered, clever rather than profound, neat instead of daring, too often the products of learning, fancy, and contrivance, to make us comfortable; they exhibit a taste that is still in its teens, one becalmed in backwater, and a mind that is seriously intrigued by certain dubious or jejune forms, forms which have to be overcome not simply exploited: fantastic tales and wild romances, science fiction, detective stories, and other similar modes which, with a terrible theological energy and zeal, impose upon implausible premises a rigorous game-like reasoning; thus for this minutely careful essayist and poet it's not Aristotle, but Zeno, it's not Kant, but Schopenhauer; it's not even Hobbes, but Berkeley, not Mill or Bradley, but—may philosophy forgive him—Spencer; it's Donne, Beckford, Bloy, the Cabalists; it's Stevenson, Chesterton, Kipling, Wells and William Morris, Browne and DeQuincy, Borges turns and returns to, while admitting no such similar debt to James, Melville, Joyce and so on, about whom, indeed, he passes a few mildly unflattering remarks.

William H. Gass. *NYR*. Nov. 20, 1969, p. 6

A dealer in enigmas and perplexities, Jorge Luis Borges is a strangely singular writer. He has created forms unlike any others in our literature, the "fictions" and the "inquisitions," his terms for his short fictions and essays respectively. The forms often seem interchangeable. His fictions, which are sometimes no more than summaries of several versions of a single work by an imaginary author, where real and imaginary authors and characters intermingle, are deceptively simple vehicles for the most complex and labyrinthine philosophical arguments about time, reality, God, the universe, consciousness, human thought— arguments which, Borges claims, interest him more for their aesthetics than for their truth. *The Book of Imaginary Beings* further reveals the formal singularity of Borges, for it elevates compilation to a potentially fictional form and suggests the encyclopedia as art.

The Book of Imaginary Beings is a fantastic bestiary, a compilation and alphabetical arrangement made up of examples taken from familiar and more distant, esoteric mythologies, as well as, in a few cases, from individual writers such as Kafka, Poe, C. S. Lewis, Swedenborg. They are creatures imagined or dreamt at different periods in time and culture, beings of the imagination like Leviathan, Behemoth, the Sphinx, Cerberus, Hydra, the Phoenix, Griffins, Unicorns, Fairies. Borges' interest in these fantastic creatures comes from how they reveal that men in different times and places share similar, if not identical, dreams, and that men dream and think into existence amazing beings that are strange, powerful, and as real in their unreality as we are unreal in our reality. . . .

The inference of a universal mind and dreamer, arguments about the self as an illusion and a dream (since we are being dreamt by someone else), the implications of extreme idealist arguments, and constructs about the nature of time and consciousness—these essential Borgesian themes manifest themselves not only in this book's encyclopedic totality but also in its choices of particular entries. Borges' entry on Bahamut or Behemoth closely resembles one of his fictions, "The Circular Ruins." Both involve arguments of infinite regression, forms of Zeno's paradox about Achilles and the Tortoise: a paradox which is central to Borges' fiction and vision. In Bahamut, God, having made the earth, then needed to provide the earth with a base, and then that base with another base, and that base with another base, and so on. In "The Circular Ruins" a man dreams another man into existence only to realize that he too is being dreamt by someone, which implies that the person who is dreaming him is also being dreamt by someone, and that person by someone else, on to infinity.

Stanton Hoffman. *Nation*. Dec. 29, 1969, pp. 735–36

Ultraísmo was Spanish expressionism, and when Borges returned to Argentina in 1921 he tried to make it into Argentine expressionism. Image and metaphor were to be retained in poetry; but "story," rhetorical devices and amorous sentiment were to be eschewed. In Borges' youthful Argentinian version, this was to be grafted onto a nostalgia, not for the *gauchismo* of Hernández (which, however, Borges praised in his criticism), but for the values of the older, *criollo* quarters of Buenos Aires. This was the programme of Borges' first three books, all of verse, and all published in the twenties. He is too subtle a man to disown a past self that is no longer, in his own terms, "him," but he has indicated that these books are forgettable and forgotten. . . .

Borges differed in one fundamental respect from other notables who, for varying lengths of time and with varying degrees of intensity, were associated with the *ultraísta* movement—among them Salinas, Guillén, García Lorca and Alberti. The source of their energy was the excitement generated by their actual creation of language. Their thoughts were posterior to their words. Borges thought with words; he was a failure as an expressionist poet—because he was not a poet. This, too, must have caused him some anguish.

It is revealing, then, that the least important feature of the work of nearly all the writers from whom Borges derived his method should be their use of language. Stevenson, the exception, wrote beautiful prose, but his achievement first sprung from a poetic failure. H. G. Wells's flights of imagination compensated him for his lack of linguistic inventiveness. Chesterton's startling and wise ingenuities sharply challenge the pseudo-genial beastliness of his poetic ungift. On a smaller scale, the same may be said of Lord Dunsany—neglected by us, but not by Borges. The influence of his fellow Latin writers has been more personal or merely technical: the semi-surrealistic, witty, but often almost middle-brow and facile *greguerías* of Gómez de la Serna—truly a Spanish Chesterton—gave Borges formal but not imaginative inspiration; so, one may venture, have the writings of the far greater figure who stands unmistakably behind Gómez de la Serna, Quevedo.

Martin Seymour-Smith. *Spec*. March 28, 1970, p. 414

It is the constructional power of the mind that moves and amazes Borges. His stories are full of the strangest architecture—the Library of Babel, the City of the Immortals, the Garden of Forking Paths—as well as examples of the endless lexical architectures to which man through-out history has devoted his time—philosophies, theological disputes, religious beliefs, encyclopaedias, dictionaries, novels, books of all kinds. The philosopher Averroës, in one of Borges's stories, is touched by "the fear of the crassly infinite, of mere space, of mere matter" and Borges has a sympathetic interest in every kind of "building"—palaces and poems—with which man seeks to cope with that fear and introduce shapes into a potentially shapeless existence.

The imperatives of pattern making and building are very clear to Borges—as are their often very equivocal results. "Funes, the Memorious" is about a young man who sees and remembers every detail of the life around him. He is incapable of generalising or abstracting and, over-thronged with details, dies of pulmonary congestion. Some system of clarification and organising is obviously essential to human life. But the nightmarish structures which can result from man's rage for architecture are vividly dramatised in Borges's vision of the Library of Babel and the City of the Immortals.

And in the story, "Tlön, Uqbar, Orbis Tertius," Borges specifically points to the dangers inherent in man's yearning for coherence. A secret society invents a complete fantasy country, Tlön, and gradually introduces into the world "evidence" of the existence of Tlön. . . . Since man made Tlön, Tlön makes sense to man; but some constructs destroy more than they clarify, their order is oppressive. We must be very careful about the constructions within which we agree to live. . . .

As [Borges] points out in a preface [to *The Book of Imaginary Beings*], a book with such a title could include "the sum of things—the universe," but he is concentrating on the weirdly fabricated creatures man has dreamed for himself. Borges reminds us that "the zoology of dreams is far poorer than the zoology of the Maker." But Borges is sensitive to the enduring human need to supplement existing creation with "necessary monsters," as necessary as Wallace Stevens's "necessary angel": "there is something in the dragon's image which fits man's imagination, and this accounts for the dragon's appearance in different places and periods."

Why such monsters are necessary emerges in the course of reading the book. They may be used as a mode of classification, as a way of giving shape to dimly adumbrated moral struggles or spiritual threats and aspirations, as a means of projecting an imperfect sense of the powers around us, of expressing our fear and awe in a universe which seems to have dimensions not directly accessible to the five senses. The book ranges over eastern cosmogonies, bestiaries, archives, legends, cabbalist works, fictions, heraldry; from Genesis to the American tall story; from the A Bao A Qu to the Zaratan. It is a book capable of giving endless delight, but it is more than another A to Z of mythical beasts. Beyond this it is Borges's tribute to the human imagination—its pathos, its humour, its fumbling grasp, its dazzling inventiveness, its wonderful excesses.

Tony Tanner. NSo. Nov. 26, 1970, pp. 960–61

Brodie's Report is the first book of new stories that Borges has published since The Aleph nearly twenty years ago. He makes no excuse in the preface for his abstinence from fiction, unless there is one to be derived from his teasing acknowledgment of the young Kipling as a model for the old Borges. In his later stories, says Borges, Kipling was an artificer of labyrinths and anxiety comparable with Kafka or Henry James; earlier he had produced some "laconic masterpieces" in a more direct manner. Borges claims to have been travelling in the other direction, declaring that in Brodie's Report: "I have done my best—I do not know to what result—to write straightforward stories. I do not venture to state that they are easy. . . ."

Thankfully, the stories in Brodie's Report do not quite live up to this dreadful promise; they may be, for the most part, simpler than the best of Borges but they are not transparent, and the agnosticism towards the ultimate nature of his own creations to which Borges holds look very much like a preliminary move in his game of withholding from readers what he wants them to think out for themselves. . . .

The majority of the eleven stories in Brodie's Report carry, as their author's letter-heading, a reference to their own source. They are explicitly "narrated," since the act of narration figures as a first episode in the story as printed: the stories have been told to the narrator before being told by him. Borges counts on this gentle alienation effect to dispossess the narrator of his story, as well as to emphasize to what extent it is fictitious. Brodie's Report is punctuated by reminders that with each successive telling a story mutates, as it is embroidered or censored by the teller, concerned with making good use of his temporary ownership of it. The story itself may have begun as a private experience but with its first transmission it was surrendered to the public world, and although the revisions made to it by the mouths through which it passes may be trivial they are the one loophole that Borges leaves for the inclusion in a literary work of those fashionable elements of style and originality.

TLS. Feb. 5, 1971, p. 149

Borges has a dialectical mind, a mind in opposition. His habit is to think in pairs and to stress whichever member of a pair seems to him to be out of fashion or unexpected. If he thinks we are waiting to hear about the meaning of poetry, he will talk about the sound of the words. When we are then ready to hear the pure music of his own verse recited in Spanish, he tells us the plots of the poems in English. Evidence of the habit can be found all over his work. So that when he suggests, for example, in his essay, "Avatars of the Tortoise," that the problem of evil is minor compared with the problem of infinity, we should miss neither the joke buried in the thought (the problem of infinity is an infinite problem), nor the polemical edge. It is because he is perfectly aware of the importance which people attach to the problem of evil that Borges tilts his interest away from it.

It is the behaviour of the dilettante, of an intellectual aristocrat, and there are plainly all kinds of dangers in it. Dialectics of this kind demand that you pick the right realities to turn your face from, and that you then turn your face towards an appropriate, mocking antithesis. Borges performed this delicate operation to perfection in the late thirties and early forties—the results are collected in *Fictions*—and has never really found his touch again. He is best seen in the context of that particular stretch of European and Latin American history—which is not to say, of course, that the meaning of his work is exhausted by that context.

There are similar perils in Borges's approach to philosophy. He is not himself a philosopher, he tells us, he is merely a magpie, taking what he wants where he finds it. This is not false modesty. And going on about how life could be a dream or how we are all someone other than ourselves, Borges can be trivial, antiquated and boring—unfortunately, many of his admirers seem attracted precisely to the feeblest moments in his work.

But mainly Borges saves himself from his own silliness by putting his philosophical finds to work. He is not, finally, interested in whether Achilles can run faster than the tortoise, and he is not even interested in the correct philosophical answer to Zeno's paradox. He is interested in imagining a world where the tortoise would beat Achilles, or rather, in revealing the ways in which our world is already like that.

Yet his very best work goes one stage further than this, for it deals not so much with individual metaphysical speculation as with the idea of such speculation itself. Metaphysics, Borges suggests, are a flight from reality, and his greatest fictions are devoted to the attractions of this flight seen in subtle war with the resistance of reality.

Michael Wood. *NSo.* May 13, 1971, p. 824

The similarities [between Borges and] Tolkien are too close to be coincidental. Both could be described, not disparagingly, as elderly fantastists. They put the resources of their considerable store of learning into creating an imaginary world with its own complicated and reciprocal structure: a world which is satisfyingly both magical and orderly. Tolkien locates his world in space (middle-earth), and Borges locates his in time. But in each case the fantasies appear to lock together securely into a recognisable landscape. . . .

A result of all this is that even the simplest of [Borges's] stories is pervaded with a philosophical idealism, which maintains that the world is in the mind and the mind encompasses all things at all times. For a man who lives through his books, in which past and present time-scales are coeval and simultaneous, this is logical enough. And many young people, with theosophies popularly ranging from Hinduism to R. D. Laing, are naturally sympathetic to an attitude of mind which denies succession and contemporaneity. No wonder that in the film *Performance*, Borges's volumes are scattered around as rather self-conscious emblems of intellectual respectability. . . .

As his popularity has risen in Europe, so it has reputedly sunk in his own country. He is accused of intolerance, lack of respect for his native traditions, and political stupidity. One "university militant" was recently quoted by the *Guardian* as saying, "When the revolution is won, I can assure you Borges will be the first to go." Without wishing to take this seriously, since there are always well-meaning revolutionaries who take a look at an ivory tower and see a battlemented fortress, there is no doubt that Borges has made some highly inflammatory remarks which reflect his belief that the evidence of facts is less important than the product of the imagination. All one can say about this is that it is a characteristic of authors who dispense imaginative justice in their writings that they should wish to impose a similarly ideal order upon the outside world. Militant spirits who forgave Joyce, Eliot, Wyndham Lewis and eventually Pound, will no doubt find it in their hearts one day to forgive him also.

Christopher Hudson. *Spec.* June 5, 1971, p. 779

As a poet, Borges has striven over the years to write more and more clearly, plainly, and straightforwardly. A study of the revisions of his early work from edition to edition of the poems shows a stripping away of baroque ornament and a greater concern for natural word order and for the use of common language. Even his ideas about metaphor have moved in this direction. "When I was a young man," Borges has remarked, "I was always hunting for new metaphors; then I found out that really good metaphors are always the same." The emphasis, then, has been away from callow, tiresome, and merely clever inventiveness (a trolley car seen as a man shouldering a gun) to the stressing of familiar and natural affinities, such as dream-life, sleep-death, and the flow of rivers and time—a turn, as Borges bitingly terms it, to sanity. There is a great deal of truth to Borges' insistence that he has been first a reader and then a writer. For it is as a peruser of books that he constantly plumps for such unabashedly old-fashioned qualities as readability, pleasure, and enjoyment, demanding in turn that the writer in him provide this same complement of unacademic and refreshing virtues in his own work. All these elements add up, I find, to endearing aspirations in a twentieth-century poet.

Norman Thomas di Giovanni. Introduction to Jorge Luis Borges,
Selected Poems 1923–1967 (New York, Delacorte
Press, 1972), p. xviii

Even acknowledging Borges' admission in "An Autobiographical Essay"—"I suppose my best work is over . . . yet I do not feel I have written myself out"—you will suspect you are watching Borges write himself out in Brodie's Report. The best stories here—"The Intruder," "The Meeting," "The Elder Lady"—are dim lusters, while the others are merely "slightly painful and trivial episodes" or, worse still, apparently vacant narratives like the title story which blankly redacts Borges' earlier "Tlön, Uqbar, Orbis Tertius," as well as Swift's still earlier travels of Gulliver. Understanding, explanation are not justification, no matter how hard psychiatrists, politicians and critics try to make us think they are. And while we can appreciate the personal value of Borges' latest revising gesture, we cannot say that it makes for great or even, in some instances, for good literature.

Ronald Christ. Nation. Feb. 21, 1972, p. 252

Until quite recently the only image of Borges in the mind of the American reader was Borges the builder of verbal labyrinths, the monstorum artifex of many fictions, the teller (or reteller) of myths linking contemporary men to Babel, Babylon, Tlön, Uqbar, Orbis Tertius. In short: a writer to place beside Kafka and Nabokov, Pynchon and Barthelme, a representative of a kind of fiction that resists the temptations of realism, of political or social commitment, of brave humanistic causes. His was a world of irony and pure alienation, of escape into the structural complexities of narrative, of a text whose only ambition was to be read as a text and not as a blueprint for the universe. . . .

In those books [between 1932 and 1952], Borges created a new genre: the essayistic short story that postulates the existence of nonexistent books and authors and proceeds to explain and discuss them, creating a reduced "model" of their work that is presented in the place of the unwritten opus. His essays of the same period dealt with real authors and subjects as if they were imaginary, and re-created them by use of the same techniques as in the short stories. An esthetics of reading emerged slowly from these exercises. Borges was the first to make plain to everyone that reading can be (and almost generally is) as creative as writing. The French new novelists and critics found in his inquisitions and fictions the stimuli to develop their own experiments. . . .

In the earlier books of poems, up to 1929, Borges is still the young poet whose ambition is to coin a verse that will be everything to everybody: The disciple both of Whitman and the German Expressionist poets, the sad, shy inhabitant of a Buenos Aires made more of dreams and loneliness than of reality. The man who continued to write poetry in his forties and fifties was no longer young, no longer so ambitious. A couple of quotations from two beloved minor English poets (Edward Fitzgerald, Robert Louis Stevenson) helped him to apologize for not being a great poet.

These apologies came at the time, it is important to underline, when Borges was writing his best fiction and his most original essays. In those days, poetry was a secondary occupation for him, and prose absorbed all his creative capacity. But his diminishing eyesight and the total prohibition to read and write that came in 1956 forced Borges back into poetry. In the long days and nights of his sightless vigil, he entertained himself by composing poems in his mind, and by repeating them to himself until the oral draft was ready to be dictated. After 1956 his poetic output increased considerably, and Borges discovered a new self. Not the young Whitmanesque poet who wanted to summarize the whole world in one poem, nor the reticent, elusive middle-aged poet who approached his craft with such diffidence. But a wise old man who worked in darkness with the same tools as his ancestors, Homer and Milton.

Emir Rodríguez Monegal. NYT. May 7, 1972, pp. 4, 18

Borges takes pains always to identify himself first as a reader; and the implication is that it is his reading which has caused his writing. I think this is true. But what Borges means by being a reader is something we are losing fast. We no longer live in books. From the earliest incursions into books in his father's library, reading has been to Borges an intense and separate life, a displacement in time, a shift to other dimensions, to a point where for him the borders between imagination and reality fuzz over and actually cease to exist.

I think that Borges, moving among languages, has always seen language itself as a separate plane of existence, on which words can manipulate everything, even the one who uses them; but at the same time, he is conscious always that language is paradox itself. Words like "forever" mock the one who utters them. The image that recurs in

Borges' writings so often—that at certain points, one man is all men, that in reading Shakespeare we become Shakespeare—crops up because it has so often cropped up to Borges in his reading. He takes in language in all forms—conversation and prayer, algebra and the tango, puzzles, maps, runes, the secret histories in objects, translation and mistranslation. He has even succeeded in making scholarship a device of the imagination.

I see three distinct strains in Borges' reading—first, the language of storytelling, of Kipling, Chesterton, Stevenson, of the sagas, the language of plot and coincidence, the unwinding of crucial events. Then there is the language of high poetry, magic, riddle and spell, words at the highest pitch of all, words as alchemy. We have only to hear Borges read poetry with the incantatory awe he gives it to realize how much it moves him. And third, the language of metaphysical speculation, from Schopenhauer and Berkeley through the curiosities of Coleridge, Quevedo, De Quincey, to Kafka and the fantastic. And, of course, it is in Borges' writings that these three strains converge—or rather in the aura given off by both his writings and his presence.

At a time when the validity of literature is often in question, Borges reads and writes as one who has no doubt at all of the power of words to illumine and disquiet.

Alastair Reid. TriQuarterly. No. 25, Fall, 1972,
pp. 100–101

The general direction of the studies devoted to Borges' writings, as well as the preferences of certain of his translators, has contributed to an unbalanced view of his total work, and has tended, for various reasons, to create the image of a countryless writer, one foreign to the literature and the realities of his homeland.

The same charge, along with those of Byzantinism and dehumanization, is one that the Argentine critic Adolfo Prieto directs at Borges in the first book devoted entirely to his work. Prieto, who writes in 1954 from a fiery existentialist perspective, is joined in his attack by Jorge Abelardo Ramos, author of a sociopolitical diatribe also leveled at Borges. To Ramos, Borges is a "systematic denigrator of everything Argentine," a man who has "lived his whole life with his back turned against the Nation." . . .

Studies favorable to Borges, by generally overlooking what is Argentine in his work, have also helped perpetuate this unbalanced view of his writings. Some have stressed the role that certain themes—time, eternity, infinity, personal identity—play in his production; others have analyzed in detail the peculiarities of his style; and still others have underlined his interest in foreign authors, tracing their effect on his work.

The apologists, finally, have emphasized the non-Argentine factors of Borges' life, education, and literary sources with the intent of stressing both his singularity in the Hispanic literatures and his importance with regard to other contemporary Western writers. . . .

I believe that an impartial and thorough study of Borges' writings invalidates all the above statements, both the condemnatory and the apologetic. There is certainly *one* Borges saturated with foreign intellectual influences, but there is also another equally important Borges deeply interested in and attracted by the landscape, the history, the human types, the language, and the literature of his country. His true literary profile emerges only when these two partial and complementary images are superimposed. A study of his view of Argentine history will reveal some features of this less known figure—Borges the Argentine writer.

Humberto M. Rasi. *TriQuarterly*. No. 25, Fall, 1972,
pp. 149–51

CABALLERO CALDERÓN, EDUARDO (1910–   )

COLOMBIA

[*Christ with His Back to Us*] is a sincere and honest denunciation of our political and social vices. If it can make our people think about the horror of such a state of affairs, the publication of *Christ with His Back to Us* . . . is fully justified. That the deck is stacked, well, that's something else. The stacking should not, however, be attributed to partisanship but to the haste with which the book was written. I want to insist on this matter of improvisation, because I think that it is the cause of all of Caballero Calderón's defects. In *Christ with His Back to Us* the failure to think things through is quite noticeable. . . .

The worst consequence of this haste has been that the author has not composed the great novel one had every right to expect from its theme. In the first place, he has not gotten inside his characters, except in the case of the protagonist; all the rest are seen from the outside without the sympathy that every artist must invest in his creations, no matter how abominable they may seem. Here he stacks his deck, so that the human flock surrounding the priest consists either of victims who have given up or of evil men who have no redeeming features. Is this the way the criminals are portrayed in the great, universal novels? Is this the way Ivan Karamazov comes off? Of course not. Clearly it is much easier to depict the struggle of the dove with the kite, of light with darkness. But there is the risk of sliding into melodrama instead of composing a lasting work of art.

This is the basic defect of *Christ with His Back to Us*. The others, such as the impossibility of fitting the action into four days, are merely technical defects of decidedly secondary importance. But the incongruities in the character of the priest *are* important, and derive from . . . the lack of a more profound (rather than more extensive) religious background of the writer. An example is his celebrating the Mass after breaking the Eucharistic fast, incredible in a spiritual man of the moral rectitude and scrupulousness that the priest is shown to possess. . . .

René Uribe Ferrer. *Universidad de Antioquia.*
No. 108, June–Aug., 1952, pp. 452–53†

When one finishes Caballero Calderón's [*Christ with His Back to Us*], he is left with the bad taste of bitter indignance. Christ chats with Don Camilo and gives him advice. But it seems instead that He has turned His back on the Andean town or that, as the other priest believes, men have turned their backs on Christ. . . .

The tragedy of Colombia (and of many Latin American countries) is the contrast presented by a democracy that is exclusively one of form, barely operating in the large cities, and the political and economic oppression in which the rest of the country lives. In this rural setting, politics is nothing but the whip which bites the living flesh of the inhabitants and which periodically makes them pay the abominable tribute of suffering and death. Amidst misery, ignorance, and fanaticism, an exhausting turmoil drives the poor deceived people mad. Caballero Calderón places us in a miserable little town, located high up in the mountain range, darkened by snow and whipped by the winds of that bleak place. In the life of the town the same old commonplace story is played out: two bosses, each one the representative of his party, struggle for control over the lands and the Indians. . . .

A second-rate novelist, who realizes that there is nothing more difficult than to represent life, chooses to go off on a tangent and talk about men as if they were static entities around whose rigidity the stream of words can be allowed to flow. . . . The characters of *Christ with His Back to Us*, however, behave in the same irrational and ambiguous ways as do men in real life. The novel's disconcerting truthfulness is its best quality. . . . Without lyricism or rhetoric, Caballero Calderón strings out his words with an easy fluency, unfolding before the reader that tragic world of the mountain village.

Let us hope that he doesn't decide to join that tradition of ephemeralism in the Colombian novel. From Jorge Isaacs to Rivera and our own time, there is a whole list of outstanding writers who have written only a single novel. And unfortunately one cannot create a literature without "second parts."

Hernando Valencia. *CHA*. No. 40, April, 1953,
pp. 133–35†

Caballero Calderón has earned the distinction of being one of the most outstanding stylists of the twentieth century. . . . The most extraordinary thing about these three volumes [forming his collected works] is the vast range of themes and genres Caballero Calderón has pursued. In a literary career of more than twenty-five years, his subjects have ranged from the destiny of man in the New World to precise descriptions of Castile, from warnings to his compatriots to an analysis of Latin American history.

Caballero Calderón established himself as a solid writer of narrative prose in 1940, with the publication of *Tipacoque*. In this work, at times with a clarity that is reminiscent of Azorín, at times with the overflowing eloquence and pensive style of José Ortega y Gasset, Caballero Calderón questioned with infinite curiosity the experiences of men. This work also established his critical reputation as a master of the language. . . .

What is Latin America and where is it going? How is it possible for it to retain the best of the Spanish tradition and at the same time develop its own personality? Is Colombia's destiny always to live under the constant threat of violent politics? These are some of the questions Caballero Calderón tries to answer in his works. . . . Caballero Calderón clearly resents the fact that, for Europeans, America is principally a place to invest capital or a place to emigrate to. Nevertheless, he realizes that he cannot deny all Latin America owes to Europe. What he most detests is affectation, the "intellectual paint" used by Latin Americans who try to forget their essential origins and their spiritual makeup. He demands sincerity; he hates hypocrisy. This sentiment is revealed in every work. . . . In *Christ with His Back to Us* Caballero Calderón authentically captures the psychology of the small towns in the midst of violence. . . . Many Latin Americans saw in *Christ with His Back to Us* their own villages, their own conditions—things that could have also happened in Mexico or in Peru. . . .

Roberto Esquenazi-Mayo. In *Homenaje a Rodríguez-
Moñino* (Madrid, Editorial Castalia, 1966), Vol. I,
pp. 167–70†

In Eduardo Caballero Calderón's novel *The Good Savage*, awarded the Nadal Prize in 1965, the vicissitudes in the fortunes of the protagonist reach an anguished climax. The young Latin American, hanging on tooth and nail to life in Paris, ready to suffer every pain and to commit every villainy in order to continue living in the French capital, seems to have reached the limit of his possibilities of staying. The great illusion that would have made possible the rejection of his literary aspirations has just crumbled around him: the love for the Chilean girl Rose-Marie (a love not untainted by prosaic materialistic purposes), a love that had seemed to him an anchor of salvation during moments of crisis. His physical and spiritual being has been reduced to a pile of rubbish. . . .

Turned into a piece of human waste, he descends the last rungs of his degradation, from which charitable souls finally wrest him. This is, without a doubt, the most compelling and dramatic part of the work.

But not even in these circumstances does the protagonist lose his faculties of fantasizing that make him imagine novel after novel, creations of an imagination turned into nothingness by the lack of other qualities. This conflict of fantasy and reality is the motivating impulse behind the characterization of the fragile human organism Caballero Calderón has made his protagonist. . . . He is a "savage," a "good savage," who runs amuck in the jungle of civilization, in accord with the romantic ideal that society corrupts natural man. He is one of those students so generously endowed with scholarships by Latin American governments out of their concern to create cadres of intellectuals and leaders. . . . Some return to their countries at the end of a couple of years with their university learning, enough to give them a place of honor in the intellectual circles of their native lands; others remain years and years, unable to respond favorably to the activities and demands of a life so different from the one in which they were brought up, attracted irresistibly by the new setting in which they have awakened to maturity. . . . The problem the book sets forth is not so much the influence of Paris on those elements of Latin America that are attracted by some aspects of its culture as it is the denial of their Latin American personality by the Parisian setting. . . .

José Domingo. *Ínsula*. No. 233, April, 1966, p. 5†

The Good Savage is a testimony. A testimony of what? The protagonist himself tells us in one of his meditations . . . "My novel will be the substitution for my graduate thesis, which I never wrote, on the psychological reality of Latin American man outside his private habitat."

In more concrete terms, it deals with a young Latin American man, the student, that is to say, one of some intellectual background, and precisely one situated in Paris during the sixth decade of the twentieth century. It is a testimony because it is not an isolated case, because it takes up the life of a Latin American in Paris. In this aspect it can be seen as part of a novelistic tradition whose most glorious ancestors are *Creoles in Paris* by Edwards Bello and *The Transplants* by Blest Gana. But neither the times nor the phenomenon is the same. The modernist, attracted to the "city of lights" and the world of aesthetes . . . has given way to another type of "Latin American in Paris." . . .

In this novel . . . several important techniques of fiction are excellently employed by Caballero Calderón. One is the use of the first-person narrator, who relates in his own voice his preoccupations as a novelist. Along with these preoccupations, he also relates his personality, his life, and the lives of those with whom he has dealings. Behind all this, there is the background of Paris, seen and portrayed with affection, that old Paris, at times a little picturesque, the Paris that has won so many men over to literature. . . . And throughout there is Caballero Calderón's style, always organized in brief paragraphs, an impressionistic technique of sensory brush strokes. . . .

Jorge Campos. Ínsula. No. 234, May, 1966, p. 11†

[*The Good Savage*] provides us with a remarkable document on Paris, seen through the eyes of a stranger, and on the life led by the international students—the blacks included—in the Latin Quarter. Add to all this an adventure, heady enough, but honestly told, in the *boîtes* of Montmartre, where the hero becomes a tout, an informer, a half-pimp. We also have his wanderings through the depths of the city and his employment at all kinds of jobs, such as being the very provisional secretary to a Moroccan delegate to UNESCO, thanks to which we are conducted to a strange reception under the chandeliers of the Crillon (we should point out that Caballero Calderón was himself a delegate from his own country to UNESCO). . . .

Let me observe, first of all, that the Latin American residing in Europe has been a literary topic for some years in South America. In contact with Europe, the South Americans seem to take stock of themselves, to discover a solidarity that they never saw before because of factional nationalisms, "cantonalisms," what Caballero Calderón . . . called an "archipelago of different nationalities, separated and isolated to the point of lack of similarity, whose people learn only in Europe to think of themselves as parts of a whole." Of a continent.

Paul Werrie. TR. Nos. 222–23, July–Aug., 1966,
pp. 138–39†

Caballero Calderón's literary production is divided between the essay and the novel. Among the former—some critics believe that Caballero Calderón's forte is in the essay—are such penetrating studies as *Broad Is Castile* and *Americans and Europeans*; among the latter the delightfully autobiographical Tipacoque series and *Childhood Memories*, as well as, and above all, *Christ with His Back to Us*, the succinct account of a young priest who in his first assignment runs afoul of the forces of religious and political fanaticism.

For anyone who remembers well *Christ with His Back to Us*, *The Good Savage* is at once perplexing and fascinating. It is fascinating because of its psychological penetration and its intellectual message; it is perplexing because it defies classification, joining autobiography, novel and essay. The subtitle of the book might well be "Notes of a Foreign Student in Paris," as it enquires into the trials and tribulations of a Latin American student who imagines himself a budding novelist. The *magnum opus* which the hero—or should we say anti-hero?—plans on page 1 and for which he assiduously collects notes in cafés and on street corners, does not materialize, but the young man's abortive attempts to come to grips with creative experience bring to life many fascinating facets of Paris. And here is the true protagonist: Paris—intoxicating paradise for some, *una enfermedad* [a sickness] for others. Not unlike Rivera's vortex, Paris seems to preclude escape for its victims. As the frustrated novelist goes down to defeat—I am referring to the novelist within the novel—the reader is tempted to exclaim: "The jungle devoured him."

While the literary devices and aesthetic criteria in this novel bring to mind the name of Marcel Proust and its title reminds us of Jean-Jacques [Rousseau] . . . there is a great deal that is decidedly Caballero Calderón. The big city smothers him, not so much by its visual impact as by its olfactory and above all auditory sensations. The candid words of confession which he voiced in *Tipacoque Diary* ring true for *The Good Savage*. The novel which has all the cosmopolitan earmarks and which in its frequent sallies into the essay genre is imbued with European literary echoes—a tribute to the author's broad cultural background—cannot conceal Caballero Calderón's nostalgic love for his native land.

Kurt L. Levy. Hispania. 51, May, 1968, pp. 373–74

CABRERA INFANTE, GUILLERMO (1929-   )

CUBA

The radicalism of Cabrera Infante both synthesizes and indicates a new direction. His novel [*Three Sad Tigers*] captures the spirit of Lewis Carroll's love of paradoxes, follows the example of Joyce in the transposition of words, and shows the influence of Borges in the global significance of the slightest episodes. But more than anything, [*Three Sad Tigers*] is a novel of intense Latin American baroqueness, and herein lies its open form. It is characterized by an antitraditionalism—a disavowal of any plot, conventional unities, credibility, drama, or psychology—and an insistence on a purely verbal reality, particularly because that verbal reality may be a requisite for oral forms. From its first to its last page, this novel is a conversation, or a series of monologues. . . .

Three Sad Tigers rejects customary structure and demands that the reader reconstruct it as he reads. . . . Its internal and external rhythms exist in the vertiginous movement of conversation, in that total verbalization which creates a porous, living language. Therefore, through all this affected, popular, elaborate, and spontaneous play there develops a nervous vitality, the physical sensation of a world that is haunted by the word. . . . Cabrera Infante is here a sort of Borges who is shaken by laughter and passion.

Julio Ortega. MNu. No. 25, July, 1968, p. 88†

At the time of the victory of the revolution, the young Cuban Guillermo Cabrera Infante published a collection of stories, *In Peace as in War.* . . . Before the Castro revolution he had added to these stories a series of short vignettes, newspaperlike accounts that are frightfully authentic in the immediacy of their portrayals of terror and power. Similar vignettes had been used by Hemingway as fillers in his first collection of stories, *In Our Time.* . . .

Here was a young man obviously taught by "Papa Hemingway." He handles Spanish almost as if he were an American. He finds himself incomparably closer to Miami than to Madrid. Cabrera Infante's reality is a corner of American dollar-imperialism, a world of gangsters wielding political power, of drunken Yankee tourists in the streets, of Negro jazz in the bars, of film thrillers from Hollywood in the theaters, of casinos and prostitutes on every other corner. In addition, there is a backdrop of native terror that gives his stories their particular aura, one of both restraint and breathlessness.

Artur Lundkvist. Utflykter med utländska författare
(Stockholm, Bonniers, 1969), pp. 217–18†

One senses in *Three Sad Tigers*, as one does in [Cortázar's] *Hopscotch*, an attempt to apprehend the totality of human existence to the extent that one vaguely suspects that the writer may be trying to swallow the chaotic totality of life. This explains in part Cabrera Infante's use of many languages, his constant word play, and his references to so many diverse aspects of human existence and culture. . . .

The freedom of its language has radically altered the importance of structure to the degree that the novel has no plot. After finishing *Hopscotch* the reader finds himself attempting to ascertain what happened to Oliveira; but after completing *Three Sad Tigers* he does not even try to guess at the eventualities, as the novel is devoid of plot. The organization of *Three Sad Tigers* is like that of a collage, or better still, a mobile, for it demands that the reader judge it as an artistic creation which has both an individual and total effect. Any meaning that the novel has is not due to an externally imposed structure, but is to be found in the interior rhythms and patterns of the language. If one wishes to argue that this results in chaotic organization, he is essentially making a case for authority; and authority, especially that represented by structure, is not accepted by the more experimental Spanish American novelists.

Raymond Souza. Hispania. 52, Dec., 1969, p. 838

Three Sad Tigers, a new Latin American novel par excellence, exemplifies the difficulty (if not the impossibility) of applying traditional critical criteria to innovative fiction without harming its aesthetic integrity. If Joyce succeeds in exalting human heroism within the commonplace through the most refined artistic perfection, and if Cortázar succeeds in reconciling the search for absolute values within the metaphysical chaos by a labyrinthine technique, Cabrera Infante proposes to bring to light (although without the usual type of probing) the complexities behind the superficial appearances of present-day life in Cuba.

At first glance linguistic pyrotechnics is the most patent goal of the work. Nevertheless, like *Gargantua and Pantagruel, Gulliver's Travels*, and *Alice in Wonderland, Three Sad Tigers* is a humorous novel of symbolic significance. Moreover, these four works present a logical trajectory from Rabelais's world of giants, through the political allegory of Swift, through the parabolic fantasy of Lewis Carroll; Cabrera Infante represents the last step, in which these fictitious worlds stop being intellectual mirrors of reality in order to be the only reality capable of being perceived or lived.

While the three earlier writers use language for philosophical and political ends, Cabrera Infante presents a world that cannot escape from the trap of its own language. The central theme, however, is more complex than *vanitas vanitatum, et omnia vanitas*. We do not have an omniscient narrator who observes the absence of existential values in the world of the characters (as in Sábato's *On Heroes and Tombs*); instead, we have creative turns around the theme of *traduttore traditore*: in other words, the book is dominated by the presentiment that the characters will betray their essences in the very act of expressing themselves. In the same way, the novelist deforms reality by re-creating it artistically.

Unlike Rabelais, Swift, and Carroll, who emphasize the absolute separation of reality and fiction to intensify their satirical intentions, Cabrera Infante totally meshes these two realms. Unlike *Ulysses* and

Finnegans Wake, in which art is a redeeming value and independent of reality, the fictional creation and the re-created world are an inseparable unity in this Cuban novel. By denying that language and art can reflect external reality, Cabrera Infante destroys the possibility of employing the technique of narrative perspective. . . . The result is a work in which linguistic play is piled up *ad nauseam*, structural novelties abound, and the characters pathetically embody a self-parody from which they escape only in death. For these reasons, *Three Sad Tigers* is truly an anti-novel.

William T. Little. RI. 36, Oct.–Dec., 1970, pp. 635–36†

[*Three Sad Tigers*] consists of the following stories: that of the author himself—the novel is autobiographical; that of Arsenio Cué and the woman who goes to the psychiatrist; that of Estrella [the black singer]; that of Cuba Venegas and Bustrófedon. These are the principal stories. The secondary ones are those of Livia and Laura, of Beba and Magdalena, and of Mr. Cambel and his cane. And we should add the story of the little girls who "do things" underneath the truck bed.

The structure of the novel does not make it difficult to read. One should keep in mind that from page 293 through the end of the book, the story of Cué and the narrator, strolling around Havana, is narrated. The Estrella chapters always have the same title, "She Sang Boleros." The story of the psychiatrist unfolds in regular order. The parodies introduced into the novel, of Guillén, Trotsky, and so forth, are bundled together and not scattered. The only time that the narrative is suspended—interrupted to be taken up again later—is in the case of the party in the apartment where Estrella falls asleep on the floor. Bustrófedon's story is also set off and is not long.

The real obstacle is in knowing, in many cases, who is talking, whether it is the narrator Cabrera Infante, or whether it is Arsenio Cué, and so forth.

This "technique of relativity," if I may so call it, consists, as its name indicates, of everything being relative—that is, the characters are and are not, even the events are and are not, which is why dream episodes are introduced into the novel. The most important incident, the one that best indicates the relativity of the whole, of the novel itself, of all the episodes, is the story of Vivian. At the beginning of the novel the man she has given herself to is Tony. Cabrera Infante lashes out against him, whom he pejoratively calls a "citizen of Miami." But at the end of the book, by a conversation with Cué, we find out that the one who went to bed with her for the first time was the narrator himself—Cabrera Infante, that is. Subsequently, after having confessed this to Cué, the narrator adds another idea of relativity: he indicates that he has lied to Cué because Cué is quite a liar himself. . . . Thus, this technique means that the reader never knows what to believe. . . .

José Sánchez-Boudy. *Nueva novela hispanoamericana y "Tres tristes tigres"* (Miami, Ediciones Universal, 1971), pp. 46–48†

Three Sad Tigers is a remarkable book. I doubt a funnier book has been written in Spanish since *Don Quixote*. Granted, that is not saying much. Literature in Spanish has not been noted for its humor. Yet this, precisely, is one of the book's strongest points: it has savagely refreshed an often portentously solemn heritage. It is also one of the most inventive novels that has come out of Latin America, and that is saying a great deal. The inventiveness of Latin-American fiction since Borges is by now (one would hope) fairly widely recognized.

Finally, its humor is fundamentally linguistic—the pun rate often runs at several per page. First published in Spain in 1964, part of its enterprise is to record the kind of Spanish that is spoken in Cuba—the kind I had imagined to be by definition untranslatable. Not only have Donald Gardner and Suzanne Levine proved otherwise. They have, in collaboration with the author, produced one of the best translations I have ever read. . . .

Superficially, this is a story of night-life in Havana shortly before the revolution. It takes us into most of the night-clubs, strip-joints, *barras* and *cantinas* the city could provide—the ones where after-hour *chowcitos* were staged, where people sang songs as if they really cared, and where one might have seen a Negro woman improvising a rumba as though she were inventing dance.

Cabrera Infante (who left Cuba several years ago and now lives in London) has no illusions about what his native island was like under Batista. The book is full of suggestive glimpses of social injustice. *Three Sad Tigers* is nevertheless an exercise in nostalgia, an attempt, to quote its Carrollian epigraph, "to fancy what the flame of a candle looks like after the candle is blown out." The nostalgia is not for the poverty most of the characters were brought up in. It is rather (I think) a nostalgia for the once-familiar bar, the familiar singer, the familiar friend, for an intensely local yet richly varied world. The novel therefore is a celebration of the small things that oblivion or time demolishes. . . .

Cabrera Infante once said he could see no difference between a writer and a bus-driver. His novel is directed against all those writers—until recently, the vast majority in Spain and Latin America—who have believed that to write is above all to distinguish oneself from a bus-driver, to fabricate sonorous, "beautiful" phrases that carry with them the signature "this is literature."

David Gallagher. *NYT*. Oct. 17, 1971, p. 5

What is remarkable about *Three Sad Tigers* has nothing to do with characters, or with sequence, and little to do with setting. The life here is in the surface, in the language itself, considered first as an extraordinary language and then as a badge for a style of living. On the title page it says, "Translated from the Cuban by Donald Gardner and Suzanne Jill Levine in collaboration with the author," and the cover of the French edition says "*Traduit de Cubain par Albert Benoussan avec la collaboration de l'auteur*," but never were such innocent acknowledgments more deceiving. What Cabrera Infante has really done is to write, presumably with the help of his translators, three similar but different novels in three different languages. The characters, scenes, and sequences are all the same, but these, as I've indicated, are not terribly important anyway. . . .

Whatever else, *Three Sad Tigers* is a very interesting book, one of the few I know that weds itself to a limited idea of a verbal medium and turns that wedding into a real marriage. If I had to try to make a simple statement of the book's limitations I would point to the obvious fact that it is a long book and finally much too long. It isn't simply that the endless punning is wearying, but that those places where it works best stand as a criticism of the many others where the attempt to gain real expressiveness is there but the achievement is not. Having finished the book one can see that the first hundred pages, which tell us of a number of people first coming to Havana, have only a structural interest, and that, for most purposes, it is only Silvestre's and Cué's last night that shows Cabrera Infante at his best. But that night takes up 160 pages, and is wonderfully sustained. To the argument that we need what precedes it to show us fully what is at stake the best reply is that that is much too long for what seems finally like preparation.

Cabrera Infante himself in an interview in Paris reveals that his pretensions are almost unlimited, and obviously *he* thinks he needs all his near 500 pages to fulfill his ambitions. Fortunately, though, that pretentiousness is felt inside the novel itself mostly in the fact that it is so long. To anyone skeptical about the very idea of a good book being written that is so self-consciously made up of words, I would suggest beginning with the last section, called "Bachata" [that is, "Party"]. . . .

Cabrera Infante's novel is backward-looking, nostalgic not just for Batista's tawdry Havana but for a pre-political world where Western culture held true, if in bizarre ways. His characters are all enormously well read, well versed in the accouterments of popular culture, and committed to the possibilities of taste, delicacy, and care. *Three Sad Tigers* is a modern novel, thus, not a contemporary one; it seems often like something written in the Twenties. . . .

Roger Sale. *NYR*. Dec. 16, 1971, pp. 24, 26

One can deduce that the life of *Three Trapped* [though "sad" is what they originally were] *Tigers* lay in its skin of Spanish, and that a creature so ectomorphic, so narrowly vital, was bound to perish away from the nurture of its native climate. Or one might, less kindly, conclude that the novel was derivative, that its excitement derived from the translation of the methods of *Ulysses* into Cuban idiom, and that, restored to Joyce's mother tongue, it shows up as a tired copy.

Three Sad Tigers offers to do for the Havana of 1958 what *Ulysses* did for the Dublin of 1904: wandering itineraries are mapped street by street, minor characters reappear in a studied interweave, a variety of voices abruptly soliloquize, a kind of "Oxen of the Sun" procession of literary parodies is worked on the theme of Trotsky's assassination, an endless "Nighttown" drunkenness episode picks up the deliberate hungover banality of the Eumæus sequence, and a female interior monologue closes the book. Unlike Joyce, however, Cabrera Infante packs most of his pyrotechnics and montage into the novel's first half and winds down into a more natural narrative tone. And, instead of attentive, soft-spoken, gradually solidifying Bloom, *Three Sad Tigers* has for its hero an insubstantial, logomaniacal trio of would-be writers—Arsenio Cué, Bustrófedon (who is dead), and the principal narrator, Silvestre. As these three compile reams of undergraduate gags ("*Crime and Puns*, by Bustrófedor Dostowhiskey," "*Under the Lorry*, by Malcolm Volcano," "*In Caldo Brodo*, by Truman Capone," "*The Company She Peeps*, by Merrimac Arty," etc., etc.) and tootle around Havana in a convertible (Bustrófedon is there in spirit, like the Paraclete, or—as Cabrera Infante might say—Parakeats), they make little significant contact with the nonverbal world around them. Havana of this era was notoriously full of prostitution and pickups, but the only instance of achieved intercourse throughout four hundred and eighty-seven pages occurs in some *tableaux vivants* staged for tourists. There is a good deal of partial undressing, and the work of one long night of seduction does jimmy a girl loose from her underpants, "*but*, BUT, where old Hitch would have cut to insert and intercut of fireworks, I'll give it to you straight—I didn't get any further than that." Later, Silvestre and Cué pick up two street flowers and proceed to bore them silly with puns and nonsense. One of the girls at last cries out, "Youse weird. You say real strange things. Both of you say the same strange things. Youse like twins, youse somethin' else. Whew! And you talk and talk and talk. Whaddya talk so much for?" To which the reader says, "Amen," and to which the author says, "Could she be a literary critic in disguise?"

John Updike. *NY.* Jan. 29, 1972, p. 91

In the original Spanish version [of *Three Sad Tigers*] Sr. Cabrera Infante gives a notice to the reader that does not appear, understandably, in the translation. He says, "The book is in Cuban; that is to say, written in the different Spanish dialects that are spoken in Cuba. The writing is no more than an attempt to catch the human voice in flight." . . . The title of the book [*Tres tristes tigres*] is a tongue-twister, like "Peter Piper" or "toy boat" in English. "Three Trapped Tigers" is a beautiful translation, I think, although I have persisted in using "sad" in this review. While I am on the subject of translation, I should note that this is rather a brilliant reconstruction of the Spanish than a translation. Some changes were perhaps occasioned by the stricter censorship in Barcelona than in New York. It must have been with the approval of the author that Gardner and Levine rendered the original "*Pues no canto, vaya!*" into "Then you can go fuck yourself, I'm not singing." . . . I get the impression that, when the translators submitted some of their work to Sr. Cabrera Infante, he became so enthusiastic about it that he told them, "Good, then, let's write it the way I wanted to in the first place, and let's use all the linguistic resources of English to enrich it." I also think that Sr. Cabrera Infante is very fluent in English, language as well as literature, and that he could help the translators with the many allusions to Milton, Yeats, Marlowe, Webster and others that do not appear in the original Spanish. Thus one is faced with the possibility that a translation is more accurate and more expressive of the author's wishes than the original. . . .

[The novel] abounds in tongue-twisters, anagrams, palindromes, mirror images, puzzles of all kinds. One of its chapters is called "Rompecabeza" ("Brainteaser"). Literary allusions . . . parodies (a brilliant one of Edgar Allan Poe in the English translation, and a more predictable one of *Guantanamero*), style imitations (Joyce and Proust predominate) and plays on words (innumerable plays on Arsenio Cué's name, which is itself a play on "arse," "arson," "*que?*," etc.) are perhaps the most frequently used devices. What I earlier called "the minor tradition in prose fiction" tells us the literary antecedents of the novel. Menippus (no surviving works, but copied by) Varro (fragments), Lucian, Apuleius, Petronius (whole works, and in paperback!)

—not the usual classics for background, though Fellini did make a big movie of the last-mentioned author's *Satyricon*. After the Middle Ages there were Rabelais, and the picaresque novelists in Spain, and Cervantes, of course, who had such a great influence on Fielding, Smollett, and Sterne. Sr. Cabrera Infante is very Sterne, and copies him in a page of mourning. Sterne's Yorick died, and merited a whole page of black mourning. Sr. Cabrera Infante's Arsenio Cué dies, and gets the same treatment—only to be resuscitated (Cué says there were blank bullets in the gun) as the very loquacious hero of the novel.

J. Raban Bilder. *CarR*. 4, 3, July–Sept., 1972, pp. 29–30

Most of the stories in *In Peace as in War* were written in the 1950s, during the Batista dictatorship, and with deep commitment to the revolutionary cause. The stories add up to a fairly coherent whole, not only because they present a picture of Cuban life that is always coloured by the author's sense of its injustice and corruption but also because interspersed between the stories there are fifteen linking sketches which describe the repressive violence that was displayed against Batista's opponents. Although the stories were probably written at random they are consequently given a coherent structure, their proposition "this is Cuba" being counterpointed by the proposition "this is how it is falling apart" offered by the terrorist sketches.

The Cuba that threatens to fall apart is not an edifying one, although the author never strains to spell the fact out. Neither revolution nor repression is mentioned in the straight stories, yet a subtly suggested sense of menace permeates them. Sometimes, for instance, a placid, almost idyllic situation is almost imperceptibly disturbed on the story's last page. Thus, in "At the Great Ecbo," a wealthy couple visit an Afro-Cuban dance ritual. The spectacle is merely a piece of diverting after-lunch exotica for them, "barbarous, remote, and alien, as alien as Africa," until an old black woman approaches them and asks to speak to the girl alone. For reasons not disclosed either to the girl's boy-friend or to the reader, the black woman's words, whatever they are, have a devastating effect and separate the couple. It is as if middle-class culture were too feeble, too vulnerable to withstand the most modest encounter with the Afro-Cuban foundations that lie beneath its respectable façades. . . .

The middle-class security which is made thus to seem so fragile in some of the stories is of course wholly overthrown in the hair-raising terrorist sketches interposed between them. They read like a litany, almost, of brutal relentless death, correcting any illusion one might have that anything in Batista's Cuba could be there to stay. . . . These sketches have, I think, had a great deal of influence on contemporary

Cuban writing, although few people in Cuba would admit it now in view of Cabrera Infante's current disfavour there.

D. P. Gallagher. *Modern Latin American Literature*
(New York, Oxford University Press, 1973), pp. 164–65

CARDOSO, LÚCIO (1913–1968)

BRAZIL

Lúcio Cardoso's work gives the general impression of pessimism and despair. It leaves a bitter taste, one difficult to forget about, because he seeks reality and does not deform it to satisfy himself or the reader. Who would not want the "ague" [of the novel *Ague*] not to decimate the town? Or at least, who would not want to present a solution, even a utopian one, for that misery. Anyone would feel tempted, even if only out of human pity, to distort the cruel reality that . . . leaves the soul oppressed and the throat dry. His lack of sentimentality in confronting reality face to face, when that reality is so painful and depressing, is undoubtedly his greatest quality as a writer. . . . Lúcio Cardoso achieves in *Ague* the most we can demand from a writer: he transplants to literature, full of blood and wounds, the living bodies of the rough men who live by the shifting banks of the San Francisco River.

Newton Freitas. In Lidia Besouchet et al.,
Diez escritores de Brasil (Buenos Aires, M. Gleizer,
1939), pp. 119–21†

I confess . . . a preference for the most recent of Lúcio Cardoso's novels: *Underground Light, Empty Hands*, and *The Stranger*. What had pleased me so much in the first phase of his career was precisely what it contained that foreshadowed his second phase. In both periods there is to be found a common element—man in struggle. In *Ague*, this struggle is of man against other men, against his environment, against pain. The struggle is external. In these three recent novels, however, the struggle is of man against himself, against his inner world, against the mysterious forces that agitate him and that guide him, "forces that are unknown, forces that persecute him night and day and entangle unaware hearts." An underground struggle.

For the form of novel adopted by Lúcio Cardoso, many labels exist: psychological novel, novel of ideas, novel of analysis. But these formulas are more-or-less arbitrary, since psychology, ideas, and analysis are general characteristics of the novel and not of any one species.

Classifications should be taken as a way of defining a dominant characteristic, not an exclusive one. In Cardoso's novels the dominant element is that of analysis. . . .

Action in the novels of Cardoso is a precarious element, too slow, more a *reflection* than a *presence*. To be sure, in all his works criminal acts and disorderly behavior are seen; to be sure, in all of his works crime seems to constitute the apex of an action. But crime in his novels is seen more as a possible surprise than as a rigorously logical consequence. The crimes occur partly by chance, partly without motive or reason, almost, I would say, *despite* his characters. . . . [1946]

Álvaro Lins. *O romance brasileiro contemporâneo*
(Rio de Janeiro, Tecnoprint Gráfica, 1967), pp. 22–23†

It is impossible, in discussing the development of this contact [between the Brazilian novel and world literature], to omit the novelist Lúcio Cardoso. Beginning with the novel *Ague*, which was in the main line of nativist literature (which modernism valued excessively), he slowly developed to the point whereby his first work seems today like an island in the totality of his novels. . . . The nativist elements, especially in the presentation of the setting, still persist [in *Willow*]. But a panoramic diluting has already begun. . . . The social webs still imprison [the characters], their Brazilian blood preventing them from moving in any deeply universal atmosphere. It is true that the psychological density, in part canceled by the force of the nocturnal lyricism, is capable of suggesting a Dostoyevskian climate. But the true shape of the problems (in Lúcio Cardoso as in Dostoyevski, they are problems linked to the power of God) will become evident later, in the strange novel, *Underground Light*. Here the problems are torn asunder, all of them, in one big sweep. One could say that, if it were not for Cardoso's language, this was the work of another novelist. And in this novel, definitively free of national limitations, the contact [with universality] is made through human nature.

Adonias [Aguiar] Filho. *Modernos ficcionistas
brasileiros* (Rio de Janeiro, Edições O Cruzeiro,
1958), pp. 86–87†

I have the impression that, like all great writers, when Lúcio wrote, his most secret and obstinate ambition was to modify the nature of people. Moreover, he, the artist, like the saint, had two ways of attaining such a goal: by persuasion and by violence. I could better define these different ways of treading the path by citing *Le petit prince* and *Journal du voleur*. At heart, Saint-Exupéry and Genet, when they began to write, had already decided to go in search of proselytes. Although each followed his own path, the fact is that they took widely different routes to attain the same goal.

I realize that Lúcio also did not attempt to attract the reader by amenities. In the literary saga he presented in *Underground Light* the most important aspect was not the part he took from life . . . but rather the way in which he expanded it at the precise moment of creating literature. I am reminded of Rhibeaudet's definition of the novelist's responsibility: to give life to the possible and never to relive the real. It is precisely in this sense that I judge Lúcio Cardoso to have been our best creative artist, the uncompromising crosser of the abyss-brink, the impulsive bullfighter whose pride does not consist in the privilege of killing bulls in the ring but in the risk of being killed by them. Because it is important to make clear that, above all else, Lúcio trusted much more in his imagination than in his memory. Hence the "lack of logic" in his characterization that some critics have objected to. Somehow, it never occurs to the critics that it is necessary to understand such characters in the light of the logic established just for them and not in the context of preestablished patterns.

Maria Alice Barroso. In Lúcio Cardoso,
Tres histórias de província (Rio de Janeiro,
Edições Bloch, 1968), pp. 10–11†

In the history of the Brazilian novel, Lúcio Cardoso stands as a solitary figure who [displayed] . . . highly romantic, highly surprising creative force. The surprise constitutes a shock in a panorama of writers who, with few exceptions, stressed economy and rigor as viable aesthetic norms. Lúcio Cardoso ran counter to everything that criticism dared to hope for in terms of polished and classical works. He was excessive, even went beyond all the limits he himself set. . . .

His poems constitute a true phenomenon. They are evidently the work of a consummate poet. . . . It could be easily affirmed that Lúcio Cardoso's poetry continues to be absolutely fresh and original in Brazil. Otávio de Faria had the following to say about his poetry: "That Lúcio Cardoso is a poet of great qualities—one of our few poets who truly deserve this title—there is no doubt of this in my mind as I read his book of poems today."

Walmir Ayala. In Afrânio Coutinho, ed., *A literatura no Brasil* (Rio de Janeiro, Editorial Sul Americana, 1970), Vol. V, pp. 377, 381†

In 1943 [Cardoso] had the opportunity to have his play *The Slave*, written in 1937, staged. It was given by Os Comediantes and later by groups of students from Paraná and Santa Catarina. This led him to focus, particularly from 1947 on, on writing for the theater (which was accompanied, almost concomitantly, by an unfortunate venture into films). This phase was to become, as he was to say later in his *Diary*, not a "derivative of the novel or a substitute for the novels I write, which I feel myself tired of," but an "act of full consciousness, with the idea that there is much possible to do in this area, which is still so undernourished in our country." Thus, after having the Teatro de Câmara put on his work *The Betraying Heart*, based on one of Poe's stories (and for which he even got to design the costumes, advise the set designer, and so on), he wrote and produced *The Silver Chord* (Teatro de Câmara, 1947), *The Prodigal Son* (written especially for the Teatro Experimental do Negro [that is, Black Experimental Theater], which presented it at the Ginástico, also in 1947), and, finally, *Angélica* (Teatro do Bolso, 1950).

But these works, without a doubt precursors of a new era in Brazilian drama, failed to achieve any major immediate impact on the public or the critics. And they were to fail to satisfy their own author, who, looking back at *The Slave*, confessed in 1949 in his *Diary* that "this poor drama did not fulfill my expectations for it. . . . And I can now see the reason for its failure to attract attention: rereading parts of it now, I can perceive its defects. . . . But by the same token, I am not sure I can accept the works I wrote later either." In 1950 he wrote about *Angélica*: "No, no, it's completely futile to return to the theater. *Angélica* definitively was my last attempt."

Renard Perez. *Escritores brasileiros contemporâneos*,
2nd ed. (Rio de Janeiro, Editôra Civilização
Brasileira, 1971), 2nd series, p. 233†

CARPENTIER, ALEJO (1904–   )

CUBA

Alejo Carpentier, a man of ambitious talent, has tried to write a Cuban novel—*Écue-Yamba-Ó!* [Ñáñigo dialect: "Praised Be, O Lord!"]. The times have not been propitious for his effort. So much attention in Cuba is directed at politics that any evaluation of the arts seems to be a forbidden luxury. . . . We lack . . . the calm moments necessary to dwell on this book with the critical attention and affection it deserves. . . . Carpentier, whose novel was conceived behind the bars of a Cuban jail, knows how prisons limit one's perspective and reduce stamina. Long months of the same spectacles, the "square sky," the slavery of windows and bars, of which the hero in the story speaks, little by little reduce him to senselessness, each night robbing him of a portion of his spiritual substance. . . .

Alejo Carpentier's novel is far removed from the usual sort of [Latin American] novel. It has the expansiveness of a symphony, with abundant and well-tuned components. We notice that from its outset it aspires to a Cubanness of essences obtained through new procedures. . . . It is a book that would initiate a rich and difficult mode, one that aspires to originality and majesty, and it deserves profound attention and careful understanding. . . . What is strictly literary in the work is excellent throughout. In this sense, it has little similarity to current Latin American literary works. Carpentier is one of the most authentic and productive artistic consciousnesses that we have, and thus it is not strange that *Écue-Yamba-Ó!* has a personal and profound structure, and an unusual narrative grace and imagery. . . .

Juan Marinello. *Literatura hispanoamericana*
(Mexico City, Ediciones Universidad de México,
1937), pp. 167–68†

For the past forty years writers all over the world have been following Proust's lead in recapturing the past, but few of them have succeeded in doing what the Cuban novelist Alejo Carpentier has done in *The Lost Steps*: create art in the process. In conception and method, as well as title, this work resembles *À la recherche du temps perdu*. Carpentier, too, is obsessed with time, conceiving it as a pattern in which the distant past and the future are fused into one, and seeing the significance of living in the escape from the tyranny of chronological time.

To break down the barriers of time as we ordinarily think of it, the author uses several literary techniques. He moves his characters between widely separated periods, from the jet-propelled present to the fourth day of Genesis, and back again through the Stone Age, the Middle Ages, and the turbulent Romantic era. As in Proust, the past is evoked abruptly through sensory perception: music, odors, the sound of a forgotten tongue all lead Carpentier's central character to recapture fragmentary memories of his childhood. In these episodes of sudden recollection, the author shifts from the imperfect to the present tense, giving the past a dramatic immediacy. The annihilation of natural or historical time is also achieved through the almost total absence of paragraphs. Page after page, the reader is held within the narrative, participating in a dimension of time that has no measurable length but extends in depth infinitely.

Structured like a symphony—Carpentier is, after all an outstanding musicologist—*The Lost Steps* presents numerous recurring themes and their variations and, like a musical composition, it may be enjoyed on many levels and admits many interpretations. The story of man's attempt to recapture the forgotten past, it also symbolizes a man's search for himself, for, as the protagonist observes, "the greatest task we face is forging our own destiny." The synthesis of Latin American civilization, it offers at the same time a cosmic vision of human history.

Bernice O. Matlowsky. Américas. 6, 7, July, 1954, p. 38

The rejection of modern urban civilization, the return to the primitive—this is a hackneyed and dangerous subject for a novelist. And Mr. Carpentier, who writes of a journey from New York City to a South American forest [in *The Lost Steps*], does not completely escape the dangers of the subject. It is not that he is cheap or superficial in what he says about the character of life in a contemporary city or about the values of a primitive society. His comments are mature and his conclusion is an honorable one. But theme and conclusion are conventional and provide little in the way of evaluation of either society that is novel. What matters in this book is the journey. It is an extraordinary trip, provoking a kind of intellectual excitement I have found in only a handful of novels. If Mr. Carpentier says very little about modern life and values that has not been said before, and as well, he does say things about the physical world, about travel and time, about the growth of culture, that are breathtaking.

William Pfaff. Com. Nov. 23, 1956, p. 211

I do not think that a novel with such qualities of magnificence as Carpentier's *The Lost Steps* owes very much that is important to habits of mind associated with a particular culture; at least I can find nothing singularly Spanish-American in its attitudes and special poetry, although a great part of the setting is South American. Its grandeur of conception, the splendor of its imagery, the powerful sweep of its energy are qualities of an individual greatness of mind. It is a mind deeply cultivated in the European tradition, immensely learned, profoundly passionate. The poetry of Saint-John Perse has something of the same "magnificence"—the vast panoramas of space and time, wrought with imagery of a similar concreteness and exotic splendor, and also a similar breadth and intensity of civilization—but Saint-John Perse's elegance is fatigued, and his cadences are like the slow shifting of sand dunes or the whispering of ancient masks, whereas Carpentier's energy is gigantic and pellmell, sweeping colossi on top of each other with ruthless, contemptuous daring. It is Balzac to whom he is closest.

Because of the anthropological character of a good deal of the materials of *The Lost Steps*, I think particularly of Balzac's *La peau de chagrin*, where, at the beginning of the story, a vision is invoked of the succession of the epochs of human life and culture, out of the chaotic dusts of a museum. Carpentier's narrative also starts in a museum, from which his protagonist then descends physically through successive cultural epochs, back to pre-history (not by any science-fiction marvels, but by a journey up the Orinoco to stone-age tribes). In both the sense of spiritual responsibility is tremendous, though Balzac arranges this by magical terrorization and Carpentier by the realism of despair.

Dorothy Van Ghent. YR. n.s. 46, Winter, 1957, p. 275

[In *The Kingdom of this World* Carpentier] condenses, compresses, crams into a sentence what a naturalistic novelist would blow up into half a book, omits acres of description but evokes a whole countryside from one leaf, and piles up trivialities which assume unexpected and powerful meanings. He creates a brilliant, improbable world which has the stylized reality of the great myths.

Specifically, the book is about Haiti from the French colonial period through the fantastic rule of Henri Christophe and on to something foreshadowing the present day. Ti Noël, who begins as a slave and ends as a vagabond, is the figure holding the story together. Ignorant, shrewd, dream-haunted, and practical, he observes the world. What he sees is a series of extraordinary enterprises that end in failure. The greedy violence of the French colonists, summed up in a wonderful comparison between wax models displaying wigs at the barber's and the waxy pigs' heads in the butcher's window next door, fails. The African magic of the first revolt, calling up old gods and the ghosts of kings "whose horses went adorned with silver coins and embroidered housings . . . bearing the thunder on two drumheads that hung from their necks," fails. The glittering Pauline Bonaparte tries to adapt magic to her European purposes, with no success. Henri Christophe's European logic and luxury vanish in the smoke of his burning palace. Even anarchic individualism fails, for Ti Noël, in his old age, makes a serious try at joining a flock of geese, who haughtily refuse to admit him.

In a moment of revelation, Ti Noël perceives that failure is unimportant: "man's greatness consists in the very fact of wanting to be better than he is. . . . In the Kingdom of Heaven there is no grandeur to be won, inasmuch as there all is an established hierarchy, the unknown is revealed, existence is infinite, there is no possibility of sacrifice, all is rest and joy. For this reason, bowed down by suffering and duties, beautiful in the midst of his misery, capable of loving in the face of afflictions and trials, man finds his greatness, his fullest measure, only in the Kingdom of this World."

Phoebe Adams. At. Aug., 1957, pp. 84–85

Alejo Carpentier is one of Latin America's most important novelists. Cuban by birth, of European family and education, he exemplifies a culture in which many nations and races mingle. He was born in Havana of a French father and a Russian mother. As a child he lived in many European countries and was educated in France where he studied music. His first works were musical compositions—ballet, cantata and choral music. Later he turned to writing novels and poetry and to films. He has written a history of Cuban music, has worked in advertising in Caracas, and he once accompanied Louis Jouror on a theatrical tour that took them to Haiti. This is Carpentier's intellectual self: a cosmopolitan jack-of-all-trades at home on both sides of the Atlantic. But there is another self: the Carpentier who was imprisoned for his political opinions in the 1930s, who wrote "Negro poetry" and whose first novel, *Écue-Yamba-Ó!*, published in 1933, described the life of the poor and oppressed Negroes of the Cuban slums and plantations.

Señor Carpentier's intellectual and social selves have never been in conflict. His cosmopolitan education, his interest in the latest literary theories and techniques have always been harnessed to a very definite social and didactic purpose: a pioneer task of aiming the Caribbean into the cradle of a new civilization comparable to the Mediterranean, and having its own characteristic epics and heroes, its Odyssey and its myths. Even his first novel, *Écue-Yamba-Ó!*, was much more than the social document that the careful observation of Negro music and rite and the accompanying photographs seemed to suggest. The family of the hero symbolized the decline in the fortunes of all Cuban Negroes and the hero himself played but the exemplary tragedy of his race. . . .

[*The Century of Lights*] is set in France, Spain and the Caribbean at the time of the French Revolution. The story closely follows historical events. One of the central characters is Victor Hugues, the French Jacobin who conquered Guadeloupe for the Revolution and helped to wage the Brigands' War in the Caribbean. Upon the basis of these historical facts Señor Carpentier constructs his many-storied allegory, for the novel is also about the vast cataclysm (the explosion in a cathedral) which followed the undermining of authority during the years of the Enlightenment; on yet another level, the novel reveals "the chaos that lies concealed," the immense variety and confusion of the world and man's attempts to impose order. On yet another level, there is a complete history and geography of the Caribbean area with all its rites and beliefs, all its historical and natural events. . . .

Nowhere has Señor Carpentier taken his "Adam's task of naming things" as seriously as here. Woven into the story is a complete history and geography of the Caribbean with its cities from Pointe-à-Pitre to

Havana, with its islands and mainland, its flora and fauna, its sea life and its merchandise. Señor Carpentier delights in catalogues; he gives us lists of the contents of a merchant's warehouse, lists of the fish in the sea, of fruits and foods. We are taken back to the Carib invasions, to the Conquest, to prehistory, until the historical events of the novel are seen as part of a constantly reenacted drama. . . .

TLS. Feb. 15, 1963, p. 105

The protagonist of Alejo Carpentier's short novel "The Pursuit" is an informer fleeing from men who would avenge the deaths he has caused. The pursuit and punishment of an informer, not a new plot, is usually developed with rapid pacing and suspense. But Carpentier modifies this traditional story of the chase by breaking it into a mosaic of fragmentary incidents and remembrances arranged without chronological sequence. Adopting certain techniques of the stream-of-consciousness writers, he reduces external action to a minimum and uses interior monologues and confused shreds of memory to show the inner life of his characters. Yet his work is not primarily a psychological study: the combination of two apparently disparate approaches to the novel (one a story line based on a closely-knit, causal-temporal progression and the other a narrative structure determined in part by the flux and shift of consciousness) creates a static and almost allegorical depiction of Betrayal in its various modes and incarnations.

This duality of presentation is also evident in the subject matter: definite historical happenings, tied to actual sites in the city of Havana, are the factual ingredients in a drama that seems to be just one possible version of a constant theme. Uniting the particular and the abstract, intertwining the external chain of events (shattered and rearranged according to noncausal principles) with pictures of internal chaos, Carpentier presents both the vision of a traitorous, degenerate world in which man plays out certain prescribed roles and the artistic or literary organization of this drama of the fall. Underlying these elements and binding them together is one of Carpentier's repeated themes—the representation, domination, or denial of time.

Frances Wyers Weber. *PMLA*. Sept., 1963, pp. 440

Explosion in a Cathedral is a work of art, a work of poetry. Yes, this is indeed not an inflated tract set against an historical background. The act of entering into the gaudy macabre scenes of that particular time [the French Revolution] gives them a surprising actuality and allows us to recognize so much of the present in this story of the past. . . . Carpentier above all else tells a story. The texture of his descriptions is as rich and heavy as brocade, closely wrought with both fantastic and realistic details and figurations, with scenes filled to the point of bursting their seams by his panoramic approach. . . .

An immense adventure emerges out of the historical reality, played out right before our eyes. The materials are so rich that . . . the reader thinks he is witnessing the hard-packed material of a hundred novels.

Artur Lundkvist. *BLM*. 32, 1963, p. 40†

Despite his hopelessness, Juan [the protagonist of "The Road to Santiago"], like Camus' Sisyphus, manages to triumph over the power of his God. By accepting the "myth" of Santiago de Compostela only when faced with death, Juan decides to shoulder his own burden, to create his own universe, however absurd his destiny may be. For a brief moment, which is his life-time, Juan curses the plague of death and deceives his God. But Juan is not the noble and tragic Sisyphus of which Camus speaks. Juan triumphs over his God only because that God has promised him eternal salvation. It is a triumph offered to him by the generosity of that God. Unlike Camus, Carpentier sees his Sisyphus as a contemptuous anti-hero, who triumphs at the expense of human dignity. . . .

Though, in its essence, this hope [of a Christian God] has no limitations, and I do not believe that Carpentier intends for it to have such limitations, it appears in "The Road to Santiago" to be directed toward the completion of the great American adventure, which, in Latin America, has been and essentially remains a Spanish-Catholic venture. For in America, Man, in his primitive state, can yet realize that morality, though it distinguishes him from his beastly cousins, is part of his primal essence. And it is this primitive morality alone which can now relieve Juan-Sisyphus of his human burden. For Carpentier, it seems that moral perfection and spiritual salvation through Santiago de Compostela —an avenue closed by man's own corruption—will remain impossible until man realizes and accepts the true essence of Santiago de Cuba, of America, of his primitive and historical being.

Ray Verzasconi. *Hispania*. 48, March, 1965, p. 74

In Carpentier, nature and culture are united only to be transfigured, to be projected into a mythic elaboration of the lost landscape between chaos and cosmos. . . . The novels of Carpentier are dialectical because they are tragic, in the sense of tragedy that Lucien Goldmann attributes to Pascal. . . . They belong . . . to universal narrative accomplishments, to movements of renovation, which substitute for the convention of characters and plot as crucial a fusion in which character and intrigue cease to be central and become buffers for a language that is in the process of developing, beginning from itself, into every direction having to do with whatever is real. Just as music has earned the right to be total sound or painting a similar right in the visual order, the novel has claimed its right to be first of all writing, the connection between language and all levels and manifestations not of "reality" but of what is "real." [1967]

Carlos Fuentes. *La nueva novela hispanoamericana*
(Mexico City, Joaquín Mortiz, 1969), pp. 50, 56†

[Carpentier's] work, in fact and spirit, spans two full generations. He has been a forerunner of our new novel and today is still one of its most distinguished proponents. Years ago, when our writers were still passing a hat around for ideas, he helped set its goals. He brought to his work an ordered resonance and sense of proportion that were a clear challenge to the atonal and the aphonic. His pronouncements, which were not meant for Cuba alone, carried well beyond its borders. He was perhaps the first of our novelists to make a conscious and concerted attempt to encompass the Latin-American experience as a whole, without undue concern for the superficial differences created by regional or national boundaries. . . .

His themes are all drawn directly—with a minimum of literary transposition—from the surrounding "contexts." His aim is to register what is specific, and at the same time archetypal, in the Latin-American experience. Every possible factor must be taken into account, he says. The Latin-American artist, if he is to measure up to his task, must be at once a miniaturist and a muralist, a moralist and a minstrel, a sociologist and a poet. Carpentier places special emphasis on the linguistic context. A phenomenon peculiar to Latin America, as he points out, is the fact that a single language will carry us across twenty different frontiers. . . .

The import of Carpentier's work must be seen in relation to his personal role as apostle and apologist for the Cuban Revolution, whose contemporary realities, in his view, embody ancestral truths of promontory significance for all of Latin America. The novelist's duty, as he sees it, is to help define these truths, then place himself at their service. Not as an agitator—our "literature of violence," as someone called it, belongs to the past—but as a moralist. What was once the novel of "social protest"—which, as Carpentier says, was unreal to the extent that it dealt with something that had not happened; the social protest framework, whatever its statistical validity, being a sort of controlled situation more or less arbitrarily assembled to prove a point—has given way to a genre more independent from immediate concerns, therefore better qualified to assess and evaluate. Carpentier is not a starry-eyed fanatic but a man aware of the complexities of the revolutionary task and the toll it takes on man.

Luis Harss and Barbara Dohmann. *Into the Mainstream* (New York, Harper & Row, 1967), pp. 38, 43, 65

The Lost Steps is a superb example of what I like to call (having attempted it myself in many a play and story) *Symbolic Action*. We read and hear a lot about symbolism in fiction these days, and some good friends of mine, admirable writers, may be found working hard at it. But all too often we find so-called symbols stuck into a narrative like plums into a cake. This is not what I mean by *Symbolic Action*, which demands that every setting, every important event, everything that happens if it has any significance at all, have symbolic depth and value. Such work can be read (or seen and heard in performance), enjoyed, understood, on more than one level. And this must not be confused with mere allegory, nearly always dreary and unrewarding, nothing more than a masquerade in which when once the masks are off all is revealed and we are left dissatisfied. . . .

On the first level [in *The Lost Steps*] we are offered a fascinating story of adventure and travel. We are told how a musician, leading an empty life doing film work he despises, accepts a commission to find some very rare primitive musical instruments in the Amazonian jungle; and how he does find them among remote Indians, with whom he lives quite happily by the side of a simple but rich-natured woman he can truly love; and how he is "rescued" and returned to a civilization he comes to dislike more and more, and then, eagerly returning to his jungle Eden, how he discovers he cannot find his way back and that the woman he loves now belongs to another man. This would be a magnificent piece of story-telling even if it had no significance in depth. Let me offer as an example of Carpentier's unusual skill in narrative what is, after all, only a minor episode. On their way to the jungle, the musician and his mistress spend some days in a large hotel in the capital city of the country. There some kind of revolution suddenly arrives with a hail of bullets. Now this is a fairly familiar situation in stories of Central or South America. As readers we have all been tourists in that hotel when the rattle of machine guns is suddenly heard, when the cooks and waiters vanish, no fresh stores are delivered, the water is cut off. But has anybody ever done it better than Alejo Carpentier does here in about fifteen pages? The monstrous tragic-farce of such a sudden eruption of violence; the suggestion of the brittle insecurity of our urban society, in which, when we discover we cannot switch on electricity or turn on water, we feel entirely helpless; it is all here in those fifteen pages.

J. B. Priestley. Introduction to Alejo Carpentier,
The Lost Steps (New York, Alfred A. Knopf, 1967),
pp. vi–viii

In three of his principal works, set in different periods—*The Lost Steps*, "The Road to Santiago," and *The Century of Lights*—Alejo Carpentier dazzles us with an authentic vision of a primitive world where there still exist positive values such as the deep collective consciousness of myths and the past, the certainty of man's identity, and a life style attuned to natural rhythms. . . .

Carpentier accepts the ancient and magical Europe, during whose distant Golden Age were created the myths of Sisyphus, Prometheus, and Ulysses, figures who still have meaning today. But he rejects the rationalistic Europe that produced the monstrous fruits of reason in our age. Thus, he proposes two different roads for his novels' characters: while present-day man finds the "shady mansions of romanticism" open, the artist becomes a sacrificial cultural hero, forced to define his circumstance and to foresee the future for those who come after. And always in the foreground, perhaps as an alternative to mechanized Western culture, Alejo Carpentier conjures up the vision of a New World that is very far from having exhausted its wealth of mythology. In America, the old aboriginal myths of the [Mayan] *Popol Vuh* flourish next to classical myths and African cosmogony, which took root and flowered with unexpected force on American soil. All reflect the intense, vigorous reality of Latin America.

Klaus Müller-Bergh. *Ínsula*. Nos. 260–61, July–Aug.,
1968, pp. 5, 23†

It is obvious that Carpentier has espoused from the start the triumph of the Cuban Revolution, although he does not seem to have participated in its preparation at all. It is also clear that Fidel Castro's regime considers him among its most distinguished writers; it has given him positions of undeniable prestige (Director of Official Publications, Cultural Attaché to the Cuban Embassy in Paris). . . .

Although Carpentier's orthodoxy vis-à-vis the Cuban government leaves a bit to be desired, at least for the most fanatic, he has firmly resisted permitting the postulates of an explicitly revolutionary literature to change his deepest aesthetic convictions. He has always rejected socialist realism, and this attitude was all the more valiant when *The*

Century of Lights was published in Cuba at a time when a faction of the literary officialdom was struggling to impose an aesthetic with Stalinist trappings. . . .

This book has not yet been analyzed with the care and the penetration that it deserves. It is, on a certain level, a delightful book, brilliant and easy to read. On another level, it is an unsettling book, an explosive book that poses problems that are difficult to assess at present with any equanimity. It is, in short, a book that rubs too much salt in too many wounds.

Emir Rodríguez Monegal. *Narradores de esta América*,
2nd ed. (Montevideo, Editorial Alfa, 1969–74), Vol. I,
pp. 283–86†

The spatial area of the Carpenterian narrative covers the expanse of the Caribbean. In his novels and short stories the Cuban writer has captured the peculiar beauty and the fascinating attraction of this American region. . . . Carpentier places as much attention on the natural world of the Caribbean (and on the nearby Venezuelan jungle) as he does on the political "becoming" that has shaken these lands since the beginning of their history.

One can see two directions taken in Carpentier's creative development. *The Lost Steps* is the novel of his that has greatest direct contact with earthly, physical America. On the other hand, in "The Pursuit" the writer directs himself to political processes. In his major work, *The Century of Lights*, both themes are fused and intermingled with an all-inclusive, all-embracing purpose. The interest in the telluric element is interwoven with the elucidation of the epic and the political in a creative undertaking of singular significance within the Spanish American novel, which, surpassing regional and indigenous limitations, reaches toward the universal. . . .

Carpentier has a dialectical interpretation of history. It is possible to observe how in his novels and short stories these dialectical laws are present: the repetition of historical cycles, the negation of an event by the one following it, the interrelation of deeds and men of different historical periods—in short, the circularity of history.

Salvador Bueno. In *El ensayo y la crítica literaria
en Iberoamérica* (Toronto, University of Toronto,
1970), pp. 257–58†

More than anything else, an ethos of action seems to preoccupy Carpentier. He does not write to reveal to us the tragedy of the human condition but to show to us a life that is badly lived, wasted, and therefore anti-heroic. Not that life has to be that way: one can choose. . . . Man does not have to be weak, helpless. He can follow another road; he can build another destiny for himself. The liberation of man depends on the effort each individual makes to conquer his weaknesses. Carpentier does not condemn terrorism. . . . One could assert that dictatorships provoke acts of violence, but in "The Pursuit" he shows only stupidity and the necessity of false idealisms. A heroism stemming from an excess of emotion or from a desire for personal glory has to be denounced as spurious, irresponsible, absurd. Man has to be heroic, but he must also reject the easy formula, must also reject the self-deceit practiced by a hypocritical society. He must reject the false ideals that the demagogues invoke when they refer to justice, heroism, and the sublime.

Alberto J. Carlos. CA. No. 168, Jan.–Feb., 1970, p. 204†

The Lost Steps, where a Latin American composer escaped from New York to an idyllic Amazonian community, seemed to me much too self-consciously literary and rhetorical. But the five short stories in *War of Time* are happily not asked to bear the same weight of philosophical reflection. One, about the arks of all the different Noahs of legend meeting on the flood, is only a dry scholastic joke, but two of them have the clarity and coolness of Aztec crystal. "Right of Sanctuary" cocks an urbane, white-gloved snook at Latin American politics. And "Journey Back to the Source" reverses the process of ageing, an idea used quite differently by Scott Fitzgerald. Here it is a great house and its master which reconstitute themselves from the rubble. We're asked to make the journey into the "*real maravilloso,*" the marvellous reality, which Carpentier seeks to create—and does here with a lightness and density that recalls the historical passages in Rilke's *Malte Laurids Brigge.* Magic and the powers of language combine to unmake the everyday.

Clive Jordan. NS. Jan. 9, 1970, p. 55

War of Time consists of five tales (masterfully translated by Frances Partridge) whose central theme is the eternal human traits that cross over all temporal boundaries.

The collection's longest and most significant work is "The Road to Santiago" (the phrase is the Spanish name for the Milky Way). . . .

"Like the Night" presents an archetypal soldier about to leave for war. In successive episodes that take place in ancient Greece, sixteenth-century Spain, eighteenth-century France, and twentieth-century Britain the author negates the idea of progress and stresses the immutability of human folly.

"Right of Sanctuary" describes the sense of timelessness experienced by an official of an unnamed Latin American country during the long months he spends in asylum in a neighboring nation's embassy after a *coup d'état*. "Journey to the Source" resembles a film run backwards, unveiling layers of memory to disclose the lost innocence of its leading figure. The last tale, "The Chosen," gives an ironic twist to the legend of the Flood.

Carpentier views our present-day circumstances as an end-product of historical forces. His quest for man's true essence, however, leads him to evoke the ever-recurring myths that fuse past, present and future into a unified whole. Because of his verbal flourishes, twisted syntax, and grotesque imagery ("when a carcass was thrown into the middle of the street, black baldheaded vultures would unwind its tripes like ribbons on a maypole"), he has been acclaimed as a master of neo-baroque prose.

George R. McMurray. SR. March 21, 1970, pp. 42–43

Alejo Carpentier is truly a writer of international reputation, though he has yet to reach the vogue which has recently come to Jorge Luis Borges. . . .

War of Time consists of five narratives which seem variations on the same theme announced by the book's opening quote of Lope de Vega: "What captain is this, what soldier of the war of time." Carpentier leads us through historical time to Biblical time and invariably to mythic timelessness. The eminently human seems to pervade the supremely magical setting of his stories. The reader need not be acquainted with Latin-American traditions because the stuff of Carpentier's world is universal and the mode of narration is suited to an author who prizes imagination over fact or history.

Carpentier has the genius to involve us in his imaginative writings in such a way that through his poetic reality we gain greater wisdom about our inadequate surroundings, spiritual or material. To attempt to describe what happens in the five stories included in this volume is to rid them of their very substance—Carpentier's art of creating literature in the "time" it takes the reader to re-create it. Whether it be in "The Road to Santiago" where he describes a pilgrimage to Santiago de Compostela or in "Journey Back to the Source" where a man "progresses" through life by returning to the womb, Carpentier successfully evokes the human condition, the passions which destroy Man across Time.

Joseph Schraibman. St. Louis Post-Dispatch.
April 21, 1970, p. 38

The sophisticated mind and compulsively idiosyncratic prose style of Alejo Carpentier have won his novels, both in the original and in translation, a wide circle of admirers, and there is no doubt that he is one of the half-dozen or so most impressive novelists in Latin America. A Cuban of French stock his novels deploy an essentially European view of tropical America. In all his novels tropical nature is displayed with wide-eyed wonder, so much so that a younger Cuban writer, Edmundo Desnoes, has felt Carpentier to be trading too facilely in exoticism. Thus in *The Lost Steps*, a disaffected urban intellectual longs to share the paradisiacal innocence of an Indian tribe he encounters deep in the Orinoco River.

Carpentier is a great deal more, however, than a latter-day Chateaubriand. There is a richly dense texture to his prose that few writers could equal. It responds to a program outlined in his book *Preludes and Differences*, in an essay called "Problems of the Current Latin American Novel." Unlike the European writer who need only mention a pine tree, say, for his reader to know exactly what he means, the Latin American writer, according to Carpentier, must show and demonstrate his landscapes.

Whatever the detail and time of the situation, there are archetypal situations that never change. The anguish of the Mother that her Son might be killed; the Parting with the Fiancée; the loading of Provisions onto the ship; the belief that Victory will Destroy Evil forever and that War will bring Glory and Medals; and the disillusioned discovery that War is Caused by Economic Factors and anyway solves Nothing. (Carpentier is liberal in his use of capital letters.)

Most of these stories [in *War of Time*] extract archetypes from particular situations in similar manner. There is one, however, "Journey Back to the Source," that marks an interesting departure for Carpentier. Latching on to the venerable tradition of Latin American literature of often gratuitous fantasy, he describes the life of a man backwards, from death to birth. When this man and his wife go to Church to be married, they "regain their freedom." One day, a party is given to celebrate the hero's minority, and "one morning, when he was reading a licentious book, [he] suddenly felt a desire to play with the lead soldiers lying asleep in their wooden boxes."

This pleasantly self-indulgent story is a worthy exponent of the inventive, thoughtful writing of a very fine novelist who has, incidentally, been well served by a translation that reads richly and fluently in English, although it could not hope to capture the eccentric syntactical and semantic convolutions of the original.

David Gallagher. *NYT*. July 5, 1970, p. 20

With a new collection of short stories, *War of Time*, Alejo Carpentier does a great deal to justify the pronouncement of Dame Edith Sitwell, quoted on the dust jacket, that he is "most certainly one of the greatest writers alive at this time." There is an essential aptness in this tribute from one literary mandarin to another. Carpentier is a Cuban, now sixty-five, who was born and educated in Havana, but he is also a member of an international literary elite that has been dedicated to the refinement of human sensibilities for thousands of years. The members of this elite belong to no particular time, and do not age, but speak directly to their readers as contemporaries in all periods. In the particular case of Carpentier, the evident superiority that justifies Edith Sitwell's words lies in the depth of his penetration of the meanings for individuals of the broad spectrum of cultural experiences that constitutes the Latinity—if it may so be called—of Latin America. He is a major contributor both to that entity's understanding of itself and to the outside world's awareness of it.

His novel *The Lost Steps*, published in this country in 1956, is the best account of the impact of the South American environment on the Latin sensibility that has so far been written. It describes that sense of being drowned in unconquerable space and overwhelmed by the obduracy of an utterly unaccommodating terrain which crushed and smothered Simón Bolívar's spirit by revealing to him the futility of the ambition, to which his Latin heritage has committed him, to create another European order in South America. Unlike Bolívar, Carpentier's hero did not find his revelation lethal but derived from it a heightened awareness of the character of the Latin-American destiny, which is not to be a second anything—European or American—but to be something new, peculiar to that place. It is a book that has been read and understood by all too few North Americans, who, when they think of Latin America at all, tend to see it in terms of a simple failure, attributable to inherent defects in the Latin character, to deal with problems very like their own—ignoring altogether the outrageous good fortune that befell the Protestant ethic when it drew the Hudson and the Mississippi, rather than the Orinoco and the Amazon, as the rivers of its testing ground.

Anthony West. *NY*. Nov. 28, 1970, p. 188

CARRERA ANDRADE, JORGE (1902–   )

ECUADOR

[Carrera Andrade] began to write when the poetry of South America had already undergone a rebellion against the decorative parnasso-symbolism of Rubén Darío which had created the "modernist" style. Part of this rebellion consisted in an emphasis on specifically Latin-American subject matter. . . . In the Ecuadorian's early work, elements of local color are present; he began by discovering his own environment. But even in the youthful verses there is a technical fluency and a consistency of tone which is to be a permanent characteristic of all his work. One feels that poetry is Carrera's native tongue.

A most important element of this poet's style, extensively discussed by the Spanish poet, Pedro Salinas, which appears even in the earliest poems, is the metaphor. The metaphor develops into his basic structural unit; it is the means by which the poet's personal vision unifies and takes possession of the objects of his environment. Carrera Andrade's metaphors are never strained or obscure, they unroll in luxurious profusion: they are a series of surprises, of aesthetic shocks which leave the mind tingling with pleasure. . . .

Coincidently with his travels, Carrera Andrade's poetic canvass broadened to include sketches of foreign cities and also poems dealing with the labor movement and the social problems which agitated the thirties. While in France, Carrera Andrade was in contact with the progressive movement of this period. There is a contradiction, however, between his art and purely social material. His poetry is born of a sensitive individualism and he is an aesthetic aristocrat. The delicate and decorative character of his poetry does not lend itself to direct and brutal statement. This awareness of social problems does, however, represent another phase of maturity and, when it is blended with Indian material, it is characteristic of a school of writing which has been called "indigenism." These poems were published in *Bulletins from Sea and Land* in 1930, antedating most of the nationalist theory which has, in recent times, stressed the cultures and economic problems of the Indians. . . .

On the formal side, there is such a feeling of ease and naturalness that slight changes in Carrera's poetical method are hardly noticeable. His earlier work tends to be written in traditional rhymed quatrains but, as he matured, he dropped the rhymes and worked in a freer but still basically alexandrine movement. He says himself:

"Poetry is *creation* rather than construction. I do not believe it should be facility or craftsmanship. The poet does not deliberately sit down at a table to manufacture poetry; the latter comes unexpectedly from the heights, like a tremendous wind, like a militant angel who shakes and tortures the man, and the victim argues with himself in his agony and stammers some broken fragments which constitute the poem. For true poetry is only that which has fallen from the combat with the angel.

"From my point of view, the poetic evolution of the world has undergone three stages: the *musical* stage (up to romanticism), the *sculptural* or *formal* stage (parnassian) and the *visual* stage (initiated by symbolism and continued up to the present). My poetry belongs to this last stage."

Reynolds Hays Hoffman. BA. 17, April, 1943,
pp. 102, 104–5

The poet in South America is not cut off from the common life, as almost everywhere else in the West he has very desperately been for a century or more. Carrera Andrade has been from his youth a polemical writer; in Spain, he took an active part in the proclamation of the Republic and for some years, being without other means, kept body and soul together by manual labor, often of the lowliest kind, all the while being engaged in the most intense intellectual activity; of late years he has been a diplomat.

"I am a man," he has recently written, "to whom nothing extraordinary has happened and who has filled his life loving things and knowing the planet on which we chance to live; above all, in fighting without respite for the liberty of the oppressed and the overcoming of injustice in the world." The need for justice has not lessened for him the immediate necessity for living. Nor has the political conscience of the man of good will ever made a coward of the poet.

It is possible to discern in his poetry three aspects. While they reflect the changing circumstances of his life, they do not strictly conform to them. Rather they lie like concentric circles, imposed one on another, about a common center. In [*Secret Country*] all three may be apparent at once.

In the first, Carrera Andrade is concerned with Ecuador and with answering the demands made on him by his country to record it in all its particularity of climate and custom.

The second corresponds to a series of voyages, in which the circumference of the circle is increased until, like the imaginary line of the Equator, it includes the world. In 1928, at the age of twenty-five, Carrera Andrade left Ecuador for Panama, on the first of those passages which were to carry him to Germany, Russia, France, Spain, the United States, China and Japan. . . .

The third is the smallest of all, for it contains only that domain which the poet has called his *Secret Country*. The book has in it poems which on the surface have to do, now with Ecuador, now with Japan. But the real subject is solitude. For there comes a time when the circle contracts and a man knows, even one who like Carrera Andrade has given himself so long and generously to breaking down the barriers of incomprehension between country and country, that there are limits to communion and that each man is irremediably alone with his knowledge and his fear. Though he has traversed the widest seas and entered into so many strange ports, each the entrance to another country, and set down all he has seen with love; though he has had his share in the struggle and exaltation of men everywhere and with them hoped to remake the world and everywhere seen the coming of dividing war and the world we know unmade, even then he must come back to himself and know that he is, beyond hope of struggle, to himself bound. . . .

John Peale Bishop. Introduction to Jorge Carrera Andrade. *Secret Country* (New York, Macmillan, 1946), pp. x–xi

Jorge Carrera Andrade dissolves the real world into metaphors so that he can re-create it in his poetry. He is a great magician of the word; he is a poet. And he is able to transmit to others his vision of the world. At times his poetry seems as if it were written for bewitched children, because it is like a spectacle of wondrous games, in which things are transformed into color, music, harmony, all moving under an atmosphere of enchantment. . . .

He finds in simple things the symbols of goodness and purity. Through love for these things, he uncovers their angelic possibilities: as he raises himself up to heavenly heights, he also elevates these simple things. . . . This is a celestial vision of reality, which cannot be reduced to logical discourse, a vision that can only be attained through a profound love of things. Carrera Andrade lives by seeing things, and seeing them with love. Thus, the waves of grain bend toward his heart, the birds fly toward his memory, and in the shadows of some forest he finds the most beautiful signs of creation. Valleys, mountains, and seas have been set aside for him like a collection of magical surprises.

Vicente Gerbasi. *RA.* 6, June, 1946, pp. 388–89†

"Notre histoire est noble et tragique." In these few words lie the key to Jorge Carrera Andrade both as poet and writer. It is likewise true to say that the succinct line: "this earth is my native land" may also be applied to this foremost Latin American poet for all he sees he makes his own and in a few imaginative words transforms a hitherto commonplace landscape. . . .

Jorge Carrera Andrade was born in 1903 in Quito. The poet's childhood was passed in a country estate, and his poetry today is coloured by his past. From his early days he learnt to use his five senses. Later he could draw on an inexhaustible treasure he had accumulated, for the mind of man is peopled, like some silent city, with a sleeping company of reminiscences, associations, impressions, attitudes and emotions. All these were to be awakened into fierce activity at the touch of words. . . .

In dealing with the impalpable, those dim objects that lie beyond the border land of exact knowledge, a poet seeks to bring them into clear definitions, to reduce them to bright concrete imagery. Life and death, love and youth, hope and time become persons. Every abstract conception, as it passes into the light of the creative imagination, acquires structure, firmness and colour. They become as flowers do in the light of the sun. . . .

But however important style, language and melody are to a poet they are but the trappings of his thoughts and ideas. Carrera Andrade is very much alive to this. He always has something to tell us, moreover in words intelligible to the least of us. He has realised that "notre histoire est noble et tragique" and he makes us see ourselves as we really are. . . . And these words are his passport to his Secret Country. It has also been said that escape is impossible from the secret country but that to enter it would be equally impossible were it not that Carrera Andrade is a poet and as he learnt to reach his secret country so he is willing to show us the way if we will but listen. . . .

[Carrera Andrade's] work is all too little known in Great Britain and those who have still to read his works for the first time have an immense treasure awaiting them. He will lead his reader to the secret country of his soul, but he will also unfold the beauties of that vast continent of Latin America.

Miriam Blanco-Fombona. SAJ. 145, April 9, 1949, p. 174

Jorge Carrera Andrade is considered one of the most important poets of Ibero-American postmodernism. His voice, together with Neruda's and Vallejo's, is one of the most original and durable of the present time. Peru, Chile, Ecuador—the countries of South America's west coast— have given us the best in contemporary poetry. In these three countries indigenous culture possesses a contemporary as well as an historical importance.

One can see similar interests and tendencies in all three poets. The influence of the French avant-garde movements—surrealism, cubism, and so forth—is quite marked. But to this they add a profound sense of the American environment, its green land and its dark men. Interestingly, these three poets have all been prominent figures in the social and political struggles of their countries. (Compare the situation in the United States: our best poets—Eliot, Pound, Cummings—have always remained on the margins of politics, and when they do hold political opinions, they are always conservative.) Imagery is of central importance to all three poets, and their use of images is daring, varied, and frequently recondite. All three have expressed a sense of exhaustion in the face of modern life, a longing for some golden age: "It's just that I'm tired of being man" (Neruda). "I was born in the century when the rose died / when the motor had already scared away the angels" (Carrera Andrade). . . .

Carrera Andrade is essentially a poet of the provinces, but he is in no way provincial. The poet withdraws to the provinces to think, to rest, to partake of the fountains of the eternal American elixir. . . . And to the provinces, to the country, the American poet must go to seek the material of his art, whether it be the Ecuadorian or Mexican provinces or the Argentine pampa.

Julian Palley. *Hispania*. 39, March, 1956, pp. 80–81†

The later poetry of Jorge Carrera Andrade shares with other literary efforts of our time the anguished conviction that solitude is the ultimate reality of man's existence, but it is not dominated, as is so much contemporary literature, by a sense of despair or frustration. On the contrary, his poetry arouses in the reader a curiously mild regret at the human predicament, and, at the same time, a calm, resigned optimism. Carrera Andrade does not achieve his effect by merely juxtaposing contradictory ideas or attitudes; instead, he fuses disparate elements so as to transmute the components into a new and unified whole. . . . Throughout his poetry insects, trees, birds, flowers, worms, clouds, and other natural objects are presented with as much care and consideration as are the specific concerns of mankind. His early poetry has a pantheistic tinge. . . . That feeling is lost after 1935, but the poet never loses the sense of delight that observation of the natural world brings him. In poem after poem he presents the world of nature to us in precise commentary such as the miniature titled "Alphabet." . . .

"Inventory of My Only Worldly Goods," which is the last poem in *World Registry*, gives us what might be taken as a concise summary of all that he found of value in his poetic voyage. . . . Two points can be made. First, the title, the structure, and the content of the poem all indicate that the poet owns these things, and he owns them because he has seen them and grasped their essential nature, or, at any rate, their essential nature as it appeared to him. Second, there is not the slightest suggestion that any one of the things listed is concerned with man or, in fact, is even aware of man's existence. The concept here is far different from the one evidenced by the poet when he wrote of the *conejo* [rabbit] who was called *hermano* [brother], *maestro* [teacher], and *filósofo* [philosopher]. Carrera Andrade is really celebrating in his poem his own vision and his own comprehension.

Here Carrera Andrade expresses his pleasure at the thought that man is free to examine the world, to experience the beauty it offers. And this consoling beauty will not turn to bitterness if man recognizes the limitations of his reason and his knowledge, and if he remembers that his problems are only small parts of all creation. Solitude, to be sure, is inescapable, but the splendid spectacle Carrera Andrade's poetic voyage revealed to him does offer consolation.

William Heald. *PMLA*. 76, Dec., 1961, pp. 608, 611–12

Jorge Carrera Andrade considers as antihuman and antipoetic the advice of the Colombian poet Guillermo Valencia: "Sacrifice a world in order to polish a line." Carrera Andrade would set forth a position diametrically opposed to this concept of poetry, taking as his slogan: "Sacrifice a line in order to endow a world with life." His method of giving life to the world rests above all . . . in the metaphor, whose richness and variety make his poetry a creation in which his intellect, his imagination, his heart, and his spirit all participate. . . .

René L.-F. Durand. *Jorge Carrera Andrade*
(Paris, Éditions Seghers, 1966), p. 67†

On numerous occasions, Carrera Andrade has defined the culture of his native country as a crossroads at which the most varied spiritual paths come together. Carrera Andrade himself exemplifies the truth of his own assertion: an ample variety of literary modalities has found expression in his poetry. If it is true that he wrote his first poems in the spirit of a waning modernism, he soon came in contact with the poetry of Góngora and the Spanish classics, while simultaneously coming under the influence of contemporary French poetry. His devotion to French culture, especially to its poetry, which he came to know intimately through his efforts as a translator, did not, however, prevent him from coming to know the poetry of other lands. Thus, as a mature man, he was apparently deeply moved by German romantic poetry, especially the work of Hölderlin, and years later he became deeply affected by the poetry of Rilke.

But it would be a waste of time to go hunting in Carrera Andrade's poetry for traces of foreign or artificially imposed elements. Both his poetry from 1926 on and his essays in literary criticism attest to his spiritual independence. This independence led him to reject not only Gongorism and surrealism, which were so much in vogue at the time, but also all aesthetic postulates that were less than compatible with the natural development of his poetry.

Enrique Ojeda. *Jorge Carrera Andrade: Introducción*
al estudio de su vida y de su obra (New York,
Eliseo Torres & Sons, 1971), p. 12†

CARVALHO, RONALD DE (1893-1935)

BRAZIL

[*Ironic and Sentimental Epigrams*] is the ideal synthesis of [Carvalho's] qualities. It is his paradigmatic book, the touchstone of his work. Here Ronald de Carvalho is almost always himself. No longer is he indulging himself as an imitator, as a paraphrastic virtuoso. He is no longer occupied with difficult combinations of rhythms, like a child with an insignificant puzzle. He has stopped indulging in pirouettes and charades. . . . Instead of writing (not without some hidden irony) in the manner of Camões or Anthero de Quental, he has moved on to write in his own austere manner. He has ceased taking pleasure in receiving from the Country of Light, like the spiritist Fernando de Lacerda, communications from dead celebrities in poetry, preferring rather to communicate in a more human way with the souls and objects of this "nether" world.

One can clearly see the spontaneity, often even the originality, of the lyrical or pantheistic motifs Carvalho uses in *Ironic and Sentimental Epigrams*. His motto has become "For silent beauty." . . . For the escutcheon of an intelligent mind, there is no better inscription. And it is even more appropriate when it represents, as in the case of Carvalho, a tendency to lose interest in sumptuous myths and heroic individuals and instead to love all that is humble, everything that other poets proudly disdain, from the simplest of souls to the simplest of plants. In this book, even if he still occasionally uses picturesque verses to characterize, say, the stylized beauty of the palm trees, he does not hesitate to have us see the sun "burning the cabbages of deserted backyards." . . .

Agrippino Grieco. *Caçadores de symbolos (estudos literários)* (Rio de Janeiro, Editora a Grande Livraria Leite Ribeiro, 1923), pp. 110–11†

Affiliated with Aranha's group and closely identified with Aranha himself, [Carvalho] did not take a position basically different from that of the novelist of *Canaan*. He was also against Beauty, Order, Proportion, Harmony [the shibboleths of the Parnassians].

Despite his academic vocation, the authentically classical quality of his writing, his temperament, his background, his clarity and grace of spirit, Carvalho rebelled against everything that represented order, proportion, and harmony, to go to the defense—no matter how incredible it may seem—of the "barbarians." And he exclaimed, in a famous lecture at the School of Fine Arts, in "Essay on Modern Aesthetics: Dialogue of the Alexandrian and the Barbarian": "Barbarianism is renovation. Only the barbarians are capable of giving liberty to the world. . . . Proportion, measurement, harmony, truth, work, and order are abstract values in flux. They are not ideograms but dynamic ideas that are perpetually transforming themselves."

[João] Peregrino Júnior. *O movimento modernista*
(Rio de Janeiro, Ministério da Educação e Cultura,
1954?), pp. 25–26†

Ronald de Carvalho was an eclectic in poetry, and he adapted his spirit and sensitivity to all of the literary genres that interested him during his brief yet important life. Ronald will have a place in our literature alongside the most cultivated writers of his generation. He left behind, as a literary historian, essayist, critic, and poet, an impressive oeuvre. . . .

The intermediary zone [between Parnassianism and modernism] —a sort of no-man's-land, the reflection of a kind of dandyism— entered literary history with a [significant] name . . . "penumbrism," a kind of whiff or smoke of symbolism. It had a function at a certain moment in the history of our poetry similar . . . to that of some of Debussy's works within modern musical symbolism. Penumbrism had its origin in an article Ronald de Carvalho wrote on Ribeiro Couto's *Garden of Confidences* (1921), entitled "The Poetry of Penumbra." The essential ideas of that article were published in a condensed form in one of the chapters of Carvalho's *Brazilian Studies*, in which, with a certain degree of exaggeration, justified at a time when Brazilian literature was going through a combative stage, Ronald asserted that in Brazil "poetry was pure eloquence" and that the poet who wanted quick triumph "had to transform himself into an able pyrotechnician, capable of putting worms and bombs in his hendecasyllables. . . ."

Rodrigo Octávio Filho. In Afrânio Coutinho, ed.,
A literatura no Brasil (Rio de Janeiro, Livraria
São José, 1959), Vol. 3/1, pp. 315–16†

Ronald de Carvalho's house was located on Rua Paissandu, where he . . . warmly greeted the youth of the literary vanguard. . . . It was a pleasure for him to have young people around him in improvised gatherings to take part in the conversation. On these occasions he often provoked debates for the sake of experiments in learning.

At the outset of his literary career, Ronald was excessively attracted to symbolism (*Glorious Light*). But later, by 1919, he was hesitatingly inclining toward the Parnassian groups. In due time he came under the influence of Aranha, who showed him that this school . . . was out of date, that it was backward and empty. Its elaborate verse, with metrical exactness . . . was purely ornamental. The skillful montage of words, with elements constituting the "sonorous stratum of a poem" . . . was purely extrinsic. Emotion was zero.

The Parnassians delighted in pompous exterior show. They took pleasure in emphatic themes. . . . They dedicated themselves to an inanimate descriptiveness, a classical culture, without color—a frieze of formal structures, with the goal of imitating Hellenic models. It was about time to insist on substituting something else for the Greek temples and to stir the deepest roots of Brazil in order to avoid the stagnation of the sensibilities of the younger poets.

In the course of these conversations [at his home] Ronald changed his course. Mário de Andrade, a personal friend of his who was pursuing the same course, also shed his Parnassian cloak.

Raul Bopp. *Movimentos modernistas no Brasil,*
1922–1928 (Rio de Janeiro, Livraria São José, 1966),
pp. 33–34†

It is precisely because of his abilities as a popularizer, his universal culture, his sensitive balance, that [Carvalho] might have been (and was, to a certain degree) the best theoretician of the [Modernist] Movement, the man who immediately inspired confidence. . . .

As a poet, and therein reflecting one of the profound tendencies of Modernism which was immediately stifled, he takes his place on the American plane rather than on the Brazilian plane. And here we find a particular semantic misunderstanding: Ronald de Carvalho encountered in Whitman, as is well known, the great master of telluric poetry; therefore, he also wanted *to sing America.* But the truth is that when Whitman sang America, he sang his own country, or rather he did something very like what the "Brazilianists" in Modernism were doing. On his part, when Ronald de Carvalho "sang America" he fled the geographical and spiritual borders of his country to create a kind of continental poetry which the North American poet had never even vaguely conceived and which, as a matter of fact, was alien to him.

Wilson Martins. *The Modernist Idea* (New York,
New York University Press, 1970), pp. 236–37

Ronald de Carvalho, after publishing *Glorious Light* and *Poems and Sonnets*, participated in 1922 in the Modern Art Week and published *Ironic and Sentimental Epigrams* in the same year. The first two books are traditional. . . . But the movement of 1922 found resonance in his spirit, principally because he had identified with the "nativist spirit," under which he wrote his *Brief History of Brazilian Literature*. Mário de Andrade called *Ironic and Sentimental Epigrams* a "crystalline work . . . clear . . . classical." There is in this book something of the Mediterranean and of the poet Anacreon, of the *Rubaiyat* and also of the [native] earth. . . . The poetry of this volume has a savagely Attic tone, as if someone seeing the earth were to feel the solitude of Theocritus' shepherds. . . .

All America, with its abundant rhythms, attempts to define the American soil, its meaning and its destiny. The resonance of Whitman in these poems has been often pointed out since the book was published, as has its declamatory air.

Péricles Eugênio da Silva Ramos. In Afrânio Coutinho,
ed., A literatura no Brasil (Rio de Janeiro, Editorial
Sul Americana, 1970), Vol. V, pp. 94–95, 97†

CASACCIA, GABRIEL (1907–   )

PARAGUAY

[*The Driveler*] is the story of life in a small Paraguayan town, and of the malicious woman whose libelling tongue destroyed its tranquil inertia. The author assiduously sets forth the most minute thoughts of his several characters, and since these are without exception selfish, depraved or frustrated types, his novel is, as a result, prolix and depressing, with a plot that tends to meander. In spite of his diffuseness, however, Casaccia frequently achieves fine emotional effects; he captures with rare skill the atmosphere of the indolent small town; and he scores particularly with his characterization of the insidious town gossip.

Kenneth Webb. BA. 28, Winter, 1954, pp. 69–70

The Paraguayan novel can be said to have been nonexistent until 1952, when Gabriel Bibolini published *The Driveler*. Despite the undeniable merit of the previous attempts to write in a genre that is today without a doubt the most complex literary form, the few tries that were made in Paraguay were never able to solidify into works of significant enough value to form a novelistic tradition, an artistic reality. At the present moment, nine long years after that date, it seems that there still does not exist a clear perception of the meaning that Casaccia's work has for the art of the novel in the country. In other words, there is no clear perception of how, through Casaccia's novel, the Paraguayan novel came into being.

When *The Driveler* was published [in Argentina] it caused an unusual stir among us. But it would be neither accurate nor honest to attribute the stir to any real appreciation of the novel in terms of what it aimed to be—a work of art. Rather, I think, the causes of this phenomenon were the raw plot, which excited the reader because it was tied to a simple and flowing technique, and the verisimilitude of the novel, whose situations at times are so realistic that they are perhaps even shocking. . . . People attempted to identify some of the characters with real people. . . .

What did Casaccia want to do with his novel? I think it was to portray in local terms a moment in the history of our society . . . a moment of frustration. . . . I feel that by illuminating this dark moment, the writer achieved the essential mission of the artist . . . bearing witness to the truth. And the truth of the frustration of human existence is symbolized and allegorized. Because identifying an evil as an evil is indirectly identifying a good, this must be then not an antipatriotic work but a moral one. This is why I believe that *The Driveler* is a true work of art.

Lorenzo Liviers (h). Alcor. No. 13, July–Aug., 1961,
pp. A8–A9†

Gabriel Casaccia's *The Driveler* apparently gave the *coup de grace* to a traditionalist and inconsequential society such as ours. . . . In this way Gabriel Casaccia revived the best revolutionary tradition, going back to [the essayist Rafael] Barrett, and gave the impression of offering the most revealing X-ray of the tumors in Paraguayan society. The novel, rejected by some bigots and political conservatives, was accepted abroad and by the newest and most volatile of the literary groups within the country. But, as Julián Marías said, for what reason does one award a prize to a revolutionary work that appears in an atmosphere of repression and silence—its moral value or its aesthetics?

I sincerely believe that the enthusiasm awakened by *The Driveler* is more political than literary, although I do not deny that *The Driveler* is one of the most solid of American novels. Did Casaccia strike a response in his psychological plumbings? Do the novelistic portraits of this writer lead to profound, vital discoveries? Does this novel inaugurate a narrative cycle? Do his later works extend the climate established in *The Driveler*? It is difficult to memorize specific situations in the "novel without a protagonist," as Josefina Pla has called it. Casaccia is a novelist of ambience, and his brush strokes are broad pictorial reliefs. . . . If he shares the moroseness of Proust, the skepticism, the icy, cutting

sincerity of Baroja, Casaccia suffers from a lack of profundity. . . .
Casaccia uses the psychological novel at a time when the world has
exhausted the devices of this school, but he feels sure of his mission
and his calling. . . .

Roque Vallejos. *La literatura paraguaya como expresión
de la realidad nacional* (Asunción, Editorial
Don Bosco, 1967?), pp. 44–45†

From the humor of *The Guajhú* through the acrid bitterness of *The
Exiles*, Casaccia has been presenting a series of . . . attitudes that end
up in mockery, irony, and an undefined sort of contained ire or anger,
in terms of which he constructs his novels and portrays his characters in
depth. What interests Casaccia in all his novels is the discovery of the
secret interior motives behind the social behavior of our people. And
Casaccia's undeniable strength lies in the vivid and lucid presentation of
the interaction of an individual's inner and outer planes.

His novels are almost always multidimensional (when he did
attempt to concentrate on only one level, the psychological, as in *Mario
Pineda* and *The Well*, the experiment was quite disastrous). As a
result, his characters move simultaneously through various times and
on various planes of existence. The complex of setting and character
forms, as a result, a splendidly authentic and vital polyphonic unity.

One should note that Casaccia is a writer little given to innovation.
His entire work is comfortably lodged in the mode of critical realism,
thereby easily enabling his aesthetic creations to have a kind of parallel
relation to reality. In other words, the world he creates is entirely of the
same matter as the world in which we live. This seems to be one of the
reasons why Casaccia has notoriously disdained imagination in favor of
observation. . . .

Francisco Pérez-Maricevich. *La poesía y la narrativa
en el Paraguay* (Asunción, Editorial del Centenario,
1969), pp. 40–41†

Gabriel Casaccia is an artist of exquisite sensitivity, obsessed with the
memories of childhood and adolescence. As a child and adolescent, he
spent long periods of time in a small town some thirty kilometers from
Asunción. It is a peaceful place on the shores of a pretty lake, Ypacaraí.
The houses, the spacious galleries, with patios and gardens filled with
leafy trees, all rise up out of the silence as though inviting one to a
calm, serene life. How did the expatriated author evoke this town,
Areguá, in *The Driveler*? Is it an idyllic place to which nostalgia has
lent added charm, even greater rustic beauty?

Hardly. Perhaps out of reverse sentimentality, Casaccia converted it into the setting of all he most hates rather than loves. In it a handful of shabby creatures, restless and gross, buzz around. With their base passions they founder in the banality of an existence that is sordid, vacuous, meaningless. The seven deadly sins have become incarnate in Areguá, the most jolting Paraguayan vision to date of their universal meanings. . . .

One Paraguayan critic, alarmed by the fact that this negative vision of the country was being spread abroad . . . judged the novel as something even worse than antipatriotic. . . . This critic was not altogether wrong: the real Areguá is not as horrible as Casaccia depicts it. But, precisely because it is not real but invented, the setting of the novel takes on an enormous power of suggestion. The artist needed to dramatize his hatred for the vices of his country and, since not even in Buenos Aires could he free himself from his obsession with Areguá, he transformed it into a pot of Purgatory in which the maggots of the base passions, his object of satire, could boil and bubble.

> Hugo Rodríguez Alcalá. *Historia de la literatura*
> *paraguaya* (Mexico City, Ediciones De Andrea, 1970),
> pp. 178–79†

In *The Driveler*, Casaccia attempts to give a realistic interpretation of modern Paraguay through the study of several urban, middle-class protagonists in Areguá, a resort town near Asunción where the author used to spend his vacations. In the story, we are introduced to a young lawyer, a Spanish priest, a widow in her late fifties, and others as they become the targets of the gossip of Ángela Gutiérrez, a middle-aged spinster, nicknamed "the driveler" for her drooling, gossipy mouth. Casaccia delves into a psychological study of several of the characters and through this study takes spiritual stock of the nation. Areguá's society, meant to be a microcosm of Paraguay, is materially and morally bankrupt. Those affected by Ángela's venom suffer because of their own weaknesses and vices, and the scandals she stirs up are catalysts that merely hasten their downfall. At the end of the novel life flows on and little has changed. "The driveler" lives on to prey on new victims.

While Casaccia primarily portrays realistically the social life in Areguá dominated by Ángela, the moral judgment passed on all of Paraguayan society moves to the foreground. What we see in the overall perspective of the work is modern Paraguay as the author judges it: politically, economically, and morally corrupt. What is indeed remarkable in his characters is their lack of ideals or sense of sacrifice. They are all anti-heroes living in a decaying atmosphere. The few educated personages, some of whom began as prospective intellectual leaders in their university days, have given up hope for a decent use of their talents and turn to immoral means to make a living. An environment conducive to morality and justice is lacking in the country. . . .

Casaccia's picture of Paraguay . . . is not a pleasant one, and his pessimism is not compensated for by sacrifice and ennobling deeds. Happiness is an elusive, almost nonexistent object, and there is noticeable lack of humor. Casaccia has chosen to live outside of Paraguay (only his first work was published while he still lived there). Many Paraguayan writers have chosen to live in other countries to avoid censorship and other restrictions to their art and livelihood.

Thomas E. Case. *JIAS.* 12, Jan., 1970, pp. 78, 83

CASTELLANOS, ROSARIO (1925–   )

MEXICO

The novel *Balún Canán* has suddenly elevated its author to the position of one of the best novelists of Mexico. The talent Rosario Castellanos had shown in the cultivation of her poetic art is prominently and decisively present in the prose of *Balún Canán.* . . .

The action of *Balún Canán* touches on violent themes but is contained within the passive rhythm of the narrative. These themes . . . form part of the nucleus of the relationship between the country gentlemen of the region and the peasants in their service. Together with these relationships, she treats the subjective conflicts of the characters and the objective ones resulting from the impact on the people of the social goals realized by the Revolution. . . .

The dialogue of the characters is adequate and clear, and everyone speaks in accord with his cultural station. In general, there is a predominance of expressions that reflect the idioms of the region, enriched by words taken from popular speech.

Rosario Castellanos comes off well in this first test in the realm of the novel. She has given to Balún Canán, the former name for the site where Comitán now stands, a novel that captures between its pages a moment in its history and a portrait of its landscape, its customs, and its beliefs.

Mauricio de la Selva. *CA.* No. 97, Jan.–Feb., 1958, pp. 272–73†

Rosario Castellanos is a young Mexican woman writer who combines passionate sensitivity with social history to make an arresting if not altogether satisfactory blend of novel. *Balún Canán* is a vivid, disorderly chronicle of landowning family life in a remote part of south Mexico during the late Thirties. It was a disturbed period when the local Indian peasantry, stimulated by Cárdenas's agrarian reforms and the official current of anti-clericalism, were beginning to kick in their own sullen sporadically violent fashion. They fire César Argüello's sugar plantation at Chactajal, and shoot his bastard nephew, Ernesto, a strange picaresque satyr of a character, disdainful of the Indians and the new threatening regime, resentful of the Argüellos to whom he doesn't quite belong.

After the fire the family moves back to Comitán, the little town near the Guatemalan border, where the novel opens. Here the curious interpenetration between Mexican Indian and Spanish Catholic superstitions is neatly illustrated when the little boy, Mario, falls ill and his mother, Señora Argüello, more than half believes the Indian nurse's warning that his spirit is being eaten by sorcerers. If only Señora Castellanos had been able to solve her story-telling problem she might have written a masterpiece. Unfortunately she puts most of it into the mouth of the seven-year-old Argüello daughter—herself, presumably—who narrates away in the breathless historic present, like an all-seeing eye. There are occasional monologues by adults and patches with no narrator. The effect is inevitably one of maddening dissociation. Even so, the vividness of the background is most impressive. This, you feel, is as near Mexico as you can get in print. And despite the extreme subjectivity, strict impartiality is preserved as between peasants and landowners. Nothing could be more tellingly detached than the laconic account of the odd masculine Aunt Francisca's brutality to her peasants.

Maurice Richardson. *NS*. July 25, 1959, pp. 115–16

Still in her twenties and generously endowed as poet and novelist, Rosario Castellanos is almost unique among Mexican writers for the respect her work inspires among the embattled cliques of both Left and Right. *Balún Canán*, her first novel to reach us in translation, shows why.

Written during a period when she was employed as an anthropologist by the Indian Bureau in Chiapas, it deals with the social upheaval of the Cárdenas period in such a way as to give little comfort to either the diehard *hacendados* or the sentimental *indianistas*. Though never explicit, the author's sympathy for the sufferings of both parties is always felt. Bedeviled by the hatreds, fears and superstitions of a five-hundred-years-old unnatural relationship, the inevitable clash of peasant and landlord was bound to end in horror; yet the reader never feels that horror is being exploited for mere literary advantage. Only in the first few pages, as a matter of fact, is one conscious of anything highly wrought: poetical descriptive passages and characters vibrating with exquisite sensibility. And this is the more remarkable in a literary tradition that is apt to strike us as excessively style-conscious. . . .

What saves this Faulknerian tale from being merely a case history in degeneracy, is the degree to which the author (like Faulkner) manages to invest the degradation of the present with a brooding sense of the meaningfulness of the past. But this, unfortunately, she does too subtly, or ambivalently. The reader unversed in the Maya background or the Cárdenas foreground would never guess that any spirit of illuminating aspiration had ever crossed this dark terrain.

Selden Rodman. NYT. June 5, 1960, pp. 4–5, 26

The Mexican Revolution, which began in 1910 and continued, more or less, until 1940, is only now becoming, as it were, externalized in its country's literature. While the Revolution was happening, outsiders such as D. H. Lawrence or Graham Greene could travel in the country, observe, comment, and cavil or commend, but Mexicans themselves were too deeply and traumatically involved to do so. Now the process of assimilation into art is going on apace, and there is in Mexico City a group of young novelists, several of whom are already being translated and appreciated abroad as well as at home.

Rosario Castellanos, whose *Balún Canán* was voted the best work of fiction in Mexico for 1957, grew up in the high Chiapas country she describes. The central conflict of the novel is between the Mexicans of Spanish descent and the Indians. . . .

The seven-year-old girl who narrates part one of *Balún Canán* is from the first aware of the hostile dichotomy: her beloved Indian nurse has a wound her own people have given her because she loved the child and her brother. "Is it wicked to love us?" the youngster asks, and Nana replies, "It's wicked to love those who give orders and have possessions. That's what the law says." . . .

It would have been a still better novel had it been all written from the child's viewpoint: the sudden change of narrator takes away from both the pace and the pathos of the story; it is almost as if the author felt she couldn't keep it up, that relating a whole revolution, even as experienced by one family, on one hacienda, from a seven-year-old's point of view, was too complex an undertaking.

Anne Fremantle. SR. June 11, 1960, p. 38

In less than fifteen years, Rosario Castellanos has produced a considerable oeuvre of appreciable artistic quality, including seven books of poetry . . . two novels . . . a volume of stories . . . and a theatrical piece. . . . Her poetry, together with that of Jaime Sabines, a comrade-in-arms from the same area, has captured the attention of the most astute critics and the enthusiasm of the reading public. Among the work of younger writers, the poetry of Rosario Castellanos and Jaime Sabines perhaps constitutes the two points between which our lyric tradition moves: an intelligence that orders appetites and tempers the perceptions of the senses, and an emotionalism that challenges the elaborate products of reason and rebuilds the real world in its own way. (The marks of both writers are more-or-less perceptible among the poets who have recently "arrived.") Among the prose writers of her generation, Rosario Castellanos has produced the best constructed and the most ideologically sound work. In her essays and literary criticism, activities which she engages in sporadically, she reaffirms the gifts that we all recognize in her: sagacity and irony.

Professionally committed to literature, Rosario Castellanos demonstrates that inspiration and talent can be complemented by patience and hard work. . . .

In her most recent work, *The Guests in August*, she reveals similar purposes and reflects characteristics that marked her previous work, but, at the same time, she follows paths she has never before traveled. Perhaps this is her best work of narrative prose, for various reasons. First, it does away with any anthropological preoccupation: her characters are no longer Indians or white men; they are human beings. Second, realism does not exclude imagination: the anecdotes allow us to see the "verified facts" and the "possible happenings." Third, the style is a rejection of poetic prose and follows the canons of narrative prose. Fourth, the writer, in telling her story, reduces the field of her observations and abandons the omniscient point of view . . . letting [her characters] act, think, and feel with a certain amount of independence. . . .

Emmanuel Carballo. *Diecinueve protagonistas de la literatura mexicana del siglo XX* (Mexico City, Empresas Editoriales, 1965), pp. 411, 424†

As in her two earlier works of fiction, *Balún Canán* and *Royal City*, [Castellanos in *Business of Thunder*] analytically lays bare the pattern of relations between Indian and *ladino* ["white"] which influences all aspects and levels of life in traditional San Cristóbal Las Casas, provincial center of highlands Chiapas. . . .

Preoccupied with the relationship between reality and myth, the work is constructed on two contrasting temporal planes. The action unfolds in a clearly historical framework—the period of the 1930's and just after, the epoch of Cárdenas and high point of the Mexican Revolution. In contrast, time for the Tzotzil Indian has the ahistorical quality of Indian legend. The opening paragraphs set the scene in San Juan Chamula, Tzotzil religious and political center, in terms of a Christianized myth, recounted in the language and images of the *Popol Vuh*, Mayan version of the creation. At the novel's end, the defeated Indian rebellion is synthesized, not in terms of battles won or lost, but in the form of newly fashioned myth. . . .

The winds of reform, in the view of Rosario Castellanos, have been blocked from reaching the valley of San Cristóbal, as though the surrounding mountains had been erected to serve the prejudices of the controlling class of aristocratic *ladino* landholders. In effect, her novelistic interpretation indicts the Revolution for having succumbed to easy compromise at Indian expense, rather than do battle with the entrenched conservative forms, including the church, which conspire to retain centuries-old semifeudalism.

Unlike earlier views of the Indian, Castellanos' vision does not gloss over the negative effects of blind superstition, of ritualistic alcoholism, of daily, relentless humiliation. But there is also consistent affirmation, especially in the hope that springs up in each generation, and in the grim, almost subconscious determination to survive the buffetings of a hostile fate, all of which form part of the Tzotzil mentality. . . .

The determinant in Indian life is the presence of the dominant society, presented in *Business of Thunder* through a series of *ladino* characters of various social classes. Most interesting are the traditional landholder and his embittered wife, their unhappy daughter, a guilt-ridden bishop, and an ambitious priest. The most striking common characteristic in all these individuals is the degree to which their entire system of values has been corroded by a blend of hatred and fear of the Indians, upon whom they depend but whom they regard as inferior, distasteful, and essentially unredeemable. In a manner reminiscent of Faulkner, Castellanos dramatizes the human equation of prejudice: perpetration of injustice upon a vulnerable cultural group can be achieved only at the expense of corrupting and deforming the institutions—social, religious, political—of the exploiters.

Joseph Sommers. After the Storm (Albuquerque,
University of New Mexico Press, 1968), pp. 167–69

The new approach toward the Indian in the Mexican novel, inspired by narrative-type works coming from some anthropologists, finds its ideal exponent in Rosario Castellanos. Raised in the midst of the Tzotzil culture in Chiapas, she began to realize in the mid-1950s her rather unique opportunity for providing a new interpretation to the long-stereotyped Indian theme. The happy result can be seen in four works she published between 1957 and 1964, two volumes of stories and two novels. The first of these was *Balún Canán*, a novel which marked the beginning of the new trend. Here she treats the Indians as humans rather than as types, and she recognizes—and makes excellent use of—the value and force of the cultural heritage of the Tzotzil tribe. Because of this her Indian novels are more complex, less superficial, decidedly more natural and convincing than [B.] Traven's. . . . Not that she solves the Indian problem any more than Traven did, but she puts it into clearer focus and, by revealing the Indian capacity for absorbing the present into the myths and traditions of the past, she shows how he can look through his eternal role as the exploited and still have the strength to survive.

This is Rosario Castellanos's special contribution to the literature of her land, yet it is but one of the reasons for saluting this rather remarkable lady. We recall the distinct merits of her other literary efforts—poetry, essays, criticism, and fiction—and add the edifying effect of her many personal qualities—serenity, peace, love, leadership—and we reach the happy conclusion that Rosario Castellanos is easily one of the most important and admirable figures in the current Mexican literary scene.

Walter M. Langford. *The Mexican Novel Comes of Age*
(Notre Dame, Ind., University of Notre Dame Press,
1971), pp. 184–85

[*Family Album*] by Rosario Castellanos, Mexico's leading woman author and presently her country's ambassador to Israel, comprises three short stories and one novelette, all of which portray feminine characters in more or less typical contemporary situations. "Cooking Lesson," the best of the collection, records the interior monologue of a young, career-minded housewife whose thoughts wander in phenomenological patterns as she inadvertently burns a steak she is preparing for her tradition-bound husband. The meat, shrunken and toughened through overexposure to heat, appears to symbolize the couple's marriage, which is constantly being eroded by friction and rapidly approaching the inevitable breakdown. Here form and content fuse, the protagonist's fleeting psychic digressions reflecting not only the deterioration of her emotional life but the accelerating momentum of change in the physical and social environment as well.

"Sunday" depicts the sterile, frivolous world of an upperclass woman anticipating her next amorous adventure while giving an informal reception, and "Little White-Head" focuses on an aging widow's extreme loneliness, the direct product of an absurdly sheltered and not atypical Latin upbringing. The protagonist of "Family Album," the book's most extensive narration, is a renowned poetess who has just returned to her native Mexico after winning an international literary award. Ironically, however, her escape from a hostile environment into the realm of art, instead of liberating her, has driven her to the point of paranoia.

Rosario Castellanos' hallmarks include linguistic precision, psychological penetration, and wry humor. Her vivid portraits of females groping vainly for identity through a maze of crumbling traditions in a male-dominated society dramatize the plight of today's alienated woman and help explain the mounting incidence of communication failures.

George R. McMurray. BA. 46, Spring, 1972, p. 275

CHOCANO, JOSÉ SANTOS (1875–1934)

PERU

In many of [Chocano's literary] efforts an abundance of apparent *savoir-faire* substitutes for direct inspiration. Where we see his skill in all its glory is in the alexandrine, which he shortens and makes nervous to express action, or which he stretches out serenely in the confidence of a musical strophe. New or renewed images, audacious and classical, are his hallmark, his lyrical stamp. . . . He has invented marvellous images because he sees the world with originality—that is to say, with the eyes of a child or a savage. What we label exaggeration is perhaps only frankness.

Having exploited his special qualities, Chocano is content to use as a motto for his books of poetry Goethe's . . . definition: "Poetry is the art of thinking in images." I would like to juxtapose to this a thought of Carlyle's that could be paraphrased as follows: "Poetry is the art of thinking in melodies." And Chocano's declamatory poetry lacks this vague, ineffable, intimate, floating music. . . . At the risk of provoking his harsh reply, I would assert that if a song tries to express the universal, it is doomed not to be able to express the individual. High-soundingness, the exaggerated daily heroism of a soul that is constantly harassed, the consonantal perfection of these polished verses—none of it ever reaches the heart. (What we would prefer, instead of supermen, are mortal creatures who cry like human beings.)

Chocano will never be the lyric confidant, the confessor to whose books we turn in our sorrow to look with devotion for the fraternal melancholy that will make us feel less forsaken. We accord him admiration, but not love.

Ventura García Calderón. Semblanzas de América
(Madrid, Biblioteca Ariel, 1920), pp. 116–17†

José Santos Chocano belonged, because of his date of birth, and the period during which he wrote, to the modernist generation. . . . But in Chocano's work there is neither affectation nor exoticism nor the influence of foreign literatures. It is almost certain that he did not study any language besides Spanish, not even French. . . .

The creative intellect of Chocano, a man who did not have a humanistic background or a solid knowledge of literature, seems to have been formed by Spanish and Latin American poets. Among the Spaniards, we should cite Balbuena, who vigorously and colorfully sang about Mexican nature; Ercilla, who wrote an epic about the conquest of Chile; and Fernando Velarde, who lived in Peru and praised the Cordillera of the Andes. Among the Latin Americans, Andrés Bello, who instilled in Chocano the literary love of the torrid zone; Olegario Andrade, an energetic precursor of the poetry of strong American feeling; and that fine writer Díaz Mirón. . . .

Chocano sings of the heroic chieftains of yesterday: Caupolicán, Guatemos, Ollanta. He sings of the conquerors: Cortés, Balboa, Pizarro; he sings of the cities of the New World: the conquered city of Tenochtitlán; the newly founded cities of Bogotá and Guatemala City; the brilliant city of the Viceroy, Lima; the modern city of Buenos Aires. . . .

Rufino Blanco-Fombona. *El modernismo y los poetas*
modernistas (Madrid, Editorial Mundo Latino, 1929),
pp. 273–74, 276†

It is a strange man we introduce to you in his first translated verse-book, the most dramatic, tragic figure of a Continent—the *Great Peruvian*, part Indian, part Spaniard, rebellious revolutionist, champion of the masses and of freedom, devout follower of The Christ, warrior like the swordsmen of old, fighting in Mexico, Guatemala—throughout Central America, suffering exile, prison, nicknamed now d'Artagnan, now Cyrano, "*poet by the grace of God*," and always *poeta bárbaro*, a primitive man, at the same time a man of the Renaissance, a man of the Age of Conquest, of Discovery, at times the opaque, hermetic qualities of Indian predominating, again royally arrogant Spaniard. . . . Sometimes when we re-read his many volumes we dream of what the Inca may have said in propitiating prayer to his Sun-God, we recall prophetic fervor of the Psalms, Biblical ecstasy, since religion and art are of the soul.

Tropic lands sweep past so richly we seem visiting some Rajah's royal garden of gigantic flowers. As to form, his sympathies were with the ancient—birds, beasts which kept something pre-glacially suggestive—and he liked the raw gold of the fabulous Indies. He was proud because he was a poet. He was arrogant because he was powerful. And his written word was direct as light. Chocano is like the condor. He confronts space, and his song is stern-fibered, wide-wing-swinging and free.

He was a bird of fire drunk with the heights where he was born, dizzy with the unshaded light of Andean suns—the only suns he knew —and tortured with the insistent picture of the prodigious past of his home, Peru, a past beyond history's accurate estimating, and that royal Spanish race at apogee of power, which other races have never surpassed.

Not since Hafiz has a poet so touched a Continent with sheer vigor. For similarity of influence upon a people we turn to the East where Song was born. And few poets, except again Hafiz (and some Chinese, Persians, Poets of India), have been born into a world of such magnificent mountain-grandeur. It is poets and madmen who are born among the mountains, seldom of monotonous mediocrity of plains.

South America sings him just as camel drivers in the desert, and boatmen on the Red Sea today, after centuries, sing Hafiz.

Edna Worthley Underwood. Foreword to José Santos
Chocano, *Spirit of the Andes* (Portland, Maine,
The Mosher Press, 1935), pp. ix, xi–xii

Chocano's life was spectacular, like that of a modern Benvenuto Cellini. He loved and was loved by many women. He knew the hard floors of prison cells and more than once faced a firing squad. His biography would make a wonderful novel, half heroic and half picaresque. From Mexico to Chile he travelled in search of gold, love and adventure. The most despicable dictators of Latin America entertained him in their blood-stained palaces. He experienced abundance, power, glory, hunger, and disgrace. There was an analogy between his life and his thought. He had no moral control and no sense of social responsibility. According to him the poet was beyond good or evil, a being with all rights and no obligations, superior to society, a superman in the most definite Nietzschean sense. There is only one redeeming feature in this idiosyncrasy: he did not have the conception of sin or crime, he had been anointed poet by the gods and as such he was outside and above all human ways and devices.

Chocano's greatest desire was to be the Poet of America. Once he wrote: "Walt Whitman has the North but the South is mine." In a way he was the poet of his continent, but alas! he was a better interpreter of our topography than of our soul. America was for him a colossal picture and he expressed it in a plastic manner. He wrote beautiful if empty lines to the Inca sun, lightning, thunder, eagles, volcanoes, condors, alligators, boas, the Andes, the Amazon. America was for him a nightmare of grandiloquence. His songs are always introduced by a music of trumpets and drums. . . .

It is true that this strange scene presented by Chocano is part of our life, of our land, and we must give him credit for having created American poetry in direct contrast with those Byzantine poets who take everything from Paris and who believe that beyond Cocteau and Paul Valéry there are no possibilities of aesthetic creation. . . .

Among the poets of the Modernista school Chocano typifies the careful Parnassian. He does not have the exquisite refinement of Rubén Darío, the dreamlike vagueness of Amado Nervo or the tortured imagination of Julio Herrera y Reissig. He liked too well high-sounding words, *wild* metaphors, cyclopean symbols. But he is a robust poet, much more vigorous than all the poets of the younger generation. As I believe that criticism is only an expression of temperaments and as I cordially dislike grandiose poets of the Victor Hugo type, I may be unfair in my estimation of the Peruvian bard, but my candid opinion is that Chocano will be entirely forgotten in fifty years.

Arturo Torres-Ríoseco. BA. 9, Summer, 1935, pp. 251–52

It cannot be denied that much of Chocano's work suffers not only from the superficiality so decried by Peruvians, but perhaps even more from his oratorical emphasis, the noise of cymbals and drums, the exorbitant heroism. In much of his poetry Chocano is like the geraniums of his own Lima, colorful, lush, springing up with tropical ease of growth even in shallow soil. . . . By contrast, Chocano can rise to be a superior painter of the seductive and exotic beauty of American nature, and he is capable of reaching occasional heights of poetic magnificence. The ego in his poetry is unrestrained. He is often bombastic, trite, and irritating. Yet amid all the glittering sequins and the tinseled verbosity there are moments when he is unaffected, natural and touchingly beautiful.

Many reproach Chocano for the lack of intimate feeling in his poetry. Certainly there is an objective, exterior quality in the major part of his poetic work. Yet in the midst of the excitement and the waving banners of his processions, there are sudden clearings of unsuspected simplicity and tender lyricism. The glimpses are brief, but they suggest possibilities in his art that never came to full bloom. The disillusions and reversals of fortune toward the end of his life enriched the soil for the flowering of his intimate "Nocturnos" and the other sensitive poetry of those years. Unfortunately by that time the parade had already passed by, and relatively few turned around for more than a glance. Chocano has never received full attention or a just evaluation of his last poetry. As a triumphant poet he had inspired awe but never affection, and there was no residue of warmth or compassion left to greet these final, moving poems.

Chocano's dramatic and premature success in his own country fostered his extraordinary self-complacency and pride, which in turn fanned his insatiable desire for fame. In part Chocano missed the heights of lasting greatness which might have been his because he squandered his energies in incessant action. Within Chocano existed the shadow of a great poet who never knew how to emerge from the superfluous.

To accept this loss of the highest laurels does not, however, justify the view that Chocano is an outmoded songster of little value, a cheap versifier of the plaza, a sculptor in sand. This is to ignore his considerable impact on Peruvian and continental poetry. The new direction which Chocano gave to Modernism and the telluric American note which he injected into this movement cannot be subtracted from his glory. With all his limitations these contributions balance the scale in favor of considering him a major and irreplaceable figure in Spanish American letters.

"Poet of America," the title bestowed on Chocano at the beginning of the twentieth century, recognized this poet as Spanish America's principal spokesman. It is a fitting title in the sense that Chocano does represent most fully the America of his time—that objective, visible, seething world of late-nineteenth-century Spanish America which continued well into this century.

Phyllis W. Rodríguez-Peralta. *José Santos Chocano*
(New York, Twayne, 1970), pp. 148–49

COELHO NETO, HENRIQUE (1864–1934)

BRAZIL

Coelho Neto has triumphed and achieved success after constant and tenacious struggle, by dint of labor and talent. He has succeeded in keeping the attention of the Brazilian public, which he so accurately analyzed in *The Conquest*, a public that is ignorant, difficult, inattentive, complex. It was a dangerous battle, to be sure, which the distinguished novelist undertook when he first started writing, a battle under ominous and unfavorable signs, which made it a life-or-death battle. This because a literary career was, at that time, a very risky business in that "lost country," as he has one of his characters say for him. . . . For these reasons I think his triumph is doubly deserved and honestly obtained, with complete nobility, a quality characteristic of someone who is generous, and Coelho Neto is generous above all else. He detests injustice as much as anyone else and has made the cause of the oppressed his own, correcting, punishing, setting right, always vigorous, honest, and fair.

And with this analysis of Coelho Neto's spirit, we come to the novel at hand, born spontaneously from the idiosyncrasies of the Brazilian author. What better could we say about *Black King* than that it is a novel that is vigorous in its form, honest and fair in its content? Let me allow its translators to speak [the review is of the French translation]: "*Macambira* [*Black King*] is a robust fresco of racial conflict and evokes the activities of the wealthy haciendas, underlining, in a setting that has [never] changed, the problem of the subjugation of exceptional beings." . . .

Félix Gallo. *Nosotros.* No. 135, March, 1920,
pp. 529–30†

For such early novels as *The Federal Capital* and such later ones as *The Conquest* I can feel no literary interest; they are, together with more than one other of their fellows, valuable for a study of the day in which they were written and for the instable temperament that produced them. Similarly, *Sphynx*, a novel of exotic mystery that begins with high promise, soon descends to the helpless confusion which threatens all dallying with other-worldly themes, particularly when the author would maintain contact with external reality rather than plunge frankly and fearlessly into the unseen realms. As to the short stories, one may open any collection quite at random; the good will be strangely mixed with the bad. Now the tale is a mere excuse for commentary, usually upon men and women and passion, with Coelho Neto in cynical mood; nature becomes a luxuriant, inciting procuress, as witness the long titular story in the collection called *Fountain of Youth*—a tale that, like more than one of Coelho Neto's, belongs rather to the liquor and cigars of stag parties than to literature. Not, understand, because it is "immoral," but because it lacks the texture, the illumination, the significance of art. That he can be sentimental he shows in "Epithalamium" of the same collection; the propaganda impulse is so strong that it overflows into tale after tale. And over it all, the fructifying ardour of his voluptuousness, as prodigal as nature itself, which scatters myriad seeds where only one can take root and thrive. . . .

As a historical phenomenon, Coelho Neto represents veritably a period in the national letters; literature becomes a self-supporting profession—it had already been that with Aluísio de Azevedo—and the production of a steady stream of novels for avid metropolitan readers is as systematized as ever in our own supposedly more materialistic nation.

As an artist, Coelho Neto is less significant; haste, disorientation and constant supply of a none too exigent demand rendered him less exacting with himself—something that by nature he has never been in any case, though he can view his labours objectively and note their demerits. A spontaneous, not a premeditative artist, achieving, at his most happy moments, a glowing union of creature and creation—a creation truly Amazonian in its prodigality of scene and sense, with creatures as unreal, yet as fascinating as itself. This is no small accomplishment, for it makes of the reader a participant, and that is what all art, major or minor, must do. Coelho Neto here expresses not only the ardent Brazilian dwelling amidst a phantasmagoria of the senses; this overflow of primitive instincts is a human heritage that, with its torch of life, makes us no less than the one touch of nature, kin to the rest of the world. . . .

Isaac Goldberg. Brazilian Literature (New York,
Alfred A. Knopf, 1922), pp. 258–60

The spareness of expression of a great many of our modern writers, principally novelists . . . who forge their verbal instrument with difficulty, explains the rejection of Coelho Neto's style, opulent and luxuriant, in recent decades. The first accusation cast at him is his overuse of difficult and uncommon words. It is true that Coelho Neto carries this at times to excess, to affectation. But in general, especially in some of his novels, such exaggerations are not damaging to the whole. Euclides da Cunha also emphatically insisted on difficult writing, and the number of unusual words is vast, without his style's suffering in its intimate structure. . . .

Then there is another accusation: prolixity. The author himself recognized that he should rid part of his work of the surfeit of words, and he attempted one day to realize this project. But the truth is that novels like *Whirlwind, Mirage, The Dead Man* did not need his pruning and others only very little.

There is a third accusation: the dominance of form over content; the words do not match the ideas exactly and the drunkenness over words interferes with the writer's ability to make his subject matter live totally. This is [José] Veríssimo's accusation of "complication without complexity," or Tristão de Ataíde's "he turns everything he touches into literature." These words give us a summarial and exaggerated judgment. One cannot say that, in the novels mentioned above, there is mere complication; these are novels in which the form is at one with the content. . . .

Brito Broca. In Aurelio Buarque de Holanda [Ferreira],
ed., O romance brasileiro (de 1752 a 1930) (Rio de
Janeiro, Edições O Cruzeiro, 1952), pp. 240–41†

Placing himself outside literary schools and currents, always faithful to artistic truth, which he was able to confirm through experience, Coelho Neto left us a vast panorama of our most intimate reality from the years that preceded the Republic through the end of the third decade of this century. It is a complete panorama, and quite an extraordinary one, one I do not believe was equaled by any other of the major writers of fiction of the period. And by speaking in this way, I am not overlooking any of the admirable portraits that Aluísio de Azevedo made—impressive in the immediacy of their truth, undoubtedly, but limited in sensitivity because of his enslavement to literary formulas that were narrow and transitory. Nor am I overlooking the profound analyses that we owe to Machado de Assis—powerful in their psychological detail, in their sensitivity, but unfortunately circumscribed by a narrow world, which was timid and limited. . . .

If one takes all of his novels, short stories, dramas, apologias, and legends as a single vision of man, of his psychological and social truth, Coelho Neto's work seems to me to be an immense *portrait* of our national life during a curious and difficult period, which began during the last quarter of the nineteenth century and reached its culmination during the first quarter of our century.

Octávio de Faria. Introduction to Henrique Coelho Neto,
Romance, 2nd ed. (Rio de Janeiro, Livraria Agir
Editôra, 1963), p. 9†

In an inventory of Brazilian fiction of the end of the nineteenth century and the first decades of the twentieth, one name cannot be forgotten, not only because of the number of works that he published but also because of the influence he exercised on Brazilian literary life for a long time. I refer to Coelho Neto, an unequaled figure in our literature, but of late somewhat forgotten. He wrote nearly twenty novels, which are quite varied; many different types populate his fictional world. . . .

Which character of his is most suited to this study of heroines of the Brazilian novel? I opt for Violante, the central figure of *Whirlwind*, a novel singled out by some critics as one of the best, if not the best, of his works. Violante is one of those frivolous and restless girls who, according to the prejudices of the period, was considered hare-brained. . . . Her habitual concerns are doing and undoing her hair, polishing her nails, spending her days on the seat of a swing, reading novels, and, in the afternoons . . . leaning out of the window to look at the trains in the Central Station (she lived on Rua Senador Eusébio), and receiving love notes that the young men slide through the slats of the blinds. . . .

She is very representative of the girl from a middle-class family that had fallen upon bad days. And the Violante type was common in all of the large cities and can frequently be encountered in the novels and stories of our urban fiction. In this book of Coelho Neto's she exercises on her declining family the effect of a cataclysm, precipitating a complete moral, social, and economic collapse. The author was cruel and pitiless with her and with the whole family. . . .

Whirlwind was a transitional novel, as were all of the works of that extraordinary writer, Coelho Neto. A product of naturalism and the first wave of realism, his books, especially his novels, are not aligned with any school and are characterized by an exuberant verbalism, by eloquence, and by formal rigor, qualities that today militate against the survival of his books. . . .

Santos Moraes. *Heroinas do romance brasileiro*
(Rio de Janeiro, Editôra Expressão e Cultura, 1971),
pp. 167–68, 170–71†

CONTI, HAROLDO (1925–   )

ARGENTINA

The great protagonist [of *Southeasterly*] is the river [that is, the Río de la Plata]. Images of it strike us persistently: the broad current of waters that are not very deep, the reeds, the mud, the ditches, all illuminated by the different hues of day and the passing of the seasons. When the novel closes, the river remains the protagonist, flowing, calm, permitting men to live on it and from it. I am inevitably reminded of another great river, great in the annals of literature—Mark Twain's Mississippi. The Río de la Plata, like the Mississippi, is given its personality through the reflection of the men who inhabit it. And one can speak of inhabiting a river because these men are to be found with their feet in the water. They live from what comes out of that water; they find shelter in floating or grounded vessels, their backs to civilization, with which they have only infrequent contacts.

Of course, there are noteworthy differences in the presentation of the two rivers. As opposed to the humor of the North American master, we have here a dry, descriptive objectivity, given nuance by poetic sentiment. Whereas Twain presented the good and bad in life, Conti presents life as inexorable—neither good nor bad but fatal, a fatality against which it is not worth the bother to act. And in this sense we can speak of pessimism in this novel.

The forces of nature, which so many Latin American novelists have enjoyed portraying, in this novel do not try to steal the foreground from the men who must suffer those forces. Not too long ago, I wrote in these pages about the struggle of a boat against the elements in a novel by Goyanarte. If we go farther back, we would come to [Rivera's] *The Vortex*. Wherever we turn, we would find a writer affirming himself as such through his ability to describe the violence of the elements, the force of the terrestrial environment, and to describe man, overwhelmed or triumphant because of it, but in any case facing up to it.

Jorge Campos. *Insula.* No. 196, March, 1963, p. 11†

In literature and art the landscape has always been of interest to the contemplator as a frame of reference on which he can project himself. He looks upon settings without objectivity, caught between the necessities of action and the urgency of his feelings. Conti . . . in his river cycle selects sites of striking sadness, the withered splendor of houses that have not changed [since the turn of the century]. His men are solitary beings in a world of isolated individuals, and they sense a companionship with boats, hold onto the dream of navigation, always a remote ideal.

El Boga [in *Southeasterly*] is alone, but he has the sky and a broad river, and there is a symphonic link between the distant current and his solitude, just as there exists a tacit correspondence between the man who departs—Silvestre [in *Around about the Cage*]—and the man who awakens—Milo [in the same novel]—a faith in the continuity of life: the old man has been saying goodbye since his appearance and the boy awakens to adventure. The contradictions—the discontinuity—are a negating, mysterious principle, opposed to inner needs but eventually corresponding to external order, which is poised hesitantly between what exists and what is latent. Examples are the attack on and burning of the boat at night in *Southeasterly*, a police persecution that is both aggressive and benevolent . . . in *Around about the Cage*, or the sinister strategies . . . with which the new prefect corners the vague "comrade" in *The Hyperboreans*. . . .

Despite the tone of supreme sadness that dominates almost all Conti's work—a feeling, according to Poe, that is inseparable from poetry—a sadness with no other modulation than an irony that is almost as melancholy, the sense of continuity (Milo in the old age of Silvestre) represents a triumph of the living, the tacit understanding that it is not worth dying.

Rodolfo Benasso. *El mundo de Haroldo Conti*
(Buenos Aires, Editorial Galerna, 1969), pp. 28–29†

Among the Argentine writers of his generation . . . whose central trait is a realism inclined toward social and political criticism, at times marked by a tone of anger or of anguish, Conti's work is distinct because of a tenuous lyricism that tempers reality. More than in politics or society, he is interested in the conflicts of individual consciences. Hence the slow and reflective rhythm we find in his books, above all in his two most important ones. The first of these, *Southeasterly*, brought a note of freshness and simplicity that were almost nonexistent in the contemporary Argentine novel. It revealed, moreover, various virtues that, taken together, represent an attitude of exemplary artistic honesty: a profound familiarity with one's surrounding and with the characters portrayed, the serious goal of creating a dignified work stripped of all facile devices; a deft assimilation of the very valid lessons of kindred older writers.

Conti's two books of short stories [*All the Summers, With Other People*] and his second novel [*Round about the Cage*] were not, in my opinion, so successful. . . . But in his latest book, *While Alive*, there reemerged the vigorous and profound narrator, capable once again of giving the full measure of his strong creative urge. If he is able in his next novel to join this strength to a greater rigor of composition and maintain his seriousness and the attention to details, he will write what undoubtedly will be his most comprehensive and accomplished work.

Fernando Rosemberg. *RI*. 38, July–Sept., 1972, pp. 521–22†

The Argentine Haroldo Conti is the author of five novels, the latest of which, *While Alive*, was awarded the Premio Barral de Novela in May 1971. Like the Uruguayan Juan Carlos Onetti, Conti writes about lives that are physically and psychologically constricted, enclosed within the city in rooms, bars, offices. When his characters venture into the open, more often than not they do so in darkness or half-light. Confined by circumstance, they seem to move without touching or changing one another. This inexorable process of alienation leads inevitably to solitude.

Oreste, the protagonist of *While Alive*, moves in a world of monotonous realities and ineffectual fantasy, a world he tries to escape by leaving the city on weekends to be with his friends. His marriage has long since crumbled, and he is alienated from his children; his fellow workers lead lives as dull as his own. He abandons Buenos Aires to live with Margarita, a whore. His circle of friends is suddenly dissolved by death, illness and absences, but these disasters seem to have little effect on his life. . . . When his son Marcelo comes looking for him, Oreste asks Margarita to deny that she has ever known him. As the disappointed Marcelo walks away, Oreste, watching him, impulsively hides—"in case the boy should turn his head." The story has come to its dismal ending, and we are left with the vague impression that a final opportunity has been met with a last denial.

Vague, because the motives of these characters are forever unclear. In Conti's unfortunate style—a hodgepodge of borrowed techniques, gratuitous crudities and awkward poeticism—the cycle of alienation extends to the reader, and whatever effect may have been intended is irremediably lost.

Raquel H. Ferguson. *BA*. 46, Autumn, 1972, pp. 630–31

CORTÁZAR, JULIO (1914–   )

ARGENTINA

The eight stories in [*Bestiary*] constitute eight . . . settings of terror. Developing them with strokes of unique mastery, [Cortázar] is the master of a style that deserves to be called personal; each setting flows from the soul of an exceptionally prophetic being, a man or woman whose impetuous sensibility feels or has a presentiment about the existence of other noises, other movements, other lives. Each situation in *Bestiary* confronts us with the boundary of reality itself, with that point at which fantasy emerges as a product of logical order, of exacerbated lucidity.

The phantoms . . . who seek out and imprison the characters of Cortázar often take the form of rodents and insects. It is not a matter then of subtle, vague presences that cannot be grasped. But these small monsters . . . do not form the bestiary. The bestiary is made up of those who unleash the fury of these insects, the ones who, upon calling them, let them in. The terrified ones are the human beings who narrate their histories to us or the histories of people they have known, and who revere their curse, finding pleasure in it; they are the ones who create the peculiar setting of panic and destruction within which these stories take place.

The monsters, like the rabbits that emerge from the entrails of the desperate occupant of the apartment on Suipacha Street, emanate from the characters and are ultimately the characters themselves. . . . The horror—the atmosphere of horror—is born [when], upon feeling themselves discovered, the characters in *Bestiary* see their inwardness fractured and feel themselves harassed by it under the animal form that represents or symbolizes it.

Sebastián Salazar Bondy. *Sur*. No. 201, July, 1951,
p. 109†

[Cortázar] attracted notice for *The Kings*, a dramatic poem in prose, a prose of noteworthy forcefulness in presenting images and ideas. In it he offered a curious variation on the myth of the Minotaur. Ariadne, in love with her monstrous brother the Minotaur, gives the thread to Theseus, not so that he could find his way safely out of the labyrinth but so that the Minotaur could kill him and escape. But the Minotaur prefers to die. He allows himself to be killed in order to survive darkly in the dreams and instincts of Ariadne [and also] in the dreams and instincts of all men. The Minotaur, from then on, will dwell in our blood, will control us like a spirit.

As early as *The Kings* we can see Cortázar's favorite theme: the monstrous, the bestial, is mysteriously attached to human destiny. It is worth noting the very significant title of the book that he published next—*Bestiary*, a collection of fantastic stories. And in *The End of the Game*, also a collection of stories, the theme reappears in "Axolotl," where the narrator thinks that he is one of the monsters that he is looking at in the aquarium. . . . It is possible that a careless reader, impressed by the sharp eye for details with which Cortázar begins his narratives, will believe that he is going to see men and things from everyday life. But he will soon discover that an air of hallucination and poetry creeps into the spaces between reality, enveloping reality and turning it into a phantasmagoria. . . .

Despite all this, his stories are not successful. One expects more from a writer who is so intelligent, learned, imaginative, and observant as Cortázar is. He seems to write them listlessly, with the sense of defeat of a young man who has arrived too late and finds himself faced with a literature—Kafka, Borges—that he admires and knows he cannot surpass. . . .

Enrique Anderson Imbert. *RI*. 23, Jan.–June, 1958, pp. 173–74†

In the course of his work Cortázar has touched upon many different topics and settings. There are figures from classical mythology, dream subjects presented as living persons, tales—very felicitous ones—some of which take place in Buenos Aires, others in Paris, and yet others . . . in pure fantasy. Yet throughout there is a clear poetic and stylistic unity. There is also a very marked Argentine and American stamp, even when the characters are not [from Buenos Aires]. They are works sprung from that cosmopolitan city, the fruit of the sharp, playful Buenos Aires intelligence, demonstrating a zest for life and the world. Intentionally or not, they are earthy in flavor.

Fanciful literature has legitimate status in Argentina. Cortázar belongs to a tradition begun by Lugones, culminating in Borges, and carried on by his successors. Without Cortázar, however, that tradition would be truncated and stunted, even though the splendid work of Borges would be enough in itself to justify any literary style. Through Cortázar's work, that tradition is reinforced, given continuity, and gains in variety and richness. . . .

Among the writers of his country Cortázar admits his predilection for two whom many consider antithetical figures—the masterful Jorge Luis Borges and the vigorous, rough Roberto Arlt. . . . For Cortázar, the influence of Borges, as dangerous as it is fruitful, found a drastic compensation in Roberto Arlt. And there were others. Almost all of Borges' admirers imitate him even to his sources, one of which is Kafka. But Cortázar has not taken that attitude. The reading of contemporary writers who use very different techniques gradually led Cortázar to synthesize the most diverse influences. Beginning with *Bestiary*, the author continually makes use of the inner monologue, a technique not common in Borges. Then we learn that long ago he read James Joyce and Virginia Woolf.

As a rule the best literature he read was in English and French. In the Spanish language the poets apparently interested him more than the writers of prose. Aside from the classics—Berceo to Góngora—he admires Luis Cernuda, Federico García Lorca, and Vicente Aleixandre. He likes César Vallejo, Pablo Neruda, and Octavio Paz among the Latin Americans; and of his fellow countrymen he prefers Ricardo Molinari and Alberto Girri. He believes that the novel and the short story are at a very high point in Latin America today. He is genuinely enthusiastic about Alejo Carpentier, Juan Rulfo, and Miguel Ángel Asturias. He is also very fond of the Mexican writers Juan José Arreola and Carlos Fuentes.

José Durand. Américas. 15, 3, March, 1963, p. 43

In theory and practice [Cortázar] seeks a total renovation, not out of an eagerness for originality but out of internal necessity. The renovation consists of the destruction of character, situation, literary style, forms ("of the formulas," he clarifies), and language. He speaks out against deceptive narrative easiness . . . padded literature, verbal clichés; and he asks for a literature that is the "least literary possible," in short, an anti-literature, which dares to transgress the total literary deed, the book. He wants to open up the closed literary order, to establish an open order that offers multiple perspectives. Even more, he chiefly wants disorder, the breaking of logical and discursive expression into a disconnected and fragmented story, which he feels can best be compared to a kaleidoscope. . . .

Cortázar does not adopt this narrative conduct only to shock the naïve reader or to be in the height of literary fashion. . . . Within the aesthetic cosmos that he wants "chaos" to be, the organization of the story and idiomatic invention have a function and are justified by the total context. Therefore, I suspect that it does not much matter to Cortázar that he is accused of snobbery or of dealing with "worn-out novelties."

Ana María Barrenechea. Sur. No. 288, May–June, 1964, pp. 70–71†

The work of Julio Cortázar seems to me to be particularly representative of Latin American literature of today: both lively and learned, at the same time worldly and very secret. . . . This literature is thus linked to Borges, but also reacts [against him] . . . no less deliberate, but with more obvious passion. Its games hide neither life nor death. . . .

This short story ["Axolotl"], six or seven pages long, casts us far from ourselves, bewildering us, leading us around, losing us, saving us again, finally placing us beyond all disquietude and repose. . . . It is the story of a man who contemplates the axolotls every day in the Botanical Gardens and who one day becomes an axolotl—axolotls are a kind of lizard and their name is Mexican. . . . One crosses through a glass, one becomes what one sees without ceasing to be oneself, while that transparent obstacle is an absolute obstacle that prevents communication even if it does open up a mysterious going and coming between the "I" and the "Other." Cortázar's story is rooted in a consciousness without memory, which perceives without losing itself. The "I" is indifferently the man and the axolotl; the "Other" is indifferently the man and the axolotl. However the "I" is also the one who is writing, the one who passes through the glass, who goes from the one to the other, who adds to consciousness a little bit of reality, shreds of memory. Because of the "I-Author" each movement has a meaning, becomes readable. . . . We are the man, we are the axolotl, we are buried alive, we crush our faces (but which face?) against the aquarium. The glass cuts us in two. We are the animal with two backs.

René Micha. NRF. No. 140, Aug., 1964, pp. 314–15†

Subtle, delicate, wavering, contradictory, the short stories of Cortázar make us marvel, but their meaning seems to slip through our hands like so much brilliant dust, like so much unstill and slippery water. The difficulties presented by his first stories turn out, nevertheless, to be almost insignificant if we compare them to the problems that arise in some of the particularly "abstract" stories of the second period. I refer to the stories of Cortázar which appeared first in literary reviews (some of the most interesting and significant ones in Ciclón of Havana) and which later were almost all grouped together to form the second part of the volume *Stories of Cronopios and Famas*.

Humor, a love for exact details of the daily life of Buenos Aires, an ironic-fantastic imagination, the creation of new words . . . are all mixed together from the first pages. "I've been working for years in UNESCO," the author confesses to us in "Possibilities for Abstraction," "as well as for other international organizations, despite which I still have some sense of humor left and especially a noteworthy capacity for abstraction—that is to say, if I don't like someone, I erase him from the map by the decision itself and while he talks and talks I go on to Melville and the poor devil believes that I'm listening to him."

When we get to the series of stories that provides the title for the collection, which carries the long subtitle "First & Still Uncertain Appearance of Cronopios, Famas, and Esperanzas, Mythological Phase," the characteristics of Cortázar's style seem to become accentuated. The most visible and surprising characteristic is the creation of neologisms. The first paragraph of the first story ("Customs of the Famas") introduces six words totally unknown to the reader (or at least unknown in their new meanings). . . . The incorporation into a literary text of such a considerable number of words invented by the writer to such an extent that we could call it saturation (the reader could attempt to decipher the first word, to imagine a possible translation of the second into ordinary language, but when there are so many, he feels overwhelmed and gives up), is not in itself something all that new. . . . It is often meant to create parody or humor. But such a goal is not quite so clear here. [1965]

Manuel Durán. In *La vuelta a Cortázar en nueve ensayos* (Buenos Aires, Carlos Pérez Editor, 1968), pp. 33–35†

[Cortázar's] *The Winners* . . . showed the extent of his ambitious seriousness. . . . By [a] somewhat creaking device, an assortment of Buenos Aires citizens are gathered in a ship; the crew behaves mysteriously; large areas of the ship are off limits; speculation, bewilderment, and resentment abound; the reader expects a large action near the end, but in fact the book peters out mildly. Fair enough; the real subject was the behavior of the passengers under stress. The book was interesting because of the wide range of characters, their depth and solidity: One had the impression that Señor Cortázar was writing about a world he knew well and viewed with considerable skepticism and wariness. *Hopscotch* is completely different in everything except its length and ambition. It is, in fact, an anti-novel.

Horacio Oliveira, an Argentinian in middle life, goes to Paris and slips easily into the floating life of a feckless expatriate, drifting from furnished room to room, holding long and increasingly vague conversations, his life measured out with books, records, and endlessly dissected love affairs. His mistress, La Maga, and his friends, a loose-knit group called "the Club," appear to have more or less coherent personalities, but it is Oliveira's ambition to fragment his personality so that he goes through life in a series of present moments which never cohere into a perceived whole. To convey his attempt to do this, Señor Cortázar has recourse to a method of writing designed to dissuade the reader, once and for all, from any attempt to add the book up; disjointed scenes, containing much the same kind of material and written in much the same manner, follow one another in a relentless procession; the interminable conversations of the Club, in which ideas are not so much discussed as washed slowly from side to side until they disintegrate, alternate with indeterminate love scenes.

Finally, the impact of definite tragic event, the death of La Maga's child, shakes Oliveira down from his perch of non-attachment. . . . He then returns to Argentina, where an old friend gets him a job in a circus. The change of scene does nothing to alter Oliveira's determination to cast adrift from human contact as before, to float in an Empyrean of disassociation, which is conveyed in the same remorseless detail. The book ends with almost a hundred short "expendable chapters," to be fitted in or not as the reader chooses; these are sometimes fragments of the story, scraps of dialogue, etc., and sometimes footnotes on the method of the novel provided by one Morelli, who seems to be a surrogate for the author. . . .

This striving towards a new mode of consciousness, the real subject of the book, will be sympathetically received in Paris, where Señor Cortázar makes his home and where the mark of an "advanced" writer is his search for a pure distillation of consciousness that refuses to concur in any conventional act such as the making of moral judgments. How a life so emptied of significance can engage the interest of a reader of novels, I don't know, but that is the sort of question one doesn't ask. Certainly, to say that *Hopscotch* is monumentally boring would not be felt by its admirers as a disabling criticism, since that, among other things, is what it is evidently intended to be, and *vive le sport*.

John Wain. *NYR*. April 28, 1966, pp. 18–19

Julio Cortázar is an Argentinian who, since the publication of *Hopscotch* in 1963, has acquired a reputation as the first great novelist of Latin America. Although this judgment is unfair to half a dozen of his contemporaries and one or two of his predecessors, his work, now widely translated, and perhaps rather too extravagantly promoted on the Continent and in the United States, certainly represents a remarkable achievement. . . .

Señor Cortázar is very interested—and he has every right to be—in structures and patterns. He sees human beings not as characters in a conventional sequence (his characterization is deliberately superficial) but as constellations in a vast structure outside time. His characters are involved in a sort of ritual dance. The more meaningless the dance, the more pleasing the patterns. In the "expendable" chapters [of *Hopscotch*], which should be incorporated into the second or alternative reading, absurd, eccentric tit-bits are collected (law reports, an elaborate plan to rationalize the world, a letter to *The Observer* on the scarcity of butterflies) and mingled with the narrative as simply part of a composite aesthetic structure. The expendable chapters also attempt to offer something of a new perspective to the original narrative, in Proustian manner, for there is a good deal of fresh background information on the characters in them. Oliveira's second love affair in Paris, for instance, only hinted at on first reading, is dealt with more roundly. Also a great deal of reflexion on the novelist's art is introduced, just in case we miss the point of Señor Cortázar's eccentric quest.

Unfortunately, Señor Cortázar is not content merely to present some sort of abstracted aesthetic pattern, but is constantly straining for meanings which this pattern is not adequate to embody. The game of hopscotch not only symbolizes the abstract dance of human beings. The hopper's arrival at the last square or "heaven" is called upon to symbolize some sort of mystical truth, an ultimate meaning beyond the false superstructure of society. The game of hopscotch is in fact a highly unsatisfactory mandala.

Part of the excellence of *Hopscotch* lies in its use of language, in its experiments with many different, some very original, types of Spanish carefully juxtaposed; the spirit of Argentina, for instance, is nostalgically conveyed in the Paris scenes by the occasional use of Buenos Aires dialect, for which Señor Cortázar has a very good ear. The translation, which is sometimes very clumsy indeed, does not, possibly could not, capture these modulations.

TLS. March 9, 1967, p. 181

All Antonioni fans should have Julio Cortázar's new book, for no other reason than the fact it contains a potent short story, "The Devil's Drivel," which the now-famous film [*Blow-Up*] used as a source. Anyone interested in witnessing a first-class literary imagination at work should have it too.

[The English collection] *The End of the Game, and Other Stories* is a selection from *Bestiary, Secret Weapons,* and *The End of the Game*, three books of short stories by Cortázar, whose novel *Hopscotch* made such an impression last year and won a National Book Award for its translator, Gregory Rabassa. The stories here, beautifully translated by Paul Blackburn, complete our image of their 53-year-old Argentine author. Most of them were written well before he started either his first novel, *The Winners*, or the later *Hopscotch*. All but one are very much in the realm of the "fantastic" short fiction so dear to Latin American writers—stories where situations tend to be resolved esthetically or symmetrically. But Cortázar's short stories really do exhaust the genre. Some of them go to the limits of fantasy, offering broken patterns which gradually form themselves into a climactic ceremonial act, where the hero finds himself living out a repetition of an age-old role.

The stories pivot on children's games, the camera's eye, labyrinths, mirrors. It is the world that Jorge Luis Borges helped open. It is also the world of what Cortázar calls "the figures." In a recent interview he said that "apart from our individual lots, we all inadvertently form part of larger figures. For instance, we at this moment may be a part of a structure that prolongs itself at a distance of perhaps 200 meters from here. I'm constantly sensing the possibility of certain links, of circuits that close around us." Cortázar's short stories are full of juxtapositions and flukes: *déjà vu* is everywhere.

Alexander Coleman. *NYT*. July 9, 1967, p. 5

Some of these fifteen stories [in the English collection *The End of the Game, and Other Stories*] justify some of the high praise I have read of Cortázar. They are quickly and credibly complex, mysterious, sad, bizarre. A few of the stories, like the title piece, seem to me to go through a mimesis of significance without really signifying much. And, unfortunately, the longest piece in the book—a novella called "The Pursuer"—is outstandingly the worst: a juvenile and crude story about a jazz critic in Paris and an American jazz musician. Overtones are attempted about the relation between creator and commentator, but it comes out a thin imitation of that spate of fiction in the last thirty years about jazzmen who have to blow it true or die, and who almost always do both. . . .

But the good stories, which are also the well-rendered ones, comprise more than half the book. Cortázar's obsessions are the intangibly oppressive, the inexplicably compelling, the imaginary, the contradictions between the imagination and the seeming world, as well as the contradictions within the imagination itself—in short, the subject of conflicting realities. The good stories are steeped in a melancholy which, so to speak, Cortázar earns. That is, he does not assume that he has a citizen's right to malaise as an inhabitant of the mid-20th century, along with the right to free speech and due process of law. The melancholic atmosphere is legitimate; it seems to have existed before the story begins. These stories would be different if there had never been a Svevo or Kafka or Machado de Assis, but Cortázar is more than a synthesizer: he has a concern and a voice of his own.

Two of the stories deal with identities that are exchanged through intensity of imagination. A man goes to the aquarium so often to watch a strange fish that he finally becomes (or imagines he is) the fish watching the man. A woman dreams of a beggar woman on a bridge in Budapest where she has never been. When she arrives in Budapest, she meets the beggar woman, they embrace, then she remains on the bridge and watches herself walk away. In a variation of this theme, a man sees a boy on a Paris bus who looks like him and figuratively adopts him as his son; the boy becomes his immortality. When the boy dies, the persistence of nature, as represented by a yellow flower—the immortality of nature as against the mortality of any one man—drives the man to become a drunkard.

Stanley Kauffmann. NR. July 15, 1967, p. 22

Cortázar defines his conception [of the figura], in *Hopscotch*, as:

> A crystallization which . . . would permit a ubiquitous and total comprehension of all its reasons for being, whether they were disorder itself, inanity, or gratuity. A crystallization in which nothing would be subsumed, but where a lucid eye might peep into the kaleidoscope and understand the great polychromatic rose, understand it as a figura, an imago mundi that outside the kaleidoscope would resolve into a Provençal-style living room, or a concert of aunts having tea and Bagley biscuits.

It is in Cortázar's first novel, *The Winners*, published in Buenos Aires in 1960, that the concept of *figura* arises. The epigraph from Dostoevsky speaks of the difficult necessity in fiction of treating ordinary people, who are uninteresting but "the chief and essential links in the chain of human affairs." Several of these *bonaerenses* [people from Buenos Aires] of different class backgrounds win a pleasure cruise (destination unknown) in a lottery and gather on the ship, areas of which are mysteriously forbidden to them. Once underway, a few of the passengers come to suspect there is an epidemic aboard, concealed by the crew, the port authorities, and perhaps the nebulous government. The threat of a hidden other dimension, which Cortázar treated individually and fantastically in his first stories, becomes now a multiple, quotidian, collective affair. Disposed by chance, evasive officialdom and the labyrinthine passageways of the ship as on an enormous game-board, some passengers revolt and try to unite and penetrate the enigma, while others retreat and socialize and protest their companions' rash disturbance of the peace; all in any case confirm or deny what is within themselves. Presented discretely by the invisible author and sur-veyed in visionary monologues by a marginal character named Persio, this promising design is cut short when one lucid passenger is senselessly killed after breaking into the forbidden area (which keeps its secret) and the rest are whisked back to Buenos Aires by official plane and dispersed at their starting point. In *The Winners*, the emergent *figura* has ample implications, serving in part as an allegory of frustrated Argentina, seen from the ground up as interlocking varieties of *mauvaise foi*, and in part as an allegory of all frustrated attempts upon Theseus-monsters and their false order. But it proceeds mostly on the level of objective presentation by fairly conventional devices. In *Hop-scotch*, however, Cortázar tries to fashion a *figura* which will at once embrace not only character, relationship and setting, but also the book itself, its devices, its sources, and the reader's perception of it all.

Though considerably longer, *Hopscotch* concentrates on one char-acter instead of many, an Argentine named Horacio Oliveira, a stub-born spiritual expatriate whatever his surroundings, whose voyage is never completed either, but in a different way. His basic movement to Paris and back, in search of a place to be, is meant to serve as a com-mon meeting ground for reader and author. It is a fable not only of all provincial pilgrimages to the City but also—as the Mexican novelist Carlos Fuentes has observed—of the deeper New World quest for a utopia, an El Dorado, or what Oliveira sometimes calls a "kibbutz of desire." Oliveira's ventures are also a version of Cortázar's own, in both an artistic and an autobiographical sense. *Hopscotch* obviously represents a radical effort by the author to overcome any fixed, com-fortable rhetoric he may have devised for himself in the past, and to realize his potentialities in the fullest way. Cortázar tries to reinvent himself as creator much as his protagonist seeks to do as human being, in a manner especially foreshadowed by the self-destructive parable of artistic creation in "The Devil's Drivel." And, as an integral part of this process, the reader is called upon to contribute a large share of inven-tion as well.

James E. Irby. *Novel*. 1, Fall, 1967, pp. 66–67

When Cortázar's most successful novel, *Hopscotch*, was published here last year, I read it with great pleasure . . . and boredom . . . and irrita-tion! Here was a man whose writing flashed with wit, superb imagery and who obviously was possessed of—and by—a fantastic imagination. But what of the endless self-indulgences? The tricks and games played not with or for—but on the reader.

In [the English collection *The End of the Game, and Other Stories*], a culling of stories from three previously untranslated collections, the shorter form allows no time for the merely tricky. Yet what magnificent tricks Cortázar *does* play. . . . Still a bright texture of reality runs through these stories. It is as if Cortázar is showing us first that it is essential for us to reimagine the reality in which we live and which we can no longer take for granted; and second, he shows us how to do this by the use of infinite variety and possibilities. (This variety, these possibilities, of course, all carry with them the threat of danger—people are always going out too far in the exercise of the imagination.) . . .

In "The Devil's Drivel," the story on which Antonioni loosely based his film [*Blow-Up*], an amateur photographer (we are all dabblers in perceiving reality, Cortázar implies) takes unsolicited, candid photographs of a woman in the throes of an embrace. Only here she is with a boy, not an older man. In a nearby car an older man sits, waiting. The woman remonstrates with the narrator about taking the photograph. The boy runs away under cover of the ensuing argument between the woman (who is joined by the man in the car) and the recording angel who is telling the story. When he develops the photographs later, it seems to him that perhaps the woman had a more sinister purpose in mind, possibly to seduce the boy for the man who waited in the car. If this was so then the intervention of the photographer actually influenced the course of events and freed the youngster. Cortázar has a marvelous way of implying much with little. The possibilities of the moral effects of art as action were totally obliterated in Antonioni's film; but this implication is what makes the work a gem among contemporary stories.

Daniel Stern. Nation. Sept. 18, 1967, p. 248

Before publishing *Hopscotch*, Julio Cortázar was principally known as a short-story writer; his first novel, *The Winners*, was considered a brilliant but unsuccessful try. *Hopscotch* made him into an international literary figure and provoked numerous comments and controversies about his boldness, his deliberate difficulty, and especially his theories of fiction, which he elucidates and discusses. In *Hopscotch* Cortázar gives central importance to the theme of the double, the literary *Doppelgänger*, personified by La Maga and Talita. It is interesting to note that this device, which has a long literary lineage, can be seen in his first stories, in *Bestiary*, and reappears with surprising regularity in the following collections of stories—*The End of the Game* and *Secret Weapons*—and later in *Hopscotch* and *All the Fires the Fire.*

In general, one could say that Cortázar does not use the double for the usual purpose of duplication of personality, or for confusion between what could be called the real character and his image. The original character and his reflection have a similar importance; one is not subordinated to the other, and . . . frequently there is no definite difference between the principal character and the newcomer. . . .

The character's "I" is diffused, or tries to be, in other destinies that are at times chosen, foreboded, or vaguely intuited as part of an atavistic legacy. The immediate result is that the "I" observes himself, sees himself as an actor and spectator, and finally situates himself outside the literary material in the most total alienation. Nevertheless, he retains his observant and narrative faculty of a reality to which he irremediably no longer belongs but which he wants to know, since he never loses the impulse to establish contact with those other possible "I's," to touch the bottom in those realities that are so similar, yet still so remote.

Marta Morello-Frosch. RI. 34, July–Dec., 1968, p. 323†

The environment and the culture in which [Cortázar] lived during his adolescence explain his predilection for a world that he knows on the basis of direct observation and the ease with which he unfolds it. Cortázar himself has referred to his fixed situation through the . . . words of one of his characters who most resembles him, Horacio Oliveira [in *Hopscotch*]: "He was middle class, he was *porteño* [that is, from Buenos Aires], he was National College, and those things can't be so easily overcome."

The dominance of the mother, even though the masculine characters are slightly more numerous, reappears constantly throughout his books set in Buenos Aires. This aspect also has its autobiographical validity; his middle-class people are seen largely in family environments like the ones he knew, in which the father figure was an insignificant or nonexistent being. This is the case in short stories such as "The Poisons," "The End of the Game," "Letters from Mama," "The Other Sky," "The Health of the Sick," "Bestiary," and in the novels—the Trejos in *The Winners* and the Gutussos in *Hopscotch.*

José Amícola. Sobre Cortázar (Buenos Aires,
Editorial Escuela, 1969), pp. 123–24†

Hopscotch has been hailed by the *Times Literary Supplement* as the first great novel of Spanish America. I do not know if this is true; but it can indeed be stated that Julio Cortázar, this tall, blue-eyed, awkward man, whose appearance belies his fifty years, has been writing . . . the most revolutionary narrative prose in the Spanish language. But to limit Cortázar to what [the French critic] Philippe Sollers calls "Latin Americanism" would be a serious error. For the North American critic and novelist C. D. B. Bryan, writing in *The New Republic, Hopscotch* is the most powerful encyclopedia of emotions and visions that the international generation of postwar writers has produced. The readers will be able to verify the validity of these statements soon after entering into one of the richest universes of contemporary fiction: the one containing the Pandora's box—play, death, and resurrection—that is *Hopscotch*. . . .

Julio Cortázar has written a novel faithful to his deep convictions: "Apart from our individual destinies, we are part of figures we do not know." Together with Octavio Paz and Luis Buñuel, Julio Cortázar today represents the vanguard of Spanish America. He shares with Paz the incandescent tension of the instant as the supreme point of the temporal tide. And he shares with Buñuel the vision of liberty as a permanent desire and as an unauthorized, and therefore revolutionary, dissatisfaction.

Carlos Fuentes. La nueva novela hispanoamericana
(Mexico City, Joaquín Mortiz, 1969), pp. 67, 77†

Although *Stories of Cronopios and Famas* was published in Argentina three years before *Hopscotch* (and caused an enormous literary stir among Latin American readers at the time), its appearance in this country post-*Hopscotch* publication though chronologically incorrect is infinitely more satisfying intellectually. I say this because I suspect that unless North American readers are familiar with Cortázar's intent in *Hopscotch*, they might think *Stories of Cronopios and Famas* a very silly book, indeed. And that's a shame, too. Because Cortázar's *Stories of Cronopios and Famas* is no more silly than Edward Lear's *Book of Nonsense* was nonsense.

If one understands what Horacio Oliveira, the major character in *Hopscotch*, was looking for, that the philosophy, the motive, and the method of his quest were those of "a destroyer of compasses," then the silliness of Cortázar's *Stories of Cronopios and Famas* reveals itself as a sublimely intricate part of Cortázar's grand design. About Horacio Oliveira's search, Cortázar wrote in *Hopscotch*: "Search is just what it is not . . . because he has already found himself. Just that the finding has not taken any shape." Nor is it "a question of perfecting, of decanting, of redeeming, or choosing, of free-wheeling, of going from the alpha to the omega. *One is already there.* Anybody is already there. The shot is in the pistol; but a trigger has to be squeezed, and it so happens that the finger is making motions to stop a bus, or something similar."

Stories of Cronopios and Famas is a textbook on how to get one's finger to make the proper motion, a lesson plan for combatting the alienation and nihilism one feels from a life of automatic acts and responses, a guide to the cronopio state of being. Horacio Oliveira was a cronopio—but not the first. . . .

My reservations about *Stories of Cronopios and Famas* stem from my uncertainty whether anyone who has not read *Hopscotch* will be able to gain any great appreciation of Cortázar's intention beyond that party-game level of determining one's own and others' categories. *Hopscotch* on its most basic level provided an extraordinary insight into the complexities of an Argentinian being and the nostalgia and longing of a Latin American for a more sophisticated culture. But *Stories of Cronopios and Famas*, perhaps because of the explosion of Latin American writers upon the North American scene . . . seems curiously disappointing, if not a bit lightweight.

C. D. B. Bryan. *NYT*. June 15, 1969, p. 4

For those who didn't realize it before, *Stories of Cronopios and Famas* should convince American readers not only that the Argentinian novelist Julio Cortázar is a major literary figure, but that he is also one of a select, disappearing breed—an intellectual humorist. His intellectuality is cultured and cosmopolitan, ironic and totally unpretentious; his *Weltanschauung*, which is coherent, is presented for the delight of the reader with no abstraction and not a trace of heavy-handedness. On the contrary, the really remarkable quality that makes *Stories of Cronopios and Famas* such pure joy is Cortázar's dry, off-beat, highly original sense of humor. He has a rare gift for isolating the absurd in everyday life, for depicting the foibles in human behavior with an unerring thrust that is satiric yet compassionate.

Stories of Cronopios and Famas is unconventional in format. It consists of a series of very short pieces, varying in length from four or five lines to four or five pages. Mostly they are about one page long. Cortázar's utter economy of means is admirable; he does more with a single paragraph than most writers manage in a full-length short story, and he does it much more entertainingly. Moreover, he creates a strange world entirely his own: a world of surrealistic bizarreness and playful fantasy the likes of which we have not encountered elsewhere. Nevertheless, Cortázar himself considers his writings to be realistic since, as he states, typically with tongue-in-cheek, "reality appears fantastic to me." . . .

Neither Cortázar nor the American publisher bothers to explain these strange names ["chronopios" and "famas"] invented by the author. In fact, there is no need to explain, because we quickly come to understand that they are elements of Cortázar's particular cosmography. Cronopios are the spontaneous, temperamental, artistic people who are congenitally disorganized and impractical, but who enjoy life and live it fully. Famas are plodders—prudent, scientific, intelligent, but unimaginative. Lastly come esperanzas, the slugs who do not think at all, who see no further than the ends of their noses, but who are nevertheless not entirely unappealing (Cortázar cannot really dislike *any* segment of people), because, like the "nebechs," they are born losers. . . .

Cortázar is masterfully incisive. Each page sparkles with vivid satire that goes to the heart of human character and, in his best pieces, to the essence of the human conditions; in its entirety *Stories of Cronopios and Famas* comprises a veritable human comedy.

Tim Bishop. *SR.* Sept. 27, 1969, p. 26

In a review of [the American film] *They Shoot Horses, Don't They?*, Paul Warshow has said that the dance marathon is "a metaphor almost a priori—one of those natural, organic metaphors which seem obvious when you see them but which take a certain 'brilliance' to discover . . . and which have enormous potential because they grow out of the common core of experience." The same, only perhaps more so, could be said of the traffic jam in [Cortázar's story] "Freeway South." It is quite obvious that Cortázar saw in [the return to Paris after weekends and holidays] a ready-made symbol for something that has been a major theme throughout his works—modern technological society and its very precarious balance. Confined in their useless metal cages, the people in the jam are obvious examples of alienated modern man. At the end, when the jam finally dissolves, each person returns to a mechanized existence controlled by machines. . . .

It could very well be concluded then, particularly in view of the slightly melodramatic ending, that Cortázar offers in "Freeway South" an alternative to modern civilization; that the story is an indictment against modern life. In short, that the double exposure creates a dialectic between the modern and primitive worlds present in the two images. Yet, while this interpretation may be valid and justifiable, it seems to me that the "topicality" of the story conceals a more profound reflection, not directly about man's condition, but about fiction. . . .

In Cortázar's utopia everything has a place because he has arbitrarily created a grammar that will contain it; everything, including the characters, has a name because he has wrought a grammar that will accept it. Toward the end of "Freeway South" snow covers the ground —winter has set in on the people who had left for Paris on an August afternoon. But this is not a break with the syntax of Cortázar's new world. The perfectly normal man in Magritte's picture is as arbitrary in his normality as the bird cage in its abnormality. The two situation signs have become one; a fiction within a larger fiction, all fictions a fiction, all fires a fire. Cortázar's "Freeway South" falls within a very rich tradition of literature whose main preoccupation is literature. At the very center of that tradition is that enigmatic figure—Borges.

Roberto González Echevarría. SSF. 8, 1, Winter, 1971,
pp.136–37, 140

There has been very little discussion of Julio Cortázar's poetry. To be sure, the author has not promoted it. A first book, *Presence*, published in 1938 under the pseudonym of Julio Denis, cannot be found today. . . . Whether or not all of Cortázar's poems are included in it, [*Pameos and Meopas* (the title is a double anagram on the Spanish word for poem, poema)] presents a representative enough selection. . . .

Cortázar, in the prologue to the book, denies that genres exist, aligning himself with an already widespread concept that says that the poetry that is found in what we understand as a poem could as well be found in writing on a wall, a happening, a song, or a theatrical work. . . . But we must give some name to these brief compositions, with their uneven lines and their very free themes. . . . Let us continue, then, to call them poems. . . .

Cortázar says other things in his prologue. He says, for example, "When my youth died, there also died in me the a priori respect for poetry, poets, and poems, which impose on us a bourgeois humanism already unmasked by an inescapable breakdown in values and systems." Nevertheless, he has not included in this book any of his poems on social or political themes. And he says, "It is then natural that these poems that follow seem to be too marginal, but that at the same time I am not sorry for having written them. A man between two watersheds of the century, I have had the bittersweet privilege of being witness to the decline of one cosmic vision and the emergence of a very different one. And if the last few years of mine are to be dedicated to this new man we want to create, nothing can stop me turning my gaze back to a region of beloved shadows, walking with Achilles in Hades, whispering those names that so many young people have already forgotten because they must: Hölderlin, Keats, Leopardi, Mallarmé, Darío, Salinas—shadows among so many shadows in the life of an Argentine who wanted to read, who wanted to embrace everything." I need not quote any more. Recently Cortázar has found it necessary in everything he writes to proclaim his revolutionary state. . . .

Horacio Armani. La nación. Dec. 26, 1971, sec. 3, p. 4†

Banality of content in *62: A Model Kit* (which is never as intellectually or emotionally rich as *Hopscotch*) provides an unobtrusive framework for a dazzling display of compositional ingenuity. At the beginning of the book, when Juan overhears a customer in a Parisian restaurant order a "château saignant" (a "rare steak" and, in Juan's deliberate confusion of "saignant" and "sanglant," also a "bloody castle"), he regards this as a "coagulation" of multiple events and meanings. The main elements of Cortázar's entire novel are contained within those two words. The paradoxical achievement of his writing is to spread out, in the time and space of linear narrative, those condensed and analogous meanings which Juan believed were violations of time and space that ruled out narrative as a mode of explication. . . .

Certainties about plot and character are sacrificed to opportunities for extending and making elaborate patterns of narrative surfaces.

Nonetheless, depersonalization in *62: A Model Kit* is not exactly psychological impoverishment. Strictly within the limits of literary play-fulness, Cortázar manages to suggest ways of achieving distance from the otherwise inescapable pressures of individual obsessions. A certain humor about the supposed boundaries of personal identity and personal mobility raises the possibility that life itself—more biological than psychological—might change the "key," the terms in which human beings think of themselves as participating in what Morelli [in *Hopscotch*] called "that flow of animated matter."

And yet . . . Cortázar's world is populated with disarmingly recognizable individuals. His work—unlike so many other attempts to subvert the humanistic faith in distinct inviolable "persons"—is an original but cautious experiment in the violation of individual differences which he has at least taken the trouble to imagine in the first place. Cortázar is the only *loving* "mutilator" in *62: A Model Kit*. It is precisely because we become attached to his characters and their absurd, old-fashioned dilemma of falling in love with the wrong people that we accept a kind of beneficent vampirism as a remedy for their anguished humanity.

A rather funny horror story about real or imaginary vampires becomes an earnest (if somewhat mystifying) plea for spiritual trans-fusions. Such transfusions (a sort of collectivizing of psychological fluids) might create a community in which the generous sharing of energies and desires would make truly anachronistic that "ontological clawing" into other people's vitality which, as Cortázar wrote in *Hopscotch*, constitutes much of what we call "endearment" or "love."

Leo Bersani. *NYT*. Nov. 11, 1972, p. 7, 43

Superficially, *Hopscotch* seems more accessible [than Lezama Lima's *Paradiso*], since Cortázar was blessed not only with the rich tradition of the literature of the Río de la Plata area but also with a permanent contact with French culture (he has lived in Paris since 1952). But if Cortázar seems to have written *Hopscotch* from the center of the western intellectual world while Lezama Lima began writing *Paradiso* on the periphery of even the Latin American world, Cortázar, in fact, used culture to deny culture. In *Hopscotch* he tried to achieve a subtraction, not a totality; an anti-novel, not a novel. Yet, though he attacked the novel as a form, he retained in the book something that is essentially a novel.

The narrative form is questioned at the start of the book itself, by the author's telling the reader how to read it. (One is immediately reminded of Charles Kinbote's efforts, in Nabokov's *Pale Fire*, to indicate a privileged reading of "his" book.) Cortázar goes a step further and proposes a classification of readers: the female reader, or hedonistic one, who reads only for pleasure; and the accomplice reader, the one willing to help in the actual creation of the novel. To this reader, Cortázar offers a bonus, the possibility of following a sequence of chapters that will entrap him in an infinite circular reading: Chapter 58 refers to Chapter 131, which refers to Chapter 58, and so on and so forth, until kingdom come. The reader thus becomes another character in the book.

In *Hopscotch* the *form* of the novel—a labyrinth without a center, a trap that is always shutting the reader within it, a serpent biting its tail—is no more than another device to emphasize the deep, secret subject of the book: the exploration of a bridge between two existences (Oliveira, Traveler), a bridge between two muses (La Maga, Talita), a bridge between two worlds (Paris, Buenos Aires). The novel unfolds itself to question itself the better; indeed, the title itself indicates its symbolic form (a hopscotch is a labyrinth and a *mandala*, in the Jungian sense). Yet it is also a novel about the complexities of being an Argentine (a man between two worlds) and about the *double* who menaces us in other dimensions of our lives. The *form* of the book has become what used to be called its *content*.

Emir Rodríguez-Monegal. In *World Literature since 1945* (New York, Frederick Ungar, 1973), pp. 435–36

CUNHA, EUCLYDES DA (1866–1909)

BRAZIL

The Backlands stands alone in the nation's literature; we, in ours, have no book to parallel it in spirit, purport or accomplishment. . . . More, a close reading of the government's application of force to a situation that might have been managed without the necessity of the final massacre—could teach something to all governmental departments that are brought into contact with alien or extra-social groups which must be incorporated into the national entity.

The Backlands is the best answer to the young Brazilian regionalists who have made the book a rallying point. Here is a volume—and a thick, compact volume it is—dealing in quasi-reportorial spirit with a brief incident in the most hidden recesses of the national interior; it was not written with belles-lettres in mind; it is strewn with terms and processes of thought that baffle the ordinary reader. Yet the man who composed it was a vibrant personality, and whether knowingly or unwittingly, he made the book a symbol—a symbol of uncomprehending persecution, of human fanaticism, of religious origins, of man's instinctive seeking after something higher. It is true that the persecution was in part necessary, that the aspect of fanaticism here revealed is most repugnant, that the spectacle of religious origins does not flatter our unctuous, supposedly civilized, superior souls. But it is true, likewise, that we must gaze into such depths as these to remind ourselves occasionally that we dwell in these interiors.

Isaac Goldberg. Brazilian Literature (New York,
Alfred A. Knopf, 1922), pp. 220–21

"A cry of protest" the author calls [*The Backlands*], and it is indeed that. A protest against what he regards as a "crime" and an "act of madness" on the part of a newly formed republican government. For him, this "most brutal conflict of our age" was the "corpus delicti on the aberrations of a people," the "major scandal in our history." A clash between "two societies," between two cultures, that of the seaboard and that of the *sertão*, the Canudos Expedition appeared as a "deplorable stumbling-block to national unity." His book, accordingly, as he tells us, is not so much a defense of the *sertanejo*, or man of the backlands, as it is an attack on the barbarity of the "civilized" toward those whose stage of social evolution was that of semibarbarians. In this connection we North Americans well may think of our own Indian wars of the early days. The author's chapter on "Man" has been seen by Agrippino Grieco as "a precious lesson in things, given by a free man to the slaves of power, by a sociologist without a chair to the governors of the nation." Cunha, the same writer goes on to say, "told the truth in the land of lies and was original in the land of plagiarism." This honesty, set off by his originality and his boldness of attack, is perhaps his most prominent trait, the one on which all his commentators are agreed.

Whether or not his primary purpose was to defend the *sertanejo*, the author of *The Backlands* certainly exhibits a passionate love of the mestizo backwoodsman and his way of life. The latter's customs, occupations, diversions, joys, and sorrows are all depicted with an affectionate wealth of detail. The "roundups," the merrymakings, the religious observances and superstitions of the region, are minutely chronicled, and the result is an authentic and unexcelled picture of the *vaqueiro*, or North Brazilian cowboy. Indeed, a Portuguese critic, none too friendly to Brazil, has said that this portion of the book contains the sixty-one finest pages ever written in the language. The description of the devastating backland droughts holds the tragedy of a people struggling with a blind fate as represented by the relentless forces of nature. . . .

Samuel Putnam. Introduction to Euclides da Cunha,
Rebellion in the Backlands (Chicago, University of
Chicago Press, 1944), pp. v–vi

What, indeed, is *The Backlands*? A poem or a sociological essay, a chapter of history or a simple military chronicle, an anthropo-geographic study or an accusatory tract against criminals?

Obviously none of these, and at the same time all of these, since all of these facets and many more constitute long, thorough, and impressive sections, admirably coordinated, with the well-defined goal of creating the most convincing and unsophisticated tract against a violent, egregious, and disconcerting national crime. . . . It is a tract in which an engineer, [acting like a jurist and a doctor] pronounces diagnoses and prescribes cures with the self-assurance of the clinical specialist, undertaking operations with the proficient technique of an able and skillful surgeon. And all of this in a style that is nervous, vibrant, restless, one that uses all of the varieties of vocabulary and syntax, of figures of speech and semantics, with a richness and a vigor that are only rarely seen in the best prose writers of the language, both classical and modern.

Without a doubt, the point of departure for the composition of *The Backlands* was the simple compiling of chronicles of the Canudos campaign, as a journalistic undertaking for the columns of an important newspaper in São Paulo. But even before he arrived at the theater of operations that he was to describe, intuition told Cunha that he should prepare himself to write a great book.

Modesto de Abreu. *Estilo e personalidade de Euclides
da Cunha* (Rio de Janeiro, Editôra Civilização
Brasileira, 1963), p. 120†

Broadly speaking, we can see four fundamental, distinguishable phases in the evolution of Euclydes da Cunha's thought. . . . [The phases represent] an unconscious evolution, dictated, among other things, by his immense intellectual curiosity, but principally by the evolution of the society, culture, and politics in Brazil. . . .

1. From the Military Academy to the journey to Canudos. This phase was marked by the clear dominance of Comtian positivism and Spencerism, with some influence of the utopian socialists.

2. From the journey to Bahia (Salvador), to observe the battle of Canudos, as a war correspondent, up through his arrival there, his stay and return, a phase characterized by a position critical of republican orthodoxy. The facts he observed took precedence over theory.

3. From the return from Canudos through the planning and writing of *The Backlands*. In this phase Cunha, now removed from the facts, attempted to strengthen his thought with theories then in vogue, which could not in any way help him understand and interpret the essence of the problem that he had witnessed in the interior of Bahia. There was a preponderance of racism in his thought—an ideological backsliding.

4. From the publication of *The Backlands* to his application for a university chair in logic. He attempted a more profound revision of his theoretical position, trying to discover, through an eminently critical attitude, new ideological and methodological postulates with which to interpret Brazil.

Clóvis Moura. *Introdução ao pensamento de Euclides
da Cunha* (Rio de Janeiro, Editôra Civilização
Brasileira, 1964), pp. 17–18†

In [the unfinished *A Paradise Lost*], a book on the Amazon region, that immense sea of fresh water and greenery, [Cunha's] attempt was not only to describe the tumultuous untamed lands of the vast area, struggling with the waters of the great rivers, which turned the verdant valleys of the fresh-water basin into islands, but also to reveal the unequal struggle of the man of the backlands with hostile nature and with man himself, among the rivers, the lakes, and the jungles. It would have been, without a doubt, a book along the lines of *The Backlands* . . . a work in defense of the rights and guarantees of a more humanized life for the worker in the forests, the fields, the lakes, and the rivers. . . .

In that marvelous world of the interior, full of superstitions and strange customs, the slavery of man was the consequence of the absence of a humanitarian and rational administration. The disorganized exploitation of natural riches had led to the suppression of man's freedom. Only through the socialization of capital and of work could there be, in Cunha's view, a control on production, distribution, and consumption of products, and an end, once and for all, to the exploitation of man through debts, as had happened to the humble and oppressed rubber-plantation workers, defenseless victims of their terrible oppressors.

Velloso Leão. *Euclides da Cunha na Amazônia (ensaio)*
(Rio de Janeiro, Livraria São José, 1966), pp. 72–73†

[Cunha] had an idea, although at first vague and barely conscious, of the affinities of temperament and style that linked him to the greatest verbal master of French literature [that is, Victor Hugo]. And if it is perhaps an exaggeration to say that Hugo was his model, the object of his greatest admiration . . . the undeniable fact is that the two are tied together by so many intimate similarities that it is surprising that these links have not yet been studied in detail. Araripe Júnior, whose virtues as a critic are slight, was nevertheless accurate when he saw in Cunha an "epic-dramatic talent, a tragic genius." Indeed, Cunha's vision of the world (as a result of his concept of style) is epic, dramatic, and tragic.

For Cunha, mediocre men and events did not exist. . . . His boundless imagination only saw things in terms of extremes: broken-down soldiers and impoverished revolutionary *jagunços* [fanatics associated with Antônio Conselheiro] are transformed by Cunha into titans, into colossal statues that symbolize and summarize the great virtues of the race. Minor outbursts between exhausted combatants are for him brilliant and rhythmic charges of Bengal Lancers. Humanity offers him only examples of creeping vermin or of exceptional beings, incarnations of the "heroes" celebrated by his old master Carlyle.

Hence . . . the natural result is that Euclydes da Cunha's style is adjectival. . . . He transforms all his words into adjectives, choosing them for the adjectival potential they contain. His images are always "qualificative" and unusual words, in which he takes so much pride; they have no other function than to serve as adjectives. In the end, a style such as this is not and cannot be spontaneous, although it can undoubtedly be instinctive. And Cunha "worked over" his style, knowing that in a certain sense it grew with the content, that it was the artistic means with which Fate could be captured. . . .

Wilson Martins. *RIB*. 16, July–Sept., 1966, p. 254†

If written by another historian less receptive to and less aware of aesthetic considerations, [*Peru versus Bolivia*] would be a difficult book to read. It would, in that case, be of interest only to those who would need to read it out of professional obligation. But its author is Euclydes da Cunha. This is enough to make us turn to this work with the attitude of a medieval knight bowing to his lady. . . . The ordering, selection, arrangement, and analysis of a multitude of facts—to be sure, this is quite a difficult task in which the ordinary historian could trip, or at least, not attain the clarity, the fluidity of thought that should characterize a work of history.

Cunha exactly followed the rules that modern essayists have established for the visualization and exposition of matters that, at a determined moment, occur and interest the historian, leading him to literary creation. In the first place, there must be investigation and examination—that is, the exploration—followed by the comparative study of data and their arrangement, and, finally, an artistic re-creation that will lead to a work of fiction, since the simple selection, ordering, and presentation of the facts necessitates a technique that belongs to the domain of fiction (Arnold J. Toynbee).

In *Peru versus Bolivia* Cunha paid perfect attention to these rules for the proper role of the historian. And when he reaches the stage of re-creating the facts, he knows how to handle Toynbee's concept that there can be no great historian who is not also a great artist. Reading *Peru versus Bolivia*, a work filled with life resurrected from a dead past, with a literary intensity that holds the reader's interest, one sees that the author has rejected those hard-working but tiresome historians whom Walter Scott called dry as dust.

Leandro Tocantins. *Euclides da Cunha e o paraíso perdido* (Rio de Janeiro, Gráfica Record Editôra, 1968), pp. 216–17†

DARÍO, RUBÉN (1867–1916)

NICARAGUA

[Darío], a precious gem, is tall, sturdy, unexpressive—small, dark, and keen eyes—a broad nose, with nostrils sensuously open—slightly curled beard and hair—"hands of a marquis." He has a grave and awkward bearing, and is slow and somewhat stammering in his speech, but he is always elegant and refined.

He is proud—"I have pride and you have vanity," he said on one occasion to Gómez Carrillo [Spanish novelist and journalist].

He is a sybarite and a gourmet of good stock. During the nine months we lived together he used to treat us—alas, the times were not always easy!—to rich golden pheasants ("The golden pheasant told his secrets"), modernistic galantines, ultra-subtle truffles, etc. In the evening there would be a "Prince of Wales" cocktail in the Continental Tavern, the one beloved by Huysmans.

For him life, full of unhappy incidents, has not diminished his inner goodness. He is kind-hearted. He is a child—a child selfish or affectionate, capricious or serene—jealous of his affections, susceptible as a violet, and on account of that very susceptibility he is capable of understanding and feeling all the shadings of a word, a gesture, or an attitude: a big nervous child. [1902]

Amado Nervo. In José Luis Martínez, ed.,
The Modern Mexican Essay (Toronto, University of
Toronto Press, 1965), p. 85

It was journalism of the Shavian sort that was produced by such reformers of prose as Gutiérrez Nájera, Martí and Darío. How remarkably little of what Darío wrote as the result of his various travels and studies is unworthy of preservation between covers! And how much our own journalists and magazine writers learn from his pages in the way of enthusiasm, patience, human insight and a sincerity that makes few sacrifices upon the altar of cleverness and mere glitter.

There is little necessity here for an extended consideration of the poet's prose works. Everywhere may be discerned the mind of the poet which never quite lost its aristocratic cast, however much it recognized the value of the crowd as a background of art. If I mention *The Rare Ones* as my favorite, it is because in that book Darío the poet and Darío the extremely sensitive human being are most evident in Darío the writer of prose. It is questionable whether such a prose would prove acceptable to the majority of English readers; the non-Spanish element in it, of course, would not bother them. What might, however, seem not fully acceptable, is the quasipoetic glow that shines from every page. It was of this book that William Archer said that from what he could half make of the work he would learn Spanish, to read it. . . .

Such is the remarkable figure who so dominated an epoch that his very name serves to characterize it. Can Darío really be pinned down in the critic's sample case like the entomologist's butterfly? Perhaps, by some refinement of the critic's art an appearance of inner unity may be imparted to the man, his life and his labors. To me, however, he is most human in his questionings, his fears, his vacillations, his wavering, his unresolved doubt. From the very first he reveals these dominant characteristics. He is of the past, of the present, of the future. From the very nature of poetry and its incapability of being transferred into another tongue it is inevitable that he will never be to other peoples what he will remain to the Spaniards; that is one of the disadvantages under which the poet, more than any other creative artist, labors.

He crystallized an epoch; he transformed a language; he infused new life into the Castilian muse; he retained his own personality while absorbing all the currents that appeared during his career; he became, as we have seen, a legendary figure even during his own life. He belongs not only with the greatest poets that have written in the Spanish tongue, but with the masters of universal poesy. For above the early Parnassianism, the later Symbolism and the final complex humanism, is the eternally human of a poet who was peculiarly of his day and, by that same token, of all ages.

Isaac Goldberg. *Studies in Spanish-American Literature*
(New York, Brentano's, 1920), pp. 181–82

Of the poets of 1900 the one whose work was most filled with pseudo-Christian motifs . . . was Rubén Darío. As early as *Profane Proses* . . . Christian symbols appear now and then, in "New Year" and in the "Response to Verlaine." But they alternate with pagan symbols and take on a purely ornamental quality, as an amplification of the mythological stock. The poet was at that time in his full youth, overflowing with Dionysian happiness, so much so that he could not linger over grave Christian concepts. Nevertheless, he already had, and always had . . . the intuition and the taste for the supernatural, the Christian—or better, Catholic—feeling for hierarchies, the respect for genius and the hero (Carlyle). . . . Because of this . . . spirit of sentimental and aesthetic Christianity, he went through phases of reverence and enthusiasm for Pope Leo XIII, to whose virtues as a poet he also paid tribute ("Letters"). And his chronicler's pen was always free of any sin of irreligious sarcasm.

But the manifestations of his Christianity through *Profane Proses* had only a sumptuous character, as in D'Annunzio, or the tendency toward a Renaissance fusion of two millenarian beauties. Thus in the "Response to Verlaine," among the purely pagan images with which he magnifies his obsequies, as if he were dealing with a Greek hero, and among the trophies with which he decorates his Hellenic tomb, he erects a cross and a nimbus of ultraterrestrial light. . . . This is pure Renaissance pseudo-Christianity and does not pretend to have any serious roots in the conscience, but rather is merely figurative language on the same level as the mythological terminology. . . .

R. Cansinos-Assens. *Los temas literarios y su interpretación* (Madrid, V. H. Sanz Calleja, 1923?), pp. 60–61†

Profane Proses and *Songs of Life and Hope* show the artist in his maturity. . . . Darío complained in his youth that the only themes of poetic inspiration in Latin America were political events and tropical nature. Thus, it is not surprising that he, in two collections, adopted subjects that enabled him to establish new sources of inspiration, especially mythology and the French eighteenth century but also including the majority of subjects popular in contemporary France. When he returned to the older subjects of Latin American poetry in *Songs of Life and Hope*, it was as if he realized that although modernism had made his reputation, he had to yield to the inevitable reaction that sets in against any literary movement.

Darío had also complained of the limitations in expressiveness of the Spanish language of his day. . . . To look for remedies, he went quite far in his investigations of contemporary innovations in France. The selection he made from among abundant choices at his disposal shows his artistic tastes clearly. Undeniably, he always remained a classicist at heart. With very few exceptions, the conception of his works is always clear and objective, the images easy to grasp, the expression precise, and the constructions logical. It thus makes sense that in borrowing from French writers he definitely favored the romantics and the Parnassians over the symbolists. For example, although he was acquainted with

Mallarmé's theories, one would be hard pressed to prove that he ever wrote a whole poem according to Mallarmé's rules of art. But he often did use symbolist techniques . . . to embellish his classical or Parnassian style and make it more expressive. In a poem like "Marine," which is a masterpiece of suggestiveness, the seascape is conceived of almost as clearly as in a Parnassian poem. But the poet communicates impressions not through detailed description but through much more subtle means, learned from Mallarmé and his followers.

Erwin K. Mapes. *L'influence française dans l'œuvre de Rubén Darío* (Paris, Librairie Ancienne Honoré Champion, 1925), p. 144†

A good many European critics are surprised to discover that our American literature does not deal with indigenous themes and that it seems so much like European literature. But nothing could be more logical. The countries of our continent are, despite the mixture of blood, eminently European. We know very little about the Aztec, Inca, and Quechua civilizations; and even if we do know something, we can never "feel" our American forefathers. Carlos V., Napoleon, and Garibaldi have much more meaning to us than Moctezuma, Atahualpa, and Caupolicán. Those who attempt to revive precolonial culture are plowing in the desert: first, because even the pure Indians of America feel themselves European; second, because indigenous culture is rudimentary compared to the one left us by the conquerors, despite all the grandeur that some see in pre-Cortés civilization.

Being cosmopolitan by necessity and using French as an indispensable tool for learning about the latest advances of the more developed cultures, our writers reveal an attitude that represents neither a breakdown nor a denial of our racial instincts. Thus, when some startled Spanish critics of the last century and in the present one—such as Valera, Menéndez y Pelayo, Julio Cejador, and Miguel de Unamuno—criticized the "Gallicism" of Rubén Darío and of the modernist poets in general, they were doing nothing more than affirming one of the fundamental characteristics of our independent life. Nevertheless, Rubén Darío was the least rootless of the early modernist poets. Julián del Casal was too close to Baudelaire; Asunción Silva did not even have a feeling for our landscape; Gutiérrez Nájera was a poet of pure feeling and therefore cannot be localized to any one region. Darío, on the contrary, was a fine exponent of Spanish genius in modern times because of the vigor of his thought, the clarity of his expression, and his realism.

Darío's refined purism is revealed in many ways. . . . His love for things Spanish was a strong attachment from his youth on, and on many occasions he sought to display this love in a concrete way, applauding Spanish art, Spain's great men, and its popular customs, as well as showing a certain disdain for the complications of Nordic art. And Darío did not love Hispanic qualities blindly, for since childhood he had been an initiate in the cult of Spanish art and literature, entering into literature through the classical doors of Moratín and Cervantes.

Arturo Torres-Ríoseco. *Rubén Darío, casticismo y americanismo* (Cambridge, Mass., Harvard University Press, 1931), pp. 129–30†

I cannot agree with Leopoldo Lugones's assertion that Darío was "nothing more than a poet, nothing more than a star" and that it is impossible to find in his works a "political prescription." The problems of America, the future of this continent, its political destiny, often occupied his thoughts.

Some critics, on the other hand, have portrayed Darío as the poet of national or racial hatred, as a prophet and the leader of an "anti-Yankee" movement. These people have stressed the fact that the famous "To Roosevelt" (which Darío once called an "innocent lyrical arrow") became a song popular in the schools of Latin America; they call this ode the clearest manifestation of an anti-Yankee movement. . . . But Darío recognized the brilliance of some aspects of the United States. He did not overlook the material grandeur of the great republic of the North . . . and as a result felt not merely a desire but a sense of necessity to learn many things from it.

J. F. Normand. *RI*. 2, Nov., 1940, pp. 435–37†

I cannot understand why there has been a quarrel over—in some cases, even a refusal to consider—Rubén Darío as an important social poet when there are so many excellent poems of his that were obviously inspired by social issues. . . . From an early age he was surrounded by politics, and the poet complained that in his country politics was approached as something provincial and vulgar. No sooner had Rubén awakened to public life than he was confronted by political problems, the most serious one being the unification of Central America.

Although it is true that social problems were not his most heartfelt concern, his career in journalism made society into a sort of professional obligation. Rubén could not allow himself the luxury of focusing on what was inside him: he was paid to observe what was going on around him and to relate it, more or less poetically, to the readers. Journalism obliged him to live the moment, to live the immediacy of politics, and, even more, to take part in it—through reporting and expressing opinions. His prose writings abound with articles of a political nature, some of them important to the history of thought, such as the ones dedicated to Spain on the occasion of the disaster [the Spanish-American War] and an attack he wrote against Theodore Roosevelt.

His trips, his sojourns in various countries, educated him in the different forms of human society, whether he lived at the foot of the Andes or on the banks of the Seine. Certain things that cannot be seen too well in America become clear when seen from Europe. And the same is true with what is European, which takes on, when seen from the other side of the Atlantic, traits and colorations imperceptible on its own soil.

Pedro Salinas. *La poesía de Rubén Darío* (Buenos Aires,
Editorial Losada, 1948), pp. 216–17†

To the generation of 1920, Rubén Darío was an artificial, courtly, Gallicized poet, totally alien to the life of his continent. His metrical reforms did not interest those new writers who proclaimed the destruction of poetic form; his verbal refinement sounded hollow in the ears of the revolutionary followers of Marinetti and Cocteau; the anachronism of his themes was interpreted as an evasion of reality.

I do not know what kind of poetry the cultured Spanish American reader of today prefers. It is highly probable that there exist as many tastes as there are cultural divisions. Besides, taste is often conditioned by elements foreign to creative production. For example, the poets of social themes—Vallejo, Neruda, Guillén, León Felipe—are read frequently just because they are of the left, even though their comrades may not understand their works. . . .

Rubén Darío was not a social poet; he did not cultivate the Negro theme; he was not a Catholic poet, though he was a Catholic man; he was not even a democratic poet. Moreover, I am certain that these characteristics have nothing to do with poetry. But the public demands such elements nowadays; literature of the moment is in vogue, and therefore Darío is not the favorite poet of Spanish Americans today.

Curiously enough, we have let ourselves be lured by García Lorca's poetry, which is really as superficial as the most shallow moments of Darío; actually, García Lorca presents a mixture of Spanish classicism with a waggish touch of the Madrilenian dandy. His is poetry for recitation, a characteristic from which the Spanish American seemed to flee in 1930, at least in the poetry of Rubén Darío. Within another twenty years all the poems of the *Gypsy Ballads* of García Lorca will seem to us merely another literary fad. The admittance of the surrealist poetry of a Villaurrutia or of a Neruda would be more logical, since that mode is currently the most accepted in Europe and since its psychological significance invades the fields of sculpture and painting.

Rubén Darío does not meet fully the demands of today's reader, but part of the fault belongs to that reader and not to the poet. I have already stated that Darío is known essentially for his most superficial poems, for those in which there is more external luster than profound sensibility, more beauty of form than vital vibration. But Darío was much more than this. Like Verlaine, he succeeded at times in penetrating the innermost recesses of the soul, in revealing the most intimate, most subtle emotions, and in expressing them without rhetoric, in the simple communication of sentiment. . . .

Arturo Torres-Ríoseco. *New World Literature*
(Berkeley, University of California Press, 1949),
pp. 122–24

These narratives [in *Complete Stories*] frequently are closer to descriptive, poetic, sensual, and refined chronicles than they are to stories. An example is in "In the Battle of the Flowers," one of the pieces that has the greatest richness of color, the greatest suppleness and lyricism— therefore, one of his most beautiful stories. In the majority of these stories, nothing happens. There is no plot, no action, not even the attempt to portray character. The poet takes the germ of the plot but he scarcely sketches it. Rather, he uses it as a springboard for meditations and reflections that are closer to the short lyrical essay than the story. . . . Some of these fantasies are like glosses in prose on themes the poet pursued in verse—one more proof of his limited creative imagination in the narrative genre. Moreover, not a few of these stories are merely commentaries on events or on the poet's personal experiences, and only a generous dose of good will could call them stories. In other cases, the author glosses biblical episodes or ones from Christian legends and saints' lives; in this material, more than subjects for stories, he finds aesthetic motifs that lead him to embroider stylistic filigrees.

One interesting aspect of these so-called stories is that they serve to corroborate what we already knew—that Darío was temperamentally saturated with Catholicism. His is not a religious soul like Nervo's or Gutiérrez Nájera's, for example, tortured by the mystery of the "beyond," a soul that doubts, inquires, analyzes, and at last forges its own faith of the rites and liturgies of all positive religions. No, Darío was a conformist and convinced Catholic. He may have moments of vacillation . . . but they are transitory, inconsequential waverings. In [*Complete Stories*], even more than in his poetry, we see him permeated with Catholicism, with the liturgies and dogmas of the Church, which he accepts blindly, without serious philosophical or metaphysical doubts. No other modernist rhapsodist comes off as orthodox and faithful as does Darío in these stories. . . .

Manuel Pedro González. *Estudios sobre literaturas hispanoamericanas: Glosas y semblanzas* (Mexico City, Ediciones Cuadernos Americanos, 1951), pp. 332–33†

Rubén Darío presents a signal case of a man who had a remarkable influence on poetry but whose own achievement may seem in retrospect not fully to deserve its first renown. That he, more than anyone else, was responsible for the dazzling revival of Spanish poetry with the generation of 1898 is beyond question. At the time when Spain lost to the United States the last remnants of her once world-wide empire this stranger from Nicaragua brought a ringing message of confidence and a range of verbal melodies such as Spain had never heard before. His metrical innovations, his rippling, lucent language, his unquestioning devotion to his art, did something to comfort Spain for her territorial losses by providing her with a new poetry. Through him men of pre-eminent gifts like Antonio Machado and Juan Ramón Jiménez found their true selves and inaugurated an era of creative activity which lasted till the Civil War.

Yet, great though Darío's influence undoubtedly was, its results were paradoxical. The poets whom he inspired reacted against his methods and were in no sense his disciples. There is no trace of his mellifluous ease in the Castilian austerity of Machado or the delicate impressionism of Jiménez. Nor has his reputation for originality weathered the years. It is true that he did something that had never been done before in Spanish and that he handled the language with a dexterity which first shocked, and then enthralled, a generation which had come to believe that poetry was dying from inanition, but we can now see that much of his work was not ultimately original but a brilliant transposition into Spanish of French images and cadences. He absorbed with uncommon skill the most prominent qualities of French poetry from Hugo and Gautier to Mallarmé and Verlaine and presented them in an alluring Spanish dress, but the substance remained French. Even in this Gallicising task Darío was not influenced by those who were the greatest forces in the development of modern poetry. Rimbaud, Corbière, and Laforgue meant little or nothing to him, and though he was an ardent apostle of the Symbolists, we may doubt if he understood their essential aims. His achievement was largely derivative, and that no doubt is why he has lost some of his first glory.

C. M. Bowra. *Inspiration and Poetry* (London, Macmillan, 1955), pp. 242–43

What Darío acquired in Chile was . . . a new concept of style, through his reading there of contemporary French writers, which supplemented his classical foundation in literature, which widened his concept of art, which led him to discover exquisite modes of expression. Darío's new concept, later baptized "modernism," was analyzed with extraordinary perspicuity by Eduardo de la Barra in his prologue to *Blue*, was defined accurately by Juan Valera when he spoke of "mental Gallicism," and was captured in a perfect marmoreal form by José Enrique Rodó in his critical study of *Profane Proses*. . . .

Darío's modernist poetry (beginning with *Blue*, of course) can be viewed as the result of three equally important cultural influences: his knowledge of the classics, prior to his trip to Chile; the contemporary ideas he assimilated first among us Chileans, and later in Europe; the direct influence of contemporary French writers. Valera wrote him: "The first thing one notices is that your work is saturated with all the latest in French literature. . . . But you do not imitate any single [writer]: you are not romantic, naturalistic, or neurotic, decadent, symbolic, or Parnassian. You have mixed it all together and have brewed it in the alembic of your brain, and from it you have extracted a rare essence."

Raúl Silva Castro. *Rubén Darío a los veinte años*
(Madrid, Editorial Gredos, 1956), pp. 205–6†

Since the name of Rubén Darío is often on the lips of those familiar with the poetry of the Spanish-speaking world, it appears strange that the poet himself and his poetry are not better known to readers in the United States. . . . Rubén Darío is considered one of the outstanding poets of his period in the New World, and by some of his admirers in Latin-American countries, one of the greatest of those who wrote in the Spanish language. Certainly, he is worthy of study and consideration in North America, where he is little known because his poems are in Spanish with few translations into English. . . .

In 1888, Darío wrote his book *Blue*, which met with a favorable reception by critics in Spain after its publication. He was named correspondent of *La nación* of Buenos Aires and, after a period of such employment, was able to visit Spain in 1892. There his triumph began.

When in 1896 he published *Profane Proses* he was saluted as a poet of great stature. He not only lived in Madrid but traveled on the continent and for a while lived in Paris, where he acquired experience which matured him and benefited his art. In 1905 his volume of poetry, *Songs of Life and Hope*, marked him as the foremost poet of his day in the Spanish language. His later books . . . served to confirm his prestige.

Although his talent began to decline after 1910, his glory took on added luster as he continued to receive recognition. . . .

During twenty-eight years of literary effort Darío had developed his creative genius, achieved a new triumph in a school of poetry developed largely by him, and had become a major poet who brought about a complete change in literary style. His place in the literature of the Spanish-speaking world would be difficult to overestimate. To Latin-Americans he is somewhat the same as Garcilaso and Góngora are to the Spanish people. America did not have before, and has not had since, a poet of his caliber in the Spanish language.

It would do him a grave injustice to base a complete critique upon his early poems, such as those in *Blue* and *Profane Proses*. One cannot consider him as a Parnassian poet who sought escape from reality or lived in an ivory tower, in the light of his *Songs of Life and Hope*, or *Poem of Autumn, and Other Poems*. . . .

Certain of his poems lack the philosophical grandeur of the search for the mystery of life, or the search for God, and yet they found wide acceptance with the public. His verses were repeated by word of mouth, they were current in the salons, at meetings of the literati, in schools and colleges. They pleased the sensibilities, they delighted the ears, and they fired the imagination, by comparing beautiful women with the agile flight of butterflies, or the quiet gliding of a swan over a mirrored lake.

George N. MacDonell. *NMQ*. 31, Summer, 1961,
pp. 105–6

[Darío's] technical perfection must have been the result of an intellectual and emotional development that his experiences as well as his studies contributed to. The disillusioned years of the life of wandering, "of Bohemian restlessness," the religious, psychological, human conflicts of the Nicaraguan all doubtlessly left permanent marks on the physiognomy of his work. . . .

His alcoholism, his enormous passions, even the vicissitudes in his exploration of spiritualism are no secrets, since they have even found their way into his poetry. . . .

All of the more-or-less trivial facts that make up [Darío's] life had a certain visible relationship, although indefinable, with the changes that occurred in his creative work and in the poetic theory that supported it. One fact of his life, however, which was a constant in his career, has not been sufficiently stressed in the study of his evolution. This is the literary success that always accompanied him, not only the culmination, the definitive success, but also the preliminary successes that won for him the name of "child-poet" and opened up to him doors and friendships during his adolescence in Chile. Undoubtedly these experiences prepared Darío to assume the responsibilities of an Hispanic poet that fell to him toward the end of the last century and the beginning of the present one. [1965]

Bernardo Gicovate. *Ensayos sobre poesía hispánica*
(Mexico City, Ediciones De Andrea, 1967), p. 125†

Although Darío found rationalist atheism repugnant—his temperament was religious, even superstitious—it cannot be said that he was a Christian poet. Fear of death, the horror of being, self-disgust, expressions which appear now and then after *Songs of Life and Hope*, are ideas and feelings with Christian roots; but the other half, Christian eschatology, is absent. Darío was born in a Christian world, but he lost his faith and was left, like so many of us, with the inheritance of a guilt that no longer has reference to a supernatural sphere. The sense of original sin impregnates many of his best poems: ignorance of our origins and our end, fear of the inner abyss, the horror of living in the dark. Nervous fatigue, made worse by disorderly living and alcoholic excesses, together with his constant coming and going from one country to another, added to his uneasiness. . . .

In "Poem of Autumn," one of his last and greatest works, the two streams that feed his poetry are united: meditation on death and pantheistic eroticism. The poem is a set of variations on the old, worn-out themes of the brevity of life, the necessity of seizing the moment, and the like, but at the close the tone becomes graver and more defiant: in the face of death the poet does not affirm his own life but that of the universe. Earth and the sun vibrate in his skull as if it were a seashell; the salt of the sea is mingled in his blood as it is in that of the tritons and nereids; to die is to live a vaster, mightier life. Did he really believe this? It is true that he feared death; it is also true that he loved and desired it. Death was his Medusa and his siren. Dual death, dual like everything he touched, saw, and sang: his unity is always dual. That is why, as Juan Ramón Jiménez said, his emblem is the whorled seashell, both silent and filled with murmurs, an infinity that fits in one's hand. A musical instrument, speaking in an "unknown voice." A talisman, because "Europa touched it with her sacred hands." An erotic amulet, a ritual object. Its hoarse voice announces the dawn and the twilight, the hours when light and darkness meet. It is a symbol of universal correspondency, and also of reminiscence: when he presses it to his ear he hears the surge of past lives. He walks along the beach, where "the crabs are marking the sand with the illegible scrawl of their claws," and finds a seashell: then "a star like that of Venus" glows in his soul. The seashell is his body and his poetry, the rhythmic fluctuations, the spiral of those images that reveal and hide the world, that speak it and fall silent.

Octavio Paz. Prologue to Rubén Darío, Selected Poems
(Austin, University of Texas Press, 1965), pp. 16–17

To have been born of mixed blood in Nicaragua in 1867, to have read in the poetry of several languages and to have written hundreds of verses by the time he was in his teens, to have gone to Spain when about 25 and overthrown the whole literary establishment more easily than Cortés took Mexico, to have given a new direction and impetus to Spanish poetry that helped make it one of the literary glories of our century—to have done all this and still have time for endless globe-trotting, for love and drinking and the artificial paradises Verlaine may have shown him, time for superstition and piety and despair—but why finish the sentence? Everything about Rubén encourages excess.

When García Lorca and Pablo Neruda paid him their joint tribute in 1933, they, too, were carried away: "He launched us on the sea with frigates and shadows in our eyes and built an enormous promenade of gin over the greyest afternoon the sky has ever known. . . . His red name deserves to be remembered . . . his terrible heartaches . . . his descent to the hospitals of hell." But they also remembered his faults: "the weeds and empty flutenotes in his bookshelves, and the cognac bottles of his dramatic drunkenness, and the impudent padding that fills the multitude of his lines with humanity."

What he brought to Madrid from his exotic tropics and his library of French symbolists was a brilliant and sensuous New World of emotion and music. And if his emotionalism sometimes darkened and turned *ojeroso* (if it had circles under its eyes) it was always vibrant. With all of his passion, he was concerned too about language and the formal richness of lines and stanzas—Rubén was never one of those who take indifference to technique as a sign of commitment and sincerity. No wonder Dámaso Alonso thinks his coming, with a whole century of French verse in his luggage, the most important moment in Spanish poetry since Garcilaso de la Vega (over three centuries before) had naturalized the new meters from Italy.

John Frederick Nims. NYT. Dec. 26, 1965, p. 16

One strong possibility of a significant debt by Rubén Darío to Leconte de Lisle has usually been denied, overlooked, or misunderstood, yet the influence of the latter's "Le rêve du jaguar" ([in] *Poèmes barbares*) on Darío's "Aestival" ([in] *Blue*), seems more obvious than various other better-known instances of French influence on Hispanic literature.

This may be considered a significant debt because "Aestival," though one of Darío's earlier and less Modernist poems, is an ambitious and dramatic work; it is a *tour de force*. In Darío's opinion, expressed in his discussion of *Blue* in *History of My Books*, it was a "bit of force." In the opinion of Juan Valera, "Aestival" is the best of the four poems comprising "The Lyric Year"—"the one on summer stands out."

Darío denied the influence of "Le rêve du jaguar," or any influence whatsoever of Leconte de Lisle on "Aestival." . . . In *L'influence française dans l'œuvre de Rubén Darío* Erwin K. Mapes discusses "Aestival" only briefly, concentrating on the presence of Leconte de Lisle in Darío's later collection, *Profane Proses*. . . .

[Critics] have rightly observed that it is the prose of the first edition of *Blue*, not the poetry, which is Parnassian, the Parnassian style not appearing in Darío's verse until *Profane Proses*, or possibly, to a limited degree, in the poems added to the augmented edition of *Blue* in 1890. Until then the cautious Darío wrote traditional poetry, neoclassic or, more often, romantic. . . . "Aestival" has thus been considered—and correctly so—a romantic, not a Parnassian poem. Any effort to search for the influence of Leconte de Lisle has thereby been discouraged. But, though Darío did not borrow the tone of "Le rêve du jaguar," perhaps he did borrow other elements. . . .

It appears that one-third of "Aestival," the framework, was borrowed from Leconte de Lisle. One-third, the melodrama of the hunt and killing, is in the style of the romanticists. One-third, the sensuality of the animals' lovemaking, was Darío's own.

Frederick S. Stimson. HR. 34, Jan., 1966, pp. 53–54, 58

Darío was interested in narrating phenomena that were (and are) inexplicable by logic and unverifiable through the methods of the natural sciences. But he believed in the existence of these phenomena. . . . His personality led him to arrive fully prepared at this frontier of reality beyond which nothing can be perceived with the senses. Once at this frontier, his imagination projected superstitious, religious, metaphysical, and humorous fiction. Humorous? Yes, this also. . . . What he sees at a distance, between two lights, seems to him grotesque, and one of the components of the grotesque is humor. In Darío, as in the masters of the grotesque—Hoffmann and Poe, for example—there is a humorist. The transition from good humor to black humor and from black humor to melancholy is too gradual to be recorded. I think that not even his friends always noticed this gradation, and thus they became too serious about some of Darío's anecdotes. I imagine that in these anecdotes Darío must have said what he did with a playful gleam in his eyes.

To repeat: Darío's imagination was not that of a madman but of a normal person. Metaphysical and metapsychical fantasies usually arise in all men, possibly . . . from the depths of collective fears. . . . Perhaps Darío would have repressed this fiction, as do many realist writers, if he had not been stimulated by prestigious writers in this genre. I refer to a literature that stresses the improbable and even the impossible, a literature whose source springs from far off. . . .

Enrique Anderson Imbert. *La originalidad de Rubén Darío* (Buenos Aires, Centro Editor de América Latina, 1967), pp. 224–25†

To call Darío the founder of modernism might unjustifiably suggest that he was a revolutionary innovator. In fact, all the elements of his creativity can be traced to recognizable sources; what is new is simply his purposeful, genius-inspired synthesis of diverse influences. His early years as a librarian gave him the opportunity to become thoroughly familiar with classical Spanish writers such as Cervantes and Lope de Vega. In his mature years he took issue with the romantic poetry of Núñez de Arce, Campoamor, and Bécquer. The decisive influence, however, was his knowledge of modern French poetry. To the Parnassians he owed his clear-cut, incisive verse technique and his love of classical mythology; to the symbolists, and above all to Verlaine, a cultivated feeling for the "inner melody" of poetry; to writers like Leconte de Lisle or Chateaubriand a liking for the exotic; and to French literature in general what Juan Valera called his "spiritual Gallicism." But the product of this assimilation proved to be something quite viable. The term "modernism," chosen by Darío himself, denotes a formal and intellectual process of refinement in Hispano-American literature: a deliberate retention of the Hispanic tradition concomitant with an openness to stimuli from foreign literatures. Darío established no rigid aesthetic principles for his school. ("The true artist combines all literary trends within himself and finds beauty in whatever form it may assume.")

Gerald Hinteregger. In *Encyclopedia of World Literature in the 20th Century* (New York, Frederick Ungar, 1967), Vol. I, pp. 270–71

Darío's success as a poet is inseparable from his personal history. From the moment when—still in his early teens—he was taken from León to the Nicaraguan capital of Managua, each new city broadened his opportunities and brought to bear increasingly sophisticated influences on his poetry. The poems in *Blue*, published in Chile, were late Romantic in style. The poems of *Profane Proses*, in which Parnassian and Symbolist contours can be traced, were mostly written in Buenos Aires; in *Songs of Life and Hope*, published in Madrid, we have the self-assured prophet who had reached the goal dreamed of by many Latin Americans—the literary conquest of Spain. If the note of inner anguish is evident in this collection and in the subsequent *The Wayward Song*, perhaps, this was only natural in a man who had achieved everything he set out to do except the discovery of his own soul. Not only his poetry but also his articles, letters and essays which poured from his pen evidence his extraordinary powers of assimilation. They pulse with the beat of the moment, now with the names of Marx or Nietzsche, now with those of Léon Bloy or Zola, now Gambetta and Gladstone. Every durable and fleeting *fin de siècle* reputation is to be found in them. Those not familiar with the relationship between Latin American and European culture might be forgiven for seeing in Darío little more than a clever mime gesturing in the manner of Catulle Mendès, Hugo, Verlaine or Leconte de Lisle.

The suspicions are deepened when we observe the disparate roles he assumed and discarded in the course of his life. Friend of the poor and oppressed when in Chile, in Buenos Aires his sympathies with the workers wavered at the sight of their faces at an anarchist meeting. In Paris, he played the bohemian and decadent; in Mallorca, the Christian contemplative. . . . Certainly he never held a consistent view even of his poetry. Sometimes he placed high value on sincerity, and on poetry as the direct expression of feeling. At other times, he regarded the poem as an artefact with tensions and inner relationships analogous to those found in experience. In his work, one style never grows organically into another. But this does not make him the minah bird of Spanish literature. Nor is his work simply a receptacle of foreign influences. Rather, the vocabulary, verse forms and mythology he took from other cultures became the weapons of a prison break-out, a break away from a stale tradition that had lost touch with modern life. . . .

The modern reader often feels a preference for those poems in which mythological or literary associations are minimal. . . . But we cannot judge his work simply on the basis of contemporary preferences. . . . For a European writer to use classical myth may indicate nostalgia or a respect for hallowed values. For a Latin American the process was more positive and creative. By means of this system of references, Darío hoped to link Latin America to an existing tradition and bridge chaos and disorder with form, elegance and refinement.

TLS. June 13, 1968, p. 620

Just as it is necessary to stress the profound Americanism of a spirit so open to the winds of the world as was Rubén Darío's, it is important to minimize or reduce to its proper proportions another element on which greater stress is usually laid—his French orientation. And, by a parallel and totally objective operation, one should point out an element that is more dominant—his Spanish orientation. This last factor . . . is by definition implicit in Americanism.

The supposed contradiction, the mistake, derives from a phrase of Valera's—the "mental Gallicism" of Rubén Darío. The expression is not inexact, but given the degree of exclusion with which it is understood, it is a distortion. For a writer as correct, for a humanist of such solid stock as [was Valera], naturally the rapid, melodious, rhythmic paragraphs of the stories of *Blue* would seem exotic, especially Gallic. By the same token Valera labeled as intrusive (and, strictly speaking, they were) the preferences for French writers of the 1890s, for very secondary ones to be sure, such as Catulle Mendès. . . . However, Valera did not fail to recognize and to admire the "Spanish background" that shone through in Rubén Darío, beyond any thematic or verbal exoticism.

What surprises us today is that the writer of *Blue* could allow himself to be awed not only by writers like Catulle Mendès, but by ones of even lesser stature, such as Arsène Houssays, Armand Silvestre, and the novelist René Maizeroy, who wrote very conventional erotic fiction.

> Guillermo de Torre. *Vigencia de Rubén Darío, y*
> *otras páginas* (Madrid, Ediciones Guadarrama, 1969),
> pp. 45–46†

Today it is difficult to relive Rubén Darío's imaginary adventure of marquises, Versaillesque gardens, princesses, and swans. We prefer to say that they died away, thank God, his visions ended forever. Eager for the simplistic formula—and wanting to pass quickly over something that no longer charms or intrigues us—we reduce it all to the statement that the poetry of gentle breezes, lyres, gardens, and marquises, was a fashion that fulfilled its function in a given moment—the end of the nineteenth century and the beginning of the twentieth—by battling against the ugliness, prosaism, and vulgarity prevalent then. But by simplifying so drastically, we deny ourselves the understanding of the high tension with which these poetic visions were charged—and still are charged—for the reader. We refuse to feel with Rubén the spiritual tension, the inner shock—beyond all changes of fashion—that drove him to dream his deliriums or chant his hymns, to find an outlet for his tremendous verbal and imaginative exuberance. We don't sympathize with this poetry because in us the organ for feeling it and enjoying it has surely atrophied. It is possible, too, that we have come to the extreme of being incapable of seeing the hunger for higher beauty and humanity that can be felt by a man born in the lowest, darkest, and remotest roots of a village, rich in sensibility but poor in fortune, justice, and happiness.

Rubén Darío was born in Metapa, an insignificant spot; all his life he walked in a dream of lakes and distant palaces. But it would be unjust to call him an escapist for this. He became a cultured man, in his own way, a way that was partly that of the Hispanic world, that is, improvised, autodidactic. He lived concerned with the great and small things that happened around him. He felt himself committed to many causes and ideas of his day. He was a modern man—more than a Modernist—and he knew as few did, in those years at the end of the century, that a flood of dehumanizing dangers was coming upon us. In a curious parallel with Unamuno, Rubén undertook a humanizing mission. He already knew, in those years, that the idea of satisfying only the material needs of the villages was inadequate. He, who had known every kind of privation, knew very well that the hunger of the poor is not "hunger" in the singular, but "hungers," in a resounding and demanding plural. Hunger for human dignity; hunger for mastery over nature, things, time, and distance; hunger and thirst for justice; hunger for beauty, cleanliness and health; and above all, the hunger of hungers, that of the spirit.

Miguel Enguídanos. In Miguel González-Gerth and
George D. Schade, eds., *Rubén Darío Centennial Studies*
(Austin, University of Texas, Department of Spanish
and Portuguese, 1970), pp. 27–28

DÍAZ MIRÓN, SALVADOR (1853–1928)

MEXICO

Díaz Mirón's ideas about the life of the proletariat, so filled with misery, are best expressed in "The Pariahs." Brimming with inspiration and realism, it expresses the hunger, the exhaustion, the bad fortune, the failure of all illusion, which the poor man sees rising up before him like an implacable specter. But Díaz Mirón does more than record the social situation; he reprobates and prophesies. Today we know of the unleashed famine and fury that have swept across the soil of our nation, and we can grasp the entire meaning contained in the vigorous lines of "The Pariahs." . . .

One feels one's thoughts and reflections stampeded on reading, in lines of such beauty, of the cruel destiny which impels the oppressed to follow a path of suffering without hope, which forces men to go into combat and spill their blood and to bear on their abused shoulders the burdens of civilization. It is a bestial inheritance of centuries past, this division into masters and slaves which still permits people to tread on the lacerated and suffering bodies of the outcasts. . . .

The portrayal of misery [in "The Pariahs"] is far from pleasant. But if one can forget his prejudices about what poetry is supposed to be—only the soft plucking of the lute, the gleanings of love and delight—he might remember that the words that stick in the mind and lead to action are those that strike deep down. One should also remember that discontent endures. Happiness can hold sway in our spirits for a moment, but discouragement and sadness are constant threats. . . . He who can witness [life's] organic process will be the only one able to feel it and express it in his art. This is why "The Pariahs" is one of the most valuable poems in all of Mexican literature.

Sergio R. Viesca. Ensayos críticos (Mexico City, Imp. Manuel León Sánchez, 1926), pp. 25–28†

In order to understand the greatness of Díaz Mirón, he must be read with acumen; one must avoid hearing his voice directly; one must cast doubt upon what he states in a direct manner in order to catch hold of what he is responding to. In Díaz Mirón there is a demoniacal interlocutor whose voice is one we like to get at by penetrating through the poet's direct words. His thought and his reasoning are interrupted in every utterance. Between the reading and the reader there is interposed an external sound which removes the text to a distance, so that it must be gone over again. A "no" is thrust in, which renders necessary an insistence, on the part of the poet, in order to answer it and to prevail over it. The poetry of Díaz Mirón is a tortured poetry, but it is tortured deliberately; it is a poetry without kindliness, a poetry with an enemy, incapable of expressing itself except in conflict, as the product of hostility. The attention he wins for himself by this effort allows one "also to hear his silence."

If one regards Salvador Díaz Mirón as "Mexican Romanticism," it is made clear what was meant by the observation that Mexican poetry, paradoxically, came to Romanticism in its search for universality, in its search for a deeper discipline; one then has the truest explanation for Mexican poetry's abandonment of the Spanish school and for its turning its eyes towards France. . . . [1934]

Jorge Cuesta. In José Luis Martínez, ed., The Modern Mexican Essay (Toronto, University of Toronto Press, 1965, p. 350

Is there any positive, internal evidence in Díaz Mirón's poetry of the influence of his tropical background, any specific element of the regional in his writing to indicate a definite awareness of his native strip of coast. . . ? The answer is decidedly yes, in one respect at least. This is the recurrent image of the palm-tree, inevitably associated with the tropic, almost universally the symbol of the kind of region from which Díaz Mirón came. The occurrences of this image are fairly limited to the earlier phases of his work, but they are so sharply drawn and frequent there as to deserve a recapitulation. . . .

The changes in his work and in his inspiration have been sufficiently commented on in lengthier examinations of his poetry. There is no doubt that a factor in these changes was his imprisonment from 1892 to 1896, which had such a saddening effect on his life. In the prologue to *Chips of Stone*, he himself refers to his "fiery adolescence," recognizing a quality that belonged to his youth, and as something out of his past. Although always a spirit in revolt, the fieriness of his youth diminished through the course of his troubled life, tending toward the final aloofness and perfection-seeking of his later verse. But in his earliest period the tropical background note was there, a part of his tempestuous spirit, perhaps not frequently enough that one could say he made a fetish of the palm-tree, but undeniably present and an indication of his identity with the *tierra caliente*.

James R. Browne. *Hispania*. 32, Aug., 1949, pp. 305, 307

An "Olympian sculptor" is what Isaac Goldberg called Díaz Mirón. [Rufino] Blanco-Fombona described his verses as "sculptured," and [Jesús] Urueta proclaimed that "he carves like Michelangelo." He caused [Genaro] Fernández MacGregor to think of "Pentelic marbles" and Renaissance "bronzes." . . . [His poems display] precision, relief, firmness. There are glimmering edges and the sweep of powerful curves. . . . Such was his Parnassianism, unchecked, the same as in Gautier, and even Hérédia and Leconte de Lisle . . . in its essential, eternal romanticism. . . .

Alfonso Méndez Plancarte. *Díaz Mirón, poeta y artífice*
(Mexico City, Antigua Librería Robredo, 1954), p. 13†

Salvador Díaz Mirón's life story could never be included in a volume of *Exemplary Lives*, nor could it be printed in a book designed for teaching purposes, unless it were to be used, like negative examples in fables, to deduce from it a model of what not to do.

If one begins to discuss the acts he committed deliberately, it would be absurd to try to explain them away by looking for motivations or by pretending that the circumstances that preceded them attenuated them in any way. Even if we omit the bloody episodes in his life, Díaz Mirón's human qualities are not stellar. Nor is his worth increased by a detailed listing of the "duels of honor" in which he was a protagonist or a second, before and after having become the idol of the American continent. . . .

Those who attempted to discuss Díaz Mirón's life while he was still alive, lacking exact information, spoke only vaguely about the poet so as not to have to talk about the man. Later, however, people forgot about the poet and, with a morbid persistence, set themselves the task of compiling statistics about the encounters in which he either wounded people or was wounded, if not both.

Francisco Monterde. *Díaz Mirón: El hombre, la obra*
(Mexico City, Ediciones De Andrea, 1956), pp. 7–8†

If the work of Salvador Díaz Mirón had stopped with the poems [in *Mexican Parnassus*, later expanded in the 1895 New York edition of *Poems*], there still would have been enough material to carve a statue of him as a great figure in Latin American premodernism. "His poetry," says [his editor, Antonio Castro Leal], "had the strength and brilliance of the blade of a sword. His inspiration became stronger through his fight with form." . . . With vigorous poetic inspiration, he denounced political corruption, sang about the apostolic mission of the parties, demanded the dominion of justice, and celebrated the advent of democracy. At times, too, his song contained intimate notes: love . . . and melancholy.

Castro Leal has also pointed out that his poetry has "greatness of line and variety of shading, which are unusual in Spanish poetry." In many ways a disciple of Victor Hugo, Díaz Mirón combined a "spirited and grandiose inspiration, a strict concern for form, a clear vision of external reality, and a willingness to sacrifice delicate nuances and lyrical finesse to a passion for his country's destiny, a desire for social justice, and a hatred for all that is ignoble and base."

Guillermo Díaz-Plaja. *El reverso de la belleza*
(Barcelona, Editorial Barna, 1956), pp. 114–15†

Díaz Mirón . . . began his adult career as a politician as well as a poet, attracting attention by his brilliant speeches as deputy from 1884 to 1885. His poetry at this time reflected the influence of Victor Hugo, and he seems to have held Hugo's view of the poet as prophet and leader. . . . This early and perhaps vainglorious phase ended abruptly in 1892 when Salvador Díaz Mirón killed a man in self-defence during the election campaign and was sent to prison where he spent the next four years of his life. The poet of worldly glory became bitter and inward-looking. . . . The poems of this period and those which he wrote on his release from prison were published as *Chips of Stone* and have a much greater range and depth than his first poems. . . .

Though Salvador Díaz Mirón is less noteworthy than Asunción Silva as an innovator, his poems do carry certain Romantic preoccupations to a deeper level than any of his predecessors. After *Chips of Stone* he wrote little, but he took up his political career again and became a deputy. He was also imprisoned again in 1910 for attempted murder, and was only released after the outbreak of the Revolution. He spent some years in exile during the Revolution but returned to Mexico in 1921.

> Jean Franco. *An Introduction to Spanish-American Literature* (Cambridge, Cambridge University Press, 1969), pp. 131–33

DÍAZ RODRÍGUEZ, MANUEL (1871–1927)

VENEZUELA

It has always seemed to me so improbable that a writer under the age of forty should succeed in making himself master of that intricately organized instrument which is our language, in stamping with his own unmistakable style beautiful medallions, in impressing his lion's claw or his soft dove-like fingers upon living pages, that I believed Díaz Rodríguez to have reached at least the aforementioned age. To my surprise I found that he was still very young, that what others acquire and master after exhausting that "long patience" which is called Art, he had conquered like an Alexander, in the flower of his years. Elegant, refined, with soft and expressive eyes, slender, with complexion slightly swarthy, slow in speech, radiating from his entire person an expression of kindliness and friendliness, it is difficult to know him without esteeming and loving him. Nothing in his actions contradicts the first impression. [1902]

> Amado Nervo. In José Luis Martínez, ed.,
> *The Modern Mexican Essay* (Toronto, University of
> Toronto Press, 1965), pp. 87–88

The novel of Manuel Díaz Rodríguez, *Broken Idols*, presents in an impeccable literary form the same problem of loosely welded nationality and antagonistic social classes on which Aranha in Brazil, Alcides Arguedas in Bolivia and other writers in practically every Latin-American country have turned the light of a living artistic criticism. Alberto

Soria, the central figure of this novel, represents that small minority which in our young people is the nonconformist element, always striving for the renewal of political ideas, for a broadening of the intellectual horizon. A trip to Europe comes to aggravate the separation between this class and the mass of its countrymen. At home democracy is not the natural development of an autonomic colonial life, but a pitiable makeshift of foreign institutions; immense differences of caste, culture and social habits separate the patrician group of pure whites from the degenerate Indian population, mixed with the negro, exploited by industry and further depressed by a torrid climate. . . .

An aristocratic, melancholic atmosphere permeates the book, changing into a pathetic smile the outbursts of protests to which a less restrained mind would have given vent. His love withered under the breath of crude realities, his statues violated by the iconoclast concupiscence of a useless revolution, Alberto turns his back upon his *Broken Idols* and returns forever to Europe, the real fatherland of his spirit, murmuring as a parting responsory the classical dictum: *Finis Patriae!*

Ernesto Montenegro. NYT. April 22, 1923, p. 24

No one, not even those of us who find the literary style and ideology of Díaz Rodríguez incompatible with his public behavior, will deny that his literary works are in the forefront of our current literature, evaluated and studied by us despite the timid or disagreeable silence of those of his contemporaries so obliged to deny the imperatives of art, dignity, and conscience. . . .

[In Díaz Rodríguez] the *précieux*, the artist of the language, consumes the novelist, the one who records the immediacy of things, souls, and settings. His novels, with the exception of *Peregrina, or the Enchanted Well*, are not poetic, despite the abundant number of poetic pages scattered through them. They are rather *literary*. The style is refined, worked like the stone lace of the medieval cathedrals. But these works are disoriented, ungainly as novels, delightful lies dressed up in reality, like many others of the same type. They present misfit characters, unadapted to life, against a background of civil war. . . . The only thing that saves Díaz Rodríguez's novels from being like all the others is the purity of the style. . . .

Peregrina is Díaz Rodríguez's true Venezuelan novel, of a caliber and a construction superior to [the rest of his novels]. . . . It is the positive proof that earlier mistakes . . . can be overcome. . . .

Rafael Angarita Arvelo. Historia y crítica de la novela
en Venezuela (Berlin, August Priez Leipzig, 1938),
pp. 61–62, 67†

Díaz Rodríguez is one of the greatest modern stylists in the Spanish language. He, Rodó, and Valle Inclán, are the Spanish-language writers who write the most elegant prose. Despite his having nourished himself on French and Italian readings, this Venezuelan writer is one of the purest that America has ever had. . . . From *Stories in Color*, in which he dazzles us with his verbal aristocracy, the excellence of his images, the poetic rhythm, the charm of the descriptions, the bright clarity and strong color, to his last stories, "Father Serafín's Sheep and Roses" and "Summer Eclogue," his prose works have been ennobling. He reached his full richness in *The Way of Perfection*, and in *Peregrina, or the Enchanted Well* he shifted from modernist prose to classical prose. [1943]

Arturo Torres Ríoseco. *Grandes novelistas de la América Hispana* (Berkeley, University of California Press, 1949), pp. 87–88†

Member of a well-to-do family, linked to the officialdom of his country, Díaz Rodríguez agreed to represent dictatorships abroad through diplomatic posts and to serve them in Venezuela in such positions of importance as that of Minister of Foreign Relations for that masquerade of a government that was the "interim" presidency of Victorino Márquez Bustillo, under the aegis of Juan Vicente Gómez, "General-in-Chief of the Army" and "President-Elect" of the Republic. Manuel Díaz Rodríguez, then, is a man whose public position made him a member of a group of privileged Venezuelans during a period of oppressive and nepotic regimes.

If we contrast the position of his daily life with his literary attitudes, we cannot fail to be surprised by the differences of tone which exist between the two. The servant of a regime of profiteers, he preaches disinterest and idealism; the civil servant of a government of oligarchs, he proclaims his faith in youth and rebellion; the collaborator of the most uncouth and most backward of American brass hats, he extols curiosity and culture.

It seems as if Díaz Rodríguez, harnessed in practice by what ideally would repel him, sought in art a means of escape, of removing himself from the situation of his country and his social group. For example, in his novel *Broken Idols*, his crudest work, he offers us the spectacle of the tragedy of his generation in Venezuela. It is the novel of a man out of step, a man of progress in a land of the creole Caesar. It is a harsh and obvious criticism of the country, but it closes with the defeat and desperation of Alberto Soria, the Europeanized artist. . . . *Broken Idols* is finally a pessimistic, defeatist work. . . . It contains some passages that appear to be an *oratio pro domo sua*, the attempt at a justification of his cooperative attitude in contrast to the despairing reaction of Alberto Soria. . . .

Díaz Rodríguez has proclaimed [in *The Way of Perfection*] his faith in a disinterested art, the "armor of ideals." In a world which, he says, is Yankeefied and which venerates only material values, the artist must seek refuge for his ideals in an elevated art, in a Franciscan, Quixotic style, both humble and proud. In light of his age and its way of life, modernism seemed to Díaz Rodríguez to be not merely a school or a purely literary movement but almost a movement of life itself, like a necessary form and a logic of expression for that new ideal art which he characterizes by a tendency to return to maternal nature, nature united with the complexity, anxiety, and intensity of the modern soul as it confronts contemporary life. . . .

Luis Monguió. RI. 11, June, 1946, pp. 50–51†

As a novelist, Manuel Díaz Rodríguez has a singularly ambivalent place in the history of Venezuelan literature. Without a doubt, his personal style contributed to the creation of a Venezuelan literary style. Few others have so well wielded prose as an instrument of creativity. Few have given to it that unique chromatism, that water-color transparency, that musicality of the sweet Central-American marimba. Few have so elevated it through imagery and the re-creation of landscapes. This is his greatest merit.

But at the same time, in the history of the Venezuelan novel, Díaz Rodríguez is an example of an anachronistic writer, the embodiment of an oligarchic caste without historical relevance, the paladin of a militant literature that attempted in vain, against every principle of literary realism, to idealize the conditions that existed in the Venezuelan countryside, stubbornly covering up the burning realities of his time. His novels are feudal novels, turned inside out by a generous dose of fantasy. And his concept of society is the shaky concept of a proprietor impermeable to the broad contemporary social currents.

Raúl Agudo Freytes. RNC. No. 67, March–April,
1948, p. 156†

Throughout [Díaz Rodríguez's] work, from the first page of *Sensations of Travel* through the last note gleaned from his explorations along the Venezuelan coast (the appendix to his last book and to his life), he never indulged in any improprieties of language. Not even the broad sweep of his novels and essays or the swiftest flow of his oratory caused him to fall into the impurities of language that so often diminish the style of Latin American writers. A foreigner wanting to perfect his Spanish, the Spanish of Castile, can trust in Díaz Rodríguez's prose, concise as the metric sounds of El Cid's spur, pure as the conversation of two gentlemen in the shade of Salamanca's Escuelas Menores. This Venezuelan from Palo Grande, born among plants and stars with exotic names, carries ounces of the gold of old Castile in his literary knapsack. When he speaks to us, our ears will not be bruised by Italianisms, North-Americanisms, Gallicisms, Indianisms, urbanisms, and other "isms." These "isms," which would make him angry, all too often have transformed the patio with noble columns of the Spanish tongue into a lobby, international and raceless. . . .

Henry Holland. Hispania. 39, Sept., 1956, pp. 281–82†

No one familiar with the works of Díaz Rodríguez could deny that the principal reason for the literary reputation accorded him is his talent as a stylist. . . . Díaz Rodríguez was considerably influenced by modernism. . . . In modernist works and in the very splendor of the tropics Díaz Rodríguez found support for his intense attachment to color. . . . Color is ablaze in his landscapes. Color, whether seen concretely or abstractly or suggested symbolically, is a dominant characteristic of his prose, especially *Stories in Color.*

Patrician Blood, more than any other of his works, shows the influence of the modernist school. Its literary value rests almost entirely on its style, since the novel has a poor structure. The style is ornate, with many images, similes, and metaphors.

Lowell Dunham. Manuel Díaz Rodríguez: Vida y obra
(Mexico City, Ediciones De Andrea, 1959),
pp. 55, 57–59†

[Díaz Rodríguez's] first books, *Secrets of Psyche, Sensations of Travel, About My Pilgrimages, Stories in Color,* take solace in European civilizations—he had lived in France, in Italy, and his views were those of Barrès, of D'Annunzio. His *Stories in Color* narrated myths and legends ("blue," "green"), allegories and parables on his artistic ideas ("golden," "pale red"), reflections on love ("pale blue," "red"). Significantly, Venezuela appears in the three stories without any color: "white," "gray," and "black." All is shading, sound, perfume, caresses, evocation, and even human suffering is phrased a little to Parnassian and a little to symbolist tastes. There are no heroes in his stories: impressionistic atmospheres are the motivating characters.

In his second group of works (*Broken Idols, Patrician Blood*) Díaz Rodríguez clashes with Venezuelan reality and repudiates it esthetically. His ideal man was the "distinguished one" of Nietzsche; but his characters do not struggle. They are pessimists, defeatists, unadaptables who go into exile or to suicide. In *Broken Idols* he shows the aristocratic figure of Alberto Soria, the sculptor, in contrast with sordid and barbarous Venezuelan masses. He wanted to regenerate his country by means of his esthetic cult; the rabble harasses and breaks the icons. But Díaz Rodríguez persists in believing that a disinterested art, proud of the elaboration of beautiful forms, can at least save the liberty of intense souls; and he writes another estheticist novel, *Patrician Blood*. His novelist aim is minimal: to present the social weakening of the upper-class Creole. What is valuable is the description of the states of the soul, and this description is not that of a psychologist but of a symbolist writer. This is odd, because the theme would have lent itself to a psychological novel; after all, it is the novel of a neurosis. . . .

In his later fiction Díaz Rodríguez attempted the Creole narrative, a form in which his artistic ideals could function, and function well, immersed in the land and its men. It is as if he took refuge from his disillusion in country life, in the direct emotional encounter with nature. Still, however, he continued to manipulate his narrative material to cast it into a coin of spectacular phrases. In other words, it was Díaz Rodríguez' phraseology rather than Venezuela that makes these last works of his spectacular. And he manipulated his material so urgently that it was not merely his descriptions that became congealed in metaphors, but the action itself took on incredible dramatic spasms. . . .

Enrique Anderson Imbert. *Spanish-American Literature,
a History*, 2nd ed. (Detroit, Wayne State University
Press, 1969), pp. 390–91

DONOSO, JOSÉ (1925–   )

CHILE

The protagonist of *Coronation* is a lady over ninety years old, Doña Elisa Grey de Abalos, who at times behaves extravagantly and in general is just plain crazy. More than a protagonist, Doña Elisa is perhaps the tutelary shadow of the novel. Beneath the ample fringes of this shadow the other characters love, rob, complain, and go mad. When Rosario and Lourdes, the two servants, play at crowning her and she dies after taking one last look at the stars, the novel assumes her point of view and then ends.

Misiá Elisita [Doña Elisa] represents an age and a world that have been lost forever, a world with rights and obligations that were absolutely prescribed. . . . Her tattered old age could seem like a triumph over death, but it is rather a disaster. Other writers (Tolstoy, Rilke) have created an overwhelmingly tragic atmosphere for a few individual deaths. Donoso presents *survival* as overwhelmingly tragic, in the shame that living too long represents.

All the psychological riches that generally become the property of old age here have no effect. The words "experience" and "tradition," to whose mythic power the elderly are accustomed to trust their expert evaluation of existence, are here worthless currency. When she is left without her reason, when she comes to see and hear everything in terms of her boundless manias, Misiá Elisita becomes the victim of an excess of life, something far worse than the lofty announcement of death. When death finally arrives, the last glimmer of consciousness she still has enables her to see that this is a time for celebration and that, although horribly overdue, it is the final piece of business in her liberation, which is, at long last, taking place.

But before Misiá Elisita can have her so-often-postponed coronation, before her violent and ineffable madness is to be rewarded, Donoso casts his gaze about, over two or three generations and as many social classes, as if searching in advance for the prototype to replace this senile and haughty monstrosity that has had the misfortune to outlive itself. [1958]

Mario Benedetti. *Letras del continente mestizo*, 2nd ed. (Montevideo, Editorial Arca, 1969), pp. 154–55†

[*Coronation*] might be regarded as an account of the decay of the upper class. Misiá Elisa, so old, so useless, so given to self-deception, so quick to inflict pain on others, could be taken as a symbol, with Andrés displaying the impotence of his class. But the representatives of the working class are no better. René is cruel and greedy, almost a personification of evil. Mario shows some decent impulses at the outset, but he is corrupted by circumstances and his brother, and there is little doubt that he will come to a bad end. . . .

Donoso, it is clear, takes a dark view of the human condition, and yet the book does not succeed in giving the reader a tragic sense of life. This is in part because the author relies so heavily on direct analysis of psychological states. The portrayal of Don Andrés, in particular, is close to a case history of regression. Despite the fact that the author has studied in America and teaches English literature, he seems to be under the influence of the French psychological novel.

In part, however, he is quite successful, Misiá Elisa in her bad mood is the incarnation of malice. The affair of Mario and Estela has its idyllic moments, though they are brief. The old servants provide an effective sort of chorus, and one can only be amused by their high jinks at the end.

Granville Hicks. *SR*. March 13, 1965, pp. 27–28

Coronation is an authentic philosophical novel by a South American writer who may not have done so well by his translator. Or perhaps the built-in difficulties are at fault. In any event, the language into which the book has been translated seems banal, at any given moment, in comparison to the broad movements of its plot, which are fine and compelling. . . .

A Chilean nobleman has reached middle age without having known passion. Surrounded by servants (Donoso is very good at rendering the life of the kitchen), he reads 17th-century French memoirs, collects antique canes, and has as his one aim in life the preservation of a queenly and demented grandmother. Her inability to die parallels his inability to live, and her Puritanism, which expresses itself in bizarre sexual fantasies, explains his own arrested growth.

Fantastically, the old woman accuses the grandson of relations with a servant girl. The fantasy takes root in his mind, inspires strange jealousies, demoralizes. As the grandmother is about to pass from this life (in a remarkable "coronation scene" arranged by her servants on her name day), he passes almost voluntarily into her state of madness in order to protect himself from the intolerable perceptions to which his tardy passions have exposed him. Meanwhile the servant girl, who has a life of her own, who is more than a mere plot device, falls into a degrading *entente* that contrasts poignantly with her master's jealous vision of her supposed sensuous freedom and innocence.

The trouble is that little of this plot-life gets into the words. The grandson's philosophical musings, which are vital to the plot, sound like badly translated Unamuno. The language of the lower classes, which must have had a tang in Spanish, sounds like American vulgarity badly imitated. One has to make up one's own language as one reads this. For the plot's sake, that is a job worth doing.

Arthur R. Gold. *BW*. June 6, 1965, p. 14

[*This Sunday*] revolves on a single axis—the family celebration of Sunday, Sunday at grandmother's. Such a subject is sufficiently flexible to permit incursions into the past and into the future, which enables Donoso to make a diagnosis for us. Because this is all we have in the end: a bitter diagnosis of the social and the metaphysical, not only of *the* family—of course, not of *a* family—but of a society and also of a way of life. The possibilities that emerge in the development of this novel, from what at first seems a limited theme, perhaps one that is even microsociological, are quite broad and lead to all of these dimensions.

A family is the protagonist of the novel: the grandfather and the grandmother, a grandson and his parents, uncles and cousins. The grandson is important in being able to gauge the others in relation to himself. There is also a servant, her daughter, the daughter's husband, and finally a prison inmate. After laying out the characters in this way, I begin to wonder if I should say that the protagonist of the novel is perhaps nothing other than the *conjunction*, the tangle, of relations. Perhaps.

In any case, what we are given is a mosaic of observations, a series of items, of *data* provided by various persons: the grandfather seen by the grandson, by the grandmother; the grandfather in his loneliness, right before our eyes, so to speak, and to a certain extent right before his own eyes; the grandmother seen by the grandfather, by the grandson; the grandmother and grandfather seen with others; and so on. We are given, in short, lives, various interrelated lives, presented with a radical fragmentation and a radical ambiguity. Of course, the fundamental mark of this novel is its complexity, a complexity in simplicity, in the *apparent* simplicity of some Sunday afternoons at grandmother's house. It is a "scalpel novel" in which a firm hand cuts an incision into our daily skins and shows the internal and *mortal* tumor, mortal because there is no solution, because this Sunday is happening right now. And on one Sunday, through a sudden alteration in the diverse elements that make up bourgeois "normality," everything will come tumbling down. *This Sunday* is a chronicle of a decadence, of a social decomposition. . . .

Julio E. Miranda. *CHA*. No. 209, May, 1967,
pp. 442–43†

The world created in [Donoso's] works is that of family life in Chile in the middle of the twentieth century, the world it has been his lot to live in. It is a world in which we find the same experience repeated: the savage discovery of the violence that lies beneath the apparently conventional surface of a society that is quite stratified and bourgeois. The writer records this world in its semifeudal, semiurban quality with a lucidity that becomes more frightening from work to work. It is a world in which the rich and the poor, the Two Nations of which Disraeli spoke in his famous pamphlet-novel, live inextricably intertwined, a world in which social categories, separable in sociological and economic analysis, are inseparable in the deepest sphere of passions, a world in which everyday superficial reality hides and releases from time to time the most horrible monsters of the human mind.

Naturalistic and dreaming, literal and symbolic, traditional and innovative, José Donoso has created in three novels and a handful of stories a whole world which indisputably bears his own stamp and which speaks for him with the same power with which the fictional universes of Clarice Lispector, Juan Rulfo, José Lezama Lima, or Carlos Martínez Moreno speak for those extraordinary artists. Rather than boring comparisons between Donoso and Latin American novelists of more epic scope (comparisons that abound these days in the Chilean literary magazines), I would prefer to link him with the writers who have succeeded in transforming the story of their lives into fiction, their personal obsessions into myths, their terrors and lucid dreams into imaginative reality, their inner universe into a land through which, both free and bewitched, the creations of their invention move. . . .

There is enough evidence to claim the presence of a profound reality in these novels and stories of Donoso's: a tortured and night-marish reality, a reality which completes the world of surfaces, which gives it a ballast of shadows, which duplicates it in a terrifying mode. This reality is a part of the work of José Donoso, and it would be advisable for readers (and critics, too, of course) not to fail to see it. Because that is where one can find the reasons for the profoundly disturbing and original nature of the creation of this Chilean novelist, who is just now approaching full maturity.

Emir Rodríguez Monegal. MNu. No. 12, June, 1967,
pp. 77, 85†

The central inversion in [*Place without Limits*], that of Manuel, sets in motion a series of inversions. . . . In this sense *Place without Limits* continues the mythic tradition of the "world upside down," which the surrealists practiced so assiduously. The theme of the novel, more than transvestism—that is to say, the appearance of sexual inversion—is inversion in and of itself: an associative chain of "about-faces," of transposed denouements, dominates the progression of the narrative.

Manuela, who novelistically (grammatically) *means* being a woman—the first inversion [in the sense that Manuela is the woman's name for Manuel]—functions as a man, for it is as a man that she/he attracts Japonesa. . . .

From within this inversion another one arises: in the sexual act the role of Manuela, a man by narrative attribution, is passive, not feminine—and this is why what we have is an inversion within an inversion and not simply a return to the initial transvestism—but a passive man who is impregnated despite himself. Japonesa possesses him by making herself possessed by him. She is the active element in the *act.* . . .

Donoso is skillful in masking the word . . . as if to situate it symbolically in the affective realm that belongs to Manuela, to attribute to her, making the third-person reflector narration serve as a form of concealment, the "responsibility" for the story, an "I" on the prowl, overlapping the real subject of the elocution. All of *him/her* is a cover up; a latent "I" threatens him, undermines him from within, splits him. As in that other place without limits—our dreams—here everything says "I." [1968]

Severo Sarduy. *Escrito sobre un cuerpo: Ensayos de crítica* (Buenos Aires, Editorial Sudamericana, 1969), pp. 44–45†

An intensely powerful, dynamic, and authoritative presentation of tragic hardships in a small Chilean society captivates the reader in this explosive novel [*Place without Limits*]. Action revolves around the lives of four principal characters: La Manuela, Pancho Vega, La Japonesita, and Don Alejo. Each is tortured mentally and physically by the devastating social and economic conditions that prevail. Introspection, psychological penetration, and self-analysis dominate this work.

An invigorating style and a brilliant new technique are presented. This primitive society living in a sordid *barrio*, is created and crystallized, stroke by stroke, with the massing of telling facts interspersed with sharp irony and satire. . . . What the reader extracts from the novel is not simply a picture of these individuals in the act of living, talking, or looking back upon specific events; rather, one perceives, feels, and identifies their internal anguish and their travail of self-discovery.

There is an aura of hope throughout the novel—conversely, a hoping for the impossible. Nevertheless, *Place without Limits* is more than a portrait of wasted life in a hopeless world. . . .

The author consistently uses ideas and characters possessing a universal vitality, thus achieving thematic unity. This work is more than a mere observation or spectacle. It is an indication of mature and profound intuition. Ideas, expression, and atmosphere are superb. Its other outstanding qualities are local color, prosaic beauty and feeling, a high moral tone, and excellent motivation and character delineation.

Edward M. Malinak. *BA*. 42, Winter, 1968, p. 81

It might be that *This Sunday* is too much like *Coronation*, not only in characters and milieu but even in some of the plotting. As a novel *This Sunday* comes off better. But what Donoso has been giving us (here and foreshadowed in some earlier stories, a few written originally in English) is the portrait of a decaying society, nostalgic for a glory that had never quite existed, with the other classes lacking the moral and psychological dominance to succeed except through violence. The relations between master and servant will elicit comparisons with the modern American South, but without the complication of race. The strength of the household servants, of the poor, of the criminal, is contrasted with the enervation of the well-to-do, but is insufficient for any real accomplishment. . . .

The central figure of *Coronation* is a man in his 50s still under the thumb of his nonagenarian grandmother. The first-person narrator of *This Sunday* hardly speaks of his parents; it is the grandparents that we see through his eyes and then, alternately, through their own. The middle generation appears as confused lists of names and is dead, whether in the grave or on their feet. The memories of the grandparents go back to their youth, passing over their young adulthood as though over a desert. As the children are deprived of parents (figuratively for the rich, literally through illegitimacy or abandonment for the poor), so parents have no children. The law professor's wife in *This Sunday*, despite her many offspring, is alienated from them and searches for a babe to suckle, like a "littered bitch." Her children are the poor, as she ambles about performing her aimless works of charity. . . . Her own destruction is brought about by the youngest generations of her surrogate children. It is the youngest of the poor who surround her and deprive her of life. And it is they, not her own descendants, who inherit her house as they overrun the abandoned mansion.

Donoso has created a more horrifying nightmare for his victims in this latest work than in *Coronation*, which at times was merely grotesque. He has now a surer hand with delineation of oddity (the aging grandson's prized walking-stick collection in the earlier novel was silly; here, the deaf grandfather attempting Händel's *Harmonious Blacksmith*, imitating [the great pianist Alfred] Cortot's *tempo*, tells us much more). He finally succeeds in making us know the full complexity of the immature and the post-mature mind with remarkable economy.

Donoso's *This Sunday* is scarcely longer than a novella. But we can take from it as much experience of human decay as we can bear.

Oliver T. Myers. Nation. March 11, 1968, pp. 351, 353

If it is true that the theme of isolation, which in the 1950s became one of the preferred themes of the new novelists, has become a commonplace in Latin American fiction, it is no less certain that its continued use constantly reveals new and more interesting dimensions. In *Coronation*, for example, José Donoso shows in detail the richness and limitless possibilities of the theme. . . .

The central theme of the work is evidently not isolation, but the decadence of a bourgeois society, trapped in its own condition. . . . But beneath this theme, as Emir Rodríguez Monegal has pointed out, is the "existential attachment between the emotional world of the oligarchy and the world of the destitute classes," an attachment, in short, that reveals an underground struggle between the oligarchic group and that of the servers, fraught with social and sexual complications. Nevertheless . . . [the] individuals are isolated not only within their own class but also within their own existence. Isolation comes to constitute, in this way, at least a secondary theme, a backdrop for the social theme. For this reason, one can assert that the overall structure of the novel revolves on two axes. The horizontal axis of the novel is the social theme (the routine of bourgeois life, the sordid environment in which the lower class lives, the conflict of the classes, and so forth); the only change possible is seen in the progressive ruin of the society that is revealed before our eyes. Tied to the horizontal movement . . . is the vertical axis, the theme of isolation, on which the action of the novel moves.

In my opinion, isolation in *Coronation* is expressed on three planes: physical isolation, emotional isolation, and spiritual isolation. . . .

Isaac Goldemberg. MNu. No. 36, June, 1969, p. 74†

In *Summer Vacation, and Other Stories* we see the beginnings of Donoso's central themes . . . although, of course, not as yet fully developed, because, in addition to being his first work . . . it also reflects literary modes of the 1950s. . . .

In the title story, "Summer Vacation," Donoso reveals what can be considered his obsession with the interrelationship of worlds within worlds, which is shown in this story through the experiences of a child. Raúl's childhood . . . is seen on three levels. The personality of the child is affected by the closed and mysterious universe created by his relations with Jaime, a youth who dominates and attracts him, drawing him toward the unknown, an impenetrable world completely separated from the daily universe that surrounds Raúl in the bosom of his family. Another subject appears in "Summer Vacation" that Donoso has taken up repeatedly throughout his career—the world of the servants. Donoso's protagonists are always finding a new, unknown world in the servants, in whom they discover an alliance they do not have in the world of their family. Or they find a relationship that ranges from the discovery of love (in *This Sunday* the protagonist is initiated into sexuality by the house servant), to an unhealthy obsession (as in *Coronation*), to the most blatant hatred (as in the relationship between Rosario and Misiá Elisita in *Coronation*). Perhaps "Summer Vacation," of the stories that make up this volume, is the one in which we can most clearly see this interrelationship among different worlds.

Ana María Moix. Prologue to José Donoso, Cuentos
(Barcelona, Editorial Seix Barral, 1971), pp. 16–17†

Against the rigidities of society, there is an ever-present oceanic sense in Donoso into which his heroes plunge. These pathetic and at times comic figures are pilgrims of their own brand of truth, vague searchers for a freer self and society, constantly at odds with the reality of their own spiritual suffocation. A groping for a sense of transcendence, a whole process that inevitably entails the encounter with the monster that is within them, engendered out of the mathematical rigidities with which societies function in apparent order. As Emir Rodríguez Monegal has pointed out in his brilliant study of Donoso, it is precisely this discovery of violence that is the obsessive and often repeated theme. It has also been pointed out that there are rarely any valid paternal figures in his work—it is very much of a matriarchy, but one in which masculine and feminine roles function nonetheless, all to the detriment of those concerned. And often, too, above all in a few of the early stories, a good story is robbed of its impact by a too obviously psychological explanation in lieu of an ending. Such a story is "Big-Scale Party," where a "Napoleonic" national pistol champion, after having engaged in some tragicomic antics at an office picnic, is lulled to sleep by his ancient mother after she has rather obviously gone through his jacket to remove the pistol, which is, of course the cause of all the trouble. But such moments are rare in Donoso's short pieces.

But certainly our sensibilities are constantly engaged by Donoso's stories—above all, because of the sheer power of the inarticulate that underlies them all. He is always careful to draw for us a miniature portrait of a society, often from the point of view of a child-like narrator who is sensitized to the significance of every detail. What draws us out as readers is the power of the unspoken in him, the deadly attraction of nothingness. It would seem that his work, glanced at in a cursory fashion, does more than its share of the reader's work, because it is so evidently a refraction of a society, but this aspect can only cloud our vision of this wholly contemporaneous literary achievement. The carefully appointed society which Donoso began to depict in *Coronation* and in the stories is for us a functioning lie possibly pointing to a truth; the words surround rather than express a reality. If they denote anything, one would have to mention a society that is itself inauthentic and false. . . .

Alexander Coleman. *SSF*. 8, 1, Winter, 1971, pp. 157–58

Death, old age, orphanhood, an asylum, a chapel that is about to be done away with, a mausoleum that is so full that it is necessary to squeeze the remains of occupants together to make room for the newcomers; a world of mortal agonies or (and this amounts to the same thing) the last death throes of our world—this is what José Donoso casts at us in the opening of *The Obscene Bird of Night*.

This novel unrelentingly presents just such a setting. It also focuses on what its writer has accustomed us to in his previous novels—the decadence of the Chilean society he was brought up in. He has sought a corner no one wanted to talk about because it is ugly, abandoned, on the inevitable and palpable road to destruction. It is a place in which the decrepit, the sordid, the grimy, the useless, and the incredible make their nest. It is a piling up and jealous guarding of things that are completely worthless, although the old ladies [who figure so prominently in the novel] think that, in fact, they are worth a lot. And in fact, these things are necessary to them in their evasions of reality, in their games of poetic and repulsive magic. And they are also necessary to the novelist so that he can provide us, in a manner also apparently evasive, with his vision and testimony of the end of something. . . .

Everything is at its end. Everything would end in the closed circle of life if the old ladies did not preserve a thread of attachment to the rest of the universe. This attachment is maintained in two ways: first, through the lady of the aristocracy, the protectress and the owner of the asylum; second, through the past, the tie between El Mudito [the narrator] and the seignorial, opulent house [of the aristocratic family]. This mansion is also falling down from within, in its morality, making inevitable the extinction of the great family, which has failed in its attempt to have a son, failed in its marriage, failed in the maintenance of a spiritual position, first established in the eighteenth century with the origin of the legend of the Blessed Inés, which had led to the erection of the asylum [both a convent and a home for retired servants].

The past, lost among the dusty corridors of the convent, has left its roots in the mansion. The decadent life of the servants is some kind of link between the two different aspects of the world [the upper and the lower classes in Chile]. The teeming mind of El Mudito keeps in the present what happened in the past and, without the characters aware of it, is capable [as the narrator] of making everything burst forth. . . . It is an entire world, to be sure, and in a more immediate vision, it is a Chilean world, the world to which José Donoso has dedicated himself in all of his works up to now, novels like *Coronation* and *This Sunday*. . . .

Jorge Campos. *Insula*. No. 294, May, 1971, p. 11†

The formula "Everything can be substituted" well summarizes the perspective that integrally controls the structure of the *The Obscene Bird of Night*. The first substitution—and in a certain sense, the primary one—is taken from the legendary past, which the novel assimilates in the form of a story within a story. . . . It is the story of witches centering on the daughter of one Azcoitía, a powerful landowner, and of her woman servant. The ending toys with a double substitution: because of popular outrage, the servant-witch substitutes for the child-witch . . .

at the same time that the child-witch, cloistered in the Convent of the Encarnación de la Chimba, becomes the protagonist of another, apparently separate story, that of the child-saint. Both situations are possible because there is a point of contact in the events. . . .

The concealing of the "true reality" is something that afflicts all of the characters . . . as well as the narrators who in turn present the story, and those who listen to it, including the reader, of course. This explains why in Chapter 21 there is an array of variants and subvariants of the story, including one that is just the opposite: the child "was neither a witch nor a saint."

Antonio Cornejo Polar. *Nuevos Aires*. No. 9,
Jan.–Feb., 1972, pp. 17–18†

There is . . . a central theme [in *The Obscene Bird of Night*], the demise of a feudal society, to which the reader can relate the many loose strands he picks up during his journey through the fictional maze. Don Jerónimo de Azcoitía, a powerful member of Chile's traditional landholding class, marries his cousin Inés who belongs to the same social elite. Their union produces a monstrously deformed child, Boy, whom Don Jerónimo's male secretary, Humberto Peñaloza, is ordered to educate at the family estate of La Rinconada. After an indefinite period, Humberto begins creating his own reality, a fictional microcosm revolving around the master's life. It is through his deranged, disoriented mind that we view the demise of the feudal aristocracy. When the secretary grows old he is sent (as all the retired Azcoitía servants have been for generations) to la Casa de Encarnación [the House of the Incarnation], a joint establishment of the family and the Church. Here, he takes on the guise of a deaf-mute, El Mudito, and in a long delirium he tells his own biography.

Around this basic plot line of the novel Donoso weaves Humberto's fantasy-ridden interpretation of Don Jerónimo's life as well as the equally exaggerated recreation of his own. Both versions are filtered through the secretary's distorted view of people and events, creating a surrealistic world populated by grotesque members of a meaningless feudal existence.

The novel begins and ends at la Casa de Encarnación but what transpires between commencement and finale falls into no logical sequence. The old people's home and La Rinconada serve as the poles of the work, each a kind of labyrinth and each an equally horrifying symbol of the decay of an oligarchical system. The temporal and spatial disarrangement is basic to *The Obscene Bird of Night* as it contributes to the overall impression of chaos, the inversion of values and myths of a way-of-life that is seen on the verge of extinction. . . .

Corresponding to the Azcoitías' place of prominence in the affairs of the Church and the nation is a family legend they refer to, myopically, as "la niña-beata" [the pious young girl]. Throughout generations the family has stubbornly preserved the version they believe will cast them in the best possible light and will more firmly cement their ties with Divine Power. In contrast, the peasants of the estate, who refer to the legend "niña-bruja" [the child-witch] tell about the mysterious metamorphosis of a landowner's daughter into a terrible bird-like head brought about through the intercession of her *nana* [nursemaid]. In both versions, the witch, who takes on the form of a yellow dog, is killed while the girl is bundled off to a convent. The contemporary re-enaction of the legend involves Don Jerónimo's wife Inés and her nurse and relative, La Peta Ponce. Donoso uses the legend to heighten the cyclical struggle between the feudal aristocracy and those elements that have traditionally threatened its authority and power.

Charles M. Tatum. *LALR*. 1, 2, Spring, 1973, pp. 100–101

Donoso's art reflects the distorted and dramatic grimace of Goya's *Caprichos* and the dark humor of Buñuel's poetic movies. But there are also definite differences. Goya's characters—the witches, soldiers, drunkards—have been pulled out of the taverns, the streets, and their vital habitats, to be torn and transmuted. Buñuel's art has its roots in surrealism with frequent projections toward allegory. The characters in *The Obscene Bird of Night*, however, are transformed by constant mutation into metaphoric figures. In Donoso's novel, transformation is a mirror of the world, and in that sense it approaches the great myths of metamorphosis: Ovid's *Metamorphosis*, Apuleius' *The Golden Ass*, and especially Hieronymus Bosch's *The Garden of Delights*, to which Donoso's cosmos is clearly related.

Two spatial contexts in *The Obscene Bird of Night* also achieve a metaphoric projection. The House of the Incarnation of La Chimba, once a convent and later a home for old women who live there in an alienated reality different from the normal one, is a place where useless things accumulate; it is nothing other than an obscure labyrinth of "patios, more patios . . . passageways, meandering adobe, empty rooms, useless chambers . . ." La Rinconada, the other spatial context of *The Obscene Bird of Night*, is a universe inhabited by monsters. It is an arbitrary place created by Jerónimo de Azcoitía in order to conceal his son's deformity, and it is governed by Jerónimo's double, Humberto Peñaloza. Both spaces in *The Obscene Bird of Night* are anarchic; both are worlds of collective alienation that acquire the meaning of an allegorical abstraction. If in *This Sunday*, one of the narrators, the grandson, placed his alienated self within the space of a crystal ball from which he contemplates the world, then in *The Obscene Bird of Night*, the whole spatial world is one huge transparent fishbowl in never-ending mutation. As in Bosch's triptych, the great crystal globe of Donoso's cosmos ends in a tableau which filters, distorts and transforms reality—where past, present and future are one. The grotesque and the monstrous free reality from its temporal bounds.

Although Bosch places his monsters of the earth, sea, and sky in an arbitrary space, there is no doubt that he gives the earth a privileged position. Bosch divided his triptych into: (1) the Garden of Eden—false pride; (2) the repressed pleasures and desires of the world—occupying the largest part at the center; (3) the tortures of Hell. It is all a game of constant metamorphosis in anarchical space. Bosch's universe, in consonance with the perspective of the fifteenth and sixteenth centuries, reflects the terror of God's absence in a world where Satan is triumphant, pointing to a destructive reality rather than to religious hope of salvation. In Donoso's world, man is a recluse who is never the Self but always the Other. Therein lies his rejection of religion, institutions, and reality. But Donoso's cosmos rests totally on earth, the only place without limits, where we are "given" heaven and hell.

Zunilda Gertel. Review 73. No. 9, Fall, 1973, p. 21

EDWARDS BELLO, JOAQUÍN (1887–1967)

CHILE

It is clear that many of the ideas presented in this novel, *The Down-and-Outer*, which serves as a prologue to his later work, do not have solidity or are simply absurd. One must consider Edwards Bello either as a capricious child or as an outstanding student of Nietzsche, who pities the man who does not contradict himself at least twice daily. Passionate, violent, without the sense of literary responsibility that every writer should have, Edwards Bello offers strong vitality as the only excuse for all the sins he commits against aesthetics, truth, and common sense.

Edwards Bello has learned certain details of technique from [Pío] Baroja. . . . In both novelists' works the good people are frequently crushed by cruelty and lack of understanding. . . . The two feel the desire to be poets and to paint landscapes for us with the sun, water, and the song of birds. Each one, a vagabond in his world, forgets about the plot in order to write travelogues: herein originates the weakness of construction, and the constant tendency of both authors to ramble. . . . Like Baroja, the Chilean prefers to express himself freely, frankly, daringly, and at times boldly. . . . And like the great Basque writer Baroja, Edwards Bello despises the cursed young men and women who are products of the stupid and hypocritical life of high society, which is filled with affectation and feigned cultural interests. . . . The Chilean and the Basque equally love all that is popular, sometimes even praising what is base.

Arturo Torres Ríoseco. *Grandes novelistas de la
América Hispana* (Berkeley, University of California
Press, 1943), pp. 104–5, 122–23†

In his quest for truth and social reform, Edwards Bello has chastised Chilean society and its behavior, focusing on the cities, principally Santiago and Valparaíso. The result has been a rich series of portraits of manners and a considerable variety of types from all classes of Chilean society. To know Chile, its anxieties and its disquietudes, one needs to turn to Edwards Bello's interpretation. According to some critics and observers, his sparse but violent propaganda has been a great impetus to political and social reform in his country.

I can understand why naturalism may not be congenial in a work of art. Its unpleasant, repulsive subjects are a profanation of aesthetics. But we must recognize in this literary movement the potential power of its social content, of its psychological study of characters, analyzed primarily from the point of view of environment and heredity. Therefore, although it is true that at times Edwards Bello's work is repellent to us because of its strong naturalistic details, we must also admit that it moves us and even convinces us because of its sociological insights and because of the apostolic mission of the writer in his fervor to better his beloved fatherland.

Chile, exposed by Edwards Bello, is revealed in all its defects, all its vices, all its internal sociological problems. But by the same token it is shown to be fully alive, sick perhaps, but not dead; struggling with a surprising energy to save its traditions, its customs, and its morals. Chileans themselves are responsible for the condition of their homeland; therefore, Edwards Bello turns his pen against them, with boldness and even with excessive cruelty. His types, passionate but real, become at times caricatures because of his desire to put before the eyes of his compatriots all of the ugliness and the vices they represent, all the evil that such individuals can bring to the fatherland if government and society do not side with him to remedy those vices. Thus, he presents corrupt and ambitious politicians, who together with the police make a mockery of the law, using it only for their own benefit. Education, alcoholism, gambling, prostitution, juvenile delinquency, matrimony— all of these issues touching the lives of the Chilean people are treated by Edwards Bello. And although he does not offer solid proposals for their improvement, he at least points them out with great sincerity and vigor, with the hope that his compatriots will not ignore his cry of alarm. . . . [1947]

> Edna Coll. *Chile y los chilenos en las novelas de Joaquín Edwards Bello*, 2nd ed. (San Juan, Ediciones Juan Ponce de León, 1965), pp. 181–82†

While Augusto d'Halmar wandered among the realms of illusion and imagination, [Edwards Bello] created works solidly based on the urban reality of our country and on the idiosyncrasies of the Chilean both inside and outside his homeland. Even though man's problems form the nucleus of his writings, he has not overlooked the physical setting in which his characters act. He is, of course, quite far removed from the landscape preoccupations of Mariano Latorre, but nothing escapes his penetrating gaze: neither the hills of Quillota, "turned the rosy color of flesh by the fall of dusk," nor the Andean peaks, "built by a Cyclopean race," nor the inhospitable coast, "without a single friendly port," nor the "pitiful rivers," stretching out over the breadth of the land like "dividing lines." The sea throbs in his writings, the sea "on which his forefathers arrived on the sailing vessel *Virgen de Begoña.*" . . .

But, as we have reiterated in our examination of his works, [Edwards Bello's] forte is the study of the organization of Chilean society, its groups and its individuals. Unfortunately, he has not succeeded in freeing himself of a huge store of a priori opinions, which get in the way of his principles. In his assessment of values, in his tireless scrutinization of any biped that comes under his pen, he applies categories he had subscribed to when too young, when inexperience still renders man audacious and precipitate. He defends the populace, deprecates the middle class, censures the aristocracy, but without renouncing the latter. In other words, every "broken man" is a hero, every bourgeois is ambitious and venal, every aristocrat is degenerate. . . . Abnormal types abound in the works of Edwards Bello, psychopaths deformed by the writer's caricaturing in his desire to symbolize the different levels of social degradation. But just as he likes to intensify the darker colors, he also takes pleasure in enhancing what is already rosy. As a sort of compensation for human degeneracy, the beautified landscape shines forth.

Julio Orlandi and Alejandro Ramírez. Joaquín Edwards Bello, obra-estilo-técnica (Santiago de Chile, Editorial del Pacífico, 1959), pp. 27–28†

ELIZONDO, SALVADOR (1932–   )

MEXICO

Farabeuf, or the Chronicle of an Instant is an experimental novel. Having said this, we have not gotten very far. Indeed, if we rely on some definition of the novel, including the most recent ones, *Farabeuf* does not fit into the genre. But perhaps it would fit if we applied Robbe-Grillet's notion of a novel without plot, without conflict, and without characters. Let us take the text of Elizondo for what it is: often excellently written prose that communicates, above all, the immediate image (if the reader wants to find something resembling a plot with characters, I refer him to Chapter Three).

First, let us gather on one side possible influences: Elizondo is tempted to push experience to limits, like Céline or Bataille; Elizondo's narration is in the second person, as is Butor's; there is a lot of the Marquis de Sade in his book. . . . The European "demonical" tradition, especially that of France, which hid Sade only to discover him later, is present throughout this "chronicle." . . .

Does *Farabeuf* have a theme? At least reiterated variations of the same motif could be brought to mind: "the concretion of our own dissatisfied desire." Desire and lack of desire, attraction and lack of it, cause the novel to play a constant game (the mirror is precisely the image of this game) between the right side and the wrong side, the head and tail of the same coin (the Yes and the No, the "Yin and Yang," which dominate . . . the whole work). . . .

Farabeuf is a "novel" about the dream that is life. But it is a dream that no one projects onto anything; it is the pure image of a dream without a subject and perhaps without an object.

Ramón Xirau. Diálogos. No. 10, July–Aug., 1966,
pp. 43–44†

It should be emphasized that *Farabeuf* is not primarily a psychological novel. The characters, their actions, and the motivation for their actions are never clearly analyzed, the author refusing to admit that he knows any more about them than the reader or the characters themselves. Elizondo's work is above all an aesthetic experiment in novelistic technique with philosophical overtones inextricably linked to its aesthetic objectives. It is similar to the "nouveau roman" that has been appearing in France since the publication of Alain Robbe-Grillet's *Les gommes* in 1953.

While the "new novel" is characterized by a reaction against rationalistic and scientific philosophical systems and psychological analysis by the omniscient author, in its quest for artistic innovations it has felt the influence of two twentieth-century philosophies: phenomenology and existentialism. In their subjective approach to reality Elizondo and other "new novelists" reveal the influence of the German philosopher Husserl, the originator of phenomenology, who influenced existentialist thought. In order to understand Elizondo's novelistic technique and aesthetic objectives, a basic understanding of Husserl's philosophy is essential. . . .

Farabeuf is an excellent fictional illustration of Husserl's philosophy. By repetition of opaque objects such as the doctor's surgical instruments, his rubber gloves, the marble-top table, the velvet curtains, the door at the end of the corridor, and the dead starfish, Elizondo captures the immediate, superficial appearance of these objects which gradually lose their false mysteries and surrender their symbolic secrets. For example, Farabeuf's surgical knives and the "sharp fingers" of his stiff rubber gloves become phallic symbols. The hall door represents the line between life and death, and the dead starfish which the woman picks up and casts aside evokes an eerie prophecy of death. Other objects merely provide compositional effect or atmosphere and appear deliberately inserted as anti-symbolic. Thus the novel contains a curious mixture of meticulously described but limited reality and of suspended, subjective awareness.

George R. McMurray. Hispania. 50, Sept., 1967,
pp. 597–98

Success is contagious, or so an increasing number of new Spanish American authors would appear to believe. They have approached the consecrated models (Cortázar, Vargas Llosa, Fuentes), pressing ever nearer to these successful fragmenters of reality and the old techniques of literary realism in the apparent hope that proximity might well produce the desired contagion. . . .

Hard on the heels of Carlos Fuentes' puzzling pop-show, *A Change of Skin*, and Luis Guillermo Piazza's do-it-yourself novel-collage, *The Mafia*, comes Salvador Elizondo's *The Secret Hypogeum* which, in turn, follows up his own interesting experiment in fragmentation, *Farabeuf*. The signs of a mental disorder suffered by the author are stamped on the latter work: *The Secret Hypogeum*, however, is more deliberate, more intellectualized, less emotional, and less interesting. It strikes me, quite frankly, as a "fad novel," a work which in its cultivated incoherence and tradition-flouting technique adheres, in a sense, to a current popular formula.

With flowing, graphic language . . . Elizondo narrates, or appears to narrate, a story about protagonists (T., E., X., and H.) whose specific character and environment are eschewed. Within the novel itself, *The Secret Hypogeum* is identified as a sort of a game; the novel by that name, which we are reviewing, is also a kind of game. By now, you know how that goes. . . .

It is interesting to reflect on how far we have come, in the literary expression of disorientation and the search for order, since Ernesto Sábato's *The Tunnel* in 1948.

That is all. There is nothing more we can say here about books that appear to be novels and are not.

Donald A. Yates. BA. 43, Summer, 1969, p. 383

Perhaps it is not surprising to note that Salvador Elizondo has spent much time (and has carried out certain studies) in Canada, France,

England, and the U.S., and that he knows European and U.S. literature better than that of his own country. Indeed it is difficult to find anything typically Mexican in his novels to date. Further, Elizondo does not write for the average reader. His works make an appeal to a special type of intellect. This is even implicit in the fact that he was cofounder of the short-lived yet most interesting literary review *S.nob.* . . .

Farabeuf, or the Account of One Moment is easily one of the strangest works to appear in Mexican literature. It reveals a direct kinship with Rulfo's *Pedro Páramo* in that in neither of them does the time element exist. Otherwise, it seems to me that *Farabeuf* and *Pedro Páramo* could hardly be more different. Whereas Rulfo is Mexican to the fingertips in his theme, setting, characters, and language, Elizondo's work has nothing in it to identify him as a Mexican writer. . . .

Only two characters have any importance in Elizondo's story: the author's adaptation of Dr. Farabeuf, a well-known French anatomist in the last century, and a woman, apparently—or possibly—mad. At various times they are *yo* and *tú* ("I" and "you") and at others *él* and *ella* ("he" and "she"), the distinction perhaps representing periods years apart, and this may be Elizondo's substitute for time. What little action there is turns largely upon a very graphic photo of the torture by dismemberment of a Chinese Boxer in 1901. . . .

The Secret Hypogeum is in its own way just as disconcerting as *Farabeuf*. At least, it is as unconventional and experimental and sure to baffle the reader who is not fully attuned to the extremes portrayed by the exponents of the *nouveau roman*. Elizondo's skill in the short story form was well established through his collection called *Narda, or Summer*, but his recent book of stories, *The Portrait of Zoe and Other Lies*, is decidedly uneven in quality, as well as unusual in nature.

Walter M. Langford. *The Mexican Novel Comes of Age*
(Notre Dame, Ind., University of Notre Dame Press,
1971), pp. 192–94

FREYRE, GILBERTO (1900–   )

BRAZIL

[In] *The World the Portuguese Created* . . . [Freyre] investigates a subject of considerable interest to all us Brazilians—the social and cultural relations among Brazil, Portugal, and the Portuguese colonies.

We believe that the time has passed for stubbornness between Portugal and Brazil, for maintaining those grudges and complaints that have kept us relatives at odds. Thus, as heredity links us body and soul to the essential and typical traits of our forebears, in both our biology and psychology, by the same token we cannot fail to see in our national spirit the characteristics of Luso-Christian culture. And since the heritage is substantial, we cannot, nor should we, allow it to become deformed or replaced . . . by other values alien to our souls and our traditions. . . .

This is the central idea in Gilberto Freyre's book. Although he sees in Brazil the "beginning of a vast plural culture," in which there was to be the mixture of cultures of the most varied origins, he finds with good reason that we must conserve the core of our culture, the Luso-Christian nucleus—or, more precisely, Luso-Catholic. He is no blind idolater of Portuguese culture, nor is he unaware of its limits, its defects, its weaknesses. "It does not seem to me," he says, "that Brazil should isolate itself within its traditional Luso-Brazilian culture. Defend it, of course, since it is our principal foundation of life and of nationhood. But defend it by developing it." [1941]

Oscar Mendes. *Tempo de Pernambuco: Ensaios críticos*
(Recife, Universidade Federal de Pernambuco,
1971), pp. 93–94†

This small volume [*Brazil: An Interpretation*], made up of lectures given in 1944 at Indiana University—the Patten Foundation lectures—constitutes an excellent synthesis of the main ideas and conceptions [of Freyre]. . . .

Gilberto Freyre stresses the role of the three ethnical elements which have contributed to the formation of the Brazilian racial amalgam: the Portuguese, the Negro and the Indian. And it is precisely the ethnic element, the theory of fusionism, and particularly the emphasis placed on the Negro's contribution, which figure among the concepts most affected by Mr. Freyre's fresh ideas. The role of the *mestizo*, his struggle for social adjustment, the stressing of the value of the common people and of regional energies, the defense of regionalism, the interpretation of the old Northeastern civilization based on aristocracy, sugar plantations and slavery; these and other themes, which are central in present-day Brazilian historiography, owe to Mr. Freyre a good deal of interpretative light.

Although one of the most enlightened and passionate pioneers of social history in Brazil, Mr. Freyre does not, on the other hand, escape certain exaggerations in his social interpretation of Brazilian history and life. In his work one finds a tendency to reduce all historical interpretation to social terms. If the social aspect is an integral part of national reality, it is not, however, the whole, nor can one explain the life of a people from a purely social angle. It is quite licit for contemporary historians to show an interest in, as Unamuno put it, "getting out of ministerial offices," opening wide windows upon the life of the whole people—in the fields, the factories, the streets.

But it is *not* licit for them to interpret the whole life of a nation through the social prism, to explain national life in social terms. This dangerous tendency is noticeable in Mr. Freyre's works, as is well exemplified in the last chapter of this book, viz., "The Modern Literature of Brazil: Its Relation to Brazilian Social Problems." If, on the one hand, one cannot fail to recognize how much is added to an understanding of literature and the arts by data taken from social history, the study of literature and the arts, on the other hand, becomes no more than external when it is reduced to the social aspect only. . . .

Afrânio Coutinho. *Com.* Sept. 14, 1945, pp. 529–30

Gilberto Freyre has not taught us only to see and to love Brazil. . . . He has shown our country as it is, and he has taught us to study seriously and honestly our specific, regional problems and to reject whatever is anti-Brazilian, anti-regional—yet at the same time to avoid an anachronistic and ridiculous xenophobia.

The suggestions that emerge from all his works have been adopted by everyone. Some openly call him a saint, the source of their vision. Others who are less honest try to conceal the origin of their "revelation," but not with complete success. . . .

I find [*Brazil: An Interpretation*] a near wonder: a synthesis of all the complexities of our social structure from the first days of our national existence up to today. And I should emphasize that sociological analysis is very much part of his method, together with a careful integration of a multiplicity of other approaches. I find this diversity his most sympathetic trait, although his detractors deplore it as anti-dogmatic. This diversity leads spiteful people to deny him a scientific basis for his studies or to accuse him of creating fiction in sociology and of presenting a man of his imagination or perhaps of his fantasy. . . .

[But he] will never allow himself to use an intriguing idea just for the pleasure of building a more-or-less sensational fiction on it, as in detective novels. . . . [1947?]

Laurênio Lima. *Crônica de letras pernambucanas*
(Recife, Imprensa Universitária, 1965), pp. 148–49†

Gilberto Freyre is a man of letters, a skillful narrative writer, but also a sociologist, well-informed and perceptive, who scientifically studies the complex social phenomena of his country. Born in Recife, in northern Brazil, he has perpetuated the traditions of north, cultural as well as political. . . .

Among Gilberto Freyre's books, *Brazil: An Interpretation* stands apart. This singular work, although only a few years old, should be considered a classic manual for anyone who would undertake a similar study. Like any classic work, it is a synthesis. . . .

Brazil is an extraordinary experiment in the meaning of democracy as a political and cultural form—or, more precisely, as a social science rather than as a political form. A unity of religion, an integration of the races, a unity within its borders—these are three things that the Brazilian synthesis has been successful in achieving. It should be said that Gilberto Freyre, no facile eclectic, has examined these issues with courage.

Electo J. García Tejedor. *CHA*. No. 85, Jan., 1957,
pp. 95–96†

The Masters and the Slaves and *The Mansions and the Shanties* have acquired a permanent place in Brazil as national classics. . . . What Gilberto's friends, followers, and admirers were celebrating, when they published a volume commemorating the first appearance of *The Masters and the Slaves*, was the work of a major creative scholar, thinker, and literary artist. In its substance and method, Gilberto Freyre's work is that of a sociologist, social historian, anthropologist, and social psychologist. He is all of these and more. He has focused a new light on the hidden recesses of the years gone by. And that light is his sense of the whole—of a culture that is infinitely complex, contradictory, riven and torn by passion, greed, generosity, love, hatred, sex, jealousy, ambition, physical voluptuousness, and the sense of art, color, music and faith—all of this and a great deal more are part of the sum.

There is a sense of detail, of the importance of all things: the food, the cooking, the dress, the odors about the kitchen, the house, the oxen, the Negro mammy, the naked little children running about the house, the sanitation, the lighting, the window, the veranda, the master, the mistress, the governor, the emperor, the law, the lawbreaker, the judge and the criminal, the fugitive, the lash. The ways of young people with one another, the church, the priest, the friar, the school—and ten thousand other matters, all part of the record—are there, concrete and inescapable. . . . One sees, through Freyre's eyes, a people emerging through time, with all of their foibles, heroism, laughter, and tears, as if through a movie camera. . . . The view is almost Augustinian, and the method infuses with life the compilation of journals, diaries, letters, photographs, newspaper advertisements, official registers, documents, books, pamphlets, songs, poems, verbal and written tradition. Synthesis, analyses, interpretation, logical deduction, and induction have gone into the shaping of this work. It has all of the craft, documentation, and "jargon" that goes by the name of science in the social sciences. But in addition it has something of the Bergsonian intuition, of the poet's insight and the artist's vision. And here form becomes almost as important as substance. The literary style that carries the subject matter of *The Masters and the Slaves* and *The Mansions and the Shanties* is like a flowing stream after a storm; it is full, deep, and sparkling. It is also intimate; it has the sensitivity of sterling verse and at the same time the richness and variety of a mosaic or a tapestry, except that it is alive, changing, appetizing, and tasteful. It reminds one of Proust at his best, but it is more robust, more vivid and all-embracing. It has a wider range and a greater depth. It reveals and embraces an entire culture in formation.

Frank Tannenbaum. Introduction to Gilberto Freyre,
The Mansions and the Shanties (New York,
Alfred A. Knopf, 1963), pp. viii–x

Gilberto Freyre, who is by far the best known Brazilian intellectual abroad, lives in Apipucos in a beautiful house from the eighteenth century: an authentic "mansion." . . . The man seems very much like his home. His spirit is noble and at the same time exotic; his temperament is aristocratic but tolerant. The knowledge of Brazil that shines in his conversation—in his sonorous and elegant speech—is abundant, generously shared, inexhaustible. To be what Freyre has always been in Brazil—a conservative, a humanist, and a scholar—is to maintain a stance more radical than that of many declared revolutionaries. . . .

Brazil is in a vertiginous phase in its development: its population is multiplying and its energies are pushing the country toward modernity. It can be said to be composed of the Portuguese sailor, the gloomy Spaniard, and an infinite variety of temperaments, colors, and secular religions: leftism and football, progress, carnival and reform. It is not a country to raise Freyre to the status of a prophet, although it honors him in other ways. . . .

His principal works . . . can be counted among the central statements of what Brazil was and is. If some do not agree with him, it is probably because they do not recognize this debt [to the past] or because they are too narrowly specialized and cannot find a made-to-order classification for works that are at the same time social history, sociological anthropology, antiquarian science, and literature. Almost all Freyre has produced in close to three decades of writing is still valid and valuable. There are few experts in the social sciences about whom the same thing can be said. . . .

Keith Botsford. *CCLC*. No. 68, Jan., 1963, pp. 3–4†

Dona Sinhá and the Father Son marks the surprising debut of Gilberto Freyre in fiction, yet a debut that could have been predicted. Gilberto could have been a writer of fiction whenever he wanted to. The [potential] novelist had already announced himself through the power of the artistic vision of the trilogy begun with *The Masters and the Slaves*, and through the prose style of *Northeast*, in which the environment is treated sensorily and poetically.

But Gilberto Freyre's "seminovel" *Dona Sinhá and the Father Son* has an interest beyond its place in the development of the writer's career. It has an intrinsic value within the context of Brazilian fiction and, more specifically, within the contemporary novel. It is, in fact, a doubly original work: because of its innovations on the basic structure of the novel; and because of its literarily and scientifically valid treatment of a difficult theme—male homosexuality.

Among the structural innovations, the following are most noticeable: the intersection of various psychological planes, both cultural and social, on a story of love that is, shall we say, timeless; the technique of psychobiography; the skillful use of newspaper clippings to re-create moments from the collective past, in which reality becomes fiction.

The complex theme of homosexuality—poorly treated in literature before *Dona Sinhá and the Father Son*—was revived by Gilberto with the impartial insight of the psychologist, the sociologist, and the poet.

. . . The novel presents homosexuality as a human phenomenon that above all demands understanding and respect instead of prohibition and scorn.

Osmar Pimentel. Introduction to Gilberto Freyre,
Dono Sinhá e o filho padre: Seminovela (Rio de Janeiro,
Livraria José Olympio Editôra, 1964), pp. xxv–xxvi†

In this era of intellectual and political upheaval [the 1920s] many Brazilians were asking themselves (often unconsciously) the question that underlay Freyre's inquiry [in *The Masters and the Slaves*]: had miscegenation done their country irreparable "eugenic" damage? This question rested on the widely accepted Brazilian belief that the country's backwardness (when compared to Western Europe and North America) could be explained by the debilitating influence of the Negro, whose sexual charms had proved irresistible to generations of Lusitanians. "Beneath the equator there is no sin," the colonists had happily reasoned. But the wages of those monumental sins, so it was later feared, had fallen on their modern Brazilian heirs, many of whom brooded over their mixed blood and hoped that European immigration might "Aryanize" the stock.

The Masters and the Slaves turned this question on its head. Far from being a liability, Freyre argued, Brazil's ethnic potpourri was an immense asset. He marshalled an impressive array of scientific evidence in support of this view. He showed how research in nutrition, anthropology, medicine, psychology, sociology, and agronomy had rendered the racial theories obsolete and had pointed up new villains—insufficient diet, and disease too often undiagnosed and untreated (especially syphilis). Indeed, studies by Brazilian scientists showed that the Indian and the Negro had made important contributions to a healthier diet and more practical style of dress. This body of knowledge, which Freyre could cite with such pride and frequency, was the product of a new and profound concern on the part of Brazilian intellectuals about the long-ignored social problems of their own country. *The Masters and the Slaves* drew on this research and its social implications, dramatizing for a wider public the country's new knowledge of its past, thereby offering Brazilians a basis for confidence in the future. . . .

Brazilians could be proud of their unique, ethnically mixed tropical civilization whose social vices—which Freyre did not minimize—could be attributed primarily to the atmosphere of the slave-holding monoculture that dominated the country until the second half of the nineteenth century. The evil consequences of miscegenation stemmed not from race-mixing itself, but from the unhealthy relationship of master and slave under which it had occurred. Freyre had brought into the open the question which most haunted the Brazilian conscience.

Thomas Skidmore. *CSSH*. 6, July, 1964, pp. 493–94

A first novel by a distinguished social historian in his later sixties need not be judged harshly. This is fortunate, for if Gilberto Freyre's *Dona Sinhá and the Father Son* were put to any severe test of its novelistic qualities, nothing would remain but a pinch of aromatic dust. Yet it is a charming book, capable of .giving much pleasure and illumination. Freyre hasn't, it must be said bluntly, any idea of how to write a novel: he is full of trepidation at his own daring in setting out on such a rickety structure at all, like a man crossing a torrent on a rope bridge. So, losing his nerve, he has added to the rope bridge a steel cable of "historical fact," this set in italic type, to distinguish it from the merely invented, so that when the book breaks into italics, we know that we are reading about "something real."

A story that can survive even this nonsense, plus the frequent asides in which Freyre whips off his novelist's mask and tell us he knows it isn't true, only it is true too, in a way, and is in any case only a semi-novel, etc.—a story, as I say, that can still hold our attention in spite of this paraphernalia must have unusual qualities. And so it has. Freyre is so interested in what he is telling us that his interest sweeps us along with him; he has such a passion for the history of his country, he finds every social detail so fascinating in the transitional period in which the events it describes take place, that it is impossible not to read on, smiling indulgently at the novelist's amateurishness and warming to the historian's somber passion. The book concerns Catholicism and the power it has over the mind of a decent, devoted woman, not uneducated but intellectually incurious, and secluded in her way of life. The boy whom she rears as a sacrificial offering to the Church is not quite a living presence in the book, nor are the mother and her disapproving brother, a backland plantation owner, who share the stage with a younger man who returns after years of exile in Paris and suffers the perplexity of the Europeanized *émigré*. As a novel, it never really begins, but two characters come across very strongly: one is Freyre's own character . . . and the other is the involuted, self-obsessed, yet generous character of Brazil itself. A bad novel; but it is more interesting and will probably live longer than more accomplished ones.

John Wain. *NYR*. May 4, 1967, p. 36

FUENTES, CARLOS (1929–   )

MEXICO

Fuentes's collection, *The Masked Days*, is a revelation. In its best stories—such as "Chac Mool"—the real world is fused with the disturbing world of the writer's fantasy. Although these stories are not altogether perfectly constructed, the transition between the two planes of fantasy and reality is not distracting to the reader. Fuentes is very skillful in re-creating the atmosphere of Mexico's past. This attention to the force of history is characteristic of the young writers of contemporary Mexico. And Fuentes uses historical elements to paint pictures with a firm hand and vigorous strokes. There is no doubt about it: Fuentes is a great short-story writer.

> Luis Leal. *El cuento mexicano* (Mexico City, Ediciones De Andrea, 1956), pp. 146–47†

Without a doubt, Carlos Fuentes's novel [*The Clearest Region*] must be considered important in its departure from the traditional form of the Mexican novel. Inspired by foreign techniques (which is not at all to be criticized), it deals with Mexican problems, people, settings, and situations. For many readers who get the book because of the propaganda and scandal it inspired, it will be just one more book they set aside after beginning it, because its technique places it among those literary productions that are for a limited public. . . . The techniques of this novel, although not new to the literature of the twentieth century, are new to our literature. Perhaps if they had been used in smaller doses, the result would have been better, for they throw the doors open to every possibility, and some of the novel ends up by being truly boring, for example, the last part of the work, called "The Clearest Region," in which Fuentes attempts a synthesis that would encompass the meaning of Mexican history through visions, allusions, names, and sayings or Mexicanisms, all in a stream of consciousness.

> Alfonso Rangel Guerra. *AyL.* 1, 2, April–June, 1958, pp. 76–77†

The Clearest Region is a *roman à clef* in two ways. First, it is a novel in which the actual persons and places appear under fictitious names. The Manuel Zamacona of the novel, for example, is the poet Octavio Paz. Second, the most valuable part of the novel, that in which the author tries to define the Mexican as a sort of mythological beast or absurd living fossil of the Dawn Man, is a direct appropriation from Paz's *The Labyrinth of Solitude*. Herein lies Carlos Fuentes's most ambitious failure. Ixca Cienfuegos, the main protagonist of *The Clearest Region*, is the creature—legitimate child of Carlos Fuentes—chosen to incarnate the philosophy of Paz concerning a Mexican archetype. But Cienfuegos lacks the reality which only a true novelist can breathe into his characters. He is a dead symbol, a stand-in for the Mexican *homo fictus* no one has yet been able to create.

Technically, the English-speaking reader will note that Carlos Fuentes has many influences that he can immediately identify—most evident are John Dos Passos's *U.S.A.*, James Joyce's *Ulysses* and the main characters and plot from Michael Valbeck's *Headlong from Heaven*. The Hispanic influences are those of Pío Baroja and Camilo José Cela in the trilogy *The Struggle for Life* and *The Beehive*. . . .

It is understandable that the translator should have had his hands full with this novel. Carlos Fuentes runs the entire gamut of the rich, the poor, the middle class, the intellectual, the lowbrow, etc., in Mexico City, and presents each one of these groups with its own linguistic habits and peculiarities. Nevertheless, it must be said that we have seldom seen a "freer" translation than this. It is not fair to quarrel with the translator's difficulties with slang. But it is hard to justify inaccurate interpretations of standard Spanish.

José Vázquez Amaral. *SR*. Nov. 19, 1960, p. 29

I cannot think of a more self-conscious culture than that of present-day Mexico, nor a literary atmosphere that is more agitated, stifling and fratricidal. This is important to know because in one of its intentions *The Clearest Region* is an attempt to extricate a living imagination from the entombed, self-devouring realities of Mexican consciousness, forever mourning its sundered past, incessantly projecting its possible future shapes, and torn between its ill-defined authenticity and the directing pressure of more advanced societies, much as the nineteenth-century Russian mind was caught between panslavism and the cultured West.

Neither a Turgenev nor a Dostoyevsky, Fuentes presses for a transcendence of the quarrel. He proceeds first by a series of bitter portraits of Mexican salon life, where writers, artists and journalists mingle with the nouveau riche and the museum pieces of the older aristocracy, in a brittle Walpurgis Nicht of sensuality, chic French phrases, complaints about boredom, gossip, jockeying for position and interminable discussions about what it means to be Mexican. As set-pieces they are among the most impressive things in the novel.

But Fuentes is only incidentally a satirist, wishing, once that preliminary labor is out of the way, to understand and create images of the metamorphoses that the Mexican soul has undergone, to work his way through old mystiques in search of a more viable one, and finally to emerge at some point where form and experience cohere and cooperate to raise an adequate structure. . . .

But it doesn't really come off. The form and the experience don't quite hold together, so that whenever the novel moves from a direct vision of behavior, manners or psychology, it slips into a solipsistic world of manifestoes, occult reveries, private myth-making and over-literary hymns to life that never attain the verbal originality and imaginative coherence that might justify them.

What's more, there are certain thematic elements which I was simply unable to grasp. They have to do with a quest for identity through the truths of parenthood and through sexuality conceived of as a differentiating principle, and I suppose they fall under the *caveat* about Mexican works not entering any order comprehensible to others that I quoted above.

I shouldn't like to leave on that note, however. Fuentes says some-where that "In Mexico City there is never tragedy, but only outrage," a remark that fixes the limits of his accomplishment. *The Clearest Region* attains to a sense of outrage, if not tragedy, but one so seriously felt and so passionately sponsoring its answering movement, that one ends by respecting its motives and at least part of its substance.

Richard Gilman. *Com.* Feb. 10, 1961, pp. 510–11

In his new novel, *The Good Conscience*, Fuentes places his scene in territory that has been conquered over and over again by the novel: the life of the bourgeois family in a comatose and smug provincial capital—here, Guanajuato in Central Mexico. Swiftly he delineates the history of three generations, starting with the small merchant who is the founder of the line; uncovering the dark ways by which it prospers: the strategic, advantageous marriages; the corrupt, opportunistic poli-tics. Remote and threatening Mexican history erupts in violence, but almost as a rumor, as Guanajuato, removed from the center of great events, merely reacts to its reverberations. . . .

The Good Conscience seems to be, in intention, a dynastic novel of epic range. Actually, it is not that at all, as quite suddenly it becomes a novel of the sensitive adolescent discovering in his agony the awful gap between dreams and reality. After the panoramic opening, Fuentes pauses with this boy, who is the last of his line, to tell his story of grow-ing awareness and final defeat. His initiation is a spectacularly full one, including phases that are rather too familiar, as, for example, the set-piece of a brothel scene in which he meets his sententious, pillar-of-society uncle-guardian; but including, also, an incestuous passion and a religious crisis dramatized by self-flagellation with a whip of thorns and masturbation in an empty church while embracing the plaster feet of the Crucified in his quest for mystic illumination.

The pattern is that of rebellion and escape, insight and repudiation. Ironically, the author makes of it a novel of mock-rebellion and ultimate acquiescence, reversal and loss, as the boy accepts his fate and patrimony. What Fuentes has written, then, is a novel of the making of a bourgeois, all dreams and hope abandoned, together with love and compassion.

The trouble is that the book cannot support its superb possibilities, failing as it does to seize the dramatic moments and establish a clear dramatic line, being, as it is, excessively panoramic and expository. It is a pity, for the book contains tremendous energy and scope, which remain latent, unabsorbed as fiction. Finally, faced with Fuentes's mixed intentions and shifting design, we feel what he has given us here is a sketch for a large-scale novel of Mexican history and experience seen as defeat and promise. This is the novel Fuentes should write, and did not.

Saul Maloff. SR. Dec. 16, 1961, pp. 20–21

Fuentes's hero-villain, Artemio Cruz—Mexican industrialist, newspaper and land-owner, millionaire—lies on his death-bed while his devoted secretary, his despised and despising wife and daughter jostle around him. A priest is trying to force on him the comforts of the last sacrament, the doctors probe and peer at his body. And he lies there in a trance of disgust: disgust with those around him, with his past and, above all, with his own physical presence. Idealism, ambition, passion, and achievement all end in one corruption, the smell of which horrifies him. He reeks in his own nostrils.

Literally so, for by an odd trick of style all Fuentes's most vivid perceptions come in as scents on the air. He is a writer with a nose and no eye. Whenever he piles up visual details, listing the goodies in Cruz's mansions, his grandiose arrays of clothes and mistresses, the writing goes dead; he sounds less like an artist than a compiler of baroque inventories. Only smells seem really to get through to him imaginatively: the smell of his skin, his breath, his faeces, the smell of girls and food. . . . Like a hunting dog, he sees through his nose. And this has a curious effect: it makes the book, for all its scope, intensely private.

This claustrophobia of the self is emphasized by the form. Cruz's story is told in three persons. "I" is the old man dying on his bed:

"you" is a slightly vatic, "experimental" projection of his potentialities into an unspecified future (you know it is experimental because the letters are in lower-case and the punctuation scanty); "he" is the real hero, the man whose history emerges bit by bit from incidents shuffled around from his seventy-one years.

The story, when you pick it out, is straightforward enough, and handily symbolic. Like Mexico itself, Cruz is the bastard son of a decayed landowner and a peon. . . . His career, I suppose, is representative of all radical movements in a country as poor and open to corruption as Mexico, where a few hundred dollars of spot cash, ruthlessly used, could be the key to millions. The chance of power corrupts more absolutely than power itself.

Since Fuentes is a sophisticated writer—at times an over-sophisticated overwriter—the gradual hardening and corruption of his hero is done with a good deal of subtlety and intelligence. He is never allowed to become a monster since the process he represents, though monstrous enough, is also natural. . . .

Fuentes, apparently, is a Marxist yet he is also literate and humane, unwilling to trust the bullies who take over revolutions; hence Cruz remains sympathetic and accepted, despite all his corruption. More important, Fuentes the Marxist is also deeply romantic. In fact, his romanticism *is* Marxist, and *vice versa*. For all his worldliness, he yearns for the pure revolution, the pure choice between right and wrong, justice and exploitation. The compromises of political reality seem insufferable.

A. Alvarez. *NYR*. June 11, 1964, p. 14

The Death of Artemio Cruz is a novel of great power and great imagination. It sweeps through the history of modern Mexico in one man's life—which is no novelty. What is unusual—I was reminded here of *The Leopard*—is the understanding of people and of history that fuses these elements into a continuously revealing whole. As the book opens, Artemio Cruz is on his deathbed. He is a rich man now. He owns a newspaper, he fixes officials, arranges massive deals for Yanqui businessmen whom he half admires and half despises. He started as a poor man, even as a kind of idealist. He has lived and hardened, without losing any of a formidable understanding of himself and his motives. The narrative of his life, presented in fragments and discontinuities, is all the time illuminated by this understanding, in hindsight and as he understood himself at the time. We see him as child, soldier of the revolution, landowner, betrayer of the revolution; as comrade, lover, husband, father. I was dazzled by the richness of this book, in texture, construction, psychology and description. I won't swear it is a master-piece; but it well may be.

Stephen Hugh-Jones. *NS*. Aug. 7, 1964, p. 189

[*The Clearest Region*] is many things: a panoramic novel of Mexico City reminiscent of Dos Passos's *U.S.A.*, a combination of post-Joycean experimental novelistic techniques; a dissection of Mexican society from the lowest to the highest levels; a document testifying to the author's disillusionment with the 1910 Revolution; an exposition of the basic duality of Mexican character, stemming from a nostalgia for the Indian past, irredeemably destroyed, and the effort to find ways to develop along Occidental cultural lines. It is all this, and much else besides, but most of all it is an indignant, frank, and moving communication of Fuentes's anguished concern over the grave problems besetting Mexico, and his anger at what he has called "the blackest part of Mexico . . . the excess of optimistic rhetoric and official tranquility" in the face of these problems. Not even Fuentes's most violent critics are unmoved by this book, nor do they doubt its passionate sincerity.

In *The Clearest Region* the last half-century of Mexican life, so closely tied to the 1910 Revolution, is recounted through the lives of numerous characters who, in effect, are Mexican archetypes. Fuentes does not side clearly with any one character or group of characters, but is concerned to show the self-interest, materialism, and loneliness he finds so prevalent among his compatriots. Most Mexicans, one gathers, never realize themselves fully. They are lost in a culture which lacks clear orientation or deep national roots, and are attracted by a glittering complex of values, goals, and attitudes most of which are foreign (American and European) and therefore difficult, often impossible, to assimilate. On the broadest possible screen, with a talent for succinct description and a magnificent ear for dialogue, Fuentes shows how the noble ideals of the Revolution have been betrayed. The new plutocrats and political aristocrats who used the Revolution to further their own ends are dominated by selfish materialism, and quiet their conscience by saying "what's good for us means 'progress' for Mexico." Fuentes's analysis of all the social classes also makes manifest the alienation of Mexican life resulting from the impact of foreign (mostly American) customs, techniques, and even language. Mexico, for Carlos Fuentes, is a country where a true national character is impossible, a spiritual wasteland. His detailed, destructive analysis leaves only one redeeming characteristic, the fecund vitality of the people. But it is an energy as yet unchanneled, dependent on leaders still unknown.

Robert G. Mead, Jr. *BA*. 38, Autumn, 1964, p. 381

Fuentes is not a political figure but a political man. There is a world of difference, which no one recognizes better than he. . . . Fuentes's kind of Marxism fulfills an inner necessity; to be connected, to hear the rush of history in the inner ear, as others hear the roar of the sea in a shell. It is, fundamentally, an imaginative, or even a literary attitude. He finds in his special literary heroes, such as Fidel Castro or Carpentier's Victor Hugues, only what he admires most: completeness and inner consistency. In this admiration is implied criticism of what we, cast in more sophisticated molds, are not: whole and true-to-ourselves to the bitter end. Like many intellectuals of his generation, Fuentes would like to do away with doubt, hesitation, and personal skepticism. His consistent search has been for a moral certainty, and as is usual in searches for a purer life, much of the impetus is negative, abnegatory, ascetic, guilty, and indignant. . . . He is not a poet, not a *vates*, but a literate young man who can write competently (and incompetently, when Mexico's version of *Time*-like vulgarity, *¡Siempre!*, demands it). He has an opinion about everything and has to have one: as the Very Model of a Major Novelist he is on constant call. That, too, is part of a "provincial" situation: the Metropolis tends to ask less, and ultimately demand more.

One could say that the reason for the random and diverse technique in *The Death of Artemio Cruz* is that the experimentation is not truly Fuentes's own, but part of a foreign tradition that he has only partly assimilated and not yet adapted to its materials. One can also concede that Fuentes is an eclectic writer, and that it is the better part of honesty for him to exploit the innate catholicity of his mind. Still my objections would hold. They stem from a *parti pris* that the novel is very much one thing; a variety of experience collected under a single view, a world ordered precisely because it has been seen in such-and-such a way and no other. This unity is what I do not see in *The Death of Artemio Cruz.*

Keith Botsford. *Cmty.* 39, Feb., 1965, pp. 66–67

Published originally in 1958, Carlos Fuentes' *The Clearest Region* must be reckoned the first of the new *genre*. Then about thirty, Fuentes achieved in this book an ambitious synthesis, fusing into a single, well-organised, subtly counterpointed vision the many different worlds of the former Aztec capital, its slums, its *nouveaux riches*, even its pagan sacrificial rituals. This is a Mexico of luxury cars and concrete speedways, of smart cocktail parties. This is a polyglot Mexico, with an upper class that has its equivalent in every part of the world, talking incessantly of its latest escapades at Acapulco, its infinite conjugal permutations. Yet at the same time it is a Mexico still very much on the margins of modern history, immobilised in its thick-blooded inertia.

The old, secret gods are not dead: that is the message of this novel which points, beneath its lucid dialectical structure, to a terrifying burden of magic and superstition. Fuentes' vigour and polemical approach do not allow him to put up with the shelving of the proclaimed ideals of the Revolution, with the sluggishness with which even the most urgent reforms are carried out. Impressive and striking are the passionate clarity with which his world is imagined, his analysis of the economic workings of society, the missionary fervour that informs his writing.

Still, it would be wrong to concentrate too much on the critical, "documentary" aspect of his ambitious novel. Beneath the social indignation, the polemical, sometimes journalistic matter of the book (the title alludes ironically to Mexico's once pure air, now corrupted by smog), Fuentes has constructed a poetical, almost apocalyptic vision of his country, a vision that goes far beyond today's city and its problems. He has attempted to reconstruct the fundamental trauma of this society so profoundly divided against itself. What Fuentes intuits with astonishing force in this novel, and has further explored in more recent books . . . is the complexity of the underlying historical trauma: the cruel violation of American soil by the European conqueror, the blood forever shed, forever crying out. This is the true origin, he suggests, of all those fantasies of *machismo*, of those apparently inexplicable bouts of cruelty and murder. Yet Fuentes sees in all this—if somewhat darkly at times—a unity in suffering, in humiliation, in expiation that is the other, Christian, side of the coin. Though Fuentes eloquently denies such an intention—insisting that his is a straightforward historical-dialectical analysis—the myth that underlies all his novels . . . is the primaeval struggle between the Spaniard and the Indian.

Emir Rodríguez Monegal. *Enc.* 25, Sept., 1965, p. 100

Carlos Fuentes' new book, *Aura*, is going to puzzle his admirers, accustomed, by his previous three, to mural-size canvases, century-long time spans, and large statements. This short Gothic tale . . . seems at first to have none of his earmarks. A competent example of the genre, it is the story of a young historian who accepts the strange but lucrative job of boarding with an ancient, bedridden woman to prepare her long-dead husband's papers for publication. The old woman's housekeeper is a beautiful young niece who comes to the young man's bed the second night of his stay in the musty rat-infested house; with each passing day—or, rather, night—the niece becomes older, until the young man finds himself in bed finally with the toothless aunt with withered breasts.

Can Fuentes mean that love inevitably involves the loving acceptance of physical decay and death? Or are Aura and the old woman the two faces of Mexico? And does it, then, mean that young revolutionaries, like Fuentes, must learn to love this sacked old hag before they can make her beautiful again? Large, windy questions like these always seem to plague reviews of Fuentes' novels, but heretofore they sat more comfortably with reviewers, given, as the cliché has it, the historical sweep of Fuentes' previous novels. For a Gothic tale must, before anything, succeed by its power to fascinate and horrify, and this *Aura* does not do. . . .

Fuentes' failures as a novelist seem obscured for the great majority—if one takes the praise of his work as genuine—by the stylistic firecrackers he sets off. I do not doubt that he is always talking about Mexico's tragedy, always harking back to what made its revolution fail, always damning its uneven capitalist development for the social and cultural emptiness of its present; but in a novel these ideas are merely opinions, unless they are so inherent in the story that plot and style become at least exemplifications of what he has to say.

For all his social preoccupations, Fuentes' work shows, with a kind of unconscious obsessiveness, that he is at least equally interested in literary one-upmanship; he can write like Faulkner, Dos Passos, Sartre, Isak Dinesen. And he can go them one better. . . . A post-Stalin Marxist, he is going to prove that the social novel can utilize all the resources of literature; a Mexican radical, that he is not provincial: he knows there are palms in the lobby of the Plaza.

For a while—maybe after his first book only—one could have said that Fuentes' faults were, primarily, the faults of excess, of reaching too far, trying for too much. . . . But we now have four books with which to judge Fuentes, and it seems clear that his genuine preoccupations are betrayed at every turn by *True Confessions* story elements, and his penchant for having a hand at other writers' styles: Yankee imperialism has harmed him more than he knows.

José Yglesias. Nation. Jan. 3, 1966, pp. 24–26

The first modern vision of Mexico City, [*The Clearest Region*] was a double revelation to Mexicans: it showed them the face of a city that, although theirs, they did not know, and it brought to their attention a young writer who from that time on would not cease to surprise them, to disconcert them, and to irritate them.

The secret center of the novel is an ambiguous character, Ixca Cienfuegos. Although he does not participate in the action, in a certain sense he precipitates it and is thus something like the conscience of the city. He is the other half of Mexico, the buried but alive pre-Columbian past. He is also a mask of Fuentes, in the same way that Mexico is a mask of Ixca's—literature as a mask of the author and of the city. Nevertheless, the opposite is equally true: Ixca is a critical consciousness—literature as criticism of the world and of the writer himself. The novel turns on this duality: the mask and consciousness, the word and criticism, Ixca and modern Mexico, Fuentes and Ixca.

The axis of verbal invention and criticism of language guides all of Fuentes's works, with the exception of *The Good Conscience*, a rather unfortunate attempt to return to traditional realism. Each one of his novels is presented as a hieroglyph. And the invisible action that animates them is an impassioned, tenacious attempt to decipher this hieroglyph. Every sign leads to another: Mexico City to Ixca, Ixca to Artemio Cruz—the anti-Ixca, the man of action—and so on, from novel to novel and from character to character. Fuentes questions these signs, and the signs question him: the author is another sign. Writing is the incessant questioning to which the signs subject one sign—man. And it is the question to which this one sign subjects the signs—language. It is an interminable task, one that the novelist must begin over and over again: to decipher one hieroglyph, one makes use of signs (words) that in turn soon make up another hieroglyph. Criticism destroys the lie of words with other words, which, barely having been pronounced, freeze and become converted all over again into masks. . . . [1967]

Octavio Paz. *Corriente alterna*, 2nd ed. (Mexico City, Siglo Veintiuno Editores, 1968), pp. 45–46†

Carlos Fuentes's *The Death of Artemio Cruz* is experimental reality. Like Beckett's *Malone meurt*, this work is centered around a narrator lying on his death bed, Artemio Cruz, whose name [that is, Cross] perhaps has a formal-technical correspondence to suffering (similar to the picture of a cross in Robbe-Grillet's *Dans le labyrinthe*). But with these similarities, the concrete analogies with the *nouveau roman* end (unless we want to include the second-person "you," which alternates periodically with the "I" and the "he," reminiscent of the famous *vous* in Butor's *La modification*, but with a totally different function here). This moribund "I" probes his past in circles of memory that move through the formal stations of distancing from the self, in the third-person singular; to self-identification, in the first person; and to the projection of himself, in the second person. In this way he achieves a greater awareness of himself, but it is an insecure awareness, partaking somewhat of the wise saying "I only know that I know nothing." In effect, what Artemio Cruz realizes is that he has disintegrated into three realities, and he cannot say which of these three realities represents him and whether or not he is the coming together of the three.

Leo Pollmann. *Der neue Roman in Frankreich und Lateinamerika* (Stuttgart, W. Kohlhammer Verlag, 1968), p. 205†

For Fuentes, Mexico is a tiger that has been artificially tamed. He appears to wish that the energies of the enchained animal be authentically unleashed. *A Change of Skin* is his most ambitious—if not his best—novel to date, because his notion of the stifled tiger is extended in it beyond Mexico to the whole of mankind.

At its simplest level, this complicated novel explores the attempts of a married couple approaching middle age to grip on to something of the initial vitality of their love. The man, Javier, is a failed Mexican writer, always ready to blame his Jewish-American wife for blocking his creative spirit with too many concrete emotional demands. Fuentes comes out with many perceptive remarks concerning Javier's and Elizabeth's problems, though one often wishes that he took this couple and they took themselves less seriously. There is a great deal of portentousness in their stylized reminiscences, their insistent exchange of lapidary phrases and dubious maxims, sometimes as bad as this: "The distance that separates us has not only more value but also more meaning than the closeness that joins us."

But *A Change of Skin* is a great deal more than just a love story. And to complicate matters, we are presented with another pair, Franz and Isabel, who accompany Javier and Elizabeth on a journey from Mexico City to Cholula. The fictional status of Franz and Isabel is more dubious than that of the first couple, Franz and Isabel being perhaps just phantom alternative versions of Javier and Elizabeth, although Elizabeth, being a generation older, could equally represent Isabel's potential future.

Just in case there is any doubt that all four characters are in fact wholly apocryphal, there is also a narrator who intervenes in their lives, yet at the same time flamboyantly exhibits his omniscience. He underlines the fact that the entire action of the novel is an apocryphal game conducted in his own mind, which is, of course, a figment of Fuentes's.

David Gallagher. *NYT*. Feb. 4, 1968, p. 5

Fuentes's basic technique [in *A Change of Skin*] is narrative disorder in which cinematographic devices dominate: flashbacks, superimposition and transition from one character to another without warning, from one scene to another, from the words of the narrator to those of the characters, to such an extent that the central thread tends to get completely lost. The goal is to incorporate and to reflect this chaotic world through its most authentic representation, pop-art—or in this case, pop-lit. The numerous references to the movies are a key to the perception of reality ("The world is called Paramount Pictures"), of the characters, and of the author's style. . . .

The result of all this is an excess of artificiality (a defect that in another way was also present in *The Clearest Region* and in *The Death of Artemio Cruz*), leading to confusions making it difficult—and even not very worthwhile—to continue reading. The novel lacks control, which gives solidity to apparent chaos in [Cortázar's] *Hopscotch* and gives [García Márquez's] *One Hundred Years of Solitude* a deceptive polish beneath which various surrealistic worlds take shape. The same is true of the novel's language. Many pages are effectively written, whether in an objective and realistic style or in an unordered monologue of rich colloquial language. But soon language runs off to one side, toward minute hyperrealistic description, or off to the other, toward unchecked chaos. The two antithetical extremes create a new paradox: by incorporating all of reality, language consumes and annihilates itself. All of this is conscious and intentional on the part of Fuentes, who has taken the side of the Furies against Orestes, the side of Elizabeth, who comes out of the water with an octopus in her arms and a cat on her head, and against Javier, who loves the circumspection of the faces in the Attic steles. . . . The literary product becomes damaged. This "personal happening" becomes exhausting. We hope that Fuentes can produce a work in which the external does not drown out the re-creation, the "revelation of what the world still has not discovered and perhaps never will on its own," which, in Fuentes's own words, is what a novel is about.

Florinda Friedman. *Sur.* No. 311, March–April, 1968,
pp. 106–7†

In Artemio Cruz [in *The Death of Artemio Cruz*] we recognize an intelligibly drawn typification of that group of men which, in the author's view, dominates modern Mexico's economic and political scene. These men found in the chaos of prolonged revolution ample opportunity for the realization of selfish ambitions and the accumulation of excessive wealth. Under their leadership, the humanitarian ideals which the revolution had gathered up in its momentum were either compromised or abandoned for the promise of power.

Artemio Cruz is also the composite Mexican. The blood of his veins is the restless mixture produced by the forced blending of three alien races. And in a very large sense his story is the story of Mexico—with representative meaning beyond the latest revolution—suggesting the many frustrated expectations, the human and political tragedies that are Mexico's history. . . . The trajectory of Artemio Cruz implies a cyclic interpretation of Mexican history in which the infamies of the past once again overwhelm the present. In many important respects the new generation, forged in fratricidal conflict, is but a familiar replica of preceding generations.

From humble origins and with a spirit of adventure, which will become nihilistic in its vehemence, Artemio goes to the revolution. He enters into the rebellion, as did his country, with a vague and undefined altruism. From the harsh expediencies of war Artemio learns the insensitive values of personal survival. . . .

If life compels Artemio to participate in forming his destiny, it also limits the range of possibilities available to him. . . . The counterpresence of unqualified fatalism in the novel significantly moves the ultimate definition of the protagonist away from a strictly existentialist position and toward a unique metaphysics wherein an identifiable Mexican cultural attitude fuses with the mood of existentialism. Accordingly, we find that Fuentes has achieved an artistic accommodation of existentialist notions with both a strongly deterministic interpretation of Mexican history and a latent, but culturally significant, fatalism which diminishes the individual's authority in the course of life.

Michael W. Moody. RomN. 10, 1, Autumn, 1968,
pp. 27, 29–30

"Old Morality" . . . in its choice of hero and theme may well have influenced such young Mexican writers as Gustavo Sainz and José Agustín, who while in their late teens and early twenties became famous in Mexican letters with their novels and short stories depicting problems of adolescents. Alberto in Fuentes' narration is a teenager who lives a life of innocence on a farm in Michoacan with his grandfather and the old man's mistress. The boy's old-maid aunts from the city obtain legal permission to liberate the boy from this degrading influence; they, in their turn, seduce the handsome youth. The latter soon becomes bored with the city and writes his grandfather, "Come and get me, please, I think there is more morality on our rancho. I'll tell you all about it." This is probably one of the most humorous pieces that Fuentes has written, although the humor tends toward irony. Alberto is presented in a very sympathetic manner as are most young men in the fiction of Fuentes. The author seems to suggest that time and society corrupt the innocence of youth. One can see examples of this in Fuentes' first three novels, where the young men Federico Robles, Jaime Ceballos, and even Artemio Cruz, all succumb to the corrupt ways of the world upon reaching manhood.

Richard M. Reeve. SSF. 8, 1, Winter, 1971, pp. 176–77

A brilliant, complex, and (in present-day political terms) risky play, *All the Cats Are Dark* stands as a significant modern literary work, and as a serious challenge to professional groups who would present it on the stage.

Never a writer who would retrace literary steps, Carlos Fuentes in his second published play continues to seek new forms and instruments of expression while mining a vein he has explored previously: the drama of Mexico's past. As in his novel, *The Death of Artemio Cruz*, the author's vantage point—morally, philosophically, historically—is contemporary Mexico. In masterful interplay, the collective tragedy of Indian-Spanish confrontation, the epic proportions of individual destinies, and the satiric impact of Brechtian "distantiation" fuse to shed light on the problematical Mexican reality of today. The historic conjunction here, however, is not the Mexican Revolution, as in the novel, but the Conquest.

Fuentes' creative approach is consistent with his earlier artistic accomplishments. He marshals the potential he finds in universal literary tradition (Shakespeare, Greek tragedy, Brecht), as well as in his innovative contemporaries (in this case the new theater movement), and fashions a work based on Mexican experience and bearing his own personal stamp. In intellectual terms, his view of Mexican history, like his dramatic technique, is universal. It transcends, while not necessarily contradicting, nationalist interpretations of the Conquest. Fuentes presents the Conquest not simply as a clash between good and evil, or innocence and corruption, but rather as a confrontation between two systems which, while differing in culture, philosophy and cosmology, were ultimately alike in their tragic impact on the lives of individual men. As is implied in the title, all oppressors look alike from the vantage point, in darkness, of the oppressed.

Individuals receive primary focus. On center stage are Moctezuma, Cortés, and Marina (Malinche). Through the first two, Fuentes elaborates the theme of power and its tragic consquences. Moctezuma, prisoner of the power imposed upon him by lineage and tradition, displays the tragic flaw of doubt, as he yearns for some personal identity independent of the determinism imbedded in Aztec time cycles and religious myths. Cortés, imbued with renaissance energy, seeks power as the only measure of personal fulfillment, regardless of the moral or social consequences of his acts. . . .

The play will be criticized as needlessly laden with sexual symbology, as blasphemous, as politically motivated. Notwithstanding the partial validity of the first criticism, it achieves, through brilliant language and imaginative dramatic technique, a level of genuine artistic and intellectual integrity.

Joseph Sommers. *BA*. 45, Spring, 1971, pp. 288–89

In 1970 the Mexican novelist Carlos Fuentes published the drama *All the Cats Are Dark*. The work vivifies, dramatizes, and supports the interpretation and criticism of society that Octavio Paz presented in *The*

Labyrinth of Solitude and continued in *Postscript* and *Conjunctions and Disjunctions*. . . .

The multiplicity of interpretive levels in this work is the basis of the process which Fuentes and Paz use, which I will call "symbolic historicism." This can be defined as a process of attributing symbolic meanings to various events, monuments, or people of the past in order to comment upon elements of cultural psychology, history, and politics in the present. And very important for this "technique" is the projection of various roles of the principal characters. . . .

The importance of [the last] scene is that Fuentes ends the work by modernizing the ancient, making a correlation between the Aztec sacrifice of the chosen ones in the Pyramids of Tlatelolco, the slaughter of the Indians in the Temple of Cholula by the Spaniards, and the massacre of the university students at Tlatelolco in 1968. In the drama the death of the student, seen in the light of the relation of Moctezuma with his death, seems to imply that the President of Mexico is to blame, up to a certain point, for the tragedy at Tlatelolco.

But a simple act of blaming or criticizing Mexico is not the only reason for the existence of Fuentes's work, nor for the works of Octavio Paz that have influenced him. These works analyze and offer some possibilities for the interpretation of present-day Mexican society as a reflection of certain aspects of its past, which many do not want to recognize.

Gary Brower. LATR. 5, 1, Fall, 1971, pp. 59–61, 67–68†

Fuentes has moved with the world and it is no longer so obsessively important to him to define Mexico or Mexicanism, or even to fight for a solution to the woes of the masses. He is more interested now in the relationship of man with his fellow man (and woman) and their situation in time. Other questions interest him—the working out of individual destinies affected by the collective subconscious, the myth, the correlation between reality and fantasy (and what these are), the merging and separation of personality with itself and with that of others, psychic alienation—all themes that transcend nationality and economics and have to do with the human condition in almost a metaphysical sense.

All this, it might be said, is simply a part of the process of maturing. Indeed it is, but the way and the direction one takes in maturing is also a result of what one has been and what one has been formed by, and we cannot understand the new Fuentes without first understanding the previous Fuentes. . . .

Daniel de Guzmán. Carlos Fuentes (New York,
Twayne, 1972), pp. 69–70

The dominant mask assumed by Fuentes [in *The Clearest Region*] is in the person of Ixca Cienfuegos. Cienfuegos, an undeniably striking feature of the novel, is a shadowy presence who is so marginal and yet somehow so central to the narrative action of the novel in his persistent appearances and in the apparently multiple functions assigned to him by the author. The mask is impressive for the man's complex—often contradictory—personality as it emerges from the long work. Cienfuegos' functions are many. He ties the immense sprawl of the novel together in several senses: his "voice" both opens and closes the novel, he brings together otherwise alien levels of society, he provides opportune interpretations of events and circumstances, and, finally, he serves as the catalyst for the central novelistic action (Robles' demise and his wife's death, both individuals examples of the ephemeral "success" of the Revolution). Furthermore, as the unifying narrative point of view, Ixca Cienfuegos constitutes the most comfortable *persona* of the author-artist engaged in creating a novel that is supposed to interpret a complex reality. This creative, dynamic endeavor, as it is embodied in the attitudes and activities of Cienfuegos, becomes highly symbolic, and the novel calls into serious question the pragmatic and prophetic functions attributed by the Western tradition to art in general and literature in particular. On the basis of the trajectory of Cienfuegos' role in the novel, a trajectory that culminates in his own abject despair and apparent abandonment of any prophetic mission which he earlier may have felt called upon to fulfill, Fuentes would seem to be not only rejecting the ability of a pragmatic art to "be useful" in the Horatian sense but as well the ability of a committed art to renovate, to "revolutionize" its audience.

David William Foster. Hispania. 56, March, 1973, p. 35

GALLEGOS, RÓMULO (1884-1969)

VENEZUELA

Rómulo Gallegos . . . has never aspired to a style . . . marked by the worship of the insignificant or oratorical paragraph and the honeyed phrase. He writes with precision, clarity, and elegance. On occasion he yields to the Venezuelan fondness for descriptive profuseness, a fondness perhaps appropriate to a people who have scarcely begun to take spiritual possession of the land they inhabit. But his characterization is not weakened by the background; the contours of the characters do not fade and become pale shadows beneath the untamed, domineering landscape. Rather, they remain firmly in front of the reader, complicated, somewhat enigmatic, illogical, and passionate—alive. . . .

Nearly all of the characters in *The Last of the Solars* are disagreeable. The protagonist himself, despite his grandiose plans and active patriotism, is a weakling, a turncoat, and good-for-nothing. . . . He lacks the Caesarean pride of other heroes of Venezuelan novels. At heart he is a sensualist; if he has a liking for great gestures, it is only because of some luxurious grandeur he chances to discover in them. His anguish is what finally redeems and transforms him. . . .

[*The Last of the Solars*], full of the contradictory truth of life, is superior to what is offered us by other regional novels, full of insignificant men making pretty speeches. The repugnant characters suggest the anxiety of the artist who finds himself in a hostile and harsh world. The spirit of the artist, like a relentless mirror, shows the deformities, the hideousness, but it does not present the antithesis, as formerly was the case in morality novels. The writer has an unfailing artistic instinct and understands that the contrast of a standard ideal with weak human characters would falsify the tale. This was not understood by earlier novelists, not even the most skillful.

In *The Last of the Solars* may be found the Venezuelan atmosphere that we have breathed since childhood. More than the characters themselves, it is the atmosphere that gives us the impression of accuracy. [1920]

Jesús Semprum. Crítica literaria (Caracas, Ediciones
Villegas, 1956), pp. 207, 210–11†

The North American reader tends to forget, in his absorption with Anglo-American literature, that another and later pioneer literature, one coming from Latin America, is emerging. Few of the works published between the Rio Grande and Cape Horn have found their way into English translation, but the best ones always appear in Spain and Portugal, and many are published in France. The United States, however, continues to pursue a policy of ignoring, so far as letters are concerned, the republics to the south.

This slight but vivid novel of ranch life on the Venezuelan plains [*Doña Bárbara*] deserves a warm welcome. . . . Now for the first time we have a picture of a new and exotic frontier life, one that is fascinating partly because of its resemblances to our own early Western frontier, and partly because of its subtle differences owing to the Latin temperament. It is illuminating to get the point of view of those finest riding cattlemen in the world—the Spanish Americans—in contrast to the opinions of the North American writers who interpret the South Americans in relation to Northern standards. . . .

The foreigner here is not the greaser, but the gringo. William Danger's contempt for the Latin American, his Nordic brutality, his ignorance of Southern honor are part of a picture which by no means spares Venezuelan justice and Spanish-Indian-American weaknesses—treachery and corruption. . . .

The character of Doña Bárbara is the chief disappointment in the tale. Her past, as related in the early part of the book, makes a good short story; but her subsequent career is not sufficiently developed to lend that sense of power which would have made this book a bigger novel.

Fred T. Marsh. NYT. Aug. 9, 1931, p. 7

It is probably true that talented writers make poor—in the sense of unsuccessful—politicians. Rómulo Gallegos, one of the foremost writers of Latin America, is no longer a senator of Venezuela; he is now living in New York, a political exile. It may very well be, however, that the influence of Señor Gallegos will prove more enduring than that of Dictator Gómez or whosoever. Not that *Doña Bárbara* is a purposeful novel in which are embedded political arguments; nor, on the other hand, is it a masterpiece. But Rómulo Gallegos will be remembered, with the Colombian José Eustasio Rivera, author of *The Vortex*, as one of the leaders in a contemporary revolt among Latin American writers for literary independence. They have rebelled against the silly tyranny of conventions borrowed from the popular literature of France and Spain. If they remain romantics, they are certainly more vigorous and honest, more aspiring and more worthy of critical attention than were their predecessors.

It would be easy to overestimate this novel, or any of the few Latin American novels that are translated, in the effort to understand their value and meaning for an original audience. *Doña Bárbara*, a lion in its native haunts, does not seem so formidable and remarkable to the Anglo-Saxon reader. It is, however, an exciting heroic tale of the life of the Venezuelan plainsmen, masters and peons, ranchers and cowboys and horse thieves; in a broadly symbolic fashion, it describes the victory of a new civilization in the barbaric last frontier of the Venezuelan plains.

Doña Bárbara herself is an evil character of lush proportions, an enchantress, an oversexed, untamed beauty. For the more ideally minded, her activities and those of the unscrupulous empire-building American named Danger, represent the corruption of the government, the primitive conditions of society. Doña Bárbara's path is crossed at last by the young Santos Luzardo, an educated aristocrat who has returned to his ancestral ranch, seeking retribution but bringing with him more civilized ways of fighting. The struggle begins immediately. . . . One should, of course, watch with approval the spectacle of civilization victorious, but one does not care very much that Luzardo overcomes Doña Bárbara and the American, nor even that he marries the illegitimate and (therefore) abandoned Marisela. The reader will prefer to remember this story of adventure in the Venezuelan cattle country for its spirit, windswept and strong, and will render thanks to its author for a day on the savannahs.

Charles A. Pearce. NR. Oct. 28, 1931, p. 304

I can consider *Doña Bárbara* one of the best novels that I have ever read. This tale is as powerful as it is polished, as bold as it is subtle, as epic as it is lyric, an expression of the innermost feelings of people who inhabit the inaccessible heart of a tropical country. . . . It is an artistic synthesis of a view of life, significant from every perspective of human existence; it is on a level with any famous modern European or American novel. . . . Gallegos's technique seems to have been influenced by three European writers of the nineteenth century: Charles Dickens, Alphonse Daudet, and, more narrowly still, Antonio Fogazzaro. Nevertheless, the novel is not at all European but is intrinsically Venezuelan. . . .

If we examine those elements on which the artistic effect is based . . . we first notice the precise description of the geographical setting—natural and cultural—unfamiliar to most people. . . . The life of the plainsman is developed before the reader's eyes as if it were a motion picture taken of reality. . . . The kind of novel that limits subject matter to the primitive conditions of human existence . . . the regional novel . . . in which the story is unfolded in the country rather than in the city, with little differentiation of characters, always is in danger of failing to penetrate depths of experience . . . of remaining on the outside, limiting itself to the strictly external. But Gallegos avoids this undeniable hazard of the regional novel—the lack of psychological interest. . . . [His characters'] continual concern with their own moral development, with improving themselves . . . that element of autodidacticism confers a spiritual interest and validity to those characters, who otherwise, lacking any spiritual anguish . . . would have instead remained below the level of human interest, ornaments on the landscape, atoms of physical life, never human beings interesting in themselves.

Ulrich Leo. *Estudios filológicos sobre letras venezolanas*
(Caracas, Cuadernos de la Asociación de Escritores Venezolanos,
1942), pp. 29, 31–32, 35†

If there is any one theme or purpose that characterizes Gallegos's novels, it is the advocacy of the amalgamation of the various races—Indian, white, and negro—that compose the population of Venezuela. *The Creeper* concludes with the union of the aristocratic Nicolás and Victoria, who on her father's side inherited both negro and Indian blood; in *Doña Bárbara* Santos Luzardo married Marisela, who through her mother was partly Indian; in *Canaima*, Santos Vargas took a wife from the wild Indian tribes of southern Venezuela; and in *Poor Negro* a young white woman of an aristocratic family preferred as a consort the mulatto Pedro Miguel to one of her own social rank.

Viewed as a whole and in perspective, the fictional output of Gallegos is uneven. Opinions and theses, while not absent from his novels, are not dominantly characteristic of them. On the whole, too, it might be said that Gallegos, like Azuela, lacks the first essential of a great novelist—the art of telling a story. Only a few of his short stories and his first two novels tell stories that interest for their own sake; best of all is *Doña Bárbara,* in which the various fictional elements are most completely harmonized; on the other hand, *Cantaclaro, Canaima*, and *Poor Negro* are almost absolutely formless in regard to plot.

Nor can it be said that Gallegos is a master of the first class in creating flesh and blood individuals, for most of his characters are personifications or idealizations. Reinaldo Solar personifies Venezuela—inconstant in purpose, impatient for results; Santos Luzardo and Dr. Payara personify the civilizing influence in the plains; Doña Bárbara, the barbarous and unpitying aspects of that region. Cantaclaro, a sort of Santos Vega, typifies the wandering ballad-singer of the Venezuelan plains; but Luisana and Cecilio are clearly idealizations. His best characters are Hilario Guanipa [*The Creeper*] and Reinaldo Solar, although the latter as an individual is almost a caricature.

Gallegos's novels have all won considerable commendation in both Spanish America and Spain, but *Doña Bárbara* has achieved a spectacular success and carried his name into a wider world. First printed in February, 1929, it was at once hailed as the outstanding contemporary Spanish-American novel. In the same year it was chosen as the best book of the month in Madrid and its author recognized as "the first great novelist of South America." For the second edition, Gallegos rewrote the work in part. In the next decade more than twenty editions were printed. Before two years had passed an English translation brought the author added praise from a new group of critics. It has so far proved his masterpiece.

Jefferson Rea Spell. *Contemporary Spanish-American Fiction* (Chapel Hill, University of North Carolina Press, 1944), pp. 236–38

I am certainly not the first to compare [*Doña Bárbara*] to an epic poem written in prose, the epic poem of the prairie, with all of its fascination, its perils, and its heroic episodes. Primitive man, the human centaur of legendary Venezuelan battles, is prominently portrayed in his particular qualities and defects, comparable only to the similar qualities and defects of the gauchos of the Río de la Plata, but distantly related to those native to the Russian steppes. This is the struggle between civilization and barbarism, described by the Argentine Sarmiento in *Facundo*, which is depicted this time on the plains of Venezuela.

The worship of courage, which still exists on the American pampas or *llanos* [the Venezuelan prairie], is magnificently portrayed in Gallegos's masterpiece, in rural scenes of vivid colors, effected by means of a language that is virile, unpolished, yet never awkward. . . . Poetry is not lacking in this immense rural novel, filled with typical characters . . . who in the Río de la Plata [region] had been delineated from the time of the romantics Echeverría and Magariños Cervantes through the moderns, Javier de Viana and Güiraldes. The narrative force of *Doña Bárbara* is comparable to that of Rivera's *The Vortex*. . . . And the conclusion, in which the permanent disappearance of the protagonist is suggested, fixes in one's memory the terrible and tragic struggle of man against the cruelty of nature. . . .

In all his novels, Gallegos, a profound artist, has respected the creole language of his characters, but he never incurs the error of imitating their grammar. Had he done this, it would have detracted from the excellence of his work without adding anything to the realism of the episodes. . . .

Hugo Barbagelata. *La novela y el cuento en Hispanoamérica* (Montevideo, Enrique Míguez, 1947), pp. 200–203†

There is a sense of the tragic in nature in the regional novel. Nature is larger and more powerful than man. Man remains on his defense against it. . . . The immensity and awesomeness of nature remain in the consciousness of the creole. The same stretch of tropical jungle that gave Hudson his subject for the pastoral poem *Green Mansions* is the fascinating stage, filled with death and mystery, for Gallegos's characters. . . .

Between . . . 1910 and 1920 Gallegos published short stories. They were serene pieces of narration, well executed, a little slow and with a general tendency toward an elusive lyricism. More than just short stories, they seemed to be, and in reality were, sketches of characters and scenes for novels. In 1920 *The Last of the Solars* was published: an essayistic novel, somewhat formless and unbalanced, overflowing with an excessive sweep of land and [with] artistic, political, and social preoccupations. . . . The book [expresses] a marked pessimism [toward] reforms. . . . But it brought many positive and new elements to the Venezuelan novel. . . . In the midst of its depictions of customs, of its theories of reform, of its inherited romanticism, there is an honest intention to re-create life within the proportions of a work of art. Much attention is given to the prose, especially in the descriptions, which at times are like elaborate enameling applied to the work. . . . This, together with the author's tendency to abandon himself to sensory perceptions, independent of his characters . . . [is] characteristic of the indisputable primitivism of one stage of the regional novel, from which Gallegos has never completely succeeded in freeing himself. . . .

Seen in the perspective of Venezuelan literary history, Gallegos has succeeded in balancing and fusing currents that had been separated into the naturalistic regional novel and artistic modernism. Furthermore, his work fulfills the great mission of bringing the Venezuelan novel to the attention of the rest of the world.

Arturo Uslar Pietri. *Letras y hombres de Venezuela*
(Mexico City, Fondo de Cultura Económica, 1948),
pp. 135–36, 143–46†

We can perceive two dominant categories of ideas in Gallegos's allusions to literary works. One category could be defined as the *search for the possible*, and it encompasses the anthropocentric religious illusion of Renan, the poetic state of Schopenhauer, the naturalism of Zola, the creed of manhood of Nietzsche—all solutions arising out of an anguished spiritual and psychic state. These solutions take the following forms in Gallegos's novels: (1) *action*, based on a *will to power*, a sense of *becoming* and a sense of *destiny* . . . accepted energetically and unquestioningly as *fate*; (2) life as an *adventure*, within the confines of nature, *in contact with nature*, and adventure as love, as a more human sentiment.

The second category could be called the *encounter with one's self* in terms of the different forms of egoism by which the search for the possible manifests itself. This category encompasses the influence of Barrès, the sentimentalism of Tolstoi, the "purified" vision of life of Andreyev. The second category of ideas takes the following forms in the protagonists of Gallegos: (1) a sense of adventure that could not be possible without a *disquietude*, an intellectualism, a tendency toward exoticism . . . (2) a concomitant enrichment of the world of *sensations*, an active use of sensuality as a way to the *absolute*, at which point one can attain a sense of self no tentative stage can offer.

José Vila Selma. *Rómulo Gallegos* (Seville, Escuela de
Estudios Hispano-Americanos, 1954), pp. 132–33†

The great poetry of the land—the Andes, the tropical jungle, the pampas, the abundant continental rivers—with its mixture of grandeur and horror, is in itself an aesthetic element capable of elevating American fiction to a universal level. . . . This literature is eminently geographical, because the other elements, the human beings who complete the picture and form a part of it, remain subordinate; nature imposes its domination. . . .

If the character of Doña Bárbara represents the primordial desert in America, the true protagonist of the novel is the desert itself, its dominant telluric force. Hence the greatness and also the weakness of the work. . . . In portraying . . . the civilized characters [of *Doña Bárbara*], representatives of the culture of the city . . . Gallegos only

briefly sketches their psychological makeup and never develops it systematically as an effective theme. . . . There is no analysis; there are scarcely
any human beings. . . . The symbols lack psychological interest; they
remain abstract. . . . *Doña Bárbara* is presented more as an epic poem
than as a novel; it is territorial observation carried to the epic plane, a
plane also reached by other great South American regional novels. . . .

Alberto Zum Felde. *Índice crítico de la literatura
hispanoamericana* (Mexico City, Editorial Guarania,
1954–59), Vol. II, pp. 66, 227–28†

Contrary to the opinion of those who consider themselves blessed with
the simple and noble qualities of country life, Gallegos conceives of
civilization as a desirable product of city life. This attitude probably
reflects the untamed nature of the South American desert as compared
with the cultivated Roman farmland, the gardens of Salamanca, and
the gently rolling countryside of New England, dotted with peaceful
farms. The most obvious and immediate definition of the civilizing force
that, in men like Santos Luzardo [in *Doña Bárbara*], flows out from the
cities, is Law: words like "law of the plain," "rights," "justice," the
"law and order" of our Western movies. In Part Two, Chapter One,
Gallegos purposely brings together in the office of the *Jefe Civil* [Civil
Chief] Santos Luzardo, Doña Bárbara, Míster Danger, Ño Pernalete,
and Mujiquita. The purpose is to have them react to the "law of the
plain." And Santos Luzardo is himself a lawyer.

The physical manifestation of Law, the law in question, is a fence,
which Santos Luzardo is determined to have erected. . . . Besides the
fence, civilization would bring other material improvements to the
plains. For all their good intentions, the appearance of these is sometimes so fantastic as to suggest the ludicrous, e.g., the locomotive as it
comes panting over the horizon. . . .

But is civilization just a matter of housekeeping? Is civilization just
a successful use of material things?

Perhaps Law is not enough. Perhaps Law is only a manifestation,
like the fence, or the railroad, of something more profound. This might
be the civilizing force.

Santos Luzardo, with his sanctified, burning light and high sights,
stands pitted against Barbara Barbarity and fear. His own personal
struggle seems to revolve around impulse and reason. . . . Santos
Luzardo, if civilized, also bears within himself the potential of barbarity.
On the one hand he is afraid of the power of the barbarous nature of his
temperament, watchful of any possibility of "a return to barbarianism"
. . . and on the other determined to direct matter by the exercise of his
intelligence. This is a very real struggle, since, as any one who has read

the book knows, Santos spends considerable time in the arms of barbarity, if not in those of Bárbara.

Ernest A. Johnson, Jr. *Hispania.* 39, Dec., 1956,
pp. 456–57

To study Gallegos deeply, one must examine his writings for the journals *La alborada* and *El cojo ilustrado,* which show the process of development of the future short-story writer, playwright, novelist, essayist, political leader, and educator. At that stage, in the form of political and social essays, Gallegos presented the preoccupations of his time and the solutions he saw for problems that disturbed him as a young intellectual at the beginning of the century. Although his horizons broadened through experience and wisdom with the passing of time, he never departed from the ideas expressed in those essays. . . .

Like members of the Generation of '98 in Spain, Gallegos analyzed his people and culture. . . . He adopted the thesis that Spanish America should follow the currents of Western European civilization whatever the difficulties. But he never reached the extreme of suggesting the repudiation of his Spanish soul as had other Spanish American philosophers. . . . On the basis of his essays, Gallegos should be elevated to his proper position as political and social philosopher. . . . In these works we see bared the heart, soul, and will of a people and its culture. His writing has integrity, intellectual honesty, without the inferiority complex that so often accompanies the Latin American when he discusses his society. . . . The essays are written in a clear and realistic style; the embellishments of the modernists play no part in Gallegos's world, a world of realities that he felt had to be faced. . . .

In his short stories . . . we can see the development of ideas and techniques he later used in his novels. . . . Although certain literary influences are seen in these stories, each one of them originates directly from the land and reality surrounding the author. Exotic though some of his characters may be, they nevertheless belong to the streets and countryside of Venezuela. And they are always Venezuelans, regardless of the technique involved in their creation.

Lowell Dunham. *Rómulo Gallegos: Vida y obra*
(Mexico City, Ediciones De Andrea, 1957),
pp. 138, 160–61, 194†

Perhaps in [Gallegos's] judgment on the dilettante conspirators one finds the most outright statement of the theme of *The Last of the Solars.* He declares that these young men belonged to an epoch of absolute disorientation; their energies, like the waters in a mountain ravine, had to seek and make their course violently. Again, he sees in the statue of the Winged Victory of Samothrace a symbol which could be applied to Venezuelan youth—it was glorious, with its wings outstretched to fly, but flight whither? It could not see. . . .

In the end, Reinaldo, a true representative of the society of which he was a part, having tried in vain to find legitimate scope for his energies and having fruitlessly exhausted himself by hurrying off in all directions at once, resorted to armed revolution, the very course of action he had condemned as being barbaric. He was not a very good revolutionist, since he was horrified at the brutality of his cut-throat companions, and finally was jailed, to be released only to die. It is ironic that Reinaldo had no better luck in reforming himself than in reforming his country. He was a knight without arms and without will, but his failure was a failure *par excellence*. Menéndez and Alcor, with talents hardly less than Reinaldo's own, also had failed, though perhaps not so spectacularly, since they seemed, if not content, at least resigned to vegetate in obscurity.

Reinaldo is only one of the many such characters created by Gallegos. This similarity in character delineation is not an accident, for it stems from the fact that Gallegos, even before he became a novelist, was a critic of the social and political scene, and that in his careful, mathematical mind he set out to analyze the causes of his country's plight and the effect which the environment offered by such a country would have upon its citizens. There is no mistaking his verdict: until the fatherland can produce the sort of emotional climate in which the abilities of its youth will have an opportunity for full and free development, there will be succeeding generations of swordless Reinaldos who will continue to squander their energies aimlessly, extravagantly and tragically. This bitter indictment of Venezuelan society is the persistent and pessimistic theme of *The Last of the Solars*.

L. Welsh. *Hispania*. 40, Dec., 1957, p. 448

In *Doña Bárbara*, Rómulo Gallegos is clearly not attempting the stream of consciousness novel. Far too much of the novel is concerned with action observable and observed externally (although Gallegos avoids interfering, officious comment) and for the most part the action is reported through the words of the author as observer. Furthermore, even when he reveals the activity in the minds of his characters, the incoherence and discontinuity so often found in the stream of consciousness novel are generally missing. But Gallegos was writing something more than an adventure story and his novel demands more than the mere reporting of external events, however "realistically" and objectively it may be done. There are times when it becomes desirable for him to give the reader a more intimate glimpse of the inner states of his characters and to make more meaningful the relationship of the characters one to the other. It is to report this psychological or inner action that Gallegos turns to some of the techniques of the stream of consciousness novel. . . .

Although introspective techniques are used throughout the novel—there is scarcely a chapter that does not offer examples of one or more of them—their use becomes more frequent as the story progresses and the decisive moments are approached. It is at times of crisis for the principal characters that these techniques are used in combination and in fair extension to reveal the essential inner action. Such is the case when Santos leaves Marisela after their first meeting, when, at the dance and immediately afterward, Marisela and Santos realize that their problem demands solution, when Doña Bárbara admits to herself that her life at *El Miedo* is ended and plans to leave.

The techniques are used for a variety of purposes. Sometimes what is so revealed makes the actions of a character more understandable and acceptable; for example, the opening of Doña Bárbara's mind to the reader on various occasions indicates that her final disappearance is due to something more than defeat. At times they are employed to supply necessary background information, as in the opening chapter where, by a combination of narrative, quoted thoughts and remembered statements, the presence of Melquíades in the *bongo* with Santos is explained. Whenever these techniques are used, some definition of character is obtained. Gallegos does not, of course, depend solely upon this method for presenting his characters, but it serves to supplement the traditional psychological descriptions. The result of many of the interior scenes, whatever else may be accomplished with them, is to stop all exterior action in the novel. In most cases, where the internal passage is of any length, it is as if the actors cease all movement and they are seen silent and motionless. One of the effects thus attained is variety in the pace of the novel.

Donald G. Castanien. Hispania. 41, Sept., 1958,
pp. 281, 287

Señor Gallegos, never prolific, has been his own severest critic. Two early novels he tore up, one when it was already being printed. *Doña Bárbara* he rewrote not once but twice. Whence, in part, his present esteem as one of the great masters of the Spanish tongue, with a style, remarkable for the intricacy allied to crystal clarity with which he constructs his architectural periods, that is a constant delight. A jury of Gabriel Miró and Azorín adjudged the same *Doña Bárbara* the "novel of the month": they could with equal truth have proclaimed it better than anything Spain had seen in years. In Venezuela Gómez's verdict, given from another viewpoint, is also worth quoting: "This is not against me: this is good."

A second excellence, developed with increasing effect in novel after novel, is his feeling for landscape and his capacity for conjuring up not the externals alone but the inwardness of it until it becomes— never indeed the protagonist, for his themes and problems are always essentially human—but an agonist that plays its part in shaping all the others. It is to be noted that the novelist's settings cover systematically the distinctive regions of his vast country; Caracas and its surroundings, the coffee lands of the Tuy valley, the rolling plains, the forest belt of the Orinoco and Guiana, the cocoa plantations of Barlovento, Lake Maracaibo and the Guajira peninsula. The European reader may thus take the feel of Venezuela as a whole and know it more intimately from his armchair than he can, through its fiction, any other of the twenty republics. And as he passes from setting to character and plot he will have constantly borne in on him the complexity of the human situation in a society where none of his own assumptions holds.

TLS. Feb. 10, 1961, p. 88

[Gallegos's work] is the basis of our national literature, because it is profoundly understood and felt by the soul of the people. . . . The writings of Gallegos are deeply inspired by the land (the country, the plain, the jungle). He expresses it as a living essence, full of creative and destructive forces. . . . He reflects the life of the man who inhabits it, expresses his conflicts, and searches into the depths of language and events for the quintessence of the native soul. . . . Gallegos takes traditional themes (human character, spiritual complexity, habits and vices, defects of society) and explores and develops them with deep feeling and creative imagination. Indeed, he develops them to a degree that makes him not only the greatest influence in the Venezuelan novel but also the culmination of the development of the Spanish American novel.

Gallegos realizes one of the most difficult artistic principles, that of expressing the maximum poetic content with the least complicated technique. . . . All [his novels] are conceived within a system of [structural] harmonies and conflicts, in a movement, full of poetic sorcery, that correlates man and nature. This sense of harmony in Gallegos's work has led some critics to characterize his style as one of great poetic restraint and balance. . . .

The novels of Gallegos follow a geographical plan that embraces all the different regions of his native country. Each . . . has its common speech, with its own features that Gallegos captures with much sensitivity. . . . If he had only given us the common speech verbatim, he would not have gone beyond folklore. [But] in all his work we find the precise and poetic form of the vernacular tongue: actual things of the animal and vegetable world . . . translated to a plane of different significance, which figuratively expresses ideas, opinions, and emotions.

Gallegos's novels are symmetrical in the arrangement of their parts and in the development of the chapters, demonstrating clearly that poetic equilibrium which many critics believe to be characteristic of his masterly technique. . . .

> Orlando Araujo. *Lengua y creación en la obra de*
> *Rómulo Gallegos* (Caracas, Ediciones del Ministerio
> de Educación, 1962), pp. 97–98, 105–106, 232,
> 234–35, 267†

Unlike other writers focusing on the clash of civilization and barbarism, who have agreed with Sarmiento's interpretation . . . that civilization exists wherever there may be found tradesmen's shops, courts of justice, and factories, and barbarism wherever there may be found anything that mitigates against change in customs and progress . . . Gallegos presents the idea that barbarism is not ignorance or decadence; rather it is youth, dynamism, human resources as inexhaustible as the fertility of his country. . . .

His advancing years have not diminished his creative integrity or his democratic patriotism. On the contrary, time has enriched the range of his inspiration and refined the integrity and clarity of his temperament as a citizen. . . . Few writers . . . have succeeded so well in reaching and penetrating the land and people of a country . . . more by intuitive procedures . . . than . . . discursive methods. Thanks to his sensitivity born of the land and his exceptional psychological gifts, he has succeeded in interpreting the essence and significance of the soul of the people.

> Richard F. Allen. *DHR*. 4, Spring, 1965, pp. 29–30†

For the most part, for Rómulo Gallegos, literature does not constitute an end in itself, an artistic creation, but an instrument of social, psychological, and political criticism. Nevertheless, his characters and some of his stories attain the universal level of vigorous creative power. . . .

Lowell Dunham has pointed out that in some of his fiction . . . there is a quest for the unusual, a characteristic of the modernist movement led by Rubén Darío years earlier. . . . Perhaps there may be some of this, yet it seems to us that the presence of *tremendismo* and *miserabilismo* [exaggeration of the terrible, stark reality, and misery] in Gallegos's work could be better explained as the influence of pre-

Soviet Russian literature, with its world of saints and devils, of down-and-out characters . . . with its messianism and symbolism. . . .

Gallegos's form is simple, even archaic compared to that of other prominent writers of Hispanic America. . . . His novels are more nouns than adjectives. . . . [His characters] are defined by action. . . . His heroes are not only cases, representatives of local, economic, social, political conditions, but *souls*, myths, actors, persons, examples of the Venezuelan human condition, and at times universal archetypes. . . .

Juan Liscano [Velutini]. *RIB*. 16, April–June, 1966,
pp. 123, 131, 142–43†

Rómulo Gallegos . . . was a member of a newly educated class that had sprung from the lower levels of the population. . . . Gallegos grew up in a generation which placed its belief in education and literary culture as a way of combating barbarism. In his youth, his main preoccupation was social and political rather than literary and this was readily understandable in a period of which one of his friends wrote: "The years of our apprenticeship seemed dark to our young minds: years of disaster, dark years in which we only wanted to think of our country." . . .

In Gallegos' hands, the novel was to become an instrument of national regeneration through the exposure of the country's weaknesses and the indication of the way to future development. . . . In a series of novels written during the 'twenties and 'thirties, Gallegos was to cover all aspects of Venezuelan life and to set his novels in many different regions—plains, jungles, plantations. But in all of them he had the two-fold aim of describing the unknown life of the hinterland and of showing how the tragic disorder and division of the country might be overcome. . . .

By incarnating the virtues and vices of his countrymen in certain characters, Gallegos criticises the root weaknesses of the nation and at the same time is able to show national virtues which could be exploited when these weaknesses are overcome. He anticipates more recent novelists in attributing many of Venezuela's difficulties to psychological weaknesses.

Jean Franco. *The Modern Culture of Latin America:
Society and the Artist* (London, Pall Mall Press,
1967), pp. 87–89

Canaima, in the hallowed tradition of Rivera's *The Vortex*, takes us to the rubber plantations in the jungles of the upper Orinoco, the haunts of savage Indians and ancestral forces that devour the civilized protagonist, Marcos Vargas, whose cause, according to the conventions of the genre, nevertheless triumphs later in his son. Canaima is an evil deity, a "frenetic god . . . somber divinity" of the local Indian tribes, personification of the demoniac, a sort of Ahriman, says Gallegos, come back to life in America. Vargas is an "adventurer of all adventures" along the road of life, on an edifying course into the heart of darkness, where the "jungle sickness" will absorb and obliterate him. But not before he enters into a rapturous embrace with Canaima. There is a histrionic encounter in which, awakening under concussion, he feels "free and alone as a man ought to be when the hour of his fate has struck"; for under his mortal skin he discovers "cosmic man, stripped of history," reunited with the original creative impulse. Meantime, he has had some instructive contacts with a local sage and tiger hunter, Juan Solito, who initiates him into primitive mysteries, and an Indian girl with the tribal denomination of Aymara, who helps him penetrate "the abysses of melancholy contained in the Indian soul." All of which is standard for the genre, which operates largely through nomenclature. The jungle is more mythological than real, a land of epiphanies, on the one hand, and colorful characters, on the other. Among the latter is another staple of this literature: the alcoholic Yank, not too unsympathetically treated by Gallegos, relatively charitable on this score compared to some of his colleagues. Here the type is represented by a Mr. Davenport, who provides comic relief with an intriguing theory he has developed that malaria is a disease of lazy people.

With *Canaima* Gallegos' creative period ends—his themes are exhausted, his scheme is complete—but his production continues unabated. In *Poor Negro* he returns to the racial problem, this time centering on the Negro race, personified by the heroic Pedro Miguel Candelas, the leader of a nineteenth-century slave revolt, who loves and eventually elopes with his mistress, Luisana, the enlightened daughter of white landowners. Luisana, a woman of the future, bears a clear message, daring for its age. So do the protagonists of *The Foreigner*, also about revolution, in this case a student uprising in the thirties that affords Gallegos an opportunity to expand on his political theories. He envisions three stages in Venezuelan political life; military warlord tyranny, oligarchic despotism, and eventually, in the somewhat utopian future, constitutional democracy. The liberal revolution in *The Foreigner* is doomed to failure—it is premature—but Gallegos, always uplifting, comforts himself with the hopeful thought that the next generation may do better, because "with every young man the world in some sense is born again." He carries his proselytism to the oil wells in the mudflats in *Upon This Same Land*, and, finally, to Cuba, at the time of the Machado dictatorship, in *A Wisp of Straw in the Wind*.

Luis Harss and Barbara Dohmann. *Into the Mainstream*
(New York, Harper & Row, 1967), pp. 10–11

The work of Rómulo Gallegos is cyclical, that is to say, it is a totality of interrelated writings . . . and not a series of independent texts. . . . The principal constants of his work are: misdirected force, with its implications of failure and sin against the ideal; the dormant soul, with its corollary of the redemptive function of awakening it; the struggle between civilization and barbarism, which includes both collective or individual cases; the subjective conflicts caused by miscegenation and marriages between persons of different social groups. . . .

Some of the criticisms made against Gallegos are: the simplicity of his characters—symbols lacking an authentic life; an absence of penetration into the depths of the subconscious; an outmoded technique; a folklore and a "creolism" that are limited; ineffective situations and conflicts. . . .

Among the motivations that animate Gallegos's characters and entwine their bodies, thoughts, and actions, is love. . . . Sex also determines the behavior of his characters. But in Gallegos's work, different from that of contemporary novelists and writers, there is no delight in or obsession with the sexual impulse. Nor is there any willful crudeness of language. By no means is there commercialized eroticism. . . .

> Juan Liscano Velutini. *Rómulo Gallegos y su tiempo*
> (Caracas, Monte Ávila Editores, 1969),
> pp. 207, 209, 223†

GÁLVEZ, MANUEL (1882–1962)

ARGENTINA

Gálvez gets caught up in excessive detail [in *The Grade-School Teacher*]. . . . His work sins on the side of abundance, with the result that concentration is sacrificed to an oppressive cargo of insignificant details. Moreover, often the details are puerile and repugnant, and therefore spoil the undeniable beauties of the work. . . .

Another element that detracts from the artistic value of *The Grade-School Teacher* is its tendentiousness and combativeness. In large part, it is a biting criticism of public education, and one that seems ultimately unjustified. . . . The author presents us with a series of pedagogues . . . who all engage in unpleasant intrigues and possess servile, absurd, or inappropriate attitudes. To what extent is all this true?

Despite these defects, exaggerations, and errors, *The Grade-School*

Teacher is nevertheless a vigorous work, one that above all shows Gálvez's talent as a novelist—in its admirable structure, harmonious and well-proportioned; in its depth of observation; in the many appropriate details of characterization. . . .

Álvaro Octavio Melián Lafinur. Nosotros. No. 69,
Jan., 1915, pp. 98–99†

"We must overcome the dreamy, lethargic spirit, the colonial *siesta* bequeathed us by Spanish decadence. We must have activity, energy, the enthusiasm of the New Argentine!" Thus speaks the winner of the prize for letters in Buenos Aires in 1920, hailed by his compatriots and neighbors as the "great American realist," the "founder of the Argentinian novel," the "South American Zola."

Manuel Gálvez has set out to produce a Comédie Humaine of life in Argentina. It is a venture of decided interest to his distant neighbors where only one of the novels has been translated and that scarcely reviewed. At times, when he hymns machinery, organization, the "go ahead" spirit, we hear our own popular prophets speaking through the unfamiliar medium of a Chesterfieldian prose. And when, on the next page, the mystic yearning, the ecstatic inner life of a dreamer assume their equal value, we halt at a new conception of the American spirit. . . .

"Sad, sane, robust, broad-minded" are the adjectives applied to this evaluation of the life of a community. The novels are realistic in the orthodox Zola sense: documented statements of human insufficiency. But something Gálvez must sacrifice to the gods of the New World. His happy ending appears in the form of spiritual regeneration. His idealistic hero, poet, social reformer, politician struggles against unconquerable odds in the lethargy and poverty of the human soul and emerges without practical accomplishment, but happy in a sort of Wagnerian redemption through suffering.

Nacha Regules, now appearing in an excellent translation, is the fifth of the series and a sequel to *The Metaphysical Sickness*. Nacha was a prostitute, noble, unfortunate, and finally saved. The search for her awakens the hero to an understanding of social injustice by leading him through "all the circles of the hell" of prostitution in Buenos Aires. . . .

Nacha and her friends are all duly repentant and anxious to get back to a virtuous life. The cause of their fall—for Gálvez, no moral revolutionary, has no doubt that it was a fall—was low wages and the unsympathetic attitude of society. Except for a Latin calmness in mentioning the details of evil, the book is reminiscent of the nineteenth-century humanitarian novel, from Kingsley to Mrs. Humphry Ward, where the solution was for the hero or heroine to share the lot of the poor and thus find salvation.

Expressionism seems not yet to have struck South America. Gálvez, alluded to in the Latin style as "a noble man of letters" and a "representative of culture" in a country where widespread reading is an achievement of the last twenty years, Gálvez has the monumental style of his monumental purpose. It is moving, however; it has the bite of earnest sarcasm, and merits the interest bestowed on the new spokesman of a new country.

Ruth Underhill. *Nation*. May 23, 1923, pp. 603–4

If any outside influence can be traced in *Nacha Regules* it is that of Tolstoy. The author, Manuel Gálvez, is described by the publishers as the leading novelist of Argentina, and *Nacha Regules* was awarded the "Prize for Letters" in 1920 by the City of Buenos Aires. It is a work of considerable power and evident sincerity. It attempts to portray one of the most difficult figures to make real and to make sympathetic in fiction—the saint who is to the world a fool. There is, to European eyes, an extraordinary *naïveté* in all the conversations. The characters are crudely contrasted. The wealthy intellectuals, whom it is intended to refute, talk of the downtrodden in a manner so absurd that it would be incredible in this country, and is not easy to believe in any. None the less, the picture of a brutal sensual plutocracy, without manners or traditions, on one side, and its helpless victims, on the other, is very striking.

The plot is not a pleasant one. It is largely concerned with prostitution. But never was vice depicted less attractively. It may, in fact, be said that the book is a crusade against that particular evil, and that to a certain extent it loses from the artistic point of view for that reason. Nacha Regules is a girl who has "gone to the bad" but loathes her calling and strives again and again to free herself from it.

TLS. Dec. 20, 1923, p. 895

Holy Wednesday . . . introduces an Argentine novelist who is new to English readers. His book should assure Señor Gálvez an unequivocal welcome, for it is a remarkable study of the confessional from the point of view of a parish priest, Father Eudosio Solanas. The book is completely objective as regards the author, who appears to have no thesis to prove; but he possesses that knowledge, sympathy, sensitiveness and understanding for lack of which the book would be a mere husk, instead of the penetrating and moving work it is.

The entire action takes place at Buenos Aires on Holy Wednesday, when from dawn onwards the confessional is literally besieged by a procession of penitents, some of whose stories are briefly narrated: children, men and women of all classes, tattlers and pilferers, perverts and adulterers. It is a terrible picture of sex obsession, which, however, throws into relief the shrewd responses of the priest and his magnificent devotion. Father Solanas, reputed to be a saint, is presented as a lonely, fallible human being, beset by the same temptations that seduce his fellow men, even to doubting his own faith; animated by the noblest conceptions of duty, but humbly aware of his shortcomings and flagellating himself for his failures. Running through the revelations of his penitents is the connecting link of his own personality, of his desires, the recollection of his one grave lapse, and his dread of once more falling from grace. The interaction between the confessions he receives and his own feelings is depicted with great skill.

TLS. March 15, 1934, p. 196

Although Gálvez thought *Nacha Regules* was at the opposite pole to naturalism, it is very much like [Zola's] *Nana* in subject, in theme, even in the enormous popular success and fame both works brought their writers. To be sure, there are differences in setting and in approach to character. Gálvez seems not to attribute much importance to heredity. Still, he is in a certain sense the observer and experimenter Zola talks about in his study of the novel, and such Gálvez works as *Neighborhood Story* cannot be explained without reference to naturalistic antecedents. The work in the packing house, the ugliness of the slums of Las Ranas, the houses of prostitution, the repugnant scenes, the hateful brutality of Chino—everything that assaults one's sensibility, hearing, sight, and smell shows that this writer, who expresses himself in a nervous, brisk, brusque, at times vulgar style, has not read [Zola] in vain.

Arturo Torres-Ríoseco. *Nosotros*. 2nd series, No. 32,
Nov., 1938, pp. 416–17†

[Gálvez's] portrayal of Argentinians and of the national capital is far from sympathetic. In fact, there are those who feel that he was unjustified in such a treatment. Claraval [in *Men in Solitude*], Toledo's son-in-law, considered vanity the national vice of Argentina and maintained that Argentinians were merely inferior transplanted Europeans. He also lamented the lack of character, energy, youth, spirituality, patriotism, discipline, and passion among his compatriots, noting that they were skeptical and entirely given over to sensual pleasures, horse racing, and drinking. He recognized that Buenos Aires was dynamic and rich but regretted that it was materialistic and that this lack of spiritual values was reflected in literature, art, social relationships, and even in love affairs.

What was woman's place in the above-pictured society? *Men in*

Solitude presents endless evidence of her inferior station. While it is true that women enjoyed more liberty in the post-war period than previously, there was still much prejudice against them. The only solution for the woman who indulged in extramarital adventures was to go to live in Europe permanently if she wished to escape the condemnation of society. Too, the idea persisted that woman's place was in the home. Claraval, maintaining that the Argentine woman lacked spirituality, felt that her only purpose in life was to have children. Martin Block, another character in the novel, declared, "In every woman there is a mother. It's the only merit they have." However, Roig, a novelist, defended women, stating that they were superior to men in sensitivity and in intelligence. . . .

The terms "civilization" and "barbarity" which Sarmiento attributes to Buenos Aires and the provinces respectively appear to have been applied inversely by Gálvez, who criticizes the resident of Buenos Aires with much more acerbity than he does the provincial. The provincial cities, because of their remoteness and traditional background, resisted new ideas longer than the capital, which turned its eyes to Europe. But they afforded a contemplation of nature and consequently a deeper religious sentiment. While the provincial is friendly, the resident of Buenos Aires is apt to be preoccupied with his own interests, lonely because he is immersed in the agglomeration of souls about him. . . .

Hazel M. Messimore. Hispania. 32, Nov., 1949,
pp. 464–65

[Gálvez's] seventeen novels and two volumes of short stories, presenting a variety of carefully studied backgrounds, interesting and human characters, some well integrated plots, and an easy style of writing, have given him a high place in contemporary Spanish-American literature. The range of the background he employs is wide. In point of time, he covers the period from 1830 to 1930; in geographical area, a large part of Argentina; and he utilizes thoroughly and realistically the political, social, cultural, and religious history of his country as no other Argentine writer has done. All this he sees and describes impersonally, as would an historian viewing the scene in retrospect, usually at a considerable distance. There is wide divergence, too, in the social levels of the characters he presents, for they range from one extreme to the other. His preference is for men rather than women, although he presents many women; and consistently in the purely fictional works he selects as protagonists weak characters who yield to love, disappointment, social or religious pressure. In his biographies and historical novels, in contrast, noble characters predominate. In his treatment of character psychological analysis enters, but there is little character development; the type is as first represented when the tale is ended. In this respect his work fails to arouse the maximum of interest.

In his technique Gálvez is the product of nineteenth-century models and far more conservative than most of his Spanish-American contemporaries. On some of his plots, especially that of *The Grade-School Teacher*, he expends great care; but others show the influence of a more modern group, for they tend toward formlessness. All are simple in structure and more like the Spanish than the French models Gálvez studied. On the whole his workmanship is superior to his inventive ability. . . .

Gálvez devotes far more attention to society than to landscape as a background. In his novels of Buenos Aires—even those in which the psychological element predominates—there is almost no description of the city; instead the emphasis is laid on social groups of various levels, which receive detailed treatment. Aside from his strong historical bent, Gálvez is a sociologist who employs his knowledge of society as a basis for his fiction. Even while he presents an individual, it is the group which that individual represents that is the author's real interest. And the plight of the group he lays bare through a typical individual.

In his work as a whole there is ample evidence that his purpose in writing as set forth clearly in *Noble Lineage* continues to actuate him. In all his works one feels his love of his native country; in several his deep sympathy for the provincial city. In the five historical novels and the two biographies is his continued realization of the importance of the "idealism and originality of the past," which alone, he believes, can save his country "without detriment to its material greatness." His portrayal of "the deadening interests that a materialistic conception of life has created" is intended to lead his people back to the calmer, traditional way of life through which Argentina became a great nation. He holds up to admiration some of their great deeds. He seeks to arouse his countrymen to an appreciation of their inheritance; to halt their hasty progress along ill-chosen ways. He tries to turn their attention to the scene about them so that they may eradicate the ugliness. . . .

Jefferson Rea Spell. *Contemporary Spanish-American Fiction* (Chapel Hill, University of North Carolina Press, 1944), pp. 61–63

Gálvez's and Mallea's approaches have differed. Gálvez, a man of pragmatic convictions, has advocated concrete action: social improvement, prestige for the intellectuals, religious orthodoxy, and discipline. At times, unfortunately, his support of these values has led him to the edge of fascism. Mallea, on the other hand, has not succeeded in finding such precise solutions. There is much compassion in his works, to be sure, but no one influences anybody else. Humility, sincerity, authenticity? He realizes that such abstractions will never placate personal torment. At one point in Mallea's development he maintained that "silence," or patient acceptance of worldly defeat, was the only solution other than madness or suicide. More recently he had tended to think that the individual can retreat to his "tower," where, voluntarily isolated from a chaotic world, he can nonetheless remain alert and in contact with the outside. . . .

Despite all that separates Mallea and Gálvez, they speak in interestingly similar accents, since theirs are both voices of Argentina. Their scopes are rather restricted, and within them they devote themselves as moralists to scrutinizing the Argentine soul.

Perhaps the world has grown tired of moralists. . . . Certainly it would not be untoward to observe that Gálvez no longer communicates effectively with the young artistic Argentine, and Mallea has recently met with resistance even among members of his own literary circle. Perhaps the floor has been yielded to more talented and imaginative writers. But it would be regrettable if people began to undervalue the undeniable contributions of these two serious minds.

G. Arnold Chapman. *RI*. 19, Oct., 1953, pp. 77–78†

The novelistic production of the Argentine Manuel Gálvez continues with almost astonishing regularity, although he is rather advanced in years and already has behind him a respected literary reputation. During the past decade Gálvez has published nine full-length novels, and there is no reason to believe that this fecund seventy-five year old writer has as yet laid down his pen. . . .

The dominant note in this recent period is the historical novel. From an early age Gálvez has evinced a special interest in Argentina's past and has sought in numerous writings to interpret his country's culture and define its pattern of life. Of particular concern to Gálvez has been the fascinating and bloodthirsty theme of the dictator Rosas. He set out in the 1930's to present a huge panorama of the Rosas era, but after two works of the proposed series were published—*The Gaucho from Los Cerrillos* in 1931 and *General Quiroga* in 1932—he apparently discontinued his efforts. In 1948, however, Gálvez came out with the third novel in this group; and in succeeding years the remaining works of the series appeared, so that by 1954 he could at last consider terminated an ambitious project begun some twenty-three years previously.

Thus the completion of the series *The Age of Rosas* represents a noteworthy accomplishment of Gálvez' recent fictional production, and at the same time seems to have satisfied an overwhelming passion of his to unmask this entire troubled era and make known his personal judgment of it. In each of the novels of the series he seeks to explain and defend his position, which in essence is toleration and justification of Rosas' generally condemned administration. For Gálvez, the dictator's Federalist doctrine meant the preservation of national sovereignty against possible French and English intervention, as well as the maintenance of order and respect for law. At the same time he vindicates the severity and cruelty of his regime on the grounds that he governed in abnormal times and could not cure his country's ills under any other system.

Myron I. Lichtblau. Hispania. 42, Dec., 1959, p. 502

The first readers of *The Metaphysical Sickness* considered the work a genuine success, a novel capable even of moving people to tears, of evoking strong feelings of sympathy for the misadventures of the protagonist, for his personal failings, his physical decline and death. Such elements of pathos affect the contemporary reader less; one could even claim that today's readers would not be moved at all by this novel. From the perspective of the current emotional climate, one could easily be tempted to suspect that the early readers of *The Metaphysical Sickness* deluded themselves, letting themselves be trapped by a number of devices craftily handled by Gálvez. Contemporary readers, on the other hand, detached from or indifferent to the "romantic life" of Carlos Riga, to his fears, his spiritual sufferings, his frustrated ideals, have tended not even to bother to judge the nature and quality of *The Metaphysical Sickness* as a novel but rather to dismiss it as a document of its period.

Adolfo Prieto. Estudios de literatura argentina
(Buenos Aires, Editorial Galerna, 1960), p. 9†

The year 1919 was decisive in [Gálvez's career]. As if knowing he was setting out on something big, he began work on January 1 on the novel that was to bring him fame, glory, and not a few uncomfortable moments—*Nacha Regules*. He later called this novel anticapitalistic and revolutionary, at least in social and economic, if not religious, matters. Its appearance in December of that year created storms of applause and outrage. There were people who denounced the work as immoral, because it dealt with the life of a prostitute. *El pueblo*, speaking as the official organ of the Catholic church in Argentina, accused Gálvez of having defected from the faith. The people at *La nación* and *La prensa* all but tore their hair out. . . .

In 1918 Gálvez had joined a Catholic political group, the Constitutional Party. . . . Because of this, people expected of him an almost total obedience to accepted forms, which were viewed as immutable for all "good thinkers." Gálvez, recollecting his act of revolt, could say many years later: "I proclaimed to many people that it was my most sincere book. That is the truth. It was wrested from inside me by an act of courage; and I cast it forth—still throbbing, still dripping with tears of blood—into the middle of the farce of life, the happy, stupid, perverse farce of life."

Undoubtedly reacting against the attacks and a little blinded by them, Gálvez turned *Nacha Regules* over, free of charge, to *La vanguardia* for publication in serial form. The following year he was awarded the Municipal Prize, which reinforced the novel's success. He had already won the approval of foreign critics.

Ignacio B. Anzoátegui. *Manuel Gálvez* (Buenos Aires, Ediciones Culturales Argentinas, 1961), p. 24†

Gálvez's Catholicism made his works too propagandistic, and thus was at times detrimental to literary considerations. There is no doubt that his propagandistic tendencies, which he gave so free a reign, reduced the quality of his work. . . . Almost all critics have pointed out as general defects his tiresome slowness coupled with an indulgence in trivial details. He certainly knew how to construct and organize but not how to polish; he lacked the ability to select and intensify. The accessory and anecdotal often block out the essential, and various kinds of interruptions—warnings, dissertations, explanations, and the like—hinder the natural progress of the story.

Nevertheless, another distinguished writer, the Chilean Eduardo Barrios, was able to state without exaggeration: "I think that the true Argentine novel begins with Gálvez. He possesses a robust style, a capacity for observation, a fine eye for setting, in short, the ability to perceive everything from the rarefied heights of the great novelist."

José Antonio Galaos. *CHA*. No. 170, Feb., 1964, pp. 346–47†

Gálvez's historical novels, or those with an historical setting, as the author has called them, form two cycles: one dealing with the war with Paraguay [during the 1870s], one dealing with the Rosas period [1829–52]. With the exception of two novels, Gálvez was engaged in writing these works when the Radical Party was in power [1916–30] and during the Perón period [1943–55]. This circumstance suggests important conclusions: during periods of tranquillity and historical equilibrium, under the influence of strong leaders, whose personalities correspond in one way or another to the model against which Argentines judge their leaders, novels appear that exalt figures from the past, men whose characteristics elevate them to the plane of prototypes of the nation.

The two cycles of novels have very similar traits, which allow general observations, through which the common elements can be analyzed, elements that are constant despite differences in subject matter. Historical revisionism molded Gálvez's determination to create historical novels that would go beyond the arbitrary formulas that Unitarian [that is, anti-Rosas] historiography had imposed over the years. . . . Gálvez insists over and over again on his impartiality toward the facts he is relating, and he almost always cites the historical sources from which he is able to reconstruct the events. But on the plane of interpretation of these facts, his impartiality disappears.

Norma Desinano. *La novelística de Manuel Gálvez*
(Sante Fe?, Argentina, Universidad National del
Litoral, 1965), p. 48†

GÁMBARO, GRISELDA (1928-   )

ARGENTINA

Gámbaro has successfully drawn from the intellectual, coldly clinical and pessimistic theatre of Ionesco and Beckett. And from Kafka, she produces precise and meticulous interpretations of the real world with nightmarish, wild situations which thwart her characters. These characters desperately try to solve the riddles of life only to be hopelessly frustrated and trapped by unfathomable internal and external forces. Gámbaro's theatre basically partakes of existentialism and the theatre of the absurd; she is preoccupied with man as an individual who seeks freedom from both himself and society. Following the existential ethic, she focuses on a few major characters, studies the individual in depth, and underplays the temporal and physical setting. Up to the present moment, Gámbaro has avoided the immediate Argentine reality and culture . . . in favor of a total concern for universal man. . . .

The Siamese Twins speaks convincingly to the contemporary audience in its elaboration of the Cain and Abel parable within the framework of modern man's schizophrenia. The work is a cold requiem for the spirit of good and evil in which the latter triumphantly annihilates the good and the weak. Written in two acts and blending a noisy and often chaotic dialogue with touches of black humor and mythic symbolism, *The Siamese Twins* [presents] two brothers, heirs to loneliness and fear, who are now bound as figuratively as they once were physically. Sadistic Lorenzo plots diabolically against ingenuous Ignacio; both characters represent the two poles of human existence, perhaps the total personality of man. Gámbaro dramatizes the tragedy of man's anguish and the futility of hope by means of a dialectic interplay in which the two brothers synthesize ideological frustration, anxieties, loss of innocence and many doubts regarding society and the new generation.

Virginia Ramos Foster. LATR. 1, 2, Spring, 1968,
pp. 55–56

[In *A Happiness with Less Pain* Gámbaro tries] to express the lack of communication within a group of human beings and the way such a lack can affect one's life. Moreover, there is an attempt to represent, through the use of absurdist techniques, our acceptance of the canons of bourgeois thought—not of bourgeois *life*, but of its *mental mechanisms*. Thirdly, by abandoning logical argument . . . the novel does away with everyday problems and strives for a continuity based on alogical and apsychological approaches.

Since the intensity of the novel makes us think again and again of the theater, one cannot help but recall [Alfred] Jarry's theory—which Jean Genet and others were to reformulate—of the need to eliminate psychological characterization in order to stress the *sign* [that is, how a character, like a word, is an element of meaning in a higher scheme of things]. The novel is written with a firmness and coherence . . . [that] gives an almost visual quality to events and dialogues. Familiar with the language of the theater, Gámbaro attempts to do what Beckett, Ionesco, Brecht, and Peter Weiss have already done in other ways: to depict archetypes rather than stereotypes and to abandon conventional approaches in the drama or the novel. . . . [One] is reminded of the theme of Boris Vian's *Les bâtisseurs d'empire*, in which, as in Gámbaro's work, all of the characters converge in a simple room in which anything can happen. But unlike Vian's work, at the end of which only a single person is left in the room, in Gámbaro's work the area becomes more and more crowded with characters, until space is devoured by a multiplicity of presences.

Elizabeth Azcona Cranwell. Sur. No. 315, Nov.–Dec.,
1968, pp. 92–93†

[In Gámbaro's *The Camp* Peter Weiss's] Hospice of Charenton [in *Marat/Sade*] becomes a Nazi concentration camp, its guests are transformed from imprisoned madmen into crazed prisoners, and the theatrical representation directed by the Marquis de Sade is converted into a piano recital by the insane Emms (Griselda Gámbaro's Charlotte Corday), organized by the very sadistic head of the concentration camp. It would not be inappropriate here to recall what Borges tells us about certain productions that "do not belong to literature but to crime: they are a deliberate sentimental blackmail, reducible to the formula 'I will present you with suffering and if you are not moved, you are heartless.'" What am I trying to say? Not that the use of concentration camps should be forbidden, but that it is an easy way out. One has the right to demand . . . either greater profundity or a focus for the poetic flight. In sum, there should be something new to say, something other than what has been already said and repeated so often, a virtue that in this case we have not been able to find.

Originality and necessity aside, the work does demonstrate a solid familiarity with theatrical devices, and not only the heavy ones, like startling the spectator with machine-gun bursts and [torture] sessions or making the protagonists run through the theater, a Pirandellian procedure that seems disjointed here. There is also a control over the dialogue, a capacity to create atmosphere and to resolve dramatic situations. . . .

Everything depends on the prior convictions of the spectator, who will thus find himself either pleased or annoyed but not indifferent, as is always the case with these didactic or propagandistic pretensions in the theater.

José Luis Sáenz. Sur. No. 315, Nov.–Dec., 1968,
pp. 122–23†

The Folly contains elements that are obviously symbolic. Lily (Lillith) represents sexual obsession; Viola, the mother, appropriately violates her son's masculinity. The strong youth stands for the working class, Luis for the selfish middle class. These symbols suggest an allegory about contemporary Argentine or Latin American society in which the middle class male (Alfonso) is fettered by his own self-indulgent sexual fantasies, by a matriarchally dominated family, and by a calloused and shallow society. The efforts of the working class, although well-meant, are arrogantly scorned by and ultimately wasted on the degenerate middle class.

Griselda Gámbaro presents her Kafkaesque tale in a very theatrical manner. By stressing physical language as advocated by Artaud, she addresses the play to the senses, not to the intellect. The iron fetter on Alfonso's foot as well as various other objects are used to emphasize his helplessness: he knocks out of his reach a ringing alarm clock; chamber pots multiply in successive scenes under his bed; the worker uses a little vegetable cart to move Alfonso about on the stage, etc. Other dramatic techniques in accordance with Artaud's theories involve the use of an oversize mannequin to represent Lily, and many sound effects, such as the annoying grating noise of the filing in the last scene while the mother is trying to entertain her guests.

Cruelty is perhaps the most notable Artaudian element in the play. There are moments of outright sadism when Luis, pretending to be playing, burns Alfonso's eyelashes with a cigarette and almost strangles him with a shawl. The incidents of physical violence and moral cruelty are very numerous. Combined, they convey a sense of despair which turns into a kind of metaphysical experience for the viewer.

Tamara Holzapfel. *LATR*. 4, 1, Fall, 1970, p. 7

Miss Gámbaro is without doubt one of the most exciting surprises that I encountered in my search for viable Latin American plays and playwrights. When I met her the first time I was impressed by her gentleness and intelligence. Her gentle disposition in no way prepared me for the quality of her plays. Upon reading them for the first time I was stunned by their brutality and vigor, their economy of means, and their cruel, almost Strindbergian assessment of life. Miss Gámbaro shows promise of becoming one of the most powerful playwrights in Latin America.

Her plays tend to be free of folkloric limitations. She is certainly as strong a writer as many of the best young playwrights in current European theater. . . . *The Siamese Twins* is, like *The Camp*, a relentless investigation of aggression and submission, of love and hatred, of dependence and independence. Some indication of the international focus that Miss Gámbaro gives to her plays is to be discerned in her amusing suggestions that the song heard in *The Camp* be altered to suit the audience for which it is translated. "What is needed is something utterly corny. I recommend that you use 'Oh Susanna.' "

William I. Oliver. *Voices of Change in the Spanish American Theater* (Austin, University of Texas Press, 1971), p. 49

GARCÍA MÁRQUEZ, GABRIEL (1928–   )

COLOMBIA

It has been said that Gabriel García Márquez's literary models are James Joyce, Virginia Woolf, and William Faulkner. But perhaps such attributions are the result more of the desire to invent for him a venerable genealogical tree than of an exact assessment of his merits as a storyteller.

If one reads the stories of García Márquez without preconceived attitudes, that is, with attention to the text instead of to categories that might, for better or worse, apply to him, it is hard to see anywhere the supposed influence of Joyce or of Woolf. And any analogies that there may be between the work of the Colombian writer and the work of Faulkner are to be found not so much in idiosyncrasies of temperament or form—things that would really justify such a comparison—as in theme. Macondo, or whatever that town is to be called on the banks of the lower Cauca, in which the majority of the events related by García Márquez take place, certainly reminds us in its sadness, its abandonment, and in the metaphysical dimensions of its tedium of the celebrated town of Yoknapatawpha [actually a county] in some backwater of the Deep South. Both towns are, so to speak, condensations of superimposed images of an infinity of similar places, the ideal-typical reconstructions of a complex reality: if the paradox can be admitted, they are concrete abstractions. . . .

As with Yoknapatawpha for Faulkner, Macondo represents for García Márquez something like the focal point of the world, but not because he is inclined to idealize sentimentally regional customs and curiosities. . . . Rather it is simply that, heeding the advice of a storyteller's healthy instinct, he is oriented toward "that point of rest amidst the perennial flight of phenomena," the axis upon which the planetary constellations of his narrative universe turn. . . . [1963]

Ernesto Volkening. In Gabriel García Márquez,
Isabel viendo llover en Macondo, 2nd ed. (Buenos Aires,
Estuario, 1968), pp. 23–25†

Leaf Storm was published the same year as [the Mexican] Juan Rulfo's *Pedro Páramo*, and both works were landmarks in their respective countries by bringing to them the new narrative techniques of Latin America. But the reception of the two works was very different. *Pedro Páramo* brought meteoric fame to its author and immediate attention to the work both in Mexico and abroad. On the other hand, although *Leaf Storm* did attract the attention of a few perspicacious critics and readers in Bogotá, it did not make its author . . . known beyond a rather narrow circle of admirers.

Despite this neglect, *Leaf Storm* did contain a true revelation for Colombian literature, comparable to that offered by Eduardo Caballero Calderón in *Christ with His Back to Us*, but one of much greater boldness in technique. Not many realized that *Leaf Storm* constituted a

small revolution in rising above the old formulas of nativism and portrayal of local customs . . . while still being as "Colombian" as
[Rivera's] *The Vortex*. . . .

Juan Loveluck. *DHR*. 5, Winter, 1966, pp. 136–37†

Leaf Storm is an embryonic book, only a crude promise of what followed, but full of fire and brimstone that provide a colorful historical
backdrop for the rest of his work. In *Leaf Storm* García Márquez was
turning the dead over in their graves. They were at the helm. The
period covered—1903 to 1928—in the history of Macondo antedates the
author. It ends the year he was born. . . . [It] is a somewhat makeshift
book, written in starts and spurts that never quite fuse to become a
single impulse and often fade out before reaching fulfillment. The
author seems to be turning his subject upside down and inside out,
without ever finding its cardinal points.

If *Leaf Storm* is a failure, it is largely because it is written in a
borrowed idiom that never becomes a personal language. Its interwoven
plots and subplots, overlappings and backtrackings, its involuted time
play, are all more or less perfunctory devices that defeat the purpose
they might be expected to serve. The separate monologues of the three
narrators are not complementary because they do not reflect separate
points of view or characterize the viewers. Whoever is speaking, the
voice is always the same. Man, woman, and child, in thought patterns
and vocabulary, are indistinguishable. Each contributes a slab of
straight narrative to a single block of events that need not have been
broken up in the first place. The result is not density but monotony. . . .

[The] doddering old Colonel of *No One Writes to the Colonel*, a
cantankerous, meteorological creature, [is] the best realized of all
García Márquez' characters in what is probably his most finished work.
The distance between *Leaf Storm* and *No One Writes to the Colonel* is
that between profligacy and absolute economy. Midway stands a thorough reading of Hemingway's stories, great favorites of García Márquez. Not that there is any direct influence. The relation to Hemingway
is platonic; a matter of general stylistic tendency. The Faulknerian
glare has been neutralized. It is not replaced by any other. From now
on García Márquez is his own master. He has pared himself down to
the bone. There are no spare parts in *No One Writes to the Colonel*.
Everything is done with "a minimum of words." Clarity, precision,
understatement, a deceptive simplicity, seduce where rhetoric never
could.

Luis Harss and Barbara Dohmann. *Into the Mainstream*
(New York, Harper & Row, 1967), pp. 320, 322–24

This capricious and intermittent contact [of Macondo in *One Hundred Years of Solitude*] with other civilizations is similar to the contact that Colombia and Latin America have had with Europe. Everything that happens in Macondo is a fantasy reflection of what has happened in Latin America. But though made aware of this, the reader never finds that allegory, symbol or analogies nudge him out of a joyful identification with the Buendías.

One Hundred Years of Solitude is primarily about the wonder and strangeness of a continent in which the fantastic is the normative. The odder the event the nearer we feel to the reality of Latin America. . . .

The Buendías bear some resemblance to the Sartoris family and none at all to the Buddenbrooks. But like both Faulkner and Mann, Sr. García Márquez immediately persuades us of the reality of his family and their environment. From the opening lines, he compels us to accept the logic of Macondo in which the violent and the strange are juxtaposed. . . .

The effect of this juxtaposition is often comic. Indeed, comic exaggeration is the keynote of the style but it is an exaggeration that underlines rather than destroys the basic verisimilitude of the story.

TLS. Nov. 9, 1967, p. 1054

While Gabriel García Márquez narrates the life of all of the Buendías [in *One Hundred Years of Solitude*], he also gives us the whole expanse of a fascinating universe, and so we gradually remove ourselves from this beautiful and simple vision of the world, entering one another, an hallucinatory reality; that of the true life of man with all his obsessions, his real and imaginary torments, his social, sexual and spiritual struggles. The novel starts with such an impulse, and so many things are said at once—linking one character with another, an anecdote to a legend, a calamity with other happenings—that when we finish reading the first chapter, we doubt the author's capability of sustaining our interest throughout the book. Nevertheless, the novel involves us more each time in an ascending rhythm, which reaches its highest point in the final chapter and resounds in our memory as an orchestral crescendo, even though the work does not have precisely that symphonic structure, because so many characters appear in it that the author almost feels forced to suddenly cut a story short in order to introduce an anecdote or to tell us the adventures of a new member of the Buendía family. Perhaps the key to the novel's structure is found in the book itself when we read that "the history of the family was a machine with unavoidable repetitions, a turning wheel that would have gone on spinning into eternity were it not for the progressive and irremediable wearing of the axle." . . .

Myth and imagination are so well handled [in the novel] that we find it totally probable and more justifiable that a character should fly, creating an unforgettable poetical vision, than that another should consume at one gulp a calf, the juice of fifty oranges and eight liters of coffee; for while the first vision is fitted into a mythical and poetical context, the second has no more than a superficial consequence which does not extend beyond its own amusement. Perhaps it is because of García Márquez's marked preoccupation with constant entertainment that his work is always dazzling, but rarely *settled down*—a lamentable fact in a novel of such dimension, for it sometimes converts the book into a magnificent *divertimento*, a tale from the *Thousand and One Nights*, but also makes it lose the transcendental, dark and moving tones, which are peculiar to tragedy. At those moments the narration becomes the astute work of a pyrotechnician, but loses the *mystery*, an exclusive gift of the poet. . . . [1968]

Reinaldo Arenas. *Review 70*. No. 3, 1970, pp. 102–4

Gabriel García Márquez was wise not to make what James called "the anecdotic concession" to his subject in *No One Writes to the Colonel*. Surely tempted by the character of his seventy-five-year-old ex-revolutionary hero to sentimentality, and by the imitative fallacy to tedium of style, this Colombian virtuoso avoids both traps by a rare combination of grace and vibrancy. Every scene, every gesture, sings life and denies death. ("Life is the best thing that's ever been invented." "You can't eat [hope], but it sustains you.")

The other eight stories [in the English collection *No One Writes to the Colonel, and Other Stories*] are gems of obliquity ("Tuesday Siesta," "Artificial Roses"); surreal, suffocating dreams ("One Day after Saturday"); or hilarious social farces ("Big Mama's Funeral"), whose inflated and mocking style and tone fit the content like young skin. Our parochialism has been compounded by the long delay in translating García Márquez into English. He is an absolute master.

James R. Frakes. *NYT*. Sept. 29, 1968, p. 56

García Márquez is a political novelist in the sense that his characters must be seen against a particular political background and we are made aware, most subtly, of the author's political orientation. But this does not imply that he is putting together a series of thesis novels in the style of the 1930s, with black and white cardboard figures and heavy-handed propaganda. He's political because his people, who for the most part are more real than is fashionable today, are operating in a context that could be found only in a place like Colombia, where a type of stability had been achieved through the machinery of a repressive dictatorship.

The character of the Colonel in [*No One Writes to the Colonel*] . . . is the most fully realized in the collection, and one of the most memorable in Spanish-American fiction. But to have become the person he is, it was necessary for him to live in a country where a talented 20-year-old could rise to colonel in a revolution overnight, and then wait around half a century for his reward; where his son could be shot down for handing out subversive pamphlets at a cockfight, and where anyone at any time could be stopped and searched at gun point by government thugs.

When the stories [in the English collection *No One Writes to the Colonel, and Other Stories*] are read as a whole, as much as they differ from one another, the central figure that emerges is not the Colonel, not Big Mama, not the hovering Buendía clan but Macondo itself. Anticipating *One Hundred Years of Solitude*, the official history of Macondo, *No One Writes to the Colonel, and Other Stories* ranges from detailed realism, through dreamy fragments and images, to political allegory. One story is linked to another by an event, or a person or merely a mood, and no one story can be fully understood without reading them all; it will take *One Hundred Years of Solitude* to understand why Macondo is what it is.

Oliver T. Myers. Nation. Dec. 2, 1968, p. 600

[The English collection *No One Writes to the Colonel, and Other Stories*] introduces the reader to the microcosmic world of Macondo, ostensibly a sleepy, hot, coastal town in which nothing ever happens, a perfect habitat for what one of the minor characters describes as the European stereotype of the South American: "a man with a moustache, a guitar, and a gun." But in truth Macondo exists only in the fantasy of the author, a town which he himself admits is born of his nostalgia for the life he lived as a young boy more than thirty years ago in a vanished Colombia, under the tutelage of his grandfather, clearly the prototype of the Colonel in the title story.

No One Writes to the Colonel is a tale of dignity in old age. The Colonel, slowly starving to death at seventy-five, is borne up through every adversity by his innate belief in human worth, by his hope of receiving a long-overdue military pension, and by his dream of an imminent victory to be won by the fighting cock he owns. . . .

The key to the meaning of the book, which is to say García Márquez's image of Colombian life as viewed from Macondo, is found in "Big Mama's Funeral," the last piece in the collection. Big Mama, whose family has dominated the region for two centuries, dies a virgin at ninety-two, and the whole town, the President of Colombia, and even the Pope attend her funeral. An era has closed. The event entails more pomp than any other happening in Macondo's history except for the traditional celebration of Big Mama's birthday during her seven decades of supremacy. . . .

All the stories communicate incidents in the lives of humble (and a few rich) townspeople, all of whom have been deeply affected by the long and bloody political strife between the liberals and the conservatives in Colombia. But politics are merely a background for García Márquez, who is concerned mainly with the mysterious inner lives of his characters, lives we intuit briefly through their laconic utterances, their actions, and their emotions.

The author's style, unusual for a contemporary Latin American writer, is well suited to his purpose. It has serenity, understatement, and compassion, and is flecked with wry humor. García Márquez possesses a special felicity for deft, succinct characterization and evocative description. His short book will have a more lasting effect on many readers than numerous longer ones.

Robert G. Mead, Jr. *SR*. Dec. 21, 1968, p. 26

One Hundred Years of Solitude, on a mythic level, is first and foremost a constant questioning: What does Macondo know about its creation? The novel constitutes a compound, comprehensive answer: to know the answer, Macondo must tell itself the whole "real" story and the whole "fictional" story, all of the proofs of a notary, and all the rumors, legends, curses, pious lies, exaggerations, and tales that no one has written down, which the old folks have told the children, which the old ladies have whispered to the priest, which the witches have invoked in the middle of the night, and which the clowns have portrayed in the center of the plaza. The saga of Macondo and of the Buendías includes the totality of the oral, legendary past; it tells us that we cannot content ourselves with official, documentary history, that history is also all the good and all the evil that men have dreamed, imagined, and desired, either to preserve themselves or to destroy themselves.

As in all mythic, aboriginal memory, that of Macondo is creation and re-creation in a single instant. The time of this novel is simultaneity. We only know this in the second reading; only then can we understand the full meaning of José Arcadio Buendía's original decision that henceforth it would always be Monday and of Úrsula's final statement that "It is as if time were going around in circles and we had returned to the beginning." Remembrance repeats the models, the matrixes of the origin, in the same way that, time and again, Colonel Buendía makes little gold fishes that he then melts down to make them again . . . to be continually reborn, to make sure that through ritual acts, harsh and deep-felt ones, there will be a permanence of the cosmos.

Carlos Fuentes. *La nueva novela hispanoamericana*
(Mexico City, Joaquín Mortiz, 1969), pp. 62–63†

José Arcadio Buendía [in *One Hundred Years of Solitude*], patriarch and founder, has undertaken, together with various other families, an exodus through the jungle in search of the sea. . . . This search, which can be seen as a search for a paradise, is not necessarily equivalent to a religious undertaking. It suggests above all the drive toward the redis-covery of the world, the need to conquer that world through a primor-dial identity, the dream of reestablishing an original reality. Thus, the journey and the founding are placed in the context of ritual. José Arcadio Buendía has expelled himself from the town in which he was living after killing Prudencio Aguilar to destroy the rumors of Buendía's unconsummated marriage. And as early as this journey, in this expul-sion, ritual begins to take form. We should not forget the implication of the fact that Úrsula, his wife, is his cousin: they are equivalent to the primordial couple. For this reason of kinship she tries to insist on not consummating the marriage, horrified by the curse of giving birth to a child with a pig's tail. The sin and punishment of an amorous relation-ship that is also a blood relationship thus appears at the beginning of this journey. The son is born without the feared pig's tail, but José Arcadio Buendía has killed a man in order to kill a rumor, and his guilty conscience drives him to undertake the journey, to banish him-self from the town.

The sense of humor with which Gabriel García Márquez relates these episodes and the way he expands them through hyperbole should not prevent our recognizing in these incidents the roots and rituals of an archetypal fantasy: the guilt of love, the expulsion, the search for another world, the pursuit of another innocence. . . .

Julio Ortega. *La contemplación y la fiesta* (Caracas,
Monte Ávila Editores, 1969), pp. 118–19†

The founding family of Macondo [in *One Hundred Years of Solitude*] carries within itself the seeds of its destruction without knowing it, and the chronicle of the lives of all of its members is an extraordinary crisscrossing without any possible exterior communication. Solitude, dis-consolateness, or disenchantment is the essence of each one of the Buendías, who are unable to live apart because all equally share the destiny of solitude that identifies and unites them. The story thus can be seen as a chronicle of the repeated failure to relieve the weight of solitude, and García Márquez has multiplied that weight in the members of a fantastic family so as to remove any notion of documentary or mere history. The Buendía family devours itself after having uselessly exhausted the possibilities of every experience. The book, then, is built around variations on a single theme, with full awareness that beneath diversity is to be found the unchanging basic unity of a common destiny.

For these reasons, García Márquez begins by destroying fleeting time as a flowing time, so that everything must be seen only as just another form of the [eternal] return or, perhaps, of immutability. He multiplies repetitions, duplications, and pairs of identical elements. Around the unifying theme of solitude, García Márquez repeats, as if he were using mirrors, similar acts in a circular time. In this way the novel rejects the linear form of development and seems to expand from within.

Isaías Lerner. CA. No. 162, Jan.–Feb., 1969, p. 188†

Trapped by a memory that is both part of the human collective subconscious and personal as well, the characters [in One Hundred Years of Solitude] strive vainly to face as best they can a Biblical "life sojourn," whose validity and relevance consistently appear to elude them. As a group, they are tortured in ways that neither they nor we can understand, sensitive always to the catastrophe and apocalypse suggested by each object, each incident of their all-pervasive environment.

The intensity and distinction of García Márquez's story produce a memorable novel in which each detail is chosen and arranged to give the unified effect of a living myth. The author's technique can be described as an exaggeration of the concept of the "novelistic correlative." The particular incidents of the story, though occasionally amusing and fascinating enough in themselves, function as segments of an immense labyrinth of magical realism and mythical vision. While we may tend to take an interest in certain incidents popularized in earlier publications by García Márquez, in the final analysis we must view them with the same objectivity that the ironic voice of the author and the magical unreality have endeavored to impose upon us. In attempting to view the book as a whole in order to appreciate its narrative and structural unity, we are faced by the dilemma of having to evaluate a literary work that requires us to penetrate the veil that conceals it. For, indeed, we are all named Buendía and Macondo is our common Biblical home, and our daily reality, if we examine it carefully, is "normal" only by dint of its monotonous repetition. How can we, as readers, dare to demand revelations—the "truth"—from a story and life that, in the end, may be our own Book of the Apocalypse?

The comprehension achieved by the last of the Buendías, which we are never privileged to share, occurs only when the prophecy has been fulfilled, only when the secret condemnation of man to one hundred years of solitude comes to an end, only when death brings with it a fusion of all reality and all time into a single point of reference. These, it is suggested, are the reasons for the very sharp irony employed by García Márquez toward the reader, an irony that at every turn provokes and betrays our imprudent, and largely impertinent, desire to know why life in Macondo is as it is. The scheme of the Biblical parable, which appears ostensibly to contain a vitally significant message, gives power to the narrative structure of the book. But more importantly, it appears to focus for the perspectives of the vision of man as seen by García Márquez, a vision masterfully realized in *One Hundred Years of Solitude*.

David William Foster. *Américas*. 21, 11–12, Nov.–Dec.,
1969, p. 41

The dominant myth in Latin American literature is that of the jungle. The jungle, whose overflowing denseness keeps one from seeing the trees, symbolizes better than any other image the resistance of nature to the ordering will of man. The jungle is the remnant of pre-creation, of formlessness proliferating in an overwhelming unchecked manner, anterior—and hostile—to the regulating hand of the creator. The jungle is the chaos of dawn, and its labyrinth. Like chaos, it is at the same time motionless and malignant, possessed of a destructive inertia, belligerent. It unceasingly hounds anyone who dares to enter into it, disorienting him and making him get lost, denying him exit and, indifferently, leaving him to perish.

The best-known literary example of jungle-nature destroying man is José Eustacio Rivera's *The Vortex*. It is impossible to overcome the ferocious antagonist without destroying it, without putting something else in its place, like a city for example. A parallel reading of *The Vortex* and *One Hundred Years of Solitude* confronts us with two imaginary worlds nourished by parallel myths, which are, at least in this sense, treated differently. But in the last analysis perhaps the novels are not as different as they might seem to be.

The most striking difference is that García Márquez transcends the American myth by incorporating it into a mythic symbolism that is even vaster: his readers, educated in the Judeo-Christian tradition, can recognize the sacred stories of their childhood and can thus feel comfortable in a novel filled with familiar references. The mythology of the Old Testament provides a suggestive framework and an underlying inspiration for the fable. Renouncing modernity (insofar as modernity demands that the writer use private symbols), García Márquez reaps the benefits of an immediate communication between himself and the reader.

Ricardo Gullón. *García Márquez o el arte de contar*
(Madrid, Taurus Ediciones, 1970), pp. 45–47†

[*One Hundred Years of Solitude*], although it reverts to an hispanic tradition (that of presenting itself as the deciphering of another work: *Don Quixote* itself professes to be a book translated from Arabic of which the author is Cid Hamed Ben-Engeli), does lay claim to its own independence: it bars and abolishes the outside world—the notion of any possible exteriorness. It does so by (a) a continuous wiping out of the spacial landmarks: within the limits of Macondo, all of the diverse geographical possibilities are synthesized; (b) a systematic telescoping of chronology: there are characters who, in order to be present where the story requires, must attain a superhuman age; and, above all, (c) the coexistence within the same instant of an entire century of daily occurrences. It is this synchronization of the action used by Melquíades in his account, which better than anything gives the only dimensions of the work. . . .

Thus, *One Hundred Years of Solitude* excludes any exterior reality from the writing, avoids any painting. But inner reality also is cast into question. The book avoids all *expression* because, whereas it sets up an interplay of passions, it remains indifferent to their code—to the psychology of inner being as well as to that of behavior; it recognizes only what Roland Barthes could call "the paper code." Here, literature is practiced as an inter-textuality; *One Hundred Years of Solitude*, according to García Márquez, "is like the secret of the puzzle to which I gave the pieces in my preceding books. Here are to be found all of the keys. One can see the origin and the end of the characters and the complete history, without gaps, of Macondo." The book, consequently, is a constant reference to all of the author's other books, books which trace and interchange the fragments, making up the history of Macondo, and the totality of which left open spaces, voids.

But the inter-texuality is more generalized. García Márquez brings in, through the subsidiary narratives attributed to his characters, the characters of other contemporary authors—the Artemio Cruz of Carlos Fuentes, the Rocamadour from *Hopscotch* by Julio Cortázar —and above all, the history of literature and its tradition emerge on each page without being expressly used, like outcroppings of an underground network of texts; Melquíades is simultaneously the "bearer" of biblical texts, books of alchemy, Nostradamus, the Cabbala, etc. The Buendía family puts back into circulation the novels of chivalry.

Severo Sarduy. *Review 70.* No. 3, 1970, pp. 173–74

"In mid-1967, a novel was published in Buenos Aires, *One Hundred Years of Solitude*, which constituted a literary earthquake in Latin America. The critics hailed it as a masterwork and the public confirmed this opinion by buying up, since then, all subsequent editions, which for a while reached the astounding rhythm of one a week. Overnight, the novel's author became almost as famous as a great soccer-player or a celebrated bolero-singer." Thus spoke Mario Vargas Llosa, a writer no less famous than Gabriel García Márquez, in a talk entitled "The Magic World of Gabriel García Márquez" at Washington State University in winter 1968. . . .

"The literary genius of our time," said Vargas Llosa in his talk, "usually is hermetic, exhausting, and elitist. *One Hundred Years of Solitude* represents one of the rare cases of a major work that *all* can read, understand, and enjoy." It is a book which most people wish would not end for at least three more times its volume. Most, but by no means all: there have been rather violent reactions against its magic (above all in Argentina, a country literally soi-disant "sophisticated"). . . .

As for the elements that make his fiction so attractive, it is difficult to single them out analytically. There is, for one thing, his style: torrid, prolific, humorous, and yet of utter precision, in *Leaf Storm* and *One Hundred Years of Solitude*; but almost obsessively pared, objective, maniacally unemotional, and nearly mathematical in the other books. Then there is the eccentricity of his characters, an eccentricity which, from book to book, progresses steadily and more deeply into the realms of what Alejo Carpentier has called the *real maravilloso*, i.e., something like marvels wedded to reality. . . .

Ultimately, his mixture of the naturalistic and the supernatural corresponds to concepts of life and history, of time and existence, of politics and violence, which are very powerful in Latin America. It is a fabulous continent on which virtually all the ages of mankind coexist. . . . It must not surprise us, then, that the inevitable friction between such extremes, the shock caused by the metaphorical jump from the gaucho saddle, say, into the seat of the transcontinental jet, should cause an ever richer and more complex sense of awe, of wonder, of "marveling," and that this in turn should give rise to the most abstruse, incredible, fascinating, and fantastic myths, legends, sagas, tall tales, beautiful lies, as well as stories of supernatural events which, as is known, are nothing but attempts by naïve—and also by educated—minds to comprehend what might be called "cultural and civilizational mysteries."

"The irreality of Latin America is something so real and so commonplace," García Márquez has stated . . . "that it is totally fused with what is meant by reality." García Márquez himself has caught this fusion by expressing his childhood experiences in the terms of his adult forms of literary expression—synchronically. His earlier books are exercises that aim at achieving the literary "marvel" that *One Hundred Years of Solitude* constitutes in Latin America and in world literature.

Wolfgang A. Luchting. *BA*. 44, Winter, 1970, 26, 28, 30

Gabriel García Márquez . . . has created in *One Hundred Years of Solitude* an enchanted place that does everything but cloy. Macondo oozes, reeks and burns even when it is most tantalizing and entertaining. It is a place flooded with lies and liars and yet it spills over with reality. Lovers in this novel can idealize each other into bodiless spirits, howl with pleasure in their hammocks or, as in one case, smear themselves with peach jam and roll naked on the front porch. The hero can lead a Quixotic expedition across the jungle, but although his goal is never reached, the language describing his quest is pungent with life. . . .

Near the end of *One Hundred Years of Solitude* a character finds a parchment manuscript in which the history of his family had been recorded "one hundred years ahead of time" by an old gypsy. The writer "had not put events in the order of man's conventional time, but had concentrated a century of daily episodes in such a way that they coexisted in one instant." The narrative is a magician's trick in which memory and prophecy, illusion and reality are mixed and often made to look the same. It is, in short, very much like García Márquez's astonishing novel.

It is not easy to describe the techniques and themes of the book without making it sound absurdly complicated, labored and almost impossible to read. In fact, it is none of these things. Though concocted of quirks, ancient mysteries, family secrets and peculiar contradictions, it makes sense and gives pleasure in dozens of immediate ways. . . .

The book is a history, not of governments or of formal institutions of the sort which keeps public records, but of a people who, like the earliest descendants of Abraham, are best understood in terms of their relationship to a single family. In a sense, José and Úrsula are the only two characters in the story, and all their children, grandchildren and great-grandchildren are variations on their strengths and weaknesses. . . .

To isolate details, even good ones, from this novel is to do it peculiar injustice. García Márquez creates a continuum, a web of connections and relationships. However bizarre or grotesque some particulars may be, the larger effect is one of great gusto and good humor and, even more, of sanity and compassion. The author seems to be letting his people half-dream and half-remember their own story and, what is best, he is wise enough not to offer excuses for the way they do it. No excuse is really necessary. For Macondo is no never-never land. Its inhabitants do suffer, grow old and die, but in their own way.

Robert Kiely. *NYT*. March 8, 1970, p. 5

The novel, as the politicians like to say, has polarized. At one extreme, super-realism, at the other extreme, super-fantasy—and not very much in between. . . . Rare is the novelist who can satisfy the novel reader's hereditary demands for a Good Story while, at the same time, coping with today's special little difficulty; that truth seems more surrealistic than fiction. What is the solution? Neat plot, three-dimensional character, palpable setting—all seen under psychedelic lighting? Nothing less would seem to do.

Gabriel García Márquez, a Colombian, deserves to join his fellow Latin-American Jorge Luis Borges among the select survivors who retain the old-fashioned charm of story-telling even as they assume the modern novelist's multiple roles; philosopher, aesthete, and general cultural problem-solver.

One Hundred Years of Solitude . . . wears the traditional look of fiction, complete to a Tolstoyan genealogical chart in the front. But in addition to being a real, honest-to-goodness, follow-the-bouncing-plot novel, it also doubles as commentary, allegory, myth—what you will—for modern history. García Márquez has devised as microcosm a remote Latin American village, and within that village, one particular family. Like a good Hispanic Galsworthy, he has followed the Buendía saga through six generations. There is domestic stuff: good marriages, bad marriages, thwarted marriages. There is public drama: civil war, the invasion of Yankee banana growers, and so on.

But this realism is sun-struck, as it were, by hot attacks of fantasy. Characters, especially the ladies, live to be 150 and are given to extraordinary feats, like levitation. A rain storm lasts four years, eleven months, and two days—to be followed by ten years of drought.

The pages crawl with spiders, lizards, and general damp rot. Omens and ancient curses coexist with "progress"—e.g., the railroad. Even prosperity descends like a sort of plague. And it does not last. García Márquez is a writer of considerable comic inventiveness, but the main theme is self-destruction.

The village of Macondo ("city of mirrors") is finally a Dantean inferno, whose inhabitants, for all their variety, have lived under a common doom. Like their town, they have, in some final sense, been cut off. García Márquez does not say what salvation is, but he makes clear what damnation means today: being severed from what Hawthorne, another dark allegorist, called the magnetic chain of humanity.

To live alone, to be self-absorbed—this, García Márquez suggests, is to exist only as a "mirage in a mirror."

He makes the point. And, as an artist, he scores another point by making it in a novel which is emphatically not a mirage in a mirror itself.

Melvin Maddocks. CSM. April 16, 1970, p. 11

García Márquez' short stories offer an immediate introduction to his work. . . . In the manner of Faulkner, many of the same characters appear in the different works, creating a kind of fictional world or family whose members come and go as they pursue their daily life in Macondo, the mythical town whose founding, completion, and eventual demise remain so vivid in the minds of all who have read *One Hundred Years of Solitude*. In much the same way that the *Exemplary Novels* reveal the gradual evolution of Cervantes' narrative technique, so *Big Mama's Funeral* bridges the gap between the interior monologues of *Leaf Storm* and the exuberant prose of García Márquez' last novel. . . .

As independent works of literature these stories continue a heritage of short fiction that is traditionally strong in Latin America, especially in this century when writers of the stature of Horacio Quiroga have modelled their work on such masters as Chekhov, Maupassant, Kipling, and Poe. But also, in the instance of García Márquez, the stories are at the same time an integral part of a much larger production, which includes newspaper articles, filmscripts, as well as novels. He himself has said that three of his works (*No One Writes to the Colonel, The Bad Hour*, and *Big Mama's Funeral*) evolved from what was conceived as one long novel, sharing the same general theme, the same characters, the same background, and written at a time when he was trying to escape from what he calls the Latin American rhetoric. In the manner of an artist's sketches, the short stories allow García Márquez to experiment with the details of his own technique. . . . Throughout his writing, there is constant evidence of these changing literary theories, and with each variation the reader is challenged to relate what is new to what has gone before, be it a second account of an already familiar scene or an additional glimpse into a character's past. Often these changes embody substantial alterations in narrative technique, thus giving an intriguing vitality to García Márquez' entire composition, and stimulating in the reader a desire to keep pace with this continuous evolution of the author's genius as a writer. . . .

Roger M. Peel. SSF. 8, 1, Winter, 1971, pp. 160–61

The beginnings and the heights of García Márquez are available to us now in [the English collection] *Leaf Storm, and Other Stories*. . . .

The novella, *Leaf Storm*, is an early work, written when García Márquez was perhaps twenty-five years old, found in a drawer by his friends
at El Espectador after the author had left Colombia for Europe, and
published to some acclaim, even though García Márquez himself had
not thought the work worthy of publication. It is certainly not the equal
in style or vision of the later work. The colonel is introduced in *Leaf
Storm*, the first intimations of the fabulist occur there, and the leftover
town is described. But *Leaf Storm* is made as much of devices as of art.
The story is told in flashbacks from several points of view, the suspense
is mere artifice, for the narrative power of a man who can tell us the
outcome of a story and leave us fascinated to know the course of it has
not yet developed. Nor is the epiphanous humor of the later work
apparent in *Leaf Storm*. . . . The story is more interesting for what it
tells us of the development of García Márquez as a writer than for
itself.

The book, however, is graced by "Blacamán the Good, Vendor
of Miracles" and two tales for children that are nothing short of brilliant. "The Handsomest Drowned Man in the World" is a Prometheus
myth for Latin America, except that this Prometheus is a gigantic, shy,
and beautiful dead body, floating from place to place, bringing not fire
or knowledge but self-consciousness. "Dear Children," García Márquez seems to be saying, "this dead culture came to our primitive village
and there was an end to innocence." The drowned body is found,
polished (like a mirror?), and given a name. Will it be Lautaro, the
name of the Chilean national hero, an Indian who fought the Spanish
colonizers? Or will it be Estéban? And by Estéban does he mean to make
us think of the first Christian martyr, stoned to death for predicting
earthly destruction and salvation through the Second Coming? Or are
we to think of the black slave who came to the Americas with Cabeza
de Vaca. . . . Estéban the slave, the perfect representative of the
exploitive nature of Western civilization, defeated once by the primi-
tives, absorbed by them, then killed by the Zunis when he led the
expedition that brought the first victorious conquerors across the Rio
Grande? The villagers decide to call him Estéban. They give him a
great funeral, they weep over him, and then they cast him back into the
sea; but when he is gone, a part of them, they feel, is gone, and they
are changed, ready to enlarge and beautify their houses, united in self-
consciousness. It is a children's tale that could have been told by Claude
Lévi-Strauss, brilliant and affecting, bearing in its simple beauty the sadness of entropy, mourning for the end of that near perfection Rousseau
called "the youth of the world."

Earl Shorris. *Harper's*. Feb., 1972, p. 102

When Gabriel García Márquez's utterly original *One Hundred Years of Solitude* came out here in 1970, I read it—I experienced it—with the same recognition of a New World epic that one feels about *Moby Dick*. Whatever else you can say about contemporary American novels, they are generally overpopulated and personally too scornful to remind the reader that ours was, until very recently, a New World. . . . Above all, the "New World" as a subject requires an indifference to the ordinary laws of space, time and psychology that enforce realism. No one who has read *One Hundred Years of Solitude* will ever forget the sensation of tripping on sentences that in the most matter-of-fact way described what happens under the pressure cooker of total "newness." . . .

However, García Márquez is not a Protestant romantic of the time when it seemed that all the world would soon be new. He is a dazzlingly accomplished but morally burdened end-product of centuries of colonialism, civil war and political chaos; a prime theme in all his work is the inevitability of incest and the damage to the germ plasm that at the end of his great novel produces a baby with a pig's tail. He always writes backwards, from the end of the historical cycle, and all his prophecies are acerb without being gloomy. The farcically tragic instability and inhumanity of the continent, where Nature is still too much for man and where the Spanish conquest is still unresolved, dominate his work. What makes his subject "New World" is the hallucinatory chaos and stoniness of the Colombian village, Macondo, through which all history will pass. What makes García Márquez's art "New World" is the totally untraditionalist, unhindered technique behind this vision of the whole—from the white man's first scratches in the jungle to the white man's inability to stave off the sight of his own end. . . .

In some of [the stories in the English collection *Leaf Storm, and Other Stories*]—"The Handsomest Drowned Man in the World," "A Very Old Man with Enormous Wings," "The Last Voyage of the Ghost Ship"—García Márquez's typical double vision of the natural world as inherently a fable, a story to be told and retold rather than something "real," expresses itself with perfect charm. . . .

In each of these stories García Márquez takes a theme that in a lesser writer would seem "poetic," a handsome conceit lifted out of a poem by Wallace Stevens but then stopped dead in its narrative tracks. García Márquez manages to make a story out of each of these—not too ambitious, but just graceful enough to be itself. He succeeds because these are stories about wonders, and the wonders become actions. García Márquez as a very young man was already committed to the subject of creatures working out all their destinies. In every García Márquez work a whole historical cycle is lived through, by character after character. And each cycle is like a miniature history of the world from the creation to the final holocaust.

Alfred Kazin. NYT. Feb. 20, 1972, pp. 1, 14

García Márquez marries realism and objectivity with a most singular sense of the fantastic and delicious fabulating gifts, often employing surrealistic clairvoyance to paint frescoes full of moral indignation and anger protesting against oppression and violence, degradation and deceit. Extolling pride, he clearly depicts certain ludicrous, even grotesque aspects, such as quixotic bravery and intransigent single-mindedness of purpose. It is a joy to encounter a poet who revels in his seductive powers as García Márquez does. And yet he is so exact in his formulation and precise in his composition. In juxtaposing the twin elements of humor and tragedy García Márquez often achieves contrapuntal heights where language and image are thoroughly fused.

Thor Vilhjálmsson. BA. 47, Winter, 1973, p. 11

GIRRI, ALBERTO (1919–   )

ARGENTINA

"Sperlonga" introduces us to [Girri's] symbolic, occasionally allegorical, world—a world at times suggestive, at times direct and explicit. . . . We are told that neither antiquity nor our age has understood the message of Christ. This may be equivalent to affirming that time does not exist. But it is also a way of noting that the eternal and the everyday have not come together, despite the intervention of Jesus. And does not all this lead us to think that such a mis-encounter has perhaps never been felt and expressed with such intensity as now? Elsewhere ("Venetian Elegy") there is an allusion to inhuman forces "that are again knocking on all the doors," and we read immediately after this that "Attila is returning. / Is the genius of the Roman enough today / to build us a refuge?"

From the first page of *Italian Elegies* [Girri] throws us into the most dramatic and tempestuous currents of our time.

Jorge A. Paita. Sur. No. 285, Nov.–Dec., 1963, p. 94†

Girri . . . belongs to a generation concerned both with poetic form and with philosophic content. His previous verse has been centered on various outlooks of human existence, against the limitations of time and death. Poems of anguished horror in the face of death were balanced by those seeking value in love or in a mystical abandonment of self-interest. In *The Eye*, Girri deepens this exploration of existence; dwelling little on the simple horrors of death, he offers more penetrating perspectives on Man's role and position. The key image of the book is the human eye; unlike the omnipotent eye of God, neatly circumscribed in a triangle, man's vehicle for insight is torn between various views which emerge from the different poems of the books. . . .

Girri's verse has been called obscure and hermetic. Some of his poems, true enough, do not offer a logically clear position; but they inevitably embody different visions in metaphors which give them coherence and turn them into concrete human experiences. Neither does Girri's work succumb to pointless literary virtuosity; although allusions abound, they become key images or devices for seizing the meanings of the text.

Andrew P. Debicki. BA. 39, Summer, 1965, pp. 330–31

The only poetic mission Girri believes in is that of expressing the painful open wound between nature and consciousness, between the spirit and matter. . . . In *The Necessary Condition* Girri comes to hate completely all art accumulated by humanity, seeing in the beauty to which it aspires a vain attempt to transcend the individual limitations and to obtain through language a permanence that cannot make us forget the "supreme evil of having been born." . . . The poetry of Alberto Girri proposes neither the rapture of ecstatic contemplation nor, as has been claimed, a thought-deciphering attempt composed out of too much premeditation. His offer is more subtle, and perhaps too difficult: Girri invites us to enter into a labyrinth of fears and hatreds, which, through its contradictions, creates a strategy, a frightful balance between two vacuums. Let us distrust poetry; reality is always beyond the word. Let us distrust reality; the chaos of appearances assaulting us during the trip in the "phantom train" that is life has sense only when organized in a reading, in a verbal construction. . . . This is the labyrinth out of which *House of the Mind* is composed. . . . In it, the only possibility is to accept our ambivalence, the ambivalence of reality. We are readers of a book that only exists because we decode it. We are readers because that book allows us to decode it.

Enrique Pezzoni. Prologue to Alberto Girri,
Antología temática (Buenos Aires, Editorial
Sudamericana, 1969), pp. 10–13†

Girri's work is a most singular testimony to the discord that gave rise to an entirely new direction in contemporary poetry. . . . With the traditional bridges destroyed between words and things . . . the poet claimed for himself absolute liberty. Reality for him no longer lay outside language; rather, it became language itself. And against the laborious undertaking of describing the world, he set up the mission of revealing the new worlds that arise, like electrical discharges, from the contact of one word with another. "Words make love," proclaimed surrealism, along with other similar, although supposedly rival, movements. The new program was to create realities through the word and to transform the poem into a conduit: the poem became an imperative to tear off the masks with which current logic and conventionalism hid the mystery of the world.

Alberto Girri began to write when this kind of poetic subversion had already permeated Buenos Aires. So-called vanguard reviews issued manifestoes condemning the soft nostalgia that had become institutionalized during its vogue of the 1940s and proclaiming a faith in the autonomy of the aesthetic act and, at the same time, a commitment to the vital reality of mankind. . . . In this context Girri's poetry seemed an isolated phenomenon, somewhat disdainful of those programs announcing the renovation of the world through art and the future brotherhood of the poet and the man in the street.

In his first book, *Lonely Beach*, we can find features that would continue throughout his work. Equally detached from those devices that had been given comfortable prestige by traditional poetry (the complacency of evoking feelings through languidly sensual melodies) and from new trends that were making their way into our midst, Girri did not set out to replace everyday reality with another one created out of unheard-of associations and new relations. . . . From the first he accepted as his mission the exposing of a world made of tenaciously irreconcilable opposites and of a language he felt had become sullied by the residues of so many attempts at futile reconciliations. . . .

> Pedro Orgambide and Roberto Yahni. *Enciclopedia de la literatura argentina* (Buenos Aires, Editorial Sudamericana, 1970), pp. 276–77†

Girri continues to exercise his subtle rhythms, muted resonances and judicious diction in these pieces of modest and nearly uniform length [in *Daily Values*]. The often considerable energy of individual poems tends to build up through angular concatenations of clauses and carefully reiterated words and syntactic elements. Reasoned statements, they nevertheless depend on metaphoric virtuosity as well as intellect. In the best instances, the reader may be convinced that the perceptions arrived at find their necessary expression in such spare but tortuous form.

"Realists are realistic," we learn; "they perform, they are there / they assign little value to the principles / that inspire their action." Not so Girri. His artistic credo makes itself felt throughout. "Mere recitative, declamation," he ventures, "would sound false, hysterical; deep emotions / have need of song." Tension and control, we conclude, underlie true poetry. Thereby the poet, a prisoner, is assured the deliverance of an "attainable garden / while he sings / that exceeds the limits of music." No easy melodies decorate Girri's vocal line, but passion as well as irony has its place in his art.

Generally melancholy, the meditations of *Daily Values* have as their ambitious subjects not only the poetic act but the nature and destiny of the self and, in the latter half of the book, themes of permanence and change. Taking nostalgic note of the passing of the age of Pisces—the Christian era—Girri views uneasily the advent of Aquarius with its "intellective and practical commotion." He is condemned to a stance on the cusp of these signs (closer, certainly, to skepticism than belief), and this is one of his affinities with the Anglo-American poets of Eliot's generation usually mentioned in connection with his work. The strengths and limitations of their idiom and their outlook remain his.

John F. Deredita. *BA*. 46, Winter, 1972, pp. 86–87

GOMES, ALFREDO DIAS (1914–   )

BRAZIL

Gomes is an author in search of a style, as is true of the majority of the dramatists who have contributed to the emergence of the Brazilian theater in a period that has succeeded worthless works and Luso-tropicalism in the drama. Gomes's problem is that of going beyond modern realism without failing to transmit to his audience a political reality. In *The Invasion* he took a firm step forward—the masses were the protagonists of the action—even though the majority of the critics complained about the lack of "profound psychological characterizations."

Modern realism attempts to merge the psychological richness of characterization with an examination of the forces that control society. . . . [Even Brecht] felt the need to strike a balance between the sociological theater and Aristotelian drama, a balance that can be seen in his most important play, *Leben des Galilei*. . . . In *The Cradle of the Hero* we can sense Gomes's desire to subordinate psychological characterization to the collective presentation of forces in collision. He makes use of . . . caricature, music, and other effects to undermine traditional realistic empathy. But he is not always successful in harmonizing these devices with the whole. . . . Gomes's stylistic contradictions, like those of other serious authors of his generation, can only be resolved through continuous contact with the audience. Only the method of trial and error, in which the audience plays an indispensable role, can produce a complete work. . . .

Paulo Francis. Preface to Alfredo Dias Gomes,
O berço do herói (Rio de Janeiro, Editôra Civilização
Brasileira, 1965), unfolioed†

Gomes, in writing his dramas, reflects and directly involves contemporary Brazil. The ignorance and fanaticism which engulf his characters are not simply stage fictions: on the contrary, they are unfortunate realities which plague the lives of an alarming number in that nation which comprises one-half of the South American continent. . . . Pointedly, Gomes deals with these problems—at the same time calling into question those time-honored traditions and institutions that have fostered their development. The result is strong, frank social drama, a phenomenon new to the stages of Brazil.

However, the playwright's social statements do not stand simply as revolutionary documents. They are basically theatre pieces. Audience involvement is dictated not merely by sensation and topical allusion. Man's dignity is more the essence of Gomes' drama than is social reform. The tragedy of Zé-do-Burro [in *The Redeemer of Pledges*] illustrates this point effectively. Though the victim of ignorance, fanaticism, oppression, and duplicity, Zé's determination to fulfill his vow, his commitment, as it were, to one course alone, attests to the fact that social conditions can debilitate but not destroy. Zé's destruction is, in a certain sense, a matter of choice. His death is tragic, but it is also victorious because he does not compromise his principles.

There is a progression from play to play in [Gomes'] thematic trilogy. *The Redeemer of Pledges* posits in very general terms man's dignity, and capacity, as it were, for victorious defeat. . . . *The Invasion* and *The Revolt of the Holy Men* deal more directly with man's response to a specific evil. For in each of these plays the protagonists realize their potential as individuals capable of asserting their own dignity. Justino and Santa strike against the overwhelming forces of corruption by abandoning the city, that which they once thought was their refuge, the basis of a new life. Although victimized by the graft and the corruption of this more complicated life, the peasants maintain their dignity by rejecting it—whereas some members of their very own family make a compromise. Bastião's reply to Zabelinha, that if it were God who killed the bull, then he was God, perhaps implies a greater victory than any of Gomes' other protagonists have known. Zé has conquered by being defeated by social forces; Justino wins by maintaining a stoical strength in the face of great odds. In Bastião's case Gomes depicts neither acceptance of the ill nor flight but open-handed war.

Bastião's slaughter of the bull, we can be sure, in no way affects the propensity for religious fanaticism that characterizes the inhabitants of Juareiro. However, he has surely struck it a substantial blow. Whether the bull is now to be canonized we cannot say: it does not matter. What is important is that Bastião has destroyed the evil at least to the degree that he was capable of doing it. Among the dramas here discussed, this play, then, is surely the most optimistic statement of social ills. From the indirect response of resignation and fight seen in the first two plays, *The Revolt of the Holy Men* is an obvious departure.

Francis A. Dutra. *Cithara*. 4, 2, May, 1965, pp. 11–12

Brazil is, in literary matters, a country that has fully embraced the experimental. . . . It has taken in, in its enormous capacity for adaptation, all ideological currents in order to submit them to a process of national adaptation. . . . The [vanguard playwright] who has been most successful with audiences has undoubtedly been the author of *The Redeemer of Pledges*. Alfredo Dias Gomes has written a masterpiece. For the theater in Brazil, it is an irreplaceable, classic work. Brazil was lacking in dramatic masterpieces of international stature. In a country that has been fortunate to have produced more and more poets of magnitude, there had been no exemplary work written for the theater. Now Brazil has one in Alfredo Dias Gomes's tragedy.

Carlos de la Rica. *RCB*. 5, 1966, p. 394†

The Redeemer of Pledges transposes the Passion of Christ to modern times. It is, in a veiled form, a dramatization of what would happen to Christ if he lived in Bahia. The external similarities are beyond question: Zé travels the roads weighted down by a cross, and in the apotheosis he is placed with outstretched arms against pieces of wood.

Zé is the only person in the work who is vitally and deeply religious. Although a theological background may be lacking and his notion of Christianity is askew, he maintains his convictions with an impressive honesty. Nevertheless, the official Church, the "scribes" and "Pharisees" of the temple, disqualify him on matters of orthodoxy, cast anathemas at him, and denounce him to the police.

One of the arguments that the Sanhedrin used to the Romans was that Jesus wanted to proclaim himself king and that he riled up the masses. The transposition into modern terms is not badly realized: Zé is accused of being a subversive and of being a sympathizer of agrarian reform. Furthermore, although there was something in Christ of the public man who attacked an unjust situation, his vital and central motivation was religious. Similarly, Zé, who divides the land up among the colonists, is guided by his beliefs in transcendent or supernatural forces.

In the play, the alliance between religious and secular power is perfectly expressed in modern terms in the alliance between the official Church and the police. And, as in the Gospel, the ecclesiastical authority delegates to the secular authority the execution of the sentence. We observe in the priest the same Pharisaic strict compliance with external juridical norms while overlooking completely the spirit of charity and profound understanding.

Fernando Millán Chivite. RCB. 22, 1967, p. 297†

After the fashion of Arthur Miller's *The Crucible,* Gomes, one of Brazil's most promising young dramatists, has written [in *The Holy Inquisition*] a moving parable on the consequences to man's freedom-of-conscience of the attempts by institutions, governments, and men in general to impose their beliefs on others. Based on a popular legend with some basis in fact, this two-act play details the destruction of an ingenuous young woman caught in the web of suspicion, accusation, and uncomprehending and self-righteous justice of the Inquisition in eighteenth-century Paraiba, Brazil. In its totality, the work is a delicate balance between the abstract, institutional fervor of the priest who sets himself the task of "saving" Branca, spontaneous and unrestrained in her simple faith and love of God's creation, and the priest as a man beset by an uncontrollable passion that is only quenched with the flames of Branca's stake.

Superficially, Gomes' play is indebted to the romantic tradition. Our sympathies are aligned securely from the outset, as we see in excruciating detail the entrapment of the "good little man" by forces which he barely comprehends and which he is incapable of checking in their relentless destruction of his being. Branca articulates with fervor the only ideal which can protect and give meaning to her suffering—her refusal to compromise with herself and her faith in the mercy of God. In this sense, *The Holy Inquisition* expresses convincingly, through the rhetoric of its art, a humanism which is one of the few protections man has against political and institutional pressure to conform ideologically.

Beyond this superficial romantic humanism, Gomes shows a technical mastery of the drama. His play takes place in a fluid world of blending scenes and shifting centers of attention. The only fixed boundaries are those of the two acts and the poetic dialogue which is circular, thus joining beginning and end into a timeless chronological time followed only in a general sense. Gomes' play is a kind of dramatic stream of consciousness with emphasis upon language and its role in the breakdown of human understanding.

David William Foster. BA. 42, Winter, 1968, pp. 101–2

The Revolt of the Holy Men is in the tradition of such works as *Path of Salvation* of Jorge Andrade, and indeed its roots can be traced back to Euclides da Cunha's classic prose work, *The Backlands*. The cases of religious fanaticism encountered in Brazilian history are reflected from time to time in its literature. (Not long ago I saw a Brazilian film, *God and the Devil in the Land of the Sun*, which also treated the same theme.) In the preface to the play, the author makes clear his objective: to produce a popular theatre, a theatre of the people. He feels that the theatre "besides being popular, is also political." One cannot be neutral: "If we indicate [to the oppressed public] ways in which it can free itself from oppression, if we arm it against the oppressor, we are on its side; if we merely entertain it—and consequently distract it from the struggle—we are against it." . . .

In [*The Invasion*] the playwright used two planes for the action, as Arthur Miller had done in parts of his *Death of a Salesman*, or even before the latter, as Brazil's own Nelson Rodrigues had done with a three-plane set in his *Wedding Dress.* . . . In a technique also reminiscent of Elmer Rice's *Street Scene* and, more recently, of William Saroyan's *The Cave Dwellers*, we have unfolded before us the conditions of a group of *favelados* [Rio slum-dwellers] who have taken over, much like squatters, an abandoned, uncompleted building (an occurrence witnessed from time to time in parts of Brazil). As in these plays, the Brazilian work leans more heavily on situation and characterization than on plot. Thus we see living in these bare quarters a range of rather colorful characters including a self-proclaimed mulatto prophet; a dashing Negro composer; a former soccer player whose only ambition is to see his son a star (in which hope he is to be disappointed); settlers from the northern part of the country who had left a parched climate only to find the inhospitable city; their daughter who finds a way out temporarily by living with a cheap politician, who, in turn, harangues the settlers and promises them everything but delivers nothing; an "operator" who insists on rent and excessive charges for slight services in a building on which he has no claims; a would-be organizer who proclaims mass action is the only way rights can be won; and again the police in an unsympathetic role. Before us unfold the tribulations, exploitation, rivalry, and comradeship of these beings "caged" in a situation brought about by a society that offers them little opportunity, and by their own inability to cope with it all. . . .

Oscar Fernández. *LATR*. 2, 1, Fall, 1968, pp. 25–26

It seems useful to read [*The Redeemer of Pledges*] as a kind of modern morality. Zé-do-Burro is the figure of the individual conscience assailed by symbolic representatives of selfish and exploiting men and of purblind institutions. The playwright himself saw the play as the conflict between the man of conscience and the men and institutions which abuse him. . . .

Gomes, instead of using Holy Church as the Comforter in his morality, has made it the most prominent of his three oppressors. The others are the State, represented by the police, and the Press, represented by the reporter. As the Church moves to frustrate Zé's single act of individual conscience, it reveals itself to be a fossil, petrified by self-righteousness born of pride and tradition; the State has become a furtive agency of repression and the Press an instrument of distortion and a tool for politicians and promoters. All of these institutions are self-centered. But so are the individuals—such as the tavern owner, the poet, the procurer, and the voodoo priestess—who try to exploit Zé. Their response to his plight is no less self-serving than that of the agents of the Church, State and Press.

In still another way, it seems useful to think of the play as a morality: there is the traditional debate between the Soul and the Body. Zé-do-Burro is the willing Spirit, his wife the weak Flesh. He has pledged himself to fulfill a promise, a promise that has claims upon him which take precedence over and chasten those of the body. As his wife, Rosa must follow him wherever he goes, but she is, up until the closing minutes of his life, conscious only of the physical: of the relentless hours of marching, of the sleepless nights, and especially of the sexual starvation to which his dedication has brought her. She represents the physical element with its temper of rationalization and of accommodation which make the body potentially subversive to the spirit.

Dale S. Bailey. LATR. 6, 1, Fall, 1972, pp. 35–36

GONZÁLEZ MARTÍNEZ, ENRIQUE (1871–1952)

MEXICO

For some time now it has been observed that in González Martínez's psychology there is a duality whose terms I have not been able to establish, not knowing the proportions of the combination of pagan tranquillity and a very slight, very intimate, and very modern restlessness. But I do not want to suggest that we continue to speak of a poet of tones, since, on the contrary, I think he has achieved a poetry of great features, one whose verses march like centaurs and sound like fulsome notes.

His tone is almost always perfect. What I mean is that he has written with a pen that is related to those of Hérédia and Samain. Has anyone yet noted the degree of relationship? I, in all honesty, have not been able to decide if the lyre bearer is closer to the pleasures of a supple language than to a slippery and formless trembling, a trembling behind closed doors because of which nearly everyone today seems to be fainting. And to make matters more murky, in his latest book [*The Death of the Swan*] there [emerges] . . . a cerebral tendency: behold the "owl sapiens" who has arrived to complicate matters. Thus, there is a mixture of the sensations of the satyr who seizes his delights fully and the trembling already noted, together with a Minervian preoccupation that perhaps somewhat weakens the overall emotional quality. . . . Do these conceptions, because of their diversity, neutralize each other; or, far from neutralizing each other, are they blended together in one unique and simple whole? This is a question for a brighter critic and for a more detailed study. [1915]

Ramón López Velarde. In José Luis Martínez, ed.,
La obra de Enrique González Martínez (Mexico City,
Edición del Colegio Nacional, 1951), pp. 48–49†

[There is] the tendency of the Republics to proclaim a literary autonomy not inconsistent with continental aspirations. Such sonnets as that by the most popular of living Mexican poets, Enrique González Martínez, in which the swan of Darío (overemphasized as the poet's heraldic bird, owing to Rodó's brilliant analysis of *Profane Proses*), is sentenced to have its neck wrung and be replaced by the contemplative owl, indicate a more sober inspiration, yet one none the less modern. . . .

Was it not Verlaine who began all this neck-twisting, in his *Art poétique*? Do you recall the first line of the sixth quatrain? "Prend l'éloquence et tors-lui son cou!"

In the reaction of González Martínez against the swans of Darío may be discerned a double effect of the Mexican's milieu and his personality. This poet comes at a time when Mexico's need is for stern self-discipline, solid culture and widespread education, rather than for effete aestheticism and ultra-refinement. The verses that he wrote as a child were probably of the same character as is produced by most gifted children; his training as a physician, however, with the necessary scientific application to concrete phenomena, must have had not a little to do with his substitution of the owl for the swan. Social need and a scientific discipline aptly merged with a poetic pantheism furnished the background for the physician-poet's new orientation of modernism. . . .

A host of contradictory influences have played upon the idol of young Mexico's poetry lovers. Lamartine, Poe, Baudelaire, Verlaine (the ubiquitous Verlaine!), Hérédia, Francis Jammes, Samain. Yet here we find no morbidity, no dandyism, no ultra-refinement. Where other poets feel the passing nature of joy and cry out, admonishing mortals to "seize the day" ere it fly, González Martínez ("a melancholy optimist" [Francisco A.] de Icaza has termed him, in a paradoxical phrase that seems to sum up modern optimism) feels rather the transitory character of grief. He is what I may call an intellectual pantheist—his absorption of nature is not the ingenuous immersion of the primitive soul into the sea of sights and sounds about him; it is the pantheism of a modern intellect that gazes at feeling through the glasses of reason, and having looked, throws the glasses away. . . .

Isaac Goldberg. *Studies in Spanish-American Literature*
(New York, Brentano's, 1920), pp. 82–84

In spite of his busy public life, González Martínez has steadily built up his literary reputation; and he early acquired a very considerable following among the younger poets of his own country. His verses have been collected from time to time and published, each new volume adding to his popularity among literary circles, if not among the masses. . . .

At first glance there might seem a bit of incongruity between the vocation of medicine and the avocation of poetry; but a moment's consideration will reveal that such a lack of harmony may be more apparent than real. To a man endowed with a sensitive, artistic temperament, intimate daily contact with suffering humanity must, of necessity, bring about one of two reactions: he will become hardened spiritually and more or less indifferent to the misery of his surroundings, or he will become, as it were, subtly attuned to mankind, seeking to fathom something of that impenetrable mystery of human existence and its significance, an enigma that is never quite solved to the seeker's satisfaction. Fortunately, González Martínez followed the second course. His poetry is intensely subjective, and his themes are frequently tinged with that mystical philosophy which comes only from profound introspection.

Robert Arrett. *Hispania*. 14, May, 1931, pp. 183–84

When González Martínez demands that the neck of the swan be twisted, which swan is he referring to? Which swan was the enemy? . . . We must also ask ourselves another question: What does the swan signify in modern poetry, that is, in romantic poetry and its successors?

So then let us return to the initial question: which of the swans (in modern literature) is the enemy of González Martínez? Doubtlessly, one is the mythical swan of Leda, the symbol of the pleasure of the senses . . . a symbol of the jubilant pleasure of life of the most beautiful of carnal surfaces. The other swan would be the aesthetic one, the swan that decorates so many of Rubén Darío's landscapes, the pure, graceful ornament that glides along in a series of languid poses on the surface of blue lakes. Both swans cultivate surfaces; they are creatures that slide over the visible forms of the world with no other urgency than to enjoy them, no other mission than to increase their beauty. And, as a result, they are ignorant of or disdainful toward the inner life. This type of swan, because it is repeated in so many of Darío's poems, incurs a certain amount of sin for being mechanistic or mannerist, and thus it turns from an animal into an aesthetic form. As soon as there is an aristocratic passage in a Darío poem . . . there emerges the outline of a lake, and we can suspect with good reason that it will not be long before we see the neck of a swan rearing up on the horizon.

Thus, we must agree that the two poets who coincided in the rash of "neck twisting," Verlaine and González Martínez, also were in agreement about the identity of the victim. When he says "eloquence," Verlaine was thinking of the pompous rhetoric of the romantics; and when González Martínez says "swan," he was taking it as the most brilliant example of the precious rhetoric of modernism.

Pedro Salinas. Literatura española siglo XX
(Mexico City, Editorial Séneca, 1941?), pp. 101–2,
111–13†

To the Modernist poets, who glean from Symbolism the least enduring elements, Enrique González Martínez opposes a deeper and more reflective sensibility and an intelligence which dares to interrogate the dark face of the world. The severity of González Martínez, the absence of any unforeseeable element, which is the salt of poetry, and the didacticism which tinges part of his work, have caused him to be considered the first Spanish-American poet to break with Modernism: the swan is confronted with the owl. In reality, González Martínez does not oppose Modernism: he undresses it and strips it of its trappings. In despoiling it of its sentimental and Parnassian adherences, he redeems it, makes it conscious of itself and of its inner significance. Gonzáles Martínez adopts Mexican originality and links it to a tradition. Thus he does not repudiate Modernism, but is the only truly Modernist poet Mexico has had, in the sense in which Darío and Lugones in America, and Machado and Jiménez in Spain, were Modernists. The attention he gives to landscape, especially to nocturnal landscape, is impregnated with meaning—the dialogue between man and the world is resumed. Poetry ceases to be a description or a plaint and again becomes a spiritual adventure. After González Martínez, Parnassian eloquence and Romantic outpourings of the heart will be impossible. In making of Modernism a consciousness, he changes the attitude of the poet to poetry, even though he may leave intact the language and the symbols. The value of his example does not lie in his opposition to the language of Modernism—which he never rejected except in its aberrations, and he remained faithful to it till death—but in his being the first to restore to poetry the sense of the *gravity* of words. [1950]

Octavio Paz. In José Luis Martínez, ed.,
The Modern Mexican Essay (Toronto, University of
Toronto Press, 1965), pp. 447–48

Enrique González Martínez's poetry was inevitably influenced, for reasons of time and place, by the sweeping lyricism of Rubén Darío. González Martínez was born four years after Darío, in 1871. He developed therefore within the same context of modernism, which, more than a school—according to Juan Ramón Jiménez—was a movement of enthusiasm and liberty in search of beauty. But González Martínez's most important contribution was that he went beyond this manner and carried Mexican poetry along new paths.

Criticism in Spanish began to take González Martínez seriously after the sonnet "The Death of the Swan," included in the book of the same name published in Mexico in 1915. Some have attempted to interpret the text of this poem as a sort of new aesthetic credo, contrary to the spirit that nourished the lyricism of Rubén. In other words, González Martínez juxtaposed to the stylized figure of the swan the mysterious and nocturnal owl, the repository of knowledge. . . . Thirty years later, during the homage to Rubén Darío at the National University of Mexico on the twenty-fifth anniversary of his death, Enrique González Martínez clarified his position by stating that it was never his intention to attack the writer of *Profane Proses*. Here is an excerpt of that memorable essay. . . . "It is painful to speak of oneself on an occasion like the present. But I feel an overwhelming need to clarify a fact. . . . I refer to my own poem, written thirty years ago, which has come to be taken as an attack on the aesthetic of a poet I have always admired, indeed more and more as the years go by. With hand to heart, I declare that when I wrote those lines I was very far from thinking about the writer of *Profane Proses*. My intent at that time was to juxtapose two symbols: that of a gracefulness that does not feel the soul of things, personified by the swan; and the questioning meditation of the owl in the face of night. Nothing more. The swan, no matter how appealing it may have been to Rubén Darío, was not his exclusive property."

González Martínez's silence of thirty years regarding this matter caused many critics . . . to perpetuate the error of affirming, in a variety of ways, an antimodernist attack in the poem, which, in fact, never existed.

Raúl Leiva. *Imagen de la poesía mexicana
contemporánea* (Mexico City, Imprenta Universitaria,
1959), pp. 28–29†

For several years prior to 1920, the two great voices in Mexican poetry were those of González Martínez and Ramón López Velarde. . . . Both poets were writing at a time when their country was struggling through a major social revolution. One of the products of the revolution was a conflict between cultural cosmopolitanism and cultural nationalism. López Velarde showed how a focus on his provincial background—on circumstances that are characteristically Mexican—could be enlarged to universal significance. For González Martínez, however, this question never arose. His poetry always transcended national boundaries, and he was keenly aware of the relationship of his work to the European tradition. His calm and absolute acceptance of this fact strengthened the position of those poets who fought to maintain the great tradition of poetry while others proposed an extreme social commitment that often produced propaganda. . . .

González Martínez was never an innovator. His favorite and most successful form was the sonnet. He did not use form very effectively; but his usage is subtle, and intended for his own purposes, rather than for stimulating other poets. Even his excellent imagery is restrained, and is used for his own discovery of communion with the universe. In the middle period, when he had come to know vanguardist poetry, he did change a bit, became more objective. But even then he was involved with the things of the universe, rather astonished by them. . . .

The last period of González Martínez's poetry is a renewal of the search for reunion, now expressed in terms of the lost beloved. It was during this period that the poet discovered fully the meaning of his vacillation between heights and abyss, and the occasional joining of the two. And on the basis of this discovery, his poetry projects us onto the bridge that extends into intuited reality, where the aspects of time become one, where all places are the same, where all created things are joined. What González Martínez says to us is surprisingly similar to what we hear from some more recent poets, Octavio Paz among them. And while it is impossible to say what, if any, direct and overt influence there is, the spiritual influence must be admitted.

In recent years the tendency has been to regard Enrique González Martínez more as a monument than as a poet. Everyone grants him a place of honor in Mexican letters—indeed in Hispanic letters generally —but few have read his work except in anthologies. These selections become somewhat standardized and, while they enable us to see some of the moments of beauty, they cannot communicate the poet's discovery of a subtle, intuited reality, or his rebellious dissatisfaction with the limitations characteristic of the human estate. . . . It is doubtful that any other poet of his time spoke as directly to what we consider to be the contemporary human dilemma—the consternation of man confronted by the question of what he really is. With González Martínez we move between heights and abyss, experiencing the eternal truth that is contained in the constant presence of choice, and knowing that if the secret is discovered, the vitality of the search will be lost.

John S. Brushwood. *Enrique González Martínez*
(New York, Twayne, 1969), pp. 148–50

In popular legend González Martínez long remained a paradoxical figure. He was the Mexican poet who both reputedly shamed the modernists to silence, with his famous demand that "the swan's neck be twisted," and nevertheless himself persisted in writing as one far longer than any of his fellows. In fact González Martínez merely moved away from the extreme estheticism of the early modernist period about the same time as Darío himself did and then simply survived longer, finally to produce superbly controlled poems in the last decades of his life.

G. Brotherston. *BA*. 46, Autumn, 1972, p. 639

GONZÁLEZ PRADA, MANUEL (1848–1918)

PERU

If we wanted to find [González Prada's] spiritual ancestors, we would have to search for them first in the Greek poets of antiquity, second in the Parnassian poets of the nineteenth century. With the Greeks he shares . . . love for nature, which is beautiful and strong; the cultivation of a simple, spare, and pure form; and the fervor for line and the passion for statuary contour. . . . From the Parnassians González Prada inherited the careful attention to details, an ability to express himself impersonally, and an aristocratic impassivity of spirit. . . .

The marmoreal smoothness of his poetry does not, however, preclude the charm of a suave and subtle melancholy. This melancholy is not, however, the sadness of disenchantment or the sorrow of memory, and certainly not the nostalgia for lost happiness. Pagan and realistic, González Prada intensely loves . . . nature and life. Nature is one of the few things, if not the only thing, in which he believes with an absolute and sincere faith. It is not only externally beautiful but also eternally young, eternally good and eternally strong. . . .

Alberto J. Ureta. In *Manuel González Prada, por los
más notables escritores del Perú y América* (Cuzco,
H. G. Rozas, 1924), pp. 82–84†

By nature a fighter, [González Prada] was born appropriately during one epoch of European turmoil and died as appropriately during another. The dates January 6, 1848 and July 22, 1918 are but parentheses that embrace a life almost predestined to struggle and opposition. González Prada was one of the great "antis" of his day and generation. The parenthesis within the parenthesis was the war between Chile and Peru that ended so disastrously for his native country; and there was yet another: González Prada's own war against Peru. He proceeded by antagonisms. He was told, as he went on, that he was nothing but a destructive critic; he was ostracized by proper society and excommunicated by the clergy whom he had himself excommunicated from his own life; by instinct he sought new enemies and launched new causes. But in the end it was recognized by a few that he was of those who make the laws, not of those for whom they are made. . . .

In [*Free Pages*] are to be found the characteristic themes of the noted polemist, and if the volume seems to flout his poetry, it but does his verse justice. González Prada began his career in the orthodox manner of the South American literatus, as a rhymester; more than once he returned to his boyhood muse, and each time with a greater freedom from the conventional shackles. It would be too unlike him if he did not try to introduce new blood into the veins of the native poetry, even though it meant violence to the spirit of the language and to its natural prosody. From one who so loudly and so eloquently proclaimed the virtues of naturalness and spontaneity, his stanzaic experiments come, to say the least, somewhat inconsistently. Yet it is not this that speaks against his poetry so much as his instinctive bias for intellectual preoccupations.

In his poetry, indeed, González Prada is rather the critical experimenter than the simple, untutored singer of untutored passions. . . . For the real poetry of the man one must go to his prose. That prose is a remarkable medium. It is, like the man himself, almost the antithesis of the *milieu* into which he was born. It is prose as consciously and as conscientiously ordered as was the life that produced it. It rejected flatly the favorite devices of the Spanish literatus: a bellying phrase, filled like sails with nothing but wind and devoid of their propulsive power; imagery that indulged in pictures for their own sake, all bright light and no vision; in two words, resounding hollowness. In that prose he created an imagery of his own that was an organic growth from the thought itself; every metaphor is relevant, an epigram in terms of sight. Time and again he paints, rather than speaks, his meaning, and in a single stroke of the brush.

Of course there are moments when he falls victim to his own virtues; at such times he launches, if but for a passing lapse, into grandiloquence such as the objects of his assaults might envy. For in González Prada was not a little of the orator that he despised; not a little of the popular tribune. There was a time, indeed, when his political opinions crystallized into the National Union party; then he ran for the presidency of Peru, meeting an inevitable defeat. For all his sympathies with the oppressed, González Prada was not a man of the crowd; his humanity was a future hope wrenched from a bitter present. He is at his best, not as a conciliator but as a polemist.

Isaac Goldberg. AMer. 6, Nov., 1925, pp. 330–31

In our literature, González Prada heralds the transition from the colonial to the cosmopolitan period. Ventura García Calderón describes him to be "the least Peruvian" of our writers. But we have already seen that until González Prada, the Peruvian element in this literature is still not Peruvian, but only colonial. The author of *Free Pages* appears as an author whose spirit is Western and whose culture is European. But within a Peruvianness that is not yet distinct and positive, why should he be considered the least Peruvian of the writers who interpret it? Because he is the least Spanish? Because he is not colonial? The reason turns out to be paradoxical. Because he is the least Spanish and because he is not colonial, his writing announces the possibility of a Peruvian literature. It represents liberation from the mother country and the final rupture with the viceroyalty.

González Prada did not interpret this country; he did not examine its problems; he did not bequeath a program to the generation that followed. Nonetheless, he represents an instant, the first lucid instant, in the conscience of Peru. . . . The devious and rhetorical prose of *Free Pages* contains the seed of the new national spirit. In his famous speech at the Politeama in 1888, González Prada says: "The real Peru does not consist of the criollos and foreigners who live in the strip of land between the Pacific and the Andes; the nation is formed by the multitudes of Indians scattered along the eastern stretch of the cordillera."

In the writing of González Prada our literature begins to have contact with other literatures. González Prada represents in particular the French influence. But in general he has the merit of having opened the way to various foreign influences. His poetry and prose show an intimate knowledge of Italian literature. His prose often rails against academicians and purists and unorthodoxly delights in neologisms and gallicisms. His verse found new moulds and exotic rhythms in other literatures. . . .

Literature is not independent of other categories of history. Who does not recognize, for example, the political purpose behind the ostensibly literary definition of González Prada as the "least Peruvian of our writers"? To deny Peruvianness to his personality is simply a way of denying the validity of his protest in Peru. It is a disguised attempt to disqualify his rebellion. The same label of exoticism is used today against the ideas of the vanguard. . . .

It fell to González Prada to announce only what men of another generation ought to do. He preached realism. Denouncing the vaporous verbosity of tropical rhetoric, he urged his contemporaries to get their feet back on the ground. . . . But he himself never succeeded in becoming a realist; in his time, realism was historical materialism. Although the beliefs of González Prada never constrained his audacity or his freedom, he left to others the work of creating Peruvian socialism. [1928]

> José Carlos Mariátegui. *Seven Interpretive Essays on*
> *Peruvian Reality* (Austin, University of Texas Press,
> 1971), pp. 203–6, 209

All of the characteristics of the capitalist system, which passed over Peru like a pestilent wind, are vigorously taken up in González Prada's works: the parasitism and the oppressiveness of a class of spoilers, with its whole entourage of military men, priests, scribblers, and bailiffs. His analysis is not complete . . . but it is the most accurate and the most courageous one ever produced in all the Americas. . . . He did not get around to revealing why the Republic could not go beyond the conditions created by the colonial period or why it could not do away with the separation between the great mass of conquered Indians and the group of conquering exploiters.

González Prada did not accomplish these things because he had a different historical mission to fulfill: he was the Accuser. His great merit rests in having demonstrated that the semicolonial bourgeoisie was as ominous as was its counterpart during the colonial period and that the contradictions in the life of a country are personified in its classes of people. He pinpointed and attacked all of the reactionary forces, and at the same time he lit a huge bonfire of hope, trying to inspire all those dynamic forces that lead to a superior state. This alone merits the gratitude of succeeding generations. But his greatest glories were having given the impetus to intellectualism in America and having contributed to the awakening of class consciousness in Peru. One can find contradictions in his thought, and many passages have overtones that are not in accord with more recent theories and feelings about society. But the superiority of his character, the sincerity of his convictions, the dignity of his every attitude will always place him among the most eminent men ever produced by Humanity. . . .

> José Eugenio Garro. *RHM*. 7, July–Oct., 1941, p. 211†

From the viewpoint of Spanish criticism of Spain, González Prada, as a thinker preoccupied with the country's problems, stands between the so-called generations of 1868 and 1898. Less bourgeois and more drastic in his opinions than the first group, he shares its exacerbated anticlericalism and goes beyond its idea of a constitutional democracy in his advocacy of an utopian anarchy. Like Joaquín Costa, one of his Spanish contemporaries, González Prada is a realistic critic of the defects of nineteenth-century Spain, but the Spanish political leader tends toward a middle-class republican solution. González Prada, on the other hand, is cautious with respect to purely "political" programs, complete and definite though they may be, and in his last years proposes a benign and humane form of anarchy as the sole answer to the problems which afflict not only Spain but any society where there exist exploiters and exploited.

What separates him from the type of thought characteristic of the Spanish generation of 1898 is his insistence on a positive vision of the problem. Dominated by a rigorous scientific doctrine and a persistent anticlericalism, he conceives the problem in terms of black-and-white, good-and-evil, and he is as though blind before every factor which does not lend itself to rational analysis. The men of the generation of 1898 realize that the complex gray of reality is resolved in another way and that it contains an immense majority of many-hued components. For them the problem of Spain has its roots not only in the race, the moment and the milieu, but also in the deep and mysterious spirit of the people and their traditional values in life. González Prada, being above all a Spanish American and positivist, does not wish to or cannot conceive that which is implicit in the criticism of this generation: the possibility of an Hegelian assimilation—a synthesis of the Spanish heritage and the cultural elements of modern Europe to form a new and different Spanish character. . . .

With the exception of his admiration for Spain's great Golden Age, he stands apart from the defenders of the traditional Spanish values because for him the only good thing in the nation, the only hope for its future, is to be found in the sporadic resistance which Spanish liberalism offers to the retrograde social and political institutions of the country. . . . He distinguishes two Spains, one moribund, the other not yet born. And yet, he cannot avoid contemplating either the first Spain, the one which is contemporary with him, or its sad legacy in America. Nor, since it is a question of Spain, can he escape to the realm of happier memories. So he seeks the only refuge which remains to him: hope. And of the three ways in which man can manifest his hope: through plans and projects, in dreams and visions, or in religious faith and expectation, the first and last are forbidden to him because of his own political and religious convictions. He dreams then—and he has told us so—of a Spain without king or official religion. . . .

Robert G. Mead, Jr. PMLA. 68, Sept., 1953, pp. 714–15

The agile and swift prose of González Prada represented a revolution in its very style. As a poet, González Prada began by imitating the Spaniards, especially Fray Luis de León and the Argensolas. Later, passing through the influence of Heine and [Gustavo Adolfo] Bécquer, he reached the doors of modernism in the books *Miniscules* and *Exotics*. . . .

He was an innovator in metrics; he planned his own method for the study and analysis of versification. He introduced into Spanish various kinds of brief compositions and metrical combinations taken from several other languages and he made use of obsolete rhythmic forms. He cultivated the rondel. . . . He worked to adapt into Spanish the English Spenserian stanza, and he adopted from the Italian the *ballata*, the *stornello,* the *rispetto* and the *pantum.* He also cultivated the *villanella* and devised compositions that he called *gacelas* and *laudes.* [1954]

> Max Henríquez Ureña. *Breve historia del modernismo,*
> 2nd ed. (Mexico City, Fondo de Cultura
> Económica, 1962), p. 333†

González Prada's concepts stress denunciation and protest—and a consequent desire for reform—of the specific social structure of Peru (and America, for the most part), which consists of economic, political, and cultural concentration in the nucleus of the white minority, and, to a degree, the mestizo minority . . . [while the indigenous masses] have been subjected to a state of slavery or exclusion since the Conquest, a situation that has not been greatly changed under the Republic. But this sharp antithesis of its historical structure—between the America of the Viceroy and that of the Incas—can only truthfully be resolved in a synthesis, in the unity of both terms, since each represents different elements and manners of a single national entity whose end is integration. . . .

[González Prada's] repudiation of the colonial tradition . . . means the repudiation of the concepts and behavior that result from a fundamentally absurd regime, inasmuch as they impose the predominance of the Latin American minority at the expense of the indigenous majority. But against the tradition he condemns, he does not uphold a restoration of the Inca reign; his banner of redress is that of modern social ideology—the Western banner of reason, science, socialism, the banner of his time.

> Alberto Zum Felde. *Índice crítico de la literatura*
> *hispanoamericana* (Mexico City, Editorial Guarania,
> 1954–59), Vol. I, pp. 280–81†

González Prada has been criticized for his bold ideas because he made literature a sounding board for propaganda and attack. But his detractors have not realized that this was the kind of literature most needed at this precarious moment in history. They have not realized that González Prada was not the only one to give priority to the social function of literature.

In spite of his critics—mostly Peruvian—the continental influence of González Prada has been recognized by the best writers of the language. Blanco Fombona recognized him as one of the fine men of the continent. Miguel de Unamuno stated that there were few American and non-American writers who moved readers as did González Prada. . . . González Prada should be remembered not only for the great influence he had on poetry and prose in Spanish: his ideology has special value in his country. There his ideas served to awaken his compatriots at the end of the nineteenth century and the beginning of the twentieth, and they established the bases for a new and democratic Peru. . . .

Don Manuel was against the capitalists who oppress the proletariat. . . . His defense of the world's helpless earned him followers and admirers in many parts of the world. The workers in Barcelona during the Civil War published *Anarchy,* Don Manuel's revolutionary book. . . . The democrats of the New World love González Prada for his protest against every king of regimentation. . . . Another message he bequeathed to his followers was a battle cry against militarism. His opposition to the uniformed oppressor reached its culmination in the excellent book *Under Opprobium.* . . .

Eugenio Chang-Rodríguez. *La literatura política de González Prada, Mariátegui y Haya de la Torre* (Mexico City, Ediciones De Andrea, 1957), pp. 118–19, 121†

The "father of Peruvian radicalism," it is generally acknowledged, was Manuel González Prada. Significantly, the critics usually refer to him as a "liberal" and, if we keep in mind the basically anticlerical connotation of the term in Hispanic America, they are quite right. Reared in an extremely Catholic environment, as a youth he reacted sharply against all forms of religious ritual and practice. . . .

In his attempt to discover the weakness which might account for his country's collapse, he isolated several factors: the unwillingness of the Indian to fight for an oppressive, vaguely comprehended national state; the backwardness of the nation's intellectuals; and the cynical self-interest of Peru's political leaders. Lying behind all these flaws, González Prada felt, was the debilitating cultural heritage of Spain— her religion, her pretentious aristocracy, her fanaticism, and her legacy of administrative inefficiency. In a series of forthright essays—*Free Pages, Hours of Struggle,* and many others published separately and then collected in posthumous volumes—González Prada boldly criticized all that was traditional not only in Peruvian society but, by extension, throughout Hispanic America.

It is quite difficult to categorize González Prada's fundamental positions, for his diagnosis of his country's ills is much more extensive than his specific remedies. It is clear that he had a deep positivistic faith in science and technology as the great deliverers of humanity. . . . It is equally apparent that he desired the complete separation of church and state, the redemption of the exploited Indian, and a more equitable distribution of the national wealth. Although he recognized the relationship of the Indian problem to those of land tenure and attacked the idea that property was sacred, he proposed no clear program of radical agrarian reform. González Prada's radicalism was personal, eclectic, and, in his later writings tinged with a vaguely conceived anarchism. He distrusted governments—even those established in the name of the Revolution. He had a wonderful understanding of human failings and of the way in which revolutionary ideals age, become rigid and, eventually, conservative. His writings will indicate at one point a fatalistic acceptance of this process (" . . . every triumphant revolutionary degenerates into a conservative"), and then, just a few pages later, he will proclaim the future success of a sweeping humanitarian revolution.

Critics who had sought consistency in González Prada's thought—particularly when his earlier and later works are viewed as a single body—are usually frustrated in their attempts. The marked nationalism of his work of the 1880's contrasted with the broad internationalism of many of the essays written in the closing decades of his life is a case in point. . . . Whether he was a Positivist or an anarchist, a materialist or romantic idealist, a Bakuninite or Marxist, would be difficult to say; for González Prada was a bit of all these. But most of all he was an agitator, an awakener of men's minds and spirits, an apostle, to use a favorite epithet of Spanish Americans.

Martin S. Stabb. *In Quest of Identity* (Chapel Hill, University of North Carolina Press, 1967), pp. 109–10

GOROSTIZA, JOSÉ (1901–1973)

MEXICO

Since *Songs to Sing on Fishing Boats* José Gorostiza has published only one book of poems—*Death without End.* In it we have, in its fullness, the world that throbbed in his first poems. Through a series of connected images Gorostiza tells us of the anxiety of man, the death of the universe and of God; he even suggests the impossibility of poetry itself. In his poems not only is man put in question, not only . . . are things placed in parentheses; there is also a doubting of the poem itself in a vicious circle that can be seen as an eternal return from being to nothingness, from the word to silence, from communication to solitude.

Since antiquity, the symbol of water has been the property of poets and philosophers. . . . In Gorostiza's poetry water is used with various symbolic meanings. In *Songs to Sing on Fishing Boats* water is a sign of the flight of time. . . . In "Prelude" water is the image of the incessant becoming that characterizes life. . . . The first strophe of *Death without End* definitively establishes the meaning of water. Man in his solitude —"besieged in my epidermis"—finds his reflection in water.

Ramón Xirau. Tres poetas de la soledad (Mexico City,
Antigua Librería Robredo, 1955), pp. 13–14†

[Gorostiza] is certainly a poet of major importance. *Death without End* is a very special achievement—a coherent search for the fundamental nature of reality. The structure of the poem and its development are logical, but the way of developing it is highly poetic, brightened by flashes of metaphors and multiple levels of communication. The result is a work of heroic proportions.

One of the most interesting things of *Death without End* is its relationship to Mexican attitudes. Xavier Villaurrutia has alluded to this in his "Introduction to Mexican Poetry": "The Mexican is a subdued being whose greatest intoxication consists in keeping himself lucid, and who, even at the hour of dreaming, likes to keep himself awake." Although one must recognize that this lucidity Villaurrutia speaks of is perhaps the most characteristic aspect of his own poetry, he has nonetheless focused well upon a characteristic, if not of all Mexican poetry, certainly of some of its major poets. Sor Juana, from whom Gorostiza borrowed the image of water and glass, differs from other baroque poets because of her lucidity. And the majority of the generation of Villaurrutia and Gorostiza shares this characteristic, although in different ways and to a different extent.

Frank Dauster. RI. 25, July–Dec., 1960, pp. 287–88†

Songs to Sing on Fishing Boats consists of twenty-five poems grouped into three sections: (1) the "Songs" themselves, three works that use sea imagery and remind us of traditional Spanish poetry; (2) the part that is called "Other Poems" and consists of thirteen rather varied poems, the majority of which also present sea scenes and scenes dealing with nature in general; (3) the "Drawings of a Port," composed of two long works and seven very short poems, also dealing with sea themes.

Nature—specifically marine nature—seems to constitute the principal subject of the book. But a careful analysis of the work leads to a conclusion that nature is not used as an end in itself, but rather as a vehicle for the expression of the human. Elements taken from the world of nature serve for an examination of the basic problems of man. . . . I would suggest that Gorostiza, by using nature to give shape to human meanings, gives nature a very important role, for through it the poet is able to preserve with a greater degree of permanence human values that would otherwise be lost with time. . . .

The passage of time underlies most of the poems in *Songs to Sing on Fishing Boats*, a theme inextricably connected with the attitude toward poetry revealed by the book. Time is the chief obstacle encountered by man in his search for universality. The temporary quality of his life deprives him of the permanence he seeks, while the changes wrought by time make his ideas, emotions, and circumstances incomprehensible and incommunicable to future generations. Time thus holds for man the worst threat—that of his complete extinction. To externalize himself somehow, man must find a way to overcome time. . . . Gorostiza finds in nature and in love permanent elements that, when used in poetry, can preserve the meaning of man and thus retard or halt the passage of time. But the reader of *Songs to Sing on Fishing Boats* nonetheless senses that no solution will be entirely satisfactory to the poet.

Andrew P. Debicki. La poesía de José Gorostiza
(Mexico City, Ediciones De Andrea, 1962), pp. 14, 35†

The contention that Gorostiza is lax and the contention that he is a perfectionist are both correct. But no one has tried to explain why he is both these things. He is lax because his intellect has convinced him that intelligence has no point and also because a love for poetry has led him to doubt poetry, to convince himself that silence is more poetic than song. He is a perfectionist for obvious reasons—because he has never confused outpouring with art. . . . He is also a perfectionist . . . in that he often goes back and revises the few poems that he has written. For example, between the first and the second time "Declaration of Bogotá" appeared—between its publication in the review *América* and in the volume of his complete poetry—it underwent six small face-lifting operations. . . .

"Declaration of Bogotá" . . . is a poem of love and a poem of events. On the one hand, it "narrates" a separation and, on the other hand, it reviews the inter-American events expressed in the Declaration of Bogotá. Hence the ironic title of the poem: like America, the "narrator" of the poem, the poet himself, is assaulted by the forces of darkness. It was a bad day for inter-American relations and for the amorous "curriculum" of the first-person speaker. Here, as in all of Gorostiza's poems, events and circumstances become phantasmal, change into symbols, and leave behind biographical material to become the common patrimony of men who have undergone similar experiences is different times and places.

Any one of Gorostiza's poems, no matter how early it was written, can give one a full understanding of his total work. There are no high or low points; instead, his poetry is like a plateau, a valley as high and ethereal as the Valley of Mexico. . . .

In his two books and in his twelve [uncollected] poems he communicates to the reader—by means of a technique so perfect that it scarcely improves from one poem to the next—several aspects of the life of a man and of the emotional and intellectual biography of the twentieth century.

Emmanuel Carballo. Diecinueve protagonistas de la literatura mexicana del siglo XX (Mexico City, Empresas Editoriales, 1965), pp. 203–5

GUILLEN, NICOLÁS (1902–   )

CUBA

It is only within recent years that the Latin American Negro has developed any poetry comparable in creative genius to that of the North American Negro. In the new poetry he expresses eroticism, love of rhythm, and typical Negro attitudes and feelings. Perhaps the most striking characteristic of this new poetry is rhythm. The Latin American Negro, like his North American brother, loves to sing and dance. And it is this festival spirit of song and dance that the new poetry reproduces. Sometimes it is the languid sensualism of the Cuban *son* [a popular dance], sometimes the mad whirl of the *rumba,* or the stomp and the shout of more warlike measures like the *batuque* [literally, "rumpus"—another dance].

One of the new poets is Nicolás Guillén, best representative of Afro-Cuban poetry. He translates the very soul of the Cuban Negro in his *sones.* He is able to express with words the contortions of the dance and the rhythm of the music. He uses the corrupt Spanish of the Negro and even some African words. But it is not necessary to understand the words because the rhythm tells it all:

Tamba, tamba, tamba, tamba,
Tamba del negro que tumba;
Tumba del negro caramba,
Caramba, que el negro tumba:
Yamba, yambó, yambambé.

This fragment from "Negro Song" recalls the "boomlay, boomlay," of Vachel Lindsay's *Congo.* The sound effect of the Cuban poem is amazing. It is based on explosives to give a characteristic "jazz" note and to reproduce the sound of the drum and percussion instruments. It is a kind of verbal surrealism and has no pictorial value at all. It is rhythm and sound, nothing more.

These dances in verse bear a certain resemblance to our "jazz," except that our "jazz," our "hot jazz," is more varied. It has certain unexpected explosions and is composed of a great variety of instruments. In the Cuban dances the music is more monotonous and primitive.

Dorothy Schons. *Hispania*. 25, Oct., 1942, pp. 312–13

To be sure, many poets in Cuba have cultivated and continued to cultivate black poetry. At one time Emilio Ballagas seemed to be the most likely disciple of Guillén. But Ballagas veered off into other lyrical directions, and his poetry is inspired by entirely subjective modalities, which are quite often surrealistic. Guillén continues to be the great black poet in Cuba, even in those poems that do not deal directly with the problems of his people (let us forget that ugly word "racial"). He has this position because of his truly dignified interpretation of the popular soul, because of his dedication to redemption, because of his feeling and his irony, because of the truly human expression he brought to Latin American poetry in his unmistakably unique works. . . .

The folklore in many of his ballads gives them something far more important than a documentary tone; folklore makes them come alive with an intense vibration. But although the popular elements in the best of his works is undeniable, one should stress that his poetry is a re-creation, a refinement. There are Cuban poems that surpass Guillén's in colorfulness and in tropical atmosphere; one need only recall "The Rumba" by José Zararías Tallet. But Guillén is the one who has given us, with the greatest honesty and the greatest strength the feeling of the Negro, the mulatto, the oppressed, and the downtrodden who are with us everywhere. And it is he who has achieved the most musical and suggestive portraits of the Caribbean. . . .

Gastón Figueira. *RI*. 10, Nov., 1945, pp. 109–10†

[Guillén] has been interested in the folklore of his people, and one can observe this interest in many of his poems. His is an ardent voice of protest against the abuses of society and politics that weigh down the Cuban people and the silent, downtrodden people of the world. His feelings, and not just his theories, carried Guillén to Spain, where he took part in the struggle against fascism.

It has been said that the only *raison d'être* of a poem is that it be understood by its readers, so that they can share in the emotion that influenced the poet when he wrote it. Unfortunately, many poets do not speak the language of the people, and they limit themselves to addressing some intellectual and cultural elite, thereby reducing the limits of their influence. Guillén, on the other hand, is a contemporary writer who almost always uses a simple, although a strong and rich, vocabulary. He paints with the words taken, still warm, from the lips of common folk. He uses beautiful and vigorous images usually taken from his environment, but he shapes them with the control over language of a true artist. His is a powerful and vital message, with the thrust of sincerity and the anguish of a sensitive and courageous man impassioned by a desire for the good of his fellow men. . . .

Guillén's obsessive subject is the lowly people—black and white—their daily worries, their poverty, their sicknesses, their exploitation, and their future. He presents them in all their misery, impotence, and confusion in the streets of the city, in the army, on the docks, in the country—wherever there are people who suffer. The only phase of life that Guillén does not touch—and its absence is striking—is the relationship between the people and the church.

Martha Allen. RI. 15, July, 1949, pp. 29–30†

Of all the Afro-Cuban writers, Nicolás Guillén was a coloured man, a mulatto, and as Cintio Vitier points out, the great difference is that he writes "from within," and the Negro theme is not just a fashion, a subject for literature, but the living heart of his creative activity. Even so, in many of his early poems, we find the characteristic atmosphere of dancing and sex, an external, plastic vision of the Negro. But in and after *West Indies Ltd.* his poetry is infused with a growing concern for the social and economic position of the Negro in Cuba, and while he does not abandon the popular tone and the general manner of Afro-Cuban poetry, he "wipes the alcohol off the guitar's mouth" and tells it to play "its full song." . . .

In Guillén, then, we find both the Afro-Cuban world of dancing, drumming, alcoholic frenzy, elements of Cuban folklore ("The Ballad of the Güije" and "Sensemayá") and poems of social and racial protest. The second phase is seen by Guillén himself as a maturing of his early manner, but still, as already pointed out, a lot of the Afro-Cuban mannerisms are retained, particularly rhythmic repetitions in the style of Cuban popular songs (the rumba, *son, guaracha*) and racy Cuban turns of speech. For Guillén wanted to reach the Cuban people through his poetry, and he felt that these elements were a ready means of communication. Although the protest against colour discrimination is constant, Guillén never adopted aggressive anti-white attitudes. His message is "Accept us for what we are."

G. R. Coulthard. Race and Colour in Caribbean
Literature (London, Oxford University Press, 1962),
pp. 34–35

Guillén does not turn to blackness out of caprice or temporary motives: the black theme is linked to the very essence of his poetic task. In that task, blackness was not a *fashion*, it was a *mode*. In white poets like Guirao, Ballagas, Tallet, Carpentier, black poetry is the fruit of the union of the picturesque and the folkloric. In Guillén, whose blood is a mixture of black and white, that poetry possesses a depth of emotion that is unmistakably his own. It is not surprising that he has himself spoken of "mulatto poetry" rather than "black poetry."

Guillén began his career with a handful of short poems, in *Motifs of Sound*, in which the persistent and primitive rhythm pulls along a hidden music. . . . The language of these poem-sounds is Spanish altered by popular phonetics, with folkloric resonances that the poet weaves in skillfully. Guillén's poetry is here . . . the simple adaptation of motifs of popular songs and dances. . . .

In Guillén's social poetry, which has universal relevance, there are revelations of great significance and high artistic value. His social poetry includes *Spain, a Poem in Four Anguishes and One Hope*, inspired by the Spanish Civil War, part of which Guillén witnessed when he visited Spain at that crucial moment as a fervent partisan of the Spanish Republic; *Elegy to Jacques Roumain, in the Sky of Haiti*, a heartfelt tribute to the incomparable Haitian poet; and *Elegy to Jesús Menéndez*, in memory of the Cuban worker-leader. . . .

Max Henríquez Ureña. *Panorama histórico de la literatura cubana* (San Juan, Ediciones Mirador, 1963), Vol. II, pp. 378–79, 382†

Much more copious and enthusiastic than the critical response to *Motifs of Sound* was that which greeted *Sóngoro Cosongo*, since its emotional and lyric sweep was of greater breadth and it probed more deeply into the sensitive open wound of the national unrest at that particular moment. Everyone was in agreement over the importance of its *appearance,* of its authentically Cuban character, and of its perfect expression of folklore, although there was criticism leveled at Guillén for the polemic points—"tendentious"—to be found in the work and for his definition in verse of mestization. "Should poetry have skin color to begin with?," some asked with alarm, although without denying the high quality and the maturity of *Sóngoro Cosongo*. . . . This kind of criticism exemplified a more-or-less conscious colonial mentality or a certain social prejudice, an unwillingness to compromise on the things of the people, even less so in the case of such a substantial part of it as were the Negroes. . . .

Today, when we can see his work and its impact panoramically and in detail, it seems to me that the critics at best only grasped

Sóngoro Cosongo in the most superficial of ways. Had not some gone so far as to fault it for being swollen with a "polemical, racial tendency"? We have already seen that it was black from the inside out—from the inside of its Cubanness—set forth with arrogance, with deceiving aggressiveness, which is the only way possible in a land such as ours, where pain has the escape valve of bitter teasing and the tone of admonition is likely to be met by a chorus of indignation no matter how much right it may have.

In even the most picturesque and seemingly most anecdotal parts of *Sóngoro Cosongo*, there is a social consciousness behind them—their background of blood and misery, the bitter root from which they spring. Guillén most certainly did not remain on the periphery of the Negro question, even if it is true . . . that his poetry strived to go beyond the pain, no matter how much it may have sprung from it. . . .

The poet of *Sóngoro Cosongo* was wrapped up in his own music, as if in waves, a music through which his people could be perceived. He was so wrapped up in it that its influence somewhat distanced him from the full human destiny of his subject: this was another criticism leveled at him [by more radical critics]. But he himself had admitted as much very perceptively: "The poet is drunk with his newly discovered rhythm and he casts his poems to the winds like coins, for the sheer pleasure of seeing them glitter in the sun. Only when he grows in inner stature, only when his body strikes roughly against life itself, only when he suffers and weeps and sees suffering and weeping around him of the most intense sort will he be able to cast loose in his vessel, now tossed about, cradled by the wind beneath the blue sky. . . ."

Ángel Augier. *Nicolás Guillén: Notas para un estudio
biográfico-crítico* (Las Villas, Cuba, Universidad
Central de Las Villas, 1963–64), Vol. II,
pp. 176–77, 192–94†

The work of Guillén is not only revolutionary but iconoclastic, in spite of his gentleness and resigned protest. His real originality consists in his introduction into his popular or academic poetry of elements that were destructive rather than reconstructive and reforming. He changed traditional "cultivated" poetry from top to bottom, from its themes and language; from the meaning and grammatical acceptance of the word and syntax, to rhythm, metrics, all the devices of poetic craft . . . and literary grammar and aesthetics. . . . He is more than an innovator; he is a radical revolutionary who attacked the feudal society of bourgeois poetics. . . .

Superficially, the poetry of Guillén can be classified into different categories: topical compositions and "Negro spirituals"; regular compositions and arbitrary compositions of capricious meter, rhythm, and length; idiomatic works and compositions of slang; social, political, and other particular themes (but never personal ones); compositions that are anedotes and playful compositions that sometimes take the form of charades, riddles, or puzzles, which hide their meaning. . . .

Ezequiel Martínez Estrada. *La poesía afrocubana de
Nicolás Guillén* (Montevideo, Editorial Arca, 1966),
pp. 6–7, 82†

Guillén is considered by many to be a great and sincere humanitarian, though a militant Communist. His love and concern for the Negro race amount to more than a superficial theme for poetry; the Negro's problems constitute the raison d'être of his life and writing. His humanitarianism, however, has led him to sympathize with the unfortunate of both races. . . . Guillén has gone beyond concern for racial and economic injustice only, however, to protest other forms of injustice, such as those he finds in Big Business, the military world, and Fascist Spain.

Three basic "color sources" may be seen in Guillén's poetry, the African Negro, the Spanish white, and the Cuban mulatto, the last being the racial group to which he himself belongs. By extension, three literary sources may also be found. Cintio Vitier lists them as, first, "the heartfelt participation in the sensuality, humor, and psychic and musical ways of the Cuban Negro"—this is his strongest drive; second, "a keen understanding of folklore," which has made possible poems as pure in contour as "Sensemayá"; and third, "a nourishing contact with traditional forms of popular Spanish poetry."

Frederick S. Stimson. *The New Schools of Spanish
American Poetry* (Chapel Hill, N.C., Estudios de
Hispanófila, 1970), p. 168

While it has always been plain to the point of commonplace that Cuba is a lively protean synthesis, so to speak, of the white Spanish thesis and the black African antithesis, no one before Guillén had advanced such a bold affirmation of the latter. Among the few Negroes who had managed in the nineteenth century to achieve some standing in Cuban letters—Juan Francisco Manzano and Gabriel de la Concepción Valdés (Plácido), for example—the tendency was to assimilate the Spanish colonial culture, to "bleach out" any strains of a darker sensibility. The twentieth century, of course, brought a deepening self-consciousness among Blacks and that much-commented white cultivation of things African and Afro-American, both of which flowered—in genuine as well as pretended manifestations—during the post-World-War-One decade in Harlem and Paris. On a popular level, Cuba's association with this flowering is through the Afro-Caribbean movement which sprang up in Hispanic poetry around the mid-twenties. But the inaugurators of the movement (Luis Palés Matos, a Puerto Rican, and the Cubans, José Zacarías Tallet and Ramón Guirao) were white. Their achievement lay principally in the manipulation of exotic sounding onomatopoeia and so-called primitive rhythm—a figure they commonly depicted is the stereo-typical Black of mystery, sensuality, and dance. They were selective observers (even exploiters) of, rather than participants in, the world their verse purported to evoke.

In radical contrast to this local-color approach, Guillén's eight "*son*-poems" offered a provocative inside picture. It is the black inhab-itant of Havana's slums who speaks here: what is more, he uses the argot and nonstandard pronunciation peculiar to his milieu, and sketches phenomena of his own daily existence. The result is a new and shocking authenticity. But gradually, through repeated confronta-tions with the text, it becomes clear that, just behind these enter-taining and often happy-go-lucky slices of ghetto life, the people of *Motifs of Sound* (1) do not have enough to eat, (2) are often ashamed of identifiably Negroid features or coloring, and (3) commonly live in exploitative sexual promiscuity. One poem tells of a *chulo*, or small-time pimp, who is compensated for his nickname, "Nigger-lips," by a good white suit, two-tone shoes, and the fact that he lives well without ever working. In another a woman is told to cheer up and try to pawn her electric iron because the power is shut off for nonpayment and the cupboard as well as her man's pockets are empty. And in one more a woman announces that, since her man steps out in fine clothes and new shoes while she sits at home eating rice and biscuits, she will defy the cen-sure of neighbors and leave him for someone else. . . .

Robert Márquez. Introduction to *Man-Making Words: Selected Poems of Nicolás Guillén* (Amherst, University of Massachusetts Press, 1972), pp. xi–xii

GÜIRALDES, RICARDO (1886–1927)

ARGENTINA

If one were to ask me if the present book by Güiraldes [*Don Segundo Sombra*] is a copy of an objective reality, accessible on sight to anyone who saw it, I would say no. If one were to raise the objection that it has obvious anachronisms regarding the material progress of the Pampa, which the writer sees with the eyes of memory and of evocation as well, I would not argue with the objection. His Pampa is, without a doubt, not the one seen by the unobservant tourist or by the rootless inhabit-ant, who is only preoccupied with the rise and fall in the prices of his products. Nor is it the Pampa of today with its railroads, industrial centers, credit institutions and cosmopolitan customs. It is the Pampa of the Gaucho, the traditional Pampa such as we understand it. Men and customs that disappear from day to day, the emotional reserve that the new breezes blow away, the profound sense of the earth created by a perennial attachment, the tragedy of the daily struggle that man and nature renew each morning—this is what the novel is about.

Güiraldes does not present an earthly paradise, at least not in the biblical sense. Man, in order not to perish, sought an ally and he found a decisive and faithful one in the horse, a conjunction that gave rise to the centaur of the Pampa. What a school for virility, independence, and even spiritual renewal was this rustic life! When the Gaucho, who can only live by forgetting, feels the jab of ideas or passions that, because they bring feelings of hatred, submission, or vengeance, threaten his carefree life, he neither despairs nor curses. He knows that the Pampa is immense and that the dust raised by his horse's hooves can bury yesterday. He puts miles behind him, and in a new place he is also a new man.

Güiraldes' prose throughout the novel has the movement and flexibility that the narrative demands. The appropriateness of the language to the characters gives his novel the powerful throbbing of life, and the dialogue achieves the naturalness of real conversation; his artistic recreation is not at all irreconcilable with the picturesque modes of Gaucho speech.

Juan B. González. *Nosotros.* No. 210, Nov., 1926,
pp. 382–83†

Güiraldes would have the Gaucho Don Segundo Sombra be so stoic—long-suffering, suited to every adversity—because he exercises a harsh occupation, that of the herdsman, in a country of oppressive conditions, the Pampa. But the occupation of herdsman is not so harsh, nor is the Pampa in and of itself so oppressive. "The most manly of occupations," Güiraldes calls that of the herdsman with a certain ingenuousness. What, then, would you call that of the roundupman in the mountain which Dávalos presents so accurately in *The White Wind*? Along the coast itself, the farming peasants carry out work that is much harsher than that of the herdsman, whose occupation, we note, does not involve the dangers or the fatigue or the violence of other occupations. . . .

The Pampa is not in and of itself a land of energy but rather of indolence. Covered in part by arable earth, with abundant water, with a climate that in the rigors of winter does not go below 5° [C] and in full summer does not exceed 30° [C], where it never snows, where the storms and the winds and the rains (with rare exceptions) never acquire a violent character, the Pampa is not a landscape destined to produce a person of such a hardened character, a soul so tempered by and accustomed to every rigor such as Segundo Sombra. . . .

Why should a segment of the Argentine bourgeoisie present the Gaucho in such a picturesque light, at odds with the true nature of the peasants that work in the Pampa? This new Gaucho-bourgeois literature tries to reincarnate long-past Gaucho values. If he had kept them, he would not have been dominated. . . .

Ramón Doll. Nosotros. Nos. 222–23, Nov.–Dec., 1927,
pp. 274–76†

Strange as it may seem, *Don Segundo Sombra* occupies in Argentinian letters a place not unrelated to that of *Huckleberry Finn* in the literature of the United States. It, too, is the history of a boy, a waif who "on his own" wanders through the country. And that country, in both books, is the frontier—an old America that had already almost vanished when the two books were written. Both tell an exciting story of adventure from the standpoint of a boy, in the boy's own language; and both lads are typical products of their respective worlds. But the books are a great deal more than good adventure stories, being classic pictures of the traditions and ideas, the institutions and the folk of the two countries.

The differences of course are enormous; and are in a large part the differences between early North America and Argentina. The gaucho had received as his heritage the Catholic tradition of Spain; and although the life of these southern cowboys was primitive, it kept a humane quality from the culture of Spain. Huckleberry Finn floats blindly down a barbarous, anarchic world in which the traditions of Old England are broken up past recognition. His friend is a poor black fugitive slave; he finds literally no one and nothing to look up to. His Argentinian brother follows a man who not only teaches him how to rope cows, but becomes his spiritual father. In all the rough work, a real culture lives in the pampa; and one feels it not alone in the lives of the gauchos, but even in the attitude of the men toward their horses and their cattle.

These distinctions are carried into the minds of two boys. Huck sees mainly the outside of events and is moved only by simple human feelings. The Argentinian lad, quite as naturally, is alive to the nuances in his adventures of colour and emotion. Mark Twain's book is written in dialects that are no more complex than the waters of the Mississippi. The book of Güiraldes is in a prose that expresses the virile, rough life of the gaucho with the sensibility of a humane culture.

These distinctions may surprise the North American reader who has been led to believe that his is a more civilized world than Latin America. The reason for this is that we in the United States have a certain kind of order: industrial, commercial, and (as a reflection of these) political; and this order is the one that we are taught to praise. The order of Argentina is more inward; it is cultural rather than institutional. It is an order of human values, much more than of business and of public affairs. But it belongs to an old agricultural world which, even in Argentina, is fast disappearing. Which explains the social and political unrest in the Latin-American countries.

But the reader of *Don Segundo Sombra* need not bother about all this. He will learn, without knowing it, all the tricks of the noble art of bronco-busting and of cattle-wrangling. He will drink in, delightedly, the savour and rhythm of the pampa. He will read the story of a boy who, like boys the world over, learns to become a man by taking life humbly, and bravely.

Waldo Frank. Introduction to Ricardo Güiraldes, *Don Segundo Sombra* (New York, Farrar & Rinehart, 1935), pp. x–xi

[*Don Segundo Sombra*] is unmistakably an American book. It has the feel of space, endless and generous and dangerous; the vigor and nobility of youth; the casual ruthlessness, the horseplay, and the enormous hopefulness of the primitive. Its thread of mysticism—the inarticulate emotions of a man riding alone at the head of thousands of cattle, across hundreds of miles—is also the sense, the excited awe, of explorers, prospectors, whalers, migrants, and pioneers.

Don Segundo Sombra, the hero of the book, rides into the life of the boy who tells the story when that boy is a small-town tough, escaping from two pious and petty "aunts" to go fishing and to hang around saloons. He has become a shrewd little guttersnipe and spends his time clowning maliciously, picking up spare pennies however he can, or brooding uncomfortably by the river. Sly subtleties in public places have made him well aware that there is a shadow on his birth. His aunts are not exactly fond of him. Yet an "uncle" whose ranch he once visited gave him two ponies and a poncho, so that when Don Segundo Sombra, the almost legendary *gaucho*, rides into his town at dusk one day, a complete vision of escape flashes into his head. He departs, with his ponies and his poncho, to lead a brave man's life, the *gaucho* life of Don Segundo Sombra. . . .

Güiraldes says Don Segundo Sombra was a real person. Frank says he met him when he was in the Argentine. But in the story Don Segundo Sombra is also a complete ideal, like our own frontier heroes. He is courageous, silent, modest, witty, and completely sure of himself. Of course he can rope, saddle, ride, break horses, dance and sing, and tell stories better than anybody else. But he was something more than these things. He was *gaucho* inside as well as out, and therefore, says the boy who took him as a model, "only Don Segundo seemed to escape the fatal law that events play with us and make us dance to every vagrant tune." As he broke green horses, as he dominated broncos, so he dominated life itself. He had "the strength of the pampas." The silent land gave him "something of its greatness and its unconcern." And because he had somehow eliminated fear, "the result was that while the rest of us were heading toward death, he seemed to be on the way back."

Don Segundo Sombra as a complete personification of young Argentina, young America, and manhood making its own fate is probably the triple reason that the book has long since become a classic in the Spanish language, one of those literary mountain peaks at once a widely popular story and a book to be studied in school. Mrs. de Onís has made a superb translation. It is informal, colloquial, and yet true.

Anita Brenner. *Nation.* Jan. 30, 1935, pp. 133–34

To Hispanic literature, Argentina has contributed three outstanding works around the life of the *gaucho*: Sarmiento's *Facundo*, Hernández' *Martín Fierro* and Güiraldes' *Don Segundo Sombra*. To the American reader desirous of a good story, *Don Segundo Sombra* offers an optimistic outlook unburdened by any intellectualism. This episodic novel will hold his interest as he reads of the herders always moving on, hiring themselves out now at one ranch, now at another, till the herd is driven to its destination or the ponies and mares are taught to accept the saddle without arching their backs or playing tricks on their riders. There is no love story, and sex is a negligible element. Don Segundo, the mentor of the boy in the story, is the surviving representative of the Pampas. The heroes of Sarmiento and Hernández were fierce fighters against the authorities and the Indians, but the hero of Güiraldes, though he moves within organized society, exemplifies only the admirable virtues of the *gaucho* outlaw. Through his disarmingly simple story, Güiraldes has built up a poetic atmosphere that illumines and justifies the ways of the Pampas.

Don Segundo Sombra is like *Don Quixote* on a different level. Both tell of the closing chapter in a people's history and the most secret yearnings of their authors. Ricardo Güiraldes, the son of a rich rancher, imaginately projects himself into the life of his *guacho* (orphan waif), who willed to become a *gaucho*. The boy, through his contact with the uneventful daily tasks of herders and horsetamers, succeeds in hardening himself to the demands of the Pampas, and when he is a master in his trade discovers he is the son of a rich ranch owner. This is not like our success stories, for the hero then feels most disconsolate, and blindly wishes to escape his fate. In spite of the three more years of life with Don Segundo, his "godfather," the young man is defeated in his will to be the poor *gaucho* of the Pampas. We are made to understand that Argentina's past, her tradition and her masculine mode of life received a deadly blow from the sudden wealth thrust upon her.

M. J. Benardete. NR. March 20, 1935, p. 166

The novel *Raucho* marks the beginning [of Güiraldes'] mastery. . . . It is the story of childhood and youth; years at school and on the ranch; the awakening of the passions and of desire. We move from the plains to the city and sense the pull of Paris, which one day carries the boy, as if in a whirlwind, away from Buenos Aires. . . . In Paris he experiences love and Bohemia, and then returns to the ranch, where we leave him asleep "on his back, his arms open, crucified calmly on the land that was always his." We lose him from sight when his "sentimental education" has been completed, when he is about to start his real life as a man. This seems like a book that should have its continuation and complement in another. . . .

[Güiraldes] was never to aspire, nor have reason to, to distillations of style that would give his sentences what we would call correctness, a pure sound. His desire is to give expression to humanity, to the feelings of the time—that other land of ours, without frontiers or traditions. . . .

The narrator of *Xaimaca*, as of *Raucho*, is named Galván, and in the dedication to *Don Segundo Sombra* . . . we find the names of a Galván as well as those of other characters who appeared in *Raucho*. How can we decide to what extent there is autobiography and free creation in his various narratives? Fortunately, it really does not matter. One should not seek a personal key in them. Conversely, even if his books were purely objective and had no connection to events and episodes he experienced, they would still constitute the most vivid part of the biography of their author.

Enrique Diez-Canedo. Letras de América (Mexico City,
El Colegio de México, 1944), pp. 338–39†

The two main characters [of *Don Segundo Sombra*], like the tale itself, are a bit romantic. Somewhat shadowy, as befits his name, Don Segundo Sombra, who possesses so many virtues—courage, endurance, moral and physical strength, leadership, the art of entertaining in various ways, and unusual skill in the work in which he made his living— and none of the vices which afflict humanity, is an idealized rather than a real character. We know him only through a source that is prejudiced in his favor, his protégé, who tells us what he is and what he does. The boy is also idealized, but he is less of one cloth than Don Segundo. Skilled, first of all, in everything that pertains to life on the plains, finally a cultivated man with a love for reading, he stands as an exemplar of Güiraldes's own ideal of a man. Of him there is, too, a side that we never see of Don Segundo, and that is his inner world, his thoughts and reflections on life, which in his rôle of autobiographer he constantly reveals.

The very effective portrayal of the background for these Argentine characters has contributed probably more than any other feature to winning for the book the high praise that has generally been accorded it. When Don Segundo's ward takes stock of himself at the end of five years, he enumerates a long list of towns and ranches, all of the province of Buenos Aires, which had seen them pass many times, "covered with dirt and mud, behind a herd of cattle." Of the appearance of this region, with the exception of the dunes and crab-infested bogs of the seacoast, there is in the book practically no description. Certain phenomena of nature, on the other hand, particularly in reference to their effect on the teller of the tale, are frequently commented upon: the cold; the heat of the summer's sun; the rain, as he is driving a herd of cattle; or the night, as he is sitting with others by the campfire.

The part of the setting, however, that is really striking is the varied panorama of rural and small-town life in the province of Buenos Aires. While there is some detailed description of places, the salient characteristic in nearly all of the various scenes is the human element, which imparts, through its lively natural vernacular, a decidedly animated tone—whether it be the coarse joking in the tavern where we first see the hero of the tale; or the bantering of the cowboy at the ranch where he obtained his first job; or the raillery of the "tape" Burgos when he tried to pick a quarrel with Don Segundo; or the love-making between Paula and our hero, when he was recuperating at the ranch. . . .

Güiraldes, however, with all of his excellent qualities as a writer —now that we have come to a final evaluation of him—is not the truly great novelist that some enthusiastic critics would have us believe. His novels, after all, are limited in scope, rather one-sided. For, while his style is poetic, while his sharp-toned pictures of certain strata of Argentine society remain with one long after his books are read, he is sadly lacking in two essentials of a great novelist: he gives no evidence of ability to develop character or to weave a plot that is much beyond that of the picaresque novel.

In spite of these shortcomings, *Don Segundo Sombra* has entered the ranks of international literature in both German and English translations and has received high praise from other than Argentine and Spanish critics.

Jefferson Rea Spell. *Contemporary Spanish-American Fiction* (Chapel Hill, University of North Carolina Press, 1944), pp. 202–4

The subject-matter and theme of [*Don Segundo Sombra*] reveal clearly that Güiraldes knew intimately and loved intensely the free, nomadic life of the gaucho and that his years spent on the family's *estancia* [ranch] of *La Porteña* were never eclipsed by his prolonged stays in Buenos Aires, his sojourns in Paris, or his travels throughout Europe and the Orient. . . .

Moreover, though he counted among his friends various contemporary French authors of note, and was himself recognized in Buenos Aires as a leader among the post-modernist writers, he retained throughout his career a close contact with *criollo* [that is, Argentine] literature. It was by fusing the techniques of the new school with native Argentine sources that he succeeded in creating the work that gave permanent literary stature to the gaucho. The "strange dual nature" of the book derives precisely from this combination of cultivated literary style on the one hand, and portrayal of primitive types and settings on the other. . . .

Güiraldes was true to the gaucho tradition in his treatment of imagery as manifested in allegory, proverbs, and other popular forms of expression. He was able to interpret the spirit and life of the pampas with sympathy and authority, not only because he knew them well, but also because he was a trained and gifted artist. The great difference between the primitive theme of the novel and the cultivated literary style of the author is in most cases skillfully reconciled by the running imagery, sometimes symbolically emphasizing or interpreting certain aspects of the thought or theme, sometimes adding atmosphere and reality to the scene. Moreover, it is chiefly by the use of imagery that Güiraldes transformed the prosaic everyday life of the gaucho into an artistic narrative possessing rare poetic and aesthetic qualities.

Eunice Joiner Gates. HR. 16, Jan., 1948, pp. 33–34, 49

Ricardo Güiraldes' *Don Segundo Sombra* is considered the masterpiece of the gauchesque novel and Don Segundo himself the perfect type of the gaucho, the last and most complete representative of a vanished class. . . . The book opens with this revelation of the sacramental presence of the gaucho in contemporary Argentina. This gaucho is the gaucho martyr, emblematical of the past. He is the symbol and the nostalgia of bygone days of freedom and simplicity. Consequently, the book has been read for the mysterious personality of Don Segundo, who has become already a mythical figure in Argentina.

Yet it is possible to read the book from another point of view and to center our attention on the narrator himself, the *guacho* Fabio Cáceres. If Don Segundo is the symbol and the nostalgia of the past, Fabio, his adopted son, is a representative of the present, the new twentieth-century Argentina burdened with a history. . . .

The education of Fabio Cáceres undoubtedly parallels the spiritual development of the author. What happens to him in the seven years of his wanderings parallels also the development of the Argentine nation. It is the education of an adolescent world begotten without love and abandoned without remorse.

Fabio, as a young boy, felt he was not wanted: his aunts did not accept his lusty boyhood and civilized townfolk mocked his irreverence. He was at the crossroads of life: fourteen years old and ready for heroism or crime. At this moment the appearance of Don Segundo starts a chain of events that will in the end bring about Fabio's maturity and his acceptance of the world inside and outside him. In Don Segundo Fabio finds his long-lost father, and it is only when he can call him father that the boy knows for the first time the truth about himself. . . .

Fabio's education takes him through all the experiences of a young cowhand on the pampas. He learns to break a horse, to deal with women and to check himself. He enumerates to himself, after five years of hardships, all the practical things he has learned from Don Segundo and then adds the realization of what they meant in moral growth. . . . Towards the end of the book, the young man thinks he has already learned all the lessons and his education is at an end. Fabio Cáceres thinks he has found his America in the way of life he has chosen and which he wants to lead forever. His pride and assuredness is yet to be tested. He must learn to accept and not to choose his place in the world. . . .

Bernardo Gicovate. Hispania. 34, Aug., 1951, pp. 366–67

Güiraldes was interested in cosmic Truth, but even at the height of his striving for a spiritual personality capable of attaining such knowledge by the direct intuitive process, he retained his concern for his concreteness and individuality, for his human experience. As he could not dispense with the concrete, the material, he sought to reduce both matter and spirit to a primary substance that would establish the identity of the two, but never succeeded in resolving the duality. In his eagerness for unity, Güiraldes attempted to find the materiality of spirit. He looked towards science hopefully, but science could not help him. He nevertheless appears to have felt that such discovery was possible. This seeming belief in the inevitability of matter was not merely a return to joy in matter for its own sake; it was the product of a rationality that longed to find unity in the universe. The rational activity in Güiraldes that sought to find the materiality of spirit was complemented by an opposite activity, that of piercing the barrier of matter through introversion, through delving into the subconscious. However, this movement in opposite directions, this attempt to reduce spirit to matter, and matter to spirit, was, in fact, but a single effort to find unity. . . .

In his efforts to regain on a cosmic plane the wholeness which he had lost in his terrestrial life, Güiraldes found himself following several paths, all leading to the same highway. Love, God, and death led to the unity which he sought, and for Güiraldes they became problems of deepest interest.

G. H. Weiss. *Sym.* 10, Fall, 1956, pp. 236–37

Don Segundo Sombra, the hero of the novel by the same name, is generally held up as a paragon of manliness and the symbol of the true gaucho; yet the more one analyzes the book, the less he seems to fill the role of this ideal man, but moves off into some other realm which results in a mere stylized portrayal.

Ricardo Güiraldes refined the Latin American novel, for he was a stylist at heart. This shows up in his sensitive writing about simple folk and his use of gaucho speech in a manner which does not strike the ear as vulgar, but imparts a distinctly Argentine and highly poetic flavor to the book. This rich and powerful prose reflects the rural speech of those limitless pampas where the spirit of José Hernández lingers under an aloof and star-studded sky. . . .

Anyone has the privilege of setting up his own ideal of manhood, but we should remember that our heritage has been amassed just as much in Athens as in Rome or among the Bedouins; Don Segundo could have been a Faustian figure striving towards higher values, and creating instead of escaping reality, but a symbol can but reflect its inventor. Don Segundo cannot be called a gentleman in the sense that he possessed refinement and knew the correct thing to say, no matter how often the author puts the telling word in his mouth. He may appear outstanding among stereotyped gauchos, but he is like no cowhand that ever lived.

T. B. Irving. *Hispania.* 40, March, 1957, p. 44

Violence is the dominant tone in [Güiraldes's] stories. Güiraldes's words show that he tried to have the voice of the narrator . . . be one with the spirit of the story. This is achieved in almost all the stories. . . . Güiraldes's stories . . . [are like] dramatic spectacles. He understood that this mode permitted him the greatest schematization and that the climate of the stories could be achieved by the action itself or by only a few telling details of the settings. Thus, some of his stories, not surprisingly, approximate little theatrical pieces, which resemble considerably the tragic *sainetes* of Pacheco and Sánchez. The constant use of dialogue makes these stories close to some of Benito Lynch's, which are also resolved with the greatest economy of means. . . .

On the basis of Güiraldes's own suggestion . . . we can group the stories both by subject matter and by circumstances of publications. Thus, we have: (1) stories of life on the Pampas—those in *Stories of Death and Blood* through "Antithesis," four in *Rosaura*, and the two interwoven into *Don Segundo Sombra*; (2) stories on city life—the group of "Grotesque Adventures" in *Stories of Death and Blood* and two later ones, "Telésforo Altamira" and "Colegio"; (3) the spiritual stories—those with . . . the title "Triptych." The stories of the first group are immersed in a strongly localized setting. . . . The second group, for the same reasons of atmosphere—in this case the city—move toward a greater psychological complexity. . . . The third group are more universal and penetrate the meaning of religious feeling. "The Judgment of God" is an open attempt at caricature. The religious element is grave and decisive in the other two stories of "Triptych." They are of particular interest in following the development of Güiraldes's mysticism from adolescence to maturity. . . .

Guillermo Ara. USF. No. 43, Jan.–March, 1960,
pp. 47–49†

Beginning with *The Crystal Cowbell* and ending with *Don Segundo Sombra*, the influence of French writers [on Güiraldes] is apparent. It is in no sense an imitation of style. Indeed, apart from the use of their poetic techniques, the style in *Don Segundo Sombra* is entirely distinct, as can be observed alone from the nearly complete absence of elliptic language and obscure imagery. The explanation lies in Güiraldes' guiding principle that the form of the expression must correspond to the significance of the subject matter. As his intent was to represent the poetic, he availed himself of the devices which best suited his purpose. Among them are those which have no connection with the symbolists. The total contribution of all the poetic techniques has given the style in *Don Segundo Sombra* the quality of a poem in prose.

Within the poetic treatment is the rustic element provided by the vernacular speech of the characters. It introduces the flavor of the gauchesque that characterizes *Stories of Death and Blood*. The expression of the countryfolk, because it is unliterary, emphasizes by contrast the polished expression of the narrator. Nevertheless, it contains stylistically significant features. These are its well-known colorful imagery and the simple form in which it is expressed. Güiraldes exploited their artistic value to advantage when he transferred them to his own narrative style. By combining rustic images with poetic techniques he poetized the vernacular. Furthermore, by casting artistic images into simple forms, he qualified his literary style with the picturesqueness and natural charm of the language of the Gaucho.

With the sensitivity of a poet, Güiraldes sought beauty everywhere, particularly in the objects of his affection. Viewing the Pampa in this light, he interpreted its emotional and aesthetic aspects as he saw them. Indeed, he represented it in three different ways. It will be recalled that these are the sensory experiences of Fabio, his emotional sensations, and the pictorial descriptions. The reality of the environment rises from the first, the intangible presence of nature from the second, and its aesthetic appearance from the third. Each is but a mere glimpse of a different aspect and is conveyed in a few words or a brief line. Güiraldes has combined all three impressions to describe a single experience. Thus with the skill of an impressionist painter he captured the essence of the moment and communicated the spell of the Pampa.

Giovanni Previtali. *Ricardo Güiraldes and Don Segundo Sombra: Life and Works* (New York, Hispanic Institute in the United States, 1963), pp. 197–98

This "autobiography of a diminished ego"—another of the titles that Güiraldes planned for his novel [*Raucho*]—traces, with more fidelity than is usually admitted, the outlines of Güiraldes's own experiences during his childhood and his early youth. The rescue of that tireless waste—Güiraldes's first visit to Paris—seemed to be, in his eyes, the aesthetic transfiguration that he attempted in *Raucho*. Still indecisive in its style, which vacillates between the intimacy of the private chronicle and the aestheticizing attempt to make poems in prose out of a few everyday experiences, *Raucho* recalls, against the idyllic background of a childhood in Buenos Aires, the adventures of an Argentine in Paris.

The first chapters trace life on a ranch. . . . Some of the themes and characters of *Stories of Death and Blood* are taken up again, but there is also a prefiguration of those in *Don Segundo Sombra*. Therefore, these chapters permit one to observe both Güiraldes's development as a writer and the strong unity, despite apparent marginal distractions, that binds his work. The key element of this unity is, without a doubt, the vision of a dazzling nature before which all overly elaborate cultural riches lose their value. *Raucho* provides us with a preliminary sketch that *Don Segundo Sombra* was to finish admirably, one in which the destiny of man is intertwined, indissolubly, with the cyclical succession of the seasons: works and days. . . .

Ivonne Bordelois. *Genio y figura de Ricardo Güiraldes* (Buenos Aires, Editorial de la Universidad de Buenos Aires, 1966), p. 64†

[In *Don Segundo Sombra*] Güiraldes chose an adolescent to express a vision of life as ritual reencounter under the protective gaze of various "good fathers" and some rather uncompetitive "brothers." Reasons for Güiraldes's choice should not be sought in a state of mind prior to the writing of the book. . . . The "narrator" of *Don Segundo Sombra* is both more and less than the "novelist" Ricardo Güiraldes. This "narrator" presents a young boy who, after a "period of latency" (Freud), enters that difficult period of human development in which there arise again the conflicting feelings toward the father rooted in earliest infancy. In the early stages of life, fantasies, especially destructive ones, play an important role, and they later engender feelings of guilt and the necessity to make amends. Güiraldes writes from the viewpoint of Fabio [his adolescent protagonist] to the extent that the urgency of the adolescent to make amends . . . influences the style and plot of the novel. . . .

The novel also reveals an exaggerated process of reparation toward the paternal figure through the different characters who play a protective role in Fabio's destiny. This creation of "good fathers" seems a way of quieting the residue of distant aggressive forces (Melanie Klein). Moreover, Fabio provides himself with a father who accords with his aspirations, a resilient master worthy of admiration ("I felt once again that strength of my godfather") in order to be effective in fighting against hatred, anxiety, and guilt.

Eduardo Romano. *Análisis de "Don Segundo Sombra"*
(Buenos Aires, Centro Editor de América Latina,
1967), pp. 40–41†

The poorness of the judgments passed on Güiraldes is astounding. Much has been written about him and his work. There has been little, very little, on who the writer was and what was the true message that he left behind. . . .

I do not believe that anyone has studied Güiraldes as a kind of spiritual centaur, half cosmopolitan man and half creole from the Pampa. The fact is that this Latin American writer first learned French and then German. And only later did he strive to master Spanish. And there are those who claim that he never managed to master it. . . . Manuel Gálvez tells us that Güiraldes, after publishing *Don Segundo Sombra*, took lessons in Spanish grammar in Paris.

Hugo Rodríguez Alcalá. *CA*. No. 151, March–April,
1967, pp. 224–25†

An impressive exercise in creating a new entity from borrowed material, Güiraldes' "Salome" is certainly steeped in the influence of Laforgue, owes a good deal to Flaubert, and is probably directly indebted to the Bible and indirectly to other versions. But he has succeeded in adapting the structure and technique to his own design.

It is a short story written in poetic prose, and it has the structure of a short story. Where Güiraldes differs from most sources is in concentrating entirely upon Salome: her dance, the desire of Antipas, her request, and her fate. . . .

The story is constructed on surprise and antithesis. After the enchantment suggested by the description of Salome's dancing and Antipas' desire, a moment of anticlimax occurs when the girl speaks gratingly and reveals a hard and untempting nature. Güiraldes reveals ingenuity in depicting her as a coquette who pouts and taps her heel while impatiently but confidently awaiting the reply to her demand. The second and major surprise closes the story. This time, instead of a descent from the dream-like to the vulgar and commonplace, as in the first instance, the surprise is a sudden leap into the realm of dream and the supernatural. Laforgue's ending undoubtedly inspired this one, but there is a significant difference determined by both the structure and the intention of Güiraldes' story. . . . Güiraldes seems to have noted [Laforgue's] description of the head [as a "phosphorescent star"] and made use of it to produce a novel solution. He reverses the direction of both Salome's movement and the surprise. While she ascends from earth upwards to death among the stars the narrative reverts from reality to magic.

The dwelling upon such a potentially morbid topic, characteristic of "decadent" literature, means that Salome becomes—to use the words of Frank Kermode—"a symbol of the pathological aspect of decadence." Güiraldes was certainly attracted to this aspect of the theme, and to Laforgue's manner of reacting through irony. But the difference would seem to be that Güiraldes remained at a distance, imitating a literary manner and exercising his own skill. The skill is undeniable and the experiments impressive, but the passage suffers a little from having the appearance of an exercise.

P. R. Beardsell. *BHS.* 46, Oct., 1969, pp. 336–37

In spite of his professed ideal of simplicity, Güiraldes also supported the validity of esoteric art. From the outset he had adamantly expressed the policy of writing according to his own beliefs, irrespective of the public's reactions ("Notes" p. 721). If the public of Buenos Aires found some of his work esoteric (for example an obscure use of imagery in *The Crystal Cowbell*) then they must make the effort required of them to understand it. The artist was not to find his means of expression limited by any criterion of acceptability in terms of public comprehension. The role of the Symbolists is important in this context. Güiraldes regarded them as the initiators of the trend towards esoteric art. . . . Finally, although he sometimes felt the superior value of a simple prose style, he could also seek more subtle effects (as did the Symbolists) by exploiting the musical quality of language and by attempting to transfer devices from music to poetry. . . .

The most convincing interpretation of this dichotomy in Güiraldes's aesthetic principles is to see his instinctive attitude to art sometimes conflicting radically with the view of writers whom he admired. Possessing a strong sense of national responsibility as a writer of the New World, and wishing to give literary expression to the realities of the regional scene, he appears to have been aware of the dangers inherent in excessive attention to style and to have considered that the ideas and content of a work were ultimately of greater value. Yet, perhaps in spite of himself, he was also attracted to that concept of art which makes a cult of beauty; style and form consequently became an end in themselves, irrespective of the subject matter for which they were vehicles. This latter aspect links him, partly through modernism, with European (and especially French) literature.

Complete contradiction, however, is relatively rare in his principles. . . . His earliest emphasis was upon his mission as a writer of Argentina. For a temporary period he partially yielded to the temptations of aestheticism. Then followed a spiritual transition. . . . The change reflected in *The Path* appears to have affected his attitude not only to his life but to his work. He now gave increasing attention to the idea of art as the expression of his personal world. In this fundamental aspect of his thought the two extremes have a logical connexion: the *pampa*, the *gaucho* and Argentina formed a vital part of that world; but so too did his fondness for beauty of form. His inability to relinquish completely the ideals of an aesthete involved him in the attempt to reconcile the two divergent ambitions in *Don Segundo Sombra*. While his attention to style has doubtless contributed to the novel's success, recent criticism recognizes that a division exists, nevertheless, between theme and style. . . .

Güiraldes's case is perhaps an acute one; but it illustrates a fairly general tendency of the early 1900s, not only in Argentina but throughout Latin America. Although they felt that Latin American realities should be allowed to find their own form of expression, many writers found it difficult to eradicate a subservience to the aesthetic standards of Europe. The result, as with *Don Segundo Sombra*, was often a less than satisfactory blending of theme and style.

P. R. Beardsell. MLR. 66, April, 1971, pp. 326–27

HENRÍQUEZ UREÑA, PEDRO (1884-1946)

DOMINICAN REPUBLIC

The theme of *Literary Currents in Hispanic America* is the unity of America—not a gray or inert unity, but one intensely blended. Henríquez Ureña first presents the differences between Europe and English-speaking America, then the differences between all that is Portuguese and Spanish in America; and within the Spanish realm, the personality of each province. His observations on aesthetic currents are no empty abstractions. Henríquez Ureña treats the complicated and contradictory features of each aesthetic period, shows two romantic generations, two modernist generations, characterizes the tendencies and works of each writer. His taste—highly cultivated and of an exceptional breadth—permits him to sympathize with generally scorned poetic forms, as when he affirms the value of Góngora in America or, in reference to Bello, when he laments that we have abandoned that fecund road of poetry inspired by science. The literary aspect appears in the foreground, but it is not treated in isolation from other aspects of American life; therefore, when Henríquez Ureña evaluates artistic ideals, he ably evokes the social climate. . . . References to music, the plastic arts, philosophy, and science also contribute to the admirable equilibrium of his study.

Enrique Anderson Imbert. *Sur*. No. 141, July, 1946, p. 44†

Henríquez Ureña's "Discontent and Promise" does not exactly present a new doctrine concerning the problem of literary Americanism, since his position is fundamentally the same as Andrés Bello's, Rodó's and that of earlier eminent essayists possessed of a lucid and balanced philosophy. In short, Henríquez Ureña stresses the unity of both elements, that is, of the formal, derived from history, from world culture, and the substantial original [native element]. . . . But Henríquez Ureña brings to literary criticism—in general a genre very neglected in all of Latin America because of the absence of intellectual discipline—a

436

generic norm, a methodology, a technique, which he most clearly expresses in the second of his *Six Essays in Search of Our Literary Expression.* . . .

The published works of Henríquez Ureña are not numerous. [Most of his work] is scattered in journals and newspapers throughout the Spanish-speaking world, and some in the United States; all should . . . be collected in a handy volume (since he never wrote anything superficial). . . .

Both [*Literary Currents in Hispanic America* and *History of Culture in Hispanic America*], fruits of a great maturity in judgment and mastery of his material, show the strengths and defects inherent in the excessive schematicism of their structure. Their virtue lies in the clear vision of the totality of history: his precise discernment of [cultural] evolution and the way he pinpoints the characteristics of each period, his exact judgment of what is most representative of each period, which he sometimes points out in a single sentence. Their defect . . . inevitably comes from their own space limitation, for he is obliged to give a resume in the only 200 pages [of each book] of the vast and complex cultural development of Latin America from the colonial period through the present. . . .

Alberto Zum Felde. *Índice crítico de la literatura hispanoamericana* (Mexico City, Editorial Guarania, 1954–59), Vol. I, pp. 547–48†

I have stated previously that Henríquez Ureña brings together and tests most of the theories—the "formulas," as he called them—on Americanism. The first formula is nature. Nothing is left out: mountains, plains, the torrid lands of the tropics, the forests, the sea, the Pampa, the desert. Curiously, some other critics—and not only Europeans—see the typical American landscape as only a tropical one . . . forgetting about the striking variety and color of the other parts of America.

The second formula is the Indian, not only the "clever and modest Indian" and the "noble savage" that the Renaissance world adopted as a literary character, but also the red Indian of the great pre-Columbian empires and the one who survives to this day. Another formula is the Creole, whose profile differs from region to region—the rival of the Indian on the Pampa, in Mexico, in Central America, on the Pacific Coast. . . .

Each of these "formulas" will provide, "at the right moments, the vivid expression that we are seeking. At the right moments, let us remind ourselves of it" [Henríquez Ureña]. Henríquez Ureña did not overlook the Europeanizers, or Spanishifiers, who, with their eyes fixed on the Old World, denied all originality to America. They were right in part, but only in part. Fortunately, the cultural ties that bind us with Spain, with the Latin world, are not and cannot be an obstacle to originality: "The original character of people comes from their spiritual depths, from their native energy, a sap extracted from the very earth." . . .

Emilio Carilla. *Pedro Henríquez Ureña (tres estudios)*
(Tucumán, Argentina, Universidad Nacional de
Tucumán, 1956?), pp. 51–52†

Culture, in any given moment of history, has both transitory and permanent values. The former . . . characterize epochs and establish the conditions of a period; the latter concern the eternity of man and his creations. Pedro Henríquez Ureña had the special capacity to distinguish one from the other and to find the sure indications of the most important moments of past culture. Particularly in the immediate past and in the culture of the period in which he was growing up, he always was able to distinguish what was dying from what was generating new dynamics for the future. Therefore, he was . . . a spectator who was always concerned with the crossroads at which we are still living: the nineteenth century, which surrendered part of its heart and soul to the ideal of reason, to experimentalism in science, to the abstraction of generalized laws, and to the worship of technology; and the twentieth century, which fights to find a new meaning of the spirit in order to restore man to his full humanity. . . .

Alfredo Roggiano. *RI.* 21, July–Dec., 1956, pp. 190–91†

Pedro Henríquez Ureña has, in his *Six Essays in Search of Our Literary Expression*, investigated the specific question of whether original cultural contributions are even possible in Hispanic America. The fact that a common history has been shared with Europe does not preordain the failure of the New World's attempts at original expression. He feels that the Old World's tradition determines to a great extent the "forms" of American culture, but that "the unique character of a people comes from its spiritual depths, from its native energy." The method by which original and authentic expression may be attained is one of deep probing involving considerable effort: " . . . there is but one secret here: work at it deeply, make every effort to obtain pure expression by descending to the very roots of the things we wish to say, to refine, to clarify. . . ." As in the case of many contemporary Spanish American essayists, Henríquez Ureña maintains that the writer or artist of the New World should, if he truly desires to attain authentic cultural achievements, embark upon a profound search of his own "spiritual depths." He does not carry this view further, as others will do. He does not, for example, suggest that this kind of intensive analysis of the self yields not only authenticity and genuineness, but that it is, in effect, the only possible method for grasping reality.

In his later writings Henríquez Ureña has distinguished himself as a literary and cultural historian of great breadth. His work as a teacher of Hispanic literature in some of the hemisphere's greatest universities—including our own Harvard—encouraged him to write two invaluable works, *Literary Currents in Hispanic America* and the posthumously published *History of Culture in Hispanic America.* Although it is probably true that Henríquez Ureña's major contributions as an original thinker date from his very early association with the Mexican writers of the *Ateneo*, rather than from this later period of activity, his role as a highly skilled synthesizer and as a devoted Americanist cannot be overstated. . . .

Martin S. Stabb. *In Quest of Identity* (Chapel Hill,
University of North Carolina Press, 1967), pp. 86–87

Pedro Henríquez Ureña grew up in a highly cultivated, literary household in the Dominican Republic. He and his equally gifted brother Max, sons of the writer and teacher Salomé Ureña de Henríquez, received a thorough education in the humanities. These studies were an excellent preparation for Pedro's valuable—indeed, trailblazing—literary activities, first in Cuba, later in Argentina, where he was a professor for twenty years. During a stay at the University of Mexico he was associated with the leading literary circle, centered around Alfonso Reyes and José Vasconcelos.

In his many essays and articles Henríquez Ureña tried to elucidate the relationship between literature and culture in Latin America. He began his investigation with *Hours of Study*, a collection of essays on Eugenio de Hostos, Rubén Darío, and the Spaniard José María Gabriel y Galán, and he continued along similar lines with *Six Essays in Search of Our Literary Expression* and other works. . . . *History of Culture in Hispanic America* was a pioneering overview of general cultural development in Latin America. . . .

Henríquez Ureña's work is distinguished by its preciseness and objectivity, qualities that could be found only rarely among Latin American thinkers before him. His style is concise, and he covers his subjects so ably that there is no need for further interpretation. According to Henríquez Ureña, the quest for an ideal combining reason and beauty motivated people to come to the New World; his own writing may be seen as a fulfillment of this quest.

Rudolf Grossmann. *Geschichte und Probleme der
lateinamerikanischen Literatur* (Munich, Max Hueber
Verlag, 1969), p. 514†

HERRERA Y REISSIG, JULIO (1875–1910)

URUGUAY

Herrera y Reissig's interest in Poe sought expression not only in the general atmosphere of all his poetry but also in very specific characteristics that reveal the direct influence of Poe's special manner and of certain of his most imaginative poems. . . . The physical minuteness of Herrera y Reissig's world, misanthropy, and his extreme sensibility to the spiritual are expressed in his line, "Live a perpetual dream! Here is the sublimest reality." Poe dedicated "Eureka" "to the dreamers and those who put faith in dreams as in the only realities." . . .

The Uruguayan poet is more particularly a disciple of Poe in his principles as to the evocative power of words, in his cult of the creative symbolism of poetry, and in his doctrine that the sole exigency of art should be its power to enslave, to thrill, to move to any extreme the most opposed sensibilities of its followers. At times Herrera y Reissig has emphasized the first two above characteristics beyond the artistic limits set by Poe. The latter foresaw the extremes in which much of French Symbolism became utterly incomprehensible and lost all contact with true poetry, when he wrote: "It is the excess of the suggested meaning—it is the rendering this the upper instead of the under-current of the theme—which turns (poetry) into prose." Herrera y Reissig, too, could very well have heeded Poe's warning.

Throughout Herrera y Reissig's poetry we meet the Poe of "Ulalume." Poe is the bard of that dim, distant land of shadows and of mists. His province is the realm of Night: Night with its mysterious murmurs and suggestive forms; Night in which all manner of deviltry, of horrible and gruesome deeds abounds; Night with all its blackness of the wings of the ominous raven. In *Wagnerians* Herrera y Reissig identifies himself with this nocturnal Poe: "Like Poe I love black." Now and then, however, Night reflects a softer hue much more in harmony with the serene elegy of Poe's "The Sleeper."

John Eugene Englekirk. <i>Edgar Allan Poe in Hispanic
Literature</i> (New York, Instituto de las Españas en los
Estados Unidos, 1934), pp. 323–25

In the last poems of Herrera y Reissig's career we sense a new direction, perhaps the result of dissatisfaction with the limitations of the private myth. This dissatisfaction is characteristic of late developments in Symbolism. The contradictory necessity for an understanding public drove the Symbolist poets, paradoxically, to attempts at reintegrating the historical myths of the race. They tried to create a new vision by associating the mythologies of the past with the life of the present.

Herrera y Reissig must have felt that his own art was becoming less communicable. His cold reception by the reading public must have warned him that he was entering the region of absolute hermeticism and that "something taken up and constructed from a tradition will be accessible to others enjoying that tradition; with the corollary that an incommunicable utterance is a bad utterance and not worth troubling about" [A. G. Lehmann in *The Symbolist Aesthetic in France*]. The conflict between expression and communication is apparent in Herrera y Reissig's attempts at self-exegesis: extensive footnoting in "Life" (written before 1904), explanatory subtitles in his collections, and epigraphs to separate poems.

As a result of this conflict, Herrera y Reissig finally turned to myths sanctioned by community traditions. "The Shepherd's Death" is centered in the symbol of the cart, still of the nature of the private myth. The fact that the cart is to come no longer is repeatedly referred to as the sign of the shepherd's death. But at the end of the poem the cart appears as a ghost cart in the imaginations of the inhabitants of the rural community, in this way providing a communal belief for a private myth.

Herrera y Reissig's most important attempts at communicability are, paradoxically, in works that have been considered least intelligible: "The Tower of Sphinxes" and *The Clepsydras*. In the first, a poem that has been a source of scandal in the criticism of his work, Oedipus is the central unifying character, equivalent to Mallarmé's "Le maître" in *Un coup de dés*, a poem Herrera y Reissig did not know. Besides this Classical myth, the poem resorts to parallel literary and legendary allusions to express the emotion of guilt. In *The Clepsydras*, Herrera y Reissig "summoned myths from widely separated periods and places to find in them a common element" [Warren Ramsey in an article on Pound and Laforgue]. This telescoping of myths in order to create a new reality developed from the Symbolists. It was a major preoccupation in the writings of Herrera y Reissig, although he seldom succeeded in organizing his fragments into a whole.

Bernard Gicovate. Julio Herrera y Reissig and the Symbolists (Berkeley, University of California Press, 1957), pp. 53–54

The desire for evasion leaps vehemently from the poetry of Julio Herrera y Reissig, whether in concrete references to an impossible escape in time and space, literally embodied in delirious visions of exotic landscapes, or implicitly in the deliberately strange form of his work. This escape motif did not arise only from a desire to startle the apathetic middle-class society of Montevideo at the beginning of the century. More importantly, what made the poet's expression disconcerting, full of surprises and consciously sought-after strangenesses, was an internal spiritual command: to flee from anything noninstinctive, conventional, or consecrated. He fled from the commonplace, from whatever was fixed by adopted and worn formulas. He preferred originality. . . . He was only a step away from what the critics were to call baroque. And he took this step very early.

The baroqueness of his poetry cannot be described as pure learned play, the product of a sensitivity and of an exuberance that were only interested in expression. The baroqueness was a consequence of a permanent disquietude, of a spirit tormented from birth. The giantism and contorted aspect of the figures that move in his lyrics are all nourished by the same impassioned fervor that agitated their creator. This is a poetry of effort, of a volcanic effort, as Cansinos-Assens has said, one that, if freed, could become uncontrollable. . . .

Hélcio Martins. RdL. No. 12, Dec., 1958, p. 161†

Like the majority of the Modernist poets in Spanish America, Julio Herrera y Reissig of Uruguay was enchanted with the exotic. Among the most important exotic elements found in Modernist poetry is classical mythology, which plays a prominent role in Herrera y Reissig's work and is treated by him in a highly distinctive fashion. From which authors he derived his mythological knowledge is difficult to ascertain with complete certainty: he knew little or nothing of Greek and Latin, but he read widely in French and Spanish literature, rich stockpiles of classical lore, and was influenced as well by the mythological poems of Rubén Darío. Along with the other Modernist poets, Herrera y Reissig turned zealously to mythology for inspiration in order to lose himself in a world suffused with beauty, splendor and opulence, far removed from humdrum actualities. To a greater degree than most of the other Modernists, he dwelt in the poet's ivory tower, wrapped up in the clouds of his subjective world and nourished by the images suggested from his readings. He shunned facile expressions and sought out the subtle, the bizarre and the glittering phrase in which to convey his thought, using mythology with more originality than most of his contemporaries in Spanish America. It is true that routine mythological allusions do occur in his work . . . but do not to the extent that they appear in the bulk of Modernist poetry. Reading Herrera y Reissig's poems, one is soon caught up and spun about in dazzling cascades of imagery, many of which refer to mythology.

Rubén Darío, the outstanding figure of the Modernist movement, devotes a considerable number of poems to specific mythological themes as well as employing mythology in a conventional decorative way. Herrera y Reissig has fewer poems given over entirely to a mythological theme. He usually weaves allusions to mythology into the fabric of his poems with little organization and unity. . . . Mythology for Herrera y Reissig is a coffer filled with treasures into which he dips at will, fashioning what he finds there into his own peculiar creations. He experiments with it just as he experiments with words. Its voluptuousness furnishes him with an abundant supply of sensory images to which he is greatly addicted, and its rich and luxuriant details provide him with opportunities for conceits and pictorial ornaments. Because of Herrera y Reissig's originality, mythology comes alive in his poetry.

George D. Schade. Hispania. 42, March, 1959, pp. 46, 48

Julio Herrera y Reissig is known as a symbolist, and various influences have been studied in attempting to ascertain the meanings and significances of certain symbols in his works. One of the most striking symbolistic techniques used by Herrera y Reissig . . . is synesthesia, the creation of one sensory impression by the use of others. Herrera y Reissig's use of synesthesia is related to, if not the same thing as, his use of religious terminology, which is encountered in his search for good and evil and his understanding of love. It should be pointed out that he uses religious symbols in the expression of profane love, but this usage is more than casual because of the depth of his Catholic heritage.

Raymond Souza. RomN. 1, 2, Spring, 1960, p. 97

Herrera y Reissig's poetry, quantitatively small, is a response, as is the case with all works of art, to factors both internal and external. The first are tied to his creative spirit and to the necessity to give a message to humanity, the validating testimony of the artist. But this testimony is also a response to external conditions, determined by surrounding reality. When Herrera y Reissig began his poetic career, American romanticism, although moribund, was still wreaking serious havoc among the most cultivated readers of the continent. The young writers—Martí, Guitiérrez Nájera, Julián del Casal, Salvador Díaz Mirón, and José Asunción Silva—who were initiators of a new sensibility, were known only to a small circle of readers. American publications at that time were overflowing with romantic poetry, bad imitations of European models. . . .

It has been said with some accuracy that modernism was a liberating, enthusiastic movement toward beauty. . . . The unchecked enthusiasm for aestheticism—the search for ideal beauty—was, however, a phase only of the youthful years of the most representative writers of the movement. Between twenty and thirty-five they were given over to it; this was true of Rubén Darío, Leopoldo Lugones, Ricardo Jaimes Freyre, Horacio Quiroga, and Herrera y Reissig. Only those who continued beyond this age achieved other forms. . . . Herrera y Reissig, who died young, did not evolve toward other, less exotic modalities. Despite this, one notes in his poetry several different attitudes, with a marked tendency toward hermeticism. But to seek in his work the expression of things that are not purely aesthetic turns out to be a somewhat futile undertaking. With the exception of "Life," a philosophical poem in which he shows metaphysical preoccupations, his poetry is exclusively a response to the aesthetic modality. . . .

Modernism has frequently been accused of deliberately overlooking certain essential moral themes and of ignoring social problems. Truth was not at issue either, since in art, as Antonio Machado said, truth invents itself: these writers created their own truth. Many important mental states—anguish, despair, melancholy, metaphysical shudderings, the search for God—were sidelined during this period, which was exclusively aestheticist. And Herrera y Reissig, because of his premature death, could not evolve toward these concerns [as did most of the modernist poets in middle age]. . . . He can be evaluated only in terms of the modality cultivated: pure aestheticism, the agonizing and tenacious search for the beautiful. . . .

Antonio Seluja. In Homenaje a Julio Herrera y Reissig
(Montevideo, Consejo Departamental de Montevideo,
1963), pp. 52–54†

Herrera y Reissig made the following aesthetic innovations in our literature: (1) the attempt at new rhythmic effects (dislocation or the absence of caesura, adapting to Spanish the revival of the [French] alexandrine . . . introducing the unknown process of alliteration); (2) the use of both rare and rich rhymes, a *précieux* vocabulary . . . [and] neologisms, including onomatopoeias.

What Herrera y Reissig renewed in Uruguayan poetry was not so much its soul, the essence of modernism, the kind of renewal seen in the mature work of Rubén Darío, the fruit of a full life, which the poet of the *eglogánimas* did not have [*eglogánimas* is Herrera y Reissig's neologism based on the Spanish words for eclogue and soul]. Indeed, beyond the specifically literary aspects that attracted Herrera y Reissig to . . . modernism, we are unable to find in the Uruguayan author the profound emotions caused by *different* passions and feelings, which would demand immediate expression. . . .

Herrera y Reissig was, and remains, an elitist poet, and his poetry is alien to the masses. This is principally because Herrera y Reissig steered away from beauty-scenery and because he made interpretation difficult, placing unusual emphasis on linguistic complexity. . . .

Hugo Emilio Pedemonte. *CHA*. No. 181, Jan., 1965,

p. 96†

HUIDOBRO, VICENTE (1893–1948)

CHILE

The two-hundred pages of fulsome prose that make up [*The Hidden Pagodas*] revolve around a theme that is quite overworked among the writers of the "sentimental Bohemia." What we have here is the exaltation of the soul of the poets, who are disdained by the multitude for their lack of balance and practical sense. It is to be noted that *The Hidden Pagodas* abounds in lyrical flights and dreaminess, which are rather empty and mawkish, somewhat reminding me of the worst books of Vargas Vila.

I believe that every writer should have a feeling for what might be called the "dignity of prose." One should only say quiet and sincere things in prose, leaving the task of communicating intimacies or fantasies to verse. Nevertheless, Señor Huidobro has chosen prose to express images such as this one: "Tree of Winter, in the middle of the melancholy landscape, thou art a prayer of melancholy, raised to God."

In sum, *The Hidden Pagodas* is a book of kitsch in which one can occasionally see that its author possesses a true poetic spirit, which, if well cultivated and better directed, could produce work of greater importance.

Nicolás Coronado. *Nosotros*. No. 89, Sept., 1916,

pp. 332–33†

Señor Huidobro tells us in a preface [to *Cagliostro, Novel-Film*] that his account of the doings of the mysterious Cagliostro is his "answer to the question whether the cinematograph can influence the novel," and it is a plain enough answer. The arrival of Cagliostro in Europe is like an appreciative burlesque of the early German film style. The story is cast in visual terms: "A coach advances towards the reader, closing upon him to the gallop of its horses, whose heavy shoes of iron make all my novel tremble." The Rosicrucians whom Cagliostro seeks are discovered in "a great room, in the film style of the Middle Ages." The influence of films may be observed in "Lorenza's head is a close-up before our eyes, swollen gigantically by our common curiosity." . . .

Certainly the exploits of Cagliostro are suitable material for a film, and Señor Huidobro's book would be a creditable scenario. There is not much save light-hearted wit, however, to distinguish his book from a scenario; and one feels in some of his incidents—such as the five prodigious tests which Cagliostro had to pass before being admitted to the temple of Isis—how much better they would be on the screen. But one need not take the book more seriously than its author does. It is good entertainment.

TLS. April 9, 1931, p. 289

The Cid Campeador thunders again through this break-neck chronicle [*Mio Cid Campeador*] that would make an excellent scenario for some Douglas Fairbanks—to whom, by the way, this book is dedicated. Now it is a question whether the great warrior were not better left to the tender mercies of legend. . . . Señor Huidobro's evident glee at the resuscitation of a superman is easily understood, but a measure of suspicion exists that the Cid, hearty figure, ferocious beard and all, was dragged down from his pedestal to make a movie holiday.

Vicente Huidobro, the Chilean poet who makes Paris his literary headquarters, and claims for himself the inception of the school of poetry known as "creationist," has produced an unusual but by no means remarkable portrait of the Spanish hero. He writes a vigorous electric prose—to judge by Mr. Wells's translation—and avails himself frequently of current idiom to secure vitality. . . . A wealth of language was squandered on this biography, and the most quotidian ideas are apt to come wrapped up in the cellophane of lyrical prose. As Señor Huidobro tosses a flock of figures from his pen and indulges gloriously in pleonastic flights, he manages that there be no trace of stiffness in his style, but, on the contrary, an extreme and disarming relaxation. . . .

His style is so fortunate that it is regrettable that he did not pull his story together. The truth of the matter is that he has combined too much material for the good of his plot; the legend of the Cid is a jointed one, and the seams are apt to show. Furthermore, since the climax occurs early in the book, shortly after the slaying of Jimena's father, the account of campaigning and exile which follows seems overlong.

Señor Huidobro has taken liberties with the tradition which states that the Cid's daughters married the infantes of Carrión and were shamefully mistreated at Corpes. He has greatly expanded the love interest which was added to the legend by Guillén de Castro, a contemporary of Lope de Vega, in his drama *The Cid's Youth*, and ignored the conflict between love and duty developed by Corneille.

Now the absence of psychological struggle detracts from the

gravity of the work. The substitution of a series of romantic interludes —Rodrigo playing Ring-around-a-Rosy with Jimena, Rodrigo climbing to his sweetheart's balcony, Rodrigo rescuing Jimena from the flames— is so much Hollywood small change.

The characterizations are adequate, Jimena is the perfect type of wife and mother, and the Cid strides through the narrative with all the subtlety of a gridiron hero. Some day somebody is going to forget the qualities which make Rodrigo Díaz such a pious Aeneas and turn out a rip-snorting novel that will show him up for the brutal and crafty old Ulysses he was.

Betty Drury. *NYT*. March 13, 1932, p. 6

What, then, is the Creationism of Vicente Huidobro? It is the author's literary self. To appreciate it, we must study Huidobro chronologically. Consider his first phase. His Chilean practicality . . . refused to be enmeshed in those mended nets of Romanticism which men were calling Modernism. Huidobro showed himself as much a crusader as "Los Diez" [The Ten] who in 1916 struck out a new line for themselves in Chilean letters. However, he would not yield to the allurements of Realism. Like his compatriot Eduardo Barrios, he takes his art too seriously to stoop to facile successes. His creative individualism was confirmed before he left Chile. He was bursting his bonds: he needed some one to interpret his own poetic gift to him. Thus commenced the second phase. For a moment, but only for a moment, Reverdy was this interpreter. Apollinaire's influence endures till this day. It were easy to name others who doubtless have strengthened the *whimsical*, the *paradoxical*, and the *Futuristic* side of his nature: Max Jacob, Jean Cocteau, Tristan Tzara, Ribemont-Dessaignes, Blaise Cendrars; but it is grossly exaggerating their influence to claim that his contacts with them have made him a Creationist. As well credit *all* his development to the reading of the Germans whom he quotes. (The mystical Unity of Nature and soul taught by Hegel and Schleiermacher has appealed to Huidobro.) Those bustling, striving, *Ultraïste* writers I have named merely furnished the needful applause or criticism for Huidobro's per- formance. The advance-guard have found him as advanced as them- selves. Their assertiveness, their revaluations, their hatred of the old commonplaces, have always been his familiars. To conclude: in the second phase, Huidobro was strengthened, not started; developed, not designed. The third phase has been, roughly, from 1925 to the present. Now the poet is acclaimed a leader, a pace-maker. Other poets come to him, talk, seek his counsel, take his ideas. A "school" is born! Mind rubbing against mind has been continually sending out showers of poetic sparks. Bread of encouragement cast on the waters to neophytes returns to him transformed into creative assurance, poise, and subtlety.

Henry Alfred Holmes. *Vicente Huidobro and Creationism* (New York, Columbia University, French Institute, 1934), pp. 34–35

Huidobro introduced European experimental writing into Chilean literature. A descendant of the Spanish aristocracy of Chile, he went to Europe at the age of twenty-four to continue his literary studies. His first two books of poetry were symbolist in tone but in Paris, in 1918, he began publishing with the cubists. At this time he was arranging poems in pictorial shapes in the manner of Guillaume Apollinaire. In 1921 he actually had an exhibition of poems in a picture gallery. He also visited Madrid while ultraism still flourished, and eventually launched his own movement, creationism. There has been much controversy over the actual origin of creationism and the poet's debt to his French contemporaries. He himself says his theories were formulated as early as 1916. They emphasize the conscious creation of new images. "The poet creates the world that ought to exist outside of the one that does exist. . . . The poet is concerned with expressing only the inexpressible."

Poetry for Huidobro is a kind of musical pattern of images, an international language independent of any specific language. In consequence much of his work is written in French. He is said to have influenced Juan Larrea and Gerardo Diego of Spain and Pablo de Rokha and Ángel Cruchaga of Chile. Several members of the most recent generation of Chilean poets also owe something to his innovations. Huidobro is active as well as a novelist and playwright. His work is extremely literary, elegant in design, and remarkable for humorous verbal legerdemain. Conservative critics disparage its value. They cannot forgive him for the picture poems, his disregard for punctuation, and his fantastic imagery.

H. R. Hays. *Twelve Spanish American Poets* (New Haven, Yale University Press, 1944), pp. 66–67

In his manifestos Huidobro fought against "infra-realist" automatism and proclaimed the lucidity of creationism and the primacy of intelligence, the latter no longer at odds with the integrity of the total man. . . . But the sign of his times was already indicated, and the surrealist epoch arrived anyway.

Huidobro, who perhaps yielded a little as a human being, was able, despite everything, to maintain himself untouched as an artist.

And his last books, like his first outpourings of creationism, remain faithful to his essential postulate, to the complete autonomy of the poem from nature. Aristotelian imitation of nature is understood by Huidobro as imitation of nature's procedures and not of its products. And his poems are created from an imaginary cell, the relationship or "rapport" of two words, like the leafy and blossomy tree is created from the simple seed. Such a radical belief in the objectivity of the poem, independent of any possible comparison with the objects of nature, was not shared by the majority of the inexperienced readers, not even by those who believed . . . themselves to be experienced. Both groups stubbornly searched in the creationist poem for the fifth leg of the cat, which does not belong to its biological make-up; thus, the simplest poetry in the world is turned into an enigma. It is true that perhaps the best thing Huidobro could have done was to replace the word "poetry" with a neologism, so as to avoid misunderstandings. But . . . the capacity of man to confuse things is limitless and incurable. . . .

In his last book, Vicente Huidobro tended more toward a refined lyricism, even though with subjective flights into unorthodox expressiveness. In perspective, pure creationism must have been unbreathable for human and sinful lungs. . . .

Gerardo Diego. Atenea. Nos. 295–96, Jan.–Feb., 1950,
pp. 16–17†

The poem *Altazor*, whose first Spanish edition had the subtitle *The Trip in a Parachute, a Poem in VII Cantos*, was conceived by Huidobro in 1919, and from that time on, it appeared in fragments in various reviews and newspapers of the Old and New Worlds, until the parts were gathered together in a final version in 1931 in Madrid. On the first anniversary of the death of the poet it appeared in a second edition in Santiago. Both editions carry Vicente Huidobro's portrait as sketched by Picasso's pencil. . . .

Altazor is the most notable work of creationism and a singular poetic composition in world literature. A complex poem charged with humanity, it profoundly investigates the nature of contemporary man. *Altazor* is one of the most extraordinary expressions of a culture based on an anthropocentric and materialist humanism. An assessment of its own time, which it condemns for its destructiveness, warning, and resultant anguish, the poem attempts . . . to transcend its time by projecting itself into eternity.

Altazor includes a poetic preface written in prose, one in which the meaning of the subtitle mentioned above is explained. Altazor, influenced by Nietzsche, proclaims himself, hesitantly . . . to be the Anti-Christ: "I was born at the age of thirty-three, on the day of Christ's death. . . ."

The first canto of *Altazor* crystallizes the entire poem. . . . Its meaning is vast, and an analysis of its content can only be undertaken summarily at the risk of filling a study with all the themes of existential philosophy. This canto begins on the extraordinary note of what we could call the existential pall of our age, with an eminently Heideggerian conception of man abandoned in the world. . . . Here we have, vividly expressed, the cosmic sense of Huidobro's poetry. Man-world, microcosm . . . wanders among the stars in pursuit of its fatal orbit in the voyage from birth to death, the dawn and dusk of existence. This polarity is always present in Huidobro's work and allows him to fuse his own creationism into a formula . . . to define the existential condition of human life. This voyage . . . is a fall into the very depths of the self in order to rebound into eternity. . . .

Cedomil Goić. La poesía de Vicente Huidobro
(Santiago, Anales de la Universidad de Chile, 1956),
pp. 203–7†

Fantasist and experimentalist, delirious and calculating, verbose and logical . . . Spanish, Creole and French, high-society boy and bohemian, *poète maudit* and *bon bourgeois,* a friend of cognac and bagasse, of cheese and metaphors, of trees and the sky, of the intangible and the tellable—how magnificently contradictory, how authentically American is this vain, genteel, adventurous and bubbly poet. . . .

The recipient of a large inheritance, of rich lands and celebrated vineyards (in Santa Rita), the descendant of two venerable creole families with titles of Hispano-Limeño nobility, the product of a Jesuit education, an expatriate in France, the husband of the granddaughter of the most authoritarian of the political caudillos of nineteenth-century Chile (Portales), the hero of unusual politico-amorous adventures, the head of a literary school in Europe and America, briefly the self-declared candidate for the Presidency of the Republic, Leninist, Trotskyite, supporter of the aristocracy, anarchist, anti-Stalinist, irascible and noisy polemicist with his equals in the Chilean Parnassus, gentle and hard, patient and restless—Huidobro appears in the literature of his country . . . as an uncontrollable man of energy, as a kind of metaphoric benzedrine . . . the destroyer of everything, save his "I," a terrible god at whose altars he would not hesitate to sacrifice even his own disciples.

His biographers and critics tend to sin on the side of excessive fervor, and this is how he wanted to be seen. . . . Vicente took with him wherever he went his Court (a quarrelsome Court, except when the poetry of the Master was at issue). . . . He worked with tension, but without fierceness, at ease in the self-assurance of his genius. . . .

Luis Alberto Sánchez. *RNC*. No. 115, March–April, 1956, p. 46†

Almost every study of Huidobro classifies the Chilean poet as a pure aesthete whose cerebral games, archetypal of the "dehumanization of art," have little to do with the personal and social problems of contemporary man. This judgment, which, to be sure, seems well founded if we limit ourselves to the study of his creationist manifestos and those on behalf of the poetry of the creationist period, is inadequate if we consider the total oeuvre of the man.

Huidobro began his career with the romantic concept of the poet as prophet . . . [but] beginning with 1925 the clash between the poet's instinct and the limitations of the creationist doctrine resulted in his abandoning creationism. In *Altazor* Huidobro proclaims the failure of the image, the focal point of creationist style, and he seeks [instead], desperately, a language that could express his metaphysical preoccupations. His overcoming of the prohibitions of creationism permitted Huidobro to speak directly in his poetry and in his prose not only of his personal problems but also of social ones. . . .

A rebellious spirit in literature and in his personal life, Huidobro did not hesitate in declaring himself a partisan of any attempt at social and political renovation. Be it for this reason or for the desire he felt to be a precursor in everything, his preoccupation with revolutionary politics was ahead of that of many of the poets of his generation in Spain as well as in America. As early as 1923, in *Finis Britannia*, he was attacking, even if irresponsibly and somewhat suspectly, British imperialism, defending the rights of colonial peoples. In *Contrary Winds* he presents the Communist as the "most noble and most elevated man human society can conceive." . . . With these beginnings it is not strange that around 1930 he inclined toward the French Communist Party or that in *Altazor* he speaks of the Russian Revolution as representing "the only hope/the last hope." . . .

The revolutionary theme inspires Huidobro's prose works published in Chile after his return from France. In *The Next One*, a prophetic novel whose theme is World War II, the visionary Alfredo Roc sets up a utopian colony in Angola with the goal of preserving Western civilization, which he sees threatened by the inevitable war. Roc's son, a Communist, refuses to accompany his father, whose efforts he sees as futile. Instead, he goes to Russia to "build the future," since the capitalist system is destined to disappear. On the last page of the novel, before the destruction not only of Europe but of the African refuge, Roc, convinced at last, shouts, "Russia, Russia, my son was right. Russia, the only hope." . . .

David Bary. CA. No. 124, Sept.–Oct., 1962, pp. 271–72†

Huidobro was obsessed by the idea of creationism from very early, long before he successfully established himself as a poet. As early as 1914, in the manifesto <i>Non Serviam</i>, read before the Ateneo in Santiago de Chile, he had emphatically declared: "We have accepted, without much thought, the fact that there cannot be any other realities other than the ones that surround us, and we have not thought about how we too can create realities in our world." This idea was to begin to appear throughout his poetic works until it came to constitute his most basic thought, the nucleus he amplified, so that creationism as a tendency became creationism as a focal point for the problems of aesthetics.

Creationism as a tendency was given programmatic form in the preliminary declaration of <i>Square Horizon</i>; that is, in 1917. It contains the following proposals: (1) adoption of the new invented fact; (2) rejection of the anecdotal and the descriptive; (3) creation of all of the parts of a poem; (4) creation of the poem as a new object. All this was to be summarized later in one sentence in the "Manifesto Perhaps" of 1924: "Make poetry, but don't put it around things." The poet was not to be an instrument of nature. He was to dominate nature so that it would serve his ends and so that he could compete against it with the <i>new object</i>. . . . Huidobro insisted that it was absolutely necessary to create a poem in the same way that nature creates a tree. . . . That is, that one should follow a process of inspiration and not one of imitation or reproduction. He thus inverted the Aristotelian conception of art: imitating nature . . . should be not copying it. . . .

Juan Jacobo Bajarlía. La polémica Reverdy-Huidobro:
Origen del ultraísmo (Buenos Aires, Editorial
Devenir, 1964), pp. 12–13†

IBARBOUROU, JUANA DE (1895–   )

URUGUAY

In the Uruguayan, Juana de Ibarbourou (a Basque name) and in the Argentine, Alfonsina Storni, there is little or nothing of the glacial Francisca da Silva. Neo-paganism may blow hot as well as cold. When, some six years ago, the poet and philosopher, Miguel de Unamuno, extended his hand across the sea to her of the Basque patronymic, he but confirmed a reputation that was already in the ascendant. This professor of Greek knew his Sappho, he knew that the chaste unveiling of her soul was a braver thing than the mere unveiling of her body. In Juana de Ibarbourou he was surprised to find the chaste spiritual nudity which, he had thought, had gone out of letters.

Since that day the poetess has grown in spiritual depth and in poetic directness. She has essayed also, as in *The Fresh Jug*, a poetic prose that does not, even at its best, wholly escape the evils of bastardy. Yet even here she displays, amidst much that lacks depth and originality, a rare nature that is stirred by stimuli to which most persons are altogether anaesthetic. Of a quiet life she has made an exciting succession of important trivialities. She has a pretty fancifulness and plays with pantheism. Yet one has but to compare her lines to water with the symphonic strophes, "Sister Water," of Amado Nervo, to realize how little she has made of an infinite theme. . . .

This is a paganism that is as young and as old as Nature. She does not imitate the classical poets; in herself flows the blood that wrote those ancient lines. In a word, the paganism of Juana de Ibarbourou is autochthonic, American. She speaks, not in terms of Francisca Julia da Silva's centaurs, but in terms of her own Uruguay and of her own days and nights. Señor Breñes Mesén thinks her a precursor [of the future] in no fewer than three ways. In the first place, she has thrown aside the masculine convention; her vision of the world is freely feminine. In the second, she proceeds without a conscious thought of the schools; her sight, in a sense, is thus virginal, and little conditioned by the work of other writers. Finally, "she is the precursor of that paganism which during this century will extend across the American continent."

Isaac Goldberg. *AMer.* 7, April, 1926, pp. 451–52

Miguel de Unamuno has stressed in an evaluation of Juana de Ibarbourou that the pessimistic, somber part of her works seems artificial to him, somewhat false, and in any event something completely literary. He considers the sincere and natural in her to be the simple joy of living and loving that she expresses in other poems. Nevertheless, with all due respect, the great Basque writer has perhaps fallen into psychological error, into a simplification, when he believes that the coexistence of the two sentiments, the sentiments of life and death, is contradictory and incompatible in the same poetic consciousness. Paradoxically, nothing is more logical or natural than that apparent contradiction. The idea of death accompanies the joy of living as the shadow accompanies the body. At least for individuals of fine sensitivity, for most people live with the philosophical unawareness of the animal in them and they do not see beyond their immediate reality.

When one most loves life, death inspires that much more terror, and that much more does its shadow obsess one's thoughts. All silence between two bursts of laughter, all rest between two dances, is filled by the presence of death. Like water, it fills all the empty spaces and the gaps in our hours. Only a belief in the immortality of the soul can overcome the horror of death. Only religious hope for a beyond can make the thoughts of our ephemeral condition less shadowy. The joy of life in one who only believes in and loves the sensory and the corporeal—and such is the case with a great part of humanity today—is similar to a merrymaking party on a sinking ship. Far from being forced, artificial, and merely literary, the pessimism of death is, in this poet of naturalism, precisely her most natural and most sincere quality.

Indeed, a poetry in which there was only joy would be forced, literary, and conventional. . . . Moreover, a totally happy poetry would be, if it were sincere, a foolish poetry. . . . The shadowy background in which graceful dancing figures move gives aesthetic value and profound meaning to poetry. Without tragic sensitivity there is no art, and tragedy in naturalistic poetry [such as Juana de Ibarbourou's] is to be found in that sense of ephemeral mortality. [1930]

Alberto Zum Felde. *Proceso intelectual del Uruguay:*
Crítica de su literatura (Montevideo, Ediciones del
Nuevo Mundo, 1967), Vol. III, pp. 60–61†

People believe Juana de Ibarbourou to be successful and lucky, but she is really a captive of life, of circumstances, of her timidity. She could have gone to Paris, to preside there as queen of poetry and of the "moment," which is the most brilliant kind of reign. She could have gone around the world by ship, lionized with triumphal trumpets. Yet she never traveled even to Brazil, which was right next door, or to Paraguay, where she was adored. When she did go to Buenos Aires, after receiving an invitation accompanied by many honors, she had to return home a few hours later because of a family illness. . . .

Juana died spiritually because of her frustrated desire to travel— to cross the sea and to cross frontiers, to hear herself called a foreigner, to see unknown horizons and to hear new sounds. And it was not because she wanted romantic freedom or had high-flown fantasies. She would probably have wanted to travel with her own people, with those who made up her beloved home. But they all had roots sunk deep into the hard soil, while she was the one with blue wings on warm shoulders.

And her poems changed, not because of new literary sensitivities but because of the impossibility of continuing to raise the burning host of hopes and dreams over her shoulders. The cry of the young and strong impassioned woman . . . has become hoarse by having struck, year after year, against the black stones of dull and heavy routine. And the inspired woman who, little by little, has let her rebellious arms fall, abandoning the sweet fruits and the red flowers, now continues to play by containing her bitter despair within the salty stones of the hostile beaches that will not let her pass.

Mercedes Pinto. RCu. 4, Oct.–Dec., 1935, pp. 49–50†

It is indeed a striking circumstance that Uruguay should have produced some of the most renowned women poets of its continent in the twentieth century. This distinction is not limited alone to its women literary artists, for Uruguay, the smallest country in South America, has also produced a galaxy of important writers, male and female, in other fields of literature. There are at least three women poets who are worth knowing intimately: María Eugenia Vaz Ferreira, Delmira Agustini and Juana de Ibarbourou. The tragic spirit of Vaz Ferreira moves us to compassion; Agustini is a melancholy dreamer; Ibarbourou, by contrast with the other two, shows a happy and exuberant nature.

The influence of these women has been great, particularly in their own country. Luisa Luisi and others of the new generation have followed the example of their predecessors but especially the inspiration of their contemporary, Juana de Ibarbourou. Juana de Ibarbourou, as well as Vaz Ferreira and Agustini, felt the current of the Modernist Movement in poetry, but instead of imitating very closely other poets of this period they wrote verses which are more individual and intimate and offer a distinct form as to content and themes. The form was free and did not conform to traditional moulds except in the case of an occasional sonnet. . . .

The first three volumes of her work . . . will probably live on and make her name immortal. In them is found the most sincere, intimate and charming part of her personality. A certain exuberance, freshness, and simplicity is apparent in them which is not found later. She expresses many of the qualities of youth: a joy, a desire to love and to be loved, and an overflowing delight in life and nature.

The work of the last period lacks the spontaneity and pleasantness of the previous poems. She has become more vague and intellectual. She is not inspired by the world which surrounds her nor does she reflect her intimate emotions and sentiments. The omission of this human element is characteristic of a great deal of modern art and poetry.

Consuelo B. Babigian. *MLF*. 25, March, 1940, pp. 9–11

Nature is the mirror that reflects [Ibarbourou's] thoughts, her emotions, her moods, her manner of expression. It is difficult, therefore, to isolate her themes and attempt to define them singly; for not only are they all interrelated as regards nature, but there is a deep inner unity of thought and concept—not necessarily premeditated—that makes each an indispensable part of the other. The thought of love, for instance, immediately evokes the desire for life, the fear of death, the pleasure she finds in offering to the lover her sun-browned, elastic, fragrant body; the thought of life summons up appetizing feasts of love, as she proffers her tempting beauty with a joy marred only by the haunting thought that youth, alas!, is not everlasting, and that death will one day extinguish the starry gaze in her eyes, will pale the bloom of her cheek, will reduce arms that embrace and lips that burn to lifeless ashes; the thought of death steals short-lived joy from what might otherwise have been cloudless hours of love, it awakens the desire for endless life as part of nature, for ever-verdant beauty; the thought of herself, fragrant with nards, and proud of her youth, her beauty, her desirability, calls up visions of the lover waiting to pluck the flowers and the fruits of love, while life still lends them fragrance and flavor—before death wilts and robs them of their power to lure. . . .

Set against a background of nature, each one of these themes is presented simply—one might almost say naïvely—without great depth of thought, without philosophical implications, but with a freshness and spontaneity which only poetry of this type can possess. For her ideas upon life, upon death, upon love, are not transcendental, but the direct, basic ones of a person who does not seek to comprehend what there is, or may be, beyond that which meets the eye. She bases her ideas of love upon her feelings and desires; those of life upon what she sees of nature; those of death upon what she knows of life. She does not attempt to pry or indagate into the unknown—or to deduce the why and the wherefore of things; for she is as simple and elemental and direct in her thoughts and in her emotions, as the flowers, the fruits, the trees and the other creatures of nature that fill her verses and with which more than once she identifies and compares herself.

Sidonia Carmen Rosenbaum. Modern Women Poets of
Spanish America (New York, Hispanic Institute in
the United States, 1945), pp. 239–40

One element that is either absent or appears only slightly [in Ibarbourou's early poems] becomes more insistent as [she moves toward] the dramatic late poems. I am referring to the sadness caused by the passing of life, the end of dreams, and the presentiment of death. The love for life nurtures the fear of death, and Juana experiences the decline with great pain. . . . The certainty of the finiteness of being inspires her to write words charged with melancholy and nostalgia for the past; these true elegies contrast with her earlier poems, which are filled with optimism and enthusiasm for life. . . . It is painful for her to accept her own destruction and difficult to foresee the pleasures of the spirit, free from bodily restraints, and to understand abstract concepts. She can only *suffer* the loss of the bodily raiment in which the soul finds itself oppressed; she does not long for the soul's emancipation, for its "setting out for the first origin," as the mystics say. . . .

[Juana's] positivism separates her from those romantics who saw in death only a repose from earthly torments, from the mystics who desired death to draw closer to God, from those Christians who accept it because of their religious convictions, and from the Greeks, who embellished its meaning. Juana speaks of death with horror, and her beliefs in returns and in future transformations [are inspired more by] poetic convention than by any authentic belief. Despite her words, her idea of death is that of someone who cannot conceive or accept it because she embraces a sensitive corporeal life. . . .

Maruja González Villegas. USF. No. 41, July–Sept.,
1959, pp. 174–75†

ICAZA, JORGE (1906–   )

ECUADOR

[Icaza] is still a young man in appearance, of affable and gracious manner, and an excellent conversationalist. His secondary education was received in a Jesuit school in [Quito]; he then began the study of medicine in the University of Ecuador, but the death of his father shortly forced him to abandon his studies in order to gain a livelihood.

He secured various types of distasteful employment, but eventually worked in the national theater. There he undertook to translate French plays for the local stage; then, encouraged by his success, he turned his hand to original productions. . . .

One of his plays, Icaza told the writer, raised such a furor that the authorities closed the theater. Although Icaza did not succeed in having the ban removed from the play, the affair ended with his appointment as censor of the national theater—a post he declined, but with the realization that his playwriting in Quito had ended. While not altogether abandoning the drama, Icaza turned more to fiction after 1933, the year in which he published a volume of short stories, *Mountain Soil*. In the main these stories tell of injustices committed by the church and the landed aristocracy against the laboring class—the Indians, the country's indigenous population. These injustices, which Icaza had observed at first hand on some of the great estates in the region of Quito, furnished the thematic material for his three novels—*Huasipungo, In the Streets, Cholos*, and a play, *Flogging*. . . .

All in all, he will be remembered as a reformer and not as a novelist. His success as a writer lies not at all in plot or characterization, but in his vigorous, cryptic, Quevedo-like style in which he reveals abuses that cry out to Heaven to be righted, and that arouse in his readers his own spirit of boiling indignation. The outstanding characteristics of that style are a brutal frankness, an almost total lack of idealism, and a use of words that are almost universally regarded as taboo. Purely from the standpoint of technique, what strikes one most in his novels is his disregard for form. Almost plotless, consisting only of a series of scenes rich in details of various phases of social life but very loosely connected, his novels move along somewhat artlessly, like life itself. Icaza's greatest personal deficiency as a novelist lies in his lack of interest in people as individuals; his characters represent the psychology of their class, but with the possible exception of Montoya [in *Cholos*] they are not flesh and blood humans. Of the two classes they symbolize, the exploited and the exploiter, the latter stands out in bolder relief. For his Indian characters, who only now and then dare to assert themselves, are so tame and servile that they seem as hopeless a lot as their masters through the ages ever have found them.

Jefferson Rea Spell. *Contemporary Spanish-American Fiction* (Chapel Hill, University of North Carolina Press, 1944), pp. 240–41, 252

Anyone familiar with the history, traditions, customs, the forms of economic, social, political, and religious life of a large part of the Americas cannot fail to recognize the verisimilitude of the episodes and characters in Icaza's fiction. Perhaps there is some impressionistic exaggeration.

But his psychological charting carries us to the farthest limits, where we can get at human nature in degradation under social coercion and violence. Misery distorts the outlines of the human soul, and hunger leads to coprophagy. But in these conditions the specimens of misformed psychology come not only from those in misery but also from those who play the roles of victimizers and despots. The social fauna and the moral atmosphere that envelops it are of interest for the scholar no less than for the artist as a portrait of the struggle for existence, with the apparatus of modernity in the heart of primitive nature. What Icaza shows us is man placed in a twilight zone in which the ghostly dawn of a native culture shines weakly and in which intruding civilization cannot wash away the ghostliness with brightness. The artist contributes in this way to the renovation of the sources of our sensitivity, and, at the same time, he opens up new perspectives for Hispanic-American literature.

J. Eugenio Garro. RHM. 12, July–Oct., 1946, p. 237†

The power of denunciation in *Huasipungo* rests, more than anything else, in its compact and direct form of execution—too compact and direct to be considered a novel; thus, it is necessary to treat it as something else, whatever features of the novel it may have. It is a revolutionary document in the form of a novel. Nevertheless, it is not a thesis work because it contains neither explicit demonstration nor preaching by the writer or by a character. Its only eloquence is that of the story itself, of these simple facts, which are sufficient to make it the most convincing allegation. One could say that there is in the work an implicit thesis, as there necessarily is in any work of a social nature. But the writer confines himself to the telling—to exposition—without commentary. . . .

One factor that contributes most to the convincing reality of *Huasipungo* is the writer's decision not to present the Indian in any falsely favorable light. On the contrary, his Indian is generally presented as a being who has degenerated into bestiality. His house and his body are nauseating things because of filth, alcohol, stench, and lice. He lives in rottenness and excrement; he beats his wife daily and bows servilely before the foreman's whip; his language is made up of crude and dirty words. . . .

There is no other book in the world that shows such iniquity, repulsion, and shame. Icaza always remains faithful to the life he portrays; he does not deceive himself into believing that he can intercede on behalf of the redemption of the Indians by glorifying or glamourizing their lives in literature.

Alberto Zum Felde. Índice crítico de la literatura
hispanoamericana (Mexico City, Editorial Guarania
1954–59), Vol. II, p. 280†

In [Icaza's work] tragedy springs from the very essence of events. And since these have been copied from surrounding reality, one could say that it is his vision of things that furnishes the sign of tragedy. But he has a very special ability to discern the fateful aspects of the trivial and the everyday, so as to order the elements in a sequence that flows toward a gloomy ending and to give those elements emotional configuration and expression. By the same token, his works, the earliest ones in particular, abound in sinister irony, a powerful weapon for destroying with mighty blows the pedestal on which great political and social lies rest.

Aware of the deep commitment an artist has to give voice and expression to the world that surrounds him, Icaza has tried to find for the lament or song of America its own accent. . . . The voices of the people have been elevated in his work, through his art, to unexpected heights. Both epic and lyric in his narration, dialogue, and description, Icaza is the greatest poet of Ecuador and one of the greatest of the Americas. . . .

Enrique Ojeda. *Cuatro obras de Jorge Icaza* (Quito, Casa de la Cultura Ecuatoriana, 1961), pp. 125–26†

First published in Ecuador some thirty years ago [*Huasipungo*] has been translated into eleven foreign languages, including Russian and Chinese. Now for the first time it is available in English. The story centers about Don Alfonso Pereira, who is in financial difficulties and has been banished, by his rich uncle, to his country estate to build a road to open up the area to timber exploiters. The problem finally becomes one of clearing away the native huts, the *Huasipungos*, which represent all the Indians possess, since these huts stand in the way of "progress" on the project.

Jorge Icaza has spared no one in his ruthless exposé. He is obviously unhappy with the Church in Ecuador, which is strongly entrenched. It must be admitted, however, that Icaza concentrates on clerical abuses rather than the Church itself. . . .

This book, like other writings of Icaza, has been the center of stormy controversy in South America. Certain critics feel that he has exaggerated the misery of the Indian, while others affirm that, even if he is realistic, it is not the function of the creative artist to depict such misery. His books do not make for amiable reading. As the translator aptly says in his introduction: "Icaza's Indians are far from being models of virtue themselves; they are only human. . . . They are not the 'noble' Indians of the European and American romanticists, but the real Andean Indians of today in all their unwashed misery. They suffer—from malnutrition, alcoholism, superstition and ignorance."

When an author is a reformer who seeks to improve the existence of the lower classes, his novels are likely to suffer from his zeal. Surely, Icaza can be compared with Steinbeck of *The Grapes of Wrath* fame, but although Icaza's book has achieved success, the conditions he sought to eradicate remain unchanged—hence his "bitter disappointment, somewhat like the shattering of a dream."

In general, this novel is Zolaesque in its realism; and though it is completely lacking in humor, it does not lack poetry and originality, for, propagandist though he is, the author has a fresh eye and an original pen to catch the naïveté of both Indian and Cholo (person of mixed Indian and white stock).

Pierre Courtines. America. April 11, 1964, pp. 517–18

The Ecuadorian village of Icaza's novel [*Huasipungo*] has all the simplicity of a Rivera mural; there are no subjective depths and all the answers are given. This, says Icaza in classic Marxist fashion, is how the upper class of a colonial country collaborates with foreign capital to despoil its natives in order to supply raw material for export. The Indians have to be dislodged from their plots of land? — a devastating flood is allowed to build up. A supply road has to be cut through a treacherous swamp? — the Church declares the job a religious fiesta, the politicians a patriotic duty, and the latifundists supply free liquor to keep the Indians pliant. The characters are sketchily drawn, the incidents rapidly developed; but the language of the Indians has an incantatory beauty, the horrors illustrate an undeniable logic, and its author's compassion and indignation are genuine.

José Yglesias. Nation. April 13, 1964, p. 377

Published in 1934, *Huasipungo* is a novel of protest against the oppression of Indian agricultural labor in Ecuador. It has been translated into English badly, but it has a force which bursts through even inadequate language. Icaza's justification for having it translated at this late date, he states, is also a source of embarrassment to him; nothing has changed in Ecuador.

The book concerns the long exploitation of a village of Indians by the complacent priest, the grasping *patron* and the lazy half-castes on a hacienda in the backlands of the country. After endless cruelty, the Indians revolt and kill some of the half-castes in a frenzy of liberty before they are efficiently machine-gunned by a company of soldiers who have rushed out from Quito.

The details are sordid. One picture remains in my mind; a cluster of desperately hungry Indians digging for the carcass of a bull, just buried by order of the *patron*, which has rotted in the sun for days.

I hope *Huasipungo* upsets you.

Arthur R. Gold. BW. April 19, 1964, p. 16

In 1934 a novel appeared in Ecuador which signaled the end of the romantic Indianist tradition and which at the same time was the culmination of a new trend characterized by a language of brutal realism, by a goal of intense social criticism, and by a revolutionary ideology close to Marxism. This novel, entitled *Huasipungo*, brought international fame to its author. . . .

In *Huasipungo* the representative figures of the horrible world described by Icaza rise up like silhouettes scissored out of stone, without any depth or psychological complexity. A road under construction slowly assumes the proportions of a myth; it is the axis on which the tragedy of the Indians revolves. Other objects also become transmuted: water, wheat, tithes, the peasant's small plot of land, his home, his *huasipungo*. In the midst of these objects the native family moves with mechanical unconsciousness, with a pathetic acceptance of its destiny that is only one remove from an animal's responses. Icaza tells a simple story: the Indian is stripped of his lands by an enemy force which he does not understand and which he cannot oppose without bringing down savage punishment on himself and his family.

To illustrate the impotence and the helplessness of the Indian, as well as the cruelty of the exploiters, Icaza accumulates extremely morbid incidents. His intention is obvious—to jar the reader through concrete images, not to argue with him or to preach to him. Icaza wants to jar the reader from his apathy by machete blows and even to move him to despair. Such a procedure is a double-edged sword. His exaggerated descriptions are so repugnant that one moves from pity to alarm and disgust; we sense that he has lost sight of the reason for his revolt. We also sense a dangerous simplification that is the sure sign of propaganda. The reader loses confidence. Icaza seems . . . to be competing with himself in an interminable selection of horrors, without realizing that the reader only needs a minimal amount of such sordidness in order to sympathize with his message.

Fernando Alegría. *Historia de la novela hispanoamericana*, 3rd ed. (Mexico City, Ediciones De Andrea, 1966), pp. 262–63†

Are the filthy, crude . . . episodes [in *Huasipungo*] necessary? No. We are of the opinion that the author would have enriched his style, would have been far more effective in his denunciation, would have been accepted by skeptical readers, if he had avoided some extremely naturalistic episodes. But we do approve and applaud the realistic approach to existing conditions as long as they are authentic and not an exaggeration of reality, for it is necessary to remember that in describing the human world, the model is not "Garden of Eden." To avoid the crude and cruel reality is as much of an escape as to avoid the ideal and sublime. At any rate, the human world has more of the former than of the latter; an eternal indulgent ignoring of the ugly will not help to cultivate and develop aesthetic beauty.

Antonio Sacoto. *The Indian in the Ecuadorian Novel*
(New York, Las Américas, 1967), pp. 223–24

First published in 1936 and premiered in Buenos Aires in 1940, *Flogging*, the last theatrical work written by Icaza, can be seen as a literary manifesto indispensable to a clear understanding of the intentions—the extent and limits of the indigenism—of this writer. . . .

The main purpose in *Flogging* is to emphasize the "aesthetic of the horrible," used so much by Icaza: this not only represents an answer to the colonial aesthetic of the "sublime." Above all, it shows Icaza's sense of necessity in revealing the nature of the ruling social order, showing its structure and effects. Moreover, Icaza does not believe it suitable to present very beautiful examples of the exploited as do other indigenist writers, because for him economic exploitation leads to ontic degradation.

Importantly, the characters in the work do not even have their own names, a detail with which the author seems to want to underline two facts: his literature is committed to the realistic-socialistic goal of portraying typical characters in typical situations, and he stresses that the Indian "cannot be understood individually but collectively," as Fernández Alborg has pointed out. So for the whites and mestizos, he is a collective character. . . .

Some of the author's basic ideas that are developed in this play will reappear in later works. First, he shows that tenderness cannot reach fulfillment in a setting such as that in which the Indian lives. This is one reason why it is absent or repressed in Incan literature. Second, he presents all the vices that can be attributed to the Indian, particularly that of alcoholism, not as natural racial defects but as strictly social defects caused by the conditions of life. Third, he offers a very fine interpretation of the "cruelty" and "sadism" of the Indian, which can be explained as follows: since the real enemy is not within his reach, initially or before the revolutionary process has broken forth, the oppressed unconsciously unleash their hatred against others similarly oppressed. . . .

Agustín Cueva. *Jorge Icaza* (Buenos Aires, Centro
Editor de América Latina, 1968), pp. 25, 27–29†

In both [*Huasipungo* and *The Grapes of Wrath*] the law enforcing agencies, soldiers and police, habitually side with the power structure.

In both novels there is, in essence, a burning question—one which is still a major ethical problem for every state and society: whether a soldier or policeman, given an inhuman command, has the moral right or duty to resist or challenge his superior's orders. Icaza would have been fairer, perhaps, had he exploited to a greater extent in *Huasipungo* the pathetic situation of the soldiers who are ordered to shoot down their own countryman. . . . Yet one can scarcely expect a total view of the Ecuadorian tragedy in two hundred pages. In this regard Steinbeck does only a little better in his much longer work. But Icaza does place blame; not only on the *latifundista* system but also personally on those individuals who choose to profit from the abuse of their fellow countrymen. (Icaza is not now, nor has he ever been, a Communist. The word "communism" does not even appear in *Huasipungo*.) In his blistering attack on *latifundismo* he does more than condemn an economic system, as does Dreiser in his most popular works (*Sister Carrie* and *An American Tragedy*). Icaza does not believe that merely removing the imperialistic gringo and the soulless landowner from the scene automatically insures Ecuador of a bright future; he still demands another type of change, a moral re-awakening among the rank and file Ecuadorians themselves. . . .

Both [Icaza and Steinbeck] essentially endorse the humane idea of helping others; they oppose the living of an essentially selfish existence which they regard with suspicion, and which they believe is prejudicial toward the rest of mankind. They are, in short, their brothers' keepers. Though both writers are obviously leftist-oriented, Icaza appears more revolutionary. His justice-for-all attitude includes specifically those depressed because of racial discrimination. . . . Even in *The Grapes of Wrath* Steinbeck's own wrath does not spill over on the economic system as a whole; he pleads only for reforms. Icaza's anger is more inflammatory.

Both novels have in common a negative regard for traditional religion although Icaza's condemnation is more ferocious by far. The priest in *Huasipungo* remains static throughout the short novel; his only growth is financial. He profits hugely from the special church fiesta occasioned by the building of the road, and, most of all, from the road itself. . . .

The readers who have been favorably impressed by *The Grapes of Wrath* will certainly note the burning similarities of theme and outrage in *Huasipungo*. Read in the original Spanish or in translation, Icaza's novel is a poetic inflammatory nightmare which makes even the wrath of Steinbeck seem almost pale in comparison.

Bernard Dulsey. *ABC*. 18, 10, Summer, 1968, pp. 16–17

In *Huasipungo* Icaza sharply penetrated the essential problem of the large estates in the villages, illuminating that hidden patronal violence within the walled area of the hacienda. . . . In the coherent frame of Icaza's novel, solutions are not given—that is the realm of sociology and politics—but the means of escape for the involved indigenous community are objectively revealed. The uprising of the villagers in *Huasipungo* is the vivid expression of a peasant subversion without political objectives or revolutionary organization; it is not a project with a "solution for the indigenous problem." . . .

The implicit message Icaza conveys . . . is one of radical change of the situation of conquest and oppression, without which change Ecuador will not be able to transform the Wars of Independence into a national revolution. . . .

Icaza's novel is not only a testimony . . . but a social diagnosis in which the characters, settings, and circumstances are integrated into one frame, one coherent problem.

> Antonio García. *Sociología de la novela indigenista en
> el Ecuador: Estructura social de la novelística de
> Jorge Icaza* (Quito, Casa de la Cultura Ecuatoriana,
> 1969), pp. 57, 80, 82

[*Trapped*] is a noteworthy novel not because it represents new departures in form, technique, or theme, but rather because it consolidates and perfects artistic accomplishments achieved in earlier novels which have not been widely read. Like most monumental undertakings, it is replete with significant successes and failures. Among the latter are several aspects typical of the author. In none of the three parts of the trilogy does one find an easily discernible structure; characters and events pour forth with the vigorous but chaotic epic rhythm that has typified [Icaza's] art from the beginning. Although much of the first-person narration is in fact autobiographical, neither the author-protagonist nor most of the other 160 fictional personages are authentic human beings, and many of them, as in previous novels, are one dimensional stereotypes. . . .

Icaza's desire to synthesize his entire life and literature is laudable, but he has been excessively prolific in reproducing themes, motifs, names, characters, and even the plot of earlier novels. Returning again are scenes depicting the degradation of the Ecuatorian Indian in *Huasipungo*, the hyperbolic extent of a capitalist's land holdings identical in form and style to its source in *In the Streets,* the transformation of lowly *cholos* into racist capitalists as in *Cholos*, the same pretentious middle class *cholos* who revert to their Indian origins when inebriated, and even the same family name Oquendo as in *Half a Life Bewildered,* ambitious *cholos* who advance in society at the expense of their brothers, as in *Huairapamushcas*, and throughout all three volumes [of *Trapped*] innumerable similarities in plot, language, symbolism, and psychology to *Romero y Flores the Chulla.*

The positive values of this ambitious undertaking are also considerable. While the flow of events and themes in each volume is characteristically unstructured and rambling, there is a clear and powerful sense of purpose in the trilogy as a whole. In Icaza's prior production, his major themes of the inhumanity of Ecuatorian society towards the Indian, the psychic instability of the *cholo*, and the necessity for collective, class solutions to basic problems were filtered through the consciousness of the novelist's stock characters: the exploited Indian, the unscrupulous *cholo*, and the urban *chulla* [hot-shot]. In this new novel these same preoccupations are mirrored in the sensibilities of a fictional "writer" who finds in his literature a weapon for bringing about changes in society.

Theodore A. Sackett. Chasqui. 2 ,3, May, 1973, pp. 62–64

JAIMES FREYRE, RICARDO (1868–1933)

BOLIVIA

The poetic art of the Bolivian bard Ricardo Jaimes Freyre is allied to Poe's in many ways. As the evocative poet of Nordic mythology, he has portrayed those elements of terror and of horror that we invariably associate with Poe. His poems are as purely subjective as those of the creator of "Ulalume" and just as liable to personal and varied inter-pretations. Suggestive as are many of the titles of his collections of verse, such as *Primeval Fountain, Dream Country*, and *Dreams Are Life*, and as are many of the individual poems . . . there are no imitations nor immediate allusions to any of Poe's work. The Poesque reminiscences that occur frequently are to be accounted for, then, mainly on the basis of affinity. Some of these resemblances may be noted in the discussion on prosody, for in the matter of verse technicalities Poe's influence cannot be gainsaid. That many of Jaimes Freyre's arrangements may have been directly inspired by Darío or by the French poets is more than likely. But in any case, whether directly or indirectly, his passion-ate attention to the rhythmical and musical qualities of verse inevitably associates him with Poe.

Repetitions of every kind, rhyming of like words, inner rhyme, in short, all of the verse artifices practiced by French Symbolists and learned from Poe, abound in the work of Bolivia's Modernista poet. His recurring phrases in such poems as "The Song of Evil," "The Elves," "Aeternum Vale," and "The Night," are as effective in enhanc-ing the leitmotif as are any of Poe's repetends.

> John Eugene Englekirk. *Edgar Allan Poe in Hispanic Literature* (New York, Instituto de las Españas en los Estados Unidos, 1934), pp. 305–6

Jaimes Freyre was the only poet of [the modernist] school who was concerned with scientifically formulating a doctrine of poetic form, which shows us that he was a reflective, conscious artist, thereby increasing his importance in the modernist movement. . . . The pre-ceding few lines [quoted from his *Laws of Castilian Versification*] show us the flexibility of versification that such a doctrine allows the poet, beyond the possibilities offered by traditional forms. But we also see that Jaimes Freyre demands the poet to have a formal plan, which he must not depart from if he wishes to produce poetry.

This doctrine of versification . . . must have been formulated by Jaimes Freyre by 1899, at least in its essential elements, to the extent that the versification he uses in *Primeval Fountain* follows the doctrine. A reading of this book of poetry confirms Jaimes Freyre's position as a writer who attempted to realize well-honed and thought-out poetry, a poetry of careful form. The poems in this volume . . . are, as the title of the work indicates, inspired by a primeval muse. The influence of the great poet of the language at that time, Rubén Darío, cannot be found in the poems of *Primeval Fountain* except in the effort at a thematic and formal liberation that the book represents. . . . [1942]

Luis Monguió. *RI*. 8, May, 1944, pp. 127–28†

The medieval Nordic world is the inspiration not only for the thirteen poems (in the main, short poems) that make up the first part of [*Primeval Fountain*]. The Nordic world of the Middle Ages is also palpably present in the second part. . . . When, toward the end of the second part, this world fades away, it yields to less shadowy colors, in other medieval sketches set, we imagine, to the south. By the third and last part, the Nordic world, so dear to the poet, becomes hidden completely.

In the first two parts (above all, in the second one) there is a rather incongruous coexistence of the classical and the Nordic worlds, of "medieval" portraits and scenes from the eighteenth century, of erotic themes and religious themes (at least as religious as Jaimes Freyre could be). But the poet redeems many of his poems by the general aura of renovation and delicacy that envelops his entire work. . . .

The poems of *Primeval Fountain*, like those of his brothers in song, appeared in its time as an emphatic declaration of a "hatred of worn poetry." . . . Jaimes Freyre emerged at an opportune moment to contribute to the triumph of modernism, and his offering to the battle was, of course, *Primeval Fountain*. Under the shadow of Darío, but not hidden by that shadow, Jaimes Freyre and Lugones were the most powerful voices at this end of the continent. . . .

Emilio Carilla. *Ricardo Jaimes Freyre* (Buenos Aires, Ministerio de Educación y Justicia, Dirección General de Cultura, 1962), pp. 47, 54–55†

In his short stories with exotic settings, Jaimes Freyre displays, together with a mastery of plot and profundity of theme, an excellently balanced and well-honed style. . . . In these stories, in which a poet uses a refined, chiseled prose, he reveals an almost oriental attitude toward the meaning of happiness and life. . . .

In "Indian Justice" the white bosses Álvarez and Córdova, who have brutally robbed the Indians of land and animals, become victims of the terrible hatred of the peasants. With the victims subjugated after a hectic hunt, the peasants subject them to a slow death in an isolated clearing. The episode is buried forever beneath the silence sworn to by the accomplices and executioners. In "A Beautiful Spring Day" Jaimes Freyre describes Pablo's revenge because of the frustration of his plans to marry Juliana. Her father, who wants to add his neighbor's lands to his own, compels Juliana to marry Marcos on Easter Sunday. Pablo, aided by his companion José, during the long nights that envelop the town, fills in a ditch dug by the Indians on the slope of a forbidding and threatening mountain. Months later, in the middle of summer, when the town is joyously celebrating Candlemas, a lethal and unrestrainable mass of moving mud descends upon them from the slope, the result of earlier torrential rains, and covers the town completely, now defenseless because of the filled-in ditch. In these two stories, the plot and concise style are joined to the spirit of social restoration. . . .

Jaimes Freyre had a free, lively, and strong spirit, He was a total humanist. . . . He used his profound historical, philosophical, and artistic knowledge and his alert sensitivity to embrace . . . the social concerns of his time; they caused him to profess advanced ideas in a period when the Argentine intellectuals were devoting themselves to the knowledge and analysis of the great foundations of dialectical materialism and historical materialism. . . .

Eduardo Ocampo Moscoso. *Personalidad y obra poética de don Ricardo Jaimes Freyre* (La Paz, Editorial Universitaria, 1968), pp. 66–68, 76†

If we can accept the idea that the child's world is the substratum on which the adult personality rests, in Jaimes Freyre we can note in at least a good part of his work the tenacious influence that the earth surrounding him as a child exercised on him [encouraging him in his "Nordic" themes].

Jaimes Freyre was not indifferent to his times, not ensconced in his ivory tower. . . . He was aware of and suffered along with the spectacle of his age. Without being a political militant, a "committed writer," he acted on the side of the people and against the oppressive men in power, the unjust who governed. He was a romantic socialist, an idealist in short. His social poems . . . written in 1906, when no one suspected that [Russia] was on the threshold of a gigantic revolutionary experience, are violent. . . .

Raúl Gonsálvez Botelho. *CA*. No. 156, Jan.–Feb.,
1968, pp. 246–47, 250†

Modernism was born at the time of postpositivism and at the beginning of idealism. Ricardo Jaimes Freyre was a good example of this era of transition: at the beginning of his career, in *Primeval Fountain*, he was, like the Spanish writers, under the influence of positivist ideas and Leconte de Lisle. But in this book, one can see him shift gradually toward symbolism, while retaining the Parnassian principles of impersonalism and the perfection of form in his ideas of beauty. . . .

His poems are like a testimony to the existence of profound laws and of moral and intellectual values that are eternal and indestructible. His language is the same as that of the tragedies of Aeschylus, Sophocles, or Euripides. It is a language that neither ages nor loses its strength. It is the language of the poet who vindicates man, the language of a man in the midst of physical or moral suffering, the unjust suffering that is our fate. . . .

Mireya Jaimes-Freyre. *Modernismo y 98 a través de Ricardo Jaimes Freyre* (Madrid, Editorial Gredos, 1969), pp. 137–38, 153†

Jaimes Freyre is a poet of spiritual anguish. Though in public life he was one of the most fortunate of the Modernists, being the son of a Bolivian diplomat and himself destined to have a distinguished career as poet, scholar, diplomat and statesman, in his poetry he glimpses the barren, bleak world of modern man. . . .

In his *Primeval Fountain*, he borrowed from Norse mythology as Darío had from classical mythology in order to create a country of the mind. But unlike Darío he wrote in free verse, creating a rhythmic effect of repetition. Among the most striking of his poems is "The Song of Evil" in which evil in the person of Lok is represented in an icy landscape with a dying victim who vainly stretches his hands towards the shadow of God. . . . The poem is much more than a description of a bleak northern scene. The shepherd, traditionally a symbol of Christ and salvation, is here associated with the God of evil, moving an icy flock and apparently indifferent to the appeal of the victim. Jaimes Freyre's poem presents us with a world without hope in which there is nothing warm, promising or alive and in which nature—sea, fog, rocks, ice—is seen in its most threatening and destructive aspects.

Jean Franco. *An Introduction to Spanish-American Literature* (Cambridge, Cambridge University Press, 1969), pp. 149–51

LEÑERO, VICENTE (1933–   )

MEXICO

Studio Q is an amusing satirical tirade against television, supported by the ironic portrait of a human being trapped in the narrow confines of this medium. It is in addition an intriguingly manipulated experiment in novelistic technique, similar in certain respects to recent literary experiments, such as those of Nabokov. . . .

In his use of evocations, complicated imagery, and psychological probings, Leñero belongs with a limited group of Mexican novelists, among them Carlos Fuentes, Agustín Yáñez and Juan Rulfo, whose works contrast with those analyzing social issues in traditional patterns. Like the French author Robbe-Grillet, whom he admires, Leñero subordinates plot development and character portrayal to the creation of a fictional world consisting of spontaneous gestures and characters rich in multiple interpretations. Instead of a systematic analysis of the character's past, he prefers to depict the ephemeral present with its evocation of the past, replacing permanent nature with momentary conditions, still preserving structural unity which he believes has been neglected by other Mexican novelists.

From the traditional, static conception of the novel, *Studio Q* could be judged harshly. Still, in this genre with its almost unlimited possibilities for expressing human reality, Leñero has carried out an experiment noteworthy in recent Mexican fiction which makes it one of the most significant novels to appear in Mexico in recent years. During the past four decades the Mexican novel has evolved remarkably, successively treating the national Revolution, post-Revolutionary problems, regionalism, and psychological studies of individuals and groups. To the growing list of fine writers such as Yáñez, Fuentes, Castellanos, Arreola, Revueltas, Galindo, and Spota may be added the name of Vicente Leñero, a fresh voice in Mexican letters whose works make us optimistic and curious about his future literary activity.

George R. McMurray. *Critique.* 8, 3, Spring–Summer, 1966, pp. 59, 61

If one compares Leñero with writers his own age, one can get an idea of some of his sound qualities as a man and as a novelist. Instead of the social attitudes of his contemporaries that lead them to form circles and coteries, Leñero offers individualism as an approach to life and literature. A solitary, introverted man . . . he avoids both pedantry and self-praise in his conversation. Someone listening to him speak . . . would not guess that he is the only young Mexican writer who has won an important international prize. Although one can hardly say that curiosity is a virtue vigorously preached or actively practiced by his contemporaries, an inquiring mind can be seen at work in each of Leñero's books. Even in *The Cloud of Dust, and Other Stories*, a book more traditional than innovative, he so transmutes his influences that one does not have the impression of plagiarism but rather of readings correctly and purposefully assimilated.

In *The Sorrowful Voice*, a novel that Leñero would like to disavow today, he successfully escapes the commonplaces into which the psychological novel seems to have fallen among our writers; he does this by blurring the frontiers separating present and past, dream and wakefulness, informal confession and clinical analysis. . . . In *The Masons*, a work that in more than one way follows the techniques of the *nouveau roman*, the successful structure is the result of mixing together elements of the novel of local custom and the detective novel, and of bringing together social themes (poverty, vice, laziness, crime) and metaphysical concerns (divine grace and pardon). Indeed, Leñero has created a single work from what could be said to be three novels: one that denounces the misery of the working class; another that relates the story of a crime; and another, universal, novel, which leaves to the infinite mercy of God the judgment of human errors. . . .

Emmanuel Carballo. Prologue to Vicente Leñero,
Vicente Leñero [autobiography] (Mexico City,
Empresas Editoriales, 1967), pp. 5–7†

The central character of *The Masons* is the detective, the "man with the striped tie." This character, who appears in the majority of the [French] novels I have cited and in Leñero's works, derives directly from a concept the "new novelists" have of the anti-hero: the detective exists only in the function of his role—with no psychology, with no history—dedicated to ordering impressions and to carrying out operations of purely mechanical deduction. The investigation ultimately fails in *The Masons*, just as it does in Butor's, Robbe-Grillet's, and Ollier's novels. The statements of the characters are not precise enough. The absence of direct causality, the indeterminateness and ambiguity of the crime give the impression that one is witnessing an eternal play, a circular situation, predestined, mythic. Other characteristics of the *nouveau roman*—the importance given to seeing, an impression of geometric form, the repeated use of symbols—can also be found in *The Masons*.

Iris Josefina Ludmer. In Jorge Lafforgue, ed.,
Nueva novela latinoamericana (Buenos Aires, Editorial
Paidós, 1969–72), Vol. I, p. 195†

The Squiggle, which can be read as an exercise for a novel or as an experiment in structures, enables us to see Leñero's narrative flexibility, his basic need to question the genre. Above all, it presents us with the most intimate theme of his entire work—the faces of chance. Life is stripped naked by the invisible violence of luck, which becomes destiny and whose laws or rules the novel attempts to capture through mathematical structure, in a rigorous assault on the ungraspable. . . .

The structure of *The Squiggle* is developed around the plurality of "authors" of the novel. . . . Various masks take over the story. (1) Pablo Mejía sends a letter to Leñero and a novel he has written—*The Squiggle*. (2) Mejía's novel introduces two characters: an established literary critic—a sort of Mexican "man of letters"—with all the obsolete formal prestige of his role, who narrates in the first person; and a young man, who, also typically, brings the critic a novel he has just written, hoping for advice or backing. Naturally, his novel is called *The Squiggle*. (3) This last novel introduces Rodolfo, a young student who seems to be the direct mask of the same young writer in search of advice. Within this game of points of view, the narrative is divided into two texts: the first-person story of the old writer and the mystery adventure that surrounds Rodolfo. Through this division, the novel (Leñero's, that is) finds its form, but the game of authors has in itself succeeded in creating the story's fundamental ambiguity. . . . Leñero plays with suspense and, as a result, with the reader.

Julio Ortega. *La contemplación y la fiesta* (Caracas,
Monte Ávila Editores, 1969), pp. 183–85†

The Masons displays a notable advance over Leñero's first novel [*The Sorrowful Voice*]. The influence of Faulkner, which had taken the form of a simple stylistic imitation, has now become also a conduit . . . to another writer—Henry James—who has made a more significant contribution to Leñero's art. James's celebrated theory of point of view, which has had hardly any application in the Mexican novel, has reached Leñero and has become a fundamental concept in this novel. Leñero's declarations notwithstanding, the influence of James in *The Masons* seems to me much more palpable, fortunately, than the more immediate influence of the ["new novelists"]. This Mexican novel is without a doubt more interesting and provocative than the precocious but wasted literary trigonometries of a Robbe-Grillet. . . .

The book does not contain an ideological statement or a social message. Rather, it is like a meeting, a montage, a superimposition, of various pantographic tracings of Mexican life. Out of the criss-crossing of these diverse tracings emerges a vision of that life which could be considered terribly pessimistic; but there is no suggestion of judgment being passed on any one in particular. Lies, duplicities, Pharisaism . . . [appear] on all social levels. Corruption extends its practiced, restless, crafty fingers. In man (not only the Mexican but all of mankind) there seems to be a bad seed, what the venerable Faulkner called "anonymous promiscuity." Thus, reality . . . perhaps cannot be grasped; one can only confront it through successive spurious approximations. Leñero seems to be suggesting that every human being—and thus every Mexican—possesses and forfeits his own truth, but that truth (or guilt) does not exist as something definitive. It is no accident that *The Masons* ends with a deliberately ambiguous gesture and that the last word uttered by Munguía, the inspector, is "nothing." . . .

Mario Benedetti. *Letras del continente mestizo*
(Montevideo, Editorial Arca, 1970), pp. 178–79†

The element of time lies submerged, unlocalizable in [*The Masons*]. Leñero seems to want the reader to grasp events simultaneously, as a totality divorced from time. Because of the temporal, linear nature of language, this becomes impossible for the reader, who, not able while reading it to perceive the grand design of the novel, has recourse, out of habit and necessity, to the only means of understanding in his grasp—the temporal ordering of incidents, which, he assumes erroneously, will reveal a logical system, an incontrovertible pattern of cause and effect. As a result, the reader, who mirrors the detective, is forced to participate directly in the work. His detective work is even more complicated and demanding than that of the investigator Munguía. . . .

The reader's efforts to establish an absolute order within this temporal chaos result in failure, or at best fragmentation, since a complete temporal sequence in which motive and action, motive and crime, fit within a logical structure is never established. Leñero has purposely left us with loose ends in the narrative so as to underline the fact that any route to knowledge—in this case, the reconstruction of the facts through time—can yield no more than a mere approximation of reality. . . .

By developing simultaneously various planes of reality, Leñero is able to confront the reader at any given moment with a kaleidoscopic vision of that reality. His intent is to give the sense of the multiple nature of everything that exists in the real world. Nevertheless, this technique, instead of achieving the desired "realism," in presenting incidents and objects, encompasses them with a shroud of chaos and irreality. For example, in the real world a single crime is committed only once by one criminal. In the novel the presentation of the same crime committed by various criminals leads to a sensation of chaos and irreality, which colors the entire work. The narrative thus confronts the reader with a sur-reality, in which multiple ways of explaining events coexist, each one apparently in conflict with the others, all nevertheless interrelated and mutually dependent. . . .

Humberto E. Robles. *RI*. 36, Oct.–Dec., 1970,
pp. 579–80, 582–84†

Vicente Leñero is a writer of awesome versatility. Among Mexicans, perhaps the only parallels are Carlos Fuentes and Octavio Paz. Since 1959, the year in which Leñero published his first work, he has brought forth a series of highly imaginative literary creations in several genres. Although he is best known for his novel *The Masons* (which won the prestigious Premio Biblioteca Breve in 1963), he has most recently distinguished himself as a playwright. The year 1968 marks the beginning of his incursion into the world of the theater, with the performance of *Rejected People*, a play that bears testimony to Leñero's social and political concern.

He is an important figure in contemporary Mexican drama for, among other things, his initiation of documentary theater. *Companion*, a play first performed in 1970, is based on the events and writings of the Argentine revolutionary "Che" Guevara. An advocate of social theater, the dramatist has continued to bring historical and sociological themes to the stage, further demonstrating his awareness of the gnawing social questions that plague our era. Leñero's latest play is *The Children of Sánchez*, based on the work of the same name by Oscar Lewis. The greatest merit of this literary version of the anthropological study is seen in the careful selection of the crucial moments in the lives of the five *barrio* dwellers, moments artistically transferred into dramatic dialogue and action.

Leñero has had equal success with his two-act play *The Verdict*, in which he re-creates the trial of José León Toral, the assassin of Mexican President Álvaro Obregón who was shot to death in 1928. As in *Companion*, Leñero has used historical documents as the basis for his play. In this case, the work is a synthesis of the court records reproduced in their entirety by the newspaper *Excelsior* during the course of the trial. As the playwright states in the introduction to his work, he has attempted to achieve the highest degree of objectivity by maintaining, where clarity permits, the original syntax of the individuals involved in the trial. Nevertheless, Leñero has seen fit to take certain liberties with the newspaper accounts, such as the elimination of minor witnesses and the reduction of several historical figures to one dramatic character. He painstakingly outlines these alterations and adaptations in an effort to remain completely forthright with his audience. . . .

Leñero has taken a dormant journalistic record and given it literary life and order. He has revitalized a crucial moment of the Mexican Revolution, and through his manipulation and selection of the documents has created a work of artistic significance. The dramatist has successfully injected into the events of the trial a philosophical element that has served to give the historical moment a much wider perspective.

Charles M. Tatum. *Chasqui.* 2, 1, Nov., 1972, pp. 55–57

[*Rejected People*] was inspired by the case of Gregorio Lemercier, Prior of the monastery Santa María de la Resurreción in the outskirts of Cuernavaca, who introduced psychoanalysis into the monastic routine. Censured by the II Vatican Council, Lemercier renounced his vows and left the monastery.

In Leñero's dramatic version, when the Prior realizes his failure in dealing with the psychological aberrations within the monastery, he enlists the help of an analyst in treating their problems of materialism, homosexuality, infantilism, and their subconscious fears. The demonic appearance of the analyst foretells conflict and the potential for negative results. Within the new system, the Prior himself vacillates between feelings of humility and pride, or in the new terms, between complexes of inferiority and superiority. Psychoanalysis produces tensions which mount as the monks lose their simple faith, and a general outcry demands that the Prior be called to trial. In Act II, the Prior's bishop pleads his case before the special Vatican tribunal, on the grounds that psychoanalysis is neither Christian nor un-Christian, but rather scientific, and the church has an obligation to be responsive as much to this science as to the technical/industrial revolution of the modern world. The analogy with the case of Galileo is, of course, called forth. A chorus of catholics denounces the Prior; simultaneously a chorus of psychoanalysts censures *their* colleague. . . . They are both found guilty; the analyst admits defeat, but the Prior resolves to build another life on his new convictions. Courageous and convinced, he attracts a group of followers in this new act of faith.

The play functions within the contemporary tradition of the documentary theatre, a form which flourished in Germany until its prohibition in 1933. Revived recently by such playwrights as Peter Weiss (*Marat/Sade, The Investigation, Song of the Lusitanian Bogey*) and Rolf Hochhuth (*The Deputy*), the form continues the styles which evolved from Bertolt Brecht's epic drama. The documentary dramatist has a double problem, for in dealing with both the historical and the artistic, he runs the risk of satisfying neither the historian, looking for the truth, nor the drama critic, searching for an artistic interpretation. . . . [Leñero] incorporates passages quoted directly from Lemercier and the proceedings of the Vatican inquiry, but it is perhaps a testimonial to his artistic talents that the principals involved discredit the historical facet of the work.

> George W. Woodyard. In Harvey L. Johnson and
> Philip B. Taylor, Jr., eds., *Contemporary Latin
> American Literature* (Houston, University of Houston,
> Office of International Affairs, 1973), pp. 97–98

LEZAMA LIMA, JOSÉ (1910–   )

CUBA

Lezama Lima's poetic inspiration led him early in his career also to found reviews, such as *Verbum, Espuela de plata, Nadie parecía,* and *Orígenes,* which for twelve years has been, I believe, the best publication of its sort in Spanish. . . . [Lezama Lima] has always had the calling of the builder, the founder, a desire for group undertakings. Thus, there began to form around him . . . a mysterious family of friends, with the inevitable countercoterie of . . . enemies, all of which has made him the center of Cuban poetic life during the last twenty years.

This phenomenon, which could be seen as a group of writers of the same generation with common interests, can only be understood completely if we make two further observations: first, there are many more differences among members of this group than among those of the preceding generation; second, the writers who can be included in this group range from Lezama Lima, born in 1910, through Lorenzo García Vega, born in 1926; even younger poets have felt completely at home under the . . . tutelage of Lezama Lima. . . . For the first time in Cuba the strictures of generational determinism were broken, not through iconoclastic or polemical stands but through a natural development. . . . This all became possible when Lezama founded *Espuela de plata* in 1939 and when, two years later, he published *Enemy Noise*. . . .

Cintio Vitier. *Lo cubano en la poesía* (Santa Clara, Cuba, Universidad Central de Las Villas, 1958), pp. 372–73†

There are those who consider Lezama Lima an impenetrable poet because he adheres to a mode of personal, arbitrary expression that clashes at times with the structure of syntax or with the demands of [syntactic] agreement. In the beginning (for example, in *Death of Narcissus* and part of *Enemy Noise*) his poetry seemed like a jungle of metaphors. But this luxuriousness of images decreased in later works because of his greater emphasis on violent juxtapositions of ideas, unusual associations that seem to come from the depths of the sub-conscious, or hyperbolic evocations that fuse the real with the oneiric. I am not suggesting that he has abandoned the metaphor; rather that he fills it out or fits it in only where it can produce just the right effect. . . . In his metrics and [rhythmic] combinations, Lezama Lima refuses to abide by any rules, although he is accustomed to making incursions into the realm of the sonnet, but without admitting any fixed measure in the distribution of the rhymes. He has been searching only for a certain rhythmic homogeneity from one verse to the next, and he entrusts musicality almost exclusively to the effects of stress.

Max Henríquez Ureña. *Panorama histórico de la literatura cubana* (San Juan, Ediciones Mirador, 1963), Vol. II, p. 434†

Reading Lezama Lima is one of the most arduous tasks and frequently one of the most irritating. . . . Lezama Lima is hermetic not only in the literal sense, inasmuch as the best of his work presents a cognition of essences through the mystic and the esoteric in all their historical, psychic, and literary forms, which are vertiginously combined in a poetic system. . . . He is also formally hermetic as much because of an ingen-uousness that leads him to suppose that the most unusual of his met-aphorical series will be perfectly understood by others as because of his very original baroque expression. . . .

Paradiso could be called a non-novel, in large part for the lack of a plot to give narrative cohesion to the dizzying multiplicity of its con-tent. Toward the end, for example, Lezama Lima interpolates an extended story filling all of Chapter 12, which has nothing to do with the body of the novel, although its mood and theme may be the same. . . . *Paradiso* departs from the usual concept of the novel because its happenings are not situated in a tangible, temporal-spatial, psychological dimension. . . . In some way all of the characters are seen in essence much more than in presence; they are archetypes rather than types. One consequence . . . is that while the novel narrates the history of some Cuban families at the end of the past century and the beginning of the present—with the most fastidious details of epoch, geography, property, gastronomy, and clothing—the characters themselves seem to move in an absolute continuum, detached from all historicity, understanding each other among themselves in spite of the reader and the immediate circumstances of the story, with a language that is always the same, because of which every reference to psychological and cultural verisimilitude immediately becomes inconceivable. [1966]

Julio Cortázar. *La vuelta al día en ochenta mundos*
(Mexico City, Siglo Veintiuno Editores, 1967),
pp. 137, 143–44†

If I had to choose a word that would define in some way the major characteristic of Lezama Lima's paradise [in *Paradiso*] I would choose *exotic.* . . . For Lezama Lima, Western culture—French palaces and parks, German and Italian cathedrals, medieval castles, the Renaissance, Greece—as well as Chinese or Japanese emperors or Egyptian scribes or Persian sorcerers, are simply motifs, objects that bewilder him because his own imagination has surrounded them with qualities which have little to do with them in and of themselves and which he uses as driving forces for his thick river of metaphors. He plays with these objects with the greatest liberty—even unscrupulously—thus integrating them into a work of purely American stock.

Lezama Lima has turned exoticism on its head. . . . In *Paradiso* the history of humanity and of traditional European culture appears summarized, deformed into caricature, but at the same time poetically enriched and assimilated within a great American narrative. [1967]

Mario Vargas Llosa. In Jorge Lafforgue, ed.,
Nueva novela latinoamericana (Buenos Aires,
Editorial Paidós, 1969–72), Vol. I, pp. 137, 139, 140–41†

Probably the most fascinating character in Cuba today is José Lezama Lima, whose major life work, the novel *Paradiso*, was published in 1966. A deeply religious man, absorbed in the contemplation of a world outside time, he is a storehouse of esoteric traditions in a country that is almost without tradition. His living space is tiny. His movements cover the shortest possible distance. He receives visitors in a small front room in which words are often menaced by street traffic, and as he talks he rocks himself and smokes his cigar under the portraits of his family and the paintings of his generation. He looks and is the traditional creole—vast, immobile, parchment-coloured, asthmatic, still attended by a servant (the Baldovina of his novel) who is now in her mid-eighties. He is "bounded by a nutshell" but there must be few minds which contain so much fantastic information. Conversing with him is like conversing with Donne, Ficino, and Sir Thomas Browne. He knows every nook and cranny of occult philosophy and eccentric religion. For him the writer or artist has a solemn, priest-like function. He is a "creator," "a creator of values, of norms, he who greets the living creator." And this same Lezama Lima, who would seem to fit more comfortably into a *fin-de-siècle* aestheticism and for whom the metaphor is not a trick with words but the key to the universe, this man has discovered in the Revolution something which is in accordance with his own aesthetic beliefs. "The Revolution is a metaphor," he says, "a metaphor of man and his future, a flash of light which illuminates the near and the far."

His novel *Paradiso*, which like leavened bread seems to have risen within him for years, is certainly destined to be one of the great eccentric works of all time, something to be read like *The Anatomy of Melancholy* or (to make Cortázar's more pertinent comparison) like *Tristram Shandy*. There is no plot, but there are circles of expanding metaphor which eddy from the different characters—José Cemí, his father, his mother, the servant Baldovina, or the friends Foción and Fronesis. Characters appear and disappear in a prose so dense that it is not unfair to compare it to *Finnegans Wake*, despite the fact that the vocabulary and word order have the appearance of being more conventional. In this novel, a song sung to the accompaniment of the guitar is likely to conjure up armies of green tortoises, fields of lettuces watered by dancing Chinamen, the water, the lettuce, and the tortoise being united by some occult and elemental significance.

Jean Franco. TC. Nos. 1039–40; April, 1968–Jan.,
1969, pp. 64–65

It is very easy to misread *Paradiso*, the now-famous novel by José Lezama Lima. . . . The most tempting error is to assume that the novel is more or less autobiographical, in the manner of Proust's *À la recherche du temps perdu*. . . . It is also possible to read the book superficially and search in it for traces of a *roman à clef*. . . .

Many times both in the book and out of it, Lezama Lima has alluded to the androgynous condition of one period of humanity. In this sense, and only in this sense . . . can *Paradiso* be allegorically interpreted as an exploration of the homosexual world—a world that Lezama Lima presents from a coordinated mythical and metaphorical point of view. . . .

To be able to read *Paradiso* with full understanding, one will have to wait several years, until all of Lezama Lima's previous works are collected in one book and circulated throughout the Latin American world. . . . Now the only thing that we can try to do is not to read him superficially and ignorantly. . . . This is a major task and, in the present context of the Latin American novel, an essential task.

Emir Rodríguez Monegal. MNu. No. 24, June, 1968,
pp. 40, 41, 44†

When the Argentine novelist Julio Cortázar recommended swimming as a way of "getting into *Paradiso*," he hit upon the only correct approach to this novel. For its 617 pages are hardly conducive to meticulous critical analysis . . . even less to a casual, straightforward reading (a mental exercise whose pleasures have already been marred by reason and force of habit). But, before diving into *Paradiso,* the reader should be warned that its waters are deep and turbulent, crisscrossed by hot and cold ocean currents, inhabited by fish that bite or pierce with their swords, teeming with carnivorous plants and with sorcerers who will turn a swimmer gone astray to stone.

In a more pedestrian sense, *Paradiso* is also an autobiography. But it is a secretive, visceral autobiography—an organism that bears some resemblance to Lezama Lima's life since it functions with the same kidneys, legs, liver and heart. In the novel, however, the legs contract and dilate, while the heart serves to separate the gastric juices and the liver pumps the blood. Lezama Lima might even admit that he is José Cemí, the protagonist, that there is a strong similarity between Rialta and his mother, Señora Augusta and his maternal grandmother, the Colonel and his father, Baldovina and his servant girl Baldomera. But these facts merely camouflage what is really going on; they are anchors with which the author holds in place the objects of everyday life (houses, glasses, cities, braided hair, noses), so that the reader is not overwhelmed by the whirlpool of mirrors and insanities on every page. However, this is in no way a concession to the reader—that victim whom Lezama Lima relentlessly harasses; it is rather an exercise in mental torture. . . .

It is no accident that every esoteric cult imaginable appears in *Paradiso*, although the images are distorted by a baroque lens that may bring together, in time and space, Verne, the tarot cards, and the graffiti of the Palatinate. The author's complete lack of inhibition, his saying whatever he pleases in any way he pleases, is one of the two principles governing the construction of this novel. The other is memory, in that Lezama Lima's superabsorbent brain cells have recorded every period and every comma in the world; and, unlike Jorge Luis

Borges' Funes, he does not reproduce them verbatim: he has chosen instead to scatter them in a vast constellation in which a period is not only a period but a comma as well.

To relate what happens in *Paradiso* would be extremely dangerous: any attempt to reduce the book to a series of anecdotes, as is usually done, would be tantamount to strangling it to death. There are some works, like this, which make one sense the utter futility of literary criticism which, in its perverted rationalism, would concentrate on the shape of the bottle without making any reference to the wine within.

Tomás Eloy Martínez. Atlas. 17, 1, Jan., 1969,
pp. 62–63

It is not easy to relate Lezama Lima to the backdrop of the Cuban revolution. Because of the influence of his mother and her family, he has been a political radical all his life. But because of bad health, he was politically active only for a brief period during his student days. His importance is as a cultural figure widely respected abroad and by Cuban writers of successive generations who differ from him greatly in the practice of their art. He is such an important figure that when the students of the University of Havana complained to Castro about the withdrawal of *Paradiso* from sale because of the demands of a few partisan factions, Fidel ordered that it be put back on sale the following morning.

Lezama Lima has benefited from the revolution to the extent that he has become a national figure without having been forced to change his work in favor of a greater degree of [socialist] realism. His increasing readership among the educated youth of the new system has reinforced his tendency to explain his poetry in terms that make it more difficult, instead of easier, to understand. Nevertheless, he has stated that he has no poetic theory to teach and that whatever theory there is springs from the poems themselves instead of preceding them. He tenaciously defends the right of the poet to be hermetic and believes that the very first poetry ever created took the form of bewitchment or enchantment, a form to which the sophisticated Mallarmé attempted to return and with which Lezama Lima has been experimenting in [the group of poems] "Reading on the Turtle."

J. M. Cohen. En tiempos difíciles: Poesía cubana de la
revolución (Barcelona, Tusquets Editor, 1970), p. 42†

Since in *Paradiso* Lezama Lima considers some of the fundamental cultural and anthropological elements of Latin America—land, man, language, religion, society, government, economy, education, the conception of time, food and drink, festivities—it is not surprising that he evokes such a penetrating and lasting vision of Cuban reality, in spite of the awe-inspiring erudite superstructure. . . .

Although the novel probably defies narrow classification, it comes closest to being a *Bildungsroman* in that it strives to present the psychic and intellectual development of the hero from childhood to maturity. We follow Cemí's growth in the Cuban educational process through hilarious scenes of grotesque sexual initiation at school, to interminable metaphysical discussions with Foción and Fronesis on the Quijote, numerology, Nietzsche, Goethe, Hegel, and Mallarmé at the university. In the end, the fact that Cemí has best assimilated the diverse elements comprising his intellectual formation determines his creole weltanschauung and gives him the strength to come to terms with the unique sense of tropical time expounded by Lezama Lima. . . .

The intellectual challenge of the novel leaves the reader exhausted. At times, the work's deliberate, unbearable obscurity taxes the limits of his patience. A monstrous, erudite overload achieves brilliant effects in some instances, and fails in others. But somehow all this seems to fit into place; the vast complexity does not matter in view of the final validity of Lezama Lima's intuition. Far removed from local color, the fundamental elements comprising Latin American culture . . . are fixed, arranged and refracted through a peculiar creole lens that captures the ultimate truth of an unfathomable, tangled, uniquely Cuban world. We might then consider that Lezama Lima's vision in *Paradiso* corresponds to that of the bard, the privileged seer of the mind's eye in forbidden zones of the intellect.

Klaus Müller-Bergh. BA. 44, Winter, 1970, pp. 38–40

The poetry of Lezama Lima (and what I say here about his poems could be said equally about *Paradiso, Tracts in Havana,* or *Clock's Analecta*) is hermetic by declaration, by intention. . . .

From *Death of Narcissus* to his most mature poems—not necessarily the most perfect ones—Lezama Lima's poetry has steadily evolved. *Death of Narcissus* is in the tradition of Góngora, in the tradition of Sor Juana, whom Lezama has called one of the great "images" of American history, and even more in the tradition of Valéry and Jorge Guillén. . . . The young Lezama Lima could be classified with other modern poets—Reyes, Alonso, Gerardo Diego, Miguel Hernández in his early works—who were encouraging a return to Góngora. Yet, none of these poets, including Lezama Lima, can be reduced, through critical laxness, to a vague modern Gongorism. This for two reasons: first, more than a "return," what they represented was a renovation of the baroque tradition; second, those who "returned" to Góngora for renovation have created their own very distinct worlds, such as Lezama Lima's in *Death of Narcissus* or Gerardo Diego's in the extraordinary *Fable of X and Y*.

Lezama Lima has allied himself with what he likes to call "that serpent, Don Luis de Góngora." But, book after book, he has discovered himself more and more. His metaphors have led him to his own *imago*, his own face as a poet.

Ramón Xirau. *Poesía iberoamericana contemporánea*
(Mexico City, Ediciones SepSetentas, 1972), pp. 102–3†

LISPECTOR, CLARICE (1924–   )

BRAZIL

The style in all of these works [of Lispector's] is interior and hermetic. In most cases the action is seen from the point of view of the characters involved, and the description is also likely to be made through their eyes. This fact places her among the new vanguard of writers who have appeared in Brazil since the end of World War II and who have taken a further step along the path initiated by the so-called "Modernist" renovation of 1922. . . .

The Apple in the Dark represents the high point in the development of Miss Lispector's work, the point toward which she was striving and to which her later novel is, in a sense, a footnote. Most of the elements that go to make up the current trend in Brazilian fiction can be seen in her work. The invention is not as obvious as in Rosa because it is less a matter of neologisms and re-creation than of certain radical departures in the use of syntactical structure, the rhythm of the phrase being created in defiance of norms, making her style more difficult to translate at times than many of Rosa's inventions. Nor is the traditional vocabulary here anywhere as rich as in the works of Nélida Piñon. It is precisely in their styles of presentation that the three writers diverge: Rosa using the primitive resources of the language for the creation of new words in which to encase his vast and until then amorphous sensations; Piñon extracting every bit of richness from the lexicon of a very rich language without falling into archaisms or other such absurdities; and Lispector marshaling the syntax in a new way that is closer perhaps to original thought patterns than the language had

ever managed to approach before. These three elements are the stylistic basis of all good contemporary Brazilian literature.

Gregory Rabassa. Introduction to Clarice Lispector,
The Apple in the Dark (New York, Alfred A. Knopf,
1967), pp. x, xii

Family Ties, a collection of short stories by Clarice Lispector, constitutes a personal interpretation of some of the most pressing psychological
problems of man in the contemporary western world. Liberty, despair,
solitude, the incapacity to communicate, are the main themes that unite
the separate stories into a definite configuration of the author's pessimistic perception of life. Lispector presents a series of characters,
"agonic victims," as Miguel de Unamuno would say, who find themselves trying desperately to maintain an equilibrium between "reality"
and their own powerful imaginations. Imagination, and by implication
solitude, is represented as a double-edged dagger, since on the one
hand deviation from the norms that society erects leads to rejection,
unhappiness, and alienation, and on the other, to retreat into a personal
fantasy world, no more than a cowardly escape mechanism.

The existential struggle, for the author, consists in a series of paradoxes with no solution. How does one establish a balance between the
need to conform and the pulsating inner life that demands expression?
If one is in constant fear of revealing oneself, how can one interact
with others on an authentic level? The main characters in *Family Ties,*
nevertheless, are fully conscious that true communication is impossible:
society is an artificial barrier that must not be transcended. Yet their
essential problem, as might be expected, is not to find a meaning for
their senseless lives, but to run from the meaning they have already
acknowledged within themselves and cannot accept. In order to feel
themselves part of humanity, in so far as they are able, they force themselves to cover up their deepest feelings with the mechanized actions
expected of them, thus perpetuating their own isolation. The outside
world, or other human beings, constitute an everpresent threat to the
precarious balance necessary in order to avoid the total disintegration of
their own personality vis-a-vis the accepted patterns. The word "ties,"
therefore, has a double significance: the chains of outward conformity
that bind each person to others by means of a false set of values, and the
ties that bind each one to the other, "sans le savoir," by the total aloneness that they possess in common. Each character lives in his own little
world, estranged from the rest of humanity, unable to be free, unable
to give, unable to be, and unable to feel solidarity with the universe.
Caught in critical moments of their existence, they prefer anything

rather than the responsibility of being what they really are—human beings.

As can be seen from this brief introduction, Lispector's mentality, rather than Brazilian, comes very close to the existentialist thought of Albert Camus and Jean-Paul Sartre. Her orientation, however, tends towards a more pessimistic outlook on humanity. Whereas both Camus and Sartre propose positive solutions within this pessimistic framework (the former, that of enjoying life to its fullest and bettering social and economic conditions; the latter with his theory of "engagement"), Lispector offers no redemption for her tortured characters. The psychological anguish from which they suffer ultimately destroys them and their only hope of salvation. It should be mentioned here that in the various stories, nothing of importance really occurs; the emphasis remains on a psychological level; the action is interior rather than exterior. The tension is maintained by use of a coherent and logical stream of consciousness method.

Rita Herman. *LBR*. 4, 1, June, 1967, pp. 69–70

Brazilian writers have been part of international literature ever since Machado de Assis, and today the number of interesting poets, novelists, and essayists in that country is impressive. Many are comparatively well known to American and English readers, but Clarice Lispector, who must be considered among the most accomplished of contemporary novelists writing in Portuguese, has remained almost unknown here. Miss Lispector, born in 1924 in the Ukraine (while her parents were en route to Brazil), published her first novel at the age of nineteen, and has been highly regarded in her adopted land for the past twenty years or more. *The Apple in the Dark*, published in Brazil in 1961, is her fourth novel, and the first to appear in English.

A fascinating and distinguished work, it more than explains the esteem in which Miss Lispector is held. Unlike much Brazilian fiction, its appeal derives not at all from its regionalism, for it is quite unconcerned with local color. It is fascinating simply because Miss Lispector is a superb writer, an artist of vivid imagination and sensitivity, with a glorious feeling for language and its uses. She employs words playfully, meaningfully, deceptively, and of course seriously, not necessarily as a poet does but as few novelists do. This makes translation more than normally difficult, and it should be said at once that Gregory Rabassa has succeeded remarkably well.

The book is about many things: the relation between speech and act, knowledge and being, perception and awareness, reality and imitation. Miss Lispector has considered the existentialists, and her ontology is essentially theirs. Superficially *The Apple in the Dark* is the story of a man who has committed a crime, which represents to him a genuine act. . . . At least that is what appears upon the surface; but an outline of the "plot" is in this instance of little value; the action is in the minds and even more specifically in the words of the three principal characters. For Miss Lispector is telling us that the mind is made up in large part of the words it knows. A feeling of "horror" about his crime, Martim [the protagonist] concludes, is "what the language expected of him" and he often "preferred what he had said to what he had really wanted to say." Each character is aware of "how treacherous was the power of the slightest word over the broadest thought."

Such conceits as these would be dangerous for anyone less skillful than Miss Lispector. Words are as elusive as the feelings and thoughts they attempt to represent, and this is true even for writers. Communication may be impossible among people, but the first-rate writer can work with elusiveness and allusiveness to create poetic meaning; and so Miss Lispector, while preoccupied with the difficulty and the danger of words, is able at the same time to demonstrate their power and beauty.

Richard Franko Goldman. SR. Aug. 19, 1967, pp. 47–48

It would be redundant for me to assert that Clarice Lispector's fourth novel, *The Apple in the Dark,* maintains the level of her earlier books, since this novelist, from the publication of her very first novel, has shown herself to be mature and controlled. What we can observe right from the start in *The Apple in the Dark* is the culmination of her conceptual process, heightened in this uncommon novel almost to a provocation. The story, with its episodic movements, is relegated very much to a secondary level, barely a tenuous thread is left, one that can hardly be called a plot, certainly not a conventional one.

It is my belief that Clarice Lispector is the first writer of fiction to make each of her novels into a continuous dramatic action, precluding any possible *historical* background on the existence of her characters. Such a dramatic action, unfolded from inside out, proceeds to reveal what is typical about temperament and emotional states. The objective events of life lose their external character and are enveloped by the senses that come to perform the action.

In any quest for analogous literary achievements, we should recall Proust, although the French novelist also stresses evanescence, without ceasing to make a document of his sensory *memories*. Robbe-Grillet's *nouveaux romans*, which also reject plot, go farther in the destruction of the traditional novel. But he [unlike Lispector] also rejects any sort of psychologizing and bases the story on the description of objects. . . . In search of a new language for the novel, Lispector parallels Robbe-Grillet, but they have pursued different experiments.

Assis Brasil. Clarice Lispector, ensaio (Rio de Janeiro, Organzação Simões Editôra, 1969), pp. 72–73†

The characters who people the novels and stories of Lispector are not at all spectral or phantasmagoric. Motivated by the desire to be, the profound spring from which their worldly desires derive, naked in their individual existences, they reveal and affirm an immeasurable restlessness. . . . This restlessness, which corresponds to the necessity to be, is sustained by the feeling of existence, whence flow all other feelings.

Associated with anguish and with nausea, the feeling of existence in Clarice Lispector's works, which implies an immediate, intuitive knowledge through the direct vision of each being . . . is primarily manifested as an intuition of the subjectivity of the self. The limits of subjectivity are not, however, the limits of existence. Kierkegaard's *thingness,* limiting reality of the human being to subjectivity, is inadequate in understanding what is contained in the experience of being and of existing as transmitted through the creations of this novelist.

Benedito Nunes. O dorso do tigre (São Paulo, Editôra Perspectiva, 1969), pp. 121–22†

[Lispector sees] existence for the majority of individuals [in *The Luster* as] a sophisticated way of being dead. The very immobility with which the characters in Granja Alta are described allows us to perceive the meaning Lispector sees in those lives. But it is not enough for an artist to understand a phenomenon with sensitivity. . . .

The imperfection of Clarice Lispector's novel results from her not having based her words (which are magnificent in themselves) on an essential concreteness. In its place she develops an immediate perception through intellectualizing divagations, which do not succeed in breaking through the limits of subjectivity or in elevating the philosophical situation. . . . The text attests to the writer's verbal talent, but it also demonstrates how her capacity for composition, rather than increasing, is annihilated. This circumstance is only a step away from romantic sentiment filled out with existentialist jargon. Therefore . . . what we have is a work of very little courage, the result of its lack of correspondence to a concrete totality, a work in which intellectualizing subjectivity usurps the place of reality and ends up by overwhelming characters and novelistic material.

Luís Costa Lima. In Afrânio Coutinho, ed., A literatura no Brasil (Rio de Janeiro, Editorial Sul Americana, 1970), Vol. V, p. 461†

Without a doubt, the most important contribution to the *nouveau roman* in contemporary Brazil has been made by the Russian-born Clarice Lispector, who came to Brazil as a child. More than her novels, her greatest achievements are her masterfully wrought short stories. These stories are surely among the best accomplishments in Brazilian literature of the 1950s and 1960s, although it must be admitted that her works have more in common with Borges and Virginia Woolf—and perhaps even Proust—than with the themes that have shaped and dominated Brazilian literature since 1956 (and before 1930).

One can discern Lispector's search for her literary identity by looking at her early novels: *Close to the Savage Heart, The Luster, The Besieged City.* These works are insecure and groping, largely without a personal style and thematically indecisive. Not until 1955, when the collection of short stories *Family Ties* appeared, did the writer find access to her own poetic world.

Loneliness and hope, passion, love and hate, disappointment and resignation . . . have become her almost constant themes. The action is almost always a spirallike process, which at the crucial point—the moment of truth—explodes the psychological tension and resolves itself in the resigned acceptance of the hopelessness of the human condition. What remains—ordinary daily life—is a disheartened plodding, in which the feelings are permanently drugged so that existence can be borne.

> Günter W. Lorenz. *Die zeitgenössische Literatur in Lateinamerika* (Tübingen, Horst Erdmann Verlag, 1971), p. 250†

In a fashion coherent with her existential vision, Clarice Lispector chooses her subjects, human and animal, from the world which she contemplates and investigates. It is they which constitute the mirror in which "I" is reflected and revealed, for the impossibility of a "pure I," as Phenomenology teaches us, leads to the verification that, although there is no "necessity of the world in order to exist," the "I" is radically linked to it.

Hence, the privileged moment, upon which Clarice Lispector bases her cosmic vision, consists, in her short stories, of the character's realization of what is happening in his immediate "circumstance" (excluding only plants) and, at the same time, in the "I" itself and vice versa. The character, upon his liberation from the mystery that inhabits his circumstance, discloses to himself the surrounding world. This sudden insight unveils both the inhabited Cosmos and the microcosm that surrounds the character. Forming a true "phenomenological reduction," the "I" and the universe meet as if for the first time, framed in a halo of original "purity," causing the mutual discovery to become suspended in time, a vision of the most intimate part of reality, without the deformation of thought or prejudice. To discover is thus to return to the Beginning, but only for a brief instant, as clairvoyance would destroy itself were it to last. Endowed with this "ingenuous" vision, the person comprehends his own secret and that of the universe, but must return immediately to his previous (un)consciousness, which allows him to live without major anxiety. He is granted single insight into the most hidden part of man and things and nothing more, as mental blindness is indispensable for him to continue living and surviving.

People (characters) and animals make up the "other," the suddenly discovered reality. As for the characters, they are submerged in an existential milieu like aquatic creatures in their natural element, static, deprived of metaphysical imagination or even of profound inner life. They are aware only of their daily existence, expecting nothing, going nowhere. Undifferentiated as people, "they are constantly reflecting upon what they feel" and they cherish an inner dialogue which, for them, is reduced to the mentalization of their senses' messages from the different stimuli of the outer world. Hypnotized by the contemplation of a spectacle that doesn't vary but occasionally presents surprises, they let themselves drift without aim or anxiety. . . .

Massaud Moisés. SSF. 8, 1, Winter, 1971, pp. 271–72

Clarice Lispector presents thirteen stories under the title of *Family Ties,* a very pertinent label for designating the relations to which she particularly turns in order to give us, on the level of literature, her vision of the world. The common bond of the different impressions released here and there is the sensation of a life that is intolerable, surrounded by dreads and fears which can lead the characters to the extreme of nausea.

The temporariness of the situations created is patent. The bourgeois family is shown in a desperate and cruel search for happiness. The family's chief value, stability, is a precarious one, entirely circumstantial; the ties which it establishes are transformed into a gilded prison, within which the mechanics of everyday life lead to ennui and disgust. The existentialist mark shows vividly in this collection by Clarice Lispector. . . .

In addition to sex, guilt-ridden and appalling, and to the revelation of a lack of conscience, the great stress of the whole book is upon nausea. Even happiness leads to this end. In the first story, the woman feels that "there were certain things that were good because they were nauseating." In the same place one finds these words about the status of a married person: "disillusioned, resigned, married, contented, slightly nauseated." . . .

All ties show themselves to be dangerous. This is seen in "The Beginnings of a Fortune," when the boy's project for wealth leads to the notion of debt and obligation.

The extreme point of nausea can be found in the story "The Meal," told in the first person by a masculine narrator. Here the narrator watches, repelled and anguished, the meal of an old man in a restaurant. As he himself says: "I am overcome by the gasping ecstasy of nausea. Everything looks huge and dangerous."

So while the narrative prose of Rosa advances towards myth, we can say that on the other hand the fiction of Clarice Lispector emphasizes the values of everyday life trying to reproduce the state of the multiple social relationships that lead to loneliness. . . .

Family Ties thus symbolizes a pessimistic vision of the world, reproducing a cell of the bourgeois family, penetrating into consciences possessed by fear and nausea, wandering in fright and fear towards an empty void. The permanent recourse to plays of contrast, to the description of sentiments in conflict, to the coupling of opposites, indicate the characters' inner vision and search for an impossible identity, within an historically dated picture.

Fábio Lucas. In Harvey L. Johnson and Philip B.
Taylor, Jr., eds., *Contemporary Latin American
Literature* (Houston, University of Houston, Office of
International Affairs, 1973), pp. 64–66

LOBATO, JOSÉ BENTO MONTEIRO (1882–1948)

BRAZIL

It was with the collection *Urupês* that Lobato definitely established himself. In three years it has reached a sale that for Brazil is truly phenomenal: twenty thousand copies. It has been extravagantly praised by such divergent figures as the uncrowned laureate Olavo Bilac (who might have had more than a few words to say about legitimate French influence upon Brazilian poetry) and the imposing Ruy Barbosa, who instinctively recognized the fundamentally sociological value of Lobato's labours. For of pure literature there is little in the young Saint-Paulist. . . .

The truth would seem to be that at bottom Lobato is not a teller of stories but a critic of men. His vein is distinctly satiric, ironic; he has the gift of the caricaturist, and that is why so often his tales run either into sentimentality or into the macabrous. When he tells a tale of horror, it is not the uncannily graduated art of a Poe, but rather the thing itself that is horrible. His innate didactic tendency reveals itself not only in his frankly didactic labours, but in his habit of prefixing to his tales a philosophical, commentative prelude. Because he is a well-read, cosmopolitan person, his tales and comments often possess that worldly significance which no amount of regional outlook can wholly obscure; but because he is so intent upon sounding the national note he spoils much of his writing by stepping onto the pages in his own person.

At his best he suggests the arrival in Brazilian literature of a fresh, spontaneous, creative power. Tales like "A Modern Torture" (in which a rural dabbler in politics, weary of his postal delivery "job," turns traitor to the old party and helps elect the new, only to be "rewarded" with the same old "job") are rare in any tongue and would not be out of place in a collection by Chekhov or Twain. Here is humour served by—and not in the service of—nation, nature and man. Similarly "Choo-Pan!" with its humorous opening and gradual progress to the grim close, shows what can be done when a writer becomes the master and not the slave of indigenous legend. A comparison of this tale with a similar one, "The Tree That Kills," may bring out the author's weakness and his strength. In the first, under peculiar circumstances, a man meets his death through a tree that, according to native belief, avenges the hewing down of its fellow. In the second, the Tree That Kills is explained as a sort of preface, then follows a tale of human beings in which a foster-child, like the Tree That Kills, eats his way into the love of a childless pair, only first to betray the husband and then, after wearying of the woman, to attempt her life as well. ["Choo-Pan!"], besides being well told, is made to appear intimately Brazilian; the death of the man, who is a sot and has so bungled his work that the structure was bound to topple over, is natural, and actual belief in the legend is unnecessary; it colours the tale and lends atmosphere. "The Tree That Kills," on the other hand, is merely another tale of the domestic triangle, no more Brazilian than anything else, with a twist of retribution at the end that must have appealed to the preacher hidden in Lobato; the analogy of the foster-son to the tree is not an integral part of the tale; the story, in fact, is added to the explanation of the tree parasite and is itself parasitical.

Isaac Goldberg. Brazilian Literature (New York,
Alfred A. Knopf, 1922), pp. 279–80, 282–83

Lobato discussed at length with Godofredo Rangel the necessity, after one has read the great writers (Zola, Eça de Queiroz, Camilo Castelo

Branco), to come away from them "more Rangel" and "more Lobato" than ever, to take from them only what did not imply plagiarism, imitation, copying of manner, and so on. But . . . a complete liberation is not possible. In some of Lobato's early works one can find traces of the style or the manner and even the vocabulary of Eça or of Camilo, of Poe, of Maupassant, of the Bible. But this is natural, because ultimately every writer is the result of all the writers before him whom he has read, plus the particular, individual coloring of his temperament, of his personality. . . .

Lobato, everything notwithstanding, formulated a style that was outstanding, original, and very special. It is possible, although unlikely, that someone could make a mistake in identifying a passage by Alencar and one by Machado de Assis, or by any other Brazilian writer. But it would be impossible to confuse a passage . . . by Lobato with that of any other writer, Brazilian or foreign.

Thus, everything is individual in Lobato—his style and his ideas. He had a very singular way of seeing things; in a word, he had a *philosophy*.

Alberto Conte. *Monteiro Lobato: O homem e a obra*
(São Paulo, Editora Brasiliense Limitada, 1948),
pp. 66–68†

Anísio Teixeira has observed that Lobato's great dilemma was not to have been able, at any time in his life, to have given "the full measure of his genius." Even in the most tragic of countries— such as India, Russia, even Ireland—a man of genius finds himself at certain moments in communion with the collective body and reaches the culmination of his efforts. With Lobato this was never possible, since he was always surrounded by the lack of comprehension of his contemporaries, which clipped his wings. A rebel and a nonconformist, he was always struggling against his environment. Hence the intemperateness of his language, the constant rages that seemed like bitter pessimism to superficial observers, the total disbelief or the absolute sense of defeat. And since there was something of the demon in him, he enjoyed the reactions provoked by his diatribes. . . . "I am tired of being hungry, so I am off to eat in Buenos Aires," he exclaimed with a mocking smile, waving goodbye to those he left behind. Anyone who knows him knows that he is obviously no glutton and that he was never obsessed by Pantagruelian dreams. But he loved to stir up the patriots, to thrust jabs at them. He defined "patriot" as "someone who lies, who falsifies the facts, who hides the blemishes, who passes on to children the sordid mess that he received himself."

The systematic falsification of Brazil's nature irritated him ever since he was a child. "National patriotism . . . is not a constructive sentiment. It is screaming, it is triteness, it is the simplest and silliest sonority possible." Lobato did love Brazil, but he wanted to love it while not seeing the things that make it ugly through rose-colored glasses.

> Edgard Cavalheiro. *Monteiro Lobato: Vida e obra*
> (São Paulo, Companhia Distribuidora de Livros,
> 1955), pp. 659–60†

A polymorphous, versatile, vibrant individual, [Lobato] seems to me a representative of the best type of Homo Americanus, that variety of Homo Sapiens which is day by day assuming a larger and larger role in the history of the species. A pioneer, a tamer, an adventurer, he had nothing of the contemplative aesthete, of the pure artist. He was a participant in all of the forms of modern life, and his books were born as if accidentally, in the in-between times of a full existence. The guidelines he set, the paths he opened, now seem more important than the books he wrote, even though the popularity of his works is justly growing. His works are comparable in many respects to those of that great North American writer Mark Twain, but this Brazilian Twain wrote no better book than his own life. [1955]

> Paulo Rónai. *Encontros com o Brasil* (Rio de Janeiro,
> Ministério da Educação e Cultura, 1958), pp. 229–30†

Lobato [sometimes] depended too much on the episodic or even on the anecdotal, and some of his stories come close to the realm of the chronicle. The writer himself was aware of this, as we can see in this fragment from a letter. "I have never written stories and I don't know if I ever can. What I thought were stories, if I reread them now, seem more like chronicles with pretensions at humor." This question [of genre], much discussed by some critics, seems to me a secondary issue: ascertaining the frontiers between genres barely has methodological value, certainly not an ontological one. What is important is to show how this technique corresponds to a basic given in Lobato's mentality, to his lack of fondness for longer forms and for deep investigation.

Within their limits, Lobato's stories are generally skillfully constructed. The various elements and planes of narrative, set forth and combined with a fine sense of proportion, fit together into a solid, harmonious, architectural whole. Our author, without a doubt, handles the techniques of the genre well, if we understand "genre" as he understood it. But it is significant that he felt more at home in dealing with jocular matters, or at least tragicomic ones, in which he could give full rein to his undeniable satiric talents. . . .

José Carlos Barbosa Moreira. Introduction to José Bento Monteiro Lobato, *Textos escolhidos* (Rio de Janeiro, Livraria Agir Editôra, 1962), p. 10†

Lobato clearly expressed [his sense of] the necessity of [style] to be natural, without alteration or deformation. Thus he said: "And to speak of style: when we allow the idea to flow from our pen, without any preconceptions as to manner or rule—when we are not able to 'make style'—this is precisely when we have style. Diagnosis: whoever would have style never attains it."

The direct, immediate putting down of thoughts—but without going to the extremes of the "stream of consciousness" and the experimental prose of a Gertrude Stein—constituted Lobato's ideal for the process of style. Following a line of thought that places him very close to Graciliano Ramos, Lobato presented an apologia for stripped-down, naked prose. He praised "direct style" in a letter to Nelson Palma Travasso. Expounding this idea, he stated: "It means saying 'sun' instead of 'royal star,' for example. . . ."

Evidently, Lobato wanted literature to be what he defended as a personal aesthetic: the perfect fidelity to being, genuineness, authenticity, the absence of artifice, the avoidance of any straying from intimate reality.

Cassiano Nunes. *LBR*. 6, 1, June, 1969, pp. 48–49†

Caricatures abound in [his] stories, usually as vehicles for Lobato's satire of human failings, stupidity, rural society, the government, etc. Sizenando Capistrano of "The Agricultural Morning Star" is a caricature of the "poet" in government. The colonels of "The 'Cruz de Ouro' " are caricatures of the rural military. Through the rural types of "The German Spy" Lobato satirizes ill-conceived and even harmful demonstrations of patriotism in an imaginary provincial small town during World War I. Lobato's small-town characters in general tend to be caricatures. It is hard for him to avoid making fun of his characters; and when he does attempt to be serious, he is apt to go over into the sentimental or the macabre. He seems to be most at home in the satiric vein. Let the reader enjoy "The Placer of Pronouns" as a satire against grammarians, but let him not try to find a flesh-and-blood human in the hero, Aldrovando Cantagalo.

However, the pitiful and frustrated hero of "Timóteo the Gardener" becomes a symbol. Timóteo, the old Negro gardener, is a lover of the old, traditional flowers. He has kept a sort of coded history of the family written in the garden, in the flowers, and in their arrangement. Every plant has a meaning for him. Then the *fazenda* [hacienda] changes hands and the new owners want to modernize the garden, replacing the traditional flowers with stylish new ones. The tragedy is that of a man ordered to destroy his life's work.

For pure comedy and entertainment, I would list the unfortunate Inácio of "The Indiscreet Liver" and the unforgettable Biriba of "A Modern Torture." Inácio as a guest must cope as best he can with unwelcome servings of a dish he abhors. Biriba is the prototype of all overworked, underpaid rural mail carriers, and a victim of local politics. He is an ideal vehicle for Lobato's humor, which is achieved through the ingenious plot with a surprise ending, quite in harmony with the mood of the story. Given a comic situation or one that can be made to yield humor, Lobato is in his element.

Lobato's secondary characters are noteworthy, particularly those of the small-town and *fazenda* stories. These are the rural personages at which he excels: the colonels, priests, maids, doctors, wives, politicians, judges, lawyers, lovers, idlers, storekeepers, etc., are usually caricatures rather than portraits, and inevitably amusing. "The German Spy," mentioned above, exemplifies Lobato's treatment of such characters; the action is episodic and numerous small-town types play their parts.

Timothy Brown, Jr. *BRMMLA*. 24, June, 1970, pp. 63–64

LÓPEZ VELARDE, RAMÓN (1888–1921)

MEXICO

The first impression one receives on reading a poem by Ramón López Velarde is precisely one of having suddenly entered a sacked house. But, immediately, out of the visible disorder, the very incoherencies begin to calm our sense of propriety. To be sure, there has been violence, but the sackers have not taken with them anything of what they came to steal. The curtain has disappeared from the door it protected, but it has not disappeared from the house. . . . The mirror has not fled from the frame that held it. It has been turned to face the wall, perhaps so as not to witness the scene of robbery that our arrival in the room—that is to say, our curiosity as a reader—has been able to prevent. . . .

Like all poetic expression that is really to the point, [López Velarde's] seems to us mysterious and difficult, like a miracle. We anxiously seek the origins of a prophecy that, in my judgment, is to be found only in the interplay of those terms in [the fragment of *Devout Blood* quoted:] the significant evocation of a tower and the quality of the word "dignitary," which, applied to the ash trees amputated by the machine-gun and joined to the stately cupola of the end of the verse . . . gives them an immediate solemnity and a resignation appropriate to the Christian martyrs. . . . This combination of devout religiousness and intrepid poetry, this subjection to the canons of dogma, and these rebellions against the canons of grammar are to be found from one end to the other in López Velarde's works. . . .

Jaime Torres Bodet. *Atenea.* No. 71, Jan., 1931,

pp. 67–69†

In Ramón López Velarde Mexican poetry is reflected upon passionately, repudiates its artifices and acquires a consciousness of its aims which is comparable, in its penetration, to the immortal poetic consciousness of Baudelaire. The poems in which this poet left the best of himself are not numerous—there are only a few—but they are sufficient to have him acknowledged as the most personal poet that Mexico has ever had. The flame kindled in his poetry is not only enough to give to his verse its brightness, but it illuminates the entire destiny of Mexican poetry. In Ramón López Velarde a sense is found in all the Mexican poetic endeavours whose originality it is difficult to perceive on account of their indecision, their reserve, or their proximity to the different schools. Even the most forgotten academic poetry recovers a value, certainly unknown to itself, when it is considered from the position of López Velarde. In this great poet, prematurely deceased, the poetic experience of Mexico is isolated, summed up, and purged; it grasps in a profound way "the American character" of its destiny, and makes that destiny universality. [1934]

Jorge Cuesta. In José Luis Martínez, ed.,
The Modern Mexican Essay (Toronto, University of
Toronto Press, 1965), pp. 353–54

Is the spiritual complexity of López Velarde's poetry real and profound? Was his obscurity of expression necessary? Was his unusual style the price of his concern for precision, or was it only the outcome of his desire to be different? Were the metaphors of his poetry sought after or were they inevitable? . . . The truth is that the poetry of Ramón López Velarde attracts and repels, pleases and displeases, alternately and at times simultaneously. But when once displeasure and repugnance are overcome, the seduction is effected, and sometimes in admiration, at other times confused, always interested, it is not possible to fail to enter into it as into an intricate labyrinth in which perhaps the poet himself had not found the guide-wire, but in which, in some way or other, the anguish of his mind was in itself the prize of the adventure.

In the eyes of everyone, the poetry of Ramón López Velarde is set in a provincial, Catholic, orthodox atmosphere. The Bible and the catechism are indisputably the ever-handy books of the poet; his love is romantic love; his only loved one, Fuensanta. But these are the general characteristics, the visible limits of his poetry, not the more special lines or the more secret frontiers. . . .

In Mexican poetry, the work of Ramón López Velarde is up to the present moment the most intense and the most daring effort to reveal the inner soul of a man; to bring to the surface the most submerged and intangible affections; to express the most painful torments and the most recondite distresses of the mind called forth by eroticism, religiosity, and death. [1935]

> Xavier Villaurrutia. In José Luis Martínez, ed.,
> *The Modern Mexican Essay* (Toronto, University of
> Toronto Press, 1965), pp. 312, 325

The poetry of Mexico in recent years (unlike the painting) is closely connected with international trends and, more specifically, with symbolism. This movement, since its birth in the nineties, has flowered sooner or later in every country of Europe and even today, in modified form, still affects the poetry of the United States.

It is not surprising, therefore, that Mexican poetry is influenced by both Spanish and French symbolism. Ramón López Velarde, acknowledged as the greatest Mexican modern, inclines more to the French tradition. The bitter ironies of Laforgue, the half-sceptical Catholicism of Corbière, the hallucinated imagery of Rimbaud are a part of his background and it is not even too much to say that in maturity of style his work is on a level with that of his French masters.

It is also said that López Velarde is the most Mexican of the Mexican poets. This indigenous quality is harder to analyze. Back of all Mexican art lies Mexican history—a story of a mixed race, Indian and Spanish, a story of a small bourgeois class with a thin colonial culture, a story of exploitation and poverty. López Velarde lived in a medium-sized provincial city in which there was very little literary or artistic life. It was a town of little adobe houses—hot, dirty—with a population mostly poor and almost primitive in their *mores*. His richly imaginative spirit, imprisoned in the bitterness, the barrenness of provincial monotony, took refuge in irony and in the adventures of the mind. The grandeur and sweep of the Mexican mountains, the patient dignity of the Indian is not reflected in López Velarde's work. He is the true poet of the Mexican petty bourgeoisie, a sordid nostalgic class existing as if in exile on the fringes of a country too great for them, a victim of forces beyond their comprehension.

Yet López Velarde, a truly great poet, creates beauty out of this poverty of soul. In "The Anchor" he has, like Rimbaud, fled in dreams from his imprisoning environment. Desperately he tries to explain his frustration to the "countrywoman" who will never understand him and in whom he will try to forget the unfulfillment of his life.

H. R. Hays. *Poetry.* 57, Oct., 1940, pp. 40–41

Two facts, apparently external, favour the discovery which López Velarde will make of his country and himself. The first is the Mexican Revolution, which breaks with a social and cultural order which was a mere historical superposition, a straightjacket which stifled and deformed the nation. . . .

The other decisive fact in the poetry of López Velarde is his discovery of the capital. The revolutionary tide, along with his own literary ambitions, brings him to Mexico City when his mind was already formed, but with his taste and his poetry still unformed. His surprise, shock, joy, and bitterness must have been tremendous. In the city he discovers women, solitude, doubt, and the devil. And while he is undergoing these dazzling revelations he comes to know the poetry of some South-American poets who dare to break with Modernism by carrying its conquests to the extreme limit: Julio Herrera y Reissig and Leopoldo Lugones. Contact with these writers change his manner and his vision. The critics of his time found him contorted, incomprehensible, and affected. The truth is the very opposite; thanks to his search for the image, to his almost perfidious use of adjectives that till yesterday were rare, and to his disdain of forms already established, his poetry ceases to be a sentimental confidence in order to become converted into the expression of a mind and a tortured anguish. [1950]

Octavio Paz. In José Luis Martínez, ed.,
The Modern Mexican Essay (Toronto, University of
Toronto Press, 1965), pp. 450–51

López Velarde's prose is not inferior to his poetic work and follows, in its totality, an evolution similar to that of his poetry. . . . López Velarde worked on his prose pieces with the same intentions and artistic insistences that characterize his poetry. His is a lyric prose: the inner form of poetry is its common denominator, although his agile pen jumps, with elegance and ease, from subjective effusion to critical observation, from literary portraiture to the presentation of ideas. Whatever the theme, his prose is subjective and maintains the same lyric tension that is to be found in his poetry.

The best moments of his prose are to be found within the genre that has been called "poems in prose," a confusing genre that I will not presume to define here. Certain fragments take on a poetic autonomy within the more linear development we demand of prose. Nevertheless, it is important to note that the poems in prose by López Velarde are not at all like precious miniatures, the kind of artificial prose that is devoid of any true lyric intention, which circulated so widely throughout Latin America toward the end of the nineteenth century and at the beginning of the twentieth. That kind of prose, undoubtedly, reflected more than anything else the influence of Darío and the other writers who contributed to the renewal of literary language. López Velarde's prose is not modernist in the most obvious meaning of the word. Prose, like poetry, always served him as a mold for the expression of authentic emotions and states of his spirit.

Allen W. Phillips. *Ramón López Velarde: El poeta y el prosista* (Mexico City, Instituto Nacional de Bellas Artes, 1962), pp. 297–98†

["Sweet Fatherland"], the most widely known of López Velarde's poems, has not had good luck. Adopted as the standard bearer of the group that has sponsored innumerable civic commemorations, and declaimed as a result at one event after another, the poem has ended up being suspected by the critics. . . .

According to [some critics], one should exclude nature, social upheaval, and heroic themes from the realm of poetry. The poet is (and to a great degree they are right) a sort of conjurer, an exorcist whose call beckons the dark and divine powers that lie in chaos. Whatever is not a flowering of the subconscious belongs to the fringe of poetry. . . .

From [López Velarde's] bones, from his blood, from his primeval vision of the world, "Sweet Fatherland" was born. What we have is not a simple objective presentation of landscapes, customs, village scenes. Rather, he gives us what lies below and what is thus the reflection of man: the drama which is immanent, which unfolds before his very eyes, which forces him to come out of his daydreaming and embrace the epic. . . .

"Sweet Fatherland" is the other side of the [Mexican] Revolution. The poet is not interested in leaders and celebrated deeds, nor in the urban and industrial upsurge that came from the new government. He nostalgically wants to fix on the collective memory the image of a country that used to be, which is beginning to pass into history. At the same time, he tries to conserve its spirit through the fidelity of tradition.

Carmen de la Fuente. *Ramón López Velarde: Su mundo intelectual y afectivo* (Mexico City, FEM, 1971), pp. 115–16†

López Velarde's poetry has as its principal theme the course of a spiritual crisis and the attempt to overcome it through the integration of the psyche. And his three books [*Devout Blood, Anxiety, The Sound of the Heart*] establish a plot for this theme which is essentially primordial and which coincides with the classic formula for plot structure. A spiritual conflict is presented in the first book, attains the level of crisis in the second, and is resolved in the last book of poetry.

This development corresponds to an archetypal plan for thematic structure, which has its origin in the confrontation of the psyche with psychological reality. It is the ancient story of Man cast from Earthly Paradise, searching eternally for the way back, confronting various threatening obstacles, and finally concluding that the reattainment lies not in this life but possibly in the beyond.

This theme can appear in various guises. Earthly paradise can be symbolized by the innocence and purity of childhood or by the sought-after comfort of the mother's lap. In López Velarde's poetry the theme is split into two series of images: one grouped around visions of the province that has been lost forever; the other around the vision of the Beloved, the unattainable Fuensanta. The result is conflict, crisis, and resolution.

Frederic W. Murray. *La imagen arquetípica en la poesía de Ramón López Velarde* (Chapel Hill, N.C., Estudios de Hispanófila, 1972), p. 85†

LUGONES, LEOPOLDO (1874–1938)

ARGENTINA

Sentimental Lunar Poems is without a doubt the most complex and disconcerting book that Argentine literature has produced to date. Once again Lugones has attempted to sound a new and strange note, and, to tell the truth, if such has been his exclusive purpose he has been completely successful. But to the extent that art cannot be equated with the rope on which the tightrope-walker executes his surprising balancing acts, or with a futile game of resolving the difficulties that one has set up for himself, however skillful the writer may have been . . . these skills are simply not enough to justify a book. To be sure, it would be wrong to deny that Lugones has put into his book much talent and patience. Nevertheless, something more can be demanded, something that can be justly demanded from any poetic work.

Roberto F. Giusti. Nosotros. Nos. 22–23, July–Aug., 1909, p. 293†

Among the [Spanish] American poets of the modernist movement, Leopoldo Lugones has his own special quality. For Rubén Darío it is elegance; for Nervo, mysticism; for Herrera y Reissig, insanity; for Chocano, spontaneity. For Lugones it is preciosity. It is also something else—rhetoric. Rhetoric in the worst sense. But despite everything, he is a most vigorous and interesting poet!

He is the most "imagiferous" and full-bodied poet of the modernist group. He encompasses the entire lyrical register, from the madrigal to the epic, from the georgic to the psychological poem. To span these areas does not mean to triumph in all of them. His nature as a poetic orator, a poet who shouts out loud . . . has made him an heroic poet. He has the objectivity, the blind faith in the people and the things of his land: cities, heroes, flocks, fields, mountains, rivers. His feeling for the land exceeds vaster feelings, such as the love for humanity; exceeds more necessary feelings, such as the love for justice; exceeds even more intimate feelings, such as the love for family and even romantic love. This feeling becomes exaggerated (and consequently less effective) in Lugones to the extent that it coincides and becomes confused with exclusivist and aggressive political nationalism. . . .

[His feeling for nature] is not spontaneous, disinterested, but the opposite: any nature one meter beyond native boundaries does not interest him. People, even less. Or if they do interest him it is only as entities to be placed in opposition to his exclusively local enthusiasms. . . .

Rufino Blanco-Fombona. El modernismo y los poetas modernistas (Madrid, Editorial Mundo Latino, 1929), pp. 295–96†

Beginning with his conversion to obscurantism, Lugones's development is marked by an accelerated fall. Generally a writer's mature works are grander and denser than those of his youth, and it is logical that this be the case. A poet, freed now from all influence . . . harvests ideas and forms with a hand that no longer trembles, with a hand that no longer makes the earlier mistakes. But Lugones offered as his final works of maturity the poems of *Ancestral Poems* and the prose of the pseudo-novel *The Angel of the Shadow*; it is better not to speak of these works out of respect for a man who was able to write, with a better control of his resources, *The Gaucho War.* . . .

No one proposes that he should have continued in his original anarchism, a position that is false because it is exaggerated and lacks any philosophical or practical basis. But he could have evolved toward broader horizons, with his face always toward the light, instead of turning his back, with increasing obstinancy, from the light. And anyone today, who like Lugones, is in the rank of the far right takes up arms against the spirit and commits a crime against simple humanity. These crimes are paid for, sooner or later, and Lugones . . . paid for them through daily decadence, through a drying up, withering and fading away, of the brilliance that had always been his true literary patrimony, until at the end he was transformed into a systematic bore, unable to write two words without repeating his tiresome mania, the same invectives against the forces of social renewal. . . .

Nydia Lamarque. *Nosotros.* 2nd series, Nos. 26–28,
May–July, 1938, p. 82†

Nothing can define the intellectual profile of Leopoldo Lugones more eloquently than the content of the seven articles that he published in as many issues of *La revue sudaméricaine*, which he founded in Paris at the beginning of 1914 in collaboration with Jules Huret and which stopped publication after only seven issues because of the universal conflagration [that is, World War I]. In the first of these articles he announced the imminent European war and proclaimed Pan-Americanism. In the second he studied the economic crisis of South America resulting from the Balkan conflict. In the third he undertook a classification of the wild plants of the southern hemisphere. In the fourth he wrote on the place of geometry in the study of mathematics in secondary school. In the fifth he presented the music and dance of the Argentine gauchos as an expression of popular art. In the sixth he was concerned with the French scholar J. H. Fabre in terms of three concrete subjects in zoology. In the last article he presented in great detail his observations on the Patagonian fossils discovered by the eminent naturalist Florentino Ameghino.

As can be seen . . . a simple listing is enough to show his extraordinary encyclopedism . . . which make us easily think of those Protean humanists of the Middle Ages and the Renaissance. . . .

Enrique Loncán. *Nosotros.* 2nd series, No. 36, March,
1939, pp. 286–87†

To the writers of his time Lugones brought a new message. When he arrived, the Argentine and Latin American [poets] were still paying homage to the worn romantic muse of whinings and swoonings. But the poet from Córdoba [Argentina] had scarcely arrived in Buenos Aires . . . when he revealed to the members of his youthful fraternity his own religion, inspired by the destinies of his people. Immediately his influence took hold. . . . Thus, first *The Mountains of Gold* and then *The Evening Shadows of the Garden* became guides to all of the advanced poets of the continent.

Pledged to the movement of renovation initiated by Rubén Darío, Lugones dominated his part of America by his mental force, the continuation and complement of his tumultuous will. . . . Darío, Lugones, and Jaimes Freyre, leaders of the uprising, had on their side the audacity and the reforming impetus of youth, not to mention the superiority of their talents, and they passed over the rhetoric and poetics of the time as one of those violent wind storms freshens and clears the heavy summer atmosphere. If they did destroy something deserving of a better fate, if the passage of time now shows us some of their errors and many of their excesses, we should not let this make us underestimate the decisive importance of their influence. . . .

Juan Pablo Echagüe. Escritores de la Argentina
(Buenos Aires, Emecé Editores, 1945?), pp. 138–39†

[Lugones] was less a thinker than a poet, and he was less a poet than an artificer: in fact, as far as I am concerned, he was not the sort of man who could or should be a poet. Anyone who undertakes a study of his works will find many supports for such reservations. Yet there can be no doubt that, from 1900 on, he was one of the fifteen or twenty main representatives of Latin American culture and that his work is linked unquestionably to the best of European literature. . . .

Because of the particular circumstances of his life, Lugones's death is important for the way in which it focuses attention on the situation of the intellectual [in Latin America]. Buenos Aires saw four suicides of writers between 1937 and 1939: Horacio Quiroga, Leopoldo Lugones, Alfonsina Storni, and Lisandro de la Torre, the last a political poet of lofty ideals and disinterestedness. And between 1939 and 1941 Víctor Guillot, Méndez Calzada, Enrique Loncán, and Edmundo Montagne committed suicide. But the symbolic suicide is Lugones's because in his death a social sickness becomes evident.

Manuel Ugarte. Escritores iberoamericanos de 1900
(Mexico City, Editorial Vértice, 1947), pp. 166–68†

Strange Forces contains twelve fantastic stories and an essay on cosmogony. Both genres recall the writer of *Eureka* and *Tales of the
Grotesque and Arabesque* [Poe]. The influence of Edgar Allan Poe is,
in fact, very probable. But neither Lugones's fantastic literature nor his
cosmogonic literature is similar to those of his predecessor. Lugones was
cultivating the fantastic story as early as 1896. In journals of the period,
one can find many examples of this kind of Lugones's writing, stories
which were not collected after his death but which bear his signature.
Of the ones included in *Strange Forces* perhaps the best are "The Rain
of Fire" (which recounts, with careful details, the destruction of the
cities of the plains), "The Horses of Abdera," "Yzur." and "The
Statue of Salt." These stories are among the best in Hispanic literature.
Lugones resolves one of the stories through the intervention of a god.
This gross device of *deus ex machina*, for which Euripides is so
reproached, achieves, through Lugones's art, a surprising and shattering
effect. Because of its popular theme and its simple style, not frequent
in Lugones, "The Toad" arouses our interest. In this story, even more
than in the others, Lugones makes full use of the supernatural.

"Essay on a Cosmogony in Ten Lessons" has a novelistic prologue
and epilogue. . . . The writer's purpose is to express an hypothesis
seriously; the narrative framework thus serves to excuse the intrusion of
a layman in scientific material. Lugones's cosmogony brings together
elements from the physics of his time—energy, electricity, matter—and
others from the Vedanta and from Buddhist philosophy: cyclical annihi-
lations, re-creations of the universe and the transmigration of souls.
[1955]

Jorge Luis Borges. Leopoldo Lugones, 2nd ed.
(Buenos Aires, Editorial Pleamar, 1965), pp. 71–72†

The vastly different criteria used to evaluate Lugones's place in Argentine culture derive, in my opinion, from an inability to make a clear
separation between the artist and the man, between the poet and the
prose writer. Those who disagree with his belligerent attitudes as a
citizen of Argentina, with a political position but without a party, pre-
judge his literary work unfavorably. On the other hand, those who
admire his extraordinary literary gifts extend their praise to all his writings as a block. . . .

It is obvious that every writer . . . must be studied and judged as
a man of his time and his country. Yet this does not, of course, imply
that being a man of one's own time and country obliges one inescapably
to channel his message into political programs. . . . The widespread
tendency of our intellectuals of all stamps . . . to consider political
action as a basic instrument of influence on society has detracted from

the efficacy and the fulfillment of almost all of our greatest men, beginning with Sarmiento. Lugones also gave in to this proclivity, and if it is certain that he did not work within any specific political party but kept himself free from obligations and obedience, his message was unquestionably political, much more so than it was philosophical, sociological, or educational. [1956]

Ezequiel Martínez Estrada. *Leopoldo Lugones:*
Retrato sin retocar (Buenos Aires, Emecé Editores,
1968), pp. 41–42†

Lugones sought a poetry free from traditional ties, one capable of expressing all the subtleties he shows in his *Sentimental Lunar Poems*, but . . . he thought that rhyme was an "essential element in modern poetry." Lugones's free verse, then, is not without rhyme. But by varying the rhythms, he created a new form suited to the humorous and irreverent tone that marks his attitude toward man. . . . Although Laforgue wanted—at least theoretically—to avoid traditional rhyme, and Lugones, on the contrary, cultivated it, there was a marked affinity between the two in their search for a rich and unexpected rhyme that would give a rarefied quality to their poetry. Furthermore, both borrowed rhymes from foreign languages. . . .

Lugones's reading of Laforgue seems to have provided him with some thematic and stylistic stimuli that directly or indirectly influenced the writing of *Sentimental Lunar Poems*, even though there is a marked difference in tone. When I stress the Argentine poet's liking for the author of *L'imitation*, I am in no way trying to deny originality to Lugones, whose verbal pyrotechnics set poetry on a new course.

Allen W. Phillips. *RI.* 23, Jan.–June, 1958, pp. 63–64†

I have already observed that Lugones sought in the security of the past protection from the instability of the present and that this desire motivated him to seek archetypes. This sort of [escape] was always accompanied by a spiritual feeling that compelled him to seek in each moment of life absolutes, which he [paradoxically] later abandoned because the need for absolutes and his restlessness were inevitably greater than the comfort offered by these modest formulas. He had a need to categorize reality, and the poet was always identifying himself with those fleeting moments that he sought so insistently. His individualism emerged in the identification with [archetypes] that seem to give an order to a troubling and deceptive reality. . . .

Lugones committed himself to dominating Argentine intellectual life through his writings and his public presence. He felt himself to be a *vates* and an oracle, and he presented ideas with an extraordinary arbitrariness. No one dared to demand an accounting from him [for his ideas], not even those who opposed them. His opponents apparently agreed with him out of a secret hope that his general acceptance would spread to them. . . . Lugones lent his support, with the best will, to the oligarchy's idea of an intellectual: someone with talent . . . who is capable of finding good reasons for bad deeds, one who would walk out when his dignity is wounded, one who feels he must be the first to speak out when the country needs to be saved, one whose spirit will not be tormented by his youthful follies, and, above all, one who is such a verbal master and accepted as a teacher by his own political enemies that they would give his feelings toward them the importance they would give an excommunication.

Of course, Lugones was disinterested, as everyone has noted accurately. But he subscribed to the notion of service, humbly resigned to not creating difficulties for those who, in his mind, were the incarnation of the salvation of the homeland [that is, the military dictators of the 1930s with whom he collaborated]. . . .

Noé Jitrik. *Leopoldo Lugones, mito nacional*
(Buenos Aires, Editorial Palestra, 1960), pp. 27, 29–30†

The meanings of silence in the poetry of Leopoldo Lugones are particularly subtle and profound. A study of Lugones' use of silence reveals that it is, like Darío's "princess," a personal symbol. . . . Using a Symbolist technique, Lugones assigns color to silence. Silence is shown again and again as pale, clear, white, silver, and gold. These adjectives give silence weightless, fragile, vague, and ethereal qualities. Reminiscent of the effect produced by Darío's "blue," these adjectives which modify silence also create for it a setting of a dream-like world of immateriality. . . .

Man enters Lugones' white abyss of silence where life, death, and love exist in harmony, and he, like Lugones, is removed from himself, but his solitude is comforting for silence is even more profound than death. Silence holds the memory of the unknown, it guards the secrets of deep thought, and it cradles eternal life.

Janice Sanders Moreno. *Hispania*. 46, Dec., 1963,
pp. 760, 763

The poems in *Sentimental Lunar Poems* can be divided into three different parts by form and content. The first part consists of thirty-four poems that are essentially caricaturist. The second part is comprised of four dramatic scenes in which fantastic beings and deeds abound. Four romantic and melancholy stories, interspersed among the first two divisions, comprise the third part.

Sentimental Lunar Poems is therefore not what we can call a coherent work in the common meaning of the word. From this point of view, its three parts could be separated as distinct books. Real relationships do not exist among the bourgeois family in "The Artificial Fires," the man in love with the moon in "The Impossible Sweetheart," and the fairy that dwells in the enchanted fountain in "The Three Kisses." The only constants within the three parts are the repetitions of certain words and the ubiquitous presence of the moon.

Why then is *Sentimental Lunar Poems* an integral work and not two or three different books? It is an artistic unity because its author always presents the same perception of life. The different surfaces of the work are internally related by the truth of the life against which Lugones wanted to avenge himself.

Marta Morello-Frosch. RI. 30, Jan.–June, 1964, p. 152†

The Gaucho War exalts episodes that were not essential to the liberation of Argentina, although they have contributed in part to the defense of the northwestern frontier. . . . Each episode concludes by pointing to the exemplary heroic individuality of the characters, although their behavior is to be explained through a generalized and dominant conscience—the idea of a fatherland—as opposed to the ritual obligations that the Spaniards fulfilled. With a procedure dear to Latin American romanticism, Lugones divides the characters into two groups: the patriots (the Creoles), and *maturrangos* (or Goths) [the Spaniards]. Nature fights alongside the first group. Lugones presents nature as the incarnation of an ancient native deity, adopting the procedure of the patriotic poems of the Revolution, such as "The March" by Vicente López y Planes. . . . [Lugones opposes] two conceptions: one alive and oriented toward the future—that of the American fatherland; the other dead and tied to formulas that have lost all stimulus—that of the supporters of the Spanish king. Among the naïve ideas of the book, Hispanophobia is the most damaging because it lessens the tensions of each episode by giving the Spaniards all the negative traits.

Nature comments on the heroic deeds. Acting somewhat like a chorus, her elements give thrust, if not decisiveness, to the action. One of the most constant natural elements in this narrative is light, especially sunlight. It is as sunlight that the symbol of the national shield and the implied reference to the Inca divinity is interpreted. The presentation of Güemes, in the episode that closes the book, ties the halo of the "Gaucho War" to solar glory. . . .

Juan Carlos Ghiano. Análisis de "La guerra gaucha"
(Buenos Aires, Centro Editor de América Latina,
1967), pp. 19–20†

Lugones's long poem, *The Mountains of Gold*, had been a Hugoesque hymn in praise of progress and poetry and undoubtedly a reflection of his view that the poet could be the leader of men in their struggle for a more just society. Soon after 1900, the extreme socialist convictions of his younger days began to waver, and he turned with increasing wonder and curiosity to his native land. At first this was expressed in his prose works . . . rather than in his poetry which still turned like a heliotrope to the sun of the European avant-garde. . . . But in 1910, the centenary of Argentine Independence, he published a very different poetry. *Secular Odes* was dedicated to his native land. Sections with titles such as "To My Country," "Useful and Magnificent Things," "To Cattle and the Wheat," indicated his intention of celebrating the rural life of the Argentine. . . . Lugones's poetry is poetry of a rural America already threatened by the immigrant horde and industrialisation. For him, the true Argentina was the countryside, its true tradition that of the *estancia* [farm] and these his poetry tried to preserve.

> Jean Franco. *An Introduction to Spanish-American Literature* (Cambridge, Cambridge University Press, 1969), pp. 163–65

[Lugones] was a poet, teacher, administrator, journalist, philosopher, and scientist. . . . In Buenos Aires he came into close contact with Rubén Darío. Lugones's motivating force was his principle of opposition to everything conventional. His political views were socialist at a time when feudal thinking and government dominated the Río de la Plata region. Later he turned toward nationalism when socialism became accepted as the world-view of the masses. When other poets were waxing enthusiastic about Mother Spain, Lugones rejected her.

His literary orientation changed every four or five years. His early poems are for the most part not easily accessible; some of them seem more like mathematical problems than flights of the imagination. . . . *The Mountains of Gold* [his first collection] was followed by two volumes, made up of both poetry and prose, which were modernist in the extreme: *The Evening Shadows of the Garden*, somewhat related to Verlaine's poetry in its decadent refinement and elegant preciosity; and *Sentimental Lunar Poems*, reminiscent of the ironic, extravagant Belgian poet Albert Giraud. . . . While his concern for form, for the refinement of meter, was slowly beginning to emerge, some of the poems [in these collections] are still so precariously perched, like tightrope walkers, above the abyss in their form, content, and diction that they seem almost like parodies. Their only purpose seems to be shocking the bourgeoisie. Other poems, however, embody the spirit of Verlaine.

After these collections, Lugones's poetry for some time was

permeated by undefined, elusive sounds and smells, but most of all by the colors the impressionists favored: violet, topaz, amethyst, and especially the famous blue of Verlaine, Mallarmé, Baudelaire, and Darío. This was Lugones's cosmopolitan period.

Rudolf Grossmann. *Geschichte und Probleme der lateinamerikanischen Literatur* (Munich, Max Hueber Verlag, 1969), pp. 341–42†

LYNCH, BENITO (1880–1951)

ARGENTINA

The more I think about the structure of [*The Englishman of the Bones*], of the way the action is developed, the more I admire the consummate art with which Benito Lynch composed it. Since he wrote *The Vultures of Florida* we have admired him as an exceptional novelist; now we can call him a master. Nothing is left to chance in *The Englishman of the Bones*, not even the smallest detail. Everything contributes to the characterization and prepares for the principal scenes. . . .

Although he works with commonplace material, simple characters, ordinary events, and lower-class language, he does not resort to vulgarity or bad taste. He has the art to distill and elevate routine material. . . .

Lynch's novels are neither all action nor all psychological analysis. They are reflections of life as it is, multiple and varied. He portrays customs with extraordinary fidelity. Indeed, it would be impossible to name any Uruguayan or Argentine writer who has written about the man of the countryside with greater truth than has Lynch in *The Englishman of the Bones* and his earlier novels. . . .

Roberto F. Giusti. *Crítica y polémica, tercera serie* (Buenos Aires, Agencia General de Librería y Publicaciones, 1927), pp. 37–38†

[Lynch's] gauchos, whether on the ranch or on the job, are men with the problems of men. He did not commit the stupid error of believing that manliness was inextricably linked to courage. His men are either brave or fearful depending on the situation. "Courage"—a word with suspect connotations—means [for Lynch] the unreal gauchos of other novels and tales, which distorted the figure of the man of the countryside.

In *A Gaucho's Romance*, for example, Lynch presents a nineteen-year-old boy, Panteleón Reyes, shy and humble like so many boys of his age (and older), who lives under the tutelage of his mother. His emancipation and his falling in love with Julia form the center of a novel in which psychological truth rather than false situations has been sought. Panteleón does not become independent through a vain gesture of courage, which indeed would only leave him irremediably under matriarchal power. Instead, like a Thomas Hardy or an Alberto Moravia character, Panteleón wins his independence slowly and timidly. . . .

This long novel, in which so few things happen, is marked by grace and charm, qualities infrequently found among our writers. When the action does become rapid and intense, it does so naturally, like the gathering of a storm. Lynch shows that beyond the clear landscape of charm and tenderness lurks horrible and ruthless tragedy. Like the characters of Hardy, those of Lynch are conquered by the land, by primordial things.

Estela Canto. *Sur.* Nos. 215–16, Sept.–Oct., 1952, p. 112†

English phrases and expressions (sometimes pseudo-English ones) are so prevalent in Lynch's books that this phenomenon is worth considering in some detail. . . . [Lynch] studies and analyzes extensively the juxtaposition of two cultures and its effects. His use of English gives nuance to a large part of his writings and influences the style of his best-known works.

Nevertheless, as opposed to his felicitous handling of the language of the gauchos, which has received deserved praise from important critics and linguists, there is an evident lack of skill in Lynch's use of English, a language that, frankly, he did not know, despite his enormous curiosity about the Anglo-Saxon character. . . . The difference between Lynch's handling of rural Argentine language and that of the Englishman is as great as the difference between character and caricature. . . .

Marshall R. Nason. *RI.* 23, Jan.–June, 1958, pp. 72–73†

[Lynch's] background was dominated by bourgeois ideology. And this ideology existed in the country as well as in the city; it was only a different branch of the same tree. The gauchos did not have a proletarian mentality. Their class condition, although it placed them in opposition to the ranchers, did not generate a theory that could both lead to critical understanding of their situation and show them the road to their liberation. . . . Where, then, could Benito Lynch find a nonbourgeois ideology? From elegant ladies, from the editorial offices of *El día*, from the Jockey Club?

Roberto Salama. *Benito Lynch* (Buenos Aires, Editorial "La Mandrágora," 1959), p. 266†

Among rural novelists, Benito Lynch . . . has been the most mature and the most nearly perfect. The sparse but intelligent criticism about him has generally emphasized four major characteristics of his work:

1. A free and spontaneous writer, he creates his work out of simple elements, professing genuine artistic modesty.

2. His work, although modern, is related to traditional realism because of the balance between character and setting.

3. He definitely stops short of naturalism because of his rejection of its seamy subject matter.

4. He straightforwardly confronts the gaucho and the countryside without being biased by his literary antecedents. He admires the gaucho, but he knows that the gaucho's stoicism, his resignation to his extinction [as a breed], does not lend itself to grandiloquent description. Lynch likewise does not demand heroic action, which we are accustomed to find in rural literature.

All these characteristics can be summed up in one fundamental attitude of Benito Lynch's: The writer looks at the peasant world to see life. This attitude shapes the structure of his novels and determines the style he uses to capture the essences of his characters and to define them through their thoughts, feelings, and actions. His most typical technique is to let his characters talk so that we can deduce their dress and gestures and infer their passions and reactions.

Carlos Horacio Magis. CHA. No. 137, May, 1961,
pp. 106–7†

There are two different styles of writing and two different types of language used in *The Englishman of the Bones*. On the one hand, there is the very correct and expressive language which Benito Lynch used when talking about his characters, describing their personalities, or giving the background for some particular situation. While much could be said in praise of this side of Lynch's literary style, it is even more fortunate that his literary skill was not limited to formal style alone. One of Lynch's greatest stylistic achievements was undoubtedly his ability to portray the personality and psychology of his characters by means of the rural dialect. He grew up among the rural people of Argentina, and their language was second nature to him. Thus, he did not need to invent or poeticize the language as other authors before him had done. Nor do we find in him the occasional lapses into cultured speech which, coming from a rustic type, seem so incongruous. Lynch's characters are definitely a part of their environment, and they express the effect of that environment in their own unique style. . . . Through the rustic speech of his characters, Lynch has managed what few other

Argentine writers have attempted, the honest and very accurate portrayal of the life and personality of the Argentine pampa. . . .

Throughout all of his novels and short stories, this language is the very heart of his literary style and is presented with perfect ease and naturalness. The psychological penetration and the vividness of his character portrayals are undoubtedly due in great part to his skill with the rural language. Its importance in all of his literary work cannot be overestimated.

Edward E. Settgast. *Hispania.* 52, Sept., 1969,
pp. 393, 400

WORKS MENTIONED

Listed here, author by author, are all works mentioned in the critical selections. Each writer's works are arranged alphabetically by the literal translation uniformly used in the book. Following each literal translation in parentheses are the Spanish or Portuguese title and the date of original publication (for poems and stories, a cross-reference to the first collection they were published in). If a published English translation exists, its title, together with the city and year of publication, is given after a colon. Collections in English of poems or stories that do not correspond to a Spanish or Portuguese title are listed at the end of the author's works.

ADONIAS FILHO

Body Alive (*Corpo vivo*, 1962)

The Fort (*O forte*, 1965)

Memories of Lazarus (*Memórias de Lázaro*, 1952): *Memories of Lazarus* (Austin, Tex., 1969)

Promised Leagues (*Léguas da promissão*, 1968)

The Servants of Death (*Os servos da morte*, 1946)

AGUILERA MALTA, DEMETRIO

American Episodes (*Episodios americanos*, 1964–65)

Black Hell (*Infierno negro*, 1967)

Don Goyo (*Don Goyo*, 1933)

Manuela, Knightess of the Sun (*Manuela la caballeresa del sol*, 1964): *Manuela la Caballeresa del Sol* (Carbondale, Ill., 1967)

Seven Moons and Seven Serpents (*Siete lunas y siete serpientes*, 1970)

They Who Go Away (*Los que se van*, 1930)

The Virgin Isle (*La isla virgen*, 1942)

AGUSTÍN, JOSÉ

Abolition of Property (*Abolición de la propiedad*, 1969)

From the Side (*De perfil*, 1966)

José Agustín [Autobiography] (*José Agustín [autobiografía]*, 1966)
Pretending that I Dream (*Inventando que sueño*, 1968)
The Tomb (*La tumba*, 1964)

AGUSTINI, DELMIRA

The Empty Chalices (*Los cálices vacíos*, 1913)
Morning Songs (*Cantos de la mañana*, 1910)
The Stars of the Abyss (*Los astros del abismo*, 1924)
The Swan ("El cisne") in *The Stars of the Abyss*
The White Book (*El libro blanco*, 1907)

ALEGRÍA, CIRO

Broad and Alien Is the World (*El mundo es ancho y ajeno*, 1941):
    Broad and Alien Is the World (New York, 1941)
Gentleman's Duel (*Duelo de caballeros*, 1963)
The Golden Serpent (*La serpiente de oro*, 1935): *The Golden Serpent*
    (New York, 1941)
The Hungry Dogs (*Los perros hambrientos*, 1939)

AMADO, JORGE

Beached Captains (*Capitães de areia*, 1937)
Carnival Land (*País do carnaval*, 1932)
Cocoa (*Cacáu*, 1933)
Dona Flor and Her Two Husbands (*Dona Flor e seus dois maridos*,
    1966): *Dona Flor and Her Two Husbands* (New York, 1969)
Dead Sea (*Mar morto*, 1936)
Gabriela, Clove and Cinnamon (*Gabriela, cravo e canela*, 1958):
    Gabriela, Clove and Cinnamon (New York, 1962)
Jubiabá (*Jubiabá*, 1935)
Lands without End (*Terras do sem fem*, 1942): *The Violent Land*
    (New York, 1945)
The Old Mariners: Two Stories from the Bahia Docks (*Os velhos
    marinheiros: Duas histórias do cais de Bahia*, 1961)
Sweat (*Suór*, 1934)
The Two Deaths of Quincas Wateryell (*A morte e a morte de Quincas
    Berro Dagua*) in *The Old Mariners: The Two Deaths of Quincas
    Wateryell* (New York, 1965)
The Whole Truth Concerning the Redoubtful Adventures of Captain
    Vasco Moscoso de Aragão, Master Mariner (*A completa verdade
    sôbre as discutidas aventuras do Comandante Vasco Moscoso de
    Aragão, Capitão do Longo Curso*) in *The Old Mariners: Home Is
    the Sailor* (New York, 1964)

AMORIM, ENRIQUE

The Backwoods Men (*Los montaraces*, 1957)
Birds and Men (*Los pájaros y los hombres*, 1960)
The Carpenters ("Los carpinteros") in *Birds and Men*
The Carriages ("Las calandrias") in *Birds and Men*
The Cart (*La carreta*, 1932)
Everything Can Happen (*Todo puede suceder*, 1955)
The Horse and His Shadow (*El caballo y su sombra*, 1941): *The Horse and His Shadow* (New York, 1943)
The Moon Was Made from Water (*La luna se hizo con agua*, 1944)
Nine Moons over Neuquén (*Nueve lunas sobre Neuquén*, 1946)
Open Corral (*Corral abierto*, 1956)
The Outlet (*La desembocadura*, 1958)
Peasant Aguilar (*Paisano Aguilar*, 1934)
Trap in the Straw Patch (*La trampa del pajonal*, 1928)
The Uneven Age (*La edad despareja*, 1939)
Unmasked Assassin (*El asesino desvelado*, 1945)

ANDERSON IMBERT, ENRIQUE

The Book of Magic (*El grimorio*, 1961): *The Other Side of the Mirror: El Grimorio* (Carbondale, Ill., 1966)
The Cheshire Cat (*El gato de Cheshire*, 1965)
The Determinist Goblins ("Los duendes deterministas") in *The Book of Magic*
The North American Woman ("La nortamericana") in *The Book of Magic*
The Phantom ("El fantasma") in *The Book of Magic*
The Prodigal Son ("El hijo pródigo") in *The Book of Magic*
The Proof of Chaos (*Las pruebas del caos*, 1946)
The Queen of the Wood ("La reina del bosque") in *The Book of Magic*
Taste of Lipstick ("Sabor a pintura de labios") in *The Book of Magic*
Tsantsa ("Tsantsa") in *The Book of Magic*
The Wall ("La muralla") in *The Book of Magic*

ANDRADE, CARLOS DRUMMOND DE

The Case of the Dress ("Caso do vestido") in *The People's Rose*
Clear Enigma (*Claro enigma*, 1951)
Death in an Airplane ("Morte no avião") in *The People's Rose*
The Death of the Milkman ("Morte do leiteiro") in *The People's Rose*
In the Middle of the Road ("No meio do caminho") in *Some Poetry*

Lesson of Things (*Lição de coisas*, 1962)

The Machine of the World ("A máquina do mundo") in *Clear Enigma*

The People's Rose (*A rosa de povo*, 1945)

Pilgrimage ("Romaria") in *The People's Rose*

Poetic Anthology (*Antologia poética*, 1963)

Poetry (*Poesias*, 1942)

Poetry up to Now (*Poesia até agora*, 1947)

Secret ("Segredo") in *Swamp of Souls*

Sentiment of the World (*Sentimento do mundo*, 1940)

Some Poetry (*Alguma poesia*, 1930)

Song to the Man of the People: Charlie Chaplin ("Canto ao homen do povo Charlie Chaplin") in *The People's Rose*

Swamp of Souls (*Brejo das almas*, 1934)

That Is That ("Isso é aquilo") in *Lesson of Things*

Tiller of Air, and Poems up to Now (*Fazendeiro do ar, e poesia até agora*, 1954)

In the Middle of the Road: Selected Poems (Tucson, Ariz., 1965)

ANDRADE, MÁRIO DE

Auction of Evils (*Remate de males*, 1930)

Dramatic Dances of Brazil (*Danças dramáticas do Brasil*, 1959)

Hallucinated City (*Paulicéia desvairada*, 1922): *Hallucinated City* (Nashville, Tenn., 1968)

Jaboti Clan (*Clã do Jaboti*, 1927)

The Little-Bird Stuffer (*O empalhador de passarinho*, no date [1943?])

Macunaíma (*Macunaíma*, 1928)

The Moral Fibrature of the Ipiranga ("As enfibraturas do Ipiranga") in *Hallucinated City*

Nocturne ("Nocturno") in *Hallucinated City*

Ode to the Bourgeois Gentleman ("Ode ao burguês") in *Hallucinated City*

São Paulo Lyre (*Lira paulistana*, 1946)

To Love, an Intransitive Verb (*Amar, verbo intransitivo*, 1927): *Fräulein* (New York, 1933)

The Troubador ("O trovador") in *Hallucinated City*

ANDRADE, OSWALD DE

First Student Notebook of Poetry (*Primeiro caderno do aluno de poesia*, 1927)

The Melancholic Revolution (*A revolução melancólica*, 1943) [Part I of *Zero Boundary*]

Pau-Brazil (*Pau-Brasil*, 1925)

Plains (*Chão*, 1946) [Part II of *Zero Boundary*]
Sentimental Memories of João Miramar (*Memórias sentimentais de João Miramar*, 1924)
Seraphim Big Bridge (*Serafim Ponte Grande*, 1934)
Zero Boundary (*Marco zero*, 1943)

ARANHA, JOSÉ PEREIRA DA GRAÇA

Canaan (*Chanaan*, 1902): *Canaan* (Boston, 1920)

ARCINIEGAS, GERMÁN

Amerigo and the New World (*Amerigo y el nuevo mundo*, 1955): *Amerigo and the New World* (New York, 1955)
Biography of the Caribbean (*Biografía del Caribe*, 1945): *Caribbean, Sea of the New World* (New York, 1946)
The Communes (*Los comuneros*, 1938)
The Continent of Seven Colors (*El continente de siete colores*, 1965): *Latin America: A Cultural History* (New York, 1967)
Germans in the Conquest of America (*Los alemanes en la conquista de América*, 1941): *Germans in the Conquest of America* (New York, 1943)
The Green Continent (New York, 1944)
Halfway along the Road of Life (*En medio del camino de la vida*, 1949)
Jiménez de Quesada (*Jiménez de Quesada*, 1939)
The Knight of El Dorado (*El caballero de El Dorado*, 1942 [2nd ed. of *Jiménez de Quesada*]): *The Knight of El Dorado* (New York, 1942)
The Student of the Round Table (*El estudiante de la mesa redonda*, 1932)

ARÉVALO MARTÍNEZ, RAFAEL

The Colombian Troubador (*El trovador colombiano*, 1915)
A Life (*Una vida*, 1914)
The Man Who Looked Like A Horse (*El hombre que parecía un caballo*, 1915)
Manuel Aldano (*Manuel Aldano*, 1922)
Mayan (*Maya*, 1911)
Mr. Monitot (*El señor Monitot*, 1922)
Orolandia's Office of Peace (*La oficina de paz de Orolandia*, 1925)
Trip to Ipanda (*Viaje a Ipanda*, 1939)
Tropical Beasts ("Las fieras del trópico") in *Mr. Monitot*
The World of the Maharachías (*El mundo de los Maharachías*, 1938)

ARGUEDAS, ALCIDES

Race of Bronze (*Raza de bronce*, 1919)
A Sick People (*Pueblo enfermo*, 1910)

ARGUEDAS, JOSÉ MARÍA

All the Bloods (*Todas las sangres*, 1964)
The Deep Rivers (*Los ríos profundos*, 1958)
Diamonds and Stones (*Diamantes y pedernales*, 1953)
Songs and Tales of the Quechua People (*Canciones y cuentos del pueblo
    quechua*, 1949): *The Singing Mountaineers: Songs and Tales of the
    Quechua People* (Austin, Tex., 1957)
Water (*Agua*, 1935)

ARLT, ROBERTO

The Deserted Isle (*La isla desierta*, 1938)
The Flamethrowers (*Los lanzallamas*, 1931)
The Little Hunchback (*El jorobadito*, 1933)
The Rabid Toy (*El juguete rabioso*, 1926)
Saverio the Cruel (*Saverio el cruel*, 1936)
The Seven Madmen (*Los siete locos*, 1929)

ARREOLA, JUAN JOSÉ

Announcement ("El aviso") in *Total Confabulario*
Baby H. P. ("Baby H. P.") in *Confabulario*
Bestiary (*Bestiario*) in *Total Confabulario*
Confabulario (*Confabulario*, 1952)
The Crow Catcher ("El cuervero") in *Various Inventions*
The Disciple ("El discípulo") in *Confabulario*
Everyone's Hour (*La hora de todos*, 1954)
The Fair (*La feria*, 1963)
Notes of an Angry Man ("Apuntes de un rencoroso") in *Confabulario*
Private Life ("La vida privada") in *Various Inventions*
Small Town Tale ("Pueblerina") in *Confabulario*
The Switchman ("El guardagujas") in *Confabulario*
Total Confabulario (*Confabulario total*, 1962): *Confabulario and Other
    Inventions* (Austin, Tex., 1964)
Various Inventions (*Varia invención*, 1949)
Verily, Verily I Say Unto You ("En verdad os digo") in *Confabulario*

ASTURIAS, MIGUEL ÁNGEL

Dry Dike (*Dique seco*) in *Theater*
The Eyes of the Interred (*Los ojos de los enterrados*, 1960): *The Eyes of the Interred* (New York, 1972)
Good Friday (*Viernes de Dolores*, 1972)
The Green Pope (*El papa verde*, 1954): *The Green Pope* (New York, 1971)
Guatemalan Sociology: The Social Problem of the Indian (*Sociología guatemala: El problema social del indio*, 1923)
Legends of Guatemala (*Leyendas de Guatemala*, 1930)
Men of Maize (*Hombres de maíz*, 1949)
Mr. President (*El Señor Presidente*, 1946): *The President* (London, 1963); *El Señor Presidente* (New York, 1964)
Mulata So-and-So (*Mulata de tal*, 1963): *Mulata* (New York, 1967); *The Mulatta and Mr. Fly* (London, 1967)
Strong Wind (*Viento fuerte*, 1949): *The Cyclone* (London, 1967); *Strong Wind* (New York, 1968)
Theater (*Teatro*, 1964)
Weekend in Guatemala (*Weekend en Guatemala*, 1956)

AZUELA, MARIANO

Andrés Pérez, Madero Supporter (*Andrés Pérez, maderista*, 1911)
The Bosses (*Los caciques*, 1917): *The Bosses* in *Two Novels of Mexico: The Flies, and The Bosses* (Berkeley, Cal., 1956)
The Failures (*Los fracasados*, 1908)
The Firefly (*La luciérnaga*, 1932)
Lost Paths (*Sendas perdidas*, 1949)
The Trials of a Respectable Family (*Tribulaciones de una familia decente*, 1919): *The Trials of a Respectable Family* in *Two Novels of the Mexican Revolution* (San Antonio, Tex., 1963)
The Underdogs (*Los de abajo*, 1916): *The Underdogs* (New York, 1929)
The Weed (*Mala yerba*, 1909): *Marcela, a Mexican Love Story* (New York, 1932)
Without Love (*Sin amor*, 1912)

BALLAGAS, EMILIO

Eternal Taste (*Sabor eterno*, 1939)
Hostage Heaven (*Cielo en rehenes*) in *Poetic Work*
Joy and Flight (*Júbilo y fuga*, 1931)

Notebook of Black Poetry (*Cuaderno de poesía negra*, 1934)
Our Lady of the Sea (*Nuestra señora del mar*, 1943)
Poetic Work (*Obra poética*, 1955)
Revelation ("Revelación") in *Poetic Work*
Situation of Black American Poetry (*Mapa de la poesía negra americana*, 1946)

BANDEIRA, MANUEL

Ashes of the Hours (*A cinza das horas*, 1917)
Carnival (*Carnaval*, 1919)
Complete Poetry (*Poesias completas*, 1940, 1948)
Dissolute Rhythm ("O ritmo dissoluto") in *Poems*
Etching ("Água-Forte") in *Fifty-Year Lyre*
Fifty-Year Lyre (*Lira dos cinquant'anos*) in *Complete Poetry* (1940)
The Key to the Poem ("A chave do poema") in *Poetry and Prose*
Libertinage (*Libertinagem*, 1930)
Morning Star (*Estrêla da manhã*, 1936)
Pasárgada's Itinerary (*Itinerário de Pasárgada*, 1954)
Poems (*Poesias*, 1924)
Poetry and Prose (*Poesia e prosa*, 1958)
Pretty Pretty (*Belo Belo*) in *Complete Poetry* (1948)
Remembrance of Recife ("Evocação de Recife") in *Libertinage*
The Toads ("Os sapos") in *Carnival*

BARRIOS, EDUARDO

Brother Ass (*El hermano asno*, 1926): *Brother Ass* (New York, 1969)
The Child Who Went Crazy with Love (*El niño que enloqueció de amor*, 1915)
Living (*Vivir*, 1916)
A Lost One (*Un perdido*, 1918)
Pages of a Poor Devil (*Páginas de un pobre diablo*, 1923)
Tamarugo Grove (*Tamarugal*, 1944)

BENEDETTI, MARIO

Death and Other Surprises (*La muerte y otras sorpresas*, 1968)
The Fiancés ("Los novios") in *Montevideans*
Juan Ángel's Birthday (*El cumpleaños de Juan Ángel*, 1971)
Montevideans (*Montevideanos*, 1959)
The Truce (*La tregua*, 1960): *The Truce* (New York, 1969)

BENEDETTO, ANTONIO DI

Abandonment and Passivity ("El abandono y la pasividad," 1958)
Animal World (*Mundo animal*, 1953)
Clear Stories (*Cuentos claros*, 1969 [originally *Grot*, 1957])
The Silencer (*El silenciero*, 1964)
The Suicides (*Los suicidas*, 1969)
Zama (*Zama*, 1956)

BILAC, OLAVO BRAZ MARTINS DOS GUIMARÃES

Afternoon (*Tarde*, 1919)
Burning Brambles (*Sarças de fogo*) in *Poems* (1888)
The Dawn of Love ("A alvorada de amor") in *Restless Soul*
Dead Virgins ("As virgens mortas") in *Restless Soul*
Poems (*Poesias*, 1888 and 1902)
Restless Soul (*Alma inquieta*) in *Poems* (1902)
The Seeker of Emeralds (*O caçador de esmeraldas*) in *Poems* (1902)
To Hear Stars ("Ouvir estrêlas") in *Via Lactea*
Via Lactea (*Via-láctea*) in *Poems* (1902)
Voyages (*As viagens*) in *Poems* (1888)

BIOY CASARES, ADOLFO

The Celestial Plot ("La trama celeste") in *The Celestial Plot*: "The
    Celestial Plot" in *The Invention of Morel, and Other Stories*
The Celestial Plot (*La trama celeste*, 1948)
Diary of the War of the Pig (*Diario de la guerra del cerdo*, 1969):
    Diary of the War of the Pig (New York, 1972)
The Dream of the Heroes (*El sueño de los héroes*, 1954)
The Invention of Morel (*La invención de Morel*, 1940): *The Invention
    of Morel* in *The Invention of Morel, and Other Stories*
The Other Labyrinth ("El otro laberinto") in *The Celestial Plot*: "The
    Other Labyrinth" in *The Invention of Morel, and Other Stories*
A Prodigious Story (*Historia prodigiosa*, 1956)

BORGES, JORGE LUIS

The Aleph (*El Aleph*, 1949): *Labyrinths: Selected Stories* (Norfolk,
    Conn., 1962); *The Aleph, and Other Stories* (New York, 1970)
"An Autobiographical Essay" (written in English for *The Aleph, and
    Other Stories*)

Avatars of the Tortoise ("Avatares de la tortuga") in *Other Inquisitions*

The Book of Imaginary Beings (*El libro de los seres imaginarios*, 1967): *The Book of Imaginary Beings* (New York, 1969)

Borges and I ("Borges y yo") in *The Maker*

Brodie's Report (*El informe de Brodie*, 1970): *Doctor Brodie's Report* (New York, 1972)

The Chronicles of Bustos Domecq (*Las crónicas de Bustos Domecq*, 1967)

The Circular Ruins ("Las ruinas circulares") in *Fictions*

The Elder Lady ("La señora mayor") in *Brodie's Report*

Fervor of Buenos Aires (*Fervor de Buenos Aires*, 1932)

Fictions (*Ficciones*, 1944): *Ficciones* (New York, 1962); *Labyrinths: Selected Stories* (Norfolk, Conn., 1962)

From Allegories to Novels ("De las alegorías a las novelas") in *Other Inquisitions*

Funes, the Memorious ("Funes el memorioso") in *Fictions*

The Intruder ("La intrusa") in *Brodie's Report*

The Maker ("El hacedor") in *The Maker*

The Maker (*El hacedor*, 1960): *Dreamtigers* (Austin, Tex., 1964)

The Masked Dyer, Hákim of Merv ("El tintorero enmascarado Hákim de Merv") in *A Universal History of Infamy*

The Meeting ("El encuentro") in *Brodie's Report*

A Model for Death (*Un modelo para la muerte*, 1946)

The Moon Across the Way (*Luna de enfrente*, 1925)

New Refutation of Time ("Nueva refutación del tiempo") in *Other Inquisitions*

Other Inquisitions (*Otras inquisiciones*, 1952): *Other Inquisitions, 1937–1952* (Austin, Tex., 1964)

San Martín Notebook (*Cuaderno San Martín*, 1929)

Six Problems for Don Isidro Parodi (*Seis problemas para don Isidro Parodi*, 1942)

Tlön, Uqbar, Orbis Tertius ("Tlön, Uqbar, Orbis Tertius") in *Fictions*

A Universal History of Infamy (*Historia universal de la infamia*, 1935): *A Universal History of Infamy* (New York, 1972)

The Wall and the Books ("La muralla y los libros") in *Other Inquisitions*

Selected Poems 1923–1967 (New York, 1972)

CABALLERO CALDERON, EDUARDO

Americans and Europeans (*Americanos y europeos*, 1958)

Broad Is Castile (*Ancha es Castilla*, 1950)

Childhood Memories (*Memorias infantiles*, 1964)

Christ with His Back to Us (*El Cristo de espaldas*, 1952)

The Good Savage (*El buen salvaje*, 1966)

Tipacoque (*Tipacoque*, 1940)
Tipacoque Diary (*Diario de Tipacoque*, 1950)

CABRERA INFANTE, GUILLERMO

At the Great Ecbo ("En el gran ecbo") in *In Peace as in War*
In Peace as in War (*Así en la paz como en la guerra*, 1960)
Three Sad Tigers (*Tres tristes tigres*, 1967): *Three Trapped Tigers* (New
    York, 1971)

CARDOSO, LÚCIO

Ague (*Maleita*, 1934)
Angélica (*Angélica*, 1950)
The Betraying Heart (*O coração delator*, unpublished)
Diary (*Diário*, 1961)
Empty Hands (*Mãos vazias*, 1938)
The Prodigal Son (*O filho pródigo*, 1947)
The Silver Chord (*A corda de prata*, 1947)
The Slave (*O escravo*, 1945)
The Stranger (*O desconhecido*, 1940)
Underground Light (*A luz no subsolo*, 1936)
Willow (*Salgueiro*, 1935)

CARPENTIER, ALEJO

The Century of Lights (*El siglo de las luces*, 1962): *Explosion in a
    Cathedral* (Boston, 1963)
The Chosen ("Les élus") in French *War of Time* (*Guerre du temps*)
Écue-Yamba-Ó! (*¡Écue-Yamba-Ó!*, 1933)
Journey Back to the Source ("Viaje a la semilla") in *War of Time*
The Kingdom of This World (*El reino de este mundo*, 1948?): *The
    Kingdom of This World* (New York, 1957)
Like the Night ("Semejante a la noche") in *War of Time*
The Lost Steps (*Los pasos perdidos*, 1935): *The Lost Steps* (New York
    1956)
Preludes and Differences (*Tientos y diferencias*, 1964)
Problems of the Current Latin American Novel ("Problemática de la
    actual novela latinoamericana") in *Preludes and Differences*
The Pursuit ("El acoso") in *War of Time*
Right of Sanctuary (*El derecho del asilo*, 1972)
The Road to Santiago ("El camino de Santiago") in *War of Time*

War of Time (*Guerra del tiempo*, 1958)

War of Time (New York, 1970): the English collection contains "The Chosen," "Journey Back to the Source," "Like the Night," "Right of Sanctuary," and "The Road to Santiago"

CARRERA ANDRADE, JORGE

Alphabet ("Alfabeto") in *World Registry*
Bulletins from Sea and Land (*Boletines de mar y tierra*, 1930)
An Inventory of My Only Worldly Goods ("Inventario de mis únicos bienes") in *World Registry*
Secret Country (*País secreto*, 1940): *Secret Country* (New York, 1946)
World Registry (*Registro del mundo*, 1940)

Selected Poems of Jorge Carrera Andrade (Albany, N.Y., 1972)

CARVALHO, RONALD DE

All America (*Tôda a América*, 1926)
Brazilian Studies (*Estudios brasileiros*, 1924, 1931)
Brief History of Brazilian Literature (*Pequena história de literatura brasileira*, 1919)
Essay on Modern Aesthetics: Dialogue of the Alexandrian and the Barbarian ("Ensaio sobre esthetica moderna: Dialogo entre um alexandrino e um barbaro") in *Brazilian Studies* (1931)
Glorious Light (*Luz gloriosa*, 1913)
Ironic and Sentimental Epigrams (*Epigramas irônicos e sentimentais*, 1922)
Poems and Sonnets (*Poemas e sonetos*, 1919)
The Poetry of Penumbra ("Poesia da penumbra") in *Brazilian Studies* (1931)

CASACCIA, GABRIEL

The Driveler (*La babosa*, 1952)
The Exiles (*Los exiliados*, 1967)
The Guajhú (*El Guajhú*, 1938)
Mario Pineda (*Mario Pineda*, 1940)
The Well (*El pozo*, 1947)

CASTELLANOS, ROSARIO

Balún Canán (*Balún Canán*, 1957): *The Nine Guardians* (London, 1959)
Business of Thunder (*Oficio de tinieblas*, 1962)
Cooking Lesson ("Lección de cocina") in *Family Album*
Family Album ("Álbum de familia") in *Family Album*
Family Album (*Álbum de familia*, 1971)
The Guests in August (*Los convidados de agosto*, 1964)
Little White-Head ("Cabecita blanca") in *Family Album*
Royal City (*Ciudad real*, 1960)
Sunday ("Domingo") in *Family Album*

CHOCANO, JOSÉ SANTOS

Avatar ("Avatar") in *Soul of America*
Soul of America (*Alma América*, 1906)

Spirit of the Andes (Portland, Maine, 1935)

COELHO NETO, HENRIQUE

Black King (*Rei Negro*, 1914)
The Conquest (*A conquista*, 1899)
The Dead Man (*O morto*, 1898)
Epithalamium ("Epithalamio") in *Fountain of Youth*
The Federal Capital (*A capital federal*, 1893)
Fountain of Youth (*Água de juventa*, 1905)
Mirage (*Miragem*, 1895)
Sphynx (*A esfinge*, 1908)
Whirlwind (*O turbilhão*, 1906)

CONTI, HAROLDO

All the Summers (*Todos los veranos*, 1964)
Around about the Cage (*Alrededor de la jaula*, 1967)
The Hyperboreans (*Los hiperbóreos*, unpublished)
Southeasterly (*Sudeste*, 1962)
While Alive (*En vida*, 1971)
With Other People (*Con otra gente*, 1967)

CORTÁZAR, JULIO

All the Fires the Fire (*Todos los fuegos el fuego*, 1966): *All the Fires the Fire* (New York, 1973)

Axolotl ("Axolotl") in *End of the Game*

Bestiary ("Bestiario") in *Bestiary*

Bestiary (*Bestiario*, 1951)

Customs of the Famas ("Costumbres de los famas") in *Stories of Cronopios and Famas*

The Devil's Drivel [Blow-Up] ("Las babas del diablo") in *Secret Weapons*

The End of the Game ("Final del juego") in *The End of the Game*

The End of the Game (*Final del juego*, 1956)

Freeway South ("La autopista del sur") in *All the Fires the Fire*

The Health of the Sick ("La salud de los enfermos") in *All the Fires the Fire*

Hopscotch (*Rayuela*, 1963): *Hopscotch* (New York, 1966)

The Kings (*Los reyes*, 1949)

Letters from Mama ("Cartas de mamá") in *Secret Weapons*

The Other Sky ("El otro cielo") in *All the Fires the Fire*

Pameos and Meopas (*Pameos y meopas* [that is, "Poemas y poemas"], 1971)

The Poisons ("Los venenos") in *The End of the Game*

Possibilities for Abstraction ("Posibilidades de la abstracción") in *Stories of Cronopios and Famas*

Presence (*Presencia*, 1938)

The Pursuer ("El perseguidor") in *Secret Weapons*

Secret Weapons (*Las armas secretas*, 1959)

62: A Model Kit (*62, modelo para armar*, 1968): *62: A Model Kit* (New York, 1972)

Stories of Cronopios and Famas (*Historias de cronopios y famas*, 1962): *Cronopios and Famas* (New York, 1969)

The Winners (*Los premios*, 1960): *The Winners* (New York, 1965)

The End of the Game, and Other Stories (New York, 1967); *Blow-Up, and Other Stories* (New York, 1968) [contain stories from *Bestiary, The End of the Game*, and *Secret Weapons*]

CUNHA, EUCLYDES DA

The Backlands (*Os sertões*, 1902): *Rebellion in the Backlands* (Chicago, 1944); *Revolt in the Backlands* (London, 1947)

A Paradise Lost (*Um paraiso perdido*, unfinished)

Peru versus Bolivia (*Peru versus Bolivia*, 1907)

DARÍO, RUBÉN

Aestival ("Estival") in *Blue*
Blue (*Azul*, 1888)
Complete Stories (*Cuentos completos*, 1950)
History of My Books (*Historia de mis libros*, 1912)
In the Battle of the Flowers ("En la batalla de la flores") in *Complete Stories*
The Lyric Year ("El año lírico") in *Blue*
Marine ("Marina") in *Songs of Life and Hope*
Metempsychosis ("Metempsicosis") in *The Wayward Song*
New Year ("Año nuevo") in *Profane Proses*
Poem of Autumn ("Poema del otoño") in *Poem of Autumn, and Other Poems*
Poem of Autumn, and Other Poems (*Poema del otoño, y otros poemas*, 1910)
Profane Proses (*Prosas profanas*, 1896): *Prosas Profanas, and Other Poems* (New York, 1922)
The Rare Ones (*Los raros*, 1896)
Response to Verlaine ("Responso a Verlaine") in *Profane Proses*
Songs of Life and Hope (*Cantos de vida y esperanza*, 1905)
Song to Argentina (*Canto a la Argentina*, 1910)
To Roosevelt ("A Roosevelt") in *Songs of Life and Hope*
The Wayward Song (*El canto errante*, 1907)
The Wolf's Motives ("Los motivos del lobo") in *Song to Argentina*

Eleven Poems of Rubén Darío (New York, 1916)
Selected Poems of Rubén Darío (Austin, Tex., 1965)

DÍAZ MIRÓN, SALVADOR

Chips of Stone (*Lascas*, 1901)
Mexican Parnassus (*El Parnaso mexicano*, 1886)
The Pariahs ("Los parías") in *Poems* (1900)
Poems (*Poesías*, 1895, 1900)

DÍAZ RODRÍGUEZ, MANUEL

About My Pilgrimages (*De mis romerías*, 1898)
Broken Idols (*Ídolos rotos*, 1901)
Father Serafín's Sheep and Roses ("Las ovejas y las rosas del Padre Serafín") in *Peregrina, or the Enchanted Well*
Patrician Blood (*Sangre patricia*, 1902)

Peregrina, or the Enchanted Well (*Peregrina, o el pozo encantado*, 1921)

Secrets of Psyche (*Confidencias de Psiquis*, 1896)

Sensations of Travel (*Sensaciones de viaje*, 1896)

Stories in Color (*Cuentos de color*, 1899)

Summer Eclogue ("Égloga de verano") in *Peregrina, or the Enchanted Well*

The Way of Perfection (*Camino de perfección*, 1910)

DONOSO, JOSÉ

Big-Scale Party ("Fiesta en grande") in *Summer Vacation, and Other Stories*

Coronation (*Coronación*, 1956): *Coronation* (New York, 1965)

The Obscene Bird of Night (*El obsceno pájaro de la noche*, 1970): *The Obscene Bird of Night* (New York, 1973)

Place without Limits (*El lugar sin límites*, 1966): *Hell Has No Limits* in *Triple Cross* (New York, 1972)

Summer Vacation ("Veraneo") in *Summer Vacation, and Other Stories*

Summer Vacation, and Other Stories (*Veraneo, y otros cuentos*, 1955)

This Sunday (*Este domingo*, 1966): *This Sunday* (New York, 1967)

EDWARDS BELLO, JOAQUÍN

Creoles in Paris (*Criollos en París*, 1933)

The Down-and-Outer (*El roto*, 1920)

ELIZONDO, SALVADOR

Farabeuf, or the Chronicle of an Instant (*Farabeuf, o la crónica de un instante*, 1965)

Narda, or Summer (*Narda, o el verano*, 1966)

The Portrait of Zoe and Other Lies (*El retrato de Zoe y otras mentiras*, 1969)

The Secret Hypogeum (*El hipógeo secreto*, 1968)

FREYRE, GILBERTO

Brazil: An Interpretation (New York, 1945); *New World in the Tropics: The Culture of Modern Brazil* (New York, 1959; a revised and expanded version of *Brazil: An Interpretation*)

Dona Sinha and the Father Son (*Dona Sinhá e o filho padre*, 1964): *Mother and Son: A Brazilian Tale* (New York, 1967)

*The Mansions and the Shanties (*Sobrados e mucambos*, 1936): *The Mansions and the Shanties* (New York, 1963)

*The Masters and the Slaves (*Casa grande e senzala*, 1933): *The Masters and the Slaves* (New York, 1946)

Northeast (*Nordeste*, 1937)

The World the Portuguese Created (*O mundo que o português criou*, 1940)

FUENTES, CARLOS

All the Cats Are Dark (*Todos los gatos son pardos*, 1970)

Aura (*Aura*, 1962): *Aura* (New York, 1965)

Blindman's Song (*Cantar de ciegos*, 1964)

A Change of Skin (*Cambio de piel*, 1967): *A Change of Skin* (New York, 1968)

The Clearest Region (*La región más transparente*, 1958): *Where the Air Is Clear* (New York, 1960)

The Death of Artemio Cruz (*La muerte de Artemio Cruz*, 1962): *The Death of Artemio Cruz* (New York, 1964)

The Good Conscience (*Las buenas consciencias*, 1965): *The Good Conscience* (New York, 1961)

Holy Place (*Zona sagrada*, 1967): *Holy Place* in *Triple Cross* (New York, 1972)

The Masked Days (*Los días enmascarados*, 1954)

Old Morality ("Vieja moralidad") in *Blindman's Song*

GALLEGOS, RÓMULO

Canaima (*Canaima*, 1935)

Cantaclaro (*Cantaclaro*, 1934)

The Creeper (*La trepadora*, 1925)

Doña Bárbara (*Doña Bárbara*, 1929): *Doña Barbara* (New York, 1931)

The Foreigner (*El forastero*, 1943)

The Last of the Solars (*El último Solar*, 1920)

Poor Negro (*Pobre negro*, 1942)

Upon This Same Land (*Sobre la misma tierra*, 1943)

A Wisp of Straw in the Wind (*La brizna de paja en el viento*, 1952)

---

* The literal translation of *Sobrados e mucambos* is "Two-Story Houses and Slaves"; and of *Casa grande e senzala*, "Big House and Shanty." Since the published English translations of these two works have more distinctive titles, we have used them throughout instead of the literal translations, in order to avoid confusion between the two works.

GÁLVEZ, MANUEL

The Age of Rosas (*La época de Rosas*, 1931–54)
The Gaucho from Los Cerrillos (*El gaucho de los Cerrillos*, 1931)
General Quiroga (*El General Quiroga*, 1932)
The Grade-School Teacher (*La maestra normal*, 1914)
Holy Wednesday (*Miércoles santo*, 1930): *Holy Wednesday* (New York, 1934)
Men in Solitude (*Hombres en soledad*, 1938)
The Metaphysical Sickness (*El mal metafísico*, 1917)
Nacha Regules (*Nacha Regules*, 1919): *Nacha Regules* (New York, 1923)
Neighborhood Story (*Historia del arrabal*, 1922)
Noble Lineage (*El solar de la raza*, 1913)

GÁMBARO, GRISELDA

The Camp (*El campo*, 1968): *The Camp* in *Voices of Change in the Spanish American Theater* (Austin, Tex., 1971)
The Folly (*El desatino*, 1964 [novel] and 1965 [play])
A Happiness with Less Pain (*Una felicidad con menos pena*, 1968)
The Siamese Twins (*Los siameses*, 1967)

GARCÍA MÁRQUEZ, GABRIEL

Artificial Roses ("Rosas artificiales") in *Big Mama's Funeral*
The Bad Hour (*La mala hora*, 1962)
Big Mama's Funeral ("Los funerales de la Mamá Grande") in *Big Mama's Funeral*
Big Mama's Funeral (*Los funerales de la Mamá Grande*, 1962): *Big Mama's Funeral* in *No One Writes to the Colonel, and Other Stories* (New York, 1968)
Blacamán the Good, Vendor of Miracles ("Blacamán el bueno, vendedor de milagros") in *The Incredible and Sad Story of Pure Eréndira and Her Heartless Grandmother*
The Handsomest Drowned Man in the World ("El ahogado más hermoso del mundo") in *The Incredible and Sad Story of Pure Eréndira and Her Heartless Grandmother*
The Incredible and Sad Story of Pure Eréndira and Her Heartless Grandmother (*La increíble y triste historia de la cándida Eréndira y su abuela desalmada*, 1972): four stories (those listed herein) in *Leaf Storm, and Other Stories* (New York, 1972)

The Last Voyage of the Ghost Ship ("El último viaje del buque fantasma") in *The Incredible and Sad Story of Pure Eréndira and Her Heartless Grandmother*

Leaf Storm (*La hojarasca*, 1955): *Leaf Storm* in *Leaf Storm, and Other Stories* (New York, 1972)

No One Writes to the Colonel (*El coronel no tiene quien le escriba*, 1961): *No One Writes to the Colonel* in *No One Writes to the Colonel, and Other Stories* (New York, 1968)

One Day after Saturday ("Un día después del sábado") in *Big Mama's Funeral*

One Hundred Years of Solitude (*Cien años de soledad*, 1967): *One Hundred Years of Solitude* (New York, 1970)

Tuesday Siesta ("La siesta del martés") in *Big Mama's Funeral*

A Very Old Man with Enormous Wings ("Un señor muy viejo con unas alas enormes") in *The Incredible and Sad Story of Pure Eréndira and Her Heartless Grandmother*

GIRRI, ALBERTO

Daily Values (*Valores diarios*, 1970)
The Eye (*El ojo*, 1964)
House of the Mind (*Casa de la mente*, 1968)
Italian Elegies (*Elegías italianas*, 1962)
Lonely Beach (*Playa sola*, 1946)
The Necessary Condition (*La condición necesaria*, 1960)
Sperlonga ("Sperlonga") in *Italian Elegies*
Venetian Elegy ("Elegía véneta") in *Italian Elegies*

GOMES, ALFREDO DIAS

The Cradle of the Hero (*O berço do herói*, 1965)
The Invasion (*A invasão*, 1962)
The Holy Inquisition (*O Santo Inquérito*, 1966)
The Redeemer of Pledges (*O pagador de promessas*, 1961): *Journey to Bahia* (Washington, D.C., 1964); *Payment as Pledged* in *The Modern Stage in Latin America* (New York, 1971)
The Revolt of the Holy Men (*A revolução dos beatos*, 1962)

GONZÁLEZ MARTÍNEZ, ENRIQUE

The Death of the Swan ("La muerte del cisne") in *The Death of the Swan*
The Death of the Swan (*La muerte del cisne*, 1915)

GONZÁLEZ PRADA, MANUEL

Anarchy (*Anarquía*, 1936)
Exotics (*Exóticas*, 1911)
Free Pages (*Páginas libres*, 1894)
Hours of Struggle (*Horas de lucha*, 1908)
Miniscules (*Minúsculas*, 1901)
Under Opprobrium (*Bajo el oprobrio*, 1933)

GOROSTIZA, JOSÉ

Death without End (*Muerte sin fin*, 1939): *Death without End* (Austin, Tex., 1969)
Declaration of Bogotá ("Declaración de Bogotá") in *Poetry*
Poetry (*Poesía*, 1964)
Prelude ("Preludio") in *Poetry*
Songs to Sing on Fishing Boats (*Canciones para cantar en las barcas*, 1925)

GUILLÉN, NICOLÁS

The Ballad of the Güije ("Balada del Güije") in *West Indies Ltd.*
Elegy to Jacques Roumain, in the Sky of Haiti (*Elegía a Jacques Roumain, en el cielo de Haití*, 1948)
Elegy to Jesús Menéndez (*Elegía de Jesús Menéndez*, 1951)
Motifs of Sound (*Motivos del son*, 1931)
Negro Song ("Canto negro") in *Sóngoro Cosongo*
Sensemayá ("Sensemayá") in *West Indies Ltd.*
Sóngoro Cosongo (*Sóngoro Cosongo*, 1931)
Spain, a Poem in Four Anguishes and One Hope (*España, poema en cuatro angustias y una esperanza*, 1937)
West Indies Ltd. (*West Indies Ltd.*, 1934)

Man-Making Words: Selected Poems of Nicolás Guillén (Amherst, Mass., 1972)

GÜIRALDES, RICARDO

Antithesis ("Antítesis") in *Stories of Death and Blood*
Colegio ("Colegio") in *Complete Works*
Complete Works (*Obras completas*, 1962)
The Crystal Cowbell (*El cencerro de cristal*, 1915)

Don Segundo Sombra (*Don Segundo Sombra*, 1926): *Don Segundo Sombra: Shadows on the Pampas* (New York, 1935)

Grotesque Adventures ("Aventuras grotescas") in *Stories of Death and Blood*

The Judgment of God ("El juicio de Dios") in *Stories of Death and Blood*

Notes ("Apuntes") in *Complete Works*

The Path ("El sendero") in *Complete Works*

Raucho (*Raucho*, 1917)

Rosaura (*Rosaura*, 1952)

Salome ("Salome") in *The Crystal Cowbell*

Stories of Death and Blood (*Cuentos de muerte y de sangre*, 1915)

Telésforo Altamira ("Telésforo Altamira") in *Complete Works*

Triptych ("Tríptico") in *The Crystal Cowbell*

Xaimaca (*Xaimaca*, 1923)

HENRÍQUEZ UREÑA, PEDRO

Discontent and Promise ("El descontento y la promesa") in *Six Essays in Search of Our Literary Expression*

History of Culture in Hispanic America (*Historia de la cultura en la América Hispánica*, 1947)

Hours of Study (*Horas de estudio*, 1910)

Literary Currents in Hispanic America (Cambridge, Mass., 1945)

Six Essays in Search of Our Literary Expression (*Seis ensayos en busca de nuestra expresión literaria*, 1927)

HERRERA Y REISSIG, JULIO

The Ancient Bells (*Las campanas solariegas*) in *Complete Works*

The Clepsydras (*Las clepsidras*) in *Complete Works*

Complete Works (*Obras completas*, 1910–13)

Life ("La vida") in *Salammbô's Necklace*

Salammbô's Necklace (*El collar de Salambô*) in *Complete Works*

The Shepherd's Death ("La muerte del pastor") in *The Ancient Bells*

Wagnerians (*Wagnerianas*) in *Complete Works*

HUIDOBRO, VICENTE

Altazor (*Altazor*, 1931)

Cagliostro, Novel-Film (*Cagliostro, novela-film*, 1926): *Mirror of a Mage* (Boston, 1931)

Contrary Winds (*Vientos contrarios*, 1926)

Finis Brittania (*Finis Brittania*, 1923)
The Hidden Pagodas (*Las pagodas ocultas*, 1914)
Manifesto Perhaps ("Manifeste peut-être") in *Manifestos*
Manifestos (*Manifestes*, 1925)
Mio Cid Campeador (*Mio Cid Campeador*, 1929): *Portrait of a Paladin* (New York, 1932)
The Next One (*La próxima*, 1934)
Non Serviam (*Non serviam*, 1914)
Square Horizon (*Horizon carré*, 1917)

IBARBOUROU, JUANA DE

The Fresh Jug (*El cántaro fresco*, 1920)
Images from the Bible (*Estampas de la Biblia*, 1934)

ICAZA, JORGE

Cholos (*Cholos*, 1939)
Flogging (*Flágelo*, 1936)
Half a Life Bewildered (*Media vida deslumbrados*, 1942)
Huairapamushcas (*Huairapamushcas*, 1948)
Huasipungo (*Huasipungo*, 1934): *Huasipungo* (London, 1962); *The Villagers* (Carbondale, Ill., 1964)
In the Streets (*En las calles*, 1935)
Mountain Soil (*Barro de la sierra*, 1933)
Romero y Flores the Chulla (*El chulla Romero y Flores*, 1958)
Trapped (*Atrapados*, 1972)

JAIMES FREYRE, RICARDO

Aeternum Vale ("Aeternum vale") in *Primeval Fountain*
A Beautiful Spring Day ("En un hermoso día de verano," 1907)
Dream Country (*País de sueño*, 1918?)
Dreams Are Life (*Los sueños son vida*, 1917)
The Elves ("Las hadas") in *Primeval Fountain*
Indian Justice ("Justicia india," 1906)
Laws of Castilian Versification (*Leyes de la versificación castellana*, 1912)
The Night ("La noche") in *Primeval Fountain*
Primeval Fountain (*Castalia bárbara*, 1899)
The Song of Evil ("El canto del mal") in *Primeval Fountain*

LEÑERO, VICENTE

The Children of Sánchez (*Los hijos de Sánchez*, unpublished play)
The Cloud of Dust, and Other Stories (*La polvareda, y otros cuentos*, 1959)
Companion (*Compañero*, unpublished play)
The Masons (*Los albañiles*, 1963 [novel] and 1970 [play])
Rejected People (*Pueblo rechazado*, 1968)
The Sorrowful Voice (*La voz adolorida*, 1961)
The Squiggle (*El garabato*, 1967)
Studio Q (*Estudio Q*, 1965)
The Verdict (*El juicio*, 1972)

LEZAMA LIMA, JOSÉ

Clock's Analecta (*Analecta del reloj*, 1953)
Death of Narcissus (*Muerte de Narciso*, 1937)
Enemy Noise (*Enemigo rumor*, 1941)
Paradiso (*Paradiso*, 1966): *Paradiso* (New York, 1974)
Reading on the Turtle ("Leyendo en la tortuga," 1969)
Tracts in Havana (*Tratados en la Habana*, 1958)

LISPECTOR, CLARICE

The Apple in the Dark (*A maça no escuro*, 1961): *The Apple in the Dark* (New York, 1967)
The Beginnings of a Fortune ("Começos de una fortuna") in *Family Ties*
The Besieged City (*A cidade sitiada*, 1949)
Close to the Savage Heart (*Perto do coração selvagem*, 1943)
Family Ties (*Laços de família*, 1960)
The Luster (*O lustre*, 1946)
The Meal ("O jantar") in *Family Ties*

LOBATO, JOSÉ BENTO MONTEIRO

The Agricultural Morning Star ("O luzeiro agrícola") in *Dead Cities*
Choo-Pan! ("Chóóó-Pã!") in *Urupês*
The "Cruz de Ouro" ("A 'cruz de ouro' ") in *Dead Cities*
Dead Cities (*Cidades mortas*, 1946)
The German Spy ("O espião alemão") in *Dead Cities*

The Indiscreet Liver ("O fígado indiscreto") in *Dead Cities*
Little Black Woman (*Negrinha*, 1920)
A Modern Torture ("Um suplício moderno") in *Urupês*
The Placer of Pronouns ("O colocador de pronomes") in *Little Black Woman*
Timoteo the Gardener ("O jardineiro Timoteo") in *Little Black Woman*
The Tree That Kills ("O mata-pan") in *Urupês*
Urupês (*Urupês*, 1918): *Brazilian Short Stories* (Girard, Kan., 1925)

LÓPEZ VELARDE, RAMÓN

The Anchor ("El ancla") in *The Sound of the Heart*
Anxiety (*Zozobra*, 1919)
Devout Blood (*Sangre devota*, 1916)
The Sound of the Heart (*El son del corazón*, 1932)
Sweet Fatherland ("Suave patria") in *The Sound of the Heart*

LUGONES, LEOPOLDO

Ancestral Poems (*Poemas solariegos*, 1928)
The Angel of the Shadow (*El ángel de la sombra*, 1926)
The Artificial Fires ("Los fuegos artificiales") in *Sentimental Lunar Poems*
Essay on a Cosmogony in Ten Lessons ("Ensayo de una cosmogonía en diez lecciones") in *Strange Forces*
The Evening Shadows of the Garden (*Los crepúsculos del jardín*, 1905)
The Gaucho War (*La guerra gaucha*, 1905)
The Horses of Abdera ("Los caballos de Abdera") in *Strange Forces*
The Impossible Sweetheart ("La novia imposible") in *Sentimental Lunar Poems*
The Mountains of Gold (*Las montañas del oro*, 1897)
The Rain of Fire ("La lluvia de fuego") in *Strange Forces*
Secular Odes (*Odas seculares*, 1910)
Sentimental Lunar Poems (*Lunario sentimental*, 1909)
The Statue of Salt ("La estatua de sal") in *Strange Forces*
Strange Forces (*Las fuerzas extrañas*, 1906)
The Three Kisses ("Los tres besos") in *Sentimental Lunar Poems*
To Cattle and the Wheat ("A los ganados y las mieses") in *Secular Odes*
To My Country ("A la patria") in *Secular Odes*
The Toad ("El escuerzo") in *Strange Forces*
Useful and Magnificent Things ("Las cosas útiles y magníficas") in *Secular Odes*
Yzur ("Yzur") in *Strange Forces*

LYNCH, BENITO

The Englishman of the Bones (*El inglés de los güesos*, 1924)
A Gaucho's Romance (*Romance de un gaucho*, 1933)
The Vultures of Florida (*Los carranchos de la Florida*, 1916)